THEOLOGY AND PRAXIS

CLODOVIS BOFF, O.S.M.

THEOLOGY AND PRAXIS

EPISTEMOLOGICAL FOUNDATIONS

TRANSLATED FROM THE PORTUGUESE BY
ROBERT R. BARR

ORBIS BOOKS
Maryknoll, New York 10545

The Catholic Foreign Mission Society of America (Maryknoll) recruits and trains people for overseas missionary service. Through Orbis Books Maryknoll aims to foster the international dialogue that is essential to mission. The books published, however, reflect the opinions of their authors and are not meant to represent the official position of the society.

Originally published as *Teologia e prática: Teologia do político e suas mediações,* © 1978 by Editora Vozes Ltda., Petrópolis, Brazil.

English translation © 1987 by Orbis Books, Maryknoll, NY 10545
Manufactured in the United States of America
Manuscript editor: William E. Jerman

Library of Congress Cataloging-in-Publication Data

Boff, Clodovis.
  Theology and praxis.

  Translation of: Teologia e prática.
  Bibliography: p.
  Includes index.
  1. Liberation theology. I. Title.
BT83.57.B59513 1987   230'.01'8   86-21671
ISBN 0-88344-416-X (pbk.)

TO THE LATIN AMERICAN THEOLOGIANS
WHO HAVE BOUND THEIR PRACTICE
TO THE DEED OF LIBERATION

Ponder well the times *(kairous)*—
then look to the One beyond time,
the Timeless One.

Ignatius of Antioch
to Polycarp, III, 2

Contents

PART TWO
HERMENEUTIC MEDIATION

Foreword

Clodovis Boff's book is not a theology of liberation, or a political theology, or a theology of praxis. It is a critical reflection bearing on the epistemological *presuppositions* in terms of which any such theology, present or future, will indeed be *theology*—and not, for example, ideology or exhortation.

It might be thought that "stepping back from one's work" in this fashion, to get a better look at it, is an indefensible luxury in the world of today. But it is nothing of the kind. We need only reflect for an instant: a scientific discipline, any scientific discipline, can render service only on condition of being what it ought to be. If it is not, then one should not disguise one's efforts with a deceptive, invalid title—however valid be its intent and message, or however legitimate and understandable such a denomination might have been in the pioneer stage of a given discipline. No, there comes a moment when a scientific discourse must either validate its rules of procedure or else admit that it is not scientific discourse at all. Theology is no exception, whatever its subject and theme.

A number of writers, among them our author, have observed that theologies of the political, or of praxis, have often manifested deficiencies in this area. It would appear that, in the majority of instances, these theologies, for want of theoretical control, run the risk of eventually failing to measure up to their original great promise. Indeed, in all cases, these critics observe, a general theory of the conditions of "theologicity" of these new theologies is wanting. And yet these conditions are necessary if these theologies, like any other, are to verify, certify, their *episteme*.

There was a need, then, for someone to undertake a commitment to this task. It would be an arduous and lengthy enterprise, and a particularly difficult one—as invariably occurs when such reflection seeks to operate in a locus where a discipline is being extended into new areas. Inasmuch as these areas are still rather unfamiliar territory for this reflection, the risk of distraction and theoretical lapse is high. I ask the reader to forgive me if I speak in clichés (are they really still clichés when they mean exactly what they say?): Clodovis Boff has carried this task to completion with a power and an excellence that will make his astoundingly well researched work a landmark in theology, and no theologian, in any area, will ever be able to do without it.

If I may use the image of a river: the course of the stream that will carry us in this book will show us the points at which we shall be called upon to exercise a special "epistemological watchfulness"—along the upper course, the middle course, and along the lower course of the current of reflection on political theologies.

Along the upper course of our stream, these theologies, we know very well, have set themselves a new object: "the political," liberation, praxis, and the like. And no wonder: this object is altogether legitimate, and we need only carry to its conclusion the logic of the so-called theology of earthly realities in order to see that it is.

But it is here—"upstream"—that the theological process must be subjected to watchfulness and control, and it is very easy to lose this control. For example, theologians may easily let themselves simply be borne along by the belief that they know what "liberation" really is. We might call this the "craftmanship" method—rather an intuitive way of doing theology. But, as the author stresses: liberation is not what just anyone may happen to think that it is. It is a reality of a social, political, economic, and cultural order, and thus has its own shape and contours. Ignorance of these contours will mean talking about everything but the subject under discussion.

In order not to fall victim to this ignorance, theologians must turn to the sciences of the social. Only these sciences will be able to furnish theologians with their proper object, the *qua de re agitur*. After all, this is their specific domain. It is not that theology has nothing to say about this reality, as the reader will see. It is only that, in a first moment, theology does not have this reality within its grasp. Theology must receive its object for what it is and will continue to be—a political, profane, truly "earthly" reality. And this reality, which is not, as such, a religious reality (isotopes must not be confused!), is not scientifically to be apprehended by means of a sort of immediatism—*extra animam,* as St. Thomas, one of our author's principal sources, would say. The theologian must apply to those scientists whose discipline has conceptualized and analyzed the reality at issue. Any attempt to approach liberation in some other way can lead only to what I would call "impressionistic" theologies— theologies that rely on the *impression* that one has a grasp of what liberation is. This will produce only illusions, and the worst sort of deception and confusion, both on the side of political reality and on that of theological reflection. It is only in a second moment—and now we have come part way downstream—that this reality (liberation, for example) can actually be *examined,* under the lens of faith, by the intermediation of theology.

Downstream, then at midpoint along the course of our river, theology, like any other science today, is specified, and contradistinguished from other sciences, by its *modus operandi*—its tools, its proper manner of grasping reality. Here, except for key variations in the use of certain new mediations and in the shaping of supplementary tools, a theology of the political need not change *status* with respect to the more classic theologies. As an undertaking of rationality, it will be characterized by what St. Thomas calls the *ratio secundum quam considerantur*, the *res* to which it directs its attention—here, political realities.

Whatever be the datum constituting the object of its approach, theology will make that approach with the operative concepts proper to theology.

Theology need not be political science or sociology. Still less need it allow itself to be intimidated by other disciplines—although it must recognize them. Above all, it must not ride the wake of discourses not its own. It has its own grammar—without which it becomes, at best, a mixed discourse, laden with epistemological unconsciousness, the price of having had inappropriate recourse to the syntaxes of other languages. Then it is that confusion sets in, and "liberation" loses all its meaning.

Theology cannot detach itself from its own pertinency. Theology has this pertinency (although it must be continually in the process of recovering it) before it applies itself to any new object. Theology has its pertinency conferred upon it in and by the concepts it has itself forged, and continues to forge, for the purpose of comprehending the realities proposed to it as the *principia fidei,* in faith and revelation: sin, grace, redemption, the divine life, creation, the kingdom of God, holiness, and so on. As we see, then, theology can change objects, but not milieu. It can move from place to place, but its milieu, its pertinency, always accompanies it. It is in virtue of its fixed domicile in its own pertinency that it will be able, thanks to a hermeneutic procedure, to assign its new object (liberation, for example) a new status (which, however, does not alter its status as a political reality): that of a reality perceived in faith and read theologically. In this fashion, by means of its own manner of theoretical practice, theology stands warranty for the place and right of the discourse of faith among the other discourses of the human being, settling upon each and every thing it addresses an *intellectus* of its own—the *intellectus fidei.*

Clodovis Boff's whole effort here consists in securing (or recovering) the path proper to theology through all the material that will permit it to acquire the "criticity" that has always been demanded of it. And this he will help it do without the least arrogance or compromise. Without arrogance, because this theology will not think that, simply by having recourse to religious subjects, it automatically and as if by magic acquires the right to be called theology. Without compromise, because this theology will not suppose that it suffices to yield, on a verbal level, to socio-political sirens and thereby win the badge of "modernity."

Well downstream, finally, a critical self-regulation continues to be rigorously imperative. Like any other theology entertains real respect for itself and its faith—after all, faith is a virtue, and calls for behavior consistent with it—a theology of the political will seek issue in practice. But this does not mean that the word "praxis" should sound in our ears like the voice of a fairy godmother, making everything all right. Practice is not the criterion of truth, any more than is any other art, and it is not by being personally committed and "engaged" that theologians create a work of pertinent theology. It is precisely a *science* that theologians must practice. It is as theologians that they must guarantee the conditions for entry into that practice for whose sake they are creating a relevant, operative theory.

Here, then, theology must, to be sure, be concerned for its purpose, which is praxis—but at the same time it must never forget that its own practice is a theoretical practice, a practice of theory, just as it has always been expected to be. Otherwise its practice is nothing.

This means, first, that theology does not transform reality as such. It would be the height of idealism to believe that a scientific construct transforms reality. Here we would have what might be called a "spellbound theology." Once more: theology does not have an immediate relationship with material reality, any more than does any other theoretical practice. Secondly, the labor of theological production effectuates a (hermeneutic) transformation on the level of ideas, and it is to this that theology should be on the alert.

Theology should be on the alert to offer Christians, when they come to interrogate their action and engagement, a tool that has not been forged in disregard of historical conditions. Consequently, the theologian's role does not come to an end when action begins. To be sure, the activity of faith calls for an epistemological and ethical leap, which no theology as such can take the place of. But once that faith decision has been made, theology must still be there, to make it the most it can be in the face of the concrete demands of social situations and opportunities. To tell the truth, these demands are such as will transform a theology lacking in rigorous rationality into (to use the author's expression) a simple ideological discourse—although of course the faith activity may continue unaltered. Theory produces an effect on practice, to be sure, but it must really be its own effect.

As will be seen, Clodovis Boff's book is intended essentially as a search for correctness in theology. This means that the question he has raised is not first and foremost, *expresso modo*, the question of truth of theological knowing (in such and such a determinate area). Rather he raises the question of the propriety of its conditions. Theology is of course a science, but it must be what the author calls a *regulated* science. Regardless of all that is said about "order"— an order that would replace method in theology—theology must maintain a continuous watchfulness over its functioning. "The lowliest operations of science, just as its most exalted, are worth just what the theoretical, epistemological awareness accompanying these operations is worth" (Pierre Bourdieu). Remarkably, however, Boff has not simply proposed a program here, drawn attention to a task to be performed. He has written a genuine discourse on method with all the rigor of which I have been speaking, and he has written it in such a way that, from this day forward, a theology worthy of the name can be pursued in these new domains.

Finally, shall we congratulate Clodovis Boff on his immense labor of research, whose fruits he here offers us in such a remarkable new application to an area in which theology is still very poor? Yes, surely. But more than this; we shall confess that, behind the theologian (and a theologian who has chosen the most formal, most thankless of theological tasks), we perceive the Christian and the human being—a human being passionately in love with his faith, and passionately dedicated to what this good news can mean for human beings and society. And this Christian, with all his concern for action and "engagement" totally retains the discipline of one who refuses to yield an inch on the terrain of intellectual integrity. This is not an everyday combination. Beneath the heart, we perceive a thought process, and beneath this intelligence passion.

ADOLPHE GESCHÉ

Preliminary Note

The work that I here offer to the public is a translation of my doctoral dissertation in theology, written in French and publicly defended in mid-1976 at the Catholic University of Louvain, Belgium, before a jury consisting of Professors Adolphe Gesché, Jean Ladrière, Jan van Niewenhove, Gustave Thils, and A. Houssiau.

Although retaining the basic structure and content of the dissertation, the present version naturally includes some modifications suggested by my own rereading, as well as by the publication of certain recent studies on our subject.

I have published a resume of this work, including the Summary of Conclusions, in *Revista Eclesiástica Brasileira,* vol. 36, no. 144 (Dec. 1976), pages 789–810. The present version includes some formal alterations in the Summary of Conclusions, introduced with a view to clearer organic structuring.

I want to take this opportunity to thank Professor Adolphe Gesché, whom I had the privilege of having as my dissertation director; and Professors Jean Ladrière, François Houtart, and Leonardo Boff, with whom I have been able to discuss some of the important points of this work.

Preface

The theology of liberation seeks to be a "new way of doing theology." It seeks out a new attitude of mind, or particular style of "thinking the faith." This style finds expression in a series of principles, in the form of propositions or theses intended to inform and orientate theological practice.

These principles, these theoretical exigencies, can be grouped into three "question areas," corresponding to the three parts of this book. The first question area refers to the relationships of theology with the social sciences. The second refers to the relationship of theology with sacred scripture. And the third question area refers to the relationship between theology and praxis.

In the first question area, the theology of liberation lays down a demand for interdisciplinarity with respect to social theories. It demands what might be called "socio-analytical mediation." It calls for a positive, contextual, and concrete knowledge of society. Hence its criticism of speculative, abstract thought, which it judges to be ahistorical and alienating. The mediation of social analyses, then, appears as a demand of the praxis of faith, to the extent that this faith seeks to be incarnate. This is the level on which the theology of liberation encounters the problem of Marxist theory, as well as criticisms of the "ideologization of faith."

In the second question area—that of the relationship of theology to scripture—the theology of liberation pleads for a reading of scripture in continual mindfulness of and orientation to concrete challenges and problems. From the very outset it rejects an atemporal or purely "spiritual" hermeneutic, along the lines of a "privatization of faith." It accentuates the political dimension of salvific events, especially the exodus and the death (by murder) of Jesus, as well as the "subversive" nature of the biblical message, particularly in the protest raised by the prophets and Jesus vis-à-vis social injustices. It underscores the fact that salvation is actualized in history, and that there is but one salvation history, embracing the totality of human beings.

In the third question area—that of the relationship of theology with praxis—the theology of liberation finds its point of departure, its milieu and its finality in praxis. Its intent is to develop an engaged, liberating theology, to which it ascribes a political option, and which it subordinates to praxis. The latter, in the eyes of the theology of liberation, holds the primacy over all theory, indeed is the criterion of the verification of theology. Liberation theology considers praxis as the fundamental locus of theology, the "place" where theology occurs. Finally, liberation theology maintains the reality of a permanent dialectic between theory and practice here: a dialectic between theological theory and the political praxis of faith.

These, then, are the principal postulates of the "new way of doing theology" posited by the theology of liberation.[1]

But when liberation theologians are called upon to propound their *method,* they only return to the above "positions," interweaving them with a variety of commentaries. Their "method" is simply the voice of their theological practice. Thus they make no distinction between "theology" and "way of theologizing," between knowledge and method. But, as Aristotle long ago observed, "It is absurd to seek at the same time knowledge and the way of attaining knowledge."[2] And even though neither of these two things is easy to grasp, as Aristotle himself immediately goes on to say, their distinction is of the utmost importance. After all, a theological theory and its epistemology—the study of the principles of its construction—are not the same thing. Accordingly, before betaking oneself to the making of theology, one ought to know how theology is made. Thomas Aquinas's position is no different: *"Oportet enim primum scire modum scientiae quam scientiam ipsam."*[3]

Until recently, simply proposing the theses of liberation theology—now by way of pursuit and now by way of defense—took the place of a methodology. The liberation theologians were content to do theology "differently," without concerning themselves with the rational justification of the original intuitions and attitudes supporting their theoretical practice. Nor did they go about establishing a critique of the technical resources that these intuitions and attitudes were to inform.

Such a situation, it seems to me, is altogether understandable. It would in fact have been impossible for the theology of liberation to rest its new discourse on a secure epistemological foundation in the very beginning. The route of this theology followed a sort of logical necessity. The history of practically any discipline, any theory, obliges us to acknowledge the inevitability of hesitant, error-plagued beginnings. In the order of knowledge, error is always first.[4]

But the moment has arrived when the imperatives of thought and action can no longer be satisfied with the mere statement, or paraphrase, of theological postulates. It should be evident that mere enunciation cannot do justice to principles governing a discourse that will have to be equal both to theoretical critiques from within and polemical attacks from without. Hence the ever increasing need to get beyond the first phase, which ignored its own methodology, and launch a basic reflection having as its goal, before all else, to supply a critical basis for the above-cited postulates—specifying the conditions under which they can be elaborated—and then to articulate the findings in such a way as to lead toward the systematization of a method. The liberation theologians themselves are gradually coming to realize the gravity of this theoretical imperative.[5]

I should like to say a word about my own intellectual pilgrimage that may help explain my choice of the theme of this work. Born and educated in the Third World, I came to the First World to do advanced studies. But I intended to return to the Third World. And so, at a certain point in time, I decided to interrupt my studies temporarily and return there, to regain "contact with reality," as they say. And so it happened that, for several years, I found myself in contact with the "unjust structures that characterize the situation of Latin America."[6] Of course, as is very well known, these same structures are characteristic of the rest of the "periphery" (Third World) as well.

Such a situation seemed to me to bristle with enormous challenges— challenges at once human, Christian, and theoretical. When the time came to resume my studies, then, I found myself doing so under the pressure of the urgency of these challenges. I felt the need to launch a theoretical attack on the problems that such a situation posed to the human conscience, to faith, and to the understanding of faith—even though, in the opinion of so many, such an intellectual endeavor would lack any real utility, indeed ran the risk of a more refined alienation: "academic alienation."

Following in the deep furrows already turned by pioneers in the theology of liberation, I was preparing to develop a theological study in the area of the "signs of the times." This seemed to me to be something that would immediately bear upon the "situation of injustice" obtaining in the "periphery"—a situation felt to the point of indignation. Suddenly our theoretical work seemed to me to be justifiable only in terms of a resolute and direct orientation to praxis.

At the same time, the evolution of my reflection and the demands of scholarship—demands, after all, being made by praxis itself in respect of the element of theory—led me to face the fact that I was falling victim to impatience here, and succumbing to theological immediatism. This attitude would surely throw up a definitive obstacle to the construction of a consistent discourse, and praxis itself stood in the gravest need of precisely such a consistent discourse. It was as if praxis were laboring under a "theoretical oedipal complex," which projected the rigor of intellectual discipline as a kind of castration of native, untamed thought, threatening to incapacitate its primitive, instinctual ebullience and thrust.

And so I had to "retreat"—withdraw to a more basic theoretical level, one that would supply a secure platform for theological, pastoral, and political practice. Thus I was in the area of epistemology, and "short of" any particular theology—on its "theory side." The construction of this platform is the objective of the present work.

It is not without astonishment that I observe how an initial concern with action finally led me, rather strangely, to a theory of (theological) theory— without having come to feel a greater distance from praxis (quite the contrary).

This, then, was the genesis of my discourse on method. As to the study itself: in its three sections, I group, respectively, the three sorts of methodological problems that seem to me to be the most important, and indeed they coincide with the three areas in which questions arise in liberation theology circles. These problems, in turn, are linked to the de facto structure of a political theology. Now, the basic elements composing this structure are:

1. The object of this theology: the *political*. This is the subject of part 1.
2. The specific manner of theoretical appropriation of this object: (political) *theology*, the subject of part 2.
3. The relationship of (theological) *theory and* (political) *praxis,* the subject of part 3.

Following is a general statement of my conceptualization of these three areas.

1. The *object* of a theology of politics—the "political"—is furnished by the sciences that bear on this object—that is, by the social sciences. The theoretical act by which the findings of these disciplines are taken up by and in theological practice goes by the name of *socio-analytical mediation.* It will be responsible for the constitution of the (theoretical) *material* object of political theology, although of course formally speaking this step can be considered pretheological. At all events, this moment surely represents a basic condition for the elaboration of political theology, and in this respect it becomes a constitutive part of the total process of the production of this theology.

2. The *mode of appropriation* in which political theology operates involves the question of *theological pertinency.* Here I am dealing with the *specifically theological approach* to the theoretical material object just mentioned. I seek to discern the precise way by which this material object is constituted in its quality of *formally theological object*—that is, how it is constituted in the form under which it appears when exposed to the light of theologizing reason. This properly theological mode consists in the interpretation of an object, in this case "the political," from a point of departure in the Christian scriptures. Hence I call this function "hermeneutic mediation."

Thus from one side, thanks to socio-analytical mediation, political theology receives a theoretical object, or "reading text." Thanks to its hermeneutic mediation it receives the means of appropriating this object in a manner proper to itself. In other words, through hermeneutic mediation, political theology receives a kind of table of interpretation for a properly theological reading. It receives a kind of grid through which it will be able to decipher its political text, which is furnished it by socio-analytical mediation.

Why do I use the term "mediation" here?

It is the concept I use to designate the complexus of *means* applied by theological thought in order to grasp its object. These means constitute a *medium quo,* giving theology an organic, not merely mechanical, link with its object. Accordingly, I hold that analytical and hermeneutic mediations are internal to theology itself, albeit not *ex aequo* with elements still more properly theological, as I shall have occasion to explain.[7]

3. Praxis, to which (theological) theory must be related, must be considered here not as a *medium quo,* but more properly, as a *medium in quo,* in the sense that praxis constitutes the de facto milieu of the actualization of concrete theological practice. I do not discuss praxis in itself, or at least I do not discuss it directly. This would be the elaboration of a political theology. It would mean taking leave of the epistemological level, on which I seek to remain in this work. On this level, (political) theology is taken as a direct theoretical object, and

thereby falls short of the theme of politics as such. What I do on the epistemological level is examine the multiple interfacing between theory and practice—but in such wise that the central subject of my study remains (theological) theory, even though this theory, in its turn, will take praxis as the object of its study, and even though the final objective of my theoretical endeavor is concrete, historical praxis.

The relationship to praxis, essential to the definition of political theology, as I conceive it—along the lines of Latin American liberation theology—ranks among the most difficult of the epistemological problems involved in the determination of the theoretical status of political theology itself. The establishment of the *theoretical* status of praxis is an undertaking beset with pitfalls. Indeed, the very formulation is distorted. But I may observe, even at this point, that, at the level of a metatheory, to which these considerations are raised, all conceptual efforts must be brought to bear directly upon (theological) theory. It matters little here that this theory must bear upon praxis. When all is said and done, praxis can attain to a metatheory only as a second step.

I must therefore point out that I am speaking here of a "theology *of* the political" generally, and not simply of "political theology." Similarly, I prefer the expression "sciences *of* the social" to "social sciences." This effort to de-adjectivize has a very precise epistemological bearing. I am trying to keep the (political or social) object at a distance from its (theological or scientific) theory. In the expressions I prefer, the key word with respect to this distantiation is the "of." Like a connecting rod, it keeps what it unites at an appropriate distance.

Schematically, the three parts of this book can be represented as in Diagram 1.[8]

Diagram 1

part 1	socio-analytic mediation	material theoretical object	(theology of) the political	seeing (analysis)
part 2	hermeneutic mediation	formal theoretical object	theology (of the political)	judging (discernment)
part 3	practical mediation of faith	praxis: real concrete object	praxis of faith	acting (action)

My intent, as can be seen, is to discuss the basic problems of a theory of the theology of the political. My concern, then, is epistemological. Hence expressions such as "theory of theology," or "epistemology of theology" will be equivalent to one another, as also such expressions as "theoretical status of theology" or "epistemological status of theology."

Let it be noted as well that, in the epistemological discussions to follow, it is not precisely the "scientific status" of theology that is at stake. Whether theology is a "science" or not depends in large part on what Pierre Bourdieu calls "cultural arbitrariety." I shall take no account of such labels. What seems to me to merit prime consideration is the question of the possibility and necessity of a *disciplined* theology—that is, a theology proportioned to its proper object and articulated in function of its new object, the political. My effort may be considered a plea for the execution of this task.

Under the concept of "epistemology" I shall range all questions arising in the course of a general critique of theological approach, whether they refer to properly methodological problems, or are merely related to basic methodological presuppositions.[9] I shall, then, have to examine the articulation of the practice of theory, the interplay of its system, and the rules of its internal relationships.

But a difficult question arises at this point. What method should be used to discuss the method?

The "method of the method," it seems to me, will have to consist in an alternating movement of critique and construction, analysis and synthesis. Accordingly, "polemical reason" and "architectonic reason" will be employed by turns.[10] Each of these two functions has its logical, or formal, aspect, and its positive, or material, aspect. Thus a considerable part of my work will be devoted to dismantling, and another large part to construction—not as distributive principles of my order of exposition, but as reflective movements in parallel, spanning the whole order of the parts as I have described them.

Accordingly, as to *critique,* on its *positive* level, I shall examine current theological practices, and those of theological tradition in general, from the viewpoint of the epistemological conceptions that support them. On the *logical* level of critique, I shall investigate the nature of the theoretical object upon which method bears. I shall, therefore, have to raise a whole series of questions, corresponding to the three parts of this book: What does the making of a theology *of the political* involve? What constitutes the *"theologicity"* of theology? How does *praxis* relate to (theological) theory?[11]

As for *construction,* I shall begin with the findings of the first moment, that of critique. I shall find that the latter has become the starting point for a series of positions defining the organizing principles of the theological discourse that I shall have been seeking. Note, however, that these positions, or theses—which I shall draw up, along with others, in the Summary of Conclusions—are not precisely the object of demonstration in the strict sense of the word, but only of rational explanation. It is not a matter of "true" or "false" propositions here, but of, so to say, "suitable" ones. These theses lay no claim to a relationship of *theoretical* adequation to a given *reality,* but to a relationship of suitability, or *operative* adequation, to a *practice*—in this case, a theological practice. Consequently, my effort in this discussion will be to produce propositions that will be genuine principles *for* theory, and not simply theoretical principles.[12] For, in addition to this adequation, I shall attempt, by *logical* reason, to bestow upon the complexus of these theses a cohesiveness such as will permit the production of actual theologies of the political. Of course, it is only in a *positive* examination of these theologies that their fecundity can ultimately be established.

This entire labor of dismantling and construction, at once logical and positive, has taken me to three distinct bibliographical sources: general epistemological works, works on the epistemology of theology, and, finally, specific epistemological studies concerned with a theology of the political.

With respect to the first of these sources, it is to be observed that, for want of adequate epistemological reflections in the area of theology, I have been obliged to look beyond the confines of theology for concepts and theories that might hold some promise of assisting me in my own reflection upon the status of the discourse of a theology of the political. And so I frequently cite Jean Ladrière, Louis Althusser, Gaston Bachelard, Pierre Bourdieu, Paul Ricoeur, and still others.

I rely very heavily on the work of Jean Ladrière for the status of scientific knowledge and its relationship to philosophical and theological knowledge. I look to Louis Althusser for the internal relationships of theoretical practice and its connections with other practices, especially with political practice. Gaston Bachelard has shown me the demands of the scientific spirit and the specific conceptuality of epistemology, especially with his concepts of "epistemological obstacle" and "recurrence" (for the critical moment), and "epistemological breach" and "recasting" (for the moment of construction). I have recourse to Pierre Bourdieu's work for the epistemology of sociology, and for its understanding on a basis of the imperatives of scientific method generally. I refer to Paul Ricoeur in the area of hermeneutics. These are the principal authors on whom I depend in this work.

Where these authors remain on the level of general epistemology, their views are applicable to theological discipline without difficulty. I may even say that the generality of their propositions will be most useful for current theology, inasmuch as the latter is sorely wanting in a solidly established epistemological basis. When these and other authors speak in a particular theoretical area, however—physics, sociology, and so on—the transposition of their concepts and theories to the theological domain naturally supposes a special theoretical operation, requiring extreme precaution, with a view to the careful delimiting of the specific conditions and modalities of these concepts and theories. This transposition can be achieved, therefore, only by means of a complete "recasting" of such concepts and theories.[13]

For this reason, my use of these concepts and theories may seem somewhat "loose." But the work of transposition must be carried out within the limits circumscribing the object of my investigation. I must content myself with indicating, in the notes especially, the sense in which I have made use of nontheological studies for purposes of theology. Thus I refrain from citing them in my text itself: their concepts are found there only after a transposition to a form that I deem correct for application to the area of theology. The fruitfulness of my employment of these concepts and theories should be judged by the concrete effects, in the form of theory, that they may have on theological practice. My propositions, then, even when they seem outrageous, should be considered as conclusions, indeed, but also, from another viewpoint, as hypotheses.

As for my second source of information, which consists in works of theological epistemology, the reader will note the great frequency with which I cite Thomas Aquinas, whom, to be sure, I consult in the area of general epistemology as well. For such consultation, certain well-known Thomist authors—namely, M.-D. Chenu and Yves M.-J. Congar—have been most useful. My repeated references to St. Thomas may seem strange, or disproportionate, considering my specific subject, which is a theory of the theology of the political. But such an impression will easily give way, upon examination of a simple sketch of the series of problems at issue, such as I have given on the foregoing pages. In all cases, I leave it to the reader to render a just judgement upon my conclusions.

Finally, in my third source of information, the works of the liberation theologians, I refer especially to Gustavo Gutiérrez and Hugo Assmann, who seem to me to be the most representative and most thought-provoking authors in this stream. But I do not neglect others: Juan Luis Segundo, Enrique Dussel, José Comblin, or Leonardo Boff, for example. I have already alluded to the nature of the methodological materials of these authors. It is intuitive and fragmentary. These authors employ a method, of course. But they do so largely *in actu exercito*—that is, largely in their tacit premises. I shall attempt to explicitate such premises when it seems necessary.

This summary presentation of the material utilized hints at the kind of difficulties that readers will encounter in this investigation, not to mention the difficulties cited by Aristotle as inherent in the very nature of foundational questions.[14]

From the complexus of problems opened up by the intent to "found" theology of the political, whose parameters I have briefly sketched here, it is not difficult to appreciate why my area of investigation, which at first was limited to the theology of liberation, necessarily increased in size. The expansion occurred in two stages. First of all, a discourse on theology of liberation ended as a discourse on theology of the political, which includes not only theology of liberation, but so many other possible theologies of the political, such as "theology of revolution," "theology of captivity," "theology of violence," and so on. Secondly, in order to understand correctly the theology of the political, it became necessary to place it within a broader context. This is what led me to make a distinction between what I call "first" and "second" theology. The former treats directly of specifically "religious" realities—the classic themes of God, creation, Christ, grace, sin, eschatology, the virtues, the commandments, and so on. The latter will have "secular" realities for its subject matter: for example, culture, sexuality, or history—including, here, political history.[15] Of course, this latter material is relatively new to theology.[16] This is particularly true in terms of the *problematic* of this subject material: the particular manner in which theology must confront these areas.

It seems to me that the whole of theology can be reordered under these two headings.

The essential difference between first theology and second theology is based solely on the respective *thematic* of each—on that upon which the theologizing is to be done, the *theologizandum*; it is not based upon any difference in pertinency—the aspect under which these respective series of material are to be approached, the *theologizans*.[17] Evidently, the technical determination of the *ratio formalis,* or pertinency, that specifies the theological method will undergo a certain "recasting" in function of the nature—the material—of the new theoretical field, inasmuch as method is a function of object. This change could be called a change in *problematic.*[18] Nonetheless, the formal *ratio* of a discipline, in this case theology, can only be one and the same throughout the discipline, because what one intends to do is theology, and not something else.

Here I must add that between these two theoretical subareas there is indubitably a dialectic at play, such that second theology reacts on first theology and obliges it to restructure itself internally, seeing that second theology is enriched by the work of first theology, even on the level of its *ratio formalis,* or "pertinency."

Thus theology of liberation comes to be considered as a particular species of political theology, whereas the latter falls within the confines of second theology—which, in turn, constitutes one of the two broad areas of theology as such.

This epistemological position does not coincide with that expressed by the liberation theologians, when indeed they express an epistemological position. They oppose what they call "theology of genitives," in which liberation would be no more than "one subject among many." Their claim, on the contrary, is that liberation is a kind of "horizon," against which the whole tradition of the faith is to be read.[19] This methodological position, and its results, as I understand them, can, I think, yield only a *rhetoric,* not an *"analytic":* discourse embroidered with many an "as to," instead of theory textured throughout with a single, powerful "in the light of."[20]

True, each of our two types of theology supposes an antecedent notion of theology itself—of what it is to theologize. That is, "*normal* theology," or the daily theology of a "theological community," is under the governance of a "paradigm."[21] A critique of this theology, however, needs no permission to inveigh against the ideology of "epistemological consensualism" that canonizes the theoretical practice of a group. What is called for at this point is a confrontation of stated intent with actual results, and then the application of the outcome of this confrontation as point of departure for the construction of a "*normative* theology."

In this spirit, then, and following my *ordo inventionis,* I have begun with the fact of the theology of liberation—or more specifically, with a concern for its epistemological definitioning, and have concentrated all my considerations on this particular point. This procedure has led me to a generalization of my thematic, though not yet to a discussion of a *ratio formalis*. And it is only by way of a sort of "posthumous conclusion" that I must here expressly assert that my open stance was a demand of liberation theology itself, in the sense of its exact comprehension and its adequate theoretical basing.

At the same time, just as theology of liberation can be defined by its relationship to praxis, both on the theoretical level (praxis as the material of discourse) and on the practical level (praxis as such—that is, as the alternative moment of theoretical practice), so too the historical merit of that theology must be acknowledged: that it has made a decisive contribution to the good of theology and of the church at large, however plausible it may be that the understanding of this relationship is as it were *extra muros,* or underground.

To conclude this Preface, let us all be well alerted to the danger of any sort of theological "epistemocracy." The danger is present. Furthermore, I regard epistemology as ancillary to theology, and theology as ancillary to the praxis of faith. This is what is meant by the celebrated maxim of St. Augustine, which resounds down though the scholastic centuries:

> *Huic scientiae tribuitur illud tantummodo quo fides saluberrima gignitur, nutritur, defenditur, roboratur.* (The only merit of this science is that from it a saving faith is born, nourished, defended, and strengthened.)[22]

Lastly, I justify the limits and shortcomings of this work with Nietzsche's pronouncement:

> Methods, one must repeat ten times, *are* the essential, as well as being the most difficult, as well as being that which has habit and laziness against it the longest.[23]

THEOLOGY AND PRAXIS

PART 1

SOCIO-ANALYTIC MEDIATION

It may be well to explain the order of my presentation in part 1. I shall begin with a discussion of what is properly at issue in the problem of the theology of the political—namely, the political itself, the object of this theology. Then I shall attempt to come to an understanding of how this object is posited with respect to theological thought.

Doubtless it would have been possible to begin with a determination of what constitutes the "theological" element in theology of the political. Such an approach may even seem per se more logical. But it is not the most logical way when it comes to the particular form of theology that constitutes for us the theoretical object at stake in the debate into which I am about to enter—namely, theology *of the political*.

For it is precisely the political that causes problems. This it is that gives rise to difficulties for a correct theological practice. It is in terms of the political, in its quality as new theoretical object, that theology is challenged to think and rethink its methods and conceptualization.

This cannot be done without first having defined the proper nature of this object, for it is on the nature of the object that the method will depend. Therefore, the aim of part 1 will be to lay down principles that will permit a response to this basic demand. Only thereafter, in the parts to follow, shall I concern myself with the hermeneutic mediation (in part 2) and, finally, the interrelationship between theory and practice (in part 3).[1]

In part 1 I follow a *modus procedendi* that will take me through four chapters:

In chapter 1 I attempt to formulate an adequate statement of the problem of a theology of the political. First I treat of the decisive and characteristic reference of this theology to praxis. Then I endeavor to form a precise idea of this reference in terms of the "two regimes" of theological practice.

Chapter 2 will touch the very nerve of part 1. I begin with a critique of certain "epistemological obstacles" that can stand in the way of relating theology to the

1

sciences of the social. Then I attempt to establish the formal status of socio-analytic mediation, in terms of its constitutive relationship.

In chapter 3 I take up the problematic of ideology, dealing with a series of difficulties that could arise from faith in the establishment of a theology of the political.

Finally, in chapter 4 I make a number of concrete suggestions intended to facilitate the choice, and actual practice, of socio-analytic mediation. This has to do with the modalities of the relationship between theology and the sciences of the social.

As the reader can see, I proceed from the abstract to the concrete, gradually enriching with new theoretical determinations the methodological instrument called socio-analytic mediation.[2]

CHAPTER 1

A Correct *Status Questionis:*
The Reference to Praxis

§1 APPROACHES TO BE EXCLUDED

The particular articulation that I now propose between theology and the social sciences calls for a careful distinction from other modes of articulation.[1] There are four principal modes to be excluded.

1. "Unity of Knowledge" Approach

It does not fall within the scope of this work to analyze how the truths at which the various disciplines arrive, from a point of departure proper to the distinct perspective of each of them, might arrive at a possible unification. This would call for an epistemological locus that would be external to each of the disciplines in question. This locus would be, to put it simply and traditionally, that of a philosophy; or to say the same thing in modern parlance, that of a "metatheory."

The undertaking of a synthesis of knowledge truly answers to a yearning of the human spirit, which, being itself one, cannot be satisfied with atomized truths. It searches for some unitive bond to link them together in a single whole, and strives irrepressibly after a totalization, be it ever so provisional, in the form of a synthesis that will be open to further internal reorganization, as it keeps apace with the development of knowledge itself.

For my part, I see in these efforts the expression of an exigency of theoretical reason rather than that of a quest on the part of practical reason. It has to do more with an interest of "intellectuals" than with one of "practical" persons. The totality pursued finds its realization in an "interpretation of the world" rather than in a "transformation of the world," although, of course, there is an undeniable relationship between them.[2] In view of what has been said, the reader can see why I distance myself from this approach.

3

2. Social Critique Approach

Nor do I intend to examine the contribution theology may potentially have to offer the sciences of the social, whether by helping them avoid what Horkheimer calls "false hypostatizations," arising from an absolutization of their methods, or by contributing to the creation of a theory of society in which the rights of subjectivity can be safeguarded.[3] This approach seems to me to be still too general, and has little orientation to praxis.

3. Pastoral Approach

Taking a somewhat opposite approach from the one just considered, I could of course consider the contribution that the sciences of the social might have to offer pastoral theology. I should have to go into the question of the utilization of these sciences in view of specific pastoral objectives. And it would not be difficult to identify which religious practices have aroused theologians' interest in the sciences of the social.[4] But neither does this perspective seem germane to my interests. I seek a horizon at once wider and more radical. I am not limiting my considerations to the pastoral—that is, to the *religious*—practice of faith. I wish to extend them *throughout* the spectrum of the praxis of faith, with emphasis on the *political* practice of faith—or, better, on a "Christian practice of politics."[5]

4. Approach of the Sociology of Theological Knowledge

Finally, my undertaking will not consist in the approach of a sociological analysis and critique of the various theologies. I grant that any theology of the political can and should take advantage of this sort of study for a fully reflective social localization of its discourse, as well as for adequate control of its proper theoretical object. However, this is not, strictly speaking, a theological pursuit.[6] It is true that I make frequent use of some of the ramifications of this approach in my study, but I do so only in indirect fashion. I do so whenever questions of the sociology of (theological) meaning are found to have some clear—or, for that matter, unclear—connection with questions of an epistemological order, precisely in order to be able to unravel these connections and articulate them correctly. The principles of this articulation are laid down in part 1, §6, to be developed in more general fashion in part 3.

These are the main approaches from which I wish to distinguish my own position, which follows next.[7]

§2 PROPOSED APPROACH: A REFERENCE TO PRAXIS

The treatment I propose to develop with respect to the possible relationships between theology and the sciences of the social has this distinguishing characteristic, that it is ultimately determined by the existence and demands of (Christian) praxis. Accordingly, it will have its point of departure in the phenomenon that may be described as follows.

Certain Christians are engaged in a multiplicity of political practices. Their faith, with the particular vision that flows from it, has encountered the question of the theoretical and practical implications of their faith in the tissue of relationships of this or that determinate *socio-historical* area.[8] These Christians now feel the need for an organic synthesis between their basic life option, expressed in and by the coordinates of their faith, and the historical options that, in one way or another, they are being constrained to make. Here, then, the "complex" question of faith and politics arises. These Christians are either resolutely engaged, or at least aroused. They wonder what their faith may have to do with political confrontations—to what it can lead, and what sense it can lend to such confrontations. At all events, for them, a faith that seeks to be lucid and effective can today no longer "bracket" concrete political mediation.[9]

In other words, the question posed to the Christian conscience is: What does it mean "to be a Christian" in a determinate historical situation—for example, in a dependent Latin America? What does this historical situation mean to the eyes of faith?

At this point another fact, flowing from the first, comes into the picture. The whole concern for a theology of the political has sprung from the involvement of Christians in politics. The discourses of the political theology have actually developed, and continue to develop, from the fact of this involvement. Here, then, we have two important pieces of data, interrelated and tacitly underlying the articulation of theology and the sciences of the social.[10]

Thus we see that it is the historical relationship between faith and politics that has occasioned the theoretical relationship between theology and the sciences of the social. In simpler terms: the practical encounter of Christians with political challenges has been the point of departure and basis of the theoretical encounter of theologians with the social sciences. Thus the relationship between theology and the sciences of the social has been and continues to be ruled ultimately by the relationship between faith and praxis. There is no such thing, then, as a theology that would have its origin and finality in praxis and *not* have socio-analytic mediation.

This socio-historical fact has decisive methodological effects.[11] To be sure, a theology of the political translates an internal exigency of the ecclesial community. It is lived by Christians—"political theology question" is purely conjunctural and confessional, perhaps even sectarian, so that it could in no way concern non-Christians, as if a theology of the political were a matter of purely subjective and arbitrary "need." On the contrary, Christians live the faith experience in politics as a matter of the lot of the human being as such, a matter of one's most profound calling—as having to do with the ontic potential of ultimate human actualization, the fulfillment of one's whole being. Christians wonder whether the challenge of political struggles perhaps involves more than appears on the surface, and more than appears to a social scientist. Here is perhaps the most radical reason why "involved Christians" show such interest in a theoretico-practical synthesis of faith and politics, the task of whose development falls to theology.

It may be said, then, that the current internal reorganization of theological discourse is the de facto product precisely of the political, as Christians come in contact with the political in their concrete experiences and practices.

Meanwhile, political tasks and practices cannot be adequately carried out without an exact understanding of their nature. Further, this understanding is possible only through the positive analyses of the disciplines whose formal object is the nature of these tasks and practices. Hence no relationship of theology to these political tasks and practices can be correctly maintained except by means of an assimilation of the findings of these very disciplines by the theologian. For a theology orientated toward praxis, consequently, the sciences of the social perform a necessary function of theoretical mediation, which I call "socio-analytic mediation."[12]

Thus when I say that praxis is the deciding factor in the articulation between a theology of the political and the sciences of the social, I mean "praxis" in the sense of the *complexus of practices* orientated to the transformation of society, the making of history. "Praxis," then, has a fundamentally *political* connotation for me inasmuch as it is through the intermediary of the political that one can bring an influence to bear on social structures.[13]

But "politics," in turn, is a concept of rather broad theoretical content. By and large it includes four components—strategic, technological, ethical, and "utopic" (in the sense of "historical project"—self-projection into the future in search of betterment). Inasmuch as my study does not bear directly on the *development* of a "political theology," but only on a *theory* of "political theology," I shall not develop the concept "politics" here, with its theoretical and practical implications. This concept will, perforce, be left with an abstract content in my exposition.[14] This is why I shall speak of "the political"—as in "the theology of the political"—and not of "politics." The former expression simply designates the political "instance," or order, itself—the locus of the power of social organization and transformation. The latter expression refers to a particular historical practice—within, of course, the same instance of power.[15]

The "political," therefore, as I use the term, will be defined in reference to power. But it must be added that the locus of this power is not only the state. More broadly, it is society. Or better: the locus of the political is the relationship between society and state. This conceptualization avoids both a minimalistic notion of the political, whereby the political would be confused with the politics of the apparatus of state, and a maximalistic one, whereby the political would absorb the whole of the social. It is true that the whole of the social is political. But it is not true that the whole of the social is *only* political.[16] Despite the discussions in progress in the sciences of the social concerning the concept of "politics," I shall have to endow it with a determinate, even if precarious, content in this work.[17]

As for the expression "socio-analytic mediation," let us, right from the start, be rid of the ambiguity it may comport. When I speak of "socio-analytic mediation," I mean that the analyses and studies of the sciences of the social are mediation for theological *theory*—that they are a theoretical mediation of theology. This is a problem bearing upon theory. It is another matter to say that studies of the sciences of the social are a (theoretical) mediation for the *practice* of faith. This is a problem bearing on practice. The reciprocal bonds linking the two problems must, of course, be recognized. Indeed, what I am here maintaining is that the second problem is at the basis of the first.

Christians feel the need of recourse to the social sciences by reason of their concrete praxis, and this touches their very life of faith. This is why such Christians experience the (derived) need for a systematic theoretical articulation between theology and the sciences of the social. This is the sense of socioanalytic mediation. In the last instance, this mediation is determined by concrete praxis—but not in a mechanical or direct way.

Here I expressly exclude other possible mediations of theology, even those ordered to the political, as for example the mediation that has been the classic partner of theology: *philosophical mediation*. Doubtless it can lend its help to a theology of the political, where the essence of power, state, conflict, society, law, and the like are concerned. And yet I exclude the notion of an articulation to be *fostered* with philosophy. I do not exclude it on the grounds that this articulation would be of no utility, but because, after mature deliberation, I have decided to engage theology in real praxis, under pressure of historical urgency.[18]

Ultimately, I have reason for refusing any primacy to philosophical mediation: it is speculative, or at least it has a tendency to be speculative. I opt to establish a relationship with empirical, positive analyses rather than with philosophical speculations, because I am afraid that, in the socio-historical conjuncture that is currently ours, especially in the Third World, philosophy would inevitably end in a mystification of the reality of the oppressed masses, and more than likely a devastating mystification. At all events, if philosophy were to be necessary, it ought to be done in accordance with de facto historical imperatives.

The interfacing of theology with praxis through the medium of socioanalytic mediation has as its objective the safeguarding of theology from the empty "theorism" that, in certain circumstances, is a trait of *academic cynicism* that ignores the crying scandal of the starving and suffering multitudes of our world.[19]

To be sure, Kant showed us that science can be "open," with infinite possibilities for development, and indeed in virtue of its own internal dynamism.[20] On the other hand, it is equally well known that, in the concrete world of sociohistorical determinations, all science is defined, and delimited, in the actual realization of its intrinsic possibilities, by the concrete objectives it is set by certain social groups—the dominant groups—according as this science acts or does not act in behalf of these groups' particular interests.

At this point, an epistemological critique of science yields to an ethicopolitical critique. Science does not float in the air. It has social existence and significance, and consequently a position of strength. Science, too, is caught in the net of power relationships. This is what is meant by a "scientific policy," more or less explicitly established and imposed on science in such a way that science may be organized and utilized in favor of the interests of particular social groups.[21]

The reason why I seek to connect theological reflection with historical tasks through the mediation of the social sciences (in socio-analytical mediation) is that I want to escape the danger of a "pure" theology, one that inevitably yields an overabundance of significations for their own sake—in a "meaning hemorrhage," an "infinitude of words," in its incontinency.[22]

§3 THE CLASSIC THEOLOGY OF "SOCIAL MORALITY"

It is true that traditional theology, too, has been concerned with "political" questions. However, its approach to the political seems unable to apprehend the political as we can today by means of the sciences of the social. This theology operates within the space offered it by its philosophical mediation. The problematic in and by which it confronts social and political questions is marked by an idealism incapable of perceiving the positive data of social phenomena and situations.

Today—and only today—we see that the traditional approach did not enjoy the conditions necessary for an appropriation of the political in its concrete, empirical, and historical expression. "Social theology" omitted from its perspective the positive determinations that are proper to the social. As a consequence, neither could it implement a method that would correspond to this particular object.

Traditional theology, first, dealt with political questions in the form of questions with ties to *ethics*. Secondly, the ethical perspective itself, by reason of its abstract nature, necessarily led theological reflection to moralism. This supplementary distortion of the social object might be called "ethical idealism." In my opinion, hence, "social morality" imposed two basic limitations or restrictions on social and political questions: *interpretation* was retrenched with respect to its object and *application* was retrenched with respect to its method.[23]

As to the first retrenchment—flowing from the concept of the *theoretical* object in question, the social—let us be content to note that for Christian faith the political is not simply an empty space for the materialization of ethical values. It is a structured space, possessing its own consistency, charged beforehand with a particular meaning that theological discourse has a duty to discover and express. Prior to any theological act, history—simultaneously the field and effect of (political) praxis—is the possible and real locus of the epiphany of God, of the coming of the reign of God, the salvation event, as the Judeo-Christian faith perceives it and the scriptures bear witness to it.[24]

Consequently, history (and therefore politics) must not be thought of only in the form of a task to be performed or a value to be pursued. Rather, also, and before all else, it is to be thought of as a revelation, or a meaning, unfolding in its own way through the course of time. Hence the work of theology is not only ethical, but dogmatic or hermeneutic as well. In its capacity as a hermeneutics, theology seeks to discover God's "truth" (God's revelation) in and concerning history and society. In its capacity as an ethics, theology, from a basis in this first line of activity, seeks to identify the socio-historical imperatives, incumbent upon Christians and human beings in general, that spring from God's plan, from the utopia of the kingdom of God—even "from the eschatological horizon." Consequently, the theology of the political is not simply an "applied theology," but is, at bottom, a "dogmatic theology" as well, and indeed especially.[25]

The second distorting limitation of "social theology" has to do with the *method* of that theology. This limitation carried its defect from its very conception. Not taking any account of the profane density of the political, and of its potential theological significance, the "social theology" approach was satisfied with a pure and simple *transposition* of the rules of private morality to the political sphere. Using a basically taxonomic model, it enunciated a whole series of norms it judged ought to guide the private life and activity of the individual Christian in the area of social practice. Thus the difference in levels between conscience and structures, between individual subjectivity and political subjectivity, was completely ignored and sidestepped.

This kind of theology, woven of pure principles (pure because abstract) did not enjoy the necessary conditions for drawing up anything more than an abstract ethical practice—that is, a morality measured by the dimensions of the individual conscience and by the intentions of the individual Christian. It was powerless to pronounce upon effective means to concrete ends. All these questions were left to a laissez-aller and a laissez-faire of private conscience, whose contradictory imperatives in the presence of other, private practices were resolved in and by an ideology of "pluralism."[26]

It is not difficult to see that such a morality was deprived of any concrete, nonspeculative perception of the social object of which it treated. The criticisms lodged against it in terms of abstractionism and ahistoricism were and are valid.[27]

I have been speaking until now of classic "social morality." If I wished to be more exhaustive, I should have to refer as well to particular orientations of that morality. Among them could be ranged the "political theology" inspired by scholasticism,[28] the classic German *politische Theologie*,[29] and the current inspired by it, which gave its stamp of approval to German nationalism,[30] and then the current opposed to it, whose outstanding figure was Karl Barth.[31] I might even go on to cite the "new political theology,"[32] and others besides.

From a strictly methodological standpoint, entirely apart from their respective ideological positions, none of these currents really adopted firm socio-analytic mediations. They fenced themselves in with hermeneutic mediations, at times succeeding in assuming socio-speculative (in preference to socio-positive) mediations.

The observations just made lay no claim to constitute a critique in abstraction from the respective historical and cultural contexts of the currents alluded

to, or from their "potential degree of awareness" (L. Goldmann). The purpose
of my remarks has been to point up the difference, and the urgency, of the relationship between a theology of the political and the sciences of the social, as I
approach this relationship here in part 1.

§4 THE CULTURAL IMPERATIVE
OF SOCIO-ANALYTIC MEDIATION

Before I proceed, it will perhaps be well to recall the theoretical locus from
which I propose to launch my reflections. I might say that I am pursuing a discourse here whose object is the theoretical practice of the theology of the political. What is at stake, then, is precisely *theological reason.* I shall be discussing
the theoretical possibility and practical necessity of the production of a theology of the political that will be rigorously scientific, thanks to a syntax that will
have borne up under rigorous examination.

It should be clear from the outset that it is not my intent to reduce the whole
language of the faith to *theological* discourse alone, and thus deny all legitimacy to other discursive practices of faith, such as the prophetic, the mystical,
the pedagogical or catechetical, and so on. There is no doubt that these discourses have their specificity, and may legitimately be brought to bear upon the
political itself, from a point of departure in their own syntax, and in a manner
appropriate to the locus and moment of their intervention within a determined
socio-historical conjuncture.[33]

What seems to me to be required today, with regard to these unquestionably
legitimate discursive practices, is the epistemological determination of the theological *logos* in virtue of which they confront political problems. Surely there
are advantages in reserving the name "theology" to a discourse built upon a
particular, established grammar. To confer this appellation on *all religious discourse,* such as those just listed, would be to betray a rather poor understanding of what is at issue. The very difference between theological discourse and
other religious discourse would be suppressed. The issue here is not just a word
whose use is largely bound up with social conveniences and conventions. The
issue here is the *denotation* of the word "theology," the theoretical demands it
signals, and the opportunities for reasoning that it offers.

It seems to me that it has been the new situation of faith today, challenged as
it is by the present historical moment, that has come to require of theology a
new theoretical rigor. In the past, before society constituted a conscience problem (in virtue of the relative coincidence of society and conscience), it was still
possible to practice a speculative discourse, whether philosophical or theological, upon social reality. By reason of the feeble degree of development of its
social relationships, society "went along by itself," in a certain sense, without
major problems. However, from the moment it became a problem for itself on
the level of practice (in its manner of organization), due to the particular historical situation that had emerged for European society at the end of the eighteenth
century, it became evident that at the level of theory as well (in the manner of

comprehension), there was going to have to be a change—society was going to have to try to understand itself in a consistent and organized theoretical manner. This appears to have been the context of the appearances of the human sciences, especially those that deal with society.[34] Thus the critical state in which Western societies found themselves, at times beset with the concrete problems of a new social reordering, sounded a very powerful call and demand for a conscious, reflected intervention of society upon itself.[35]

Christian reflection, for its part, reacted to this phenomenon of civilization from a point of departure in the idiosyncratic determinations of the ecclesiastical institution. The latter was tied to the old order of things. It was bound up with feudalism, which was precisely what was being called into question. The manner in which it reacted consisted in a leap into the past—into the Middle Ages—appropriately idealized. In the area of Catholic intellectual life, the neo-scholastic movement is partly to be explained by this yen for the past. The church had assimilated the movement of history only slowly and reluctantly; now the same occurred with respect to the corresponding movement of culture, expressed in the nascent human sciences.[36]

At all events, today theology can no longer afford to remain a stranger to the new *episteme*—under pain of having to remain prisoner of the prehistory of the human sciences, and thus of being condemned to accept as the ideology of tomorrow what is already outdated today. For that theology must be considered "ideological" that is content with a philosophico-anthropological discourse, and remains mute vis-à-vis the social relationships of human beings—for example, their class situation, political position, and the like—reducing itself to the detection of the common traits of all human beings in their transcendentality.

In these terms, any humanism supported by such anthropological theology can only be an ideology.[37] Not that a transcendentalizing theological reflection is deprived of all titles of legitimation. Such reflection can even be necessary, in the capacity of a philosophical mediation for a first theology. What I am saying is that theological humanism can *no longer* occupy the place of a theology of the political having a bond with praxis. It can no longer arrogate the *whole* space of the theological problematic. Unless it acknowledges the appearance of a new series of questions, with which the human sciences now deal, and accepts its place in a dialectic with this new positivity—for example, in its capacity as socio-analytic mediation for a second theology—it will probably take flight for the cloudy skies of ideology and disappear.

Thus an approach like that of Augustine's *De Civitate Dei,* or Thomas Aquinas's *De Regimine Principum,* is clearly far from adequate as a response to the current socio-historical problematic. The integration of the new positivity of the sciences of the human being—socio-analytic mediation—is the indispensable *theoretical* condition today for rigorous theological discourse, and the essential *practical* condition for the insertion of such discourse into (political) praxis. This is the opinion, for that matter, of the most capable theologians today. But it is especially the stance of politicized Christians who are making an effort to reflect on their faith in a manner appropriate to their new historical tasks.[38]

§5 MARX'S CRITIQUE OF THEOLOGY

The need for an essential relationship between theology and the sciences of the social is felt in a particularly acute way when we examine Marx's critique of the Hegelian theology of his time—accusing it of mystifying real problems by being speculative and abstract.

We can still draw profit from this critique today.[39] I shall not discuss the specific case of the Marxian critique of religion here. Rather I shall direct attention to Marx's criticism of theology, specifically the theology of the "young Hegelians," notably Bruno Bauer and D.F. Strauss. Let us note that Marx works from a standpoint of praxis. His aim is to work out a real solution for the real problems of his times.

Marx's program can be summed up in this formula:

> We do not turn secular questions into theological questions. We turn theological questions into secular ones.[40] The *criticism of theology* [turns into] the *criticism of politics.*[41]

Marx's principal complaint with respect to theology, which he likened to Hegelian speculative philosophy, is that it offers a spiritual, ideal solution for material, real problems. According to Marx, theology "de-reifies" concrete contradictions, volatilizing them, dissolving their material density, in such wise as to transform them into spiritual entities, entities "outside reality." Thus theology operates as an abstraction from the world and from reality, a withdrawal from reality—in a word, a phantasmagoria. This form of thought, Marx says, is "the transcendent, abstract expression of the actual . . . state of things and real human beings."[42]

For Marx, theology is a religious system—a "theoretical ideology," as his disciple Althusser would later say. Religion, for Marx, is an alienated theory—alienated in the second degree, because it is the alienation of an already alienated world. Theology, in sum, is *the (inverted) science of the inverted consciousness of a perverted world.*[43]

In Marx's eyes, discourses on morality[44] or love[45] disguise the reality of alienation, and deceive human beings, constituting "the phantasmatic expression of the existing world."[46] And he continues:

> From the religious viewpoint, the answer to all real *questions* can consist only in certain *images* full of religious emphasis, which stifle all meaning in a thick cloud. It can only consist in grandiloquent titles, like "human race," "humanity," "species," and the like, and in the transformation of any real *action* into a *fantastic verbal formula.*[47]

Illusory, spiritualizing solutions of this kind demobilize human energies, Marx holds, and consequently fail to produce any results. The old world goes on as before.

But what is Marx's own solution for this problem, which, he thinks, theology is powerless to explain and resolve?

His first step is to *de-theologize* problems. We see this in his approach to a particular problem, "the Jewish question":

> Since Bauer . . . saw in [Judaism] "merely" a religious significance, it could be foreseen that the emancipation of the Jews, too, would be transformed into a philosophical-theological act. . . .
>
> We are trying to *break with the theological formulation of the question.* For us, the question of the Jew's capacity for emancipation becomes the question: What particular *social (gesellschaftlich) element has to be overcome in order to abolish Judaism?* . . .
>
> Let us consider the actual, worldly Jew, not the Sabbath Jew, as Bauer does, but the *everyday Jew.*
>
> Let us not look for the secret of the Jew in his religion, but let us look for the secret of his religion in the real Jew.[48]

Here we have the spirit of the Marxian critique of speculative theology. It is simply "ideology." It explains things the wrong way around. Theology, Marx holds, simply explains nothing at all. It does nothing but give a *symbolic* solution for *real* problems. But real problems call for real solutions, and the only way to provide them is by learning the real causality of these real problems. By taking care of this first step, one acquires the tools to apply a real remedy to problems equally real.

In Marx's opinion, theology does just the opposite. It dissolves concrete problems by giving them an abstract solution. It effectuates a *metabasis eis allo genos,* an (illegitimate) extrapolation to another order of things. And human beings and their world go on unchanged.[49] The effective suppression of prevailing life conditions, however, entails the suppression of theology, as an illusory system for explaining these same conditions—which in turn engender theology.[50]

Faced with this criticism theology generally reacts with an apologia. And this is justifiable, in part at least, inasmuch as the spiritual imperialism—the "spiritualism"—that it is accused of creating in religion is countered by Marx with a materialism that in theologians' eyes can be no less imperialistic. Still, we must give Marx credit for enabling us to see that a theology (or, antecedently, even a faith) that fails objectively to recognize a given real historical situation and do it justice, necessarily spins out a vacuous discourse bereft of any credibility—a "mystifying" discourse.

Consequently, *since Marx, it is no longer permissable to theologize as before with regard to social problems.* And to the extent that theology continues to ignore an etiological approach to these problems, this critique will be justified. It will have no alternative but to continue its own basic antitheological position.

The touchstone of the authentic response of theology to this critique will be whether it will be able to accept the truth it contains without losing out entirely. And this is just exactly what the challenge of socio-analytic mediation is all about.[51]

§6 TWO REGIMES OF THEOLOGICAL PRACTICE

My position on the relationship of the theology of the political to praxis by way of socio-analytic mediation raises a series of problems concerning the very concept of a theology of the political as an articulate discourse. For the thesis linking theology to praxis can lead either to the *empiricism* of a theology drawn immediately from praxis and directly treating of praxis, or to the *pragmatism* of a theology directly oriented to praxis or managed directly for the benefit of praxis. Theology can be conceived in such a way that it seems to have no other determinations than those of praxis as such. Its rules of practice would be dictated to it by praxis itself. Thus it would be no more than a simple "reflex" on the part of extrinsic interests.

At the other extreme, it can happen that theology is considered as absolutely disconnected from any historical context. It would transcend history and praxis, as if it had no relationship to them. This, in my view, is an *idealistic, speculative* conception of theology.

Let us note that this is not a specific problem of theology, but one common to other disciplines, as well. This is the debate that so vigorously agitates scientific circles today, especially where any *political implications* of science are concerned. Indeed it would appear that no science of our day has escaped involvement in this discussion.[52] Positions in the debate are diametrically polarized between the two extreme points just cited: empiricism or pragmatism, and idealism or theoreticism.[53]

In sum, then, such are the characteristic positions of the two orientations, each depending basically on an option—the one for justice and the other for truth, the one for political practice and the other for scientific practice. It would be simplistic and pretentious to deny either of these positions its partial truth. The task is to grasp the articulation of these partial truths.

In order to shed a little more light on this twilight zone, I shall here propose a thesis—one whose exact comprehension will be of capital importance for the whole remainder of this study. When I take up the question of theory and practice in general (in part 3), I shall have occasion to resume and amplify the schematic observations that are about to follow, because theory and practice are precisely the subject upon which this thesis bears. But it will be important to set forth the principles of this problematic right from the start. They are essential to a correct delineation of the theoretical status of theology, on the one hand, and of its social and political position, on the other.[54]

With respect to praxis, theology is both autonomous and dependent.

This formulation will at first seem self-contradictory. But even a casual second glance at the semantic content, or at the etymology of the key terms "autonomous" and "dependent," will suffice to reveal the possibility of their relationship, and thus dispel the initial impression.

Autonomy is simply that property of a being in virtue of which it is self-governed, or moves according to its own law. This notion attaches to the internal structure, the immanent logic of the being in question. Autonomy regards the "within," the essence side of a thing.

Dependence, on the other hand, regards the "without" of the thing, its existence side. It suggests an extrinsic relationship, in the form of the effective conditions for setting in motion the logic to which I have just referred. And so an autonomous system can very well be in dependence upon external factors, to which it is related in its concrete effectuation, as in other determinations of existence.

Moving now to the application of these two categories to the practice of a given discipline—in our case, to theological practice—I may say that the first term, "autonomy," is the note attaching to the proper mode of the functioning of theology. Its set of norms is not bestowed upon it from without, is not dictated from a point of departure in extrinsic instances. Theology possesses, interiorly, its own constituents and raison d'être, even when its chosen purpose is to spin in a vacuum. From this standpoint, then, theology need render no accounting of its practice to any exterior instance, be it politics, science, or what-have-you. It is self-constituted. Thus theology is *auto-nomous* in the Kantian sense—that is, it is subject only to the law that it imposes on itself.

And so I take a position against the pragmatist conceptualization that attempts to avail itself of the theological enterprise as a purveyor of one or another type of pastoral or political service. If this were legitimate, theology would be no more than the *voice of praxis*. It would have no other name than that of ideology, precisely in virtue of its inability to stand on its own feet without immanent, consciously-established determinations. Indeed, from the moment this "theology" might congratulate itself on having been "realized"—consumed—in and by praxis, it would have lost all interest for this very praxis, becoming nothing more than a "simulacrum," a lifeless instrument available for all manner of utilization, even contradictory uses.

My theses must be clear from this point forward, even though their demonstration will have to wait until part 3. First, then: it is not the social positioning of a theological production, or its political teleology, or even its thematic relevance, that will determine its *theoretical quality*. A theological practice as such is the only "culprit" when it comes to the criteria of its grammar—the conjunct of rules organizing its discourse. Thus a judgment on its "truth" can be pronounced only within its own epistemological perimeter, even with respect to "experimental verification."

Now let us move on to the *dependence* of theology with respect to praxis, to society—to the world, that is, and history. On this level, theology is a concrete praxis, effectuated by concrete agents, and issuing in concrete results, thanks to theoretical and technical tools that are equally concrete. Thus the discipline of theology, like that of any other science, is inserted in a complex network of material and historical determinations that situate it in a particular location within the socio-historical field. All theory is susceptible of geographical location and historical dating. Consequently, all theory is dependent on multiple conditions of production: materials, cultures, policies, politics, and so on; and hence its results can be directed toward this or that social, political, or other objective, and so on.

Consequently I must assert: unlike the internal relationship of autonomy, which is defined as a *theoretical-truth relationship,* the relationship of dependency is defined as a *practical-function relationship.* It can take many forms, such as that of technical application, political utilization, ethical mediation, and so on.

Let us observe, however, that the distinction between the internal regime of autonomy and the external regime of dependence in a given discipline is a purely formal distinction, even though it does enjoy a *fundamentum in re.* Obviously both aspects coexist. It is only by means of an abstractive operation of the mind that they can be differentiated for the purpose of better perceiving the articulation, with its implications, prevailing between them. My distinction is drawn with a view to watching how they work together. We "distinguish in order to unite," as Maritain would say. And this is how any science can be said to be at once *neutral* and *committed.*[55]

When it comes to the concrete order of existence, therefore—the level of actual theoretical practice—these two dimensions are difficult to contradistinguish in their respective specificities. For the moment I shall have to be content with having set forth the viewpoint from which, it seems to me, the question lies a little more in the light. I believe that the analytical distinction I have suggested will furnish a conceptual tool calculated to enable me to put a modicum of order in my delineation of the epistemological identity of theology and its relationship to praxis.[56]

Here an objection may be raised. Someone may say that theological language bears upon meaning and value, not facts and structures, which is the preserve of the positive sciences; therefore "theological truth" is necessarily "functional" (it is "salvific truth"), but it is ordered to finalities external to knowledge.

Here I must simply respond that knowledge of a thing is not to be confused with the thing itself. Theology indeed treats of values, but it does not follow that theological knowledge is identical with such values.

Further: theology speaks of *the good* only under the aspect of the true. This is a necessity flowing from the very nature or structure of reason, whose transcendental object is precisely truth.[57]

It is possible, therefore, for the intelligence to exercise its function upon meanings and values with the aim of judging their "truth," and of thus determining "true" values, "authentic" meanings. It is not legitimate to reduce the responsible, serious exercise of reason to the area of the positive sciences alone. Theological reason has at its disposal a syntax of its own, proportioned to its theoretical object, which prevents it from saying simply everything imaginable.

In this sense, it is always necessary to apply the capital distinction between *real* object and *theoretical* object. The God of the theologians is and can only be a *theoretical* object, and the theologian cannot pretend otherwise; whereas the God of the believer is and can only be a *real* object.[58] To confuse these two levels is to be prevented from doing theology. On the strictly theological level, one simply must say: knowledge of salvation is no more salvific than knowledge of sugar is sweet.[59]

§7 IDEO-POLITICAL VIGILANCE AND OTHER CONSEQUENCES

The relationships of any science—be it explicative (as a study of structures) or comprehensive (as a study of meanings)—to the socio-historical reality around it constitute a kind of network, whose lines of intersection possess multiple functions—technical, strategic, political, ethical, and so on.

The internal and external vectors of a discipline are not, however, without their interconnections. Any given science or body of knowledge is constituted, and effectively exists, only within a society, at a definite moment in history, with a view to concrete interests, and so on. The sense of a "scientific policy" is precisely to govern the production, distribution, and consumption of scientific and cultural products in general. This makes "truth" a kind of commodity. Its status as such may be readily gathered, first of all from the fact of the "scientific policy" of a state, and then from manifold social practices—for example, in pedagogy (where the level of instruction is conformed to the personal development of the learner), diplomacy (for instance, in the matter of state secrets), professional work (professional secrets), the media, or trade.

Thus there is no such thing as total science, any more than there is such a thing as total truth. Not the most scientific theory, not the most metaphysical speculation, not the most mystical discourse can avoid concrete insertion within a mesh of socio-historical determinations. There it will exercise an objective function, perhaps even develop an objective meaning distinct from the subjective intention of its surroundings.

The absolute control of knowledge is doubtless an ultimately unattainable goal, by the very fact that it presupposes what it would control—knowledge.[60] However, this does not militate against the fact that the procurement of knowledge will be marked, at least implicitly, by all sorts of conditionings.

Applying this general condition of science to the science of theology, it is evident that it too is subject to the play of particular historical and political determinations. From this it follows that theologians must pay careful attention to external influences on their practice. Theologians will have to exercise an *ideo-political vigilance* with regard to institutional incursions, political or other, on their research or findings. Theologians are called upon to acquire the ability to view less and less ingenuously their socio-historical context, and to relate to that context in a spirit of critique of the political conjuncture of the moment.

In virtue of its double capacity in terms of the normalized interpretation (hermeneutics) of revelation and the inculcation of moral attitudes (ethics), theology is absolutely incapable of remaining insensitive to the ethico-political effects of its own discourse.

Further: theology is likewise called to take account of the distinction to be made between subjective intentions and objective results.[61] In no case are the latter subject to total control, owing to the very nature of social mechanics. Therefore political theology, watchful as it must be with regard to the political effects of its practice, must also, in virtue of this same watchfulness, be on guard against any voluntarism that ascribes to intentions a power for change that they do not possess. Here is a norm that cannot be codified—recipelike—in formularies, but must be learned in practice as such.[62]

In order that the principle of ideo-political vigilance be grasped in appropriate terms, it will be most helpful to notice something else here. In terms of its autonomy, theology, in order to be constituted theology, prescinds from its relationship to socio-historical mediations. This it can do in virtue of its methodological *epoche,* which opens it out upon a space and a time that are specifically theoretical.[63] This is a function of the intellect, which "brackets" the world around the empirical "I," in order to develop, in the realm proper to reason, its own text, according to the laws of a particular syntax.

In terms of its dependence, theology cannot practice a *real* abstraction from the world, for it is inevitably incorporated into the world. Not merely its raw material, but its product, the conditions of its operation, and the like, pertain to the factuality of the historical world. Everything that constitutes the material body, as it were, of a discipline—agents, places, estimates, plans, resources, and so on—is bound up with the conditioning of its socio-historical reality. Endowed though it be with a logic of its own, theoretical functioning is not possible in reality except as articulated upon a determinate social space.[64]

It will not do, then, to separate—still less, to confuse—*theoretical locus* and *sociological locus.* The former is found on the level of reason, and appeals to its faculty of transcendence with respect to the world. The latter occurs on the level of society, as locus of historical inscription of all practice.

My explanations here are intended to show how a theology concerned with its relationship to society can spare no theoretical efforts to take cognizance of this relationship. Otherwise the relationship itself will be disturbed and distorted, and practice will be served by an unreliable, fragile instrument. To be sure, it is precisely the relationship to praxis that ultimately drives theology to reflect upon its own theoretical status. But it is no less true that only on condition of so reflecting can theology be of any genuine use to the practice of the faith.

With this fundamental distinction established between the regime of autonomy and the regime of dependence, I trust that we are now in possession of the conceptual means to arrive at a somewhat clearer understanding of why a theology seeking to be "rigorous" and "scientific," and therefore ignoring and even denying its relationship to history, cannot complain if it is accused of being "alienated," "irrelevant," or "reactionary." After all, it is enmeshed in history in a fashion that really deserves these labels. Even if it manages to construct "true" and "orthodox" theories, this "serious" theology, ignoring as it does the imperatives of the historical moment, will be sweeping real problems under the rug, and directing its thinking far off course with respect to the urgent, and sometimes dramatic, challenges and opportunities of certain social situations.[65]

On the other hand, I am equally well aware that it is possible for a theology to take up a correct strategic position in the face of a historical movement and at the same time display a lack of any adequate theoretical quality. In this case, there will be the real danger that this theology will totally submit to the exigencies of immediate objectives, and fail to take a satisfactory critical distance.

Let it be noted that I am leaving out of account here the extreme case of the use and abuse of theology, without the least respect for its proper content, when its products are played with and manipulated at will. This malpractice does not even merit the name of "ideology." We ought to come right out and call it what it is: "theoretical vandalism." Political vigor is not another name for theoretical rigor.

If my theses are tenable, then it is possible to be a "good theologian" and still be on the "margin of history"—just as one can very well be "committed" and yet be a mediocre theologian. There are two distinct sorts of problems here, as Nietzsche once observed: "Objectivity and truth are two things having nothing to do with each other."[66]

Finally, I must add that the two aspects we have been considering can subsist in concrete mutual articulation, so that theological truth can be practiced in history, and political practice can be a "true" practice. Here we have a dialectic, at full throttle. Only in motion does theology stay healthy, true, and historically fertile. But I shall take this up in part 3.

CHAPTER 2

Formal Establishment of
Socio-Analytic Mediation

§8 EMPIRICISM: ABSENCE OF SOCIO-ANALYTIC MEDIATION

The preceding chapter intended to demonstrate that, if theology seeks to articulate praxis—first that of Christians, then that of human beings in general—it will have to be mediated by the sciences of the social.[1] But the relationship between theology and the sciences of the social is determined, in the last analysis, by praxis as such. I have also singled out the principles that will permit the relationship between theology and practice to avoid both empiricism or pragmatism, and idealism or "theoreticism."

In the present chapter, I proceed to the formal establishment of socio-analytic mediation. How, or in what terms, is the relationship between theology and socio-analytic mediation to be founded?

First, however, I must deal with certain "epistemological obstacles" that hinder the correct and orderly establishment of this relationship. The value of this preliminary investigation will lie in its heuristic potential—that is, in the help it can provide in identifying the real configuration of my discourse, which is a theological discourse, and still more specifically, a politico-theological discourse. This discourse is susceptible of detailed analysis.[2]

I see five principal types of "epistemological obstacle" to a theology of the political: (1) empiricism, or the absence of socio-analytic mediation; (2) methodological purism, or the exclusion of socio-analytic mediation; (3) theologism, or the substitution of theological methodology for socio-analytic mediation; (4) "semantic mix," or badly done socio-analytic mediation; and finally, (5) "bilingualism," or poorly integrated socio-analytic mediation.

First, then, let us consider the obstacle posed by empiricism, which seems to me to be the basic one for a theology of the political.

I begin with an example. Take the case of a theology that would undertake a reflection on a determinate historical situation or political practice. This theology might simply undertake to discourse upon its chosen object as if it had immediate contact with its reality—as if its gaze had penetrated it directly and

20

in depth—so that it could start out immediately with its own discourse. This intuitionist position is actually due to an empty impression, an illusory impression: that of the pseudo evidence of immediacy. This is at the basis of all empiricism.

My own position is that there is no such thing as an absolutely immediate reading of the real—here, of the social. No object of cognition offers its truth completely naked. Even when, and especially when, it presents the appearance of overwhelming, absolute transparency, the reading of reality is still the reading of a code, and this code is read in alphabets whose seeming immediate spontaneity is merely the product of "habit"—that is, of the degree of internalization of the culture to which these alphabets belong.[3]

Thus any theological reading of any socio-historical phenomenon whatsoever will include or imply a conscious or unconscious theory to make possible and define that reading. Nor is all this a matter of option. It is bound up with the structure of cognition itself—the structure of the way that thinking accosts the world.

The potential distinction, and therefore the possible option, is not, then, between a theology that has recourse to socio-analytic mediation and a theology that dispenses with all interpretation of the social. The only real alternatives are a theology mediated by a *critical* reading of its proper object and a theology mediated by an *uncritical* reading of the same. The first alternative outfits itself with adequate tools for its (real) approach to the (social) real, whereas the second merely apprehends the real through a reading grid of which it is unconscious. A critical reading is equipped for approaching the real, whereas a noncritical reading, unthinkingly dispensing with any mediation, actually captures only its own illusion of the real.

In other words, there is always mediation—critical or acritical, disciplined or spontaneous.

But, then, what of the oft-repeated enjoinder to "start with the facts," to "take your point of departure in concrete reality," and so on?[4]

This may be mere polemics, wielded by observers who see a real problem but who are powerless to understand it. Lacking analysis and critique, this sort of theoretical stance can lead to manifold misunderstandings, and can end by depriving theology of all hope of substantive language.

The benefit of such exhortations is that they encourage theological reflection to take up a position in contact with concrete praxis. They provoke thinking to get to work on the real urgencies that constitute a challenge to faith and to thinking the faith.

Meanwhile, as we say, the facts do not "speak for themselves." Facts are mute. Before they can speak, they have to be questioned. The "concrete" object of "concrete thinking" does not exist in a raw state, does not exist in some absolute "in itself," as an absolutely immediate datum. *"Les faits sont faits,"* says Bachelard—facts are made. *Les donnés sont donnés,* I might paraphrase—data are indeed *given,* not found "as is"—and objects are "objected," cast athwart thinking by thinking itself.

There is no such thing, then, as "zero degree subjectivity," some objectivity so complete and total that the knowledge of a thing would coincide with the thing itself. This is an exclusively divine privilege. Human cognition, alas, can be activated only from a point of departure in objects that have been subjected to some antecedent elaboration or other. The whole sweep of the cultural history of humanity is witness. This is valid for the spontaneous awareness of common sense, and it is valid a fortiori where critical awareness is concerned. The latter begins with an object that has already been "worked." But it takes it up in order to *re*work it. In this sense, scientific reason *constructs* its theoretical object, making use of its own proper instruments, in a manner calculated to produce reliable results in the form of knowledge. Knowledge is not gathered, and still less is it assimilated, by reflex. Knowledge is produced.[5]

We must realize, then, that critical mediation operates at the very heart of scientific practice. "Criticity" is the constitutive property of the scientific exercise. It enables science to create a distance between thinking and its object, in order to be able to regard it as ob-ject indeed. To this end it constructs a concept, by which it apprehends the object in its own way—that is, theoretically, which is the only way it can apprehend it. This is the process of "objectivization."

A theology, therefore, that would seek to grasp "the facts," grasp "concrete reality," and so on, without the "detour" of the appropriate nontheological disciplines, would not really grasp "the facts" at all—would not really grasp "concrete reality," however it might think it were doing so. What it actually grasped would be certain current, ideological images that common sense forms of facts. Thus, for example, a political theology that assumes it can overlap the profane disciplines that give access to the political, and believes that it thereby places itself in the very heart of the political, would necessarily only come up with assumptions disguised as facts, and concern itself with them instead of with the real.

In the present state of development of the social sciences, such an attitude on the part of theology is anachronistic, if not simply ignorant, even granting the still problematic state of these disciplines.

Just so, one may well wonder whether the theological gaze is not a particular, proper gaze, situated *alongside* other "gazes"—rather than behind them as if spying across their shadows.[6]

Here we doubtless have a defensible thesis. But in the case of a theology having the political for an object, the adoption of a *lateral* position relative to the other disciplines will have a tendency to distort the autonomous, profane nature of the object that it has so assumed. Deprived of a criticized content, this object will, like so many other related instances of "evidence," run the risk of evacuation of any theoretical content but that consigned it by the dominant culture.[7] Therefore "natural" (scientific) knowledge must be considered to constitute the basis of theological cognition—as indeed theological tradition itself has always admitted.

Theological practice as such has no means whatever of coming to know the "profane" fabric of the political object it proposes to "work." In its capacity as a hermeneutics, theology undertakes to deliver religious significations—not causal structures or concatenations. But significations can arise only from a point of departure in the real as really known. If theologians read a faulty text, there can be no doubt that their interpretations will mirror the defects of the text.

In the area of the potential political practice of Christians in search of an expression of their sense of faith, then, it is plain that a theological reading of a badly restored text can only obstruct comprehension of the political situation in question—can only constitute an obstacle to lucid intervention by theology. Such is the fate of a theology that would cheerfully dispense with all mediation, which it feels is an embarrassment to the spontaneous thrust of its own discourse.

At the same time, let us bear in mind that we are dealing here with an object falling directly within the domain of another discipline. We are dealing with the political. Surely we must assume that the theoretical mediations to be engaged by theology must evidently themselves be mediated by the structure of the theoretical object in question. In treating of a first theology, then, it is clear that socio-analytic mediation could be irrelevant, and have to yield to other mediations, such as the historical, the philosophical, the philological, and the like, according to the case at hand. Would the epistemological status of the "auxiliary sciences" be any different from socio-analytic mediation? It would seem not.

To summarize what I have said in this section, then, for the purpose of clarifying the placement of the various moments of the real in a scale of degrees, which, although seeming to distance us from the real, actually lead us to it, in inverse proportion to each successive degree:

a) At zero epistemological degrees from the real, we take the real simply and utterly as itself, in its absolute *in se,* inaccessible as such to all thought other than a thought perfectly coinciding with it, if not indeed actually constituting it: the divine thought.
b) At one degree of distance, we have the idea of the real extracted by everyday "common sense," which will be the content of the current, perhaps dominant, ideology.
c) At two degrees of distance, we have the critical cognition of the sciences, which breaks with ordinary knowledge and opens up its own special route to the real, in virtue of the concept and the theory that it constructs for this purpose.
d) At three degrees of distance, finally, we have theological cognition—for us, the cognition of a theology of the political.

This schema may be summary, perhaps indeed distorting, rather like the empiricism it is intended to combat.[8] But it will serve as a basis from which to renounce, most emphatically, a false opposition between abstract and concrete, between theory and practice—the illusion that lies at the heart of all empiricism. My schema shows how illusory this false opposition really is. It spawns a great number of "critiques of theology," which would not be so disconcerting were they not so frequent and widespread. We actually hear of an opposition between "concrete theology" and "abstract theology," and even "revolutionary theology" and "reactionary theology," which is absurd.

What is objectionable in such language is not its possible ideo-political justification, its conjunctural correctness, which of course is what it is concerned for—but precisely its nature as jargon substituting for analysis, and especially its theoretical claim, which is actually contradictory. This is a language that confounds politics with theory, denunciation with critique, sincerity with logic, struggle with rigor. In a word, it confounds the two regimes of knowledge, of science—and baldly exchanges the code of one system for that of another.

The empiricist ideology of concrete versus abstract, practical versus theoretical, throws up an epistemological obstacle to the foundation of socio-analytic mediation, and of a disciplined theology generally.[9] The fact is that political reality in its absolute purity, which political empiricism claims to grasp, of itself yields up neither its political secret nor its religious mystery. Anything it delivers is only in virtue of, respectively, a political or religious "grammar" masquerading as the "natural feeling" to which its internalization has given rise.

§9 METHODOLOGICAL PURISM: EXCLUSION OF SOCIO-ANALYTIC MEDIATION

The notion of a mediated theology, the subject of our discussion, encounters numerous difficulties, especially at the most basic level: that of the construction of a method.

Having examined empiricism, I turn now to another epistemological obstacle—an obstacle to theological method. It might be expressed in the form of an objection: theology has its own proper status, and has had, all through tradition. Therefore it has no need to address itself to other disciplines, to ask their permission to theologize, and still less need to ask them how to do so.[10]

It must be acknowledged that it does indeed belong to theology to say what it thinks, as well as how to say it. Its own foundational discourse, a kind of metatheology, enables it to be autonomous in this regard, and no epistemological extrinsicism can be legitimate for it. It is perfectly true that theology is possible only in its element—faith: it is revelation that furnishes it its principles for theorizing.[11]

There is something to be added, however. The purist observation addresses only part of the truth. Theological purism ignores the other side of the question, and the other side of the question touches the theology of the political in a very particular fashion. After all, when theology comes to treat a determinate raw material, it must take steps to inform itself precisely as to what it is about to treat. And it is precisely here that the need arises for socio-analytic mediation as an integral part of the theological process—integral in the sense that this mediation prepares the text for theology to read, the raw material for it to transform.

Theological purism, rejecting the "intromissions" of other disciplines within the theological field of operation, corresponds in the area of epistemology to the *sola fides* attitude in the area of dogmatics.

What exactly is this self-styled "methodological purity"? Indeed, where is this "pure theology"?

As human discourse, *sacra doctrina* (to use the medieval term) is constructed from top to bottom of human material, in its workings (theologizing reason) as in its conceptual instruments, in its subject matter as in its concrete findings.

If by "pure theology" it is classic, first theology that is meant, then I must point out that, unlike faith itself, the disciplined discourse of faith does not and cannot have direct access to the objects of first theology. Theology disposes of no particular system of symbols or transparent concepts for dealing with these objects. Its language is not that of angels. Theology takes images, likenesses, and analogies drawn from human experience, already "worked" in some fashion by human culture, and weaves them into a discourse, in such wise as to suggest—point to as if with a finger—realities that faith actually possesses. And to this purpose theology can have recourse only to spontaneous reason—"common sense"—or critical reason—philosophy—such as it finds them at a given moment of historical development, and not as it would like to find them in some *hyperkosmos*.[12]

As a result, even on the level of a first theology, mediations of reason are ever present, however veiled or disguised.[13] No theology is without mediations, and if it thinks it is, it is deceiving itself. Here as well, the line of demarcation passes between a critically mediated theology and an acritically mediated theology.

Doubtless it is owing to a persistent confusion of the realities of faith with its scholarly discourse upon them that has caused theological consciousness to go astray here, and take itself, and hold itself forth, as transhistorical language. Suddenly knowledge of God is endowed with the very attributes of God, and the distinct, autonomous orders of reality and thought are confounded.[14] I shall return to this question below.

Of course, if "theological purity" is spoken of with respect to ideological or ideo-political intrusions into theological discourse, then we must indeed emphatically insist that theology is really "pure"—in the sense of being "autonomous": it is the legislator of its own law.

But in its capacity as a discourse of the *human being* on God, theology must be mediated. It was mediated in the past by philosophy. Now it is invited to be mediated by the sciences of the social when it treats of the social. This is the price of its fertility and validity.

Unless theology espouses, correctly and appropriately, the spirit of the new rationality of the sciences of the human, and casts off the false shame of its "methodological purity," it will not be able to provide for its future. It will be like a "virgin dedicated to God and barren," to quote a phrase used by Marx.[15]

§10 THEOLOGISM: SUBSTITUTION
FOR SOCIO-ANALYTIC MEDIATION

The epistemological obstacle that I call "theologism" has to do with method—the method used by theological *theory*.

Theologism consists in considering theological interpretation as the only true or adequate version of the real. This spirit leads the theologian to set up an artificial opposition between theological reading and other readings, as if the only legitimate reading were its own.[16] It criticizes the "materialism," or the "partiality," of other interpretations, as if the theological reading were total, and exhaustive of reality. Obviously, with this position there is no way to speak of socio-analytical mediation.

Theologism reigns where a theology pretends to find everything it needs to express the political within its own walls, whereas in fact it is missing something: the silent prerequisites available only in the sciences of the social, which are implied in any approach by theology to the political. Theologistic theology considers the political to be a simple self-evident reality. But by this very fact, such a theology can only be an ideological theology: it serves as the vehicle of the "immediate evidence" of the prevailing conceptualization of things.

Let us follow this singular theology, and try to see how it operates. What is it actually doing? Drawing its inspiration from certain supposedly "interesting" or "relevant" subjects or themes drawn from the "deposit of faith," or from the thematic arsenal of traditional theology, this thought simply takes up one matter after another as each seems to be suggested by the one that has gone before. Its method consists in a *free association of ideas,* replacing an *organization of ideas* from a point of departure in tested, verified principles.[17]

In a word, theologism in the theology of the political is a thinking that starts out: "Incidentally . . . ," and the only outcome can be a religio-political rhetoric. There will be no way for political notions not to settle in here, under the weight of content circulating at random in the symbolic market of the prevailing culture. The only result can be a sticky heap of ideas, of such a nature that theology must ask itself how it can make some sense out of a given socio-historical situation in order to intervene, in the light of faith, when and where the need may arise. But the language of this self-sufficient theology is left dancing on air, borne along as it is by "fluctuating significants," down river toward "significants on the loose."[18]

For want of a syntax to preside over the internal density of its discourse, we have a theology molded of empty, hollow sentences, reminding us of nothing so much as persons who can recite a message they do not understand, yet think it is they who are actually composing it.

For us today such a discursive practice can only be a kind of ideology. Today we are able to look at things in the rational consciousness of the human sciences. This is a practice, therefore, that, although justifiable and legitimate yesterday, today is so no longer. It *becomes* ideological, and this is how it appears to criticism that strips it of its mechanisms of dissimulation and pronounces it vanquished—ideological.

Thus we are led to see in theologism a basic epistemological obstacle to the formation of a suitable theology of the political. If theology regards with a jaundiced eye the other disciplines that bear on its material object—here, the political—how will it be able to articulate an enlightening discourse on this subject, and thus be able to inspire an appropriate praxis?

I shall leave this important matter to a later discussion. Still, even at this point it can be said that theologism is the *theoretical* correlative of the *practical* attitude that has come to be called "supernaturalism," or "spiritualism," or simply "mythology."[19] And so we find ourselves faced with a theology that performs the function—a specifically ideological function—of rationalizing a distorted practical orientation. This theology straddles a mythical conceptualization of the world, a two-story world of natural and supernatural, material and spiritual, temporal and eternal, earth and heaven, freedom and grace, body and soul, human and divine, and so on. These antithetical elements form, respectively, two universes, which if not contradictory, are at any rate isolated, like twin monads.

In a like mythologizing conceptualization, realities such as God, the Spirit, Christ, grace, sin, heaven, faith, judgment, *agape,* and so on, are as it were substantialized, transformed into separate, supernatural, autonomous entities situated on "the other side." The relationships they are presumed to maintain with the "sublunar world" are submitted to the jurisdiction of religion, which administers them through its system of dogmas, rites, and hierarchy.

Such a distorted understanding of the relationship between God and the world can only distort this other relationship, of the epistemological order, between theology and the sciences of the social. It is present, anonymously, in the ideologies of "Christendom," or "apoliticism," or even "faith without ideology."

Probably no one will acknowledge my description as a description of herself or himself, perhaps not even the unlettered Christian. This is unimportant. My viewpoint, that of the theory of theology, authorizes me to interrogate not theoretical intentions or declarations of orthodoxy, but products of reason and the de facto rules of their production. Thus, for example, despite criticisms of "demythologization" and "secularization"—criticisms that practically all will accept (nor is such acceptance very difficult)—we are still at considerable distance from a discourse governed by a grammar that does these phenomena justice.

Further: my "typical" descriptions claim no more than a "characteriological" value. Their intent is to permit me to sketch the profile of the obstacles I have cited, which, after all, is one of the objectives of this chapter.

§11 SEMANTIC MIX: FAULTY ARTICULATION OF SOCIO-ANALYTIC MEDIATION

It can now be seen, and demonstrated, that no theology concerned with the social in general and the political in particular can be "innocent of sociology"—some sociology.

Let us say, then, that a theology of the social has taken up the sciences of the social (in socio-analytic mediation) in a resolute, active way. (It may not be allowed to do so passively, taking up "social subjects" under pure historical pressure, cultural impregnation, or logical inevitability.) But it can happen that the "social theories" in the socio-analytic mediation of a given theology remain uncriticized, and are not appropriately assimilated, thus constituting foreign elements in the body theological, which for its part remains indeterminate and nondetermining.[20] In this case we have not an obstacle excluding socio-analytic mediation, but one nevertheless failing to permit its firm, correct articulation.

This type of discourse is adopted by a goodly number of the productions of the ecclesiastical magisterium bearing on "social problems."[21] But some political theologies, as well, fall prey to it, not locating their methodological instrumentation, their socio-analytic mediation, with exactitude. And so it fails to operate efficaciously.[22] This type of discourse is a *semantic mix*.[23]

In this case we have a group of discursive practices deprived of the spinal column of a socio-analytic mediation, leading to the development of a system of mixed language, drawing on resources in two distinct knowledge universes—the one of religious symbols, and the other of "profane" representations (social, political, and so on). The relationship between the two universes is neither exterior nor interior. They are simply mixed. But the resultant semantic mixture is always organized under the domination of the logic of one of the languages in question. In the case at hand, it is the system of the universe of religious discourse that presides over the whole. There is a tendency to empty the notions of the "profane" discursive universe of their proper content, in order to be able to fill them with a "spiritual" content. The process is not always obvious, but it can always be identified and examined.

As practiced by hierarchical jurisdictions of the church, this hybrid discourse seems to rely on an epistemological spontaneity, in virtue of which the magisterium would be in possession of a divine science received directly from God by way of revelation, in such wise that, through an act of substitution, the theology of the magisterium is suddenly considered as invested with a divine authority, and deemed to hold the keys of the secrets of the destiny of history and the world. Hence the confidence of these magisterial assertions.

This way of thinking considers timeless truth the only essential, important truth. Historical reality and empirical existence are devalued to the rank of contingent and secondary. And when judgement is passed on them, the analysis is empiricist, the explanation of the facts moralistic, and the solution therefore necessarily incapable of transcending the level of technocratism. This thinking is built on a refusal to acknowledge scientific mediations—doubtless a symptomatic refusal.[24]

What we have here is a certain ignorance with respect to the particular epistemological identity of a given discourse, or a consequent erroneous epistemological consciousness. The distortion comes to be expressed in a zeal for orthodoxy, indicating a basic insecurity in the face of the instability of external reality.[25]

These summary indications should be sufficient to afford an idea of the mixed status of certain theological discourses.

§12 BILINGUALISM: UNARTICULATED SOCIO-ANALYTIC MEDIATION

Closely related to "semantic mix," indeed scarcely distinguishable from it, is another epistemological obstacle dependent on language systems. I call it bilingualism.[26]

Bilingualism consists in practicing two readings of the real synoptically, as it were. It juxtaposes socio-analytic discourse and theological discourse, thus seeking to play two language games on the same field simultaneously, and hence contradictorily.

This epistemological intent seems viable at first sight. But unquestionably, it fails to be maintained over the long term. Inevitably the moment arrives when different interpretations come into conflict. Then the socio-analytic language attacks the theological language, "de-totalizing" and disorganizing it.

The outcome of this confrontation will take different forms. The language introduced the more recently may triumph, and finally occupy practically all the theoretical space formerly governed by the old language.[27] Or the theological language, dismembered but not destroyed, will shift elsewhere, take on a new, temporary identity, and so recoup the status of a uniform discourse.

The second case evidently constitutes a positive solution of the conflict in favor of theology. But the price is a more or less profound *recasting*.

Besides the two "solutions" just mentioned, other types of compromise can be invoked. One is the case of mixed language, which we have already seen, in which one of the competing discourses always prevails. But another is that of a sustained bilingualism, in which the contradiction is not dialectically resolved, yet the terms abide in mutual confrontation. Can such a position long be maintained? Will it not constitute a moment in a dialectical movement whose dénouement in favor of one or other of the two solutions, positive or negative, is sooner or later inevitable?[28]

I shall later have occasion, in part 2, to propose and explain a possible articulation between theological discourse and the discourse of the sciences of the social. It is enough for now to have identified the obstacles to this articulation, and to have given them a rough characterization. In so doing, I have opened the way, I think, to a statement, perhaps even a solution (at least by way of a first approximation), of the epistemological question of a harmonious, regulated relationship between theology and the sciences of the social.

§13 THE CONSTITUTIVE RELATIONSHIP BETWEEN THE SCIENCES OF THE SOCIAL AND THE THEOLOGY OF THE POLITICAL

Having removed the principal obstacles to a correct relationship between the theology of the political and the sciences of the social, I now propose to establish the formal terms of this relationship. To this purpose, I shall make use of a distinction whose power of elucidation seems to me adequate to express the manner in which theology integrates the contribution of the sciences of the social in the process of its practice. I refer to the distinction between a *relationship of application* and a *relationship of constitution*.[29]

A relationship of application obtains between any tool and any thing. It is an instrumental, technical, mechanical relationship. It supposes the autonomous duality of the elements that enter into reciprocal contact. This relationship consists in an "adjustment," a fitting together, extrinsic in nature—a simple juxtaposition. The relationship is extrinsic, a relationship of exteriority.

A relationship of constitution, by contrast, consists in an organic interchange in which each of the terms of the relationship shares in a vital way in the whole of which it is a part. In this type of relationship, the subject forms a real part of the object. It enters into its internal constitution. Here, then, we are in the presence of an intrinsic relationship, a relationship of interiority.

Let us ask ourselves which of these two types of relationship articulates the sciences of the social with the theology of the political. It seems to me that it is the second: the relationship of constitution, or interiority.

Where a first theology is concerned, it seems clear to me that a theological practice will not necessarily have to be mediated by the sciences of the social, although it is always possible for these sciences to be used here in the capacity of "auxiliary sciences" (from the side of the object), perhaps even in terms of a *recasting* (from the subject side).

On the other hand, it seems to me equally clear that in the area of a second theology—for our purposes, a theology of the political—the sciences of the social will be genuinely constitutive of the theoretical organization of a corresponding discourse. Indeed this is implied in the very name, "theology of the *political*." Now, if we consider the political here not as a merely speculative essence or material, but primarily under the formality of the historical, concrete praxis of concrete Christians and human beings, then we shall have to say that, owing to its particular, proper structure, the political will be knowable by the theologian only through the approach of the sciences of the social. *Hic Rhodus, hic salta!* What can a theologian say, not about the abstract nature of power or society, but precisely about that altogether determinate power or society in or under which Christians and human beings generally live, struggle, and die?[30]

I repeat: if theology seeks to address itself to, and pronounce upon, politics, it will have to know in advance what it is going to be discussing. It can fulfill this condition only through the mediation of disciplines furnishing positive knowledge. It becomes evident, therefore, that theology must first of all incline its ear to the sciences of the social if it hopes to escape the reproach of *ignoratio elenchi*. Otherwise it will be able to do nothing but fill the air with words after the fashion of a rhetoric. Its concepts will emerge reduced to pure phraseology, and so lose all credit.

It is true that theology has its own proper object. Its material object, nevertheless, can be offered, and even enriched, by other disciplines. The latter inform theology about what it is to treat. Thus the instruction of the theology of the political by the sciences of the social marks the former *intrinsically.*[31]

The reason for this is that a theological reading does not settle upon a sociological one by way of affixation or superimposition, but in a vital assimilation, a kind of metabolism. The articulation implied in such an assimilation remains under the regime of theology. Otherwise it is no longer theology. I must insist most emphatically on the constitutive character (at their own level) of the sciences of the social with respect to a theology of the political. But I must insist just as emphatically on the exact manner in which the relationship between the theology of the political and the sciences of the social is established.

The correct way to pose this relationship, in order to render it articulable, means, as we shall see in part 2, posing it in the following terms. The sciences of the social enter into the theology of the political as a *constitutive part.* But they do so precisely at the level of the raw material of this theology, at the level of its *material object*—not at that of its proper pertinency, or formal object. Thus although the theology of the political must lend an attentive ear to the sciences of the social, in order to gather from them information necessary for its discourse, neither this attention nor this gathering may be taken for what they are *not*—theology in the formal sense of the term. The undeveloped insertion of sociological material into theology without the care to rework it in accordance with the formal object of theology, so as to integrate it organically in an articulation of the whole, would be to betray both theology and the sciences of the social.

It must be said, then, that the sciences of the social furnish theology only with that upon which it is to ply its practice. Thus what for the sciences of the social is product, finding, or construct, will be taken up in the theological field as raw material, as something to be (re)worked by procedures proper to theologizing, in such wise as to issue in a *specifically* theological product, and one so characterized.

Until the "specifically theological" is produced, the work of the sociological deciphering of a social reality or phenomenon continues to be for theology a "not-yet-theological," or a "pretheological."

In sum: the text of a theological reading with respect to the political is prepared and furnished by the sciences of the social. Theology receives its text from these sciences, and practices upon it a reading in conformity with its own proper code, in such a way as to extract from it a characteristically, properly, theological meaning.

Consequently, it must be denied that the sociological and the theological subsist in the same continuum. A qualitative transition is at play, which may be called an *epistemological breach* or rupture.

§14 EXTENSION OF THE THEORETICAL FIELD OF THEOLOGY

In part 2 we shall be returning to the various moments of the articulation under discussion. In this section of part 1 my intention is to argue from the foregoing reflections to the following thesis: theology is theology of the nontheological.[32] The theological does not subsist *in se*. The theological is constructed, is won, *becomes* theological. The theologizable object (*teologal objeto*) is not the theological product (*teológico resultado*). This is precisely why there is such a thing as theology.

After all, a theologian reflects on a determinate object precisely in order to understand its theological signification. This is not found just lying there as if printed on the pages of an open book. It is extracted, through an effort of description. Theology, therefore, is not to be conceived as something static, like a deposit, or a sum-total of knowledge—but as something dynamic, a practice, a process, a labor, a production. Theological effort transforms the nontheological into the theological.

The basic ontological postulate for the nontheological to be able to become formally theological is its materially theological character. If God is actually the Meaning of the world and of history—and God is—then, in very principle, there cannot exist any object or event that cannot be theologized. Everything is theologizable.[33]

A theology of the political can exist only in virtue of this utterly basic, "principial," condition: that the political is susceptible of being theologized. Here is the essential postulate of the fertility of the political with respect to theology. Any political object must be able to be "theologically thought." Armed with this principle—that theology is theology of the non-theological—I shall now attempt to measure the extent of the theoretical field of the various possibilities open to a theology of the political.[34] As the limits of this field are staked out, we shall at the same time discover the thematic breadth to which a theology of the political can, in principle, lay claim.

To begin: a theologizing limited to the already-constituted theological would remain, in my opinion, in the order ranging from repetitive reflection to rabbinical commentary.[35] A theology of the political seeks precisely to break free of the narcissistic circle of this kind of theology, and brave the frontier country of a field where no formally theological object lies prepared, such as the field of a second theology.

We shall not have advanced far, however, if we take for our material the political object produced by biblical or theological tradition, and limit political theology to commentary, examination, and criticism of the various views of the past, or even present, concerning this political object. Doubtless this is a necessary labor. But by no manner of means is it the only one, or the most important one, if we seek a theology of the political engaged in the historical. Even changing the subject matter will not guarantee that we shall be able to avoid a theology constructed in as traditional a spirit as ever, with all the old risks of falling for the fads of the moment.

The root of this shortcoming is certainly to be found in the absence of a vital linkage with the historical moment and its challenges. This is a theoretical deficiency, suffered in virtue of a deficiency in practice—evidently not a deficiency inherent in the theory itself. At all events, the "thematic" of this parasitical theology is obviously overnarrow. At bottom, what we have here is a "theology of theology." There is no point in its attempting to develop into a theology of the political. What it will produce will be only a "political theology."[36]

A theology of what is non-Christian can be practiced, as well—not in the traditional sense of a Christian reflection on what is non-Christian, but in the more engaged sense of a "non-Christian" reflection on the virtual Christian element (the "christic" element) in other religions.[37] The task here is to construct a theological reflection capable of reflecting on the Christian element through and in the categories of a so-called pagan culture, with the objective of an "acculturation" of Christianity, especially in mission lands. This effort is linked to the political by the intermediary of the cultural.

Here I am not treating directly of political practices, but rather of cultural, or significative practices. This is an area of theological exploration that is really new and vast, but not yet sufficiently radical and open.[38]

Let me note further, within the current of second theology, another tendency, which, although willing to work in a fairly broad field of vision, seems not to recognize the whole extent of the horizon of which theology is capable. This is the case with a theology that indeed reflects on the issues of the day, but grasps only the (real or potential) political content of religion—understanding religion here as the *manifest* dimension of the Christian faith in a given culture. This tendency conceptualizes Christianity as a socio-historical phenomenon whose empirical quality is perceived through its dogmatic corpus, its forms of worship, its institutional power, and its ethico-utopic function. All theologizing is done upon expressly, patently "Christian" elements. The addressees of this discourse can only be Christians.

This theology seeks to discover the Christian meaning of Christian practices or the practices of Christians. Its themes are the church, its doctrine, its historical tradition, its practices, and perhaps popular piety. One or another subject from among the subjects reposing in the great store of Christian or popular "symbolic capital" is selected, and its resources searched in terms of political, transformational significations. This tendency is certainly possessed of a very broad horizon of reflection, and seeks resolutely to be inserted in the urgencies and challenges of the age. Still, it adheres to the clear element of religious awareness and its products, without looking for more, and without looking deeper.[39]

My own position is that theology should be assigned the task of developing what is contained in the expression "theology of the political." My position is that the political *turns* theological, *becomes* theological, not by absorption, but by enrichment.

Paradoxically, therefore, theology demonstrates its vitality when it is able to think an "atheistic" politics (as well), and think it not only under the sign of sin (*sub ratione peccati*—ethics), but also under the sign of grace (*sub ratione gratiae*—hermeneutics). Theology must be able to uncover the properly "christic"[40] signification even where it is ideologically denied, as in certain historical movements and in the practice of certain non-Christians.[41]

Thus the competency of theological language extends not only to the political element of the Christian phenomena but, more broadly, to what is or can be the christic element in political phenomena. In principle there is no political phenomenon absolutely destitute of a potential theological sense. It belongs to the jurisdiction of theology to "show" this theological sense.[42]

To such purpose, one must "say what the said does not say." Bachelard's maxim is apropos: "All science is of the hidden." Christian theology exists for the sake of the "parousia" of the divine sense of history in the province of the *logos*.

What is important is whether theology is in possession of a sufficiently mature awareness to know its identity and measure its own potential. If it is not, perhaps what is lacking is a better-defined epistemological awareness, and one better suited to its new tasks.

The objective of the reflections just presented has been to uncover the still latent capacities and opportunities of theology.[43] For the rest, the concrete socio-historical situation will have to be examined in every case, to see what theological or religious discourse is culturally possible, politically desirable, and fertile on the level of faith. But none of this can be determined except within a dialectic of theory and praxis such as will be taken up in part 3.

CHAPTER 3

Difficulties on the Side of Faith: The Ideological

§15 SOCIO-ANALYTIC MEDIATION: IDEOLOGIZATION OF FAITH?

In the foregoing chapter I treated epistemological obstacles to the articulation of a theology of the political with the sciences of the social in terms of socio-analytic mediation. Now I shall examine the obstacles that arise on the side of faith itself.

The theology of the political is the target of a particular, basic criticism that questions the very legitimacy of a theology having the political as its subject matter. This criticism consists in the censure of the theology of the political for an alleged "reduction of the faith." The theology of the political is said to reduce the faith to a relative, transitory expression—for example, to some particular political undertaking. In the same vein, we hear of an "ideologization of the faith," meaning an absolutizing of the "relative" historical dimension of faith. Faith, then, would be a transcendent, absolute reality of such a nature that any attempt to "lower" it, to bring it beneath its proper level, would be an assault on its very essence. And this, we hear, is what is done by a theology of the political, in its quality of a "socializing theology."[1]

My own undertaking, then, will appear, to the eyes of this criticism, as reprehensible a fortiori. Not only am I dealing here with the theology of the political, but I am actually attempting to welcome an epistemological assent to this epistemological deviation. After all, am I not seeking a methodology of a theology of the political—a systematic organization in function of its principles?

I feel obliged, then, to delve into this objection for a moment. It raises a complex issue, and touches the very foundations of what I am trying to do.

To my mind, the objection lacks depth and rigor. Perhaps it would be illusory to expect to be able to find a satisfactory solution to this problem, for it implicitly involves the questioning of *truth* on the theoretical or speculative level, and of the *good* on the practical or ethical level. But, as we shall see, these are pre-

35

cisely the two areas where ideology functions. To boot, neither the question of truth, nor that of the good, can be adequately handled apart from the question of being, the ontological object.

Still further: the theological approach to ideology is especially problematic in view of the fact that, even outside the area of theology, this is a question that is the object of the most burning polemics.[2] Stirred up especially among and by Marxists, this thorny problem is not merely unresolved, it has not even begun to be discussed in a balanced way. Indeed one begins to doubt whether this will ever occur.

As for the theoretical content of the concept of "ideology," it would be desirable for all users of the term to determine expressly what they mean by it, lest we have a discourse that is a "carnival of meanings," as we frequently do.

For my own part, I shall attempt, first, to delineate the question under discussion, strictly in function of my larger theme, the theology of the political, and (especially) socio-analytic mediation. Next, I shall set forth the terms that seem to me appropriate for a proper use of the notion of ideology.

The objection to what is called the "ideologization of the faith," which is usually formulated as an accusation, does not offer the defined theoretical contours that would permit a correspondingly defined response. It seems to me that, until now, confrontation has never gone beyond the stage of an ideo-political polemic.

Thus, theologians of first theology, with their classic orientation, accuse theologians of second theology, those of the "new theological problematic," of falling into a "relativization of the faith," by identifying the faith with a determinate political content. This, we are told, is the very definition of ideology.[3]

For their part, "political theologians" call first theology "ideological," for not reflecting critically on the social function that belongs to it and that it cannot deny it has, and for consequently holding itself forth as the sole, self-sufficient translation of the faith, whereas in reality it is nothing more than an essentialist, atemporal version of that faith. Such a procedure, we hear, will lead precisely to the reinforcement, in all innocence, of the prevailing relationships of power.

This debate is present even in second theology—between theologians of the center (the "developed world"), and those of the "periphery" (the Third World).[4]

Thus in the eyes of the theologians of the periphery, the North Atlantic political theologians perform an ideological function, for lack of an unequivocal determination of their political option on the levels, respectively, of (theological) theory and (political) practice. Granted, the North Atlantic political theologians are striving for transformation. Still, says the periphery, their theology ultimately consolidates the status quo.[5] For their part, theologians of the center tend to consider "ideological" the close bond with which the theologians of the periphery link the transcendent content of the faith to the historical imperatives of liberation.[6]

Such, it seems to me, is the general panorama of the debate on ideology.

§16 SOME PRECISIONS

To begin by taking my position at the level where all these objections begin—the level of theological theories—let me note from the very outset that, as it seems to me, it is most improper to speak of a true "reduction of the faith" simply by reason of its theoretical (theological) expression. If faith is to be conceived as being substantially a *basic life option,* including a consistent ethical practice (love, justice, and so on), then it will have to be said that faith realizes its transcendence only in the order in which it is realized itself—that is, in the existential order. Before being a confession or, a fortiori, a theoretical affirmation, the transcendence of faith is linked to a life option, implying corresponding practices. Faith is first and foremost, although not exclusively, *orthopraxis.* Only something concrete—concrete injustice, for example—would be opposed to this transcendence, for only this would signify, in the concrete order, that closing in upon oneself that we call, in more existential terms, selfishness, hatred, death.[7]

The question of the formulation of the faith, or its theorization, is a derived question, a second question. If it is at this derived level that discussion is joined, as is the case in this book, then it must be kept in mind that when I speak of "reduction" here, I mean a *theoretical* reduction, not a *real* reduction. We are dealing here with *orthodoxy*—with a *correct* understanding of the content (positivity) of faith. Here the consequences of an error or deviation will be primarily and directly of a *noetic* order, with the practical order remaining relatively unaffected.

It is true that faith is possessed of its positive determinations—in the creeds—and that the confession of a creed is more than a simple theoretical expression of truths. It engages the living subject of its enunciation, in and by the very act of enunciation. The profession of faith is *self-implicating.* Furthermore, true theology exists only where justice is done to the content of faith. Nevertheless, it seems to me that this confession of faith—standing with one foot in (theological) theory and the other in (ethical) practice—is *ultimately* situated on the theory side, or at least it "pulls" to that side. In any case, the self-implication of the confession of faith is effectuated only under the essential condition of ethical commitment—as the church has always taught. On the other hand, the door is always open to "magicalism" or religious formalism. After all, apart from works, faith is only words! Faith without practice is sermonizing.[8]

Here we must once again recall the distinction between *practiced* faith and *theorized* faith.[9] If this distinction wobbles, theological theory swims in *idealism.* It will mistake the adventures of *reasoning* on the faith (theological theory) for the adventures of *faith* itself (experience and practice). Theology is not faith; it is the discourse of faith. Saying and doing (doing what you say) are not identical, but they can dovetail. The theologian, especially the theologian concerned with the political, must not ignore this dovetailing.

At the root of the question of an "ideological" or "ideologizing" theology we find a concrete problem, and one meriting close attention. It may be expressed as follows. Faith, as a theological virtue, a "gift of God," signifies an absolute openness to an absolute meaning: the Meaning of meanings. Faith is not and cannot be adequately identified with any of its possible or real human expressions, be they in the theoretical order or in the practical. Exuberant dynamism that it is, faith is not exhausted in any of its manifestations.

To be sure, all this is valid in the order of the (abstract) *essence* of faith. In the order of its (concrete) *existence,* faith is nothing without the particular realizations of its aim and intent. It exists *in concreto* only in altogether determinate structures. Apart from its historical concretizations, faith, for a human being, is but an abstraction, or, better, only the transcendental possibility of particular realizations.[10]

Consequently, it is the intrinsic dynamism of faith that necessarily impels it to assume concrete "incarnations." Thus faith is historically real only in and through its "incarnations." Hence we can say that the transcendence of faith is its immanence in history and in the existence of human beings, in the form of realizations ever to be renewed, radicalized, and deepened. Faith, consequently, like practice, is necessarily particular, historical, and relative.[11]

Transcendence and immanence, absolute and relative, are not opposed in faith. On the contrary, they call for each other. A theology of the political must do justice to both aspects. When the theoretical self-projection of faith concentrates on immanence in the political, faith may be tempted to horizontalism, to the neglect of the transcendent. This temptation can also be called "secularism": it consists in the *mundanization of the divine.* All one need do, it is felt, is transform the religious into the political or vice versa. Here we always have an instance of (theoretical) reduction, which accordingly must bear the name of "heterodoxy." Such a temptation is all the more real when the existential affinity of the religious and the political orders of reality stands out.[12] If theology yields to this temptation—it is more than simply a tendency—to take the one order for the other, theology loses its own identity, and earns the name of "ideology."[13] The theology that falls into this trap will be theological in name only.

History, then, is theologically legible only *sub specie aeternitatis.* Immanence has a theological meaning in strict proportion to its solidity on the horizon of transcendence. It could scarcely be otherwise. Any and all theology is founded on the affirmation of the absolute sovereignty of God as expressed in the First Commandment and (what is tantamount to the same thing) on respect for the primacy of the kingdom of God as ever the *proton*—the first thing to seek (Matt. 6:33), in virtue of its quality as ultimate and definitive cause of the political itself. Is this not the sense of Metz's "eschatological reserve"?

Stepping back for a moment from the theological level, even on the level of philosophical reason it must be said that the human being is not defined entirely by politics, as totalitarian regimes would have it.[14] According to Thomas Aquinas:

Homo non ordinatur ad communitatem politicam secundum se totum et secundum omnia sua. . . . Sed totum quod homo est et quod potest et habet, ordinandum est ad Deum.[15]

In virtue of being a person—that is, open to all reality, even the Absolute—the human being is defined (in the abstract) as the indefinable (in the concrete). To attempt to know or define the human being exhaustively is to usurp the place of God, and to run the risk of reducing the notion of the human being to the level of a "thing." Hence Marx's Thesis Six on Feuerbach: the human being is "an ensemble of social relationships." To advocate a metaphysical status for human nature inevitably involves a contradiction.

Even without appealing to the properly religious dimension of the human being—"vertical transcendence"—it is a commonplace to observe that, besides the political dimension, there exist other human dimensions, possessed of their autonomous practices, such as sexuality, celebration, esthetics, friendship, and so on. True, these dimensions are articulated upon the political—they have reciprocal relationships with it. But this does not mean that they are reducible to it. In this sense the political is under the obligation of acknowledging its "other," and paying it due honor. Otherwise, the way is left open for hybris, with its cortege of insolences.[16]

These positions must be firmly maintained by any theology of the political seeking to remain what it is in actuality: theology, not ideology; elucidation of the truth of the human being and history, not the imperialistic monism of a part over the totality.

With this well in mind, let us now return to the proper terrain of our work in this book. I think that I shall not be contradicting all that has been said thus far if I assert that, at the level of the concretions of faith, there could be moments of crisis, of particular historical urgency or special political stress, that would call for total engagement, and this in the name of the transcendence of faith, hence precisely in the name of a call coming from "elsewhere." Thus in the gospel (Luke 10:29–37), for the one going down from Jerusalem to Jericho, love (the theological virtue, if you will) is totally "reduced," in the case of the unfortunate man lying by the side of the road, to "treating him with compassion." In this particular act, love as such is "identified" with one of its expressions, as a species of "concrete universal" (Hegel).[17]

In my view, what is to be feared today are not the notorious "reductions" of faith, but rather the danger that the "transcendence" of faith may serve as a pretext to justify a doctrinaire apoliticism and escapism, when it comes to any and all faith commitments. Need we recall that, for the whole of scripture and for Jesus himself, a "pure" faith, faith devoid of all concrete mediation, is hypocrisy pure and simple?[18] In my opinion, this is the *hic* of the question under discussion.

The simultaneous particularity and legitimate plurality of "pistic" (faith) practices and theological theories have roots in the very transcendence of faith.[19] The kingdom, however it may and must be historically identifiable with such or such a practice, is nevertheless always irreducible to this practice. It is ever the *proton* in intention and the *eschaton* in hope.

Accordingly, I assert that a theology of the political respects, as it must, the transcendence of faith only to the extent that it is developed on the following absolutely necessary practico-theoretical condition: *the acknowledgement of its particularity according to the particularity of its historical condition, and the consequent acknowledgement of the possibility of other theologies in other historical circumstances.*

I may say the same thing using a negative formulation: a theology will be reductive of the faith, and hence ideological, if and only if it puts itself forward as "theology itself"—as the only legitimate or valid theology for all persons and times, to the exclusion of any other, whereas of course it is only a particular theology, the theology of an equally particular socio-historical situation.

Meanwhile, it must also be observed that the opposite attitude is no less ideological than the one that is the target of its critique. I refer to a theology that today presents itself as the adequate expression of the faith merely in virtue of its enunciation of its strictly dogmatic content, with the express renunciation of any competency to render decisions on the historical or "incarnational" determinations of faith, calling this "ideology."[20] Such an attitude will effectively consign the political definition of the faith to the will of the given social forces at play. This theology has nothing political about it but its intention. Ignoring its inevitable relationship with the culture and the society in which it develops, it is prevented from recognizing the quotum of its own "ideologicity," and so deprives itself of the ability to control it.

Finally, I must add, the improper and probably unconscious (but not innocent, as the unconscious may be in other cases) passage from *a* theology to theology *simpliciter*—the passage from reality to the desired—is precisely what I might call "theological ethnocentrism." This ideology is precisely what European theology, ignorant of its own identity, practiced for so long—not without a connection (unconscious, as always) with the European colonial enterprise.

Summing up what has just been said: every theology develops de facto as a particular—and in some way political—theology. The theology that recognizes this condition, and presents itself as what it is de facto, at the same time acknowledges the transcendence that belongs to the faith by right and permits it a potentially infinite manifestation of concrete possibilities, as well in the theoretical as in the practical order. By contrast, a theology that ignores its historicity and its political nature, and presents itself as *theology itself*—the rigid, dogmatistic expression of the meaning and imperatives of faith—this theology, which claims that it coincides with the voice of revelation itself, can only be an ideology. It adopts an erroneous position, be it in the area of theory (illusion) or politics (lie).[21]

What has been at issue in the above considerations are particular theological discourses with a defined content. I have sought to establish the conditions under which they can or cannot be called "ideological." On another level, that of the *formal* analysis of theological discourse, it must be said that theology is no more historical in virtue of thinking history than it is transcendent in virtue of thinking transcendence, for the simple reason that knowledge is one thing and known reality another. It is only in its semantic objective that theology is transcendent. In other words, it is only from a point of departure in the *epistemological locus* from which it is given to speak—revelation—that theology is transcendent. This is as it must be. Otherwise, theology would not be theology, but some other language.

This circumstance of a formal order pertains properly to all theology, hence also to the theology of the political. By the same token, from the moment it undertakes a discourse, theology—all theology, including first theology—can do so only in a concrete locus (historical, cultural, and political). As discourse, consequently, theology is fated to be human, cultural, and historical; but in respect of the meaning intended by its discourse, theology, all theology, is necessarily transcendent.[22] I shall have to return to this point.

To conclude the present section, let me say one more thing about the case of divergent theological interpretations of the same, given situation.

Bracketing the enormous problematic this question implies—pluralism, catholicity, church unity, orthodoxy, authority, and so on—and limiting myself to the aspect relating to socio-analytic mediation under consideration here, I shall say only that, in the case mentioned, it does not appear to me that it is socio-analytic mediation as such that is the problem. Rather it is its theoretical content, or, subsequently, the manner of its articulation with the content of the faith. It would not be the suppression of socio-analytic mediation, then, that would resolve the problem. On the contrary, this would result in nothing but the disappearance of that upon which one is to produce a judgment, in recognition of causes. It would be an example of discursive prestidigitation.

It might also be objected that it is unacceptable, or at least dangerous, to subject the faith to a dependency on the analysis of a situation. But in my view it is still more unacceptable and dangerous to analyze simply nothing at all, for this would mean that the only way to be on the "right side" would be to ignore the whole question, after the manner of an ostrich. The real problem would still be there. In fact, it would grow worse, after such a pseudo solution had been applied.

§17 TOWARD A RIGHT USE OF THE NOTION OF "IDEOLOGY"

In order to state the question of ideology in theology in a form that will permit me to rise above the level of polemics and mutual recriminations, I want to suggest some basic propositions.

Let me utilize the distinction made above between the internal regime (autonomy) and the external regime (dependence) of a science or body of knowledge. What needs to be done here is to apply these two notions to the particular case of ideology.[23]

Under the heading of "autonomy," the term "ideology" can be defined as *error occurring under the appearance of truth*. This is the pitfall of a science or body of knowledge constituted in immediate relationship to the concrete life and functions of empirical existence. Having almost no critical distance from concrete life, this knowledge seizes phenomena in their sensible appearances. What is acquired in this case is what the Greeks called *doxa: seeming* knowledge, "opinion." Ideology fabricates a veneer of knowledge, a false knowledge. Stopping at the superficial level of symptom, of the obvious, of what "goes without saying," it explains nothing. Here, then, we have not error pure and simple, but illusion—error (mis)taking itself for truth. I shall designate this order of pseudo truths "first ideological" or "ideological 1."[24]

However, I must immediately make a reservation. Spontaneous knowledge is not always illusion. But a rationalist, aristocratic mentality, in its contempt for "common sense" and "popular maxims," may pretend that it is. To speak with all rigor, I should have to say that spontaneous knowledge is divided into false knowledge (preconceptions, errors) and acceptable opinions. In all cases, only the judgement of reason as critical arbiter can render a corpus of knowledge "ideological," by declaring it such.[25]

On the side of the rubric of "dependence," I must say the following. First, to affirm without qualification that the notion of "ideology" refers to any idea whose function is the justification of a practice of an interest simply gives us no information. Surely every idea will have some relationship to determinate interests or practices.[26] To my mind, the real question is: *what* interests? *Cui prodest?* Is the interest legitimate or not? Now we are dealing with the relationship between knowledge and (ethico-political) function. Here the designation "ideological" connotes the "unjustifiable"—not the simply unjustifiable, however, but the *unjustifiable in the guise of the justifiable*. We are dealing with the immoral in the guise of the moral. In a word, "ideological" will be synonymous with "feigned," indeed with "lie." This order of procedure I shall call "second ideological" or "ideological 2." This acceptation will be verified in the social field, especially in the political field, and even more so in the ideo-political field—in the sense of the political function an idea may serve.

The common element in these two acceptations of "ideological" (what I have called "first ideological" and "second ideological"), and therefore what will justify the use of the common term "ideological," is the aspect, or better the appearance, of what is "natural" or "spontaneous"—as well in the gnoseological use of the term as in its political use—in relationship respectively to the practico-practical real and the politico-political real.[27]

Now let us attempt to apply these two acceptations, as I have delineated them, to the area of theology, in particular to the theology of the political.

As for our "first ideological," this would apply to any religious discourse expressing a "problemless" relationship with life experience or pistic experience—a discourse of empiricism. This will be the case with a language constructed with a direct view to the immediate imperatives of existence or of the historical moment—the language of pragmatism. We are then before a discourse that does not have available the instruments of its own internal self-critique, or at least is not concerned with applying them. Thus it represents as "true" what is simply "practical." It has recourse to religious significations with a view to determinate practices: pastoral, ideological, pedagogical, and the like.

Let us take, for example, the formula: "To be a Christian is to struggle for justice"; or again: "Faith means change."[28] Thus expressed, without qualification, leaving out any consideration of the socio-historical context in which such expressions could acquire an acceptable ideo-political sense—and this by neglect of socio-analytic mediation—and brandished at times as slogans alleged to have a theoretical basis (dogmatism)—assertions of this kind are evidently inadmissible in the area of theology as rigorous discourse. The religious discourse that makes use of them will see itself automatically deprived of the ability to furnish the theoretical support that would legitimate the saying of what is being said.

How can the term "justice" be simply predicated of "being Christian" if the discourse in question is incapable of assigning a minimal theoretical content to the subject of the proposition? The question is not as abstract as may appear. Experience has shown its practical implications in the order of a "Christian practice of politics."[29]

We shall see all of this more in detail in part 2. Here I shall only say that any discourse having a connection with praxis (pastoral, political, pedagogical, and so on) must be called "religious discourse," in contradistinction to "theological discourse," which latter, as such, is characterized by a *direct* relationship to knowledge, not to action. It will therefore be detrimental to both types of discourse to mix them, and invert their respective "language play."[30] The theoretical language of theology cannot have its work done for it by the practical language of prophecy, homily, or the like. These languages are no less legitimate; but let us note that only theological language properly so called is of such a nature as to allow the others free play without the danger of abuse. Without the critical vigilance of theology, the language of practice—ideology—will find it difficult to keep out of reach of the unbridled manipulation of religious significations at the direct, indeed exclusive, service of concrete needs. This is a theoretical servility that theology, in the name of faith, must refuse.

Now let us move on to our "second ideological." However "orthodox" it may consider itself, a theology is always open to the objective possibility that it may exercise an ideological function. Indeed its "truth" may very well have the role of justifying a morally indefensible social situation—or perhaps simply of masking this situation by a discourse that is doubtless "true," but that is irrelevant or inopportune, because it distracts the mind and "detours" the attention of the faith vis-à-vis the urgent tasks of a given conjuncture. Just as a science, without ceasing to be science, can have an ideological function, so also can a theology, without ceasing to be a theology—however rigorous and disciplined it may be—have the same ideological function. It is for this reason that theology has the need to control its relationship with praxis by what I shall call "ideo-political vigilance."

It is clear from what has just been said that it is absolutely insufficient to claim not to be ideological, or to wish not to be, in order actually not to be. What is important here are not intentions, but deeds, be they theoretical (as in first ideological) or practical (as in second ideological). For the rest, the temptation to remain in the "absolute of faith," together with the will to keep clearly out of reach of the historical determinations of the faith, does not of itself guarantee the "nonideologicity" of a discourse or practice, whatever this discourse or practice may be. Correlatively, no symbolic system, be it philosophical, scientific, or religious, can be considered completely immune, in virtue of an effort of internal organization of its significations, from ideological manipulation for objectives that it may indeed have previously and explicitly rejected or removed. I may assert, then, this general principle: any idea is susceptible of an *usus ideologicus.*[31]

As we come to the end of these reflections on the formal status of the concept of "ideology," and its "correct use," we have a better grasp of why the allegation of "ideologization of the faith" can be leveled, indiscriminately, and with justice, against either camp in the debate. Thus first theology, or "traditional" theology, seems to me to be more exposed to second ideological, whereas second theology is more likely to be tempted by first ideological.[32]

Perhaps we are now better equipped to unravel some of the confusion and introduce somewhat more intelligibility in the area of a notion that looms with a truly Protean shape in contemporary culture. And indeed is it not the role of reason, as Hegel said, to "bolster the trembling"?

§18 THEOLOGY: A REGIONAL LANGUAGE

Certain difficulties arising out of the relationship between the absolute of faith and the relative of a theology of the political mediated by the sciences of the social have now been prepared for. Next, then, let us examine certain other difficulties of the same order. First we must resolve the seeming contradiction between the total or totalizing, universal or "catholic," eschatological or ultimate, character of the faith or revelation, and the regional, particular, ephemeral, relative character of the productions of theology of the political.

Along the lines of what I have already attempted to elucidate in this chapter, and for the purpose of delimiting the terrain of this question more precisely, I shall set up two "stakes" here in the form of two pairs of distinctions, the one on the theological plane and the other on the epistemological plane.

First, then, on the plane of a theological *theory* of the faith, I propose a distinction between two levels of faith: that of its essence and that of its existence.

On the level of its *essence,* faith can be likened to an absolute *openness* to the Absolute, a real possibility—that is, a demand—for inexhaustible realizations. Faith on this level must be seen as abstract, relative to the concrete determinations that it can assume in history. We may say, therefore, that, at the level of its essence, faith is universal, absolute, transcendent, totalizing, and so forth. We are not dealing with a simple concept—with Aristotle's form without matter, or Plato's subsistent entity—but with a palpable, perceived aim, a demand. It seems to me that it pertains to first theology to articulate this sense.

On the level of its *existence,* faith must be thought of as an *actual* realization in history, in praxis, in life. It is faith realized, concrete, determined. It belongs to second theology to treat of this relationship.

Note the difference in the passage from the level of essence to the level of existence: faith can be determined. This is why there is no real opposition between the absolute and the relative of faith. The absolute of faith exists only in the form of the relative. Of its essence, the absolute of faith is an abstract absolute, whereas in its existence it is a concrete absolute, or a concretized absolute.[33]

The same will hold with respect to the total(izing), ultimate, or decisive character of faith.

Moving on now to the properly *epistemological* plane—the point of view of a theory of the theology of the political—I find the following distinction to be of capital importance: that between

- the real (the "theologizable," the *teologal,* or "materially theological")
  and
- knowledge of it (the "theologized," the *teológico,* or "formally theological").

As can readily be observed in considering the two regimes of a discipline, the structure and logic of knowledge, with its *autonomy,* are not the same as the structure and logic of the real, in respect of which the knowledge is *dependent.* By this very fact, the properties of the real are not and cannot be the properties of knowledge. A rock is material; the concept of rock is immaterial.

Applied to theology, the distinction between real and known, theory and world, is equivalent to the assertion that theological knowledge is not endowed with the qualities of its object. Thus, first theology, which bears upon the absolute of faith, is not *eo ipso* absolute, just as second theology, which bears upon the relativity of the political, is not automatically political. As knowledge, theology is and always will be human, historical, concrete activity, and it is absolutely not *in virtue of* its bearing on the divine, eternal, and transcendent that it would have these same predicates. A pari, or perhaps a fortiori, theology remains a partial, precarious, defectible, "aspectual" knowledge—in a word, a *regional* knowledge.

Even with the Absolute as its theoretical object, theology is always relative. This is because the theoretical object is not identical with the real object. If this is valid for all knowledge, it is valid with very special reason for theology. The idea of God will never be God. To assert an equivalency between the two would be to fall into idolatry.

Thus theology can take the viewpoint of the totality of its object only in a "sectorial" manner. In brief, theology is not absolute discourse. It is discourse *of* the Absolute. Even if it is defined as "religious" science, or *sacra doctrina,* it is only in virtue of its (real) object that it is so denominated—not in virtue of its discursive formality. It would actually be preferable to "disambiguate" these expressions, by a systematic process of "de-adjectivization," and speak, more rigorously, of a "science *of* religion," a "doctrine *of* the divine," and so on.[34]

The same observations will be in order in the area of a theology of the political. Here, too, we must distinguish the political real from the knowledge of it that theology may furnish. On the one hand, theology extracts the "meaning" of a given situation or practice by placing it in the light of faith, or *sub specie Dei*. Evidently, one result is that the meaning intended has a totalizing, radical, and absolute dimension. This is precisely what is proper to theological discourse—to give an account of the (totalizing, radical, and absolute) manner in which faith lives history. On the other hand, when theology undertakes to express the absolute of faith, it can do so only by means of human language— that is, something relative.

Such is the *absolute* nature of pistic *meaning,* and the *relative* character of theological *discourse*. It is this that constrains me to assert: theology is not the absolute language of the political—it is, more precisely, the language of the absolute of the political. In other words, it places in evidence the ultimate, transcendent cause that is operative in (political) praxis, in the sense that the latter, within and beyond the humanization of the human being, pertains to the inauguration of the reign of God.

Unless they are careful to keep the distinction between *pistic meaning* and *theological expression* operational, theologians will be led to a dogmatist sclerosis of historical, transitory viewpoints, to the creation of closed theological systems, and to the absolutizing sacralization of conjunctural politics or political policies. This is tantamount to the (theoretical) denaturing of the political, as well as to that of faith and theology.

I take it that I have sufficiently called attention to the epistemological deviation that is the pitfall of the theologian more than of any other theoretician, and which consists in the tacit attribution of the qualities of the object of knowledge to the knowledge itself. Here theology begins to masquerade as faith, and we assist, as it were, at the usurpation of the place of the significate by the signifier. We must therefore always be vigilant with regard to this idealistic tendency, which deems itself to have the thing itself in virtue of having its idea.

By reason of these precisions, I think that I have presented some of the elements of a response to the difficulties cited at the beginning of this section. The assertion, then, that a theology of the political, and a fortiori a theology of the political socio-analytically mediated, would be incapable of being realized, or illegitimate, by reason of the fact that the faith is absolute, transcendent, or totalizing—or, still worse, on the pretext that theology is an absolute, ultimate language—is a confusionist position, which, interchanging as it does the predicates of the *res* with those of its knowledge, automatically obstructs the acquisition of any genuine knowledge.[35]

Let me add just one more thing apropos of theology as a totalizing language. I acknowledge the many difficulties arising from this concept, especially in view of a discourse as decidedly regional, even from the standpoint of its material object—not to mention its formal object, which is a priori particular—as is the discourse of the theology of the political.[36]

To be sure, theology attempts to express the absolute and total meaning of praxis, of the world, and of history, for it is in this that the theologicity of theology consists. But let us observe, first of all, that this is but an attempt at, a *votum* of, totality. Next, let us observe that this attempt is not totally vacuous. It does produce synthesis. Only, its syntheses are always provisional, open. They are theoretical syntheses in process, never definitive, closed systems. Even when it is a matter of Christ as the "absolute revelation," or of Christianity as the "absolute religion," any conceptualization suggesting a monophysitelike system of identity is carefully to be avoided, in favor of an ever analogical, asymptotic conceptualization—one that unflaggingly refers to an ultimately ineffable Mystery.

What has just been said refers to content. As for form, I need only repeat what has been said above. It is true that theological discourse intends totality. But it can do so only in the *form* of partiality—that is, it can do so only through a particular discourse that obeys postulates that are never anything but relative (to the totality). The vision of theology does not have the faculty of seeing things in all their facets, of embracing them from every side. Theology is but a viewpoint—even though it is a viewpoint that opens out on the totality of a material object. Theology, therefore, is a regional discourse.[37]

An awareness of its limits—and they are constitutive limits—is the sign of the epistemological health of a theology, and an essential condition for an appropriate articulation with other disciplines. Socio-analytic mediation obliges theology to listen to what the sciences of the social have to say. The word of theology comes later, as "second word."[38] Not that it belongs to theology to pronounce the "last word." The "last word" of theology will never come. Its "last word" will be such always, and only, in the sense of the last word so far enunciated. Theology speaks after the other disciplines have had their say, yes—not in order to shortcut their circumnavigation of the real, however, but to fill their sails still fuller.

Like any (particular) knowledge, theology is open to the temptation of hybris, which would here assert itself as the will to power over the other "knowledge" with which it will come into confrontation.[39] What is relatively pardonable in the case of another discourse, however, will be less so in the case of theology—which is merely the attempt to articulate the word of the "stammering community of the faithful."[40]

I should wish to go on record, meanwhile, as having said that these considerations of an epistemological order may not be allowed to serve as a pretext for invoking, abstractly and *mal à propos,* "pluralism," or "dialogue," with the purpose of placing obstacles in the way of the resolute effort of rationality and political efficacy to respond to the challenges of a concrete socio-historical situation, even if this response might lead to real confrontations. When wolf meets sheep, no one must be deceived as to the ideological value of calls for "cooperation" or "dialogue" or "pluralism."[41]

Accordingly, a theology of the political ignorant of its own ideo-political position, and of the "weight" this position necessarily "pulls" in the taking of a position and the determination of a project, its objectives, and its strategies, is political in name only. A theology of the political is perforce involved in its own theoretical projection. It cannot be simply aseptic reason. Rather it must be combative reason, a *dezidierte Vernunft.*[42]

Thus, although it is given to a theology to be genuine theology only on condition of being at the same time a theology *of the political,* the converse is no less true: there is no theology of the political that is not at the same time a *political* theology.

§19 THEOLOGY OF HISTORY

Theologies of history are typical examples of theoretical syntheses, or totalizing discourses. At the same time, these theologies have this in common with the undertaking of a theology of the political, that they also seek to interpret the historical present. The difference is that they situate this present on the horizon of the general march of history.

The connection of the theologies of history with political subject matter is a matter of historical record. The most typical case is that of St. Augustine's *City of God,* which has exercised such an influence on the whole West down through the centuries.[43] In this section I shall be asking what the relationship of this kind of discourse is with the subject of my study.

The general characteristic of the classic theologies of history is surely their speculative or contemplative aspect. These theories give a grand religious interpretation to the course of world history.[44] The attitude of mind at the root, and the summit, of these discourses is theological hope, divine hope.

To my view, these elaborations are the product of a nonhistorical consciousness. They answer to the subjective demands of the moments at which they have arisen.[45]

For its part, theology of the political takes up an expressly active objective. For theology of the political, what is ultimately important is "making history," rather than "interpreting history." The theoretical moment is invoked only as a necessary mediation of praxis. It is for this reason that the theology of the political is possessed of the constitutive exigency of appropriating beforehand the empirical weft of the historical moment, in socio-analytic mediation.

On the other hand, theology of the political does coincide with the theology of history in that it too seems to suppose a certain general vision of that history. Indeed, praxis also seems de facto to involve some form of hope in a transcendence of historicity as such, in a transcendence of pure facticity.

The substantial results of a theology of history that would be of potential service to a theology of the political might seem to lead us back to affirmations corresponding to the very essence of theological hope: that history has a meaning, and that this meaning pertains to Mystery.[46]

In the elucidation of the relationship between the history of God and the history of humankind, there are two opposing positions that sin by oversimplification, the one optimistic, the other pessimistic.

The former posits a relationship of *parallelism,* or term-for-term correspondence between God's history and human history. This is the standpoint of all evolutionisms, be they Hegelian or Teilhardian. Systematically and on principle, they draw up the equation: human victory = God's victory, and human failure = God's failure.

The other orientation is that of pessimists, be they apocalyptical, or simply negativist, as is the case with the Reformers, for whom God ever appears in history "in the shadow of cross and contradiction," *tectus sub cruce et contrario,* or *sub specie contraria.* Here the operative principle is: human victory = God's failure, and human failure = God's victory.

It seems to me that the very course of history forbids the systematic, a priori application of principles of this kind. The only legitimate a priori is that, in the Christian interpretation of history, there is no hermeneutical a priori. What can be said is that all historical activity is connected to the plane of God (though it is not possible to know the exact nature of the connection). In other words, we know the *quid,* but not the *quomodo.* The discernment of the "wheat" from the "chaff" is essentially eschatological. It is of the nature of "harvest," and, furthermore, is a matter of divine judgment.[47]

This does not mean that there are two histories. It only means that the divine logic is not always the same as human logic in respect of the one history. The logics can coincide, or they can be opposed, depending on the individual case. It is not legitimate always to see salvation where there is success.[48]

So much for hermeneutics. But for ethics the case seems clear, and ethics is what ultimately matters. In terms of ethics, we may confidently draw up the equation: God's will = human will—with the equal sign designating an "ought" in the sense of an ethical yardstick.

At all events, no particular historical action reveals its whole meaning apart from the horizon of global history. So long as history is in course, the signification of a particular historical action remains in some fashion suspended in the *pleroma* of history. On the other hand, we cannot but see the fondness of the human being for anticipating the end of history, by a kind of prolepsis, so as to be able to mark out an orientation, a sense, for praxis.

Theologies of history are attempts to subsume history in a necessary, if provisional, synthesis. These theoretical totalizations, and the objective hope that corresponds to them, are found in implicit form, or lived, in praxis. They may not advertise themselves explicitly, but they are present and operative.[49]

It may happen that, at moments of upheaval or sharp turns of history, the theoretical need may be felt to explicitate the coordinates referred to, with the objective of conferring upon the historical moment then being lived a broader and deeper signification, through its linkage with total history and its plero-matic or eschatological sense. Then a theology of history may impose itself upon the reflection of a theology of politics—on condition, however, that that theology always remains an open synthesis, constructed from the memory of the past, critically appropriated, and intending nonutopian, antichiliastic pro-jections with respect to the future.

As we consider the degree of historical awareness so widely developed today, and as we reflect on current historical tasks to be performed, it seems rather doubtful to me that a theology of history in the classic mold could offer the required means to the end of a theory and a praxis of the sort of which we stand so sorely in need today. Such discourses remain ever abstract from history-in-becoming as it must be critically grasped (in socio-analytic mediation). Thus they are unable to furnish concrete criteria for defining the socio-historical content that Christian hope should assume in terms of practices in a determinate historical conjuncture.[50]

At the same time, however, it remains true that a theology of the political can always find, in these broad visions of a theology of history, the sap of a hope that can nourish its own *logos*.

CHAPTER 4

Some Concrete Details: Practice of Socio-Analytic Mediation

§20 THEOLOGY OF THE POLITICAL, SCIENCES OF THE SOCIAL: A DEONTOLOGICAL CODE

Having discussed the more theoretical questions implied in socio-analytic mediation, I shall now treat of questions bearing more directly on the actual practice of theology of the political as articulated with the sciences of the social. To this purpose I shall first have to ask: In order for theology to establish its socio-analytic mediation, what cautions are to be observed with respect to existing sciences of the social? What is the code that ought to preside over this relationship?

It seems to me that this relationship should be governed by two principles: (1) respect for the autonomy of the discipline in question; and (2) critique vis-à-vis all manner of dogmatism.

The first principle refers primarily to the rules relating to the evolution of a science. The second refers mainly to its conclusions.[1]

With the first point, we touch upon the problem of secularization, which sets in relief the (relative) autonomy of earthly values.[2] The notion is a legitimate one. Here theology would be incompetent to pronounce upon the internal regime of the sciences. The play of the sciences is one in conformity with their own rules, as they search after their own proper truth under the guidance of a "spirit" whose most radical law is summed up in an ethic of objectivity.[3] They are strictly within their rights to work with what is called a "methodological atheism." The sciences operate in function of the axiom *Etsi Deus non daratur*—with a maximum economizing of transcendency, then.[4]

This being the case, to criticize science for bracketing realities such as God, spirit, the human being, and so on, and to accuse it of atheism, materialism, or antihumanism because it does so, is to betray an ignorance of science and of what constitutes science. It is like criticizing birds for having wings.

The theologian has nothing to say about the specific procedures of other disciplines. The theologian has no competency to tell the sociologist how to do sociology. What the theologian may legitimately do is censure the sociologist's unwarranted premises or extrapolations, as shall be described below.

Further: for its own good, theology should concede science the whole extent of the area of investigation of which it will have need in order to draw up its hypotheses. Bold scientific positions that are partly the product of imagination can turn out to be false. But theology possesses no supplementary illumination of a scientific order that might qualify it to invalidate scientific hypotheses. Such hypotheses may or may not pertain to the "core" of a body of theory.[5] But this does not mean that they are not constitutive of its system and its process, after the manner of an atmosphere, making it possible for the theory as a whole to acquire an intelligibility proportionate to the nature of the science that frames it.[6]

Confronting the scientific process, theologians must wait, in an attitude of attention. They have nothing pertinent to say until they are correctly instructed as to what is transpiring "out there," at a distance from them.[7] To proceed as if theologians should issue commands to a foreign discipline is not only an anachronism, and a useless one at that, but also the expression of an excess to which any science is tempted, and which in theology takes the shape of "theologism," as has already been observed. In contact with other sciences, "theologism" is characterized by a "panlogistic" need to explain everything, and explain it totally, through exclusive recourse to spiritual forces or supernatural factors. Nary a suspicion is harbored of the need to introduce, between the phenomena in question and their theological meaning, the innumerable mediations furnished by the sciences.

Religious discourse may and even should permit itself the *via curta*.[8] But theological discourse may not. Theological discourse is a discourse toughened by long peregrinations, one accustomed to arriving by roundabout routes—by the *via longa,* coming at last to the point where religious language has arrived and is waiting.[9] Confusion of these two languages is the essence of "theologism," and theologism is as prejudicial to faith, which is alienated in this fashion, as it is to theology, which ends by no longer knowing its own name.

Theological discourse, therefore, may not be allowed to sin by vague concepts, or merely chatter about the divine subject of its enunciations. The various discourses of the sciences on matters of religion can help it contemplate the subject matter of its reflection on the level at which it holds its own competency.[10] In this way theology will refrain both from secularizing the divine, and from deifying the world. The concept of a *deus ex machina* like the god of miracles, unceremoniously interfering in the affairs of the world, is incompatible with the possibility, indeed the actuality, of science. Such conceptualization can no longer have theological warranty, if indeed it ever should have had it. A critique by way of secularization and demythologization, therefore, should be systematically applied to theological discourse, and maintained in it, in full vigor.[11]

Thus the superiority flaunted in the face of scientific knowledge by certain theologians who consider such knowledge "fragmentary," of little importance, or even compromised, and consider their own knowledge transcendent, absolute, or divine, is the index of an idealistic spirit ignorant of the relativity of the theoretical and political status of all knowledge.[12]

Even with respect to the raw material that was so long their exclusive terrain—distinctly religious phenomena—theologians must now accord their *nihil obstat* to the explorations of other sciences. True, they cannot accept possible or actual absolutizations from these sciences in this area. But they may not, for all that, neglect to profit by the findings of the latter in order the better to situate their own discourse, both in theory and in political practice, as well as the better to establish the text that will be submitted to their own deciphering.[13]

These observations concerning the relationship of theology with the sciences in general will of course be valid for the sciences of the social in particular, although the theoretical status of these latter leaves much to be desired, as shall be pointed out below. Of course, particular precautions on the part of theology are in order, owing to this theoretical circumstance.[14]

Now something should be said about the second principle that theology should call into play in its relationship with another discipline. We can call this the principle of *antidogmatist critique*. Here we have a more active attitude than that suggested by the first principle, the principle of simple respect for the status of each particular science. We are not dealing here with the need a science may have of the critical service of theology for the purpose of maintaining itself within its proper limits. But the fact is that the limits of a science can also be drawn from without, with the assistance of another science. After all, this is what occurs in any definition: "omnis determinatio est negatio," as Spinoza says. There will always be border clashes, inasmuch as borders shift with the course of history (the history of the sciences)—whence the previous discussion of the "confines" of a discipline, a terminology I prefer to that of a "division" of the sciences. We must recognize, however, that it is only by way of an effort of self-definition that a science may take shape and make progress, as experience attests.[15]

Theology will be particularly sensitive to whatever touches the theoretical area it claims for itself—not in the sense of the "materiality" of this field (the "religious," or the "Christian"), to which all manner of approaches are a priori possible and legitimate—but primarily when it comes to questions of its exclusive competency. Let me explain what I mean. When any discipline, constituted in its autonomy, becomes "scientificist"—rationalistic or positivistic—and denies all foundation to any other possible approach to the object in question, especially to a theological approach—a mind-set that is visible in reductionist formulas such as " . . . is nothing but . . . "—this is the moment for theology to block the way to such an illegitimate pretension. Theology cannot accept reduction to silence easily, just as it cannot brook the pretensions of another language to speak the word that theology alone is competent to speak. There is nothing for it but to smash the fictitious *clausura*—closure—of this totalitarian, "ultimate" language.

As we move closer to the question of socio-analytic mediation itself, we must observe that the particular form of "scientificism" that can be met here is "sociologism." Sociologism consists in attempting to exhaust the signification of a social phenomenon in the "sociological." Here we have a new version of closed science, closed knowledge, without exteriority or "otherness."

In this case, too, one question suffices to unmask this (epistemological) totalitarianism. What is the theoretical status of the science in question? To put it in other ways: What is its object and method? What are the conditions of validity of its assertions? How does it come to say what it is saying? A philosophizing, critical reflection of sociology upon itself ought to be able to lead it to acknowledge its status as a particular, historical body of knowledge.[16] On the other hand, if it fails to conduct this reflection and make this admission, it will devolve upon other disciplines to remind it to do so.

Theology, of course, is not the only science to have the right to de-absolutize "scientificist" thought, in all its forms. But it has a powerful contribution to make, in virtue of its specific nature as a knowledge bearing precisely upon what, by definition, escapes all *clausura,* precisely by being supremely intelligible: Mystery.

Theology can construct its socio-analytic mediation only from the findings of a discipline whose conclusions are susceptible of articulation by and in a properly theological discourse. Consequently, these conclusions cannot present a closed, finished, or absolute character. If they are the findings of a system that presents them as closed, finished, and absolute, theology can utilize them only after a process of discernment, in which all exorbitance is sifted out of these claims, so that they are reduced to their legitimate proportions.[17]

To be sure, in dialogue with the sciences of the social, theology cannot pretend to regulate their discourse, any more than it can rest content with simply echoing their word. Theology must hear them, of course—but hear them in order to make *its* own voice resound, and say what *it* has to say. To this purpose, theology will rely on the other sciences, but will advance beyond their limits.[18] Dialogue of theology with the sciences of the social is not possible with a "scientificist science." It is possible only with a "scientific science." In other words, theology cannot dialogue with a mad science, but only with a sane one.

Will theology alone, then, to the exclusion of every other body of knowledge, be the only dogmatic, absolute body of knowledge to be able to lay utterly legitimate claim to the name of science? Indeed, will this claim not be an essential attribute of theological language?

The first thing to be said in answer to this question is that dogmatism is a general deviation of mentality, of which scientificism is but one form—the form pertaining to the modern sciences in particular. Theological reason, then, is not immune to the temptation to dogmatism. If theology can "stand up to" another science that is putting on dogmatic airs, it is not in quality of being the sole depository of dogmatic knowledge. It is precisely in virtue of the fact that theological discourse, more than any other, ought to be sensitive to the precarious character of all cognition, and consequently sensitive to the need always to keep an open mind—in its own case, a mind turned toward the ineffable. As a disciplined body of knowledge, theology of course sets in motion a whole system of formal steps for saying, in all rigor—its own rigor—what it has to say. But the rigor of its discourse is not for the sake of comprehending the incomprehensible, for grasping the ungraspable. No, paradoxically, it is for the purpose of comprehending the incomprehensible precisely as incomprehensible. Its discourse is therefore not representative but significative. That is, it is shot through with the energy of symbol, and must finally end in apophasis. Confronted with Mystery, the theologian is reduced to the role of servant or guardian in the area of *ratio*.

As a consequence, theology is not, or at any rate ought not to be, a "dogmatistic" science. At most it can be a dogmatic one, in the sense of constituting a knowledge *of* dogmas—provided it keeps in mind that dogmas are open formulas referring to Mystery as such: Mystery as incomprehensible Reality, comprehended only as incomprehensible.[19]

§21 HISTORICAL MATERIALISM

Now let us take the case of Marxism, with a rapid discussion of certain problems posed for a theology of the political that might seek to utilize Marxism as its socio-analytic mediation. My choice of this current of thought as an illustration of the positions developed above is not a random one, seeing that today the most straightforward practices of socio-analytic mediation are connected, remotely or proximately, to this particular theoretical tradition in the area of the sciences of the social.[20]

Let us, then, apply here the norms of the deontological code that I have just expounded: respect for scientific autonomy with critique of any dogmatism.

The distinction implied in this double principle corresponds to a distinction to be made within the Marxist corpus along a decisive line of demarcation between its *philosophical* aspect—its dialectical materialism, unacceptable by reason of its reductionist or dictatorial character—and its *scientific* aspect—historical materialism, which, as a method for the analysis of society and history, is, in principle, legitimate.[21]

Under this aspect, Marxism will deserve the opportunity to attempt to prove the credibility of the cognitive material that it will have been able to produce as a scientific theory. Thus Marxism will not enjoy any a priori privilege where the proper exigencies of all scientific method are concerned. It will be valid only to the extent that it actually "makes one know," that it is "scientific." And it will "make one know," in all rigor, only under the quite precise conditions that, of validity like any other science, it will have to define.[22]

On this exclusively scientific level, the problems that Marxism raises are enormous. As a "science of history," Marxism posits as the essential epistemological principal of its theory that this theory is to be verified through historical practice. Society, then, becomes a vast laboratory of social experimentation, and the hypotheses of Marxism are a function of the development of history itself.[23] One sees immediately the consequences to which such a conceptualization will lead. Questions of this nature relative to the scientific status of Marxism are far from having met with even minimal consensus, even among Marxists. The very concept of "science," applied to and by Marxism, appears problematic, if not completely set on its head.[24]

Clearly, then, Marxism can serve as socio-analytic mediation only on the level of *scientific theory* (and only to the extent that it is scientific), and not as an all-explaining *Weltanschauung*. As to theology, it cannot allow itself to be measured by the yardstick of Marxism and accept the place Marxism assigns it, a place in the superstructure. Theology would then cease to be theology. (I am speaking here of theology as such, not of particular theologies.)

The spirit that has animated theological tradition in confrontation with so many cultural mediations down through the course of its history, as exemplified so well in Thomas Aquinas and his attitude toward Aristotelianism, should likewise prevail where Marxism is concerned. This is precisely why the "theological word" can only come "after." It is pronounced from a point of departure in, and in transcendence of, any other "word," Marxist or non-Marxist. Articulation between a theology of the political and historical materialism is valid only in so far as this rule is observed. The contrary is fraud.[25]

One may well wonder, for that matter, whether the problem of the scientific status of Marxism has been well posed. The historical success of Marxism may be much less the result of its theoretical virtue than of other factors—such as ideological, ethical, or utopic, connected with praxis rather than with theory.

Faced with this theoretical and practical situation of Marxism, theology would be well advised to adopt a reserved attitude where the manner of evaluation of the theoretical results of this current are concerned. At the same time, given that theology acquires its theoretical urgency from the practical urgencies of the time, and is constructed, so to speak, at the behest of and with a view to praxis (although always only in the last instance)—theology sees itself forced to make a choice among the socio-analytic systems that are de facto at its disposition in the current phase of cultural development.

It still remains to ask whether it is possible to disconnect historical materialism from dialectical materialism. Without entering into a discussion of the theoretical possibility of this undertaking, let me speak for a moment from the standpoint of Christian praxis. Here the case seems to me to be perfectly clear. After all for Christians there are two and only two solutions here, and they are mutually exclusive:

1. Either the two cannot be severed—and then Marxism must be completely rejected, along with any theoretical and practical resources it may claim to provide where capitalism is concerned.

2. Or they can be severed—and then the Christian cannot continue to be a Christian without rejecting the totalitarian face of Marxism as expressed in its materialistic, and consequently atheistic, profession (of faith).

With this simple statement of the terms of the problem, the choice "makes itself." After all, theology must bend its efforts to assimilate the theories that most satisfactorily explain the situations to which it is particularly sensitive in virtue of the faith. This is precisely what I observe in the current "political theologies," all of which use Marxism as their socio-analytic mediation. They see in Marxism the theory that gives the best account of the current socio-historical situation, a situation challenging the conscience of Christians (capitalist exploitation on a worldwide scale, and so on).

However, an extratheoretical element intervenes in the choice of this orientation, one tied to faith and implying an antecedent ethical option. It is this extratheoretical element that will finally determine the choice of the actual theory. At this moment, then the question arises: How is the criteriology of this choice to be established? This will be the subject of the next section.

§22 CRITERIOLOGY FOR THE CHOICE OF SOCIAL THEORY AS SOCIO-ANALYTIC MEDIATION

Seeing that a theology of the political must necessarily have an articulation with the sciences of the social, the question then arises: Among existing theories, which method of concrete analysis, or which "social theory," is the "political theologian" to select for socio-analytic mediation?

The answer is not so simple, for the various "social theories" are not only in competition, but contradictory.

Let us enter upon this question a step at a time.

The various orientations of the contemporary sciences of the social can be distinguished in reference to various criteria. Still, it is relatively easy to discern two basic orientations:[26]

1. There is a *functionalist* tendency, which assigns the primacy to a concept of order, harmony, or equilibrium, and which attempts to analyze society in the form of an organic whole with complementary parts.

2. There is a *dialectical* tendency, which centers around the idea of conflict, tension, and struggle, and which sees society as a complex, contradictory whole.

In the concrete world of today, the first of these two basic functions or orientations is represented by the liberal tradition. The second is represented by Marxism. The former reads society from above, from where society appears under the idealistic aspect of harmony and complementarity. Clearly, this is the vision of dominant groups. The dialectical orientation reads society from beneath, hence from where it is defined first and foremost as struggle and confrontation. Naturally, this is the vision of dominated groups.[27]

The question that arises for a theology of the political is the following: Of the two orientations, which is the more satisfactory? In order to respond to this question two sorts of criteria can be advanced: *scientific* criteria and *ethical* criteria.

As to scientific criteria, the theory that explains the most will be preferred.

As to ethical criteria, the preferred theory will be the one that best responds to the values considered to be decisive, and that can be included in a practical plan for personal or political action.

As to the first type of criteria: let us note that the scientific character of the sciences of the social is at least very problematic. Here we are very much before a still open question.[28]

Even so, it may be said that functionalism satisfactorily answers the questions with which it is concerned, involving the regular functioning of a social system that it judges good and to be maintained. Likewise, it may be said that Marxism largely takes into account the problems of a people that suffers as a result of conflicts and seeks to resolve them, even at the price of revolution.

At this point, then, we must move on to the second type of criteria—ethical criteria. The question of "scientificness" raises an antecedent question, one concerned with ideological options and determinate political undertakings, and finally leading precisely to ethics. Before a judgment can be made on the explicative value of a theory, one must determine the *concrete problems* this theory claims to explain. The actual determination of these problems implies a decision of an ethical sort (though not exclusively of an ethical sort).

First of all, then, there is an ethical option concerning the concrete problems that are presented to awareness as questions to be resolved. Secondly, there is a choice of the means to resolve these problems—theoretical means and practical means. As we see, then, it is in a second moment that the choice of a theory occurs. This choice is made in function of a previous ethical option.[29] Let us note as well that the two moments in question are dialectically connected, describing a "methodological circle."[30]

Thus, for example, if an option is made for the "liberation of the poor" (in virtue of an ethical norm), or for the "emancipation of the working class" (in virtue of a political or ideological norm), it will not be in functionalism that we shall find the necessary theoretical tools for an understanding of what is at stake in this option—the so often traumatic reality of the exploited masses.[31]

It will not be in order to confuse these ethical options and theoretical arguments. We have two orders of questions here, and they are by no means interchangeable. A desire for the liberation of the oppressed will be no automatic guarantee of possession of a serious analysis of their wretched condition. Such a desire is a *condition* of the analysis, indeed, but it is not the analysis itself. The latter will be the result of a specific practice—a theoretical, or scientific practice. Nor will it be enough to be a good social analyst to be able efficaciously to assist the "development" of a country for which the ideology of "developmentalism," still in fashion in our days, so eloquently pleads. Besides—and antecedently to this act of assistance—it will be necessary to make one decision as to the finalities of "development," and then another as to which groups shall be the beneficiaries of this "development."[32]

If I wished to formulate all this in terms of my distinction between the two regimes of a science, I would say that the question of "scientificness" and its criteria is a matter of the *internal regime* of a science, whereas the criterion of the ethical choice—or better, the ethico-political choice—is located on the side of the *external regime*. To the former regime belongs the task of explaining a given series of problems by a "social theory," whereas the latter must determine whether these problems are to be constituted the raw material of the theory in question.

Perhaps this distinction will shed some light on the question of the "axiological neutrality" of the sciences of the social.[33] These sciences de facto presuppose ethical choices (the aspect of dependency). But *at the same time* their scientific density is by no means justified by the correctness and justice of these choices (the aspect of autonomy).

With these observations behind us, we may now ask which of the two basic "social theory" orientations the theologian ought to select, in terms of ethics, to serve as socio-analytic mediation. A concrete response may be given to this question in the form of a reference to the practices of engaged Christian communities. We may then say that the solution is given *in actu,* in the ethico-political option that these communities have made in the name of Christian faith.

At the same time, on the level of the content of Christian faith, the theologian is not deprived of certain precise, referential criteria for the selection of a determinate social theory and a determinate social practice. These will be found above all in the gospel—which, although of course manipulable, is not so manipulable as to render any and all effort at concrete ethical demarcation simply ludicrous, although this demarcation and its corresponding realization indeed in all cases preserve their "kairological" character, in the sense of remaining relative where the historical moment is concerned. Thus we hear of Jesus' preference for the poor, his imperious, polemical attitude toward the prevailing order in the world, his message of justice and fellowship, and so on.[34] These criteria are too clear and certain to confuse the Christian communities that are the most aware of the problems of the periphery, along with their pastors and theologians. Suffering and struggling side by side with non-Christians and the most alert of scientists, these Christians have resolutely chosen a conflictual reading of the reality that is theirs.[35] And they have done so on the basis of criteria furnished by their very faith, in articulation with analyses of the sciences of the social.

The criteriology in question could appear too precarious to justify the sort of methodological imperative I am proposing for the choice of an orientation of theology in the field of the sciences of the social. I respond to this anticipated objection by an appeal not to the commonplace of "pluralism," but to realism. The mediations of the language of faith are and will ever be historical, and consequently relative. One seizes upon the rational tool furnished by the cultural present, not upon one alleged to carry a guarantee of infallibility, or eternity. Such an instrument exists only for the illusions of idealism. From the moment one is forced to a choice, under pressure of circumstances that cannot be postponed, one must simply select the most adequate means—or, negatively, the means that constitute the lesser evil.[36]

That a risk exists is undeniable. Risk is the price of all growth—human, historical, or scientific. But it can be a *calculated* risk, a risk with a likelihood of success. I trust that I have now shown this with sufficient clarity. When all is said and done, the absolute that fears the relative shows that it is not so absolute after all. And God has run the risk of the relative—in incarnation, passion, and death. So why not the church and the Christian, why not faith and theology?

Finally: of all the organized bodies of knowledge, theology has the least reason to fear the perils of sharing the destiny of all human existence, especially political existence. Otherwise its vaunted title of "political" will be no more than a simple ornament—or worse, the mask of its impotence.[37]

§23 TOWARD A SAVOIR-FAIRE OF THE PRACTICE OF SOCIO-ANALYTIC MEDIATION

Something must be said about the mode of the practico-practical implementation of socio-analytic mediation. Am I not demanding too difficult a theoretical articulation—perhaps even an impracticable one?

In the response to the difficulties of the practical implementation of socio-analytic mediation, we may no longer invoke the theory of a theoretical practice, but must have its savoir-faire, its methodological technology. To this purpose, the concrete practices of socio-analytic mediation, recent though they be, can point us along certain paths. Let us stake out certain signposts along these paths, claiming no more authority for them than that of mere suggestions.

1. Socio-Analytic *Habitus* [38]

It would seem that "political theologians" will have to provide themselves with a sufficiently developed critical awareness of society in order to be able gradually to withdraw from the grossest of the naiveties, unmask current ideologies, appraise theoretical "novelties"—in a word, "get a solid idea" of the socio-historical conjuncture in which we are situated. Even more than a critical awareness, it would be preferable for "political theologians" to possess a (critical) science, whose theoretical domain will enable them to be genuine producers of knowledge rather than simply consumers.[39]

2. Concrete Analysis of a Situation

Social analysis should take place in *interdisciplinary* collaboration[40]. In such collaboration, theology speaks its own specific language, such as I have endeavored to define it in this study. Accordingly, theology must exercise caution, in respect for the otherness of other discourses, and in maintaining its own proper difference.

There are those who judge "interdisciplinarity" an impossible undertaking. But it will be impossible only for those who consider their specialty to be the last, if not the only, word of reason. What is certain is that scientific discourses are irreducible as such. At least it pertains to their nature and dynamic to stake out their own specificity in the clearest manner possible.

There are, however, zones of convergence—for example, questions that touch on philosophy (metaphysics), ethics, and the solution of concrete problems. In such cases, it is difficult to imagine that questions as complex as political ones should be manageable by theologians alone, or especially that theologians should be able to provide solid, concrete orientations with regard to this kind of problem. Theologians would readily lapse into a totalizing, generalizing verbalism, sometimes merely useless, sometimes demobilizing.[41]

The theoretical elaboration of political themes should be done by teams composed of those who, Christian or not, share a common front in the struggle. Theology can neither claim to be a total science nor a complete guide to action. Theology is only theology, a regional discourse.

3. Theological Elaboration as Such

The qualification "theological" belongs to reflection that articulates a conjunct of mediations in such a way that a metabolic, as it were, assimilation of sociology, or of any other discipline, transpires against the theological horizon.[42] Thus, the "sociological" can belong explicitly to the corpus of theological elaboration, just as it can also be simply presupposed by theological elaboration—but always in such wise that the properly theological word takes flight only from this previously prepared solid base, which makes it proof against clandestine penetration by an "unbridled" sociology disguised as properly theological knowledge.

4. External Circumstances

Finally, it remains to consider the external, secondary aspects of a determinate theology of the political—the selection of content, form, language, addressee, mode of publication, and the like—aspects very dependent on the material conditions of production of any theoretical practice.

Being subject—relatively speaking—to the contingencies of the political—that is, of history—this reflection will have to assume the task of self-interrogation as to the actual conditions (material, political, cultural, ecclesiastical, and so on) of its possibility, and even as to its opportuneness at a given moment.

For it were better to deliver oneself, in full cognizance of cause, to discursive practices that are not properly theological (prophecy, homily, catechesis, and the like—even sociology, and the like) than to seek improperly and illegitimately to misname these same practices "theology," in the hope of bestowing upon them a credibility and warranty that otherwise they would not enjoy. These religious (or even "profane") discourses, having no further theoretical pretensions, may actually be more important than the theological discourse itself. But indiscriminately to denominate as "theology" any and every concatenation of cognitional materials or religious recipe is to suffer the blemish of rationalism, by implying that the *ratio fidei* is more important than *fides* itself or, therefore, more important than its revealing word.[43] It is not evident by what privilege the discourse of science would be superior to the discourse of lived experience, nor therefore why theological discourse would be the acme of any and all religious language.

When all is said and done, as the great Portuguese poet of the century, Fernando Pessoa, has sung:

> *O mais que isto,*
> *É Jesus Cristo*
> *Que não sabia nada de finanças.*
> *Nem consta que tivesse biblioteca.*[44]
> (Greater than all this
> Is Jesus Christ,
> Who knew nothing of high finance.
> And had, it would seem, no library.)

PART 2

HERMENEUTIC MEDIATION

In conformity with the general methodological model I am following in this work, I now propose to treat of questions relating to the properly theological aspect of the theology of the political.

In part 1, we entered into problems touching on the *material* object of a theology of the political—that is, touching on the political as such, as including in its notion the ideas of praxis, society, history, and socio-historical conjuncture. I came to the conclusion that a journey by way of the mediation of the sciences of the social, in socio-analytic mediation, is an obligatory detour for a theology of the political with any aspirations for adequation to its new theoretical object. This conclusion, we saw, is imposed all the more forcefully in view of the fact that it is precisely the imperatives that praxis addresses to Christians that take shape against the horizon of this same theological theory. It has not, therefore, been a mere ambition to know for the sake of knowing that has animated the program of a theology of the political in the last instance, but the problems of the actual life experience of Christians engaged in social confrontations. Accordingly, social analysis is an indispensable element of this theology: it permits the apprehension, within the limits of the possible, of the positive, autonomous structure of the situation within which faith must operate.

This first step—socio-analytic mediation—pertains integrally to the nautical chart of the theological voyage. The mediation itself, then, will need to be situated precisely within the purview of the theology of the political.

Having arrived at this point, we shall have to set sail once more, and investigate the actual horizon or "purview" just mentioned. In other words, I must now pose certain questions with respect to the *formal* object of theology, with respect to theological pertinency: What constitutes the "theologicity" of a determinate discourse? What founds the particular approach to which the name of "theology" is given? What is the proper element—*to idion*—of theological discourse?

63

In terms of the precise object of this book, it may appear that I am distancing myself too far from my specific objective. May we not consider this more general question already resolved? In a way, yes we may. Second theology supposes first theology, which considers the problem of its epistemological legitimation resolved with such questions as: Can God be known? Can God bestow self-revelation? Under what conditions? And so on.

The more general question of "theologicity" has its answer, then. But only *in abstracto. In concreto,* we have to face the fact that theological practice in general is suffering from a profound identity crisis in our day. Hence, the schizoid mien of so many of our current theological discourses.[1] This is owing in large part to the secularization of thought provoked by the human sciences. The crisis of theology does not need to be verified; it needs to be resolved.[2] Hence the necessity for a genuine epistemological *recasting* of theological practice.[3]

As we know, periods of crisis drive reflection back to its launch pad for a new lift-off. This is verified for all science, indeed for all knowledge. Theology, in my view, enjoys no privilege of exemption from this condition.[4]

Thus I find myself obliged to posit anew certain truly radical questions. But, in the wake of an orientation that seems generalized today, I, for my part, hold that the questions called "radical" deserve this qualifier, not in virtue of their intending any directly new theoretical objects, through the development of new theological theories with radical intentions, but in virtue of their bearing on actual theological elaboration—that is, the manner of apprehending and "working"—of these new objects.[5] For me, what makes a question radical is not the problem but the problematic, not the subject but the method, not the theological theory but the theory of the theological theories.

It is precisely "fundamental" problems, in the etymological, material sense of the term, that constitute the thematic of my investigation, especially in this part 2. These problems have not been selected abstractly, in some aprioristic fashion; they arise out of theological practice such as I see at work on the level of second theology—namely, in the theology of liberation. I single out a certain number of these problems—the ones that seem to me to be the most important, the ones that take the form of basic mental patterns that trammel the healthy development of theory. I have already characterized these procedural difficulties as "epistemological obstacles."[6]

My procedure is akin to that of the medievals. For me as for them, the point of departure is in the problems the theologian faces in the de facto historical and cultural situation. For the medievals it was *question.* For me it is *obstacles.* And, like them, I try to arrange a series of difficulties in a certain logical order.[7]

Thus my choice and order of obstacles is somewhat arbitrary. It would have been possible to compose a systematic classification of these obstacles and problems of method in general, first by a selection of the obstacles, together with their corresponding theological productions, and then by an analysis and critique. However, properly epistemological productions bearing on a theology of the political, as well as the general tenor of their discourse, seem to me to be so deficient in comparison with the demands for rigor made in other areas of learning that I have resisted the inclination to develop my study in direct and systematic contact with such productions. Such a point of departure would surely have been impoverishing. I prefer to take my distance from these productions, so as to be able to focus upon certain basic problems implicit in their theories, even though the relationship of the problems to the theories may not appear at first blush.

Now I can trace out the development to which I propose to subject the material in the four chapters of part 2.

Chapter 5 will attempt to bring into sharp focus the question of theological *pertinency*—the precise formality that authorizes a language to proclaim itself "theology." This step will necessarily be an abstract one, for I shall be attempting to carry out a *formal* analysis in respect of the "theologicity" of theology. My theoretical exploration will, however, rely on (1) a particular historical study, focusing especially on Thomas Aquinas, and (2) on a critique of certain current theological modes of practice. Thus the formalism to which I allude will not be so formal after all, because its "concretizations" will be evidenced in the two instances to which I have referred.

In chapter 6 I propose to establish, in terms of theology, the *fundamental* distinction (in the twofold sense of "founding" and "foundational") between the "real" and the "known"—that is, between the *teologal* and the *teológico* (the "theologizable" and the "theologized," or the objectively and the reflexively theological). This distinction will posit the real object of faith, and consequently the real object of theology, as antecedent to, and independent of, any awareness of that object. Such awareness, for its part, will appear as a merely derived event, as a "phenomenon" in respect to its "noumenon." It will therefore be determined by the anteriority, in all senses, and the absolute otherness, of the real, proper object of faith and theology. This thesis seeks to found the proper "objective" character of theology, and radically to exclude any vestige of theological idealism.

Chapter 7 will draw a second line of demarcation, this time not between the real and awareness of the real, but within this very awareness. The new line will split this awareness, this conciousness, "right down the middle." On the one side we shall have *faith*—our awareness as experience of its "Real," our awareness as simple awareness. On the other side we shall have *theology*—critical cognition. Thus theology will be distanced from faith, from its word, from its immediate, spontaneous language, which is precisely religious discourse.

In chapter 8 I shall reflect on *hermeneutics,* with respect to the epistemological status of the word of faith as the starting point of theology. Through hermeneutics I shall attempt to grasp the relationship uniting revelation to the texts of scripture and of its tradition, in and through Christian writings generally. Thus hermeneutic will appear as one of the necessary epistemological moments, although not the only one, in the process of the construction of a theology— here, a Christian theology. From a point of departure in this conception, then, I shall approach the question of a hermeneutic adequate to a theology of the *political.* The underlying question of this last chapter in part 2, which will have been prepared for by the preceding chapters, then, is the following: How is scripture to be read when what we are doing is theologizing the political, and theologizing a determinate politics?

As I have already had occasion to observe, this sequence is not purely taxonomic. There is a more or less logical connection among these four chapters, which may be expressed in the following way. After having treated of the material object of a "theologicity" of the political (the political itself, as given in socio-analytic mediation), it remains to study its formal object: the precisely theological element of this theology (in the hermeneutic moment). This is what I call "theological pertinency," and it is the concern of chapter 5. But at once a question arises as to the justification of this particular theoretical object. I must speak, then, of the "ontic" bases of this pertinency—which gives us chapter 6. Then, from a reflection on the (real) being of theology, the question of the status of the (theoretical) knowledge of this same being arises, for being relates to an order of its own, and knowing relates to its own, and we are into chapter 7. But the relationship between being and knowledge becomes possible, in theology, only by means of hermeneutic mediation—hence chapter 8.

As can be seen, then, I shall be touching on all the basic themes of a theological epistemology: the pertinent, the real, the theoretical, and the hermeneutic. My plan may seem ambitious, even overambitious. But I serve notice from the outset that I shall be attempting to grasp only the general articulations of the material to be handled.

It is my conviction that the appearance of a kind of theology for which I have coined the name "second theology" is a shock to the very concept of theology, and calls for an epistemological recasting, by a redefinition of the essential elements of its practice. The elements I have just indicated seem to belong precisely to the internal constitution of the theological process. On this level, it is by no means enough to treat each term in isolation. All the force of reflection, in my view, should be brought to bear upon relating each term to all the others, as the structuralist method would suggest.[8]

I am of the number of those who think that the time has come to go beyond a voluntaristic, impressionistic, or declamatory epistemology, and finally set ourselves to analyzing the organic structure of theologizing, even at the price of seeming, or indeed being, "abstract" or "formal" or "dry" or "bland."[9]

Such, in my view, is the high price that praxis (of the faith) imperiously demands of a (theological) theory that would undertake to deal in that praxis.

CHAPTER 5

Theological Pertinency:
Word of Revelation

§24 THEOLOGICAL NONPERTINENCY

I have said that the state of theology today is one of "epistemological unconsciousness"—an inability to put its finger on the differential of its own discourse, to construct a self-definition. In order to appreciate the seriousness of the situation, we need only glance at some of the discourses that go by the name of "theology." The appellation would seem to be claimed solely in virtue of the fact that these discourses bear upon a "religious" or "Christian" *subject*. If we take care to examine the *manner of treatment* that these discourses bring to bear upon this subject, however, we have reason to doubt the legitimacy of their claim to be "theological." After all, what determines the category of a discipline but its *pertinency*—that is, its own proper "language project," its characteristic outlook or perspective? A proposition or question will be called "pertinent," then, under the *conditio sine qua non* that it pertains to the area of that "project" or "outlook." Thus the pertinency of a discipline will be logically defined in relation to its *formal* object.[1]

Assertions of this kind may not seem to go beyond the level of truisms, even tautologies. But cases of deviation and misunderstanding in theological discourse are too frequent and obvious for us to suppose that these truths, elementary though they be, are known, or that any conscientization has occurred in theology in their regard. At all events, it seems to me to constitute an abuse of the word "theology" to use it to qualify any and all religious discourse indiscriminately.[2]

I can distinguish three areas where this abuse seems to stand out most clearly:

1. The level of simple religious discourse.
2. The level of the philosophy of religion.
3. The level of the "human sciences" of religion.

As to the first type of discourse: I shall be speaking of this more *in extenso* throughout the development of part 2. Here let me say only that, although theology can be considered a religious discourse as well, it is nevertheless distinguishable from the others in virtue of its critical and systematic nature. It seeks to map out its route clearly, and to acquire the means of checking and verifying all the steps that lead to its object. The case is different with other religious discourses. They are characterized by a direct and immediate relationship to lived experience. They adhere to their object. They construct no theoretical instrument, no method, that would enable them to contemplate what they say at a distance from their saying it. If they are called theology, it is only a spontaneous, "undisciplined," theology that is meant, if not indeed a "theology" in some merely analogous, impoverished sense.[3]

As for philosophies of religion, here again it is not its material that determines the pertinency of a discourse, but the manner in which it develops its material. Briefly, it may be said that it is faith, as their particular horizon of understanding, that distinguishes theologians from philosophers. The theological mode of approach is in a relationship of dependency (to be determined further) on what faith allows to be seen (revelation). To use the classic expressions for theological practice, the theologian sees "in the light of faith," whereas the philosopher sees "in the light of (pure) reason," so that the theologian's formal object is God, whereas that of the philosopher is being.[4]

Moving closer, now, to the problematic of the theology of the political, the discourses of the nontheological religious human sciences must be treated under the various aspects of the religious factors they bear upon: experience, organization, language, history, and so on. Hence the proliferation today of sociologies of religion, psychologies of religion, analyses of religious language, and the like.[5]

The material object of all these undertakings is "the religious." But it is not their material object that confers upon them their epistemological identity. It is their modus operandi, their point of view, as has already been stated.[6]

When we consider the principal subject matter of the theological undertakings today that claim to be in dialogue with the human sciences, we perceive that, in the majority of cases, this subject matter is constituted by a (material) "religious object" that supposedly lends these undertakings their specificity: analyses of religious language, histories of religion, psychologies of religious behavior, sociologies of the church, anthropologies of myth, analyses of biblical texts, and the like.

All these investigations are surely legitimate. Their validity is measured only by the methodological limits that found and establish them. Thus, for example, when we examine biblical language simply as one language among others, or when we analyze the history of the people of Israel simply as one social group among others, we are conducting a legitimate investigation, for we are conducting it according to methodologies specific to each such undertaking. The key expression is that specifying "as." It denotes the particular perspective from which the material under consideration is examined. This formalizing particle signals the willed, originative abstraction of one aspect from among so many others in the totality of the real.

The theologian must insist on the bracketing of the "supernatural" in and by the other disciplines. This aspect is "nonpertinent" there, and because it does not appear in the premises of a discourse, neither may it appear in the conclusions. It would constitute an unwarranted, improper interpolation.

It frequently happens, however, that a specific order of question is thus duly placed in a state of suspension as a line of argumentation opens—but then insidiously works its way back into the reasoning and makes its appearance in a final statement, apparently allowed in by a kind of "theoretical fatigue." But this phenomenon always involves a sophism—a sophism to be denounced for the sake of the soundness and health of the discipline in question, as well as for the sake of the truth of the real object under consideration. Thus the notorious critiques of religion by Ricoeur's "masters of suspicion" must be apprehended theoretically at the very root of their approach, on the level of their methodological constrictions.

In accordance with the positions maintained in this book, "extraneous" or "lay" analyses of religion, faith, church, and so on, today constitute an indispensable mediation for a theology that hopes to avoid shouting to the four winds after the manner of an ideology (a "first ideology"). Recourse to such mediation is all the more urgent today, when what is at stake is precisely the practice that Christians take up in politics, a practice that they want to be lucid in its intelligibility and its efficacy.[7]

I use the word "mediation" in this context because the analyses in question here are a means (a *medium quo,* an instrumentality) by which theologians gain a correct understanding of the signification of the faith whose theory they have taken up the task of organizing.

Thus, for theology, "extraneous" interpretations of religion like those cited above are presupposed, are antecedent—and hence are mediations, and necessary ones. At the same time, mediations they are, and only that. They do not make up the field of properly theological reference. The theologian who means to do theology, then, may not stop at the level of these religious studies. They are no substitute for theological theory. They must be taken up by theologians and reworked, according to the properly theological mode of production, in order to become specifically theological products—the results of a specific labor. I shall return to this point in more detail below.[8]

Besides studies of the human sciences concerned with "religious objects" but not themselves theological studies, there are also those that take theology itself as the proper object of their analysis. This is the case, for example, with the sociology of theological cognition, the analysis of religious language, the history of theological thought, the criticism of religious ideologies, and the like.

These studies will of course be of interest to theologians. Theologians should take their findings seriously. But theologians must be on guard lest such studies come to replace their particular task. They have no discriminating relationship to the word of God that founds (Christian) theology, and hence cannot be taken for constitutively theological analyses.[9] They must be taken for what they are. For the theologian they are mediations, both with (direct) respect to (theological) *theoretical* practice, and with (indirect) respect to the *political* practice of Christians.

Coming now to the epistemology of theology, we know that this, too, takes theology as the object of its discourse, constituting the metalanguage of theology as its language-object. Still, we shall have no difficulty in placing it within theology itself, as the watchful conscience of that theology. The epistemology of theology is vigilant theology, or theological vigilance. It is theology aware-of-being-theology, and aware of its nature as distinguished from other sciences or ways of knowing or bodies of knowledge. The epistemology of theology is theology staking out its otherness in their respect, establishing its determinative pertinency.

This has been a very summary sketch of the panorama of discourses that, bearing the likeness and sometimes the name of theology, seem to me to be deprived of a properly theological specificity. I hope I have succeeded in circumscribing—from without, as it were—the specific terrain of this study, and for which I shall be seeking a clearer definition in the remaining sections of this chapter.

§25 THE PROCESS OF THEORETICAL PRACTICE

In order to approach the question of theological pertinency in a clear and methodical manner, I shall now propound an explanation of the process of theoretical practice in general as delineated by Louis Althusser.[10]

I justify this choice, first, by the heuristic value offered by the Althusser model of theoretical practice; and secondly, by the objective I have here of showing that theological knowledge or science can appeal to a structure that is homologous with that of any canonical science, or discipline.

By "canonical science" I mean a body of knowledge structured in a discourse articulated by precise principles that govern its process and that can be identified. I mean a critical, reflexively conscious, and self-regulated approach. I mean, then, an approach that is distinct from that of other kinds of knowing—the prescientific, the rhetorical, or the ideological—each of which in turn has rules of its own, but rules that operate, so to speak, clandestinely.[11]

I am not proposing other sciences as a model for theology, in the spirit of ambiguous expressions like "as scientific as the natural sciences." I simply wish to show that theology pursues, *in its own way,* the formal approach that any discipline pursues in its own way.[12]

Before moving on to Althusser's description of theoretical practice, it will be in order to ask why I speak of "theoretical practice" or "theological practice," instead of simply "theory" or "theology."

I employ the expression "practice" (theoretical or theological) because it better corresponds to the truth of scientific theory itself. A science must first of all be understood as a particular practice. A science must be considered principally as a "science-in-becoming," not as a "science-become"—as a process, not as a system; as a project, an enterprise, a task, a labor, rather than a body of knowledge, an aggregate of conclusions, a stockpile of concepts and theories.[13]

Science in act is a labor—a *production of cognition*. It is an operation of *transformation*.[14] That is, it is genuine *practice*. Its material, means, and products are, of course, *sui generis*. They are of a *theoretical* nature. Contrary to the idealistic conceptualization, a theoretical practice does not transform external things, at least not directly. It transforms ideas. This does not mean that ideas have no substance, or that they do not yield to a genuine process of production and transformation.

On the other hand, science is not a simple reflection on reality, a passive gathering up of the world, or its purely symbolic representation. Science is essentially an effectuation of the world, in thought. It is performance. Science is not the duplication of the world. It is critical autoproduction.[15]

Even when it is articulated upon society and praxis, a theoretical praxis, like any other praxis, has its own autonomous rules, and this from a point of departure in its internal structure, as we shall shortly see.

Following Althusser, then, the process of a theoretical practice comports three "moments" (levels or instances): a "first generality," a "second generality," and a "third generality."

What is a "generality"? Here it will suffice to say that the process of cognition bears properly upon the universal, not on the singular or the "concrete" existing "outside the head" (Marx) or *"extra animam"* (Thomas Aquinas).[16]

After all, the real object, the *res,* and the object of cognition—the idea, the concept—are totally distinct. The former is a *real concrete,* and the latter, at very best, is a *thought concrete (Gedanken-Konkretum*—Marx).

I say "at very best," because I am thinking of a "third generality," a *concept*. Theoretical generality is not homogeneous. It is distinguished, in its internal structure, into first, second, and third generalities, as we are about to see.[17]

Theoretical practice, in its three instances, "takes place entirely in knowledge."[18] There is no question of a direct cognition of the "real," the "concrete," or the "thing in itself," as a simplistic epistemology would have it, be the latter called empiricism, intuitionism, sensualism, or positivism, all of which naively oppose the "abstract" to the "concrete," the "theoretical" to the "practical."[19]

The process of scientific cognition formally begins not with real or concrete things, but with general, abstract, and ideological notions that it encounters in a given culture.[20] These constitute its "first generality"—that with which it knows or theorizes, the matter it has to rework and transform into knowledge, into the "thought concrete." Real things remain behind the cognitive process, as presupposed by this process and as the somehow asymptotic object of this process. The concept *(Begriff)* seizes the object only theoretically—that is, in its ideal form. Only the hand may grasp the thing in its material concretion.

The first generality, in theoretical practice, plays the role of raw material. But as generality, it is "matter already elaborated and transformed," down through history, by various social practices—esthetic, technical, ideological, scientific, and so on.[21] There is no question of practicing upon an absolutely "raw" material, a brute, "pure" fact, an object "in itself." This raw material already belongs to the conditions of the production of cognition.[22]

The "second generality," in turn, is the instance that does the work. Here we have the theoretical means of production, the "corpus of concepts," or the "theory" of a science in a given phase of its development. The second generality is that by which the first generality is "worked." In the process of transformation called cognition, the second generality holds the "primacy," and so determines the specific type of a science—being the vehicle of identity or pertinency of that science.[23]

Finally, the "third generality" is the "product," the "thought concrete," or "concrete thought," the no longer abstract, but now concrete generality, the no longer generic but specific, the no longer ideological but scientific generality. In this moment we no longer find ourselves before a vague, general idea, a simple notion, but precisely before a concept, or scientific theory. The third generality is the theoretical result or product. In more idealistic language, the third generality is what the second generality shows, as it "makes knowledge" (scientific). If the concepts of the instance of intervention (the second generality) can be called "theoretical concepts," those of the third generality ought to be called "empirical concepts."[24]

To sum up what has been said thus far: theoretical practice produces third generalities by the operation of a second generality upon a first generality.[25]

It is to be noted that theoretical practice genuinely transforms: it produces something new. In epistemological theory, a third generality is of a different order, a different form, from a first generality. To be sure, a third generality proceeds, emerges, from a first generality. But between these two generalities an "epistemological severance" occurs, an "epistemological breach," or "rupture" (Gaston Bachelard).[26] Between the (abstract, ideological) notion and the (concrete, scientific) concept, a real discontinuity prevails.

The important thing here is to appreciate the position of each term in the structure here being analyzed. It is this position or place that determines the function of the term in question relative to the other terms.

In accordance with this formal ordering, what was originally a third generality can perfectly well occupy the place of a first generality in a subsequent movement, or even of a second generality.[27] What we are dealing with here are positions, not elements with an independent content.[28]

Should I wish to schematize the three articulated levels of theoretical practice, it could be done in the triadic form depicted in Diagram 2.

In terms of Althusser's analysis, which we have just seen, it is clear that certain conceptualizations of the process of cognition are guilty of simplism and ought to be criticized: for example, the conceptualization of knowledge as a simple relationship between two or three terms, subject and object, or subject and object connected by method; or that of science as a relationship between a theory and a thing (a phenomenon, an experience, a datum, and so on); or even the classic representation, of positivistic hue, of scientific construction as occurring in the simple moments of observation, hypothesis, and experience or verification.[29]

At all events, it is absolutely imperative that we be rid of the "mirror myth of

Diagram 2

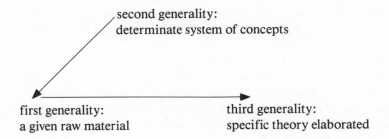

second generality:
determinate system of concepts

first generality:
a given raw material

third generality:
specific theory elaborated

knowledge as the vision of a given object or the reading of an established text, neither of which is ever anything but transparency itself."[30] Theoretical practice must be understood for what it is: a practice of the production of cognition. Hence, a "materialistic" language is more suitable for expressing the activity of the cognitive practice than is an "idealistic" language, which inclines more toward a model of epistemological passivity, inasmuch as the former is based on a production model, and the latter uses the analogy of vision.

A presentation of theoretical practice, as well as a critique of its distorted, and distorting, images, can concur only when it comes to an exact understanding of the epistemological identity of theology itself.[31]

§26 THEOLOGY AS DISCIPLINED KNOWLEDGE

I am of the opinion that the process of theological cognition obeys the same structural laws as any other theoretical practice, as such practice has just been described.[32]

After all, theological practice comprises a first generality—its "subject," or material object—a second generality, which is the body of its asymptotic or analogical concepts, and finally a third generality, the theological theory produced.

The structure is the same: we have the same loci, and the same interplay of relationships among the terms occupying these loci. Only the nature of the terms is particular to theology, as is to be expected.

In order the better to appreciate this structural configuration, let us turn to history. Let us dwell for a moment on Thomas Aquinas, the first theologian to raise theology to the level of a discourse having a rigorous theoretical status of its own.[33]

Thomas Aquinas's model of science was clearly Aristotle's. For both philosophers, science was a deductive knowledge, proceeding from a number of self-evident principles. In the case of theology—for Thomas, then—these principles were furnished by revelation, and received by faith. These faith-principles are for theology what the first, self-evident principles are for the other sciences.[34]

It is not difficult, however, to understand Aquinas's epistemology of theology in a framework of the process of theoretical practice just explained. When Thomas speaks of the *principia* of theology, and identifies them as the *articuli fidei,* we recognize these as occupying the position of a second generality—the instance that gives shape to a first generality, rendering it a finished product in the form of third generality.

In order to ground a second generality, theological theory, according to Thomas, has recourse to faith—or to revelation, which is tantamount to the same thing. The principles of theology, then, are the truths of faith.[35] It is not necessary, therefore, to create them, or deduce them by a particular cognitive process. The justification of faith will of course be another matter—evidently a pretheological one, which theological discourse takes for granted, just as it takes the truths of faith, the doctrinal content of revelation, for granted.

It is, then, the *principia fidei* that constitute theological pertinency. They constitute that by which theologizing is done, the light in which theology is practiced, the horizon of theological cognition.

To designate this pertinency, Aquinas employs the classic expression *objectum quo,* as distinguished from the *objectum quod.* It is in virtue of the former that the latter may be contemplated. The *objectum quo* constitutes the *formality* of the theological gaze.[36] *In concreto,* this pertinency is constituted from a point of departure in the message of revelation, as identifiable in scripture.

Obviously, things are not so simple that we might simply draw up the equation: revelation = second generality. In theological practice, a second generality, too, must be produced, and produced through a process homologous to that described in the foregoing section. I shall call this particular process "hermeneutic," and I shall return to it in more detail in chapter 8. In any case, the content (positivity) of Christian faith may not be conceived in positiv*ist* fashion, as if the mysteries of faith were something like meteors—*veritates e coelo delapsae,* simply.[37] In theological tradition itself, a second generality has always appeared as the object of a particular procedure—"positive theology"—which, as theoretical process, is also a process of transformation.

At the same time, it is evident that, when one does theology, one enters into a movement that is already in course, and is sustained by the social activity of the community of theologians, in such wise that one attains this movement at a given moment in its historical development, without the validity of the presuppositions that nourish this dynamic theology having to be verified at each successive moment in time. Still, it remains true to say that the productive instance of theology—a second generality—needs to be examined each time theological practice enters into crisis.

Let us now speak of first generality—the raw material, or subject matter, of theology. Here, I must repeat, there is nothing, in principle, that cannot become the (material) object of a theological treatment. Theology can become interested in anything. But this "anything" is "pertinently theological" only when it is considered under a certain *ratio formalis*—that of divine revelation.[38]

As a consequence, it is "in the light of revelation" that anything in (Christian) theology is contemplated. And it is precisely this specificity that renders a particular gaze the theological gaze.[39]

Let it be noted, that, following Aquinas here, I employ mainly the classic terminology, whose lexicon is, so to speak, "idealistic." Theology is conceived here in the form of "theory" in the Greek (and etymological) sense of "vision," or "contemplation," where the aspect of receptivity predominates. If I wished to use a more "materialistic" lexicon, and express myself in terms of "practice," or "production," or "transformation," I would describe the theological process in these terms: the content (positivity) of faith, already constituted as second generality, works upon a given raw material (first generality), in order to transform it into a finished theological product (third generality).

Thus one can certainly say that "it all depends on the point of view.[40] That theory alone is theological that is produced in accordance with the theological process. And because this process cannot be effectuated without an essential reference to the positivity of faith, there is no theology that is not in the element of faith. Here, we come to the "third generality"—the term of the process of theoretical transformation, of which Aquinas's *Summa Theologiae,* like any other theological production, is an illustration.

Thus, the work of theological *ratio* consists in placing a second generality in relationship with a first generality, so that a third generality may be produced. The third generality is a first generality reworked by a second generality.

On the basis of what has been said, one may easily resolve the pseudo opposition in theology between salvation history and speculative science. To my mind, one need not choose between the two. The terms are mutually inclusive. True, each has its particular function. The former is located on the level of first generality, and the latter on that of second generality. Thus, to borrow an example from Thomas Aquinas, "faith believes in the Passion [first generality] to the extent that it is the Passion of God" [second generality].[41] There is no *salvation* history apart from a faith vision capable of reading, in history, the salvation event. Correlatively: (Christian) theology exists only to the exact measure that it is precisely salvation *history* that is being described. Indeed biblical history as such has a pistic, hence a theological, signification only with reference to God's action within it. Without this reference to God, history has no (theological) meaning.

Consequently, what makes a determinate discourse a theological discourse is its formality—and this is a concrete tautology. Aquinas observes that the *subjectum* of theology—its formal, or proper, object—is not to be defined by its subject matter, or *"ea quae in ista scientia tractantur."* It is to be determined by the *manner of treating* the subject matter— *"rationem secundum quam considerantur."*[42] It is precisely this *ratio secundum quam,* or *ratio qua,* this "as" that renders a given discourse *such and such* a discourse, and no other. For a theologian, it is the light of faith that confers upon a discourse its theological qualification.

One must beware, however, of attempting to "freeze" the moments of the theological process. These elements can move about, for their loci or instances are defined in function of the articulation of the whole, as we shall see in the following section.

Let it also be noted, that, once the specific "point of view" of theology has situated it as a science among others, as a particular science, we may say that the regionality of its language, besides supplying the basis of its social and historical inscription, is now configured in its actual epistemological status itself, just as happens with the other sciences.[43]

It must be added that the process of properly *theo-logical* cognition does not, any more than any other disciplined discourse, begin, or at all events does not begin *immediately*, with "life," or "the facts," or anything else exterior to thought, as empiricism would have it. The theological process begins with the "ideological," be the latter a word, an idea, an abstract notion, an intuition, or again some particular question—or finally, anything already perceived and "thought" in a first approximation and approach. From a point of departure in *these* primary data, the theologian proceeds to transform them into a third generality. That is, the theologian effectuates an "epistemological breach" with respect to their first, primitive form, to arrive at the production of the formally theological.[44]

This being the case, theological discourse cannot be of the same fashioning as the "word" of the (nontheologian) believer. The theologian does not speak *in the way* that the (nontheologian) believer speaks. Root and flower have the same texture here, to be sure. But they do not have the same structure. This is what I shall be discussing in chapter 7.

Obviously, the (formal) *pertinency* of a discourse is found in some fashion translated into a concrete *method,* for which its part appropriates an adequate *technology,* into which the pertinency of a language is as it were incorporated in the form of directives and tools of research. A technology without method is lame; a method without theory is blind. A second generality—as we see—is an extremely complex and contradictory unit, as Althusser says. It is also partially opaque. It has its inevitable blind spots, which cause incompleteness in its systematization.

The second generality is composed of two basic integral parts, one of a theoretical nature, and the other of a technical nature. The study of its internal constitution, its function, and its matter of operation can be considered as belonging to that part of epistemology called "methodology."[45]

At all events, it is the second generality that is responsible for the identity of a determinate theoretical approach. Here is the locus in which a discipline acquires its name, its proper signature. We have seen what this means in the case of theology.

For an identification of the "theologicity" of theology, I have recourse to Thomas Aquinas. The intent of this recourse, this *recurrence,* is to grasp the project of theological rationality objectified in this author so as to be able to gather his intentionality, and prolong it in some way in our own times. For, it seems to me, the concept of "theology" ought to be as justifiable today as yesterday. Surely changes in the theological problematic need not be regarded as constituting an absolute, definitive breach between classic theology ("first theology") and modern theology ("second theology"), to the point where they would no longer have anything in common at all.[46]

At all events, it seems to me that it will surely constitute an epistemological advantage to conceive the *officium theologi* after the manner of Thomas Aquinas.[47] But in order to do so, it will be necessary to resume, in our own day, the effort expended by Thomas in his time to establish a theoretical status for theology.

The concept of "recurrence," mentioned above, suggests the substitution of one term for the other in the relationship that it establishes between the history of theological practice (here, that of Aquinas) and an analysis of its current state (here, that of the theology of the political). This permits us to focus on the necessary connection between the two terms.[48]

In this fashion, we can ask whether, in theology, epistemological reflection has made any really substantial progress since Thomas Aquinas.

Here we may not ignore the contribution of Melchior Cano.[49] As is well known, Cano sought to take the question of theological methodology a good deal further, and give it more formalization, pretentious as his effort may have been.[50]

Without entering into a discussion of the historical relevancy of his undertaking, or of its concrete results, I venture to suggest that Cano's methodology is, today at least, culturally obsolete, if indeed it was not so from the beginning.[51]

In particular, I would contrast Cano's *topical* methodology with the *analytical* methodology of Thomas. Thomas's is fundamentally a practice that "shows" — a scientific practice, then — whereas Cano's is substantially a heuristic practice. Cano's "topical" methodology is production only in the juridical sense of the term — it places a series of items in evidence as exhibits. It is concerned with the loci of knowing, functioning as a kind of deposit of theoretical resources for the justification of the faith, the church, and the magisterium.[52]

My own position is that this epistemology of loci should be abandoned. It is capable of providing only a technology for rhetorical discourse. It is powerless to furnish a critical theory of theology. A "topics" of this kind appears to me to be insufficient for the development of theological thought, especially in the case of a theology that means to be in contact with history, and a fortiori a theology of the political such as we are seeking here. Furthermore, this method tends to produce repetitive discourse, and with time shows itself to be involutive and impoverishing.[53]

To be sure, the loci methodology is useful for gathering material for compiling the positive data of faith. But it can never be more than a *moment* in the global theological process. To elevate it to a complete method is, to my way of thinking, a retreat from the milestones erected by Thomas Aquinas himself.[54]

The usually negative influence of this heuristic epistemology on contemporary theological research, especially in the area of second theology, is evinced at the very level of language, when we hear of "life," or "history," or "experience," and the like, cited as "theological loci," or even as the *"locus theologicus* par excellence."[55] The moment this notion of locus is restored to its original conceptual system, the astonishingly "technicist" nature of this epistemology betrays itself unreservedly. One after another, it threads together such disparate loci as scripture, reason, history, life, and so forth, in a taxonomy that is nothing short of surrealistic.

My position is that this topical terminology is to be transcended, along with the epistemological presuppositions of which it is the vehicle, if we are to refloat theology and take it to sea once more.[56]

It seems to me profoundly open to criticism to assert that "life" is a locus of theologizing. The frankly sensualist, intuitionist, or empiricist brand of such thinking cannot be disguised. For this assertion to have any truth, either "life" must be considered as the element in which the theologian, like everyone else, lives—and then it is a *medium in quo*—or as the *materia prima* of the doing of theology—but it is surely not its *medium quo*.

"Life" as such says nothing. It is we who must make it speak. It explains nothing. It is precisely what is to be explained. It is not the *revelans* of theology; it is its *revelandum*. It does not occupy the theoretical place of a second generality but that of a first generality. Life speaks Christianity only in the one who teaches Christianity.

Accordingly, it will be to our distinct advantage to take our distance from Cano's methodology and head out along Aquinas's course, thus in some sense returning to the point where Cano began.

Besides the paradigm of Cano's theology, we have another—one that antedated Thomas, developed during his time, and outlived him. It was a conceptualization of theology as *scientia affectiva,* as *sapientia, contemplatio*—in a word, as a language of the living experience of faith. I refer to the monastic and mystical currents, especially that of Augustinianism, which found its greatest expression in the Franciscan school.

But I question whether this paradigm can occupy the place of an epistemology. On its face, it seems to me more or less to exclude, or at least to fail to maintain, a rigorous rationality. Therefore I must distance myself from this conceptualization as well.

Finally, we must ask ourselves whether the labor of assigning theology a better-defined and better-articulated theoretical structure is not perhaps more urgent than that of working with merely effusive, or even "revolutionary" theologies—and whether, in our historical conjuncture, faith does not have more need of head than of heart.[57]

§27 THEOLOGY OF THE POLITICAL AND ITS ARCHEOLOGY

We establish theological pertinency from the data of faith. The theologian works with categories whose content is constituted by the *auditus fidei:* salvation, sin, grace, spirit, Father, Christ, eschaton, kingdom, *agape,* and so on.[58]

In the case of the theology of the political, I have said that the political functions as the raw material upon which a second generality must be brought to bear in order to rework it. Now, the second generality is the theoretical equipment of production, in which the positivity (content) of faith has been as it were "invested."

If we were to analyze, then, how the process of a theology of the political is concretely effectuated, we should see that it presupposes at least two disciplined discourses: (1) the discourse of first theology, on the side of hermeneutic mediation; (2) the discourse of the sciences of the social, on the side of socio-analytic mediation. Let us examine in more detail how these discourses relate to a theology of the political.

The Discourse of First Theology

Does second theology replace first theology? If not, then what is the relationship between them? Is second theology established in direct reference to the data of faith—that is, does it apply scripture directly to the political text—or must it pass by way of classic, or first, theology in order to do so? Finally, what end is served by traditional elaborations where a theology of the political is concerned?[59]

I shall leave an *ex professo* treatment of the constitution of the second generality of a theology of the political for later (chapter 8). It may be observed here, however, that first theology contributes intrinsically to this constitution.[60] Surely a referral to scripture is the identifying function of any theology, hence also of a theology of the political. But scripture itself yields its meaning only on condition of being read *in community*. The community is at once the guardian and agent of a tradition. But this tradition embraces theology as well, in such wise that it will be impossible, without deceiving ourselves, to seek to have direct contact with the very meaning of scripture without passing by way of the history of this meaning—that is, without turning our attention to the course of the transmission of this meaning. Thus the second generality of a theology of the political will be a structured composite, with traditional theology among its composing agents—this theology being evidently articulated with biblical content and being under biblical dominance.

Doubtless the theology of the political, for its part, exerts a discriminating retroactive effect upon tradition, and upon the classic elaborations to be found incorporated within it. This is verified whenever a "return to the sources" is undertaken. But what we have is discrimination, not annihilation. It does not seem to me that second theology excludes or replaces first theology, as certain contemporary polemics imply or even state.[61] Epistemological thinking must make rigorous provision for a certain differentiation. It must be able to explain, for example, what justifies the claim of a European discourse to be "theology" with equal right to that of a discourse from somewhere else, say, from Latin America. Of course, the opposition here can only be one of a difference of identity, or then again of a differentiation in the interior of one and the same homological structure.[62]

If a theology of the political began by opposing "classic" theology, it was precisely in order to gain a place in the theological sun. As a result, first theology itself, in some sort, underwent a more or less profound alteration in resisting this attack—underwent a "recasting." For those who know the history of the sciences, there is nothing abnormal here. Has Bachelard not shown that the logic of scientific progress is dialectical, in the sense that it is necessarily achieved under the sign of resistance to knowledge already constituted, against which the new knowledge must struggle in order to establish itself?[63]

For the sake of completeness, it remains to say that we discover, even deeper in the foundation of a first theology, the discourse by which believers must give an account of their faith in the revealing word that is certified in scripture and testified to by the ecclesial community. This discourse is that of a transcendental reflection, having the function of guaranteeing the possibility of revelation, and hence of the faith that corresponds to that revelation. This kind of investigation is situated, so to speak, at zero degrees on the theological scale. In the classic tradition it bears the name of "natural theology."[64]

Thus when we address ourselves to a theological interpretation of the political, we need to be assured beforehand of the possibility and legitimacy of the viewpoint that will be at issue. In other words, before anything else, and independently of the political itself, it is necessary that "Christian truth" be guaranteed, for it is this that makes a theological reading possible, as has been explained.

Theology is a point of view. This is clear. But if this point of view is not based, is not founded, then it is nothing but the superfluous reduplication of another discourse. Theology then ends by acting as the ideological substitute for a science that is simply not there. In this case it is better to take off the theological mask and show one's face.

Thus in order to be able to posit a relationship between, for example, salvation and liberation, we need first of all to be able to secure the theological content to be ascribed to the concept of "salvation." For theology, the real content of "salvation" has nothing in common with the equally real content assigned by the social analyst to "liberation," even taking the latter content at the absolute limit of its extension and intensity. Social liberation may be as radical as you please, yet it will never be the salvation offered by God. There obtains between the two a difference of order, or nature, and not simply of degree. There is no "quantum leap" that can bridge this gap.

On the *conceptual* level, the only relationship that can obtain between "salvation" and "liberation" is an *analogical* relationship. This does not mean that *real* salvation has nothing to do with *real* liberation, but only, and precisely, this: that in order to have an *idea* of (God's) salvation, we can certainly make use of the *idea* of (human) liberation.

Here is where a first theology "has its work cut out for it." The scope and limits alike of a first theology appear where the question arises: What does the *fact* (and now no longer the idea) of (real) liberation have to do with the *fact* (not the idea) of (real) salvation? Here we are on the concrete, or historical, level. First theology is only the condition of the *theoretical* possibility of a second theology, in the sense that its scope is to guarantee second theology the formal locus from whose point of departure this second theology can make a (theological) interpretation of the political. The limitations of first theology are immediately evident: first theology is not endowed with such a nature as to be capable of setting up a possible relationship between the reality of salvation and the reality of liberation. Here, then, we must move to a higher level.

This is where second theology takes the helm. Second theology does not work *upon* the concept of salvation (as a first generality), but works precisely *with* that concept of salvation as *its* second generality, which first theology has produced and placed at its disposition (in a third generality). Second theology has recourse to this concept to establish the relationship between its content and the reality of liberation (first generality of second theology).

If I may be permitted to speak in Platonic terms, first theology is the "transcending" gaze that, though situated in the empirical world, pierces its limits, contemplates the divine realities, and says: "God's salvation is *like* human liberation." Then, for its part, second theology is the return glance, which, although certainly in the world, yet from a standpoint within those divine realities returns to the world and, seeing this world "divinely," says: "Human liberation *is* God's salvation."[65]

To be sure, the sociologist's liberation abides, throughout the process, as a "presupposit": it is maintained in second theology as the object to be seen (in socio-analytic mediation); it is maintained in first theology as the second term in an analogical mediation. To say, then, that the theological gaze (of first theology) is necessarily "mystifying," merely because it loses *real* liberation from its sights—understanding "real" to mean historical, political, human liberation—is to fail to grasp that what is being drawn up here is an equation of metaphysical, transcendental values, whereas the real, by contrast, is the historical. Such a procedure is the effect of an abstraction, be this abstraction implemented by a particular discipline, by an ideology, or even by a culture.[66]

A theology (or a faith) that allows itself to be pulled into this "game," disguising itself as sociology or political science out of a sense of shame, in an attempt to rehabilitate itself and gain credibility, only demonstrates in broad daylight the symptoms of its morbid state and hence of its approaching demise.[67] Political science does not know what to do with a "political theology" like this. Only a "theological theology" can become a genuine "political theology."

The positions defended here posit an articulation between first and second theology of such a nature as to avoid, on the one hand, a dualism, whose epistemological species is semantic mix and bilingualism, and, on the other hand, a monism, corresponding for its part either to the "ideologization of the faith" or to secularism. By virtue of thus avoiding both of these extremes among epistemological pitfalls, my positions seem to me epistemologically sound.[68]

Next, let us consider how the discourse of first theology, and a fortiori that of natural theology, which I have situated at "zero degrees" on the theological scale, constitute, in different degrees, the theoretical groundwork for a second theology. We need only try to think what would be left of a second theology were the content of Christian faith—the "Christ question," substantially—to be shown to be false—or, more radically still, were the "question of God" as discussed in "natural theology" to be decided in the negative. The answer is clear. Second theology would fall to pieces.

We must conclude, then: if a theology of the political pretends to be more than a purely ideological construct for disguising certain practices—if it means to be, on the contrary, a theory revealing the truth of a meaning—then it must be able to rely upon the foundations whose solidity has rational warranty. We must say, consequently, that the truth of a theology of the political draws its sustenance from the (hidden) energy of the discourses of first theology and of "theology at zero degrees," even when it does not explicitate its vital relationship with them.

Let us be very clear, however: these observations have validity only at the level of a *theory* of theology. Where theoretical *practice* is concerned, the discourse that history imposes at the given moment must be enunciated concretely. We may not pretend to be able to think all things for all purposes and keep them all in good order, as will be gone into in part 3. In all cases, the "truth" of a theology having a political signification is a function of the truth of the discourses that form the groundwork of this theology by serving as its "archeology." The analysis of this groundwork by a discourse in a march to the rear, and operating as a foundational discourse, becomes urgent the moment a given discipline enters into crisis—or indeed, the moment it is called upon to justify its theoretical status by the explicitation of its presuppositions.

The Discourse of the Sciences of the Social

So much for the "archeology" of a theology of the political from the side of hermeneutic mediation, or its second generality.

As for socio-analytic mediation—the first generality of second theology—it will be necessary to return to what has been said all through part 1 of this book: that the theology of the political begins where the discourse of the sciences of the social ends. In other words, the first generality of a theology of the political is an "ex-third generality" of the sciences of the social. Thus besides the discourse of first theology in the instance of its second generality, the archeology of a theology of the political embraces the discourse of the sciences of the social, as well, in the instance of its first generality. A theology of the political has no more access to society apart from the sciences of the social than it does to revelation apart from an adequate interpretation and understanding of scripture.

For want of a sufficiently clear idea of the structure of theoretical practice, the theology of the political has provoked sometimes useless, and often confused, polemics, which have deprived it of the possibility of producing an elucidating, adequate response to objections.[69]

We see, then, the regulated articulation that prevails between the first and second generalities of a theology of the political, as also between the theology of the political and the antecedent discourses that enter into its foundation. Perhaps it will be helpful to represent these various articulations graphically, keeping in mind that what is important here are not the terms of the relationships but their structural interplay.

Diagram 3

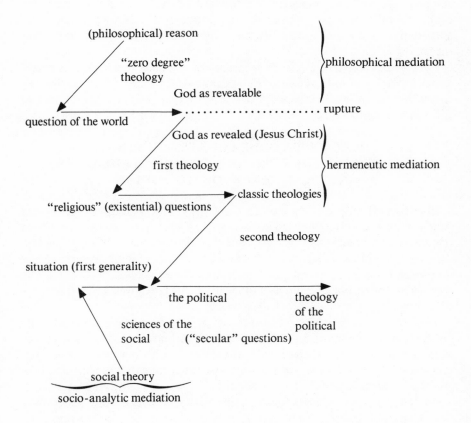

Diagram 3 outlines the "archeology," so to speak, of a theology of the political. It is limited to a sketch of the main levels of this archeology. The archeology itself can be complexified, according to the demands of rationality.

Let us note first of all that philosophical mediation comes into the picture on the lowest level of theological reflection, from the moment one begins radically to question what the "world" is. This mediation can be discerned as well on the side of the first generality: the question of "existence." But the philosophical mediation can also be seen on the side of the first generality of a science of the social. This is the position of a "social philosophy." It is true that I have shown a certain reserve vis-à-vis this mediation. But this has only been for fear lest, in the current situation of the theology of the political, this mediation come to occupy the place of the sciences of the social, as still frequently occurs. I am well aware, however, that this phenomenon corresponds to a *parti pris*—a particular strategy—in the element of (theological) theory.

Observe the line indicating a "rupture" between the third generality of a "theology at zero degrees" and the second generality of a first theology. After all, between the rational possibility of a revelation of the Absolute, and its historical effectuation, there is a humanly unbridgeable gap. Accordingly, the revelation of Jesus Christ founds an "existential rupture," or "leap" of Christian faith, to which there corresponds an "epistemological rupture" or breach in Christian theology, the former acting as "foundational breach" with respect to the latter.

Finally, we come to the second generality of a second theology. It is represented as resting on at least two archeological layers: the one, a second generality of Christian revelation (by hermeneutic mediation), and the other, a second generality of human reason (by philosophical mediation).[70]

§28 COMPLEX ORDER OF ARTICULATION BETWEEN THE THEOLOGY OF THE POLITICAL AND THE SCIENCES OF THE SOCIAL

In virtue of the fact that one and the same first generality is open to treatment from a number of different pertinencies, this first generality can become a bone of contention among these pertinencies. This occurs when one of them neglects its constitutional particularity and behaves as a system of identity, denying any otherness, hence any plurality, of significations, and holding itself out as the sole vision, the absolute vision, as if other pertinencies enjoyed no truth content whatever.

This is a type of problem to which theology is particularly sensitive. As discourse upon the Absolute, theology will have an acknowledged locus and place only on condition that no discourse take itself for the absolute discourse. Even theological discourse is relative discourse despite the fact that it bears upon the Absolute as such as its object.

As we know from what has been said above, the diversity of third generalities from a point of departure in a single first generality is owing to the diversity of second generalities. Thus, for example, the social situation in Latin America is susceptible of a sociological interpretation in terms of "sin."

The validity of these two interpretations, and consequently their compossibility, depends on their respective pertinencies, as may be seen in Diagram 4.

One must do justice, then, to the legitimate difference among plural readings, as each meaning, for its part, seeks to found and acquire its own legality to the extent of its rational and historical possibilities.[71]

Diagram 4 illustrates the compatibility of a theological discourse with a sociological discourse, in such wise that we observe that one can coexist with the other without either one of them necessarily excluding or opposing the other.

It is only in reference to praxis that we see the order obtaining between these two theoretical practices, in virtue of distinct principles. If we focus on a common praxis, and if this praxis ultimately determines the organization of theoretical practices, then the latter are finally ordered within a strategic framework that assigns them their locus in the logic of the imperatives of the praxis in question.

It is precisely in accordance with obedience to praxis that I have posited the theological discourse in quality of a second discourse, posterior to that of

Diagram 4

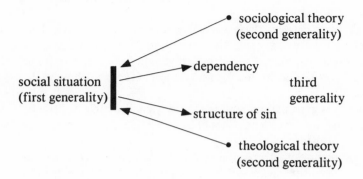

social analysis. A theology of the political can have nothing but an ideological effect (on an earlier generality) if it proceeds in a methodologically premature fashion, without being sure, in advance, about the text it undertakes to interpret.

At the same time, I raise the question whether, after social analyses have had their say, theology may not have a word to say upon the content of their productions, over and above their conclusions—a word held in reserve, but a word that theology alone is qualified to pronounce. Not that the discourse of theology is meant to complete antecedent discourses, or, still less, replace them. It will rework them, in the area of the gratuitousness of faith.

This potentiality of (Christian) theology is based on its quality as discourse upon Ultimate (eschatological), Absolute Meaning—the God revealed in Jesus Christ.

The modus operandi of theology does not lie in a search for the causes, laws, or internal structure of its raw material in the manner or place of the disciplines whose object belongs to the empirical world.[72] Theology "works" its object, seeking to *understand* it, "grasp" it, find its *sense,* its meaning—its meaning par excellence, *kat' exachen.* This does not dispense theology from the theoretical effort to *know* this sense, to possess its knowledge, to produce it theoretically. This sense is inscribed in the body of a fact, a phenomenon, a situation, and so on, in the measure that such data bear within them an objective orientation or structural relationship to the proper object of theology, the God of faith.

Hence the com-possibility of theological discourse with socio-analytic discourse is measured on the basis of the com-possibility of a sense and a fact—here the absolute Sense and the political fact. Conflict arises when one of these discourses usurps the place of the other—when an "interversion" of their epistemological loci, and respective pertinencies, occurs, in a situation that we might sum up in the popular Brazilian metaphor, "selling cat for rabbit."

The ultimate reason why theology *follows* social analysis is that the understanding of the sense of a fact can be satisfactorily effectuated only on the basis of an explication of the fact in question from a point of departure in its internal, "profane" structure. Sense arises only from structure.[73]

Such is the strategy to be adopted in the construction of a theology of the political. It will take everything as a reading text to be deciphered in accord with the "syntax" of faith.

There is a break, then, between the levels of theological and sociological discourse, even when both "work" the same first generality. This difference in levels is twofold: it is *epistemic,* in that the same text is read from different points of departure; and it is *strategic,* in that the same subject is spoken about in different "moments."

This break in levels is to be maintained. It assigns each discourse its "track," its specific aspect, and thus obviates clashes of interpretation, or any confusion of the "game rules" proper to each.

Thus I take a different position from the model of articulation between a theology of the political and the sciences of the social that has been proposed for overcoming "semantic mix" (confusion) and "bilingualism" (separation) by way of a "Chalcedonian method" or "Chalcedonian dialectic."

The "Chalcedonian dialectic" is perfectly epitomized in the formula "union without confusion, distinction without separation."[74] We hear of a "fertile tension" of "continuity and discontinuity," of an "ongoing dialectic," between the theoretical dualities whose articulation is under consideration. In conformity with the principle just enunciated, it will be said, for example, that "faith implies politics and politics is consummated in faith," or that "complete evangelization embraces humanization, and integral humanization implies evangelization," and so on.[75]

What is to be said of this model? First, that it sets us on the right path to the articulation of theoretical dualities such as salvation/liberation, sin/oppression, kingdom/society, and so on. The Chalcedonian model therefore corresponds to a correct approach to the problem at hand. However, the approach does not go beyond a *first* approach. It yields only a *first* approximation of the solution being sought. It stays on too general and abstract a level to be able to take account of concrete situations. In virtue of its vague, oversimplifying tenor, it does manage to hold semantic mix and bilingualism at bay; but it does so in a purely formal, even verbal, fashion.[76]

Let us take, for example, the case of liberation theology (which I shall here simplify for purposes of illustration). Its theoretical commitment is evident from its name: liberation. Now, the problems of this theology revolve about the question of what content to confer upon the notion of liberation. What liberation is meant? Political? Economic? Cultural? Spiritual? Or all these together?

On this concrete point, the Chalcedonian method betrays all of its weakness. It permits us to go no further than the simple observation that there is a reciprocal relationship linking salvation and liberation.[77]

In the de facto theological polemic concerning this relationship, the answer has been decided from the beginning of the debate, in a determinative fashion.[78] One must ask, then, to what purpose is it to theologize, if everything is already resolved in advance by the alchemy of a Chalcedonian dialectic totally contained "in a single sentence" (Hegel): union without confusion, distinction without separation?

To my view, a theology of liberation must, on the contrary, *begin* with its particular object, "liberation," as a first generality, and hence as an object enjoying the autonomous constitution of a first generality. "Liberation" will then be understood in accordance with its historical materiality—that is, in accordance with the real texture that the sciences of the social seek to teach us to perceive in it. From this point of departure, it can be grasped that "liberation" is said in respect of real oppression, of an economic, political, and ideological order, and in respect of real historical thrusts in the direction of an emancipation of the same order.[79]

In this initial moment, a theological decision that begins by speaking of "redemption" as "spiritual liberation," or "structures of sin," or the like, appears on the scene prematurely, and thereby impertinently. This is to jumble up everything with everything else—the work of mystification. To justify this conceptual procedure by saying that all reality is somehow one is to betray a total lack of understanding of the nature of reason. Ever since Anaxagoras, we have known that the logic of things is not the logic of reason.

In my opinion, therefore, the theologian must start out with the primary datum of oppression/liberation conceived in all its material, "profane" density, and in the security of socio-analytic mediation. Only subsequently can there be any theology. The theologian will now theologize from a point of departure in, and with respect to, this datum, so constituted. In this second moment, *res agitur:* What do I have to say on this subject?

Plainly, the Chalcedonian model is inadequate to the task. We need to construct a richer, more articulate model. This model will be none other than that of the theoretical practice of theology—a model ordered internally in conformity with the logic of all theoretical practice, and externally in conformity with the only logic that the nature of theology comports: the logic that its first generality be an "ex-third generality" of the sciences of the social.[80]

Accordingly, although "sin" and "exploitation" enter into the discursive structure of theology and sociology alike, they never occupy the same place in that structure. Their "play" is different, in function of the respective pertinency in which each "player's" science is inscribed. Only when epistemic regimes are mixed or juxtaposed does ambiguity prevail and comprehension evaporate.

Nor therefore is "liberation" a properly theological concept, or the theologian's second generality. It is a sociological concept, and belongs in theological practice as a first generality—the object upon which theology is to be practiced. The theologian does not work *with* the concept of "liberation." The theologian works *upon* the concept of liberation. For the theologian, "liberation" is not an operative concept, not a second generality. It is a passive notion, a vague, general one, whereas for the sociologist it may be a very precise empirical concept, a third generality. The process of theological articulation consists in this: to transform, with the help of the properly theological concept of "salvation" (second generality), the sociological concept of "liberation" (first generality) in such a way as to produce a theological proposition such as: "liberation is salvation" (third generality).[81]

But the price of a theological finding from a point of departure in sociological data is an inescapable "breach," or "rupture." It is only beyond the "breach line" that "liberation" will appear in its entirety as a "pistic event." For this it is unnecessary that it be endowed, either de facto or even de jure, with a supplementary "spiritual dimension." In its own historical body, with all the ideologies of its practitioners bracketed from consideration, liberation will be seen to be charged with an *objective* salvific signification of grace or sin. This signification is not the imaginary creation of faith or theology. Faith becomes aware of it only from the word of revelation, and theology produces its theory only from the awareness of faith.[82]

This is the moment—when the profane third generality has finally been posited—that the theologian's work can begin. The yardstick by which the rigor of a theory is measured is not of an authoritative kind, but is precisely *rational*—among theologians, at any rate—as Thomas Aquinas teaches in his great *Quodlibetum* 4, article 18.

Thus instead of a simple, abstract, indeed dualizing articulation, I propose a complex, unitary one—that of a theoretical practice indeed, but in twin form: in the form of an articulation of articulations, illustrated in Diagram 5.

Diagram 5

1. Articulation on the Chalcedonian Model

dependency ◄——————► sin

---

2. Complex, Ordered Articulation

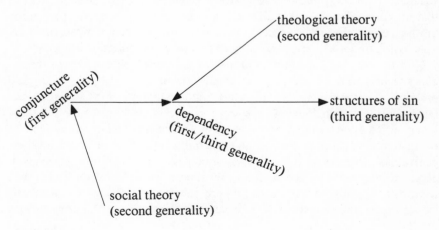

I take the liberty of closing this chapter by once more turning to Thomas Aquinas. I am not suggesting that Thomas reflected on the kind of theory that concerns us here, or that his theology can still be "applied" today. Thomas Aquinas is and always will be a theologian, a contributor of his time, and his theology will always be a theology of its time. Nevertheless, it seems to me, Thomas posited the articulating principles of theology vis-à-vis the sciences of his time so well that these principles are still open, in some manner, to the kind of position I have just taken. Restricting my considerations to question 1 of the *Summa,* I shall now present a rapid sketch of this "openness in principle."

First: Thomas establishes the "regionality" of theological rationality. For him, theology is not a universal discourse. Theology, like any science, has its own pertinency.[83] It is this pertinency that creates the difference and the homogeneity of its discourse. This is the sense of article 3: *"Utrum sacra doctrina sit una doctrina?"* The question, then, is the thematic identity of theology. The answer is that indeed theology does possess this identity: it relates everything to a single focus, God.

But are there such things as theoretical objects that are "worked" by other sciences? Indeed there are, Thomas responds, and there is nothing to prevent theology from taking these objects up as its own, for it subjects them to a particular treatment—its own proper treatment. It therefore receives them as raw material, whether they proceed from philosophy or from any other science.[84]

As we see, then, Thomas Aquinas's theological epistemology is in accord with what I have called socio-analytic mediation (in a second theology), and even with philosophical mediation ("theology at zero degrees"). But in either case theological practice always has the task of reworking these other discourses. It handles them as material for transformation, and in this quality they are subordinate to theology.[85] It is not because theological discourse is conceived as some manner of regulatory discourse over all the others that the others are thus subordinated.[86] It is because if theology means to be what it is— theological—then it has no choice but to subject them to itself in this manner, be it in order to transform them (when a third generality of another discourse becomes a theological first generality), or, as may also occur, in order to assimilate them (when a second or even third generality of a given discourse includes the instance of a theological second generality). Owing to the ontic excellence of its object, says Thomas, theology can in no wise be subject to other disciplines. On the contrary, in virtue of its own proper internal structure, theology can be related to other disciplines only in order to make use of them.[87] To be sure, theology comes only after the other disciplines, and this is a sign of its incompetence. But it is the sign of its strength to be able to pronounce "one more word"—its own—when other languages have fallen silent.

The epistemology of Aquinas can even enlighten us with respect to hermeneutic mediation. *"Haec scientia,"* Thomas says, *". . . non accepit sua principia ab aliis scientiis sed immediate a Deo per revelationem."*[88] I shall have occasion later (chapter 7) to question the pretentions of theology to immediacy where revelation is concerned. For Thomas, however, the relationship between the two is without intermediary. Be this as it may, Aquinas does consider revelation to be the *conditio sine qua non* of (Christian) theology.

Finally, with respect to the articulation between first and second theology, Thomas offers an indication I consider to be very instructive. He tells us that theology treats *"principaliter de Deo"* (and this is what first theology does). As to creatures—all other existents, then—it treats of them *"non ex aequo,"* but *"secundum quod referuntur ad Deum."*[89] And he adds, in conclusion: *"Unde unitas scientiae non impeditur."*[90] And then the whole of article 7 bears on the articulation of God and creatures. At the basis of this articulation is always the epistemic identity of the formal object, or pertinency, of theology, where these creatures are concerned: the *"ratio secundum quam considerantur."* For they are considered only *"secundum ordinem ad Deum."*[91]

By way of my own conclusion: the epistemological principles established by Thomas Aquinas, although restricted in their application to a first theology, show themselves capable of supporting an articulation where a second theology is involved, as well. Therefore they afford adequate evidence that the political is in principle theologizable.

CHAPTER 6

Objectivity of Theology: Order of Salvation

§29 THE EPISTEMOLOGICAL APPROACH

In this and the following chapter, I shall be dealing with certain basic concepts that one discovers in the foundations of theological discourse in the real order. These concepts are: salvation, revelation, grace, *agape,* faith, religion, and theology.

At first glance, this investigation would not appear to belong to the area of epistemology—to the particular discourse that bears on the *principles* of theological theory. It would appear rather to relate to theological theory itself.

As I have stated, however, the emergence of a new problematic—the theoretical object of a second theology—has provoked a reaction in the form of a total rearrangement of the theological scenery. The theological scene itself must now be restructured—"recast." For it is impossible to construct a theology of the political that will be adequate to its object without first rethinking theology, in its theoretical bases and in the system of its fundamental concepts. Upon the success of this task will depend the very possibility of a theology of the political: we are dealing here with the theoretical prerequirements for the production of that theology.

At the same time, we know that between epistemology and theory there is a crucial dialectical relationship. A methodological change here will entail a change in object, and vice versa.[1]

At all events, we see that method and knowledge describe a circle, one that ought not to be ignored—one that it will be well to recognize in order to be able "to come into it in the right way."[2]

Contemporary epistemology has accustomed us to this idea. It resists the utopian attempt to reduce knowledge to its absolute, ultimate foundations, the project fostered by the Greeks, the medievals, and the moderns.

At the same time, it is no less true that it is always the object that ultimately determines the method. Heidegger reminds us that instead of imposing a particular method on a particular object, as the technologistic mentality prescribes, we should rather let the object of our research be manifested to itself.[3]

Surely this assertion does not go beyond a simple expression of the scientific spirit, which is characterized precisely by "obedience to the real." It implies a calling into question of the methodological apparatus each time that dysfunctions occur between it and the object of its application.

Aristotle had already warned us, as I referred to briefly in the Preface, above (p. xx):

> One must be already trained to know how to take each sort of argument, since it is absurd to seek at the same time knowledge and the way of attaining knowledge.[4]

This epistemological directive, laid down by Aristotle as a determination of method, was invoked time and again by Thomas Aquinas, precisely in treating of theological method. *"In qualibet scientia, oportet supponere de objecto quid est,"* he says.[5]

Still, Thomas himself, concerned with the search for the indemonstrable-but-demonstrative *prima principia*—in conformity, then, with the Aristotelian model of *episteme*—had also discerned, as Heidegger would, that there was a circle at play here: the object is determined only by an appropriate method, and the method, for its part, is determined only by its adequate object.[6]

It is clear, consequently, that questions of epistemology are linked to a consideration of the theoretical constructions upon which they bear. This is what we shall be seeing in this chapter.

The considerations that follow are not an attempt to alter the content of the faith in function of viewpoints exterior to it—in function of a preestablished epistemology, and, indirectly, in function of the theoretical or ideological needs of militant Christians. This sort of "adaptation" is indeed to be rejected. What I seek to do here is to interrogate Christian positivity, not in any spirit of theological dilettantism, but from a point of departure in questions arising within "Christian" practices on the front where struggles are being waged.[7]

What I am about to present will be found to lie along the lines of what has already been observed vis-à-vis theoretical practice. I shall attempt to elucidate a *system of concepts* in the form of a theoretical structure that, by the play of its internal relationships, will afford an understanding of the place and function of each of the elements comprising it, and particularly the place and function of theological theory as one element articulated with others in the same structural whole. As will appear, my focus of interest is ultimately epistemological.[8]

The complex structure of which I speak can be expressed in a simple fashion in the form of two theses, each the respective object of one of the next two chapters. The two theses are connected: the first comprises the second. They serve to *direct* theological reflection, and in this sense they are metatheoretical:

Thesis 1. *A distinction is to be drawn—a basic distinction for the objectivity of faith and theology—between the real and awareness of the real.*

Thesis 2. *On the level of this awareness, a distinction is to be drawn—a basic distinction for the theoretical status of theology—between faith and theology.*

This twofold, articulated distinction can be represented diagramatically:

FAITH (awareness) / THEOLOGY (science)
ORDER OF SALVATION (real)

This diagram reflects the structure to which I shall be referring. It will afford an understanding of the theoretical status of the three concepts it represents, in virtue of the respective place occupied by each and the relationships of difference, or opposition, obtaining among them.[9] They therefore have *relational* determinations (determinations according to function), not *qualitative* ones (determinations according to properties).[10] Consequently their content is their respective position in the structure to which they belong.

As to the terms themselves, the base of the structure consists in the "order of salvation," or simply "salvation." This term designates the "real" upon which Christian awareness—faith—and the scholarly intelligence of faith—theology—bear. This base is the "objective" of the superstructure, in both senses of the word. Philosophically, this "real" could be defined as being of the ontic dimension, or, more precisely, of the theo-ontic dimension, in history (the history of salvation).[11]

In the transcendental approach à la Rahner, one speaks of the "supernatural existential."[12] Theology has other terms as well, such as "supernatural order," "Christian order" or "christic order" or "plane," "mystery," "economy of salvation," and the like.[13]

We may likewise cite Paul Tillich's philosophico-religious concept of the "unconditional," from whose point of departure, and within which, Tillich would understand the content of Christianity.[14]

But most, if not all, of these notions have a theoretical content inclining them toward a particular theological conception, and so I prefer the term "salvation" or "order of salvation," which seems to me to be neutral vis-à-vis any ulterior theological formulation, and yet precise enough to found its distinction from, or opposition to, the other terms of the structure: as "real," this "salvation" is distinguished both from "awareness" (faith) and from "science" (theology).

Thus the other terms are automatically identified and situated. *Faith* is the first level of salvation awareness, and *theology* its critical cognition.

Let these remarks suffice for our purposes as far as the terms of the theses are concerned, and let us now move on to the explication and theoretical foundation of the theses themselves.

§ 30 ORDER OF SALVATION: THE "REAL" OF THEOLOGY

That there is salvation apart from and independently of an awareness of that salvation is the thesis at the basis of the objectivity of theology.[15]

I speak of "salvation." I could just as easily speak of "God" as Savior. Indeed, we begin from a position in *Christian* theology, which bears upon the salvation in Jesus Christ that our faith confesses.

The thesis under consideration here is surely not new or original. It claims a whole tradition of theological reflection.[16] It will not be necessary to rehearse here the arguments that have been presented in its favor. Suffice it to draw the consequences of this thesis for a correct thinking of a theology of the political.

The thesis under immediate consideration here has long borne the name "supernatural order." Today the tendency is to designate it under the appellation of "mystery of salvation," or "Christian mystery."[17] The name is surely much less important than the theoretical content of which this notion can be the vehicle, and which I must now undertake to circumscribe more precisely.[18]

First, there is a way of understanding the supernatural that seems to me erroneous. This erroneous conceptualization may be expressed in the following equation of proportionality:

$$\frac{\text{supernatural order}}{\text{natural order}} = \frac{\text{order of revelation}}{\text{order of reason}}$$

The paralogism here consists in the unwarranted parallelism posited between the *ontic* level of the first ratio of the equation and the (onto)-*logical* level of the second. This parallelism seems to me indefensible. On the contrary, the latter ratio is to be understood as standing *toto quanto* within the supernatural order. The natural order, for theology, is never anything but an abstract, artificial concept, in utter contrast to the case of the nontheological, or "natural" disciplines. In theology, the "natural" has an exclusively *logical* value. It is applicable only *to* (natural) reason (in contradistinction to "revelation"), and *by* (theological, or super-*natural)* reason.[19]

By rejecting the theological idealism of this first conceptualization, we bring out the distinction between the real and the known clearly and distinctly. We can now assign the distribution of these categories—a distribution on *logical* criteria—in the following manner:

$$\frac{\text{revelation} \ / \ \text{reason}}{\text{(supernatural) salvation}}$$

There is a second way to conceptualize the supernatural, one that seems to me equally erroneous. It might be put in the form of an equation:

$$\frac{\text{supernatural order}}{\text{natural order}} = \frac{\text{order of grace}}{\text{order of sin}}$$

In actuality, the second ratio in this equation should be included in the first term of the first ratio: "supernatural order." "Grace" and "sin" are actually two concrete modalities into which the supernatural order is resolved in virtue of the intervention of human freedom. "Supernatural order" thus appears as an abstract concept, looking to its two basic concretions. Consequently, from a point of departure in a criterion now not logical but *existential*—therefore from the concrete alternative in which salvation as an ontic possibility for the human being is decided—we may construct the following diagram:

grace/sin

salvation

As we see, then, the terms of our first two conceptualizations of the supernatural shift at random, to weave a self-styled theological discourse, but one that has not tested its semantic content beforehand, and allows itself simply to be borne along by the free association its terms arouse in virtue of their "stereophonic force" (R. Barthes). This is no longer the practice of theory, but a game played with "fluid signifiers," so that the actual production of any intelligibility whatsoever is out of the question. Unless there is agreement on the determination of the sense of the terms, there is nothing to guarantee to a discourse that seeks to be (theo)-logical the ability to manage such a determination, even in function of its own internal consistency. And yet this is something it will have to succeed with if it means to render its theoretical effects subject to maximal check and control.

But how, then, is the supernatural to be conceived? It may be thought of as *the natural itself, as elevated to the plane of its divine destination*. In this very definition, we may observe the effect of a minimal theological elaboration, whose first generality is "the natural itself," and whose third generality is "elevated to the plane of its divine destination"—it being understood that the second generality can only be revelation/faith, the sole font of this "cognition."[20]

The category of the "supernatural" is better understood if we oppose it semantically to the category of the "natural," or of "pure nature."[21] It has already been emphasized that, in theology, this concept is a mental construct, a conceptual fiction, created by (Christian) theology for itself, in view of an understanding of the novelty of history as *sacred* history, and especially in order to confer intelligibility upon the novelty of the existential status of the human being as called to divine filiation, or divinization.[22]

Consequently, no pure "natural order" really exists for the eyes of faith. It is only that this pure nature *could have* existed and been historically realized, and this is what the concept of "nature" attests in its constitutive purity. The "reality" negatively indicated by this *Hilfsbegriff* (Karl Rahner) is an unrealized possibility, forever vacated—a history dead from all eternity. The positive virtue of this negative concept consists in its bestowing upon theological reason the theoretical conditions for reflecting upon the originality of the Christian faith. It is the solid line drawn athwart the foundations of theology, marking the point where the properly (Christo)-theological horizon emerges.

One of the conclusions to be drawn from this conceptualization is the rejection of all dualism: two orders, two histories, two destinies, and so on.[23] And with the rejection of all dualism, epistemologies based on a dualism go by the board as well: bilingualism and semantic mix.

For theology, therefore, there is no such thing as "pure nature." Only its concept exists. In (theological) truth, what has existed from the beginning is a (human and cosmic) nature seen in the light of divine salvation, a nature destined for salvation, a nature existing historically under a soteriological regime, existing historically in a supernatural situation.

The concept of (pure) nature, then, for theology, is a purely operative concept, whose theoretical utility is to keep theological thinking on its proper level. It is an artifact, with an analytic function, a residual concept—that is, one obtained by subtraction. It defines what remains of total "reality" after an *epoche* has been referred to salvation or divine calling.

The idea of "nature" is therefore theologically comprehensible only with the soteriological reference bracketed. The soteriological reference does not obtain as to the *metaphysical* status of nature, to be sure, but it does obtain as to its *historico-*(salvific) status. This reference or relationship possesses an *objective* density, such as is capable of founding a specifically theological objectivity. It is not that the "theological viewpoint" creates this relationship, but rather that this relationship renders the "theological viewpoint" possible, once it is shown from revelation that this relationship exists.[24]

But how is the supernatural precisely to be conceived—this relationship of nature to salvation? Will it be a *simple* relationship to the Transcendent, a *potential* destination, a *pure* orientation to salvation? Or must we not rather conceive of it as "something" constitutive of being itself, as an ontic dimension, such as will render the human being a being-open, a being-called, a being-hoped-for, a being-for-the-future?[25] Does this relationship not mark the human beings in their existential depths?

In the latter case, the teleology of the soteriological plane will be objectively inscribed in the ontological, and the relationship to God and God's salvific will will have to be conceived of as Leibnitz's *vinculum substantiale,* a vital bond. Has not the word of faith always proclaimed that grace marks and transforms human beings in their innermost depths? Is grace anything other than a *relationship* with the saving God?[26]

Of course, this ontology is more precisely a theo-ontology, in the sense of being a reading of nature *from above,* from a point of departure in revelation. Nature is revealed and understood as that of being turned toward God, so that God is conceived as its *telos,* its sense, its direction. At all events, it appears to me that this is the only thinking that can render the actual possibility of salvation *thinkable.*

And yet these theo-ontological considerations are not the main concern for faith. What is important for faith is that the destination of nature to salvation springs from God's pure initiative (and is therefore antecedent to any awareness of its existence), as God's free gift (and is therefore independent of "works").

Here is where I see the function of the basic theoretical demarcation established at the opening of this chapter, which posits a distinction between the *real* and the *known* where theology is concerned. Here this distinction wins the name of "salvation/revelation."[27] Salvation touches every person, whereas revelation is specific to those alone to whom it has been *given* to become aware of this same salvation—to Christians, as shall be explained in §35.

Now let us go one step further, and assert that the concept of "supernatural order," real as its content may be—the human being's historical situation—is nevertheless still an abstract concept. It does not yet enable this situation to be thought as concretely realized. It only sets us on the right path. In order to think the concrete state of human beings in a supernatural economy, we have to have recourse to another conceptual pair: grace and sin.

As we have already said, it would appear to be an error to confuse this still abstract order with one of the terms of the alternative into which it is positively resolved: grace. If we do, it becomes necessary to identify the category of "sinner" with that of "natural human being," which is manifestly false.

Another conception that seems to me imprecise consists in conceptualizing salvation in terms of "potency" or potentiality, openness, ordering, or destination, to grace or revelation. This idea rests on the supposition that the said possibility is actualized *when* the explicit message is accepted.[28] Now, were this to be the case, how would one view "pagans" but as "natural human beings"—which is simply absurd? Here the confusion is between the supernatural and revelation.

This last confusion, or so it seems to me, lurks at the heart of the theology of salvation history, a theology that seeks to be much more biblical, patristic, and "existential" than was "classic" theology. Actually, however, this theology rests on a system of speculative concepts of which the principal one is that of the "supernatural." In any case, this "biblical" theology must be required to answer the decisive question: Is the supernatural calling or destination to the divine life universal or is it not?

For my part, I propose a recasting of "salvation history" as revelation history—as the history of the *revelation* of salvation. I base my thesis on the fact that salvation has always been under way. This (theoretical) groundwork is furnished us precisely by this second level, the level of the history of the revelation of salvation. "Salvation history" would then be the history of salvation manifested, acknowledged, proclaimed—not the history of salvation as such.[29]

Revelation should then be conceived as a derived moment in the global history of humankind—a second moment, a moment "with a lag." But as revelation, it would not actually reach the universality of human beings. Far from it. It would perhaps pertain to its essence to be, and necessarily, a sectorial phenomenon only—charged, however, with a *metonymic (pars pro toto),* symbolic *(sacramentum salutis)* value.[30]

The towering question raised by this conceptualization of the "supernatural order," a conceptualization that postulates a distinction between salvation and revelation, is the function of the economy of salvation. How are we to theologize the faith statement that salvation has been effectuated in the "salvific events" attested in the scriptures, particularly through the deed of Jesus Christ? Likewise, how are we to understand the sacramental economy of the church as a "means"—medium and milieu—of grace?

These questions can be solved if and only if it is possible to demonstrate that scripture, and the events reported there, as well as the whole salvific order of the church, are, where salvation is concerned, not of the order of its *constitution,* but of the order of its *manifestation.* Thus we would be dealing with a *hermeneutic* of salvation, not a *history* of salvation. Christianity would then be the *interpretation* of the salvation of the world, and not the salvation of the world itself, or even the exclusive instrument of this salvation.[31]

More delicate is the particular, and central, case of Jesus Christ, whom faith confesses as savior, and not merely as prophet, sage, or saint.[32] Here we must recognize that the church began very early to theologize the salvation brought by Jesus in less than totally intimate linkage to its proclamation (revelation) and explicit acceptance (faith). Even the apostolic church understood that Jesus' salvific deed was of an essentially *eschatological* nature. Salvation spanned history from end to end, and so was universal. This is not the place to enter into the details of these universalizing interpretations, held as canonical because they were presented by the New Testament, and more or less prevailing ever since. Suffice it to recall, for example, the parable of the last judgment in Matthew 25:31–46, the soteriological scope of love (Luke 10:25–37; Gal.5:6), the universality of the "natural law" or "ethical conscience," by which God's (salvific) will is manifested (Rom. 2:6–16), the universality, again, of the salvation wrought by Jesus (Mark 10:45; 1 Tim. 2:3; and esp. 1 Pet. 3:18–22; 4:6), and finally, the pancosmic and panhistorical outlooks on the redemption wrought by Christ in the letters to the Ephesians and Colossians.[33]

This New Testament position—implying, to be sure, the need for explicit faith, but divorcing salvation from revelation—has remained a constant in the history of Christian thought.[34] We find it in the apologetes with their theory of the presence of the *Logos* among pagans, we find it in the church fathers with their conception of the *Ecclesia ab Abel justo,* we find it in the scholastics with their theory of *fides implicita* and invincible ignorance, we find it in the moderns, to our own day, and we find it in contemporary theologians.[35]

We are thus led to admit of a salvation *antecedent and exterior to revelation*—antecedent to and outside the historical Jesus—not, however, independent of the *Kyrios* of glory. We shall see, throughout the remainder of part 2, the important conclusions to be drawn from this conception to the profit of a theology of the political.

In this sense, the thesis concerning "anonymous Christians" is altogether defensible, not in its name, and not in its *usus ideologicus* for recouping a tattered *extra Ecclesiam nulla salus* theory, but in its solid dogmatic substance.[36]

Thus the theological concept of the "supernatural" would be no more than a (theo)-ontological translation of the biblical notion of "covenant," in its own historical record.

For we can distinguish two broad types of interpretation of Christianity. One is *historical*. This interpretation, in conformity with biblical and even evangelical tradition, sees salvation as an event realized, unfolding, in historical time. The other is *ontological*. It sees salvation in terms of the order, economy, or situation of salvation, present in every age.

The second approach seems preferable to me, for many reasons. First of all, the ontological interpretation is richer and more powerful. It has the capacity to include the historical interpretation, in the form of revelation or hermeneutic. Further, the second type of interpretation has the advantage of bringing out into the open any confusions that obtain between the reality of salvation and its cognition. Finally, it permits the resolution of many a theological aporia, as I have been able to suggest.

My preference is corroborated, as it happens, by the fact that the deeper New Testament reflection goes, beginning with historical description and moving toward theological interpretation, the more it tends to dehistoricize salvation in favor of ontologization. We need only compare Mark with John, or Romans with Ephesians and Colossians.

As I close my discussion of these points, it may be well to represent its more salient features in a kind of diagram:

0. **theo-ontological plane:**
   (natural order)/supernatural order
1. **existential plane:**
   $$\frac{\text{grace/sin}}{\text{salvation}}$$
2. **theoretical (logical) plane:**
   $$\frac{\text{revelation/reason}}{\text{salvation}}$$
3. **epistemological plane:**
   $$\frac{\text{faith/theology}}{\text{salvation}}$$

These four schematizations do not coincide. An order of level-differentiation obtains among them, indicated by their numerical order. Of primary importance here is the reality of salvation, whose truth is at the basis of the objectivity of theological discourse.

In subsequent reflections I shall be verifying the fecundity of these perspectives for a theology of the political. For the moment let me say only that the identification of salvation with consciousness or awareness of salvation (revelation, faith, church, sacraments, theology, and so on) obliges a theology of the political to adopt an ideological position. Such a conceptualization is much too narrow. It functions as a pair of blinders, preventing its subject from seeing the saving presence and practice of God apart from explicitly Christian practices — if not indeed apart from ecclesiastical practices. In the former case, theology will have a tendency to become a *sectarian* theology—a religious doctrine of a small number of dedicated Christians. In the latter case, it will run the risk of being taken for an *ideological* theology, inasmuch as it is developed in terms of the ecclesiastical institution. How, then, will one interpret all the rest—that is, nearly everything? How will one theologize the great historical movements that haul the masses along even as they are hauled along by the masses, that raze the established social forms of organization to establish others? The main thrust of these, for all intents and purposes, at least for the last two centuries, would seem to bypass the institutional framework of the church, and even the Christian symbolic universe.

To break this bottleneck of theological thinking, we must be rid of the theoretical mortgage that weighs upon the Christian conscience in general and theological intelligence in particular, a mortgage consisting precisely in the intimate connection, indeed near identity, between the order of salvation and the order of revelation—in other words, between salvation history and the awareness of that history, and finally, between the kingdom of God and its sacrament, the church.

§31 APPROPRIATION OF SALVATION: PRACTICE OF *AGAPE*

In the section just concluded, salvation has been posited as an order that has always existed, and in which human beings are historically situated. Now the moment has come to ask ourselves how this order concerns human beings in their destiny and activity.

I may respond to this question by saying that salvation concerns human beings on the level on which they resolve the salvation alternatives positively or negatively. And it is in virtue of the concrete practices that express and realize their freedom, capacity for decision, and life purpose, that human beings concretely resolve the salvation alternatives in favor of a positive or a negative solution. It is thus that human beings respond to the salvation that always has been and always will be proposed to them.

The response to salvation presents itself in a *religious* form—for example, that of a particular faith—or in an *ethical* form. In the first case, the absolute demand appears in the guise of the personal Absolute, manifest as such. In the second case, this same imperative or exigency declares itself in the guise of abstract values to be pursued or, more concretely, in a definite face—that of one's "neighbor"—as an appeal for acceptance, justice, and service.[37]

In either case, for theology there can be no doubt: here is where salvation is decided. And salvation is not decided "punctually," but in accordance with a whole series of practices, a "pointillism" designing the unified figure of a basic life project.[38] In this sense it is fair to say that human beings *make* their salvation. Their (future) being is made and fashioned in and by their qualified practices.[39]

The ascription of a soteriological density to ethical engagement may seem to imply an underestimation of the importance of the visible economy of salvation—religion, precisely—structured by its own system of practices connected to a profession of faith, sacraments, and membership in a church community. I shall be taking up this question at greater length below. For the moment, let me simply say that there is no contradiction, but actually an articulation, between the order of religion and the order of ethics. This articulation has a dominant term, however, and it corresponds here to the second term of my equation: the ethical.

At the same time, even the religious, or cultic, version of salvation has always admitted, in language of its own, the substance of what is affirmed in ethical practice—namely, that salvation in the last instance (that of the divine judgment) is decided on in the practice of love. And it is in virtue of this sometimes tacit ethical principle of religion that theology acquires the potential to understand and recover theoretically the soteriological value of ethics, by way of the theory of "implicit faith," or the *unknown* presence of grace.[40]

The concept of a universal salvific order absolutely forbids us to think of this order as a "thing in a certain place," something somehow deposited in the human being, or again something in which the human being somehow becomes situated, simply. On the contrary, the salvific order is to be thought of as an existential situation, whose parameters are the locus of the effectuation of the destiny of human beings from the first movement of their freedom. There grace or sin acquires a body, composed of human decisions, in such wise that there is no human act, in the proper sense of the term, that would be neutral, or devoid of all qualification in terms of grace or sin.[41]

Thus it is in and by concrete, definite practices, unified in a basic project, that salvation (or its rejection) comes to the human being, and to every human being, whether under the sign of grace or that of its opposite. We may not, then, imagine works as being only the *expression* of an essence that is *antecedent* to them. Rather it is the works themselves that concretely constitute this essence: grace. In this moment, there is no problem with the reconciliation of nature and grace. Both realities become one, however possible it may be to grasp them in their respective formalities from different perspectives.

In this order of ideas, the doctrine of justification by faith "without works" will belong to the area of *religious interpretation* of what *actually happens* on the level of salvation. This doctrine has no reference to the domain of *ethical prescription*. It only says that what is embodied in agapic practice—salvation as grace—does not occur in virtue of these same practices, which of themselves are radically powerless to achieve salvation as grace *(de congruo),* but that it occurs by the vital power of grace itself *(de condigno).* Whether a person knows this or not in no way modifies the theo-ontic relationship that binds *agape* and salvation: this relationship is based on the sovereign decision of God in the form of the "economy of salvation."[42]

Faith without *agape* is dead (James 2:14–16; 1 Cor. 13:2). But *agape* without faith still has meaning (Matt. 25:31–46; Luke 10:25–37). Therefore salvation can be independent of awareness, but not independent of the practice of *agape.*[43] Inasmuch as it effectuates the appropriation of salvation, this practice is not anything adequately distinct from that salvation. As belonging to the existential plane of salvation, in terms of decision, *agape* is salvation itself, in its historical body.

Praxis must therefore be understood as located on the side of the *real,* as object of faith and of theology, and not on the side of the awareness they represent. And then, given that agapic practice is the appropriation of salvation as grace, *agape is the (asymptotic) concept available to the theologian for understanding political practice in its soteriological signification.*

But our manner of positing this problematic does not yet permit us to transcend the horizon of individuality. We are considering the human being in the political, but we are not yet considering the political as such. For a theology of the political, it is of basic importance to get beyond the level of a purely humanistic or anthropocentric reflection, in which the free subject or agent still occupies the central place. Otherwise praxis necessarily suffers a certain shriveling and becomes restricted to a crippled, one-sided ethics.

Then salvation also suffers a reduction. It appears under the form of a *private* appropriation, and we are once more in the classic tradition of first theology, where in the last instance—in the ultimate practico-practical norm—ethics is an affair of the private conscience, and where salvation in the last instance—in the Last Judgment—consists in "saving one's (own) soul," regardless of what may happen to others.

It can be seen, then, that according to this view the concept of the "political" as such, be it in its own structure, or be it from the point of view of the praxis corresponding to it, is practically obliterated, although it does preserve some interest *ratione peccati et ratione gratiae,* with sin and grace being likewise understood in individualistic terms.[44]

And yet when we move up to the properly political level, sin appears in the form of inhumane, unjust situations. It can be conceived as a power developing in history and permeating the network of interhuman, social relationships—permeating structures themselves, as scripture, in its fashion, gives us to see.

It is only at one remove, based upon this foundation and within this framework, that we might perhaps be able adequately to understand personal decision in the area of politics: what an individual person can and ought to do when faced with such and such a situation in respect of politics. For the individual is summoned by revelation, in the full sense of the word, within this situation. Thus also the individual's faith response, in the theological sense of the term, will be able to materialize only within this same situation, and according to the degree of awareness of the person in question, as also according to the objective and subjective potentialities and opportunities inscribed within a given conjuncture. The notion of "original sin" may very well provide the key to the articulation between structure and person, and various attempts in this direction can be seen in theological writing today.

The positive resolution of salvation—grace—may be approached in the same manner. Here, on the structural level of the natural element of the political, images such as that of the reign of God are pregnant with meaning. Transcending the narrow horizon of the personal, interior "state of grace," it would be possible to conceptualize salvation as a "state of social grace," thereby designating the whole complexus of objective conditions that realize the image of the reign of God.

These suggestions only reflect vectors already rather well established today in theologies of the political. However the case may be with these particular approaches, at all events it is clear that, if a theology of the political means to be proportioned to its object, it cannot be built on Robinsonizations.[45] That is, it will not be able to situate the (social) structure in solitary function of the (private) individual, and thus posit the abstract individual in the place of the concrete structural. This would amount to a complete misunderstanding of the specific project of a theology *of the political*.

Of course, theology of the political cannot pretend to the status of an integral theology. As a particular theology—one of the political and of nothing else—it has the "right to neglect" what does not belong to its defined theoretical field.[46] Thus for it, "the individual is an abstraction" (Comte). The concrete object of its reflection is the political, and in the political it is collective praxis that counts. The task of the theology of the political is to theologize the salvific value of this practice, not *in abstracto*, but *in concreto*: in the concrete real of determinate historical practices.

At all events, it is through the intermediation of an effort to develop categories and theories adequate to its object that "political theology" will acquire the means to see the "materially theological"—the "real of salvation"—manifesting itself in history, right where this "materially theological" does not yet declare itself, and there produce the "formally theological." For the theologian, the political involves more than what "natural" awareness and science might know. For there is a dimension of the political that only the theologian is competent to qualify in its ultimate truth, and that is in what the political holds of the absolute, as decisive salvation or radical perdition.[47]

From these considerations, I find that praxis is to be located on the side of the "infrastructure": that of salvation as the personal, historical appropriation of salvation. But this is known only through a theoretical labor. The theological *logos* constructs the relationship between praxis and salvation as a relationship of pertinency and even identification.

Praxis as such is not a theological category. It is "theologically opaque": it cannot pertain to the second generality of a theology of the political, but only to its first generality. Praxis is not a theologizing, but a theologizable, category. If theology of the political is possible, it is because the meaning of praxis—a determinate praxis—is not religiously or theologically evident. It is therefore necessary to theologize it, and this is done by applying to it the theological *organon*, as when we ask: What is the pistic or soteriological sense of such and such a practice? How is God present there? How does the kingdom come by means of such a practice? What practice expresses and realizes *agape?*

There is no such thing as a *Christian* practice as such, a practice with the name "Christian" written on its forehead as constituting its particular essence.

What really exists is a practice *inspired* by faith and *interpreted* as being "Christian," or "supernatural," or "salvific."[48]

The objection may be raised here that these considerations are "ideological"—that they posit praxis in function of a supposed religious meaning, thus turning social practices away from their specific objectives and thereby emptying them of their proper substance.

The appropriate rebuttal here will be the retort *ad hominem:* Does the objectant's notion of the political exhaust the totality of the signification of the political? Is practice nothing more than what a particular discourse can say about it? Or does praxis instead have a greater volume than that gauged by a simple sociological interpretation? Does praxis not perhaps permit, indeed demand, other readings, readings that disengage a plurality of significations, disengage new dimensions?

If the political is no more than political, then neither is there a theology of the political. But in that case neither will there be a genuine political as such. The political, *in order to be and remain political,* has need of a jurisdiction that can judge it and save it. Otherwise it "goes mad"—loses its reason—and becomes unbridled hybris.

Further to the retort sketched above: Is it not just as "ideological" to "repress" theological thinking upon the political as to practice it capriciously? Is it not just as "abstract" and "reductionist" to abstract from the "religious" dimension, which one holds for decisive, and supremely decisive, as to limit oneself to it?

Theology becomes impossible when a (profane) theory of the political holds itself out as the last word, as the discourse *ne plus ultra.* If this happens, theology will not hesitate to break with the dictatorship of such a discourse and liberate its space—that of the God question at the heart of the political, as has been shown.

To be sure, the pistic sense of political practice can be rigorously and critically stated only by the one equipped to do so: the theologian. And this sense can be attested only in and by Christians who are really living in the practice of *agape* on the political level. This means that, in the last analysis, theological discourse is comprehensible only in virtue of the credibility of the practice of the Christian community. Thus theology is a theology of the political first and foremost with and for that community. But theology can be with and for this community only in function of the approaches and actual concrete interests of the concrete community, in its struggle for or against other social groups that may have other theories and other practices.

Here, then, is the concrete complexity from which arises the urgent appeal for a theology-of-faith-lived-politically—that is, a theology of the political.

§32 THEOLOGICAL LOGOCENTRISM

The theological hypotheses expressed on the foregoing pages are certainly not those expressed formally in scripture or classic theology, although I have had recourse to both in this study. I say "formally" because, in my opinion, my theses accord with the content of faith, as well as give an account of it.

Surely it is evident that, both for the Bible and for theology in general, salvation is bound up with faith, the sacraments, and the church.[49] The fact that faith as well as theology provide for salvation without (explicit) faith, without the sacraments, and without membership in the visible church, need not really contradict this, and theology has sought to render scientific the connection between salvation and these elements. But it would not be unreasonable to ask whether it has done so in a really articulate and organic way. Its conclusions seem less than totally secure, and they would not, apart from certain dogmatic pronouncements, appear to have won a broad consensus.

The reason for such theoretical shortcomings is to be sought, I think, in the epistemological presupposition that allows for the utilization, *as architectonic concepts,* of biblical notions just as they are reported—that is, with the theoretical content with which the sacred writers themselves have invested them. This theoretical content is not always homogeneous. More often than not it is plethoric, turgid: semantic superfluity "lays down the rules." And theological discourse, failing to take an appropriate distance from its object by means of an adequate theoretical instrument, wanders now in one direction and now in another, at the whim of biblical language, which is a living, vital language, showing the disorderly ebullience that is the mark of all life.[50]

Idealism or Logocentrism

The immediate adhesion of theology to its object is particularly to be seen in the idealistic view of salvation that the classic tradition seems to foster. Or, instead of "idealism," we may speak of a "logocentrism," in the sense that it is the content of awareness itself that occupies the central place in the question and controls the final decision.[51]

In conformity with this tendency, theology has come to think of salvation as being realized in and by the word received in faith, in and by participation in the sacraments, and finally, in and by membership in the church community. Thus salvation has come to appear as intimately bound up with religion, when in fact religion is but the visible, phenomenal aspect of de facto salvation. And so we still have vestiges of intellectualistic, sacramentalistic, and hierarchicalistic "ruts" in the church, which have occasioned a great deal of criticism.

The conceptualization of faith as knowledge has recently encountered opposition from the conceptualization of faith as experience. There has been progress, then. Yet one wonders whether we are not still mired in *awareness*—(subjective) awareness of salvation.

To be sure, one will not often meet with the flat declaration that individuals realize their own salvation. On the contrary, this is what we regularly hear denied. Nevertheless, the status of those who call themselves non-Christians, and who constitute the majority of humankind, past and present, remains to be explained. The intimate nexus posited between salvation and awareness of salvation—faith—leads to two impasses, to which attention has already been called: (1) that "pagans" are in the situation of "natural human beings"—which is quite indefensible—and (2) that "sinners" are in the same situation—which is even more indefensible.

It is true that the old theory of "implicit faith" has recently been rehabilitated in a new guise—that of "anonymous Christianity." But here a problem arises as to how this concept can be reconciled with the logic of the traditional concept of faith as decisively conditioning salvation.

Let us take St. Thomas Aquinas. The very first question of the *Summa* is symptomatic. There Thomas asks whether revelation is necessary. The response is loud and clear. Revelation is necessary for salvation, because without *knowing* God it is impossible to attain God.[52]

Here faith receives its familiar intellectualistic connotation.[53] Theology, for its part, acquires the status of a "science." It continues to bear upon faith and revelation, "noeticizing," as it were, their proper object.[54] And here appear the criticisms leveled at Thomas's logocentrism by the Franciscan school and, later, by the Reformers, as we shall see in §34. Perhaps this logocentric tendency was the price to be paid by theology for the Greco-Christian synthesis.[55]

I shall therefore qualify as "idealistic" or "logocentric" the theological conception that establishes a bond of dependency between salvation and revelation (or faith). The logocentric conception is idealistic because it prioritizes the aspect of awareness—not because it prioritizes it in religion, however, because there it is precisely awareness that is essential, but because it prioritizes it on the level of a general conception of christic reality, or the supernatural order.

Further: the distinction between faith and religion, whose pertinency is exclusively theological, as we shall see more clearly later on, is always to be found in the area of a logocentric identification of salvation with revelation. Indeed, the distinction between faith and religion, too, confers the primacy on the aspect of Christian awareness, just as does theological idealism.

Idealism manages to conceive things only where they are "said" and *by reason of* their being "said." Where they are not "said," neither do they exist. The pitfall for idealism consists in positing knowledge as a condition of being. Thus idealism sees salvation in and by its expression, its *dictum:* religion, which enunciates salvation (in doctrine), celebrates it (in ritual), and organizes it institutionally (in a church).

According to this conceptualization, then, salvation is, first, *knowledge.* It depends on the reception of a message. The verbal/auditory element is utterly decisive. Secondly, salvation is bound up with a *ritual* complexus, by which it is communicated. Thus the sacraments are held to be causes of grace, and liturgy is considered to be actualized salvation. Thirdly, salvation is tied to insertion in a *community,* according to the well-known formula *extra ecclesiam nulla salus.*

The idealistic conception draws the content of Christianity over to the side of the historical movement and sociological reality that bear the name of Christianity. When all is said and done, everything else, everything non-Christian, is always understood in relation to a Christianity primarily conceptualized as the "significate," not just the "signifier," of salvation.[56]

The consequences of this tendency for a theology of the political are easy to foresee:

1. On the level of *doctrinal* expression, Christianity will be simply and impertinently set in opposition to other currents and ideologies, such as Marxism.

2. On the level of *cultic* expression, Christianity will be opposed to other (non-Christian) religions, and even to other (nonreligious) social practices.

3. On the level of *institutional* expression, the only alternatives before Christianity are (1) sectarianism, which opposes the church to the world; (2) clericalism, which seeks to impose the religious forms of its own organization on society as a whole; and (3) apoliticism, which seeks to establish a "religious sphere" alongside the "political sphere," or "economic sphere," or what have you, having a function of its own, and completely independent—which would not be false if faith were nothing but religion.

Theologism and Physicalism

Moving on now from the theology of the political to its (epistemological) theory, I discern two major negative consequences of a conceptualization of salvation or "christic reality" such as we have been examining. These two consequences are theologism and physicalism.

For *theologism,* history and society can be correctly addressed only by theology. Thus the duality of salvation and liberation, which is legitimate as a linguistic and analytic duality, becomes a genuine hermeneutic dualism, in which two interpretations engage in an antagonistic "standoff." Because it is urgent to articulate them, however, theologism sets them in fictitious, mutually contradictory contiguity. Theologism posits their mutual opposition aprioristically, based on a radically vitiated religious conceptualization.

Physicalism, subscribing to a primitive conception of religious language, considers theological "entities" after the fashion of empirical, historical realities, as if they were substances apart, opposed, or at best parallel, to the realities of our world. Simultaneously, "religious" realities, such as the church, the sacraments, sacred writings, instances of authority, and the like, are conceptualized as entities having a double, "humane-divine," nature. Physicalism thus falls within the sphere of influence of mythological thinking, which endows its own products with life and then takes them as distinct realities, when they are actually only vectors of reality. Would it not be more fair to say that these "realities" are at once human and divine, depending on the vantage from which they are observed, whether from (pure) reason or from faith? Thus, for example, for a historian Jesus can only be a human being, whereas for a believer this man Jesus is truly God.[57]

In a word: the idealistic or logocentric conception, which identifies salvation with revelation/faith, issues directly in the ideological identification of church with kingdom, or religion with salvation.

We must therefore draw a hard line of demarcation through the cluster of interacting, articulable concepts that this view confounds. This demarcation will furnish us with the wherewithal to define the theoretical conditions for saying that the church is the kingdom only sacramentally or metonymically—that faith, to be sure, proclaims salvation, but that this salvation is to be found elsewhere as well, and not only where the faith is confessed—and that grace can be present in the agapic practice of any human being, and not just where this grace is identified, as in the church.

The content of the theological concepts here proposed, with their position among the theoretical mechanisms that provide them with their field of operation, evidently does not correspond to the manifest content of the notions that bear the same name. Their names indicate how they function in the language of the content of faith and theological tradition in general. What is important is that, from a point of departure in a broader interpretation, the concepts we have advanced will answer for those other notions, in virtue not only of what they say, but of what they leave unsaid.

CHAPTER 7

Theological Theory: Order of Knowledge

§33 THE THEOLOGICAL DIFFERENCE

In the foregoing chapter, I have propounded the theo-ontic status of salvation as object of faith and theology, in contradistinction to the awareness of this object as faith and theology. On this quite basic level, faith and theology are still indistinct, lumped in a general unity that might be termed "superstructural," for we are here dealing with the conscious forms of the appropriation of salvation.

I now propose to trace a line of demarcation between faith and theology, marking out a difference within this general unity. The interest this distinction holds for me is that it will permit me to distinguish the specificity of theology from that of faith, and the mechanisms proper to theological discourse from those that govern religious discourse.

Just as we saw in the distinction between salvation and the awareness of salvation, the distinction between faith and theology will make it evident that the methodical awareness of salvation is something different from its nonmethodical awareness, and that this otherness is expressed in the "language play" proper to each.

First, then, let me attempt to define the various epistemological mileposts along the road the language of faith must travel.

1. First of all we have the level of the word of revelation or faith—faith being the human "other side of" revelation. In order to open up the field of theological thinking, a previous intervention by revelation, correlate of faith, is necessary.[1] This intervention may be thought of as a *historical breach* (with respect to revelation) and an *existential breach* (with respect to faith)—to which there corresponds an *epistemological breach* of reason relative to its natural forces. Reason and faith do not lie along the same continuum. Reason can, at most, dispose itself for the leap of this "breach" (from "theology at zero degrees"). It cannot actualize it. Between faith and reason, then, there obtains a discontinuity.[2]

Let us not tarry longer at this level. My thesis presupposes it as central, as has

109

been said repeatedly. However, let it be noted here that the "breach" of which I speak has a particular application in the case of a second theology. For, whereas the sciences of the social furnish the theology of the political with its raw material, this theology must break with this first datum if it means to arrive at the production of a genuine theological theory.[3]

It is clear, then, that there is *mediation* on the level of the first generality—socio-analytic mediation—but *breach* on the level of the third generality. It cannot be otherwise with a theology (second generality) of the political (first generality).

2. A second level is that of *religious discourse.* Here we are within the purview of the word (of revelation, or of faith). Here a relationship of *continuity* obtains between faith and reason—which is not the case with the inverse relationship of reason to faith.

Religious discourse—the human response to the word of faith—is "diffracted" into a multiplicity of discursive practices: kerygma, catechesis, homily, prophecy, testimony, magisterial teaching, hymnology, ritual, and so on. Religious discourse is situated just at the intersection of the word of faith with theology. It is the word of faith on the way to becoming theology.

These observations will suffice here; this is not the place for a further development of the particular status of this type of discourse.

3. The third level is that of *theology.* Theology arises when the *ratio fidei,* already present in various degrees in religious discourse, becomes systematic, methodical, disciplined. This is the difference between theological reason and religious reason. Both, of course, receive the object, or content, of cognition from the word of faith. But theology is distinguished from religious discourse by the *mode* of cognition of the same content—that is, by its method. This may be shown by analysis of the "language play" proper to it. It is by the "play" of its language that theology is differentiated from simple religious discourse. The difference is not one of kind or nature, but of *degree.* Theology lodges the demands of reason in the degree of *critique* and *system.*[4] I shall examine all this in detail in §36.

Again, on the level of *cognitional content,* a substantial identity obtains between word of faith, religious discourse, and theological theory. But on the level of *rational elaboration,* expressed in a particular "language play," the case is no longer the same: the words of faith and religious discourse are closer in kind to "ordinary language," whereas theological theory belongs to the genus of "normed language." It is this difference that is the subject of the present section.[5]

It is in the sense of this difference that theological discourse acquires all the mediations that build distance between (theological) reason and its object. And it does so by way of the mediations proper to it in its capacity as a theoretical language: its first generality will be socio-analytic or philosophical mediation, and so on; its second generality will be hermeneutic or philosophical mediation, and so on.[6]

From the above considerations, we can distinguish among:

1. The *theory* as such—that is, the object or content—of theological cognition, which is identical with the object or content of revelation, or with the object or content that one is given to see *(theorein)* in faith.

2. The *method* of theological cognition—that is, the rules of its own proper practice (discursivity, criticity, systematicity, and the like).

3. Finally, the organization of its *language*—the form in which this particular theoretical practice called "theology" is expressed.

In the present chapter I am emphasizing the last two aspects (which are intimately connected). It is here that theology demonstrates its difference from the word of faith (which of course is its theoretical principle, or point of departure) as well as from all other religious discourse (which, in terms of language or discursive practice, are on the same plane as the word of faith).

As I have already noted, discursive practices of a religious nature are governed by rules no less than is theological practice. The only difference here is that their rules, unlike those of theology, constitute a *regularity* rather than a *legality*. The rules of simple religious discourse are as it were buried within the discourse itself, so that the one enunciating the discourse does not advert to them. By contrast, the rules of theology are explicitly laid down, positively established, and critically controlled. Here we are dealing ultimately with a self-regulating discourse, as has been stated.[7]

The varieties of religious discourse listed above are all concerned with *direct practice*. They express life as actually experienced, and are developed with a view to the solution of concrete problems. Accordingly, they set in motion a type of language that corresponds to life experience, and to practice. They are largely, although not exclusively, constructed on the basis of *"performative," self-involving* elocution, charged with a *forensic* force of greater or lesser strength.[8]

Theological practice, on the other hand, has no immediate objective in life experience. It is not built in direct function of a practice. Its immediate objective is the *cognition* of that of which faith is the experience and simple consciousness: God's salvation.[9] Theology is more theoretical, or scientific, practice than it is ideological practice.[10]

This is particularly evident from the fact that the rules governing religious language permit and even encourage inconsistencies, hyperboles, substitutions, contradictions, and, very particularly, condensations (metaphors) and dislocations (metonymy)—in a word, all the possibilities of symbolic language for expressing the metasensible by the use of polysemy.[11]

By contrast, the theological *logos* is a work of distinction and unification. It is a linear, not a contrapositive, discourse—a surface discourse, not a discourse in density. It seeks consistency, precision, semantic constancy. In brief, it is organized by a canon of legislative, executive, and judiciary power.[12]

Theological language is composed of propositions in the indicative mood—not in the optative or the imperative, as with religious discourse.[13] Theology is a language of theory, not the discourse of passion or action. It is the theory of salvation, not the expression of its subjective experience.[14] I shall return to this below, in §§36 and 37.

True, the *articuli fidei* are the *principia* of theology, in virtue of the fact that the truth of theology receives its force from revelation itself.[15] At the same time, it must be said that these *principia* only constitute the indispensable conditions of theological practice, and do not replace the work of the theologian, which depends essentially on rational "discursivity." Such indeed is the proper sense of the term "principle."

In the word of faith, theological reason finds an absolutely virgin field of exploration. The word of revelation is there; its exploration remains to be carried out. Here, reason is challenged. And it is only at the moment when this challenge is accepted that theology begins. Indeed, in no other area of knowledge is so much demanded of reason.

To say that faith means a *sacrificium intellectus* is completely to fail to comprehend either the nature of faith or the power of reason itself.[16]

But here a legitimate question arises. By virtue of its adhesion to its objects, is theology not liable to be taken with them, and in their stead, and thereby represent itself as something that it is not (its own first generality) and as something that it cannot even give—salvation as reality, appropriated in and by the praxis of *agape,* and faith as revealing word and founding experience?

Here, the theological difference performs the function of theoretical warranty, both with respect to the reality of salvation, and (therefore) with respect to its experience. The enterprise of differentiation has the singular effect of yielding up an unambiguously modest conclusion: theology is only theology. Theology is only a particular practice, a determinate language, and nothing more. This can only clarify the nature of theology. Theology is neither salvation, nor praxis, nor even faith or revelation. It weaves a theoretical relationship among these terms, in such a way as to render intelligible the manner in which salvation is to be found in *agape* and experienced in faith. For the rest, *"sileant theologi a munere alieno."*[17]

These considerations lead to an examination of the classic definitions of theology. Theology has been called the "science of faith" (*Glaubenswissenschaft),* the "intelligence (understanding) of faith" *(Glaubensverständnis),* the rational "discourse of faith" *(ratio fidei),* "faith in the state of science," "faith cogitated" or "faith reflected on," or even "faith thinking" (faith in the act of reflecting), and so on.

These definitions, by reason of their objective, are all within the great tradition of *fides quaerens intellectum,* which spans the whole history of theology from the agnostics of the Alexandrian school, to Augustine, to Anselm and the Middle Ages, and down to our own day.

It seems to me that the positive element in these expressions is, first, that they offer the occasion for a first step in the *autonomization* of theology as a theoretical practice, and as a differential language vis-à-vis the word of faith; and secondly, that they express the *dependency* of theology *in principle* on the content of faith.

However, owing to the very close bond they posit between theology and faith—a bond felt with particular acuteness today—they tend to conceal the difference proper to theology and, by this very fact, its autonomy as well. *They do not name theology for what it is:* theory *upon* faith, not theory *of* faith—knowledge, not acknowledgement. They conjure away the distance that exists between faith, as event and word, and its rational, critical theory.

As already stated: in order for faith to be faith and theology to be theology, and continue to be such, a line of demarcation must be drawn between them. This line of differentiation will pass between the discourse *of* faith and the discourse upon, or concerning faith—between the believer's word and the theologian's language.[18] True, the former is the sine qua non of the latter. Indeed this is what I mean by "dependency in principle." But it is not, for all that, its reality. Theology retains its discursive autonomy.

This identifying difference—its concept, and what it provides—can never be overemphasized. For what it guarantees is the autonomy of theological practice, with all its intellectual demands.

"Epistemological vigilance," then, is all the more to be recommended in theology, which is particularly exposed, more than any other theoretical practice, to entanglement in the mesh of "spontaneous" religious discourses of various kinds.[19]

If theologians mean to live up to their name, they must hold these discourses at a distance, interposing, between their practice and its object, the tools of their method, which are technical mediations.

Indeed, when all is said and done, faith itself will be the gainer, for it will then be able to be understood in its true identity, instead of being taken as a simple acknowledgement-in-ignorance, or even a phraseology pure and simple. No one can be satisfied with a theory of love as a substitute for love itself. Thus the best theology is the most theological theology—the one that neither seeks to substitute for faith, nor allows faith to substitute for it.

Of course, although the theologian's task is not formally of the order of the word of faith, there is no reason why it should not be conceived as a charism in the church and a profession in society. Theological practice can become genuine expression of faith and *agape*. And it will be such to the precise extent that it will be informed by this faith and this *agape*.[20]

But on the level of our considerations here, we shall do justice to our subject only by distinguishing theology from faith, taking the former *for what it is*. We shall do justice to theology only by postulating its difference from faith, as this alone will assign it its proper space of realization.

Finally, I want to stress that the theological difference is not first and foremost an (internal) demand on the part of the reality of salvation, or even of the experience of faith. It is rather an (external) demand of the historical moment in which we find ourselves. For, in my view, it is precisely our age, with its practical problems and theoretical questions, that calls for a new effort of theological intelligence.

It would not be appropriate, therefore—at least it would not be germane to our considerations here—to attempt to judge other times and other cultures in terms of the theological standard by which our own era must be judged.[21]

§34 THE THEOLOGICAL DIFFERENCE IN THE THEORETICAL PROJECT OF THOMAS AQUINAS

I have had repeated occasion to refer to Thomas Aquinas, and here I turn to him once more. How did he handle the specific difference of theology?

In his short, absolutely remarkable history of theology, M. -D. Chenu traces the evolution of the theoretical struggles of the Middle Ages. He does so in order to be able to ascribe to theology a precise theoretical status—obviously, within a framework of the sciences of the time.[22]

As we follow, under Chenu's guidance, the development of these controversies to their denouement, we realize that Thomas, in conferring upon theology a rigorous epistemological status as a science, and drawing the corresponding conclusions for theoretical practice, attained a revolutionary theoretical achievement—something whose effects, as we know, have been incalculable.

I am of the opinion that the determination of the theoretical status of theology has not changed substantially since Thomas's time. True, it has undergone some remodeling, and even development. But these modifications and developments have been homogeneous with Thomas's original positions.

Much could be said about the historical lot of Thomism as a *system* of Christian philosophy and theology rather than as a *method*. What I intend to discuss here, however, is not Thomas Aquinas's system, but his epistemology. The simple substitution of a so-called scholastic, speculative theology for one seeking to be more biblical and existential, without a resolution of the theoretical problem posed by this substitution, may very well constitute a practical advantage in, for example, the pastoral area. But it would certainly mean ignoring the problem of theology itself, or at least presenting it in so confused a fashion that there could be no hope for its solution.[23]

The reason why I think it necessary to take Thomas's trajectory—not repeat him, but develop him—is that I see no other way of pursuing, in some fashion, his decisive, irreversible theological undertaking, as well as emulating him in his concern for scientific rationality. I am not seeking to turn back the clock; I am only seeking to go further in the direction of a spirit whose level later theological tradition did not always maintain.

The thought of Thomas Aquinas is characterized by an extremely ambitious application of (speculative) reason, and this in full self-awareness—that is, expressly and systematically.

History shows that the effort to raise theology to a scientific status did not fail to meet with heavy opposition.[24] And no wonder: this is the price of every new discovery. It is part and parcel of the logic of the evolution of all science.

Thomas Aquinas succeeded in constructing a most precise definition of the position of theology as a science among other sciences. He did so from a point of departure in the intellectual culture of his age, bestowing upon theology a solid epistemological "assent" through the intermediation of precise concepts. Among these concepts, and in a preeminent position, is that of *subalternation,* borrowed from Aristotle's theory of science. Thus far, we have Thomas's contribution *in actu signato. In actu exercito,* he took these foundational demands to their logical consequences, as we may see from an examination of the corpus of his writings.[25]

In order to set theology on an epistemological pedestal "cut to size," Thomas readily refers to various bodies of knowledge of his time. It is in reference to this corpus of scientific rationality, that of his era, that he seeks to define the regional rationality of theology. On the map of the contemporary *episteme,* he limns the boundaries of theological knowledge as one knowledge among others.[26]

Thus he conceives theology as a full-fledged science, with all the rights accruing to a science. The objective of theology, in Thomas's thinking, is not action, but knowledge. Theology is a speculative, theoretical science. Only in a second moment is it a practical science.[27]

In assuming these theoretical positions, and thereby basing theology as a science, Thomas Aquinas delineated a true difference between theology and religious discourse. The latter was lacking in intellectual pluck, and failed to place all the resources of reason in the service of faith.

My concern here will be to identify the exact terms of this difference. For Thomas, the theological difference consisted in the resolute, methodical use of speculative reason in an understanding of the content of faith, following Aristotle's model in this matter. In this fashion, Thomas broke with the theological tradition inherited from Augustine, according to which theology was conceived as a *sapientia,* or *scientia affectiva,* in which a rational discourse upon faith was really a ventriloquistic discourse of faith upon itself, in terms of *cogitatio* or *meditatio.*[28]

This is Thomas Aquinas's truly basic epistemological contribution to theology.

However, the differentiating demarcation laid down by Thomas includes, for us today, some rather incomplete lines. The "unfinished" part of Thomas's theological difference is aptly represented by the expression *sacra doctrina,* in virtue of the contradictory unity to which it points. This is my hypothesis; I shall attempt to support it with the following considerations.

Not only theology as such, but sacred scripture was included in the meaning of the expression *sacra doctrina.* Thus a basic, barely discernible, oneness was established among certain distinct terms; thus: revelation = faith = Christian doctrine = scripture = creed = tradition = theology. Distinctions and nuances are delineated only in different discursive contexts: they are not posited in their own right, even though they shape the organization of Aquinas's theological discourse.[29]

My claim is that one will discover, in the notion of *sacra doctrina* in Thomas Aquinas, a heterogeneous whole—whose theoretical components I have individuated above, redistributing the same elements in a new order.[30] In Thomas, *sacra doctrina,* and the concepts composing it, are posited in terms of truth, knowledge, cognition. Thus revelation is the communication of truths inaccessible to (natural) reason; faith is the assent of the intellect to the revelation of mysteries, and theology becomes a systemization of the content of Christian faith. "Christian reality," or the supernatural order, is in some way "noeticized," and faith as an integral whole is elevated to the plane of *sacra doctrina,* and covered by it. The knowledge attained by *sacra doctrina* is invested with a soteriological and even eudaimonic virtue. We are dealing with *veritas salutaris* (cognition = beatitude).[31]

In a word: the theological difference marked off by Thomas vis-à-vis all other religious discourse failed to take into account the type of autonomy, and consequently the legitimacy, of the latter.

By this very fact, Christianity, conceived as order of salvation, is posited in its entirety within the cognitional element, and thereby idealized. In its journey to the plane of science, *sacra doctrina* took with it, within itself, faith and everything else, including salvation.

But this unity can only be self-contradictory. Witness the aporias of Thomas's thought, the controversies of Thomists surrounding the meaning of *sacra doctrina,* and especially the historical resistance thrown up by, first, the contemporaneous "epistemology" of a Franciscan *unctio,* and then, later, the Reformers' "epistemology" of *fiducia* or the humanists' *sapiens et eloquens pietas.*[32]

These last two epistemological positions have recognized (but not *cognized),* felt (but not theorized), the "unfinished" element in the identification of theology. They perceived the Thomistic definition of theology as injury to or reduction of Christian (or, better, christic) reality. It seemed abusive to them to distill the whole content of faith as rational knowledge. These positions show us the limitations, and even the error, of Thomas's epistemological project.

Unfortunately, this reaction is as mistaken and lopsided as the Thomist position it criticizes. It derives from the same premise that damages Thomas's conclusion: these positions too are prisoners of the complex unity of theology whose self-contradictory nature conditions their empiricist position. Instead of opposing theological discourse to religious discourse, tracing within the contradictory unity of *sacra doctrina* the difference or quasi breach between the two discourses, these positions oppose one type of theology to another (leaving it clear, of course, that both deal with faith). And so Bonaventure would still like to speak as a *theologian,* but *secundum pietatem,* and Luther still wants to talk theology, but *sine Aristotele.*[33]

Just as Thomas Aquinas, then, toppled "christic reality" over into philosophy (in order to have it "science"), so these later tendencies pulled it down on the side of faith (and it becomes ideology—a religious discourse upon christic experience).

To Thomas's credit, however, it must be said that the line of distinction of theological rationality had been drawn by him once and for all. After him, Christian theology could never again be the same.[34]

These simple observations, rather sketchy, are the product of the concept of "recurrence": it is from my particular epistemological position that I reread the history of theological thought; and contrariwise, it is from a point of departure in this history that I determine my position. This constitutes the solitary novelty of my retrospective reading.

The Thomistic framing of religious discourse upon theological discourse is "legible" for us only in reference to our cultural and historical conditions, in whose context indeed all reflection is necessarily articulated in all its forms and methods. From this point of view, it can be seen that the language of theology will never be able to constitute itself in its specific difference.

For my own part, I am convinced that theology of the political forces all theology to rethink and reconstitute its theoretical platform in a more precisely defined way. The conceptual instrument for doing so is furnished by the scientific spirit of the times that are ours.

It was ever thus with theological rationality, which has always been forced to measure up to the *episteme* of its time in history. Today is no exception. Quite the contrary. Theological reason today is challenged, ultimately, by the imperatives of praxis. The enterprise of Thomas Aquinas ought to be continued, then—not so that we may think we have finished it, because we never shall, but in order for theology to measure up to the intellectual and practical demands of our time.

And so the stroke that must be delivered to *sacra doctrina* today will be to sunder the self-contradictory unity in which Thomas Aquinas left it, and in which he could only have left it. We must thrust theology, which lies in fetters on the wrong side of the line of demarcation, back across the line, and keep faith distinct from theology. At the same time, and very especially, we shall need to keep the common object of both—salvation—at a distance from either, in the sovereignty of its own reality.

The epistemological alternative that I propose does not consist in a simple return to Augustinianism—which has not qualified for inclusion in Thomas's irreversible epistemological edifice in any case.[35] Nor is it a contribution to Thomism by way of a synthesis, which could only be fictitious and formal.[36] Nor again is it a return to Thomas Aquinas, except in the sense of the recurrence mentioned just above.

The task I here propose consists in a kind of division, tending to the following effect: on the side of Augustinianism, that a *scientia affectiva* renounce its claim to the status of a theological discipline, and recognize its reality as simple religious discourse; and on the side of Thomism, that a *fides in statu scientiae* cease to identify itself as religious discourse, and come into its own as *methodical science.*

§35 FAITH AND RELIGION: CHRISTIAN IDENTITY

In my reflections thus far, there is a certain lack of definition, and precision, in one of the notions that I have been using, but which I have not yet subjected to any formal treatment: the notion of *faith.*

In order to circumscribe the content of this concept, we might apply the very simple rule that comes down to us from Anglo-Saxon analytical philosophy: *the meaning of a word is in its use.*[37] We have only to examine, then, in what linguistic context, and in what circumstances, the word in question is being employed. This rule will be seen to be quite fertile for determining the sense of such a polysemous notion as that of faith. We have only to insert our term in its discursive context—be it that of scripture, or the fathers, or popular usage, and the like—in order to learn its signification.

At the same time, if theology would be a "well-made language" (Condillac), or "exactly specified" (Tarski), it will be incumbent upon it to define, as far as possible, the meaning it assigns to concepts and the cognitive use made of these concepts.[38] Having fulfilled these conditions, theology will be in a position to organize a clear, and clarifying, discourse.[39]

It is true that faith is not subject to control with respect to its object. But this is no obstacle to the perfect "controllability" of that discourse having faith as its theoretical object—for the simple reason that the real is not reflection on the real, as I have emphasized (in part 1, §18).

To resort to an obscure discourse on the pretext that the object upon which it bears is "mysterious" is to confound language and world, theory and reality. It is not impossible to speak clearly of obscure things, any more than it is impossible to speak obscurely of clear things. Why? Because—once again—the laws of thought, like those of language, are not those of reality. The order of being is not the order of cognition.

The price of having forgotten this has often been, for theology, a fall either into "speculative idealism," which means "reducing the real to thought," or into "empiricist idealism," which is "reducing thought about the real to the real itself."[40]

As a consequence, it is perfectly possible to ascribe a precise, operational sense to the notion of faith. I shall seek to do so from the theoretical structure that I have already proposed, in which the definition of a term consists in the expression of its relationship to other terms in the same structure.

Placing faith, then, among the concepts of this structure, we perceive that it receives its semantic determination partly from the concept of salvation, and partly from the concept of theology. This twofold relationship, however, is composed of incommensurable formalities, as will be seen shortly.

Faith, then, is a bridge. Or better, it stands at the intersection of theology and salvation.

faith/theology
<hr>
salvation

Hence the two essential components of faith: *fides qua,* with respect to salvation; *fides quae,* with respect to theology.[41]

The first component is expressed in the form of a spiritual "experience," a meaning "event," a "discovery" of Truth, and "encounter" with Someone.

This is *fides fiducialis*. Here we are viewing faith from its subjective side, its living, experiential, sometimes mystical side. This component is always accompanied by a more or less important psychological content.[42]

The second component may be defined as the objective, phenomenal pole, where *fides qua* is in some manner in suspense. This is the side of the content of faith. Here we are dealing with the content of "revelation," with "doctrine" — in a word, with "religion." This is the dogmatic, positive, historical side of faith. This component is always charged with a more or less clearly pronounced sociological (cultural and historical) density.[43]

As can readily be grasped, these two aspects are dynamically interrelated. Faith is the *dialectical unity* of both. Faith is both an experience of Meaning, and meaning experienced.[44] It is both a lived Truth and a true life. Only analytically can we distinguish a *Du-Glaube* from a *Dass-Glaube*.[45]

Faith is not salvation. Salvation is not exhausted in the *experience* of faith. For this is precisely what faith is, and it is an experience that is inevitably ambiguous. Nor is faith its own *theory*. This is precisely what theology is—critical knowledge of this experience and, thanks to this experience, of salvation.[46]

This does not militate against the fact that it is only through *fides qua,* realized in *agape,* that the reality of salvation comes to the totality of the human being.[47] At the same time, it is only through *fides quae* that the truth of salvation reaches the knowledge of the human being (in revelation). Faith, therefore, is the first and absolute condition of all theology.[48]

The relationships of these three structural terms can be summed up—the better to appreciate their differences—as follows:

Salvation is the real apprehension of (the reality of) God in and through the practice of agape.

Faith is the conscious apprehension of (the experience of) God in and through religion.

Theology is the theoretical apprehension of (the idea of) God in and through a conceptual system.[49]

There is no better way to demonstrate the nature of faith as an "experience of" than by analyzing the word of faith itself—a word that effectuates what it expresses and expresses what it effectuates. This typically *performative* character of the word of faith appears most luminously in the word of the sacraments.[50]

The experience of faith is an experience of meaning. Faith reads and lives history (that of the world) and life (one's own) as having a meaning. But it reads them as having not just any meaning. The meaning of faith is absolute meaning, ultimate, decisive, definitive meaning, the only meaning that can be spelled with a capital letter—Meaning—the only meaning that can be used antonomastically.

For the Meaning that is the object of faith, and is experienced in and by faith, we might perhaps also use here the philosophical term "transcendent," in its most vigorous sense—or the New Testament term "eschatological," in the sense that the primitive community understood it, as the term of that most painful experience, the postponement of the Parousia.[51] Perhaps indeed we might also say "divine meaning," or "sacred meaning," or even "religious meaning," provided that we still intend the same thing.

Here, however, a distinction is to be made. In the matter at hand, "meaning" as general *sense* must be taken as *telos,* and even *skopos,* whereas "meaning" as *signification* is to be understood as the *development* of "sense," in the progress of the latter toward the *telos.* Thus the notion of "meaning" as *sense* touches on the notions of *value* and *behavior,* and religion prolongs ethics.

For its part, Christianity holds—this is its faith—that Meaning as Sense has appeared in Jesus Christ, eminently and gratuitously (John 1:14; Heb. 1:1).

The human being, meanwhile, is of such a nature that sense—all sense, and therefore the (eschatological) Sense of history as well—can be apprehended only through *signs.*[52] Signs are things ensconced in other things, objects superficially indistinguishable from other objects, but objects with a difference: they are "things-toward," indicative objects, pointers, "addresses."

Faith, therefore, as significative, and supremely significative, existence, or as the orientation of existence in the direction of its absolute Sense, presents and expresses itself in the form of an *order of signs*—as a symbolic or sacramental realm, which may be called *religion.* Thus we arrive at another notion to be explained in this section—religion.

Faith is the phenomenon of salvation on the level of *individual* consciousness, and it is the deed of revelation. Religion, on the other hand, is the phenomenon of faith on the level of *social* consciousness—that is, on the level of the culture of a particular society.

Inasmuch as it occasions a cultural and social institution, religion occupies a determinate place in society, and reserves to itself particular moments of personal and social existence.

Faith, whose social expression is religion, of course has reference to the Sense of the whole, and of each thing in the totality, precisely to the extent to which each thing refers to its decisive, and final, End. Furthermore, this reference, in its own way, is objective and structural, in such wise that experience of it or thought of it are but secondary, derived phenomena, which testify to and acknowledge the absolute anteriority of Meaning-from-all-eternity.

Meanwhile, in virtue of the symbolic, and symbolizing, structure of the human being, both (revealed) Meaning and its (pistic) apprehension can be expressed only in a human and social manner. Religion is precisely the human, social status of faith.

Religion, then, is of the order of signs, referring to, pointing to, revelation/faith. It is faith, in a cultural, social, historical regime. It is in virtue of the fact that sign and meaning are on different levels that religion possesses its autonomy. Religion is organized in "creed, cult, and community." This is how we understand the visible church, or Christianity, in its empiricity. From this viewpoint, religion is but one historical phenomenon among others, as a social sector or system alongside others; it is not everything. Consequently, from the institutional standpoint, the separation of religion and politics is not only a social demand, but actually flows from the very nature of the two terms.

In virtue of its autonomy as "profane" reality, politics, even good politics, can be practiced without religion and the church, as experience demonstrates. For its part, religion can be practiced and justified in its quality as an autonomous social entity. Thus the church can be considered as one social institution among others, having its own particular origin, structure, and functions. And this is verified by everyday experience.[53]

Political power, then, can never be the direct objective of the church. The church is concerned with power only to the extent of its own interconnections with the social body as a whole, and thus with other social systems, including political systems such as the state.

A Christian has every right to see the church differently from the way in which a sociologist sees it as sociologist, and to apprehend more there. But what the Christian sees and apprehends will not invalidate or replace what the sociologist sees.

Further: it is possible, even permissible, for Christians to acknowledge the existence of good politics in "atheistic" regimes, just as they may recognize the existence of evil politics in "Christian" regimes, however anxious such regimes may be to have the "Christian" label for their ideology. After all, for jurist or Christian, what counts in politics are the actual *practices,* and not what their agents say of these practices in terms of ideology or even faith.[54]

The human sciences, therefore, consisting in the celebrated "decentration of consciousness," find their application, and a particularly rigorous application, in the area of theology.[55] To know what is evangelical, the theologian need not ask those chatterboxes we call human beings and expect to learn the answer from their overgenerous mouths. No, the theologian must read it in the body of their practices, which manifest their own proper being. The self-proclamation of a "Christian" is less important to a theologian than whether the "Christian" (or "non-Christian") does the "works of Christ." The theologian need bend no ear, not even the most benevolent, credulous ear, either to professions of faith or proclamations of atheism. The theologian's theoretical duty is to break with *manifest* sense—which is always suspect in any case—and heed the *latent* sense, which is almost always genuine. Just as a social analyst can situate a "Christian" in a determinate social and political position independently of the consciousness that that Christian may have of that position, so a theologian— with more modesty, and less commotion—can situate a self-styled "atheist" in relationship to the kingdom regardless of what the "atheist's" awareness of that kingdom may be.

These considerations touch the very root of what is called "clericalism." Here one must hold fast to the fact that the religious is not the political, even though the two are interrelated in one and the same complex social totality. Thus the political sphere is open to the practice of *agape,* the practice that appropriates salvation, whether it be exercised by a Christian or by a non-Christian. If salvation does not coincide with faith, a fortiori it does not coincide with religion, the emblematic regime of faith.

But what, then, will the positive function of religion be?

This question can be answered by seeing religion as the locus of the social identity of faith, the space in this world that permits the objectivization and acknowledgement of faith, and thereby enables faith to declare itself aloud and publicly.[56]

In religion, and by religion, the awareness of salvation—faith—is organized and condensed, as it were, to the point of visibility, so that it becomes diaphanous and apophantic.

Religion is faith declaring itself. Religion is the unveiled countenance of faith. It is its specificity, not its substance; its name, not its essence. Just as a person's identification card is not his or her identity, but its socially recognizable sign, so religion is not faith, but its socially recognizable sign.

It is precisely *in the Christian church,* therefore, that Christian identity is read and recognized. Just as the signifier stands for the signified, so the church stands for salvation, in the form of sacrament. The church has no specificity of its own. It borrows it from the specificity of the world, just as the theological definition of Christian implies that of non-Christian.

How may this conceptualization be justified?

Resuming what has been set forth in foregoing sections, every human being enjoys a de facto relationship to Jesus Christ. This is the sense of the single real order of salvation—the christic order. Thus there are ways of conceptualizing a *constitutive* reference of the human being to the person of Jesus Christ. We are dealing here with an ontic dimension, established in and for human beings, on the plane of their divine calling, and independent of their awareness, as has already been explained.

The Christian is precisely that human being in whom this constitutive reference emerges on the plane of consciousness. In the Christian, the ontic dimension is rendered onto-*logical:* the implicit reference becomes explicit, the latent reality becomes patent. This conscientization is faith. Faith is realized in virtue of an event that may be called revelation. Thus the Christian is the *person who knows.* Christians know their reference to Jesus Christ, and know that all human beings have this same reference.

This conceptualization, which posits the identity of the Christian on the side of *conscious* reference to Jesus Christ—that is, in the order of the *manifestation* of salvation (revelation/faith)—suggests that we might do well to rethink two essential traits of the church as we have them in ecclesiology: its *sacramental* character (as liturgical, priestly, and vicarious), and its *missionary* nature (as kerygmatic, pastoral, and prophetic).[57] I must rest content with having called attention to this implication; it will not be further delineated here.[58]

Thus the distinction between faith and revelation appears as a minor, inadequate distinction.[59] It is that between a whole and one of its parts. As to salvation, let us be clear that it is in no way identified with its phenomenal expression, however privileged that expression may be. Salvation is *in* the Church, but the church is not itself salvation.[60]

The reason for this is that the sense, the Meaning, that comes to be expressed in our signs of religion in no way coincides with these signs. It overflows them on all sides. Religion—more precisely, the church—can be thought of as a sacrament: as the symbolically consummated realization of the world, the proleptic image of the eschatological kingdom, the parable of the divine sense of history. So conceived, the (Christian) church is not the locus of some random interpretation of the world or of history. It is the locus of preservation of the *hermeneutic code,* or reading paradigm, thanks to which it is possible to read the "christic" sense of history (even though the very code may also be a "text").

Consequently, I may make the following statement. *Faith is not a landscape to be seen, but eyes for seeing. It is not a world, but a gaze upon the world. It is not a book to read, but a grammar for reading—for reading all books.*

Thus also with the church: as "sacrament of salvation," or "sacrament of the world," it can be understood as a theological metonymy, *part for whole,* or *pars totalis.* It represents/realizes, performatively, the salvific sense of the world and of history, even where this sense has not yet "come to word." And if we conceive this sense under the figure of the kingdom of God, we shall then say that the church is, to be sure, not yet the kingdom, but rather precisely its acknowledgment and proclamation.[61]

Therefore the Christian community can be defined as *gens prophetica,* a "people-metaphor" (G. Cattaui), the *interpreter of the world* and the *prophet of history,* in the sense of the agent of the hermeneutic of which we are speaking.[62]

It should be noted that I consider the church strictly as *sacramentum tantum,* the *res* being God's salvation or grace. The church is *res et sacramentum* only very relatively—that is, to the extent that salvation, which so far surpasses it, is also to be found within it.

That the system of signs comprising religion should come to replace the meaning (salvation) to which it refers, is nothing to be wondered at, in light of the history of all religions and the history of all signs.

As to the former, I have nothing to add to the already voluminous material on the subject.[63] As to the latter: sign, of course, possesses an opacity that will always tend to replace what it signifies. It resists, in varying degrees of stubbornness, all transcendence of itself. It refuses, at times violently, the passage to meaning. And yet, we know that meaning is never apprehended "in itself." Meaning itself is radically inapprehensible. It is the horizon that recedes with our approach. Ultimately, we find ourselves simply amid signs, as with the twin-mirror game, in which each mirror reflects the other indefinitely. It is as if we were caught in a "net of signifiers."[64] We see, from the nature of sign, then, how the symbolic order of revelation can become opaque and self-sufficient.

Further, religion is not the ultimate sense of history. Salvation is. Religion is no more than a sign, or signifier, of this meaning. It is not even experience of salvation—faith is—but only its voice and name. As that voice and name, religion is the space in which world and history come to radical self-expression, self-recognition for what they are *when all is said and done*—that is, *sub specie aeternitatis.* Without being the substance or essence of the secret revelation of the world, religion is its repository.

The dogmatic block represented by the identification of salvation (grace, kingdom, God, and so on) with the historical phenomenon of Christianity and the social phenomenon of the church, constitutes a genuine obstacle to theological practice.[65] It is only at the price of its dismantling, which we have but sketched in rough, that one may win the right to produce a theology of the political that is proportioned to its object. It will be a *theology* because it will rest on defined and identifiable principles. It will be *of the political,* because the subject matter indicated by the term "political" can now be related to any and all praxis, inasmuch as this praxis may be read by the code of the faith.

Then, once the code of faith is objectified in this symbolically structured space called religion, it will be incumbent upon theology to effectuate the theoretical formalization of religion, from what it sees in the proper place in the code, as church.

There is no theology, therefore, without church.

§36 "LANGUAGE PLAY" OF THEOLOGY AS A WHOLE

I shall only briefly pause on the problem indicated in this title, because it does not constitute the proper object of this study. But it does imply that object, and by implying it modifies it. Hence it merits a rapid, and so of course elementary, treatment.

Theological *pertinency* is defined as constituted in relation to the word of revelation. The concrete manner in which this pertinency operates is its proper *method,* and still more concretely, the *technology* of this method.[66] On this level, pertinency will vary with the degree of development of a culture. At the same time, theological reason cannot be altogether reduced to the cultural concretizations that form the underpinnings of its objective. Theological reason is a particular gaze cast upon things, or to put it more dynamically, a manner of producing things in the element of theory.

Theological functioning or practice has as its effect an *argumentative* discourse. This discourse elucidates the content of faith through the intermediation of the development of its discursive concatenation, from a point of departure in the *articuli fidei.* We are dealing, then, with a speculative discourse, producing intelligence concerning the "truths of faith." As Thomas Aquinas puts it in his celebrated article 18 of *Quodlibetum* 4: "Its reasons instruct us as to *how* what it proposes is true."[67]

Thus theological discourse appears as possessing a distinctly *critical* character. It gives an account of faith *(quae* and *qua)* in response to difficulties thrown up to that faith, as it may also give an account of its own process, testing itself and allowing itself to be tested.[68]

To such purpose, theology can avail itself of all the tools and techniques open to its assimilation, although it will order them within the larger scope of its proper pertinency. Among these techniques I must name, here, *hermeneutic,* in the sense of a set of norms of (exegetical) interpretation of the inspired texts. One of the essential moments of the theological process as a whole is the construction of the "datum" of faith, the establishment of the positive content of

Christian belief. It is thanks to this that the second generality of theological practice can be projected. I shall return to this more extensively in the next chapter. Here let me simply state that I am dealing with a first, indispensable moment in the theological process.

Here, however, we are still on the level of a *fides quae*. In order actually to have theology, there must be a second moment—the theoretical, or speculative moment, which is the one most characteristic of the integral process of formally theological production.[69]

I must, however, admit a circularity between these two moments—between "positive theology" and "speculative theology," between "exegesis" and "dogma," between "Bible" and "reason." It may be said that, whereas for *fides fiducialis (fides qua)* it is the first term of each pair that is the more decisive, for theological theory it is incontestably the second that marks the process.[70]

Let me be somewhat more specific concerning the manner of this process, the rules of this "language play." I shall begin with religious language and then come to theological language properly so called.[71]

First of all, what specifies a religious language is not its vocabulary but its grammar. Such language has no "divine" or "revealed" concepts available. Indeed, if it had, how should we understand them? Religious language is a texture of human words, invested with the significations, experiences, and the history of human beings.

However, thanks to a grammar of its own, religious language can "work on" these words. It renders them capable of calling attention to its own field of reference. The field of reference proper to religious discourse lies beyond the empirical horizons of the world. It is metaempirical. Clearly, if when it says "God" religious language points to the "Sense of the world," this Sense "must lie outside the world."[72]

But for the truth of the intentionality of religious discourse, two basic conditions are necessary:

1. That the proper field of reference of a religious language can be justified. This it can be by the intermediation of a transcendental discourse.

2. That the terms employed by the religious language have available an internal semantic structure capable of rendering them suitable for a metaempirical "dispatch," a sort of transgression of the sensible limits of the world. This is possible in virtue of the intrinsic polysemy of words.[73]

From this we may conclude that religious language can only be *meta-phorical,* or more precisely, *ana-logical.*[74] It is its *manner* of organizing words that imposes a different sense. It is not a matter of abstract, formal signs being the vehicle for empirical things, as is the case with scientific language. It is a matter of *symbols*—things taken up in the form of signs evoking "other things." Consequently, for religious language, the world acts as a "vehicle of meaning."[75]

What determines the religious sense of a discourse, then, are not its words—which refer univocally to concepts, whereas these latter refer to their empirical referents—but rather the *articulation* of the terms employed. It is not their dictionary, it is their syntax. It is not the predicates, it is the predication. The religious sense does not lie in a word, it moves in a phrase—or better, in the sequence of phrases. That is, it lies in discourse.[76] This sense emerges between words, in the interstices of the sentences, rather than in the words and sentences themselves. Thus the religious sense is "spoken between"—*inter-dit*—because it is "forbidden," *interdit*.[77]

Thus far, I have been speaking of religious language, not of language that is properly theological. How do the two differ?

As has already been stated, the difference between religious and theological language consists in the *criticity* of the latter. What form, then, does theological language take?

To be sure, this language springs from symbols. By them it is inspired, and on their wings it flies to freedom. But its flight is its own. Theology consists in a reflection developing within the thrust of the word of faith. But it beats its own path. The point of departure of theology is in religious symbols indeed—but it is a point of *departure,* whence it sets its own course for its own goal. If it extends to analogies, it is not thereby caught up in them. It interprets them, but does not reduce them to allegories. It criticizes them, defining the limits of their validity, and seeks a possible internal consistency of the universe of symbols itself.[78]

In this fashion, religious language only appears as such by virtue of its contradistinction to theological language, and vice versa. To understand the laws that structure religious language, we might refer to two essential mechanisms of ordinary language: *condensation,* corresponding to the figure of rhetoric known as metaphor; and *displacement,* corresponding to metonymy.[79]

I have already spoken of the former. It is characterized by a detachment from one reality (the signifier), and attachment to another (the significate).

Displacement consists in taking a part for the whole, an effect for the cause, a container for the contained.

Religious discourse, we know, is governed by an "economy of the unconscious," whose chain of meanings imposes its own laws—free association of ideas, immediate reference to objects, which is metaphorical or phantasmal, if not actually fantastic, and so on.[80]

The mechanisms of condensation and displacement will generally fashion a discourse with identification such as: salvation = God = faith = revelation = word = sacrament = church = kingdom = fellowship, and the like; or even: liberation = salvation; or, for that matter: revolution = redemption; and so forth. Underlying all of these identifications is the fundamental identification in ordinary language between the real and the known.[81] Let me add that this language has no fear of contradictions or antinomies.

Theological Language

So much for a sketch of the mechanisms that govern religious language. Theological language, by contrast, is given its structure by positive, elaborated, at once controlling and controlled, rules. Here we are dealing not with simple regularity, as in religious language, but with *regulation*.[82]

Theology, therefore, is not simply a restatement of religious discourse. This discourse, to be sure, has its privileged characteristics and effects. But in theology we no longer have the believer speaking, praying, or giving witness—we have the theoretician reasoning, discoursing, criticizing. The agents of religious discourse are "parenthesized" in theology. If they continue to play a role in theology, it is simply to keep theological discourse on the correct side of the boundary line drawn by faith itself.[83] The agent of religious discourse is no longer at work (in theology): this work has now been done and reason has been elevated to a level that of itself, by its own strength, it could not have attained. And yet, of course, even "elevated" reason remains what it is. Therefore it does not cease making its voice heard, and raising its demands, on the new plane to which it has been raised.[84]

The function of theological practice is by no means to assume the role of faith, or to abolish faith and replace it with rational intelligibility. This would be to misunderstand faith completely. The function of theological practice is simply to explicitate the intelligible content of faith through the formation of analogies, and to keep up the struggle to maintain the boundaries of the universe in which faith is maintained—and this "to give reason to," render an account of, faith itself. Here theology must enter into dialogue with the theoretical positions (or questions) and practical positions (or problems) of the age in which it is being produced (in its own "epochality").[85]

§37 SPECIFIC "LANGUAGE PLAY" OF THE THEOLOGY OF THE POLITICAL

We come, then, to our own problem—that of a theology of the political.

How, in light of what has been said, does theological language operate? Essentially, of course, it operates in the way that has just been explained. Still, in view of the fact that it is a particular form of theology that we are considering, the specificity of this form must be taken into consideration. How, then, does theological language *specifically* operate?

To answer this question, I must first discuss the language of the theology of the political in relation to traditional theological language, which indeed it presupposes.

In the first place, at the level of "theology at zero degrees," the world—nature—is apprehended by theological *ratio* in the form of *symbols* of the divine.[86]

For a first theology, revelation as such can come only by way of the mediation of mundane symbols. There is no other way for it to come. In Jesus Christ, to take the central example, God will be said to have given a self-revelation in and by the humanity of Jesus—that is, by the way in which Jesus lived, spoke, died, and rose.

Where second theology is concerned, the process is the same. Human history functions as symbol of divine history.

At this point an important observation must be made. The symbol I speak of must absolutely not be understood as a sort of empty, unsubstantial "as if," like a utilitarian sign whose sense is exhausted in its function of indication—for example, the letters of the alphabet when printed in a book.

Nor are we in the area of the culturalists' symbology, where symbols are no more than indices evoking, through themselves, something that cannot be apprehended in itself—for example, an eagle as a symbol of strength.

What I mean by "symbol," when I speak of religious symbols, is in the line of sacrament—an efficacious symbol, an expression-and-realization. Here, the symbolizing thing is more than itself. There unfolds within it an energy, a presence, a signification, that can be evoked in an appropriate language—the word of faith. Between symbol and symbolized there obtains a co-pertinency of content. Thus human history is not only the text where something else—salvation—is read; nor is it a pure sign, evoking, after the fashion of a gesture, some other thing—divine history. It is the sacrament of divine history, in the sense that it is in some manner divine history itself. Divine history transpires in human history—without, for all that, being another name for it, and without being exhausted for it.

Immanentism? How? The believer knows that none of this would have come into the human mind if God had not freely entered into self-revelation (1 Cor. 2:9–16). Revelation only lays bare what has always been fact: the history of the world is a history of salvation.[87]

But to pronounce it, to read it, to interpret it as such—nothing less than a *code* is necessary. Now this code is furnished us precisely by revelation. Second theology, therefore, presupposes this revelation—as "reworked," to be sure, by first theology—in the same way that a text requires a code in order to be deciphered, and in the same way as a first generality needs a second generality to "work" and transform it.

On these premises, let us now approach the question of the language of a theology of the political. First, we shall have to recognize that this problem presents particular difficulties. To be sure, a study of this "language play" will mainly depend on the manner in which the content of faith, and the relationship of this content to the political, is understood.

Here I shall take a moment to examine this latter aspect—the relationship of faith to politics, which will be in the form of the relationship of a second generality to a first generality. Once I am within my theoretical model, I shall endeavor to analyze the manner in which a second generality "works," or "works upon," a first generality. I shall attempt to set forth this relationship in a way that will be simple yet enlightening, leaving for the next chapter a treatment of the way in which the content of faith is to be understood as second generality.

I shall begin, then, with four formal models, which translate four ways in which faith and politics can be interrelated.[88] Let me formalize them, in order to facilitate their treatment and use, as well as their explanation, as follows:

1. Relationship of *juxtaposition* between faith and politics, as between two equal quantities or two homogeneous "substances," as in the "liberal" conceptualization of religion.

2. Relationship of *opposition* or exclusion, as in the Marxian conceptualization of religion.

3. Relationship of *identity,* as in the model of secularism or horizontalism.

4. Relationship of dialectical *reciprocity* between different terms, as in the model of "political theology."

My own view is that none of these models is satisfactory from the viewpoint of theological practice. At the same time, I acknowledge that the last of them holds more theoretical promise, on condition that it be enriched and better defined, and this is the direction in which I shall be working.

Along the lines of my critical observations with respect to the so-called Chalcedonian method (§28, above), I must now move toward more precision in the relationship between a second generality and a first, which is the relationship between faith and politics.

I have stated that the Chalcedonian method tends toward bilingualism. It recognizes a mutual relationship between the content of faith and the content of politics, but it fails to produce this relationship, or produces it purely abstractly and formally. It is expressed in formulas such as: "Faith *implies* politics, and politics is *completed* in faith," or "the gospel has a political dimension *too,*" or "the church includes a social type of mission *too,*" or "human liberation *and* salvation in Jesus Christ," and so on.[89]

To enrich this model and make it more precise, we must in the very first place recognize the exact nature of the terms we are relating. Thus we must identify the autonomous structure of each, and the level on which each is originally found. Only subsequently can we establish the types of relationship that they can maintain with one another.

After all, as I have shown, before a method can be proposed, the nature of the object to which we hope to "apply" the method must be determined. Were we to fail to respect the appropriate mediations, then, and their order of articulation in the process of theoretical practice, we would run the risk of positing the terms "faith" and "politics" in an oblique relationship that would "strangle" all discourse and render it inarticulable.

An articulation between faith and politics becomes possible only on condition that one avoid a mixture of pertinencies and effectuate a genuine conversion of one term into the other, according to a logic that is defined (or to be defined): according to a "transcodage," then. In this fashion, instead of thinking of the terms "faith" and "politics" in a vague, "bilingualizing," way, by simply pointing to a mutual reference, we should think of them as follows: How is a faith meaning to be produced theologically from a raw material of politics in general—and then, should we wish to apply this to a given concrete situation, from the raw material of this particular political situation? In other words, how may one show the kingdom of God in such and such a determinate society? How may one think salvation history in human history? Thus instead of speaking vaguely of an articulation of faith with the political, or vice versa, we should speak more precisely of an articulation *upon* the political.

Framing the question in these terms means asking ourselves how faith, as second generality, clarifies ("works") the political as first generality. As can be seen, I am here following the hierarchical order of the process of theoretical practice. In this order, it is faith that commands the political. Now, the work of the second generality of a theology of the political is to show how political practice (as first generality) can form a salvific action, an action constructive of the kingdom, and thus produce a third generality.

But does not such a posing of the problem fall victim to a Platonic ontology, for which the essences of empirical things preexist those things in another world? Shall we not have to distinguish here a "supernatural" essence (kingdom, salvation, and the like), from the "natural" phenomenon (society, politics, and the like)?[90]

I answer that these objections would be telling if a Chalcedonian model were at work here—with its latent, Platonic, essence. It is the Chalcedonian model that functions in terms of "image," "reflection," "likeness," "anticipation," "proclamation," "promise," and the like.[91]

A second theology, however, as we have seen, presupposes the work of a first theology. But in a first theology, "christic realities" differ *toto coelo* from the Platonic "ideas." Thus we find ourselves operating in an entirely different conceptual structuration.[92]

The relationship of faith to politics is to be conceived as that of a second generality to a first. This relationship is an *operative* one: it produces the relationship of a first generality to a third generality, in the form, for instance, of politics as related to *agape,* or again as liberation related to salvation.

Thus, the relationship of faith to politics does not have the same status as the relationship of politics to *agape,* or as the more concrete relationship of liberation to salvation. Let me illustrate this statement with the following diagram:

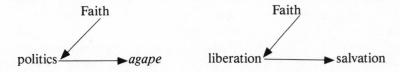

Faith, of course, is *fides quae* here—consciousness of salvation. *Fides qua*—a living experience of salvation—is invested in the Christian's first generality—that is, in an actual political practice.

Consequently, faith and politics are terms articulated in a determinate form from a point of departure in their specific positions. These positions define, between the two terms, an *asymmetrical* relationship, reflecting the asymmetry of any relationship between a second generality and a first generality. By contrast, the relationship between liberation and salvation is *symmetrical*. Of course, its symmetry is in virtue of its production by faith, which sees salvation in liberation.

Faith and salvation are commonly confused. This is like confusing a thing with its shadow, or a glass with the liquid it contains. Salvation depends on faith only in its identification, as I have explained above.

The model I here propose is reducible to the model of theoretical practice. The other model of faith and politics concealed an ambiguity: besides its own content *(fides quae),* "faith" included its real object—salvation—so that there actually were three terms: faith was related to politics, and this conjunct was in turn related to salvation.

That faith can produce salvation from politics is clear from the fact that faith (theoretically) contains salvation. Otherwise the simplest process of transformation would be impossible. After all, a second generality can transform a first generality into a third generality precisely because it in some manner contains the third generality within itself.

Liberation and salvation can be simply identified only to the "eyes of faith" (second generality). Faith, on the (antecedent) level of a first theology, already holds salvation as an absolutely sovereign reality.

Finally, a word of warning will be in order. The schema proposed here has an incontestable value in terms of ethics. But the case is not the same with hermeneutics. Here we must be extremely circumspect, lest we superimpose the resounding event of the fall of the Bastille on the obscure fact of the crucifixion on Golgotha.[93] This allusion will suffice to show the enigmatic manner in which the relationship of faith to politics, and this pair to salvation, really operates.

The analogical nature of all theological discourse is to be taken seriously, then, even in the case of the discourse of a theology of the political. Theological concepts are asymptotic.[94] And those taken up by a theology of the political from a point of departure in the sciences of the social, in virtue of socio-analytic mediation, finally suffer a kind of refraction—inevitably, in function of their semantic "transvaluation."[95] But such is the price of any metamorphosis.

CHAPTER 8

Hermeneutics: Constitution of Theological Pertinency

§38 THREE ACCEPTATIONS OF HERMENEUTICS

I have defined theological pertinency as the essential reference effectuated by a determinate theoretical practice, called "theology," to revelation. I have likewise stated that such pertinency operates theoretically in and by the formal disposition of a second generality. In the present chapter I must sketch the theoretical constitution of this identifying instance of theological thought.

I shall begin by asserting that the activity of this instance belongs to the order of *hermeneutics,* as indeed my definition of theological pertinency indicates. Whether it be formulated as "reflection in the light of God's word," or "reflection in the perspective of faith," or even "theory from the viewpoint of revelation," or the like, it always refers to *Christian positivity*—that is, to the objective (dogmatic, historical) aspect of faith, with its ties to the order of the "given," the "right there."

This positivity does not float in the air as an abstraction. It is found inscribed, witnessed, translated, and deposited in the corpus of the canonical writings of the ecclesial community, the *Christian scriptures.*

The series of canonical texts whose scope is "fontal," inasmuch as they constitute the font of all other Christian writings, consists of the Old and New Testaments. The superiority of their value for the Christian community is indicated in the very name they customarily receive: "Bible" or sacred "scripture."

Other texts or fonts of Christian positivity must be seen under the ordination of the writings just mentioned, which always occupy a central place and perform a cardinal function. At the same time, however, within the Bible itself, a certain hierarchy can be discerned. The New Testament takes precedence over the Old.[1] Within the New Testament, the gospels hold the primacy over the other writings.[2] Scripture, then, must be conceived as an articulated whole, and this is a fact carefully to be taken into account in hermeneutic practice. I shall have occasion to return to this point.

132

The foundational texts of faith are subjected to a process of interpretation. Their sense is not simply open and plain. Time has interposed a distance between them and us. The process of decoding that seeks to overcome this distance, and thus reappropriate the original sense of the written message, goes by the name of "hermeneutics."

I take "hermeneutics" here in the sense of an interpretive activity bearing on *written* texts. I thus take up a position in the ongoing "war of hermeneutics."[3] Below, I shall add greater detail to my position.

From the outset, we are in the theological area. The hermeneutics I speak of is *theological*. It bears upon the Christian scriptures.[4] In the theological area, the notion of "hermeneutics" can have three distinct acceptations, in increasing degrees of extension:

1. Hermeneutics may be understood as a set of *canons of exegetical interpretation*. Here we have the etymological sense of the term *hermeneutike techne*.[5]

2. Hermeneutics may be understood as *interpretation as such:* exegesis itself, as the operation of decoding, along with its result. Here we may speak of a *hermeneia,* in contradistinction to *hermeneutike techne*.[6]

3. Finally, hermeneutics can be simply considered as synonymous with *theology,* inasmuch as theology has the task of understanding an original sense today and for today. In this maximal acceptation, theological hermeneutics would correspond to what I have called "theological theory."[7] Thus, for example, there would be a hermeneutics of the "signs of the times," a hermeneutics of history, a "political hermeneutics," and so forth.[8]

When I speak here of "hermeneutic mediation" of a theology of the political, I refer to senses 1 and 2—although a theology of the political can always be considered as a hermeneutics in the third sense, in virtue of the fact that it designates a theory of the "Christian" sense of politics—that is, in virtue of its quest of an understanding of (political) praxis in the light of faith.

By "hermeneutic mediation" I mean the necessary relationship of a theology of the political with the Christian "fonts," which furnish this theology of the political with its proper identity. In this perspective, the Christian scriptures constitute an *obligatory and constitutive theoretical resource of any theological process.*[9]

But let us recall once more that hermeneutic mediation is not constitutive of a theology of the political *ex aequo* with socio-analytic mediation. Obviously, these two mediations must have an interlocution. It is for us to delineate this interlocution, this articulation. Their relationship is governed by a logic: the logic of theoretical practice in general. In accordance with this logic as I have described it, socio-analytic mediation occupies the position of a first generality, and hermeneutic mediation that of a second generality, whereas the theology of the political will be considered a third generality. Thus, in the expression "theology of the political," socio-analytic mediation takes charge of the "political" side, and hermeneutic mediation takes charge of the "theology" side, with the "of" indicating the articulation between the mediations.

This, then, is my position with respect to the sense and scope of hermeneutic mediation. This too is how my position is to be distinguished from that of others.

I shall now point out other positions taken with regard to hermeneutics, very sketchily, and at the risk of a certain oversimplification.

First there is the position of H. G. Gadamer, who conceives hermeneutics as a sort of ontology. His important *Wahreit und Methode* (1960) bears the subtitle, *Grundzüge einer philosophischen Hermeneutik*.[10] The criticism to which this conception is vulnerable is that of its arrogation of universality, by which it exempts itself a priori from all analytical criticism. Gadamer permits a teeming anarchy of every sort of reading. Too much meaning is terribly strong light.[11]

Rather too broad as well is Aristotle's conception of *hermeneia* in his work *Peri Hermeneias*. It is applied to any linguistic enunciation affirming or denying anything of anything. Here, hermeneutics has the extension of language itself.[12]

Then there is the undertaking of Wilhelm Dilthey, who attempted to base an epistemology of *Geistwissenschaften* on the notion of "comprehension," which, he held, makes it possible for us to apprehend a human sense or meaning in the actions and deeds of human beings. Thus we have the "hermeneutic sciences," of which one is theology. This epistemology is losing ground, however, and today is considered obsolescent or passé.[13]

Coming to Paul Ricoeur, we find interpretation assigned the task of deciphering the "double-meaning" language that constitutes the language of symbol. Thus interpretation will bear on "texts," in a broad, even analogous sense: a myth, a dream, or even a whole culture.[14] Here we have a conceptualization that obviously extends far beyond the notion of a theological hermeneutic.

Finally, we have the conceptualization, already referred to, that identifies theology with hermeneutics, in a tradition coming down to us from Friedrich Schleiermacher.

In the present chapter, I shall limit the sense of hermeneutics on two sides: on the side of its *object,* a (theological) hermeneutics will bear solely upon the Christian scriptures; on the side of its *method,* a (theological) hermeneutics will be limited to the exegetical interpretation of these Christian scriptures.

To be sure, the (original) exegetical sense of these scriptures is animated from within by a thrust that continues into the present, and this justifies the use of the term "hermeneutics" in another sense as well—that of the recovery of meaning not just within the actual bounds of the text, as *techne hermeneutike,* but beyond them as theological theory. However, I deem it preferable to restrict its scope to that of hermeneutic *mediation.* Thus, hermeneutics, as I employ the term, will not correspond to the totality of (political) theology, although it will still be an essential part of (all) theology.[15]

When all is said and done, the important thing will be a precise grasp of the distinct acceptations covered by the notion of hermeneutics, lest we confuse them.

§39 THE HERMENEUTIC CIRCLE

It will be in order to take a glance at theological hermeneutics as such, in order to determine both its scope and the manner of its use in the development of a faith datum.

To this purpose, I shall be guided by the notion of the "hermeneutic circle." I begin by noting that "positive theology," taken as final result of a labor of hermeneutics and exegesis, can be developed only if there is a relationship, however implicit, between itself and "speculative theology," and *e converso.*

This inescapable circle does not contradict—indeed it actually explains—my attempt in the foregoing sections to sketch a theoretical version of the key concepts of theology—notions originating with the Bible, but thereupon coming to be organized in a specific conceptual network.

Now it can be seen that we are involved in a full hermeneutic circle.[16] In the following sections, this circle will appear and reappear in various forms.

It does not suffice, however, simply to point out the existence of this circle. We have yet to analyze the actual form of its presentation, so as to be able to "insert ourselves into it in precise fashion" (Heidegger). For this circle subsists according to particular rules. It is not a perfectly circular trajectory between homogeneous terms. On the contrary, the constitutive relationship of the hermeneutic circle is of a dialectical nature. We are dealing with a tense, critical, indeed dramatic relationship, effectuated under the governance of one of its terms, which rules the rhythm of the dialectical movement. After all, there is dialectic and there is dialectic—one must always identify the rules of its process.[17]

There are many forms in which the hermeneutic circle can appear, once we have set about theological, and especially biblical, deciphering. Among the manifold forms it can take, I would single out those that obtain between the following pairs of terms:

> word of God—scripture
> creation of meaning—acceptance of meaning
> structure—meaning
> present—past
> technique—interpretation

Let us examine these forms one by one.

Hermeneutic Circle: Scripture and the Word of God

The terms of the first relationship to be considered are often simply identified. But they are on different levels, and we must recognize the difference between them. It is not for nothing that, in the determination of the *regula fidei,* the meaning context, or pragmatics, within which scripture has its value, is explicitly named: "The norm of faith is scripture read *in the church.*"[18] The prepositional phrase at the end of the formula inserts the biblical text into church tradition.[19] This means that its sense can be apprehended only in relationship with the *sensus fidelium*—the living spirit of the living community.[20]

Scripture is surely the *norma normans* of faith. But it is likewise in some manner a *norma normata.*[21] This is clear from a study of its historico-literary genesis, as well as from its "canonization" by the charismatic authority of the church. I shall have occasion to return to this point later on.

And so, strictly speaking, the word of God is not to be found in the letter of scripture.[22] Nor is it in the spirit of the hearing or reading community.[23] It is precisely *between* these two, in their mutual, dynamic relationship, in a back-and-forth that is never perfectly objectifiable.[24]

Hermeneutic Circle: Creation and Perception of Meaning

To clarify the dialectic operative between creation and the perception of meaning, let me cite the two extremes to which nondialectical, or dogmatist, thinking leads: hermeneutic improvisation and semantic positivism.

By *hermeneutic improvisation* I mean the attitude, and corresponding practice, that consists in taking from scripture simply whatever serves one's own interest, without any concern but that of making use of biblical passages as "proofs" for a preestablished theoretical project or practice. This is precisely the way of *bricolage* (improvisation or tinkering or makeshift): it makes use of the tools at hand for the needs of the moment.[25] The relationship it sees between the store of "useful pieces" at hand and a work plan is purely utilitarian. It can be a forced relationship.

Hermeneutic improvisation translates into pragmatism in the interpretation of texts. The right meaning is the useful one. Obviously, this is an open door to a riotous carnival of meanings.

At the other end of the spectrum from hermeneutic improvisation is *semantic positivism*. Semantic positivism endeavors simply to gain control of meanings, catalogue them, and store them, so as to be able to use them at will.

It is not difficult to perceive what interest these two extreme positions have in common: control of meaning and its utilization at whim.

The danger for Christian theology—less today than yesterday, it is true—is precisely that of transforming Christian positivity into textual positivism. This creates a "meaning metaphysics," or semantic dogmatism, that freezes any living meaning in its tracks. The images that spontaneously arise in association with semantic positivism are those of the refrigerator, the museum, and the cemetery.[26]

Both of these hermeneutical tendencies, instead of dialecticizing their terms, flee to the extremes. My own position is that meaning can arise only from a sustained relationship between reader and text, between questions and answers.[27]

Hermeneutic Circle: Structure and Meaning

Now let us consider the hermeneutic circle between explanation and comprehension with respect to a written text—here, with respect to the Christian scriptures. Various linguistic theories can offer us a particular service here, precisely in the order of a structural explanation of texts.[28]

Inasmuch as the letter of a text, like any sign, has its titles of nobility, it is important to grasp exactly what the autonomous structure of this letter is before attempting to gather its sense and meaning. Meaning needs structure for support. Structure serves meaning as its vehicle of communication, thus imposing upon it the confinement of its own determinations.

In the case at hand, dialectic proceeds in such a way that explanation becomes a preliminary moment, whereupon the work of "comprehensive reading," a reading with understanding, supervenes.[29]

The same type of relationship is operative between cause and meaning, fact and meaning, the law and meaning—all modalities of the same fundamental pair of structure and sense, structure and meaning.[30]

Hermeneutic Circle: Present and Past

The text never ceases to be open to the world and history. It dispatches all its readers, real or potential, on one assignment after another. Indeed, this is why there is such a thing as writing. It exists to last, to be read and reread.[31]

The written text is the channel of a meaning through a succession of historical moments. This is the case with any text, and especially with the Christian scriptures.

But the Bible does not enjoy such a special and important place in the eyes of believers in its status as a literary text.[32] It does so by reason of the meaning it simultaneously conceals and reveals. The reason it invests in faith is that faith has already been invested in it. And the circle returns.

At bottom, the ultimate reference of the Bible is to the present, to the reader's current history. The biblical sense regards precisely this. It is the reader, then, who occupies the center of attention of the text.[33]

Thus, although in a first moment, a basic one, to be sure, sense or meaning is obtained under sign, word under writing, spirit under letter—now, in another moment, sense is obtained in the present, word in time, spirit in history. But all of this comes through the meaning of scripture.[34] The hermeneutic circle is not broken.

This means that the entire work of exegesis can and should be conceived as a moment in a complex process bearing upon the hearer's or reader's present moment. Now word ceases to be simply text to be interpreted, and itself becomes interpretative code. *Now word is no longer world to be seen but eyes to see, no longer landscape but gaze, no longer thing but light.*[35]

The theory that seeks to take account of this reading is called "theology." If we are dealing with politics, then we are of course in the presence of a theology of the political.[36]

Hermeneutic Circle: *Techne Hermeneutike* and *Hermeneia*

The hermeneutic circle, whose modalities have just been described, shows how impossible it would be to construct an interpretative technique such that its application to a text would lay utterly bare, once and for all, its integral meaning, and obviate all further questions a priori, as hermeneutical positivism dreams of doing. All we would need would be "interpreting machines"!

It so happens that the very openness of ex-sistence is an irreducible fact, one that is always "there," like a wound that never scars over, or a leak that cannot be plugged. The human modality of being-in-the-world is one of comprehension, of endless interrogation—an interrogation that places the world in the balance of a critique, one that seeks to deal with the very Absolute.[37]

This "analytic" may not, however, be allowed to furnish a pretext for the notion that the hermeneutic effort falls back to zero. The objective of the awareness furnished by this "analytic" is only to deliver the interpreter from any kind of "hermeneutical millenarianism"—the illusion of having exhausted, or of even being able to exhaust, the signification of the positivity of faith.

Sense arises in the interstices of the relationship between the twin poles of the decoding process. Sense cannot be seen directly. It can be seen only out of the corner of the eye when the pupil is focusing on its sign.

Thus the hermeneutic circle functions subject to the following restrictions: (1) meaning cannot be fixed once and for all; but (2) neither can meaning be random.

In principle, hermeneutic technique has the capacity to fix the spatial limits of the appearance of meaning or sense. There are incompatibilities, impossibilities—in a word, thresholds impossible to cross.[38]

At the same time, however, hermeneutic alone, with its own tools, however perfected these may be, is incapable of deciding what the "right" meaning is. At this point, an act of creation is performed: a *Sinngebung*. For the "bestowal of meaning" is not to be understood as capricious invention, but as a decision and determination of meaning in the space that "hermeneutic reason" has opened and circumscribed.

This is what occurs, for example, in the relationship between scripture and the reading community. This relationship must be conceived as one of *communication*. Scripture evokes an appeal, an invitation, a provocation, an interrogation. Its text is persuasive. It persuades acceptance, openness, availability. But there remains the task of the one invited—personal response.[39] For meaning is realized only in and by response. Further: it is only in concrete life that meaning unfolds, and "comes to itself." And here hermeneutics flowers into ethics.[40]

Thus there is no escaping the fact that all interpretation is innovative, more or less arbitrary, and always personal—without, however, the necessary exclusion of the contraries of these qualifications.[41]

Here, then, in strokes that are still abstract, and perhaps individualistic, I have set forth the lines of a general hermeneutics, drawn from the notion of the "circle," and developed especially with an eye to biblical reading.

In the next chapter, I propose to entertain some considerations on the question of the relationship of the historical present to Christian writings, and, still more particularly, on the question of the relationship of the political to scripture and the positivity of faith generally.

This will be the *punctum saliens* of part 2.

§40 A HERMENEUTICS FOR THEOLOGY OF THE POLITICAL: POSSIBILITY AND NECESSITY

I have now set forth the principles of interpretation of Christian writings—principles located within the force field of hermeneutic circularity. We have seen that this circle is of such a nature as to be able to include historical currency. Let us now take the present, the political present, expressly as the term of hermeneutics.

What are the implications of reading Christian writings from a point of departure in a determinate political situation? What exactly does it mean to define theology as a "reading of the praxis of Christians in the light of God's word"?[42]

In order to respond to questions of this kind, we shall have to transcend the phase of a simple posing of the problem and move into the area of propositions and hypotheses—to the extent of our means and capabilities, of course.

The questions just posed can be rephrased: How may we establish a hermeneutic mediation for a theology of the political?

First, however, let me delimit the problem and its conceptualization. When I speak of "hermeneutic mediation" here, my direct and primary intent is a hermeneutic mediation with regard to sacred scripture; secondarily, I intend Christian tradition generally, inasmuch as its texts refer to sacred scripture. It is this conjunct that I denote by the expression "Christian writings."

Plainly, it is impossible simply to leap with both feet into the original sense of sacred scripture. It is absolutely necessary to go by way of Christian tradition. Further, any hermeneutic practice supposes a tradition, and takes a position within the flow of that tradition.[43] This being the case, a hermeneutic of the Bible may not neglect dogmatic tradition. Its modus operandi—the hermeneutic circle—forbids it.[44]

It is within these parameters that hermeneutics is to be understood when hermeneutic mediation is spoken of.

Before going further into these considerations, certain difficulties arising from the nature of Christian positivity should be addressed.

Method is a function of its object. We may well ask, then, whether Christian positivity indeed lends itself to an actualizing type of interpretation, such as a theology of the political aspires to, without having its nature distorted.

There are questions that no hermeneutics worthy of the name can sidestep. Especially, in our case, there is the question of the *ephapax* (the "one-and-only" quality) of the salvific event, with its eschatological sense of the consummation of history.[45] And then of course there is the related question of the *clausura, "closure,"* of revelation.[46]

We shall see that such difficulties become insoluble only for an immobilistic, antidialectical approach, which raises them in such a way as to falsify their terms from the outset and thus preclude a correct response.

I have asserted above that the written text remains open to future readings, and that it is illusory to think that one has direct access to the original sense of a text. This is a notion that comes to us from myth. Myth, of course, takes itself for a secret witness to the genesis of a meaning *in illo tempore,* and pretends to make present that original meaning.

What is valid for any text is all the more valid, for specific dogmatic reasons, for Christian writing. These cry out in every word for their own effacement, erasure, *Aufhebung,* sending us back to the Risen One, whose currency renders the sense of these scriptures current as well. They send us to the voice of the Spirit present in the community.[47]

At the same time, we know very well that the writings that make up the Bible, in the phase in which we find them and in which they can be analyzed, are themselves the result of an "updating," a going-beyond the "letter" in favor of a free amplification of the "spirit."[48]

Revelation, of course, is never closed. But it is *canonized*—fixed as an exemplar, model, or code. *Revelation is closed only and solely in order to render possible a multiplicity of readings in later historical moments.*[49]

The closure of scripture is a closure of its *script*-ure alone. Closure does not imply a prescriptive meaning, but only a *negative* meaning (prohibitive of a certain meaning), or at most an *inductive* ("allusive") meaning.[50]

Strictly speaking, we ought to say that scripture is to its interpretations as a language is to its various possible discourses. "Hermeneutic competency" is analogous to Chomsky's "linguistic competency." The only difference is that scripture is a code only in the form of a *paradigmatic message.*[51] Scripture is obviously not a set of formal rules with a view to a set of virtual interpretations. Scripture appears as a model interpretation, and thus as an *interpreting interpretation,* a *norma normans ut normata.*[52] The hermeneutic circle works from the inside out, in the sense that *this hermeneutic paradigm grows richer as such through the interpretations that it permits.*[53] Its "letter," in its very unchangeability, is in some sense *further determined* by the significations that it has itself engendered. This is the very meaning of tradition. We see, then, that the "circle" is inescapable. It reappears at every turn in the hermeneutic process.

The concept of scripture as a *norma non normata,* then, must be transcended, first of all by exegesis, inasmuch as our current exegesis takes no account of the complex archeology of scripture, and then by hermeneutics, inasmuch as our standard hermeneutics is a one-sided, dogmatic tool that kills instead of giving life.

Scripture is therefore made to be taken up and given currency, and this is a principle woven into the very writing of scripture itself. This circularity—this "virtuous circle"—lays waste with one fell stroke the myth of a "return to the beginnings" as a resumption of the original sense of scripture in all its morning freshness. The present is entirely in the reader's eyes.[54] Indeed, this is why the reader does not realize it. The present is not only that which is read, it is also that *by which* the reading is done. This fact is the *condition of the possibility* of any reading, not its obstacle, as historicism, or any other type of empiricism, would have it.

The obstacle, if such there be, consists in this sort of prejudicial presupposition, which dogmatically anticipates the sense to be produced. On the other hand, presuppositions that open out upon comprehension, such as interrogation, intuition, hypothesis—resource tools that remain subject to the reading process—are presuppositions only so long as interpretation itself allows them to be. The first kind, the prejudicial kind, should be minimalized. The latter kind should be enriched to the maximum.[55]

The primacy to be conferred on the present, with its questions about the past and its texts, must be inserted in the "circle" in such a way that the actual density of these texts (their constrictions and their inductions) will be rigorously secured, thus avoiding all "rerouting of scripture."[56] The history of Christianity is too filled with instances of an ideological and manipulative use of scripture for us to continue to be so offhanded in its regard.[57]

Still, we must also take account of this general situation: that it is apparently impossible to install adequate theoretical precautions and sufficient technical arrangements to render a given corpus of ideas inaccessible to all "use against nature." Scripture is exposed to the most surprising uses.[58] It can always become a *scriptura ex machina,* and offer excellent services as such.[59]

But this is not an argument in favor of "misosemy" ("hatred of [multiple] meaning").[60] Rather, we become persuaded of the need for a *hermeneutic watchfulness* that will be all the more on the alert. The word of God continues being what it is—a reality developing throughout history. Otherwise, a theology of the political would simply be impossible.

By this very fact, the word of God is a *historical concept.* Its objective can never be decisively determined, whether it be faith, Christ, the Father, or anything else. Scientific work on the texts is not enough.

To seek to determine *in aeternum,* the "essence of Christianity," or the "essence of the faith," or the "essence of the church," and so on, is to fall victim to the illusion of essentialism. Such an endeavor only succeeds in canonizing what is no more than one historical, cultural form of "Christianity" or "faith" or "church." This lack of a sense of history is actually a failing in humility. It is the sort of metaphysics that leads inevitably to inquisitorial intolerance and the spirit of domination.[61]

Far from yielding to the tendency to control and dominate the pretended "essence" of a text, we ought to conceptualize the text as a *spring* of meaning rather than a *cistern,* a focus of energy rather than a traffic light. The text of Christian scripture is pregnant with all the virtual senses that will come to light upon contact with historical currency. I repeat, therefore: these senses are to be taken as an integral part of the text itself, a demonstration of its kairological virtuality.[62]

§41 TWO UNACCEPTABLE MODELS
OF HERMENEUTIC MEDIATION

Having established the possibility of hermeneutic mediation, we must now take some steps in the direction of a concrete use of written matter, both sacred scripture and Christian writings in the broad sense.

As long as we are dealing with general prescriptions, everything seems to proceed without major difficulties. We have been moving among abstract entities—"Christian positivity" simply, "the" political situation, "the Bible" as such, "the" theology of the political, and so on. Problems begin to abound, however, from the moment the "virtue" of these prescriptions begins to be felt—that is, when we move on to concrete determinations such as a particular Christian truth, a given political situation, or this or that biblical text. For what we are now asking is: What theology can be practiced upon such and such a political situation? And this is not such an easy question.

What I am about to say has meaning only in terms of this passage from the abstract to the concrete.

At the same time, let it be noted that until now I have accorded a primacy to the relationship of faith to politics in terms of *sense,* or meaning, using the equation form, oppression = sin, or liberation = salvation. But the question of *value*, which is gathered from *sense* with a view to *action,* has scarcely been considered at all. I hope, then, that the practico-theoretical aspect of ethics and strategy will become a little clearer in the course of this section and the next (§§41–42).

In order to have a better circumscription of the difficult terrain over which we are moving, I shall work with some diagrams. What I need to do first, then, is to develop models. In the present section, I shall discuss an interpretation model that I shall call the "classic model." Actually, it is a relatively recent one—but it has become so generally used in "political theology" that it can have this title by right. I shall make some critical observations in its regard, because, as it seems to me, it is open to criticism in its very foundations, and I shall take a moment to say why.

The Gospel/Politics "Model"

But first let me quickly describe another "model"—not really a model, because, as will be seen, it is too unnuanced to deserve prolonged consideration, but the claims that have been made for it are so strident that I have to refer to it, even if only briefly. This is the gospel/politics "model."

This "model" is cast in the general mode of the relationship of "rule to application." But such a relationship is mechanical, automatic, and antidialectical.

Here the gospel is conceived as a code of norms to be *applied,* and suddenly we are back with a "rabbinical" conception of the gospel, with its essence as the good news completely negated, and Jesus a political *Moises Moississimus!*

Referring to this construct in terms of "scripture/diary" or "God's word/history" fails to confer upon it any greater heuristic and operative substantiveness. It is actually so vague and general that, in seeking to "say it all," it finally says absolutely nothing. It is powerless to respond to the elementary requirements of articulate theological thinking. It dismisses out of hand both the internal complexity of scripture—which requires hermeneutic mediation—and the complexity of the historical situation in which this scripture is to be "applied" and lived—which needs socio-analytic mediation.

In terms of theoretical practice, we may well ask how a "model" of this sort can posit a relationship between a system of biblical significations, whose consistency is at least problematic, with the continuous flow of historical events, whose unity is anything but a matter of prima facie evidence. It is easy to see how open this "model" is to abusive, uncontrollable manipulation of the gospel, and to the "mystification" of the political. In other words, in matters of hermeneutics, it is obliged to plunge headlong one way or the other into improvisation or positivism (§38, pp. 132–34).

If we analyze the history of Christianity in search of lessons for our own time, we easily see that the "model" in question can equally well be perceived as a map for social organization, or as something politically impracticable.[63]

This vague, limp manner of positing the problem of the relationship between gospel and politics is therefore not so much to be rejected, as to be transcended—all the more so in view of the fact that this "application model" passes over in the most complete silence the *historical context* of each of the two terms of the relationship.

The Model of "Correspondence of Terms"

I now turn to the model that has become the classic one. It has the merit of being *richer* than the other, in virtue of including just what was missing before—historical context. It might be called the model of "correspondence of terms."

In the simplest of schematic terms, I could say that this model seeks to establish the following proportionality:

$$\frac{\text{scripture}}{\text{its political context}} = \frac{\text{theology of the political}}{\text{our political context}}$$

The exodus theme has been developed similarly:[64]

$$\frac{\text{exodus}}{\text{enslavement of the Hebrews}} = \frac{\text{(theology of) liberation}}{\text{oppression of the people}}$$

More recently, liberation theology has taken up the exploration of the theme of captivity, with regard to the current, seemingly insoluble, situation in Latin America.[65] Here is an equation for this pursuit:

$$\frac{\text{Babylon}}{\text{Israel}} = \frac{\text{(theology of) captivity}}{\text{people of Latin America}}$$

In conformity with an analogous schema, still another effort has been launched, this time to read the New Testament with an eye to the problem of Jesus and the politics of his time.[66] This undertaking might be formalized in the equation:

$$\frac{\text{Jesus}}{\text{his political context}} = \frac{\text{Christian community}}{\text{current political context}}$$

In the model of a "correspondence of terms," two ratios are set up and equivalated. Then the sense of the first ratio is transferred to the second, by a sort of *hermeneutical switch*.

I shall not discuss here the various theological elaborations that have implicitly followed such a model. In my opinion, the majority of these elaborations, even apart from their contradictory findings or ideo-political position, have basically been worked out under the sign of the double correspondence I have just cited. All seek to establish an "equal sign" between the two "ratios," each with its bi-level pair of terms. It seems to me that, on the level of a theology of the political, the place and function of this equal sign presents problems that call into question the validity of the model of "correspondence of terms."

Let us take the special case of "Jesus and the politics of his time." There are two extreme positions here: that of *pacifism,* advanced mainly by Oscar Cullman and Martin Hengel, and that of *zealotism,* maintained especially by Robert Eisler and S.G. F. Brandon.[67]

To my view, both positions have been conditioned by the political situation of the historical moment in which they have been developed. True, each set of investigations appears to bracket its respective political situation. Their conclusions, however, or their manner of evaluating them, show that this is not exactly the case. At all events, each reading assumes an undeniable parallel between its respective "ratios": if Jesus can really be shown to have been a Zealot, the Christian participation in a revolutionary process is justified; if, on the contrary, he can be shown to have been an out-and-out pacifist, then "revolutionary Christianity" does not have a leg to stand on. Let it be noted, however, that in either case the mode of inference, in terms of "political theology," is the same: it is based on a parallelism model, or better, that of a "correspondence of terms."

My hypothesis, therefore, is that the substance of the exegetical and theological discussions provoked by these studies has not really been of the order of *his-*

torical cognition, but rather of the order of the *political results* that might be obtained in terms of Christian social behavior.

I think that my hypothesis gains further credit from the fact that this polemical situation has been implicitly or explicitly supported by the "evident" correspondence between the situation at the time of Jesus and that of the critical period of the moment, especially at certain moments (as in World War II, or the upheavals of the 1960s) and in certain countries (such as Germany or the Third World).

Here are some of the summary parallels that have been drawn to support the model in question:

Roman power	=	imperialism
Sadducees' power	=	power of dependent bourgeoisies
Zealots	=	revolutionaries
Jewish people	=	oppressed peoples
Jesus	=	Christians

And the list could be lengthened.

This type of correlation seems to me problematic and vulnerable in the extreme.[68] I shall now raise certain questions with respect to this model, with the objective of preparing to propose an alternative.

Questions Leveled at the "Correspondence of Terms" Model

As to the Figure of Jesus

Has due consideration been given to the singularity of Jesus' earthly career— to the special character of his human, historical destiny?

Have the historical, cultural, political, ideological, and especially religious conditions (for example, the influence of apocalypticism) influencing Jesus been respected?

What might have been the degree of politicization of Jesus' human consciousness?

Was the political context in which Jesus lived really as much like ours as would at first appear?

Has the figure of Jesus not perhaps been taken in a mythical, ahistorical way?[69]

As to the Type of Relationship between Jesus' Political Stance and Ours

Does the model of "correspondence of terms" not perhaps suppose that Jesus is the "model" for Christians in the sense of an example to copy in every last detail?

Can a model of political conduct valid for today be deduced exclusively from an analysis of Jesus' political conduct?

Supposing that it could be shown, incontestably, that Jesus was indeed a revolutionary—will this, simply of itself, legitimate participation by Christians in a revolutionary process?

Supposing, instead, that it could be clearly shown that Jesus positively renounced all recourse to violence—as would appear to have been the case—will this fact alone make all recourse to violence on the part of the Christian "nonevangelical"?

Finally, supposing that it might be shown (as the "eschatological school" claims to have done) that Jesus had no interest in politics whatever—would this constitute a motive for the Christian to do exactly the same at all times and in all places?

As to the Basis of the Model in Question

Is the comportment of Christians linked to the behavior, teachings, examples, and occurrences found in the Bible in such a way that there must be, as it were, a "term-for-term" correspondence between the Bible and the situation in which Christians live?

Has due consideration been accorded the extreme complexity of our society, and the degree of development of political awareness to which we have attained, on the level of analysis and on the level of ideology, during the twenty centuries that separate us from the gospel events?

Can our political context be so closely identified, thematically, with the political contexts of the Bible that resemble them, that we should read "oppression" for "Egypt," "liberation" for "exodus," and "political assassination" for "cross"?

Will the correlation that this model attempts to posit be a sufficient criterion for the selection of biblical passages that can be inserted into the relationship laid down?

Will it be necessary to prescribe a precise relationship between such and such a pericope from the gospels and such and such a political fact of our history, or again a particular event and such and such a political text? Will such a one-for-one correspondence be the sine qua non of the functioning of the proportionality?

These questions show the direction I would take in criticism of the model of "correspondence of terms."

§42 ALTERNATIVE MODEL: CORRESPONDENCE OF RELATIONSHIPS

The alternative model that I here seek to present is suggested both by the hermeneutic practice of the primitive or apostolic church and by that of Christian communities generally.

A number of writings of the primitive church came to constitute the canon of Christian faith, or foundational message of Christianity.[70] The work of the

Formgeschichte and the *Redaktionsgeschichte* schools has taught us that the biblical writings, in their final form, are the result of the superimposition of successive redactional layers—a fact that introduces a distance between the texts as actually presented and the *ipsissima verba Jesu,* in consequence of the concrete situations and needs of the various Christian communities, or what is customarily called the *Sitz im Leben* of these texts.[71]

Further: we know that these texts, once they had been fixed, kept on being lived and commented upon by Christian communities, and that this is a phenomenon that continued down to our own day. In fact, this is precisely what constitutes the work of tradition.

We realize, then, that there are at least two great phenomona separating us from the original deeds of Jesus, in the very act of bringing us in contact with them: the Christian scriptures, and the tradition of the faith.[72]

That the very text of the gospel constitutes the product of a tradition—that is, that it is the result of a labor of reading on the part of the primitive community—is a datum that, although not written into the gospel text itself in just these terms, is nevertheless the *external vehicle* of the gospel message, and this in its entirety.[73] Besides its considerable dogmatic importance, therefore— with respect to the value of tradition, the authenticity of the church, the role of the Apostles, and so on—this fact has a very special hermeneutic scope all its own, and this is the aspect that is of interest to me here.[74]

This hermeneutic scope can be represented in the model depicted in Diagram 6.

Diagram 6

"Correspondence of Relationship" Model

$$\frac{\text{Jesus of Nazareth}}{\text{his context}} = \frac{\text{Christ + the church}}{\text{context of the church}} = \frac{\text{church tradition}}{\text{historical context}} = \frac{\text{ourselves (a theology of the political)}}{\text{our context}}$$

$$\text{reduced:} \quad \frac{\text{scripture}}{\text{its context}} = \frac{\text{ourselves (a theology of the political)}}{\text{our context}}$$

Let me explain the relationships operative in this model. The model itself takes its inspiration especially from the manner in which the primitive church understood, interpreted, and committed to writing Jesus' original words and deeds. Hence the towering interest of the work of exegesis, which permits us to adopt, with respect to scripture, an attitude analogous to that of the first community with respect to the words and behavior of Jesus of Nazareth. Their attitude was one of creative fidelity—as they attributed to Jesus even later developments undergone by his message and work, based on the identity of the Christ of glory with the historical Jesus.

Provided, therefore, that they be accompanied by a hermeneutic concern giving priority to questions of the historical present, studies of the "form history" type can help us to reconstitute the articulation represented by the first two ratios in the model (Diagram 6). This articulation could then serve as a hermeneutic model for us today in our use of scripture.

Moving on to the third ratio—representing the relationship between church tradition and historical context—the articulation between the first and second ratio is repeated between the second and third—that is, between scripture and the later tradition of the church. This, by the way, is easily recognized as something that happens in current, indeed daily, *hermeneutic practice* of Christian communities. This hermeneutic practice is expressed in homilies, catechesis, liturgy, and other discursive or symbolic practices, even with little or no explicit intent.

This brings me to the second point of reference in my attempts to draw up an alternative model—in my attempt to "solve the equation" in Diagram 6. What do we observe in the ongoing hermeneutic practice in our communities? We observe that Christian communities seek to "apply" the gospel to their particular situation, just as the primitive community sought to do. We further observe that, in this effort, both the text, and the situation to which they are to be "applied," are taken *in their respective autonomy*.

At the same time, for an ordinary hermeneutic, the "transposition of sense" from text to life proceeds in spontaneous fashion, so that, even when the "application" becomes difficult, the *need* for the "application" is always felt by Christian communities as normal. As a consequence, here too, as for the primitive community, a kind of creative fidelity reigns, with the result that a genuine "spiritual sense" continues in substantial identity in the most diverse experiential contexts. Perhaps this is the "spirit" of the gospel. It is not meaningless, then, for these communities to call these "applications"—as they do so call them—"word of God," or "message of salvation," or the like. Thus, meaning transpires, "comes to light," in historical currency, through and beyond the letter of the text of the past.[75]

To be sure, a hermeneutic practice of this type has been and continues to be subjected to abuses. But this cannot constitute a motive for its abandonment. On the contrary, it constitutes an invitation, and a challenge. This hermeneutic practice must become the subject of greater theoretical interest, with the objective of furnishing it with the tools that will enable it to overcome these abuses.

At all events, the effort of the church community to be faithful to the gospel in a diversity of historical situations indicates that a *basic identity of significations* obtains throughout the successive readings. It is this identity that I represent by the equal sign (=). The sign does not designate an equality between *terms* of the hermeneutic equation, but precisely between the respective *relationships* between pairs of terms. The equal sign refers neither to the oral, nor to the textual, nor to the transmitted words of the message, nor even to the situations that correspond to them. It refers to the relationship between them. We are dealing with a *relationship of relationships:*

An identity of senses, then, is not to be sought on the level of context, nor, consequently, on the level of the message as such—but rather on the level of the *relationship* between context and message on each side respectively. It is this homological relationship that is the vehicle of sense. It is this relationship that produces a "homosemy," by virtue of serving as the vehicle of the same "spiritual" sense. This is why I have called the model the "correspondence of relationships" model.

The key element in this model, then, is not this or that particular text of scripture, in correspondence with such and such a precise situation. Still less is it a number of texts to be produced with a view to this or that particular behavior, or this or that particular meaning.[76] The key element here is the global, and at the same time particular, "spirit." This "spirit" may, of course, lead to the selection of a particular passage from scripture—but without invoking a correspondence of terms, or a fortiori, a relationship of application. These two models, as we have seen, are insufficiently flexible to effectuate an adequate articulation.[77]

It seems to me that the basic hermeneutical principle called the "analogy of faith," or "principle of totality," or even "canon of the canon," functions and can only function along the lines of the correspondence of relationships model.[78]

We need not, then, look for formulas to "copy," or techniques to "apply," from scripture.[79] What scripture will offer us are rather something like orientations, models, types, directives, principles, inspirations—elements permitting us to acquire, on our own initiative, a "hermeneutic competency," and thus the capacity to judge—on our own initiative, in our own right—"according to the mind of Christ," or "according to the Spirit," the new, unpredictable situations with which we are continually confronted. The Christian writings offer us not a *what,* but a *how*—a manner, a style, a spirit.[80]

Such a hermeneutic comportment is equidistant from a metaphysics of meaning (positivism) and a surfeit of meanings (improvisation *ad libitum).* It lets the hermeneutic circle have free play, which is the only way to arouse meaning.

After all, the hermeneutical equation I have drawn does not "travel a one-way street," or "read from left to right," from scripture to ourselves. The relationship is circular, like any genuine hermeneutic relationship. I might speak, then, of a "dialectical hermeneutic," or vice versa—were the expressions not indeed pleonastic.

But, once more: this circularity functions within an *articulation with a dominant term.* The thrust of the dialectic-hermeneutic movement comes from *scrip-*

ture and is measured, in the last instance, upon scripture as *norma normans*.

At thus juncture, let me return to the familiar model of theoretical practice, which I may seem to have allowed to fall by the wayside, in favor of other models. In fact, however, these other models have been no more than concretizations of the other, more basic one.

The first term of my equation (Diagram 6, reduced)—scripture/its context—occupies the position of a second generality (as hermeneutic mediation), whereas the second term—a theology of the political/our context—holds partly the place of a first generality (in socio-analytic mediation) and partly that of a third generality with respect to the first of its elements (a theology of the political to be produced).

This, then, is the functioning of theological in the production of meaning. But there has never been, nor will there ever be, a *historical* effectuation of a so-called *sensus plenior*.[81] This is the preserve of the eschatological. What we have is a "plentifying" sense, a fulfilling sense, a development of unfolding of meaning—at best, because there is nothing to prevent a "repression" of sense, either.[82]

In any case, the advantages of hermeneutical dialectic scarcely dispense one from pursuing normal investigations and applying classic techniques, with all their advantages (material means, team or joint research, and the like). At the same time, the functioning of hermeneutical dialectic implies a "pneumatic" reading of scripture, consisting in the agent's compenetration with the meaning that informs scripture, and a sustained familiarity with the word dwelling in it—whose enigmatic syntax is anything but connatural with our own at first.[83]

§43 TWO ATTITUDES TOWARD HERMENEUTIC PRACTICE

A correct articulation between scripture and a given human situation—in other words, the correct relationship of hermeneutic mediation with socio-analytic mediation—cannot be constructed on the model of a correspondence of terms, so that our relationship to politics would be parallel to Jesus' relationship to the politics of his time, or so that our relationship to an oppressive power would correspond to the relationship of the Hebrews to the pharaoh's slaveholding regime. And so I have given methodological indications for an alternative model, which I have defined as a "relationship of relationships" obtaining between the terms of a hermeneutic equation and bearing upon the "homosemy" or "pneumatic sense" of scripture in terms of a determinate situation.

For the sake of even more concreteness, I here suggest two basic attitudes of guidance in the solution of the hermeneutic question.

Priority of the Christian Community

Priority is to be accorded to the value of the real practice of the community over that of any theoretical elaboration.

The "political theologian" should be more alert to what is occurring in the community and in society in general than to the past meaning of the pages of scripture. For this theologian, it is more important to theorize "what the Spirit says in the churches" than to apprehend what the Spirit said "once upon a time."[84]

To be sure, theologians cannot do this without having recourse to scripture itself—to the thesaurus of the principles of their theoretical practice. At the same time, this undertaking, in its very roots, is charged with the intent to decipher the historical *present*—to read *kata graphas,* and not the *graphai* as such. Indeed, this is how the church of the New Testament acted with respect to the Old Testament. We can speak, then, with all justice, of the "hermeneutic value of the work of the Holy Spirit."[85]

As a consequence, the theoretical solution sought by the "political theologian" for a determinate situation is in some sort already given in the actual practice of Christians, who, like other human beings, endeavor to bring an adequate solution to the problems with which they find themselves confronted. The theologian need only take account, in the element of theory, of the solutions already in process in the element of practice. I have already called attention to this, first and foremost in the question of the choice of a "social theory" for socio-analytic mediation (in part 1, §22), and shall do so again, in the question of the choice of a model of hermeneutic practice (part 3, §62). These questions have been "solved" by an analysis of the de facto practices of Christians, who, of course, do not wait upon the verdict of the theologian in order to set to work.

Then, too: even the most cursory glance at history will show from what direction the Holy Spirit comes. Without any doubt, the Spirit comes from the direction of Christian (and other christic) practices, and not—at least not principally—from that of theological research, however serious this research may be. And even if such practices are contradictory, their real object—God's salvation—continues to operate in history, thanks simply to not being tied to theology.

This is valid, I should be careful to note, not as a methodological principle, but as a basic directive, or fundamental orientation, on the level of the *attitude of mind* accompanying hermeneutic practice. The priority of practice is a practical, not a theoretical, priority. Therefore, it is not and cannot be a principle of theory, governing the theological process. Indeed, when theologians undertake to theologize the consciousness and practice of the community, they obey only the norms of theological practice—norms that, after all, exist in virtue of a "breach" with those of the spontaneous language of this same community, as I have stated and demonstrated.

I must admit, however, that the word of revelation is bestowed upon believers in its immediacy in virtue precisely of the presence of the risen Christ, and of the ever living word of his gospel. The awareness, especially the theoretical awareness, of this practical fact is only a second phenomenon (not, of course, a secondary one).

This observation supposes, and simultaneously demands, that theologians work in close relationship with their own local community. They should live its concrete life in concrete political terms. It is their office to fashion its theory.

Pursuit of Hermeneutic Prowess

The relationship with scripture, and with Christian positivity in general, ought to tend more to the acquisition of a hermeneutic habitus *than to immediate practical applications.*

Here I call for a hermeneutic *habitus*—prowess, skill—paralleling the socioanalytic *habitus* of socio-analytic mediation.[86]

Thus exegetical studies, meditation, or the reading of scripture and the Christian fonts, cannot be conducted with an exclusive view to concerns of immediate, practical application, or with a direct view to a repertory of defined problems. Otherwise, there lurks the danger of one or the other of two extremes—improvisation *ad libitum* or hermeneutic positivism.

At the same time, one may legitimately search out, for purposes of a general directive, texts that clearly manifest a strict or proximate relationship with the situation in question.[87] But this is as far as it is legitimate to go in the direction of a one-to-one correspondence; nor may these particular applications be invoked as incontestable in the face of other interpretations. It may be that we should admit, as a principle of hermeneutic practice, a basic suspicion when it comes to parallels between the Bible and politics that are too obvious and too facile. Such parallels are often deceptive, and fail to reflect the thematic unities of the Bible. As I have said, the Bible must always be taken as a complex hermeneutic totality, and the same thing applies to the body of the other Christian writings, the writings of tradition.

Reference to scripture should be by way of *creative* memory, and the readings of scripture should be a *productive* reading. Instead of being a technical relationship of application, reference to scripture should, at bottom, be a *pedagogical* relationship, in the sense of having the purpose of forming in the community the *nous Christou* (1 Cor. 2:16), or the *diakrisis pneumaton* (1 Cor. 12:10).

In any case, Christian consciousness—that vital element of theology—can be maintained as such only if it is steeped in the *memoria Jesu,* if it is activated by his "dangerous memory."[88]

Further: the toil of exegesis, the inquiries of history, and the investigation of Christian fonts generally, must continue, if we are to guarantee theology an *objective basis* in hermeneutic mediation.[89] This is all that these efforts can furnish, but it is a great deal. For want of this secure base, the Christian corpus risks becoming a kind of cafeteria, where everyone can find something or other to suit her or his particular taste.[90] There are limits within which theology must keep lest it seek to be "anything and everything."

And yet, a theology of the political cannot rest content with registering, or simply gathering, the results of such studies, or with broadening their conclusions and nothing more. It must actually produce the relationship (third generality: a theology of the political) of the concrete situation in question (first generality: socio-analytic mediation) to the content that these studies disengage (second generality: hermeneutic mediation).

Theologians can never be completely equal to their task. Their office is that of setting in confrontation, in the field of the *logos,* the positivity of faith and the course of the world. After they have exercised this office, they shall have to make their own the words spoken by Jesus: "We are useless servants. We have done no more than our duty" (Luke 17:10).

PART THREE

DIALECTIC OF THEORY AND PRAXIS

In the first two parts of this work, I have posited the terms of the problem of a theological *theory* that would undertake to reflect on a "Christian practice of politics."

Here in part 3, I propose to take the same problem from another viewpoint. I shall now move to a consideration of (theological) theory from a point of departure in praxis (of faith). I shall ask in what sense and manner praxis exerts an influence on theological practice as such.

I do not yet wish to begin the construction of an actual theology of the political. I shall still be on a metatheoretical level here—I shall still be engaged in an examination of the methodological presuppositions of a theology of the political. Here, however, instead of positing the epistemological (internal) *principles* of a theology of the political, along with the methodological *rules* in which these principles are invested, I shall be particularly concerned with the (external) *social conditions,* and, more precisely, with the political determinations, of theology of the political. This theology, then, will be considered *ab extrinseco*—from the standpoint of praxis, its vital milieu, its *medium in quo*. I shall be dealing, then, with the *pragmatics* of politics.

I must take care not to seek to situate this study precisely along the lines of a sociology of theological cognition—an approach ruled out from the very beginning (§1). My concentration upon the social determinations of theological thinking is strictly limited to the implications of these determinations for theological practice as such. I seek, then, to determine here, as far as I may, the properly *theoretical* effects of political practice.

Thus the ultimate interest of my analyses will be to fix the principles, or rather the cautions, with which a theologian of the political must be outfitted in order to develop a theological cognition that not only "speaks of" politics, but does so politically. To this purpose, it will be necessary to carry out a scrupulous examination of the *practical conditions* of the production of theological meaning—conditions permitting theology of the political to go beyond a cri-

155

tique of the theoretical density of its propositions, and actually be capable of criticizing and controlling the political signification that such propositions may have in the social sphere.

The subject of part 3 has already been broached several times in parts 1 and 2, especially with reference to "political watchfulness" (§7). But the moment has now arrived for a treatment of this material *in extenso,* with a formal explicitation of its implications.

The subject matter of parts 1 and 2 has been of an expressly epistemological nature. I have been propounding the notion that the exigencies of reflective thought on the part of Christians living out their faith in practice imposes upon theology a change in the norms of its internal practice, a restructuration of its own field of operation, in view of its new theoretical objectives. I have called the redistribution of tasks and techniques implied by this historical imperative of a reflection on faith an "epistemological recasting."

I have sought to contribute to this "recasting" by proposing the adoption of theoretical operations at two levels. The first level has to do with research techniques. I have urged the integration in and by theology of the contributions of the sciences of the social, in socio-analytical mediation. On the second level, in more intimate contact with theology itself, I have proposed a renewed employment of theological hermeneutic.

In this present part, part 3, I discuss praxis. However, it can be wondered how praxis can be the subject of an *epistemological* discussion. Here, apart from the indications I have already given, I can only note that, for the interim, an answer to this question cannot be given until it, along with others, has been subjected precisely to the present examination. For the moment, then, suffice it to say that I have decided to include it in this study because praxis is of overwhelming concern today for the basing of a theology of the political.[1]

This question, it must be recognized, has not yet been subjected to any very significant studies, especially where its theoretical, and practical, implications are concerned. But a lack of lucidity in questions as important as this, and the indefinition of their theoretical status, conceal certain "epistemological obstacles," to whose removal I have sought to make at least a practical contribution.

A treatment of the problematic involved in a consideration of praxis is a particularly arduous one, by reason of the very nature of its coordinates, and the complexity of the interrelationship of these coordinates.[2] This problematic is all the more difficult when one must face, as in this investigation, questions of the cognition of the *political,* and then questions of the *theological* cognition of the political.

Accordingly, by way of a methodological caution, I cite the perspicacious words of Aristotle with regard to the status of what we call "political science," at the beginning of his *Nicomachean Ethics:* "Our discussion will be adequate," he says, "if it has as much clearness as the subject-matter admits of, for precision is not to be sought for alike in all discussions. . . . " And after recalling the great "variety and fluctuation of opinion" in the area of political knowledge, he continues: "We must be content, then, in speaking of such subjects and with such premises to indicate the truth roughly and in outline. . . . " Then, addressing the learner, Aristotle adds: "In the same spirit, therefore, should each type of statement be *received;* for it is the mark of an educated man to look for precision in each class of things just so far as the nature of the subject admits."[3]

It is evident, then, that my treatment of praxis in these pages cannot pretend to constitute a systematic exposition, cannot form a finished, balanced whole. On the contrary, I neither can nor wish to abstract from the situation in which the theory of the theology of the political finds itself. It is in explicit reference to the present difficulties of such a theory that I present my considerations. Whatever contribution I may make, then, will be in the area of *theology,* and will be in terms of the actual problematic of the *current* situation.

This, then, will be the general tone of the reflections of this third part of my work. It must be said, however, that, where the current state of theology of the political is concerned, my reflections shall all have to be made under the previous condition of a further, broader determination. This will explain the use of a generic vocabulary of "theory" and "praxis." What is meant by these terms is always "theology" and "faith," respectively—or, better: "theological theory" and "political practice of faith" (or "in faith").

Still on the generic level, let me try to sound out the essential layers of this level, its various strata. Let me turn the notion of a "dialectic of theory and practice" in various directions, and mark off, as best I can, the nature, modalities, and laws of this dialectic. These "variations on a theme" will entail some repetition—justified, however, by different applications of the same fundamental principles on new terrain in each case. Thus these fundamental principles will demonstrate their scope and fecundity.[4]

I discern, within the problematic of praxis, a series of questions bearing on theological practice. They may be divided into the following points:

the theologian's social engagement (chap. 9);
the thematic relevance of theology (chap. 10);
the political finality of theology (chap. 11);
praxis as criterion of truth (chap. 12);
the dialectical relationship between theory and practice (chap. 13).

These seem to me the main problems raised by theology of the political today, where praxis is concerned.

There is no a priori logic in these chapter divisions. There are reasons for their order, however, and they will appear in the development of the material. For now, I may remark that the first three chapters are much more closely related structurally. They represent three manners in which praxis is related to theory—namely: according to the mode of the theologian's social position, according to the mode of the subject matter of a given development, and according to the mode of the political function of a theological theory.

As to the latter two chapters—chapters 12 and 13—the first addresses the question of the nature of the relationship between theory and practice—the relationship to be studied according to the three "modes" just mentioned. More precisely, I shall be asking whether praxis has any jurisdiction over theological discourse—and if so, in what sense. The last chapter will prolong this interrogation at a broader level: that of the dialectic of the relationships between theory and praxis.

This problematic is certainly not of interest to theologians alone. It will interest, as well, any scholar concerned with the possible relationship of knowledge with power—of scientific practice with political practice. Theologians, however, will feel questions of praxis very acutely, by reason of a more immediately perceptible relationship between faith and politics, ethics and power, church and society—especially in the current critical and challenging socio-historical conjuncture in Latin America.

I am moving onto "slippery ground" in part 3. I must measure its extent, and try for a firm footing. I harbor no illusions of being able to reconcile the contradictions or resolve the aporias of the problematic of theory and practice. But I shall make an attempt to introduce a modicum of order into a theoretical area that is still "under construction." I am convinced that, in finding its proper relationship to praxis, the theory of theology of the political will be clarified.

CHAPTER 9

The Theologian's Social Commitment

§44 THEOLOGY AND SOCIAL CONTEXT

Efforts in the area of a theology of the political, especially in Latin America, draw attention to the importance of a correct social positioning for those who elaborate this theology—in order that they be able to apprehend correctly the real problems challenging the conscience of Christians in whose midst they live and whom they are meant to serve. Thus we hear of the theologian's "engagement" or "commitment," and of an "engaged," "partisan," or even "classist" theology. We hear of the "place" or "locus" from which a given historical situation is being interpreted.[1]

However, this exigency is more often than not expressed in the form of a slogan or bald assertion. We look in vain for the *rationes* that define and sustain it. Deprived of the "signature" of rationality, this demand can only remain on the level of an ideological claim. Reflections built up around the postulate of "commitment" generally consist in paraphrase and commentary rather than in precise explanation. It will be necessary, then, first, to establish a diagnosis of this postulate, starting with what I take to be its symptoms; and secondly, to evaluate the tenor, nature, and potential methodological scope of this postulate.

What might be meant by an "engaged" or "committed" theology? In what, or to what, might a theologian be able to be, or obliged to be, engaged or committed? Finally, what is the value of this sort of aphorism in terms of cognition? This is not the place to discuss the various conceptions of the "engagement" of which we hear so much, simply because these conceptions have not been sufficiently developed by theologians.

Words like "commitment" and "engagement" suggest that their user is dealing with the *topos,* the locus, of a theologian's social insertion and action, and consequently of his or her work within a determinate *socio*-historical situation.[2]

It is a truism that theologians are social agents—that they "do theology" in and from some determinate social locus, make use of the means society offers them, and formulate cognition and meaning endowed with a determinate social

159

existence and finality. This is of course the situation of any scholar in the social field.[3]

This being the case, *any* theology, in its quality as a determinate social practice, and as a "signifying" product—just as *any* theologian, as someone working in a specific area of knowledge and signification, and as a social agent—is socially situated, inserted, indeed "engaged"—*sciens nesciens, volens nolens*—in the articulation of a social conjunct, regardless of whether this theology or this theologian be "traditionalist" or "progressive."

What leaps out at us is that the motto of "engagement" is voiced by a very specific group of theologians: the theologians of second theology, especially the "political theologians." In listening to them, we come to perceive that the imperative of "engagement" they proclaim is not simply to be identified with the primary sociological *datum* just outlined: that all theology, and any theologian, is socially situated. They intend rather a position *taken*—a very determinate *option*.

We may ask, however, whether this intent is backed up by adequate theoretical formulating or whether, instead, its margin of incognizance is sufficient to allow theoretical and practical error. A theology claiming to be "engaged" may not perceive the spontaneous sociology upon which its claim rests. Thus we would have a theoretical presupposition that has not been explicitated, and eludes the awareness of "engaged theologians."[4] It is possible to have such a presupposition only in virtue of current usage, when language confers upon a key concept such as "engagement" or "option" a content presumed to dispense with any need for explanation.[5]

It is also possible that this tacit sociology is reducible to the empirical and undeniable evidence of a state of affairs—for example, the lamentable spectacle of the disadvantaged masses of the Third World—whose "truth" stands in need of no major theoretical "proofs," and which spontaneously moves consciences to take a position, *some* position.

Here the call for engagement means, concretely, an urgent invitation to take sides with the abandoned and oppressed. What is being called for in this case is not the recognition of a political position held by a particular theologian, but rather a particular, specific partisanship, a conscious insertion into a movement for liberation—in a word, an active, indeed militant, political action for a concrete political undertaking.

Nevertheless, this practical conception, however justified, especially in ethical terms, leads to pragmatism. It is too vulnerable theoretically. It might well be asked what the strategic effectiveness is of an "engagement" that has no base in an antecedent analytical evaluation of what is at stake in the struggle. But I shall not further pursue this consideration here: it does not fall within the scope of my investigation, which bears specifically upon the theoretical tenor of the "engagement" slogan.

It must be recognized that the spontaneous sociology referred to just above is also indisputably at work: it does not have the means to see the possibility, indeed the reality, of an objective engagement on the part of the ideological opposition. The "engaged" theology fails to perceive that the theology it accuses of "alienation" and "connivance with the establishment" is no less really engaged than itself, with all its talk of "engagement." The only difference is the content, or cause, of this actual engagement—in other words, the respective ideo-political position of each theology.

To the spontaneous sociology of "engaged" theology, it appears natural that the "alienation" of theology from "real problems" would be based on the absence of theology from historical reality. This position is simply absurd. Only in the imagination is it possible to be absent from history.

The vacuous analytic or critique latent in the ideology of "engagement" is unmasked in the flawed political effects it is likely to engender. The "engagement" assumed by this theological consciousness, the moment it has wakened from its "ahistorical sleep" (to paraphrase Kant), has often taken the form of "progressivism," or "modernism": it delivers itself body and soul to the realization of tasks that, far from concretizing an effective position in favor of a well-identified cause, only leads to impasses and contradictions.[6]

The elementary sociological precisions I have just made are themselves enough to permit us to relegate to the category of ideological discourse the indiscriminate and acritical use of the term "engagement" and its cognates. "Engagement" is a type of practice—not analysis. It calls for action, not for inquiry. It appeals for action, not understanding. In and of itself, it will be of no use for qualifying a theology of the political such as I have conceptualized it. If it has no operationality in sociology, a fortiori it will have none for a theology that lays claim to an express relationship with the sciences of the social.[7]

To my mind, the real political problem for a (theological) theory is not that of "engagement" as such, but that of an analytically predicated engagement: *What type* of engagement is to be undertaken? *What* social position must the theologian take? And, inasmuch as a theological discourse is always situated in some particular locus in social space, *which* locus should a given theological discourse occupy?

These questions bring out how the relationship of a social agent with society has a double character. It is objective and subjective, static and dynamic. Its objective and static aspects translate a state of fact—an agent's social *situation*. Its subjectivity and dynamism express the contribution of this agent's consciousness or decision—so that we are now dealing with (the assumption of) a political *position* on the part of a given social agent.[8]

As a consequence, we must conceptualize the theologian's social position, as indeed that of any social agent, not only statically, but first and foremost dynamically. It must be conceptualized as engaged in an interplay within the activity of social groups, at the heart of the unstable configurations of power relationships. We perceive, then, that the theologian is always engaged and always has been, in one manner or another.[9]

The impression of "alienation," or "absence," or "indifference," that a social agent may give, in confrontation with particular groups, is nothing but the (conscious) effect of a social position so identified with the dominant group that it no longer manifests an immediately apprehensible difference in respect of this group. For this agent, it is enough to be borne along by the current of force relationships in order to cease to feel (actively) "engaged."[10]

By way of conclusion: the postulate of "engagement" is equivocal. It is equivocal in virtue of the fact that we are always—ultimately—engaged, whether it be passively or actively. The real question, then, is: What engagement is meant? Engagement for whom? Option for what cause?[11] Taking sides with whom? Struggling for which class?[12]

It should be evident, then, that in theological work the answer to a question presupposes recourse to socio-analytic mediation. On the other hand, this mediation operates for the sake of a *theoretical* development of a given theology of the political (part 1)—and on the other, for the sake of a *practical* position to be assumed by a "political theologian" (part 3). I need only add that this process is always effectuated in a dialectical circularity, which we shall be examining more closely.

§45 DIFFERENCE BETWEEN SOCIAL LOCUS AND EPISTEMIC LOCUS

As explained above (§6) we must hold fast to the distinction between the *regime of autonomy* and the *regime of dependence* in respect of any body of knowledge—in our case, theology.

There is a *chorismos,* a difference, between these two registers. This difference defines an area, a precise place—a *chora*—that affords "room" for a discourse, and precisely a "differing" discourse.[13] This difference draws a line of demarcation between two areas. The former is the space of *epistemology,* or theory of knowledge; the second is the space of *Wissenssoziologie,* or sociology of knowledge. The *history of science,* or of a distinct science, can be situated between the two.

It is obvious that, from the moment a discipline is taken as a social reality—in our case, theology—this discipline, precisely as social reality, is susceptible of a legitimate analysis in terms of power, interest, or social and political function. Once it is seen in this manner—from without—it will avail theology nothing to vaunt its position as a "science of the Absolute." It has not, for all that, ceased to have an empirico-social existence and reality. This is the aspect in which scientific engagement, like so many others, such as that of a laborer or an office worker, is social engagement. The theologian too, then may be legitimately perceived as a social agent, alongside so many others in society.

Consequently, the kind of relationships that can obtain between theologians and society is governed by a different code from the one that applies within a discipline—which of course will be in the form of the relationship of theologians with their theoretical object. Here, theologians act as epistemic subjects. In the exterior set of relationships, they act as social subjects. Internally, what is important are relationships of objectivity; externally, what is important are relationships of power. Within, the tools used are theoretical; without, they are political. Internally, the result is cognition; externally, the result is power. The list of antitheses could be lengthened.[14]

Any community between these two orders will be, at most, that of a structural homology.[15] Each of these orders is endowed with its own rules and content. This specificity demands respect for what it is: it is not legitimate to confuse it with its homologue.

Thus when theology is taken in its formality as social object, it functions as any other social object, as does economic production or, for instance, any institution. Consequently, what we are dealing with here is a sociological problem — which, as such, is independent of the epistemological instance in terms of the theoretical quality of the theology in question (its rigor, consistency, verification, and the like).

Rudimentary as these observations are, to the point of banality, they enable us to apprehend the difference obtaining between two orders of questions. This difference is all the more to be respected as it is seen to be neglected in current debates on the status of theology, especially that of the theology of the political.

I must add, however, that this neglect is to be found not only where theology is concerned, but in the area of the sciences of the human being generally. The reason for this is, in part, the indefinition of the theoretical status of these disciplines. We need only cast a glance at the multiplicity of tendencies and techniques prevailing in these areas. In my view, internal, specific questions of a discipline ought to be severed analytically from the external, social questions that it raises. Failing this precaution, one order of problems is judged by the code pertinent to another, and confusion reigns. As Hegel put it, at night all cows are black.[16]

Thus has arisen the "theoretical monstrosity of the double science" — the Manicheistic dichotomy between a "bourgeois science" and a "proletarian science." History warns us that the theoretical commingling of knowledge and power is disastrous, even catastrophic, for both of the elements in question.[17]

As can readily be seen, I am seeking to emphasize the *legality* of theological theory. This is the legality by which theology as theology (theology in its internal, epistemological regime) must be judged. I leave for the next section (§46) any discussion of the relationship between theologians' theoretical engagement and their social engagement (in the external regime of the sociology of cognition).

If my position here be admitted, then what is to be said of appellations such as "Latin American theology," "North Atlantic theology," "African theology," and so forth? From the epistemological standpoint, such adjectives are *determinative,* not qualificative. They designate an external — I might even say extrinsic — determination of theology. They do not touch on the actual *nature* of the theology to which they point. They have to do with functional identification, not analytical evaluation. Recognized for what they are, then, these labels are indeed justifiable.

They entail a disadvantage, however. They open the door to theoretical ambiguities and practical consequences of which history offers us the most regrettable examples. Consequently we must be careful not to ascribe to such expressions the status of concepts supplying information about the level of a theological discourse as such. It is enough to simply acknowledge their function as convenient designations, which have more to say about the ideo-political stance of the discourse to which they are linked than about the intrinsically scientific quality of these discourses.

The same observations will be in order for other denominations, such as "engaged theology" and "alienated theology," "revolutionary theology" and "reactionary theology," and so forth. These are simple references to the social exteriority of a given theological discourse. They have nothing to say about the cognitive content of the theologies in question.

The same remark, once more, will apply to *determinative* adjectives of geo-political locus, such as "theology of the center," "theology of the periphery," "metropolitan theology," "Third World theology," and so on. These designations point to the place where these theologies are forged, and even to the ideo-political causes they serve, but are incapable of responding to any question concerning the *truth* of these theologies.

We must take into account the pertinency of a language of this type: it pertains to the area of sociological judgment. It takes a discipline by its body—that is, in its institutional signification. It is off the mark, then, to represent a judgment of this type as a judgment rendered by a theoretical or epistemological critique. This would constitute an unacceptable extrapolation, or what Aristotle would call a *metabasis eis allo genos*. This illegitimate move from one pertinency to another falsifies all discourse and renders it unintelligible. It is like uncoupling the cars of a train.

My critical demarcation is not intended to disqualify sociological or ideological discourse. Both have their legitimacy and legality, their function and importance. I seek only to do justice, according to my means, to both: *suum cuique.* My overriding purpose is to restore to theological discourse its identity, its rigor, and its own legality—this is the object of my study.

But someone might object: what is of interest today is precisely the political position of a theology, not its theoretical substantiality. My reply is that this may indeed be the case, but the objector will still have to answer the great question: What will the meaning and scope of a political position today be without the support of a solid theoretical basis?

§46 RELATIONSHIP BETWEEN SOCIAL LOCUS AND EPISTEMIC LOCUS

Now let us ask whether there might be a possible relationship between the epistemic (theoretical) locus, and the social or political locus. These loci are of course positions, engagements, practices. Indeed, these terms are more expressive, inasmuch as they connote movement. These loci (or levels, or instances) are the "places" precisely of "positions," "engagements," or "practices."

The tendency of "political theologians" is to posit political engagement as an antecedent *epistemological* condition for the development of an appropriate or consistent theology. This is a delicate problem, and calls for an adequate elucidation. Let me pose a number of propositions relative to this problem, and thus orientate this discussion toward a pertinent solution.

Before proceeding, however, it will be well to step back for a moment and raise a question that is antecedent to my entire study and concerns the discourse I am conducting here: How is this discourse to be understood? To be sure, I am speaking of (theological) theory and of politics (the politics of faith). But under what formality am I considering them? What standpoint am I taking in my pursuit of this manner of discourse?

Let me answer these questions briefly by saying that I am speaking from the locus that classic tradition has denominated "philosophy."[18] This locus is based precisely on the nature of the human mind, one of whose essential faculties is re-flection: the ceaseless, indefinite reappraisal of its own presuppositions. I might add that this self-transcendence of the mind, far from dispensing with the material support constituting the series of extrinsic conditions of the mind, such as social locus, education, techniques, and the like, actually presupposes it, because this mind is an "incarnate" one, a "situated" one—a human one— not an absolutely free, creative mind or spirit like the divine mind.[19]

This being said, I can now address the subject at hand—the articulation between theoretical locus and political locus.

I begin by setting aside two theses representing extreme solutions to the question under consideration.

1. There is *no relationship at all* between (theological) theory and (political) practice. In this hypothesis, we would be dealing with a false problem, an imaginary one, one that asks us to compare the incomparable. After all, we are dealing with an essence (a theory) and an existence (a politics). The attempt to relate them would be the very prototype of the bi-level relationship, the inarticulable articulation. The relationship between theory and praxis would thus be a false, or at best a fictitious, relationship.[20]

I think that this position is difficult to maintain. The fact is that a discipline or theory can develop only under certain conditions. We see this in the history of the sciences, as well as in the empirical practice of a given science.[21]

2. *A direct and intimate relationship* obtains between theoretical position and practical position: that of cause to effect. In my view, this position is likewise indefensible. I have had repeated occasion to observe that the logic of science is not the same as the logic of politics. Consequently neither is engendered or regulated by the other.

But then how *are* we to conceptualize the relationship between science and society, or between theory and politics? After all, it seems that such a relationship does in fact exist, enigmatic though it may be.[22]

My suggestion is that we might conceptualize it in the oppositional categories of "permission" and "prohibition."[23]

By "permission" I mean that a given political engagement permits, renders possible, the realization of a corresponding theological discourse. This relationship is neither equivocal nor bi-univocal.[24] It is a *reflex* relationship. "Permission," of its very concept, excludes the notion of "cause," at least in any mechanical sense. It corresponds to the concept of a *conditio sine qua non.* "Permission," then, designates a factor that is necessary, but insufficient.

"Permission," accordingly, confers upon a scholar a determinate political position, but does not of itself produce the corresponding theoretical event. For the latter to come about, what else is necessary?

Everything. That is, it is still necessary for the intended theory really to be effectuated. But if the political "prohibits" it, neither can theological theory come to be.[25]

Let me attempt to delineate this problematical relationship more clearly. To this purpose, let us ask what might happen in terms of theoretical production when a theologian takes an active part in social conflicts. Would the positivity of the faith—the substantial *content* of theological discourse—change? It would not seem so. But it does seem that the theoretical *expression* of revelation would be modified, by reason of the political cause for which the theologian is struggling. But between the two—between political cause and theological expression—there is no direct, immediate, continuous relationship. There is a leap, a break—the "epistemological breach." The passage between the two terms points to the intervention of the human mind, with its dynamism, its generative force. This is what philosophical tradition has meant by the very notion of "mind" or "reason."[26] Now Bachelard has reasserted it in his epistemology, especially in the concept of the "epistemological act."[27]

Thus under one aspect we have discontinuity between theoretical locus and political locus. And yet under another aspect we have something connecting them. First there is the *subject,* who, although existing now in this locus and now in that, is nevertheless always the same subject, according to the celebrated axiom *actus sunt suppositorum.* In the second place there is the *object,* which, however much its form may alter, remains materially the same, now as conceptual object of cognition, now as real object of political struggle.

Still, the concepts that allow us to see the relationship between social locus and theoretical locus are themselves paradoxical. The notion of "permission" has enabled us to appreciate the continuity between the two loci, and that of "break" or "breach" has shown us their discontinuity. In order to grasp the totality of the phenomenon, however, we must make alternating use of both of these concepts, and hereby we see that they are complementary.[28]

Let me dwell a moment on the continuity manifested by the first of these concepts. Science has its own legality, to be sure, as an autonomous system. But science does not thereby cease to be articulated upon social history, from which it receives decisive impulses. A discipline progresses both in virtue of a (logical) force that it exercises upon itself, and in virtue of the counterblows it receives from historical factors, as indeed the history of the sciences teaches us.

What I have been saying of science in general is proportionately valid for theology as well. Augustine theologizes differently from Thomas Aquinas. Thomas theologizes differently from Luther, who theologizes differently from Newman. And yet a basic epistemological identity abides, and we may refer to the reflections of all four authors as "theology." It is his relationship to his time, and to the culture of his time, that constitutes each one's difference from the others. But the objective uniting them is identical. This unitary objective occasions realizations marked by a certain degree of success—this is why each is reckoned as a great thinker—and at the same time by a certain degree of failure—which is why each one's work must be improved. The common objective consists in the demand for as close an approach as possible to God's truth—revelation. After all, God can be understood only within the purview of our historical possibilities, especially our cultural possibilities.

If one may be permitted to speak of "Absolute Knowing" (Hegel), this can only be in the mode of an eschatological horizon, against which and toward which reason is moving.[29] As long as the course of history continues to unfold, there is no place for a parousia of Hegel's Consciousness or Kant's Reason.[30] This conviction lies at the very heart of the theological *logos*.[31]

Moving closer, now, to the question under discussion in this section, it may be stated that a political position interferes in a theoretical position first and foremost in virtue of the *common subject* of both positions. This interference is observable in the *style* of the language in which a theological theory is couched.[32] It is interesting to observe how antecedent political options leave their marks on the written style of a social theorist, and, even more, on that of a "political theologian," betraying the "social locus" of the discourse. These signs are observable in a turn of phrase, in the choice of vocabulary and examples, in emphasis on certain subject matter, in the relationship that the author assumes with the reader, and so on. Thus the personality of the theologian emerges from within his or her discourse in its language, and the epistemic subject is as it were hypostatized upon the social subject.[33]

But there is still another way in which the political influences the theological. It (also) does so, as I have asserted, on the level of the *common object* of the two corresponding practices. One chooses one's subject in view of the causes in which one is politically engaged. The political action project then becomes a theological project of reflection as well. One's practical position furnishes one's theory with the "materials" with which to work.[34] I shall make this point the object of a special treatment below (chapter 10), and so suspend further consideration of it here.

It is clear from these reflections that there is indeed a relationship binding (political) practice with (theological) theory. And yet this relationship somehow eludes our grasp. It is made of breach and bond—as if it were a leap at once succeeding and failing.

I shall rest content, then, with the following conclusion. *Political engagement in a given cause within a defined group or class, although failing to guarantee the intrinsic quality of a theological theory, nevertheless constitutes a necessary condition for the selection by this theological theory of a determinate and adequate theoretical object, or thematic, as well as that of a style proportioned to its task of communication.*

Now it can be understood how theological practice can be, at one and the same time, although not in the same respect, political practice and (political) practice of the faith. It can be, at the same moment, knowledge and participation, cognition of the political and the exercise of "political love."[35]

For purposes of *theological investigation,* the *analytical* distinction between the twin loci we have been considering must be respected. We must distinguish between the *theoretical* (or, more generally, the epistemic) locus, upon which the social agent *as such* is incompetent to make any pertinent judgments, and the political (or, more generally, the social) locus, in respect of which the theologian *as such* possesses no competence whatsoever.

At the same time, *in historical concretion,* it must be recognized that these two loci are always found bound together, in the unity of a single person and a single basic object. I shall now attempt to see how this bond, or better, this articulation, between theoretical engagement (theology) and practical engagement (politics), can achieve a relatively successful realization in the concrete existence of a militant theologian.

§47 MODELS FOR A VITAL SYNTHESIS OF THEOLOGY AND POLITICS

Thus far in this chapter, the following have been determined: (1) the *positive existence* of social engagement on the part of every theologian and every theology (§44); (2) the *analytical difference* between social engagement and theoretical engagement (§45); (3) the *real bond* between these same differentiated engagements (§46).

In the present section, I shall endeavor to draw the practical conclusions to which these principles will lead. If these principles are correct, then what follows for the theologian? If these are the coordinates of the problematic, then how is the theologian to act? What fruit or profit can the theologian draw from these propositions? Or, more directly: How are theologians to concretize their political engagement while continuing to be theologians? Under what conditions can the theologian actually realize a synthesis of theology and politics, theoretical practice and political practice, science and justice? How is the theologian to take a position in these two distinct loci?

Let me respond to these questions by proposing three possible models for a synthesis, arranged in ascending order of complexity. The closer the terms of the synthesis to each other, the easier the synthesis—but, by this very fact also, the less rich. Conversely, the more distant and complex the terms of the synthesis, the more difficult the synthesis itself will be—and therefore the richer.

The three models of progressive synthetic complexification that I wish to suggest are: (1) the "specific contribution" model; (2) the "alternating moments" model; and (3) the "incarnation" model.

The "Specific Contribution" Model

According to this model, the synthesis between theology and politics is realized *in and by* theoretical engagement itself. In other words, a (political) position is taken within the intellectual field as such. The theoretical locus becomes the real battlefield on which political battles are fought. Thus theoretical practice as such comes to be conceived as one social practice among many others. It contributes, after its own fashion—that is, theoretically, according to its own rules and from its own locus—to the complex praxis developing along the various fronts of the social whole, of which one is the theoretical front.

In its capacity as conceptual translation of concrete political struggle, theoretical struggle represents political struggle where the theoretician is concerned—in our case, the theologian. As can be seen, then, theory, as theory, will here be susceptible of an intrinsic, positive investment with a determinate political dimension. The theologian will still be a social agent, engaged within the complex network of power relationships. The theologian's (political) position-taking, and the shifts and movements implied in it, will "play" in the theoretical area itself. This will be possible first and foremost by the choice of *questions* to be treated (the theologian's "thematic"), and then, secondarily, by the determination of a *style* adequate to this selection, as has been explained.

For some theologians, such a political engagement in the element of theory may entail a change of theoretical terrain, a genuine intellectual conversion, by which these theologians pass from one theoretical front to another. This theoretical engagement, endowed with a political signification, is discernible in these authors' theological writings. That is, it is discernible in theological theories that correspond to their political position.

The possibility of a political commitment in the sphere of theory can be understood only within a *dialectical* comprehension of the social totality, in which totality the social factors (the economic, the political, and the ideological) are divided from one another in a mutual articulation and compenetration. Thus, if the political can have an ideological dimension or effect, the ideological for its part can very well have a political dimension or effect. This is what is called, quite properly, the dimension of the "ideo-political."

In this model of engagement, the epistemic subject coincides wholly and adequately with the social subject. Nothing remains of the difference treated in §45 except the outlines of a purely formal operation. The theologian is the agent who performs, on behalf of a group or political movement, the specific task of reflecting upon its activity precisely in its theological meaning. Thus, in and by the intellectual or scholarly *profession* itself, the theologian performs social work and exercises a political option.[36]

It must be added, however, that this model is practically unrealizable in a pure form. It supposes, to a greater or lesser extent, elements of the models to follow—assuming, in the concrete, certain of their modalities. The latter—as we shall shortly see—are naturally extratheoretical. Accordingly, pure theory can have a political implication only on condition that its producer also stands in relationship with the extratheoretical domain, through, for example, meetings, collaboration, or various contacts with a given political movement. The theoretical position is conditioned by the practical position, and so a more or less direct participation in concrete practices is necessary for the well-being of the theory itself.[37]

The "Alternating Moments" Model

In this model, the synthesis between theology and politics involves the taking of a political position in the political field itself. A kind of split occurs within the actual person of the theologian: the theologian acts now as epistemic subject, now as political subject, with the person of the theologian providing the permanent, self-identical supposit of alternately theoretical and social practices.

Here the theologian does not always act as theologian. The *actualization* of theological competency is not, evidently, continuous: it is necessarily intermittent, even though the competency itself, which, by definition, is a constant positive disposition, endures.[38] Accordingly, this theologian performs now the role of a scholar, now that of a militant. Unity can be established on the level of the all-embracing *project* undertaken by one and the same person, and this is generally accomplished in terms of transcendental language taking the form of an ethical, even religious, discourse. We should say, then, that the overall engagement of this theologian is marked by two alternately recurring moments: the theoretical and practical moments of one and the same engagement. Hence the name, "alternating moments" model. We are dealing, then, with two basic practices relative to two moments in the realization of one unitary, synthesizing project.

This duality—not dualism—is observable in the double bond this theologian may maintain with, on one side, political, or simply social, organizations and movements, and on the other, with cultural institutions that provide what is needed for the practice of theory. This alternating, rhythmic shift—this, as it were, diachronic bilocation—is effectuated in virtue of the specific configuration imposed by the play of the social dynamic in a determinate conjuncture.[39]

The "Incarnation" Model

A third level of synthesis, at once the most complex and most arduous of the three, can be lived in the form of a social insertion comporting an organic and even physical participation in the existence of social groups or classes with which the agent in question is bound by an antecedent ideo-political option. This model presupposes the very strictest solidarization on the part of the agent with the life conditions and general lot of the group in question.

I give this model a name having a clear-cut religious connotation: that of "incarnation," seeing that this form of synthesis generally translates properly (although not exclusively) Christian and evangelical inspirations—a thrust toward identification with the oppressed, a sharing in their condition of poverty, a thirst for justice.[40]

Such an option, more existential than political, is visible in the objective dislocation effectuated by the theologian within a given social structure, and even within simple geographical space (by a change of domicile, breadth of activity, and the like).

The model of incarnation, or communion of life, a fortiori comports the modalities of the other two models—the modalities of political participation (as found in the second model) and those of a taking of a theoretical position (as in the first model).

The main problem of this third model, especially on the periphery, is whether, when one lives with and as "the people," one still has the necessary, even minimally necessary, *material conditions* for continuing to do theology, and "good theology." Of course, it may also happen that one finally decides that theological practice is "inopportune," or perhaps "irrelevant," for a given pastoral or political strategy in view of the urgency and gravity of certain real problems that one may be facing. Here the limits of theological practice are drawn in view of the correlation of forces that may be operating in a given situation. The upshot can even be that the problem we are discussing is suppressed with the suppression of its very terms.

Here, then, are the three circles normally followed by models for the concrete juncture between (theological) theory and (political) praxis. I trust that they will enable us to make some response to the imperative proclaimed so insistently by so-called engaged theologians, especially by liberation theologians.[41]

We must recognize, however, that taken *in abstracto,* our three sketches cannot be made the object of a theoretical or political prescription. They can be selected only in the concrete of particular situations. Why? Each is a *living* synthesis between a person and a locus. In order to remain living, any such synthesis must remain open to modification, in accordance with the continuous, enigmatic circularity prevailing between its terms.

An ad hoc, even superficial, analysis of the phenomenon of concrete political engagement demonstrates that it has not been in obedience to any theoretical ukase that "engaged" theologians have "chosen" to become such. It is rather the dynamic of events, operative within a given conjuncture, that has placed them in that situation, and led them, as a result of personal existential views and options, to take such and such a concrete political position. Consequently, the synthesis here proposed becomes actual only at the heart of the interactions at play among situations and options, between objective conditions and subjective conditions.[42]

The living, vital totalization of which I am speaking is the deed of praxis, where the objective and the subjective coincide.[43] Hence the actual processes that would lead to its realization cannot at all be prescribed. Theory is not life. All we can do is testify to the manifold elements that must be set dialectically in motion in order to emerge in a definite form of commitment. Let us be content, then, with indicating the elements, or, better, the moments, in this vital totalization.

In the process of vital synthesis between theory and practice, we can see that three dialectical circles emerge, all interlinked and forming a single large circle—the circle, or circularity, that I have just described between socio-historical conjunctures and subjective decisions (Diagram 7). The reason I call the relationship obtaining between these two terms "dialectical" is that each term is defined and redefined only in confrontation with the other. Thus, in the case of theology, the subject is engaged only within a network of given structural possibilities—and conversely, these possibilities are real possibilities only insofar as a subject is inserted in them.

Diagram 7

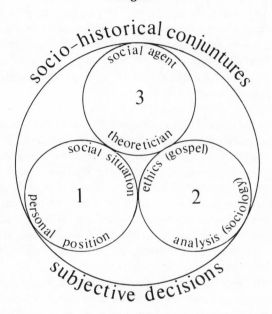

Here, then, are the three circles normally followed by theologians on their journey toward the determination of a concrete engagement:

1. There is a dialectical relationship between the given social situation and the personal position adopted in respect of this situation. Here we encounter the old question of *individual and society.* In function of this dialectic, the nature and extent of one's "theologizing" is determined not so much by free choice as by force of circumstances. In other words, one's social locus is the measure of the "permission" or "prohibition" of theological practice.

2. In order to be able to make an option—in order to be able to take an active place in the network of open possibilities within a given conjuncture— theologians must consider the terms of the cause with which they are confronted. They must relate the desirable to the possible. Thus we have a circle between *analysis* and *ethics,* between sociology and gospel. This is the circularity of socio-analytic and hermeneutic mediations in the ambit of the theology of the political. Thus we observe a sort of homology between the methodological

structure of the theology of the political and the form of practical engagement of the "political theologian."

3. By committing themselves to a determinate political position, theologians find what they need for confident reflection on the real in correct and accurate terms. They have taken a (political) position from which they can adequately theologize a given situation. However, they must still simultaneously secure the material and socio-institutional conditions permitting them to reflect, with all rigor, on the material to be reflected on. Here too, therefore, a dialectical circularity prevails, this time between *theologian as social agent* and *theologian as theoretician.*

Given the complexity discernible in the problematic broached here, what I have just outlined is of very modest scope. Indeed I have merely posited, in terms that are still only abstract and approximative, the implications and conditions of a commitment that strives to be as lucid as possible. The theory of a given socio-historical conjuncture has still to be developed and related to a possible theology. Finally, one must still take the decisive step—that of actually making the proposed commitment. That is, one must still actually accomplish the vital synthesis of which I have been speaking throughout this chapter. This is an act that suppresses simple theory, carrying it to realization beyond itself.

Let me close this chapter by advancing some propositions—which, to be sure, as hypotheses, stand in need of confirmation and development, something I cannot give them here.

1. The *correct* way to approach the problem of the theologian's political engagement is to do so in accordance with the *nature and structure of the political itself.* Both the speculative and the individual must be transcended, then, if one is to avoid the quixotism of political voluntarism.

2. As a specifically *political* question, "engagement" must be reflected upon from within concrete praxis itself. It must be articulated upon an overall strategy, within which the theologian's *own* space of political engagement is defined as being the *area of theory.* This area is to be considered as *one* of the fronts along which a multifaceted political practice is to be embraced, or as one of the functions that must be performed organically within a given social movement.

3. The *extratheoretical* engagement of the theologian, then, has a *subjective and individual* meaning only in view of *theoretical engagement.* On the other hand, the *objective and collective* sense of a theologian's practice is the realization of a *political* self-projection (a self-projection of liberation).

If my theses are defensible, then I must also deny that the intensity of the political engagement undertaken by a theologian can tolerate the abandonment of theoretical rigor, or a certain economy of thought. On the contrary, the *political* intensity of the theologian must become sensible, must appear, *in the very element of theory.*

Indeed, in the perspective of a complex, articulated praxis, the particular practice of the theologian is seen to be only one of the elements, or one of the tactical moments, in a broader strategy. I must add that, except in rare cases, theological practice today no longer plays a dominant or hegemonic role in the social area, or even in the specifically ideological area.[44] At all events, the theologian must be careful to avoid the idealistic, or theoreticist, pitfall of thinking that the key to political problems resides in theological knowledge.

One must be careful not to reverse the terms of the global strategy, and posit the terminal objective of praxis in the construction of theological theories, no matter how "political," or even "revolutionary," they may be styled. With this attitude, the theologian's political engagement would risk losing all seriousness, and falling back to the level of *theoretical opportunism,* which takes social practices—possibly a matter of life and death for a great number of persons— as simply occasions for proclaiming to a fad-loving audience some "new theology" as the banner of salvation, if not of the very eschaton.

After all, "what counts is not liberation theology, but liberation."[45]

CHAPTER 10

Thematic Relevance of Theology

§48 WHERE THEORY BEGINS

In the foregoing chapter I have discussed the implications, for theological practice, of the theologian's social *topos*—the implications of the theologian's engagement, taking of a position, even "taking sides." The influence of this engagement is observable in, among other things, the selection of a theological thematic, in the sense that the material of the engagement in question has become the raw material of the theologian's theoretical work.

In the present chapter, I take praxis as the object of consideration, but from another point of view: that of history. Hence I shall now be speaking not of a *topos,* but of a *kairos*—the propitious moment for a question, its favorable time, the moment at which it presents itself and calls for examination, calls for a response. This is the sense in which I shall be speaking of "thematic relevancy." One must make a commitment in order to grasp the "right questions for theologizing." Well and good. But how is the "rightness" of these questions to be understood? How are they to be regulated and governed?

Ever since the publication of *Gaudium et Spes,* it has become a commonplace to say that the "signs of the times" are the new "place" for theology today.[1] Contemporary writing abounds with assertions to this effect. Formulations may differ, but their content or meaning is the same. This new "place" goes by various names: "the life of the church," "the experience of the faithful and their Christian communities," the "base," or "the exploited," "the oppressed," "the poor," the "praxis of liberation," the *sensus fidei,* "church history," "the other," "lived experience," "Christian existence." And the list could be lengthened.[2]

Postulates of this kind have a positive function. They call for a distinct, new theological practice. Their function, then, is ideological, not epistemological.[3] They are bereft of any very great theoretical vigor. They are pointers, signposts. They call attention to a new theological field. But once we enter this field, we perceive that these postulates are no longer of any help. I must repeat: they lead to empiricism. They engender a thinking that mires itself in the concrete. We

175

must therefore criticize these postulates, measure their scope, explicitate the questions they imply—in a word, formulate very clearly the terms of their problematic. As we know, "an insoluble problem is an ill-posed problem."[4]

First of all: What does it mean to propose history, for example, as a *locus theologicus?* After all, ask history no questions and it will remain mute. Or worse, it will simply echo the voices of each and all.[5] It is the same with "the poor" as a locus. How can such a locus become the object of theological concern? "The poor" do not go about with the words of revelation written all over their faces. "The poor" are seen to be the "sacrament of Christ" only by the one who is attuned to this manifestation. And this is called "faith."[6]

Accordingly, we must say that, taken in the immediacy of its formulation, the imperative that renders "life," and so forth, the *locus theologicus* par excellence is a failure as a guiding principle for the organization of theological discourse. At the same time, however, it must be acknowledged that such an imperative is not bereft of all "truth," even with respect to the theory of theology. The "truth" it holds must be carefully discerned, in order to be recognized—that is, that "an account be given" of this truth, that it be "rationalized," in terms of the *ratio,* the reason of which it is the "symptom," in all its empiricist wrappings.

However true it may be that any reading of history—any interpretation of the signs of the times—is an outfitted interpretation, an interpretation clothed in a determinate theory, it is no less true that this theory comes only after the fact. Prior to the theory, outside it, and independently of it, history follows its sovereign course. It presents human beings with challenges, and these human beings are obliged to respond, even when their consciousness of these challenges is minimal, distorted, or nonexistent. Theory as such must be capable of acknowledging that history is ultimately the material, not the result, of its activity.

And so if we step back from theoretical practice, in the direction of the general articulation of theory and praxis, we are constrained to admit the priority of praxis, of life, of world, of history, over their representation in the field of awareness, even in the field of the rigorously scientific.

Underlying this assertion, we have the classic postulate of critical realism, which implies a distinction between cognition and reality, between the logical order and the ontic order, between awareness and world, with the primacy in the genesis of cognition lying with the second term of each pair. The postulate, "Start with the facts," although it cannot be admitted as a *theoretical principle* (as we say), nevertheless contains its truth—the truth of a *practical principle,* with a view to the exercise of theory, or thought.

This rudimentary thesis bears mention, for the "theoretical" is always exposed to the temptation of "theoreticism," that aristocratic form of idealism that seeks to explain everything in concepts, seeks to place everything under the lock and key of the ideational, finishes by taking theory to be the perfect replica of the world, and substitutes it for the world.

But here theory only succeeds in showing its ignorance of what its own constitutive "breach" has separated it from.[7] It has forgotten that its very nature as theory is constituted precisely by the "rupture" of the concept in virtue of an artifice going by the name of "abstraction," or *epoche*. This "bracketing" or parenthesizing operation is no more than an expedient by which the theoretician acquires entry into the "immaterial" area of theory. But to ignore what has been left behind is to vitiate one's enterprise in its very "genes," as it were. In virtue of this neglect, theoreticians will end by claiming independence of all praxis, as if *they* were the constitutive subject of the world (Hegel).

Even on the prosaic plane of concrete scientific research, we see that life often cheats the logic of scientists when it comes to their "discoveries."[8]

Further: we are obliged to acknowledge a more *original* form of relationship to the world than that of the scientific concept and what that concept depends on. The scientific concept depends on the human being's *sensibility*, depends on human perception.[9] To be sure, the sensible is always found shot through with culture, and history, and steeped in the ideological significations that social groups, especially the dominant classes, have deposited at its heart. This is true, and hence susceptible of analytic treatment, such as that which historical materialism seeks to accord it.[10] Nevertheless, it is the *Lebenswelt* that constitutes the sole provender of all further relationship to the world, including scientific relationship. Without experience, science would not be possible.[11]

It follows from this that the "breach" that establishes scientific discourse is never "done," is never a "per-fect(ed)" act, a finished act once and for all. The effort of the "breach" permeates the totality of scientific procedure. It is not, then, a "punctual" act—one by which we take our leave of the phenomenal world, to take the "Milky Way" leading to the "world of ideas." On the contrary, a sustained effort is necessary to keep us on the level of theory.[12] Then too: the success enjoyed by the enterprise of the concept is only a relative one. Ideology—first ideology—dogs the steps of all science like a shadow.[13]

Finally: all science presupposes an act of foundational decision, consisting in the practice of arbitrary amputations within the living framework of the "real" and experience of the real. Science opts to neglect all else, to fix the mind on one circumscribed sector alone, and to make of this its "epistemological region," its chosen province.[14] Consequently, every science focuses on a mere part of the integral real, and so cannot pretend to be total knowledge, total science, unless in the self-contradictory form of a dictatorship.

Where do I seek to "go" with these general observations on the status of the scientific approach? I seek only to do justice to sensibility—to establish the "truth" of "facts," or "experience," the truth of "everyday." Such truth seeks to be acknowledged rather than known, respected rather than inspected, lived rather than thought. This is precisely the level on which one must grasp the most "primitive," the most "archaic" (in the structural, not the chronological, sense of the word) form of an approach to the world. Here is where "original truth," the truth in which all other truths merely participate, is to be found.[15] It is only by "forgetting where it came from" that conceptual thinking can become the most arbitrary of totalitarianisms. After all, even though science as science *begins* at the outer edge of the "rupture," it nevertheless has its *origin* just short of that rupture.[16]

Science, then, like any other thinking, must be situated within a totality vaster than itself. We call this totality "life," "existence," "history," "world," and so forth. Thought is but an island in the ocean of the real.[17] And just as it arises from within that real, so also it will return there. The ultimate finalization of all theory is its reabsorption into the bosom of the life that generated it. Thought terminates in its "return to things." Theory is completed in praxis.[18]

To attempt to live exclusively in the stark light of science, furthermore, or even consciousness, is an impossibility for the human being. Here we have a project that, although ever frustrated, is ever reborn: its name is "rationalism," or "scientism," and it seeks to assume the guidance of history, believing itself capable of carrying it to term. But scientific reason is not the only form of reason. It is not even its most eminent form. Scientific reason is in competition with ethics, religion, and other forms of expression of the human-being-as-reason—that is, as "openness to the world," or "ex-sistence."[19]

§49 NOTION AND ESTABLISHMENT OF RELEVANCE

Certain observations made above lead to the understanding of an important notion that I wish to introduce here. It figures in the title of the present chapter. I refer to the notion of "relevance."

This notion is applicable to subjects or questions pertaining to the theoretical field indeed, but regarding praxis. It will be said of an issue that it is "relevant" when it is "apropos"—that is, when it arises from a point of departure of the perception of a given situation. Then we are said to have a "genuine issue," or a "real issue" or question. A relevant subject is a subject that, relative to a given critical conjuncture, can answer questions like: What is *the* question? Where is *the* problem? What is *really* at issue in such and such a situation?

These questions try to find out "where it hurts," try to identify "what is causing the problem," try to determine the exact spot where things "cross paths" along the road of history. They seek as it were to "palpate" time for its "swollen spots," for the "saliencies" of a given historical situation. Relevant questions are the ones that touch on where the future exerts pressure on the present. They are the interrogation conducted by the present moment. Vatican II calls them the "signs of the times" (*Gaudium et Spes,* nos. 4, 11).

Relevance and Pertinency

Relevance expresses the relationship of a theory to a historical moment and its causes. This concept is the correlative of that of *pertinency.* The latter points to the relationship of a question with a given *theoretical* problematic, to which precisely a question "pertains." The notion of relevance, in turn, regards the relationship of the scientific process with a given historical problematic. It seeks to set in relief the strategic character of a thought—its mode of presence and action in social relationships of force. Thus it concerns the relationship of knowledge with power.

The notion of pertinency, then, regards epistemology—the *internal* regime of a discipline. The notion of relevance regards praxis—as defining the *external* regime of this same discipline.[20]

Unlike pertinency, therefore, which circumscribes the area of questions susceptible of being raised within a given discipline, relevance is situated *short of* the repertory of these questions. It seeks to relate these questions to *history,* simply. It asks: In what respect do these theoretical questions concern this historical moment? What do they have to do with the present and its concrete problems? In what respect does this particular body of knowledge bear on human existence? Relevance poses a type of question that "questions the questions" of a given science.[21] We can call this kind of interrogation, then, which arises at and out of the heart of life, and which calls the (pertinent) questions of a given science into question, the "question of the questions."[22]

Relevance does not qualify a question *of* theory. It qualifies a question *for* theory. It is history, designating, for thought, the tasks of thought. A series of problems is relevant when it represents the agenda inscribed by history in the intention of thought. To use Heideggerian language, the "relevant" is what is *zudenkend,* or *fragwürdig,* or *denkwürdig.*

A relevant interrogation is situated short of the "breach" of a discipline, but it points beyond the breach. After all, on the one hand, we think of "problems" as the real crises, difficulties, and contradictions of real existence; and we consider as "questions" these same "problems" as taken up in and by theory—that is, theoretically. Thus it is clear that relevance designates precisely the *passage from problems to questions.*[23]

Now I can pose this basic question: If what I am saying is true, must we not question the existence of theology itself in terms of today? In other words, are theological "questions" really relevant for problems of today? This is the "question of (theological) questions" raised by modern atheism.

To answer this question I shall pose another. How can history become *problematic* except for a consciousness that lives problems, names them, and seeks to solve them? Such consciousness is already "worked" by history and culture. It never occurs as a *tabula rasa,* simply ready to receive the universal discourse of history. Hence we must always take the measure of the reciprocal conditioning of history and consciousness. Thus on the theological plane, we must take consciousness as being already "worked" by "religious questions." Theology speaks *from* these questions. It supposes that the religious content of consciousness corresponds to answers to questions antecedently raised by history itself, from a point of departure in real problems. This is what gives religion, faith, and theology their actual "relevance." They possess their *own* relevance.

Thus to speak of "relevance" in theology is meaningful only when and if (theoretical) questions, translating (real) problems, are actually *posed within theological pertinency.* Theological relevance will therefore be expressed in questions like: What (theological) problems demand the theologian's attention today? What is the real problematic presenting itself to theology as *fragwürdig?* What is the task of theology today? What is the theologian's *zutheologizierend?*

As we see, then, the category of "relevance" regards praxis, but only in proportion as this praxis regards theory. Relevance, therefore, is a category of the *theoretical* relationship between theory and praxis. Doubtless it has a reference to the theoretical practice of theology as well, but only in the measure that this theoretical practice is invested with (real) praxis and its problems.

Let us observe that the negative correlate of the category of relevance is "irrelevance." The latter properly attaches to, first of all, secondary problems, those on the margin of the course of history. Next, it also qualifies questions corresponding to these—the "nonessential" questions, or "alienated" subjects, however fashionable these may be. Obviously it would also cover frivolous, mundane, even cynical questions.[24]

The Operative Scope of Relevance

Now that the content of the category of "relevance" has been defined, we may proceed to an evaluation of its operative scope. We are dealing with a notion that raises a whole series of questions to be analyzed.

These questions may be formulated as follows: How may one establish what is relevant and what is irrelevant? By what means may we know what to "think about"? How shall we decide which subjects to accord priority? By what criteria may we determine which investigations are to be undertaken? What, or who, is to decide the "question of (theological) questions"?

Theology itself, within its own confines, does not have the wherewithal to answer these questions. The reason for this is that theology is already in a certain sense a species of limited repertory of answers to a determinate series of questions. And yet theology has always given answers to the questions posed above, through its own exercise—*in actu exercito*. But it has not always taken the care critically to guarantee the principles that it applies in order to carry out this selection of its questions. That is, it has not always been critically careful to establish its problematic, to decide what is relevant and what is not, what deserves to be theologized and what does not so deserve. This is a matter of simple historical record.

Very well, then—how is one to control, to check, the relevance of theological subject matter? How may we identify which subjects are worthy of the effort of the theologian's study?

In order to respond to this difficult question, let me begin, first of all, with two observations: one historical, and one theological.

Historical Aspect

It is easy to see that the theological problematic has not always been the same. A "relevance" of one era became an "irrelevance" in another. Theological interests have changed, then, obviously in function of the historical context, cultural as well as social, of the theology in question. Theological thought, then, possesses an undeniable historicity.[25] The "accents" have not always been the same. The material of theoretical concern of the fathers of the church was different from that of the scholastics, and both of these differ, respectively, from recent theologies, such as those of second theology.

But to assert that the scholastics developed an "alienated" or "irrelevant" theology is to commit a genuine anachronism: it means that one ignores the relationship that binds a theological production to its history. We know, for example, that the metaphysical questions of christology and the doctrine of the Trinity were exciting and stimulating for those who lived in the age of the great ecumenical councils. Likewise angelology and the question of universals were for the medievals subjects of such "relevance" as actually to set in motion not only minds, but social groups and political forces of the times as well. It is equally erroneous, then, to cling to scholasticism today or to deny it all historical merit.

In order to understand change of accent, then, or fluctuation of thematic relevance, their respective eras and their particular problematic must be taken into consideration.

Sociological Aspect

In the world of today, relevance is de facto defined in terms of the contradictory interests dividing society. Theological production continually suffers the blows and counterblows of the conflictual relationships of opposing groups, be they groups within the church or groups dividing society at large. Theological relevance is ultimately determined on nontheological criteria—namely, on sociological criteria. Not everyone is interested in the same theology. Theology considered "relevant" by one group will be considered "irrelevant" by the opposing group.

It would appear, then, that "relevance" is finally only the index of contradictory interests that are in dispute over theology. In this case, it must be recognized that the use that is made of the terms "relevant" and "irrelevant" takes on a frankly ideological hue. It is nothing but a function of silent interests, so that, when all is said and done, this terminology is bereft of any critical content whatever.

Even those who speak today of an "engaged" theology, or a "militant" theology, can do so only on the basis of a given social interpretation, in light of which interpretation a traditional theology appears "alienated" to them— "irrelevant." Consequently, we must say that, in the evaluation of a theological theory in terms of "relevant" and "irrelevant," a latent, anonymous sociology is always at work. It may not publicize itself, but it is present and operative.

To qualify traditional theologies as "irrelevant," then, is to renounce the opportunity to perceive the real relationship of *functionality* maintained by these theologies with the status quo. Vis-à-vis the prevailing social system, these theologies are altogether "relevant," in their way. It is only that the nature of their "relevance" remains tacit as long as the socio-historical situation to which they refer goes unchallenged. But the moment their dominant position encounters competition—that is, once disparate ideo-political tendencies emerge and enter into confrontation—it immediately becomes clear "which side" these self-styled transcendent theologies are "on" when it comes to politics. This is the moment at which they are forced to reveal their political locus, their real social weight, and the "relevant services" they provide the prevailing system.[26]

In strictly sociological terms, there are no absolutely "irrelevant" or "alienated" discourses. Relevance is always the function of a given situation or set of interests or determinate undertakings, and this is the condition of any theological production, whether it be "revolutionary" or "reactionary," and whether it be styled "relevant" or "apolitical." It is not a matter of (subjective) decision. It is a matter of the (objective) structure of discourse in the social field.

This puts a different face on things. Now it is no longer a matter of knowing what a "relevant" theology is, and under what conditions it becomes such. This becomes an abstract question, and admits only of an ideological answer, such as: "Irrelevant means the other kind." The correct state of the terms of the problem is: "Relevant" to *what* social situation? "Relevant" for *which* political cause? "Relevant" to the interests of *which* class?

§50 RELEVANCE AS A CRITICAL POSITION

According to what principles should theological subject matter—a theological "thematic"—be selected? Here we touch on the problem of the "political vigilance" of a theory—the relationship of a given theory to its external regime, or its dependence with respect to social conditions.

In order to answer this question, it seems to me that it will be necessary to take into consideration two basic factors, whose synthesis—a difficult but not impossible one—will be calculated to lead to a more and more critical or "adjusted" *prise de position*. These two factors will, as I assert elsewhere, maintain a mutual dialectic. The first factor will be in the order of *sensibility*—the order of experience. The second will be in the order of *analysis*—the order of rationality. Let me explain how.

1. The term "sensibility" designates, here, that global experience, in varying degrees of reflexivity, that is had in a given social position and amidst the interplay of practices that that position implies. The term translates what are commonly called "the facts," "the situation," "events," "life," "history," or "praxis"—along the lines of the reflections given at the beginning of this chapter. There I stated that the referent of these terms must be represented in the form of an all-embracing, living, totalizing synthesis. The dismemberment of such a totality into its constitutive elements can only be a deed of the mind, by way of an abstraction, and this is done at the price of the equally abstract destruction of that open, ever processual, totality of existence.

The actual, intimate experience of a determinate situation *permits* the perception, the sensation or feeling, of what is "relevant" in that situation. The "peaks" of history become palpable. This perception is most often expressed in the discourse of experience, which translates reactions of indignation, criticism, denunciation, stimulus for change, the mobilization of hearts and minds, and so on. Ethical judgments emerge on the scene, arising from the expression of moral consciousness called "conscience," which breathes a mighty wind upon the whole experiential complexus. This first moment may be called the ethical, or better, the prophetic moment.[27]

It has thus been established as a necessary, though of itself insufficient, condition for a positional, or engaged, theology, that it be committed to, and even identified with, the things or causes that make up the object of its theoretical concern. It is only in praxis and in its existential or illocutionary language that the theologian acquires the capacity, or "permission," to discern the historical relevance of the imperatives of the moment. The fact that this experience and the language that is its vehicle are not constituted in a formal theory, and hence are not theology, is of importance only in the eyes of a crypto-rationalist mentality.

2. At the same time, it will not suffice to immerse oneself in praxis in order genuinely to be inserted into the flow of history. It will also be necessary to have the capacity for analysis or criticism. Now, and only now, will views be confirmed, impressions tested, and projects defined. It will therefore be necessary to examine and establish relevance in the most critical manner possible, in all its complex levels—sociological, axiological, strategic, tactical, and so on. Thus, for example, in a particular situation it will be perfectly legitimate to have recourse to an analysis of social class in order to be able to define the relevance of the theology corresponding to that situation. Whether theology "should" be "classist" or not is a secondary question. The fact is that, here, it cannot help but be.

Without "sensibility," on the one hand, analysis can become pure technique—and degenerate into *cynicism*.[28] On the other hand, without analysis, sensibility can remain blind—and wander into illusion and empty protest. Consequently, the determination of a *theological* problematic passes by way of a determination of the *historical* problematic; and inversely, the definition of the *political* position of a theology passes by way of the definition of its *theoretical* position. That which is to be theorized—theology—must first be practiced—*agape*—and vice versa. Thus, thematic relevance can be constituted only by actual historical relevance. In order to act adequately, as well as in order to think correctly, care must be taken not to prescind from analytical mediation in favor of total immersion in existence.[29]

Between the prophetic moment and the noetic, an incessant dialectical movement must be established, in such wise that thematic relevance appears as such only in function of a given historical situation; and inversely, that the latter appears as the occasion of just confrontations only in function of the theory or thematic to which it gives rise.

In other words, the relationship of a unit of theoretical subject matter to a historical situation—its relevance—is not directly apprehensible, at least not at the level of theology as such. This relationship comes to light only through and within the dialectic between theory and praxis, between experience and reason, and, for our case, between agapic and theological practice. It is evident that, in virtue of the very dialectic involved, a pure instrumentality of the positivity of faith is out of the question. One of the poles of the dialectic would have to be sacrificed: faith itself. Admittedly, the problem would be thereby "resolved" — by one stroke of the sword through the Gordian knot: the problem would be laid waste.

Finally, it is always possible to "dialecticize" the transcendence of faith and its historicity, revelation and its political transcription, perennial values and their transitory concretions.[30] Indeed, this dialectic draws its vitality from the inexhaustible nature of faith: Mystery is the Ever-Retreating—that which ever holds itself in reserve.

Perhaps these conceptualizations have succeeded in "de-simplifying" the problem/question of relevance, and stripped them of the ideological veils that mask their real complexity. It may be relatively easy for an engaged Christian conscience to decide in a single instant what is and what is not relevant in a given context. But the matter is not that simple for a reflection that seeks to be critical, hence founded on arguments and proofs. Then too, contrary solutions are proposed for the same political problems today, so that theology today is challenged more than ever before to carry out a work of serious penetration and laborious explanation, always in the knowledge that history is no vast, peaceful ocean, but a tumultuous torrent, one that sweeps theology and the theologian along in its wild sweep.

It is therefore impossible to remain content with subjective, empirical "views," or with generic statements like: "You have to have the Bible in one hand and the daily newspaper in the other," as Karl Barth or Paul Lehmann would have it. Maxims of this kind may not be allowed to serve as a pretext for facile theories of a positivist mold. Serious practices are at stake here.[31]

The simple repetition of the creed, in season and out, is not the same as its efficacious proclamation. One must also, indeed especially, see to the procurement of a theoretical and practical language that will render the creed credible. Neglect of the socio-historical content in which the gospel finds its sounding board is abstraction from history. It is the vain attempt to grab hold of some utopia, perhaps placing one's faith in the magic power of the simple enunciation of the word of the gospel. A concern for the objective political effects of the kerygma, then, is foreign neither to the kerygma itself, nor, a fortiori, to theology.[32]

On the other hand, the principle of relevance may not legitimately be reduced to the will to "follow history," or to be "au courant" without a critical examination and concrete engagement to give form to this velleity. Otherwise the theologian falls victim to the illusions of progressivism, reformism, or even of theoretical opportunism, which last is absolutely to be rejected.[33]

The discussion just concluded has done no more than posit the terms of the question and suggest paths to its solution. I am well aware that I have remained in the realm of generalizations, and have not addressed the contemporary socio-historical situation, thus detouring a search for what is "relevant" for theology in this situation. This is because such an undertaking cannot be realized from a point of departure in the *theoretical* locus in which I have taken my position—but only from the *political* locus, parenthesized in this chapter.[34]

Finally, let me observe that the discussion begun in parts 1 and 2, concerning the theory of the theology of the political, has been resumed and extended here, in terms of the same articulation (by way of socio-analytic and hermeneutic mediations)—but alongside praxis, and with a view to praxis. This has been done in strict proportion to the obligation imposed by praxis upon theology to become, as well, and simultaneously, a political act. I shall employ the same formal approach in the next chapter.

CHAPTER 11

Political Objective of Theology

§51 DISINTERESTEDNESS OR INTEREST OF THEORY: AN ANALYTIC DIFFERENCE

In an investigation of the relationship between (theological) theory and (political) praxis—the object of part 3—I deal with two modalities according to which such a relationship obtains. The *first* is that of the social *topos:* the theologian is necessarily a social agent. This relationship has been shown to be possible in virtue of the fact of its articulation upon the basis of an identical *subject,* who maintains two distinct practices, one theoretical and one political. It has also been shown how political practice concerns the theologian, occasioning a "shift" in properly theoretical practice.

A *second* modality of the relationship between theory and praxis is implicit in the first, and has already been touched on when the first was discussed. I have spoken of "thematic relevance," which consists in according a privileged status, in the element of (theological) theory, to questions arising out of a confrontation with the (concrete) problems of praxis. I there referred to a *kairos,* in the sense that instances of historical urgency become instances of theoretical urgency. A synthesis appeared feasible, by reason of the *matter* common to both practices—the theoretical and the social.

Now I want to point out a *third* modality in the relationship between theory and praxis. This modality is constituted in function of the "destination," the end or scope, of a practice or a theological theory. I shall ask, then, what occurs, on the level of theology, when the question is posed: In view of what interests is theology done? In the service of whom or what is theology undertaken? For what causes is a struggle waged in the realm of theology itself? Obviously, then, we are dealing here with the *telos* of theological theory—its finality, its objective.[1]

The categories I use in part 3 in order to reflect correctly upon the relationship of praxis to theory are precisely the categories of "engagement," "relevance," and now, "objective." These are not categories pertaining to theory as such for the sake of theory, nor are they categories of praxis for the sake of praxis. They are precisely categories—theoretical, of course—of the *relationship* between theory and praxis. "Engagement," "relevance," and "objective," then, are *categoriae mediae,* articulating the *dialectic* of theory and praxis. Let us, however, be aware of the theoretical difficulty of initiating and maintaining a theoretical discourse respecting praxis, especially with regard to the precisely *theoretical* effects of the latter.

When the question of the social objective of theories is posed, when the practical interests of science are interrogated, when it is said that theory is a function of praxis—instantly we run into an objection. This, we shall be told, is precisely a thesis of "theoretical pragmatism," or "technocratic thinking."[2] And we are confronted with the celebrated maxim, "knowing is for the sake of knowing," or "knowledge is a value in itself," a *Selbstzweck.*[3]

But there is another side of the coin. The sociological critique of science has shown the extent to which all knowledge is, in fact, power, in virtue of its factual insertion into the fabric of social interests. Governments know this very well. It is precisely with a view to the "common good" that they promote scientific activities, and organize "cultural policies" corresponding to "social needs." This is also the reason why they seek to control the sources and channels of information and culture generally.[4]

There is, consequently, no body of knowledge or science, however pure, metaphysical, or mystical it thinks it is or seeks to be, that is not socially situated and politically orientated, in one manner or another. This is valid both for society in general and for social groups in particular, not excepting the church. For the latter, one need only think of the program of studies, especially theological studies, and its corporative and ideo-political finalities.[5]

How are we to understand this two-sided datum: the *disinterestedness* of theoretical research and the inherent social *interest* of all research? How may justice be done at once to the position maintained by scientists and theoreticians in general and to that of politicians and critics of scientific and theoretical knowledge?

If we begin with certain principles often cited in this work, we shall find that we are already well on the way to the answer. Let us note, first of all, that we are confronted here with two series of propositions, in no way incompatible with or contradictory to one another. They answer, as it happens, to two series of totally different questions. Accordingly, their pertinencies are not identical.

The thesis of the disinterestedness of science proceeds from the internal critique of science itself—from epistemology. Epistemology interrogates the scientific approach as such. It analyzes the process of theoretical investigation and research. In a word, it examines conceptual finality and modus operandi. As is evident, then, the aim of scientific research can only be knowledge. A science is a science only to the extent that it "makes one know;" the "scienti-fic" is that which *facit scire*. The more it shows, the more scientific it is. Accordingly, the interest of science can only be an interest *immanent* to the scientific process itself. Indeed, the essential, constitutive element of a science is not its body of particular results (its third generality), and still less its raw material (its first generality) but the operative and motive instance of its cognitive process (its second generality). Science, therefore, is first and foremost undertaking, projection. At this level, science obviously aims only at the production of instances of knowledge—not the production of reality or history (praxis), except indirectly and partially (that is, "for its part," making its partial, specific contribution to that reality and history).

The seemingly opposite thesis—to the effect that science is not neutral, that it always serves definite social interests, and that therefore it is not as "innocent" as it pretends to be—places us on a different level. These propositions answer another series of questions: precisely the questions that concern the "dependency" vector of knowledge—its external, extroverted regimen. These questions bear upon science considered as a social reality. They speak to the social function of this social datum within a determinate social whole. Here, then, it is no longer a matter of a relationship of *cognition,* but of a relationship of *function.* Knowledge is here taken in its social positivity—as a something-there, objectivized in conceptual elaborations or as the technological toolbox of such elaborations, and consisting materially in their cultural results. Here knowledge has the shape of a social instrument, of which its agents can avail themselves for the realization of their concrete pursuits. Here science has altogether the character of the social object: it is "as a thing" (Durkheim).

According to the thesis of disinterestedness, a theory is, and can only be, neutral, apolitical, and even atheistic. The scientific approach as such "does not know what to do with" political, ethical, and religious questions. Science *as science* is no more revolutionary or reactionary than it is religious or atheistic. These determinations are extrinsic to its epistemological status. They designate a "nonpertinent" relationship vis-à-vis what is proper to science as science. None of this is of interest to it. Or if it is, it can be so only in a privative sense: science is areligious, amoral, apolitical.[6]

With the thesis of interest, or nonneutrality, we have just the opposite. Here, science indeed draws its predicates from its social orientation, from its mode of social presence, in its capacity as "social thing." From this viewpoint, science is qualified to pass judgment regarding how it is to be employed, who is to employ it and for what purposes, who are to be its addressees, and so on. Here, science enjoys the properties attaching to any social reality: political destination, ethical option, religious signification, and the like. In this sense, there is no science, theory, or theology that is neutral, apolitical, impartial, pure, and so forth.

This distinction, let us take careful note, is of an analytical character. It regards aspects, dimensions, or levels of a single complex reality. It serves to further an adequate understanding of the problems cited. Despite its clarity, however, this distinction is not always grasped or observed in current discussions bearing on the relationship of science to society. Scientific neutrality is invoked in order to prevent a discipline from rendering a political or ethical judgment. Or, just the other way about, a theory may be credited with a coefficient of objectivity in direct proportion to its degree of determinate political, ethical, or religious engagement. In either case, there is confusion of two codes of pertinency, and consequently of two orders of questions.

Let it be noted, however, that such contradictions sometimes stem from the desire to have science "on one's side," or from the desire to find oneself "on the side of science." Still, in either case, we are dealing with the discourse of interest—with ideology.[7]

As for theology in particular, we shall have to deny that its position is any different in our cultures. Where the question of disinterestedness or interest is concerned, theology is found in the same conditions as are other disciplines. Its theoretical practice, too, obeys a canon of its own; it is disinterested, but it does not for all that cease to be in the service of (other) concrete objectives or interests.

I shall offer only two examples of this two-sided—theoretical and practical, epistemological and social—status of theological discourse.

The first comes from patristic theology. It is a matter of record that, generally speaking, the church fathers wrote with very precise pastoral needs in view.[8] Indeed, this was also true of the New Testament writers and the apostolic fathers. We are dealing, then, with "interested" writings. But let us ask: Does this fact exhaust their meaning? No, it does not, and the proof is that these writings continue to be read and understood today. This shows that they are not integrally of their time—that they partly transcend that time. They contain an element of "truth" that has not been completely consumed by the practical finalities that occasioned them.

The second example comes from the scholasticism of Thomas Aquinas. Here too we can discern the two-sided status of theology, although the ordering of priorities is diverse. Thomas's theology, of course, was constructed, on the one hand, in the form of a systematic body of knowledge, all of it informed by a speculative, or theoretical, finality.[9] On the other hand, it is equally clear that the scholastic edifice objectively performed an ideological, an "interest-ed," role, in the sense of justifying the social relationships of the feudal society of the time.[10] These two data, far from being contradictory, coexist perfectly well in one and the same discipline.

It is clear, then, that a "disinterested" (or "scientific") theology is not opposed, in principle, to an "interested" (or "pistic") theology. One must only know how to distinguish these two dimensions, thereupon to join them together congruously.

§52 DISINTERESTEDNESS AND INTEREST OF THEORY: A REAL RELATIONSHIP

Is there a relationship between the two questions I have just distinguished, and if so, how is it to be understood?

This brings us to the heart of this chapter. The answer to this question may be formulated in the more general and familiar terms of theory and praxis. Two modalities of this relationship have already been established: one articulated on the basis of a single *subject* (engagement), the other on the basis of a single *object* (relevance). Now we need only found the unity of a homologous relationship in terms of *finality* (destination).

In virtue of establishing the specific *difference* of the two orders, I have been able to speak at one and the same time of theoretical practice and its internal logic, and of political practice and its corresponding "normatics," or set of norms. Let us now turn to the question of the relationship between these two practices—or, more precisely, the question of the relationship between disinterestedness and interest.

To this purpose I now advance the thesis of the primacy of praxis over theory. I maintain that it is praxis that "gets theory going." It is practice that "fires" the logical mechanisms of the cognitive process. This may be conceptualized in the form of the *challenges* directed by praxis to theory.[11]

Not that theory is therefore reducible to the order of pure "reflex," or epiphenomenon, of praxis. Doubtless theory can appear on the scene only in response to the appeal of a concrete problem of praxis—in function of which it "gets under way." But this it does in conformity with its own axiomatic. And there is more: it is theory that actually makes it possible to pose problems in the form of questions. The interrogation arising at the heart of praxis does not transpire apart from theory. Between these two terms, therefore, an inevitable, necessary dialectic obtains—but with the reservation that (historical) priority must be ascribed to praxis.

In accordance with the terms of our particular problematic—that of disinterestedness and interest, and their mutual relationship—although epistemic subjects go "disinterestedly" in quest of cognition with respect to a given problem, it is only because they have been led to do so by real exigencies or concrete problems that necessitated theoretical investigation. Conversely, it is no less the case that cognition, for its part, arouses new interests. Therefore a dialectic must be exercised in order to render an account of the articulation between the disinterestedness of knowledge and the interest of action.[12] At the same time, attention must be paid to the principle that it is precisely praxis that leads the way in the dialectical movement in question, standing at the beginning point and the end point of this movement—theory being no more than a necessary resource, an indispensable detour, never the decisive term.[13]

Thus, we see, the maxim "knowledge for the sake of knowledge" is valid only for scientific practice—*one* of the forms of (overall) praxis. Within praxis, knowledge is not finalized in itself, but in function of the solution of concrete problems, or the satisfaction of real needs. To sum up, then: within the dialectic of praxis (history), the *immediate* end of theory is cognition, but its *mediate* and terminal end is praxis itself.[14]

Nor does this depend upon the volition or awareness of the theoretician. The logic of this dialectic is inscribed objectively in the structure of the relationship between theory and praxis. The good subjective intentions of theoreticians are inadequate to prevent their toil, or the fruit of their toil, from being utilized for ends repugnant to their consciences. History is not some vast, peaceful, uniform ocean, over which one may sail just as one pleases. History is much more like a great torrent, with a set course—the "course of history"—from which the prudent helmsman will know how to profit.

By way of a summary of what has been here expounded: all knowledge, including theological knowledge, is interested. It objectively intends precise finalities. It is finalized, mediately or immediately, by something external to itself. The true problem, consequently, does not reside in the alternative: interested theology or disinterested theology. The true problem lies in questions of this kind: What are the objective interests of a given theology? For what concrete causes is it being developed? In a word, *where* are its interests?

Posing the question in these terms, we are thinking of the *objective,* structural, sense of a theology within the domain of praxis. This sense can coincide, but not necessarily, with the *subjective,* conscious sense applied to theory itself. To appreciate this disparity of levels is to provide oneself with the means of drawing as much profit as possible from the objective dialectic that presides over the relationship of theory and praxis.[15]

Now we must inquire into the manner by which the finalization of a determinate theological discourse can be controlled. What principles must be set in motion for a determinate theory to preserve the conscious signification assigned to it? In other words, how may the gulf separating—on the social plane—subjective interests and objective interests, goals and outcomes, conscience and consequences, be narrowed?

In order to answer this question we may have recourse to the principles applied earlier in studying the form of the theologian's political engagement and choice of theological thematic.

It was determined that the answer to such a question could only consist in a living, vital synthesis between two distinct terms: on the one side, a *sensitivity,* including ethical and religious conscience, and on the other, an *analysis,* or critique, at its various levels.

The two aspects are complementary. At the same time, they are mutually irreducible. Nor can they be completely separated. Sensitivity alone is not enough: it can degenerate into irrealism and inefficacy. Likewise, pure ratiocination will never mobilize practice. Only a synthesis of the two will permit an efficacious, lucid input in the determination of which political interests a theology should prioritize.[16]

Thus we are dealing with an existential attitude, giving rise to a synthetic judgment. This judgment does not, then, proceed from analytical reason. It proceeds from the reason that defines the human being as such, is coextensive with the realm of the human, and of which analytical reason is but the expression—indeed a partial, lesser expression. The *ratio* of scientific *rationes* is not itself scientific, nor can it be. Classic tradition has long since identified a particular function of reason with respect to ends. It calls this function "wisdom." In these terms, we are constrained to say that, although the reason of wisdom cannot replace scientific reason, it does not, for all that, fail to provide scientific reason its final objective, which, of course, must be situated out beyond its immanent, direct objective, which is cognition.[17]

If we have learned our lesson from the social sciences regarding the fabric of which society is woven—that web of relationships of force obtaining between (opposing) classes—we shall perceive that today the political objective of theory does not lie on open, level terrain, as it would in a society understood as a harmonious, balanced organism (functionalism), but in the arena of struggle (Marxism). Reason, therefore, will have to choose between exclusive alternatives, and cast itself into the sea of social confrontations—a true *dezidierte Vernunft.*[18]

If this is indeed the case, then we must maintain that theology can only be, in a broad sense, "partisan"—can only be "sides-taking." Inasmuch as, *in concreto,* it has always found itself in a situation favoring one "party" or "side" with respect to one or more others, there is nothing for theology to do but become aware of this, and to define, with all lucidity, the possible and desirable ends of its finality. And although the logic of its internal process is not in dependency upon its external finality—and on this terrain the "sides" question neither is nor should be taken up—nevertheless theology does not cease, for all that, to share, in its capacity as a particular social practice—and, hence, in an objective manner—in the finalities and causes of politics. Consequently, the theologian must exercise watchful care that the signification of the *opus operantis* lie as close as possible to that of the *opus operatum,* that the instrument of truth may come to be likewise an instrument of justice.[19]

Therefore a theology with a political finality must not be less theological, in the epistemological sense of the term, than any other theology. On the contrary, the vigor of the fray must be matched by the rigor of the inquiry.[20] Hence the social responsibility attaching to the work of the theologian, and to the destiny it may have in the play of history and the dynamics of society.[21]

Further to our consideration of the relationship between theory and praxis, an important remark must be made regarding the paradoxical nature of the finality of theory, particularly of theology. Within the vaster context of praxis, theological theory intends a terminal realization in it own transcendence. Although this transcendence is not of a logical or theoretical order, nonetheless it is real: it is of a practical order. The practice of faith—*agape*—is the realization, and at the same time the suppression *(Aufhebung),* of theological thinking. To seek to realize the ultimate aim or intentionality of theology by dint of "strokes of theory" is to go around in circles, and is illusory, be the name of the illusion idealism, theoreticism, or scientism. Thus the theoretical transcending leaps of praxis are seen to be actual, practical realizations. After all, it is only praxis, in its quality as action inspired by faith—action in the form of *agape*—that can effectuate the accomplishment of the intention of the theological word.[22]

But to arrive at this—to pass from (theological) theory to (agapic) praxis—

there is no continuous, straight road to take. The road of theory is different from the road of praxis. There is, then, no analytical, theoretical passage from theory to praxis.[23] Just as theory is constituted through a *breach* with praxis, to establish itself "on its own"—in its own house, as it were—so also, in the opposite direction, the return from theory to praxis is reliable only through an analogous "rupture," a *leap in the opposite direction*. Each of these two breaches is the deed of human de-cision—human decision as sovereign act of creativity, the prerogative of spirit alone. No theory can replace practice.[24] What theory can do is represent praxis (which, after all, is its definition).

This means that no theory, be it ever so rigorous or profound, will ever of itself engender praxis. The same holds for the inverse calculation: no praxis, be it as radical as you please, will ever, just on that account, issue in a theory. Praxis no more springs from "theoretical strokes" than theory from practical strokes. Thus theory and praxis represent irreducible orders.[25]

Even when a realization of theory occurs in and by praxis, this realization is never total and "traceless." It remains ever historical and unfinished, in such wise that the movement from praxis to theory must now resume its course. And we are swept up once more in the endless ebb and flow of the dialectic of theory and praxis.[26]

§53 CONCLUSIONS FROM THE PRECEDING THREE CHAPTERS

As can be seen, each of the last three chapters has treated of a different modality of a single basic theme, the relationship between theory and praxis. These modalities—*topos, kairos,* and *telos*—have been described and studied according to the same basic principles. Now it is time to explicitate these principles.

1. For purposes of *analysis,* one must guard against confusing two differential orders: the orders of theoretical practice and political practice, respectively. One must allow each its own proper system of connections, and consequently its specific pertinency. Thus, for theoretical practice, one may speak of a *constitutive employment* of reason, inasmuch as reason is a necessary mediation for the constitution of the *object* of a given political practice, whereas for *political* practice, one must speak of a *regulating employment* of reason, inasmuch as, here, reason orientates this political practice in the direction of a determinate *objective.*[27]

2. In its capacity as *social function*—that is, in its social status—theological practice is de facto always marked by a given political position, by a schema of thematic relevance, and by a set of defined interests. This is a general *datum,* which demands, first, to be *recognized,* and then to be *known*—that is, apprehended progressively in its concrete determinations (which engagement, which theme, and which interest?).

3. The knowledge and assumption of this datum permit the emergence of a "new theological spirit,"[28] characterized by a *sense of ideo-political responsibility* on the part of the theologian. This spirit is expressed in the attitude that I

call "political vigilance," understood as due attention to the political and social implications generally of theoretical practice and its products, in such wise that these may be controlled as much as possible.[29]

4. Finally, this active orientation of theory on the social level can be properly established and maintained only through the *dialectical relationship* that must be operative between the proper poles of the theology of the political—that is, between situational analysis and faith discernment, political vigilance and epistemological vigilance—in a word, between socio-analytic mediation and hermeneutic mediation.

CHAPTER 12

Praxis as Criterion of Truth

§54 CONTEXT OF THE QUESTION: THE COURSE OF "POLITICAL THEOLOGY"

I have been treating of the relationships between (theological) theory and (political) praxis. It has been explained that what we have here is a situation that has always been in effect. A deepened awareness of it has led theologians to take a critical and conscious position vis-à-vis their own activity of research and publication.

But here certain questions arise: Is this not to maintain that practice is the norm of all theory? And will this not be dangerous? Will politics not now come to constitute the critical tribunal of theology? Are we not faced with a questionable inversion of relationships here?

These questions have some foundation. Current theology of the political, of course, has indeed spoken much of praxis as the "criterion of truth."[1] This theology is beholden more to *orthopraxy* than to orthodoxy, as one of the essential themes of its concern.[2] It has even been presented as akin to praxeology.[3] That is, it has been defined as being a "critical reflection on praxis."[4]

We see here the signs of a new sensitivity—not in the field of culture generally (witness Marxism today), but in religion, and particularly in theology. We do not yet find, in this last area, reflections sufficiently developed and systematic to enable us to grasp this new conception in a more precise fashion. Given the novelty of the "discovery," we are not surprised to find a mental attitude of psychological content (opposition to dogmatism, to abstract thinking, to essentialism, and the like), rather than one of critical content properly speaking (confrontation of positions, origination of new concepts, an effort at precision, "speculative boldness," and the like).[5] In brief, the "political theologians" have been content with an empiricist discourse, verging on impressionism. This discourse has been constructed with such terms as "the real," "the concrete," "facts," "occurrences," "praxis," "experience," "history," "life," "material," and so on.

Such notions are credited with a theoretical content so very evident that it

195

does not seem necessary to ask for their analytical credentials. They slip, part and parcel, into theological works without having been subjected to the comprehensive examination that ought to have been made at the outset. Not that theology does not have, or cannot illustrate, its system of concepts, and the rules of its elaboration. No, theology possesses its own intelligibility: that of the theological. But what is disquieting in all this is the *quality* of the new materials that theology is introducing into its spectrum and with which it is being constructed. I refer to the absence of the necessary theoretical mediations, especially that of duly articulated socio-analytic mediation.

Has the course of the theological process been inverted with the appearance of this new vocabulary? Yes indeed it has, if we may believe its theoreticians. A "deductive" theology, we are told, has been replaced by an "inductive" theology, "speculative" by "practical," "abstract" by "concrete," "alienated" by "engaged," an "archaic" or "medieval" theology by a "modern," "progressive" theology, and so on.[6]

However, when this new thinking is challenged to show what it has actually produced, to propound the grammar of its new language—what are we offered? Usually, mere protestations of theoretical volition, in place of a missing theory. We get a voluntaristic epistemology, exhausted in phraseology like: theology must reflect upon this, or upon that, it must speak a different language, it must be understandable, it must begin with the facts, reflect with a view to praxis, be revolutionary, submit to the judgment of concrete praxis, and so on.[7]

One would think that the current theology of the political were concerned less with *methods* than with different theological *practices*. It will suffice to analyze the *opus operatum* of this current of thought to realize that its "new way of doing theology" is not really as radical as it makes itself out to be. Doubtless second theology has realized genuine progress vis-à-vis the old way of theologizing. It has put itself in a position to be able to deliver up a new thematic, with its corresponding theological problematic. It draws a good sketch of the tasks that are needful and urgent in theology today, and it is headed in the right direction with them. But its concrete manner of practicing the demands it champions is still rather disconnected.

In proposing to "begin with the facts," then, and "do an inductive theology," what is it that this theology of the political claims? It claims to be leaping with both feet right into "facts" themselves, thereupon to decipher in them, in black and white, the theological meaning they are supposed to have written all over their faces. It seems to hold the belief that with a few biblical keys it would be very easy to lay bare the message of faith that lies right on top of the "concrete."

And so we read things like: "hope as the motive force of history" (Moltmann), "the church as institution of social critique" (Metz), the gospel as radical revolution, faith as a factor for change, love as the transforming dynamism of society, Christians as vessels of permanent revolution, and other slogans of this kind.

It is not difficult to see that the subjects of these theological propositions are always the same—hope, church, gospel, and so forth—and the predicates are precisely the materials of the new thematic of second theology—history, society, revolution, and the like. But, because this new discourse is being enunciated without a precise knowledge of the rules of its own play—that is, of its predication—the identifications made are hasty, one term is absorbed by another, and what we end up with is language congestion.

We must recognize, of course, that this situation is in some sort a natural one. It belongs to the process of the emergence of any new discourse, as its first phase. After all, this is the way a new language is learned: by making mistakes, stammering, correcting oneself, and going on.

This initial phase is already calling for its own transcendence, even today. It feels the need "to be gone beyond." A need is felt for a methodological mechanism to guarantee the theoretical appropriation of this new terrain that second theology is traversing. We lack a critique of the theological process, and a tool to guarantee its validity. We need a theological *technique*, and, underlying the technique, a "methodique."

To this end, however, yet another step back must be taken, in order to return to the "primary verifications" of theology, its *prima principia*, its foundational elements. This is the direction of my efforts in this study, especially in my insistence on the question of theological identity (hermeneutic mediation), and on the question of mediations generally and their articulation in theological practice.

For the specific case of praxis, of which I must speak here, the question must be put quite straightforwardly: What does it mean when one says that praxis is the "criterion of truth" for theological theory? What do the other rough-hewn propositions, cited at the beginning of this section, mean, with their vague, nebulous denotations?

If we were to study the sources of the slogans cited above, and the origins of their theoretical pretensions and claims, it might be that we would find accounts to settle with the three following currents:

—With *scientism*, where the *internal* criterion of "scientificness," consisting in the formation of operative codes of validation, extends its credibility, ideologically, *out beyond* the space of theory into culture in general, with such propositions as: this is scientific, and so there is nothing to object to.[8]

—With *pragmatism*, where the validity of an idea is judged by its concrete, external results.

—Finally, with the *Marxism* of the young Marx, who insisted so much on praxis as opposed to theory.

Let us pause for a moment on this last point, which calls for some clarifications. Marx's *Theses on Feuerbach* have exercised an evident influence on "political theology" generally. Again and again we find references to this work of the young Marx in recent theological writing, especially to Thesis Eleven: "Philosophers have been content to interpret the world in various ways, but what matters today is that it be changed."[9]

In support of this thesis, "political theologians" have adduced a great number of biblical passages, such as those presenting works as the expression and test of faith, works as testimony of the presence and action of the Spirit, works as confirmation of the divine truth, and so forth. They have underscored the dynamic conception of "truth" in Judeo-Christianity—for which, we read, truth is a task, something to be done, something accomplishable and verifiable.[10]

The approach of "political theology" to Marx's theses on Feuerbach is, in my view, all too symptomatic—all the more so because it reflects a most intimate spiritual affinity between Marx's thought during the years 1840–45 and post-Vatican II "political theology."

After all, Marx was at that time on the point of loosening the ties that still bound him to the young Hegelians, especially Feuerbach.[11] The *Theses* appear, in this context, as a discourse of breach. But they are written in a language that cries out to be left behind, transcended. They are like flashes of lightning, enabling us to discern a new "problematic," however vaguely and provisionally.[12]

For its part, political theology today finds itself in a situation analogous to that of the young Marx. It too seems not quite sure of what it confusedly sees in the dark. It lacks a syntax of its own that would enable it to articulate its new discourse. Hence its strident, demanding manifestos in behalf of praxis. It exalts the "epistemological destiny" of praxis to the point of threatening the autonomy of theoretical practice—to the detriment of praxis itself.[13]

Taken in depth and to their ultimate consequences, these claims for praxis lead from misology to "theoricide." They end by simply prohibiting speech—by prohibiting the "doing of theology" at all. In order to give praxis its due—in order to recognize that praxis can be "right," can *avoir raison*—current "political theology" empties praxis of its rationality.[14]

Even this, of course, is a product of reason—but of a senseless, mad reason—mad because contradictory, and not just nondialectical. Impatiently, this "reason" goes so far as to de-articulate, dismember, the living movement of the dialectic of theory and praxis.[15]

§55 THEOLOGICAL CRITERIOLOGY

As a prelude to embarking on the epistemological enterprise, let me make it very clear that the thesis that "praxis is the criterion of truth" has to be correctly posited, in that its unelaborated formulation is ambiguous and erroneous.[16]

From the viewpoint of theological practice, (political) praxis neither is nor can be the criterion of (theological) truth. The reason is simple: political practice is of another order than that of theoretical practice. Thus neither has anything in common with the other. The thesis that praxis is the criterion of truth is theologically nonpertinent. It seeks to compare the incomparable.

In the purely scientific ambit, the problem of verification is one of the most burning questions confronting the critique of the sciences, with regard both to the concept of "verification" generally and to its application to the various branches of knowledge.[17]

On the other hand, the assertion that praxis is the criterion of (theological) truth entails the basic, persistent ambiguity that I have been denouncing all through this study, and that I am making an effort to dispel. This ambiguity revolves about the possibility of a theological discourse as a particular theoretical discipline and practice. It consists in the identification, indeed the confusion, of the real with knowledge of the real, of agapic practice with theological practice, of pistic experience with its educated discourse.

Where criteriology is concerned, it is important to note that each of the two orders mentioned—the theoretical and the practical—possesses criteria of truth corresponding to itself (respectively, theoretical and practical). Thus we have, on the one side, faith and its "marks of credibility"—the "signs" that manifest that faith. On the other side we have theology and the manner peculiar to it, which *it adopts*, of legitimating *itself*.[18] It will be in order here, then, to contradistinguish *theological criteriology* from *pistic criteriology*. The former is of an *epistemological* order, and concerned with the rules of the *theoretical* practice of the *theologian*; the latter is of an *existential* order, and springs from principles that orientate the *concrete* practice of the *believer*.[19]

It is only when a mistaken or "warped" relationship is introduced between these two levels that orthodoxy is disqualified in favor of orthopraxy. This is the misdeed of a pragmatist ideology, which only sows confusion and is powerless to understand that two distinct orders of question are present here.[20]

Just as with the other disciplines, theology is exempt from any wholly external criterion of truth, any jurisdictional "tribunal" having the right to pronounce from without on the validity of its propositions. Theology is a *self-policed* practice.

Let us view the question under discussion as follows. Like any science, theology comprises two fundamental instances: a *logical* instance, comprising the totality of its formal conditions, and a *verificational* instance, corresponding to the totality of its material conditions. The former is responsible for the internal consistency of theological constructs. The latter is responsible for their validation.

When it comes to the criterion of consistency, theology bends its efforts toward the organic development of the understanding of revelation in a given era and in accordance with the cultural resources offered by this era. This is its most important task, as indeed its best epistemologists have maintained.[21]

Not that the *ratio theologica* must establish the truth of revelation. No, revelation is entrusted to the believer, who responds to it by faith *qua* "existential decision." Theology comes only afterward, to explain, explicitate, and render intelligible, in the measure of its capacities, the order that obtains in the universe of significations opened up by revelation.[22] This is the "theoretical" function of theology, in the sense that it "clarifies" what is already believed (Thomas Aquinas).

As for the second criterion—that of *verification*—we shall do well to keep in mind that it depends on the nature of the discipline in question.[23] For our purposes, it is by an examination bearing upon its conformity with the canon of faith that a theological production is to be judged.[24]

It will be objected that, in the case at issue, the *norma normans* is in some manner a *norma normata* as well. I respond: that is as it must be—nor is this a predicament peculiar to theology, as a comparison with the canonical procedures of verification of other disciplines will quickly reveal. After all, such procedures have a twofold—theoretico-empirical—nature. By the same token, it is impossible to establish, for a determinate science, an absolute, definitive, and immutable "canonics." This would mean the end of all knowledge. Further: in order to measure the conformity in question between "theory and empiry," one would have to resort to theories that themselves would have to be verified. In such wise, one would enter upon a process in which one verifying theory would have to be verified by another verifying theory, and so on *ad infinitum*.

My point is that, when all is said and done, there is no way to escape the sphere of theory altogether, or even measure it, and that a circularity obtains between normative and normatized particulars, just as between their own proper relationships.[25]

What is to be gathered from all this? That theology can be organized in conformity with the formal structure of scientific knowledge. It too is susceptible of measurement from a point of departure in two criteria: one of a *logical* order, and the other of a *positive* order—controlling, respectively, the (internal) rigor of a theological production, and its (external) concordance with the positivity of faith (with the creed). These two criteria correspond formally to the constitutive principles of scientific knowledge—logic and experimentation—and they occupy their place in the specific field of theological knowledge.[26]

One could object, at this point, that, in the presentation of theological criteriology, the historical and current experience of Christians does not come under consideration, as it would appear to offer no interest for theology.

To be sure, the living, current praxis of Christian communities is not an *immediate* norm for theology. How could any direct relationship be established between such and such a faith practice and such and such a theological proposition? Here we have to pass *by way of* the mediation of the foundational message, which is the *norma normans* as well of faith as of theology. The living practice of Christian communities, therefore, will have to be considered only an *indirect* norm for theology. And so the living gospel—which is what matters "when all is said and done" (in the eschaton!)—does command theology in the measure that theology falls in line with the imperatives of the historical gospels.

On the other hand—as already explained—praxis (that of Christians, first, and then of human beings in general) is not, as such, *what explains* (the second generality), but on the contrary, is *what is to be explained* (a third generality) in terms of theology. Praxis prepares the agenda, the repertory of questions, that theology is to address. Practices in general are not proofs of "theological truths." Otherwise it would be legitimate to ask which practices are proofs of which truths. The case is rather that certain practices are possible "signs" of faith, in the subjective and objective sense. They are not, then, the dis-course of faith, they are its course. They are invitations to theological deciphering, but they are not the deciphering itself. They are on the side of the (objectively theological) real, not on that of its (subjectively theological) knowledge.

Furthermore: it is perfectly conceivable that there could exist a faith practice accompanied by a very elementary, even heterodox, theology; or conversely, that there could be great theological progress without a corresponding increase of sanctity or *agape*.[27] History, past and present, is replete with examples of both. There is no necessary correlation, then, between theology and holiness. We are confronted with two relatively distinct orders here. Their dissensions must appear before different tribunals, to be decided in conformity with correspondingly different codes.

As for the traditional practice that considers the ecclesial community as represented by the hierarchy to be the highest judicative tribunal relative to the "doctrine of faith"—orthodoxy—I maintain that the above-cited principles governing the theological process remain intact. They do not fall under the jurisdiction of any institution, even where second generalities are concerned. The magisterium is no more than the *guardian* of the "deposit of faith," and, although it is the legitimate tribunal in the discernment of the faith, its determination in this function proceeds in the manner proper to it—that is, by the *via authoritativa*—or better, *prophetica* or *martyrica*—and not *via argumentativa* or *theoretica*. After all, its "authority" proceeds from faith, which indeed is the vehicle of the magisterium rather than its cargo.

Accordingly, the relationships among church, faith, and theology are in principle organic, not independent, much less contradictory. They must be dialecticized—not, to be sure, in purely formal fashion, but in accordance with the specific nature and function of each of the three. And within this dialectic, the role falling to theology is that of the *theoretical* tribunal of the faith.[28]

§56 PISTIC CRITERIOLOGY

In order to shed more light on the theme of "verification," I shall now approach it from the side of faith. I do not wish to treat here *ex professo* the question of the "proofs" of the faith.[29] I seek only to stake out certain guidelines that will be helpful, I trust, in a consideration of the particular problem of the political *practice* of faith.

First of all it will be necessary to work out a correct concept of the notion of faith and of its "proofs." I leave out of consideration the problem of the "reasonableness" of faith. This is rather a speculative, secondary question. Instead, I shall fasten upon another aspect, one more proximate to our problematic: that of the *capacity of faith for social transformation*.

Current theology prides itself on its capacity for social transformation, vaunting this as one of the signs of its authenticity. Actually the self-evident character of this oversimple formulation is illusory. A theologian should be mistrustful of the "self-evident"—of what is presented as something that "goes without saying."

And indeed the formula cited entails a tangle of problems. How is the expression "social transformation" to be understood in this formula? What is to be "transformed"? And how? And to what? Next, with respect to the term "faith," there are more questions. What is being spoken of when faith is referred to as a transforming dynamism: the gospel? the church? Christian teaching? Christians? What is the social status of faith?

Here we cannot be satisfied with the acritical, superficial criterion of *pragmatism*, which assigns primacy to practical effectiveness.[30] We must always assign a *moral qualification* to an action, even a successful action.

The path of history is strewn with victorious irrationalisms and vanquished idealisms. Over the theologian's own path hovers the cross—a perennial reminder throughout the march of history that divine logic is different from human logic, although not necessarily contrary to it.[31] One must not be too quick, then, to draw up the equation: liberation = salvation. The kingdom of God, many times down through the course of history, is left *tectum sub cruce et sub contrario*—to adopt one of the formulas of the Reformers. Thus the *crucial* test, literally, of any faith-life, as well as of any theological *ratio*, is, in the realm of concrete reality, the *experimentum crucis* (Roger Bacon). Least of all may theologians be allowed to forget this—any more than they may be permitted to "dig in" behind this truth, using it as an alibi for noncommitment. The theologian is equally a "realist of the cross" and a "political realist."[32]

The insistence with which "political theologians" call for political action cannot replace a theoretical effort, in the twofold sense in which it is taken here—provision of *ethico-critical determinations* (by hermeneutic mediation), and definition of *analytico-strategic positions* of political action (by socioanalytic mediation). The function of political theologians is to determine *what ethical quality* a political practice ought to assume, as well as to evaluate the *concrete political action* put forward as responding to this ethical quality.

If we pay close attention to what is going on in current "political theology," we know what is implied in its urgent appeals in favor of praxis. No one doubts that it is a liberating action that is being called for. This is a theology struggling for the transformation of a state of affairs whose injustice has no further need of demonstration. However, all this is charged to the account of (implicit) "evidence" that stands in need of correct and appropriate examination.

It may be that there are political situations that are so urgent that they dispense us from all rigor of thought and make a very direct appeal for indignation and action. Still, when an individual or group is *satisfied* with crying, "Praxis, praxis!" or "Political action, political action!," thinking that thereby something has been done, we must recognize that this individual or group has scarcely gone very far, in terms of either theory or praxis. If truth be told, this is the road leading directly to that impatient, truncated form of pragmatism called "doing *something*."[33]

Such an attitude satisfies neither the imperative of genuine political efficacity, nor that of ethical evaluation.

In respect of the former: the complexity of current socio-historical situations is not such as to recommend dispensing with cool, rational calculation—not to mention that sentiments of rebellion and deeds of protest frequently lead to a hardening of the status quo and are consequently inefficacious.[34]

As for ethical evaluation, it is evident that political efficacity cannot constitute moral value. Rather it is efficacity itself that must be "justified." Its ethical character derives from the causes inspiring it. In other words, to assert that politics, simply, is a value, is to imply value in a reactionary politics, and thus deprive oneself of the option of proposing alternatives.[35]

The incessant invocation of politics is vain. It remains to know *what* politics is at issue. And this presupposes an ethical resource capable of furnishing the criteria of a political practice that is indeed liberating, humanizing.[36]

This would be the point at which it would be in order to develop the theme of *ethical mediation*. It could be understood as a function of a broader mediation—the philosophical, which, for its part, would be linked to hermeneutic mediation, in the sense that it would enter into the second generality of a theology of the political and enrich it with its specific determinations, especially in the form of natural law. But I shall not pause longer here on this particular question.[37]

It is clear, then, that we may not embrace the ideology of orthopraxy, or praxiology, dispensing ourselves from a thorough reflection on the ethical content of a given practice and from a critique of the idea of efficacity and the "theoretical short-circuit" that it tends to provoke.[38]

Without entering into detail on this question, let me refer once more to the dialectic that I have been proposing in all these matters. In the formulation "social transformation: verification of faith," we actually have a continuous reciprocal relationship, according to which faith measures, criticizes, stimulates, and orientates social transformation, which, in turn, expresses, realizes, and verifies the truth of faith and its values. Thus we do not have "faith in one pocket and transformation in the other," to speak in the spirit of Hegel. What we do have is a vital connection established between the two terms, which "proves" or confirms the one by the other.[39]

On this level, yes, works are the "criterion" that judges someone's faith. This criterion is in a way *interior* to faith itself, in the sense that works are faith *qua operata*—*qua* lived, "realized"—and faith is works *qua good* works, *qua liberating* practices. This reciprocal relationship is dynamic, and preserves the good health of its members by means of its ongoing dialectical "circulation."[40]

Let me complete the definition of my position by placing in evidence this datum of the positivity of faith: when all is said and done, the definitive verification of the truth of faith and the practice of justice is of an eschatological nature. It remains suspended, *fine finaliter*, until the Last Judgment, when "every mouth shall be closed."[41] Then shall the "apocalypse"—the revelation of the sense of history—be realized. But this supreme, final verification is the exclusive prerogative of God, the sole judge.[42]

Hope in the divine promise, however, may not be allowed to serve as pretext for the renunciation of practice in politics. The Christian community is challenged, by this same hope, to live and transform history, that the kingdom of

God may come, and that God's will may be done "on earth as it is in heaven."[43] For, although the kingdom of Christ is not *of* this world—is not of terrestrial origin and fashion—it is nevertheless *in* this world, which is the space and material of its realization. Thus too, although salvation is not (simply) liberation, it can and must be *in* liberation. Hence, where the historical verification of faith is concerned, the church always bears the burden, not so much of scrutinizing the "signs of the times" as of itself being a messianic sign, not so much of a practice of hermeneutics as of a practice of ethics, not so much of doing theology or even "religion" as of doing *agape*—the sign par excellence of salvation-in-history.[44]

§57 ARTICULATION OF THEOLOGICAL CRITERIOLOGY WITH PISTIC CRITERIOLOGY

The clear-cut difference between faith and its criterion, and theology and its criteria, has now been established. This difference must be carefully maintained for the sake of the discipline of theological thinking—that is, with a view to epistemological vigilance.

Now let us try to see the relationship obtaining between the truth of faith and the truth of theology, the pistic order and the theological order, the work of theory and the work of praxis.[45]

The articulation of this relationship has forced itself on our attention many times so far in this work, however much it may have been in the "course" of other considerations rather than in a "discourse" of its own. I shall devote the next—the last—chapter of this study to an exposition of this relationship in formal, systematic fashion.

In order to remain confined strictly to the matter under discussion here, let me say first of all that there is no immediate, direct, term-for-term correspondence between pistic criterion and theological criterion. The latter is not the mirror image of the former, or its shadow, or its reflex. The reason for this is that the order of theory is not the same as that of praxis (recall "auto-nomy").

At the same time, theology, however self-regulating it may be or claim to be, is not for all that any less *dependent* on (agapic) practice. This is kept in mind in my consideration of the three distinct modalities of praxis: social position, thematic relevance, and political interest. The same is the case with regard to "verification."

In brief, let me observe that a rigorous and genuine theology receives its effective sanction only from a practice consistent with its own thematic. A theologian's praxis is a necessary, although of itself inadequate, condition for public credibility and ecclesial reception of his or her theses. *In concreto*, a theology is judged also by its progenitor's commitments and causes, and what these produce in terms of historical and political action.[46] Indeed, the canons used to validate a theological theory inevitably have a social and historical aspect, in virtue of the fact that they must be formulated in a conventional manner. Hence theological practice is concretely bound to agapic practice.

Consequently, theologians who fail to present, besides theoretical titles of credit, pistic and agapic ones as well, in terms of faith engagement, evangelical witness, and love "tried and true," place obstacles in the way of "theological truth" itself—their own elaborations, however scientific they may be.[47] Such is the mutual "overlap" of the truth of faith and the truth of its theory.[48]

Nor will it be of any avail to appeal ultimately to the contemporary "crisis of theology" in this respect. The "crisis of theology" today is the product of a crisis of faith, which appears to consist in a crisis of the concrete "proofs" of faith in terms of praxis as the production of social and historical reality. It will not be only, or even mainly, by dint of theory, therefore, that theology will be able to regroup its forces. There is no theoretical *Putsch*, however spectacular or revolutionary it may think itself to be, that is capable of restoring theology to its vigor. No, theology remains dependent on a more fundamental and mysterious determination, one bound to the historical *kairos* of revelation itself.[49] I shall return to this in §63.

At the same time, there is a second movement, an inverse one: that from theology to praxis. In this direction, a praxis is "credited" only when it answers to criteria. There is no practice possessing absolute self-evidence. All practice must be evaluated.[50] Efficacy will not do as a pistic criterion: otherwise the scandal of the cross would be removed.[51] The credibility of an agapic practice *qua* agapic, therefore, does not "go without saying"—least of all in the social field, with its abundance of complexity and contradiction.

Consequently, the intervention of theological thinking in the political action of the Christian community has its importance. Not that the function of theology is to solve the mystery of the cross. On the contrary, it is to safeguard it. Thus the human *logos* comports itself before the cross as "shepherd of Mystery."[52] The human *logos* is the "guardian of the transcendence" of the cross.[53] Its function is not the solution of mystery, as if "mystery" were tantamount to "problem," but, on the contrary, the maintenance of mystery in all its vigor and vitality.[54]

Accordingly, pistic truth—a truth of praxis—and theological truth—a truth of theory—call for each other, and interact upon each other.[55] And they do so in a rhythm that is not purely linear, but is ultimately measured by the basic "scansion" or yardstick of the reality of faith. For the dialectical balance always leans toward the practical dimension.

Thus, we see, the dialectic is not exhausted "in a single proposition." Contradiction continually recurs, in the form of mystery, to set in motion, once more, both theology and the practice of faith *(agape)*, thrusting them toward the eschatological *telos*, which is nothing other than Mystery itself in its divine *pleroma*.[56]

CHAPTER 13

Dialectic: Its Modes and Norms

§58 INITIAL DEFINITIONS

It now remains formally to circumscribe the relationships between theory and practice that constitute the subject of part 3 of this book. The proper mode of these relationships has been given the name "dialectic." In the present chapter I shall make an effort to clarify the precise manner of this dialectic. And I shall do so exclusively in function of the particular theme of my thesis: the theology of the political.

Dialectic must not be conceived of as a particular method, in the sense of a precise technique of investigation or research. More basically, it is a particular manner in which reason operates, a fundamental attitude of the human mind. This attitude is characterized by the *dynamism* of thought—by the indefinite effort to transcend all fixed points. Dialectic is the perpetual motion of reason. It is a style of thinking marked by the will to shatter all static rigidity, to burst the conceptual frames that imprison the mind, that the mind may assert itself as a force of negation and creation. Dialectical thought renounces definitive conclusions and eternal truths once and for all. It is essentially antidogmatistic. It is perpetual commencement, transgression of limits, journey through the desert endlessly.[1] This is the figure by which we should represent what might be called "dialectical drive," perhaps the sublimest of the possibilities of the exercise of reason.

But a thesislike treatment, although necessary for the understanding of dialectic, risks stopping at too formal a level, and yielding up propositions deprived of all content, if not of their very form. Therefore I must take a further step, and say that dialectical movement is not a pure play in absolute, free space. On the contrary: we are dealing with a "play" that is regulated, and regulated in more than one register or "key."

Keeping in view the project with which we are here concerned, I shall try to identify the registers and rules of this dialectical "play." Inasmuch as the foregoing chapters have already resorted to the principles of dialectic and demonstrated their usefulness, it remains only to establish them *ex professo* in this chapter.

"Political theology" invokes the dialectic of theory and praxis as one of its specific principles. But, just as in the case of other methodological postulates, neither has this one been given an adequate definition. It has remained on the level of a general aphorism or abstract description.

Unless it means to constitute itself a sterile formulism and, in the extreme case, spin away in an unbridled, suicidal career of thought, dialectic must submit to an examination of its actual constitution and of the rules of its employment.[2]

I shall not review here the various formulations of the notion of "dialectic" that have sprung up in the course of the history of thought.[3] Nor is it my task to report and discuss the manifold positions taken vis-à-vis the dialectical relationships obtaining between theory and praxis.[4] I shall rest content with availing myself of these relationships for the purpose of opening up a field where a theology of the political can be produced that will be in possession of an awareness of the dialectic that it can and must exercise, as well as of the dialectic in which it is caught up.

My position is that a dialectic "plays" in two distinct and coordinated registers or "keys." The first is a minor key, the second a major key. The minor key is that of the restricted field within which the process of cognition occurs: the sphere of theory, or theoretical practice. The "major key" is that of the broader terrain in which historical movement unfolds: the world of praxis, in its capacity as producer of social reality and by this very fact the abode of theory. This is my initial thesis.[5]

The price of ignoring this difference, which basically resumes that between theoretical practice and social practice, is to fall victim to generalizations and confusions altogether out of place in a question as important as the one that concerns us here.

§59 TWO "KEYS" OF DIALECTIC

The Minor "Key"

In its minor "key," dialectic operates between terms constituting cognition itself. It expresses the movement of theoretical practice, which oscillates between the logical and the positive levels—or, more precisely, between the theoretico-theoretical instance and the theoretico-empirical instance.

Let it be noted that, in these last formulas, the rational element performs the *predominant* role in science. It is precisely the work of the mind that is primary, and that guides the process in question. The empirical, or positive, moment is at play only to the extent that it is somehow determined beforehand by the mind itself. Still, the empirical element is a necessary one in the dialectic of knowledge itself.[6]

When it comes to the "human sciences," this dialectical circuit is no less valid than for the "natural sciences": it operates in every area in a manner tailored to that area. That is, dialectic always depends on the manner of approach assumed by a discipline in obedience to its formal object, or pertinency.

It must be noted that, in every discipline, there is a reciprocal play between the moment of logical construction and the moment of empirical verification—between subject and object. This dialectical reciprocity appears to reproduce, at different stages, what might be called the "circle of truth."[7]

For theology too this dialectic is at play—but, naturally, to the measure of theology. To take the case of the theology of the political, we may say that the terms to be dialecticized are, on the one side, the political, presented by socio-analytic mediation, and on the other, the theological, which is furnished by hermeneutic mediation. Theological intelligence is born of the mutual confrontation of these two elements, within an interlocution regulated by an appropriate syntax, as I have proposed in parts 1 and 2 of this book.

Let it be recalled that, where theology is concerned, it is altogether out of order to subject a theory—in our case the theology of the political—to the jurisdiction of the tribunal of concrete praxis. No, the praxis to which this appeal is made is itself to be established theoretically. There is no way out of the circle of theory, then. Praxis is already subsumed within theology as the material of its labor, the material "upon which" it works, in such wise that its manner of presence in theological space is that of *theoretical* form, which is the only form that can take up that space. Consequently, one must be armed with the necessary epistemological vigilance in order to avoid an oblique relationship of terms—oblique because set up between *disparate* terms, pertaining to two distinct orders.

The better to clarify the case of the relationship between (theological) theory and (social) praxis, let us examine the manner in which theory and praxis appear on the social scene. There is a clear-cut disparity of level between them. This disparity is observable in the manner of organization of various social practices. Cultural institutions generally, and scientific institutions in particular, exist in parallel with and alongside a large number of others. Theoretical practice is performed in parallel with economic practice, political practice, ideological practice, and so on. Each of these practices has its field, its materials, its rules of production, its agents, its specific products, and so forth.

From this viewpoint, theoretical practice, like any other, enjoys a relative autonomy (vis-à-vis other practices). Intellectual labor exists alongside manual labor. The theoretician is a social laborer: a mechanic works with nuts and bolts, the theoretician with ideas and concepts. And the same analogy can be drawn for other types of labor.[8]

The minor, or lesser, circle of dialectic operates only within theoretical practice. It moves not from the concrete to the abstract, but rather from the "thought abstract" to the "thought concrete," from the unknown to the known, from the less known to the more known. This movement arises on the basis of an (epistemological) breach, which signals the passage of nature from one form of reality (an ideological form) to another (a scientific form).

The dialectical process has no final term. Nothing achieved is achieved definitively, but is set in motion in such a way that the pendulum of cognition never comes to a dead stop. When movement comes to a halt at the pole of the subject, we fall into empiricism. When it comes to a halt at the opposite pole, that of theory, we fall into idealism and its like.[9]

Theology is no exception. Theology has always been considered one function among others in the church and society. True, the task of the theologian has been variously evaluated in the course of history, in terms of the importance attributed to symbolic activity by the church and the importance attributed to the church by society at large. But it is equally true that theology has always been considered as a practice, among many others, not to be neglected in the church, and the theologian has always been viewed as having an ecclesial "charism" and a social profession, alongside so many others.[10]

The mode of relationship between specialized function or practice and the totality of ecclesial or social praxis has already been treated, when I dealt with social locus, thematic relevance, and political finality, and even "verification" between theory and praxis. Here we come to a distinction that I have been able to treat as established ever since part 1 (§6), and has been formulated in terms of the *autonomy* and *dependence* of a discipline—the first marking the (formal) *breach* between theory and praxis, the latter marking the (material) *continuity* between the two.

As for the norms by which the relationships between these two terms function, they will be taken up *ex professo* when I broach the question of a *regulated* dialectic.

The Major "Key"

I pass to an examination of the major "key" in which the dialectic of theory and praxis plays. As will become evident, I shall now be speaking of theory and praxis not as processes, but as products. Although the relationship between these two terms is here treated in a broad or extended manner, and we find ourselves on the terrain of the general, it will be useful to stake out part of that terrain—or better, to mark out its confines by distinguishing its respective terms.

At this stage it seems to me appropriate to employ the current vocabulary of theory and praxis without further determinations: my intention is precisely to understand, as far as possible, what these terms mean even in their generality.

In treating this question, I must call attention to the level of discourse to be practiced here. Account must be taken of the fact that a dialectic of theory and praxis can be spoken of only *theoretically*—that is, from and within the element of one of the poles under discussion. There is no other way. Consequently, we must studiously eschew the idealism that, silently insinuating itself under the cloak of discourse, ends by conferring upon ideas the aspect of the reality they designate, even without the thinker's knowing it.

In the course of the extended realization of dialectic, a relationship is established between consciousness and the world, between all manner of thought (reflection, discussion, science, poetry, and so on) and all expression of the real (work, experience, practice, and so on). This distribution remains fluid. It corresponds to what common sense designates as theory and praxis, respectively.[11]

But this is only a beginning. We must now attempt to discern the profile of these immense "continents."

The "everyday" distinction between theory and practice is not, to be sure, purely arbitrary. But neither is it as clear-cut as its terms might suggest. My task will be that of describing the modalities in which the relationship between theory and praxis presents itself in its major key. I distinguish two fundamental modalities here: mutual inclusion, *perichoresis*, and difference, *chorismos*. This is what I shall be examining in the section to follow.

§60 *PERICHORESIS* AND *CHORISMOS* BETWEEN THEORY AND PRAXIS

Perichoresis

If we look closely at the terms "theory" and "praxis," taken separately, we shall observe that, on the one side as on the other, we find common elements or forms, constituting an area of coincidence in which these two spheres are in some fashion mutually inclusive. There obtains, then, a kind of *perichoresis* between theory and praxis.

With respect to theory, there is first of all this basic fact: that it possesses a structural homology, or homomorphism, with other practices. The brain works as much as hands do. Next, there is the fact that theoretical activity can be carried on only when it takes, as its proper material, the world as sensibility, history, practice.[12]

Further: any and every mental activity comes enveloped, *in concreto*, in a whole series of external factors that accompany it and render it possible. Such factors permeate the practice of research, writing, teaching, apprenticeship, and so on—in a word, that whole complexus of material, even technological, apparatus that is necessary for the production of a thought, however metaphysical, poetic, or mystical it may be, and this even without speaking of the general economic and social conditions of any cultural elaboration.

These summary indications will suffice to show that the forms of theoretical work involve, on a greater or lesser scale, material and technical elements by way of support.[13]

Praxis, for its part, understood in the broad sense of any human activity calculated to transform the world, always includes its theory—its reasons, its motivations, its finalities, and so forth. As human, praxis comprises the senses, the meanings, that the individual or transindividual human being, consciously or no, invests in it, in the form of theory, latent or patent. The simple fact that human praxis is intelligible demonstrates that it harbors *rationes* proper to itself.[14]

Similarly, praxis is often accompanied by word, which is the voice of meaning. At times, word actually achieves the realization of the meaning it expresses, in virtue of its *illocutionary* force. At that moment, word—mediation between the regions of theory and praxis—moves unequivocally to the side of the latter.

It is this mutual "overlap" that provides the possibility both of a theory of praxis and of a praxis of theory. Indeed, either can perfectly well be considered as a moment of the other. Theory is in praxis in the form of significations, principles of action, ethical norms, guiding notions, and the like; praxis is part of theory in the form of problems, a desire for change, search, utopia—in short, as question.[15]

Thus the possibility of a vital bond between these two terms must be admitted. I am not yet examining the rhythm of the dialectical relationship. For the time being, I am content with verifying the presence of this relationship and discerning its possibilities.

Let me add only that the dialectical movement can be derailed, both on the side of praxis, and then it will fade into pragmatism, and on the side of theory, where we then have idealism.

Chorismos

Although we must acknowledge a kind of circumincession between theory and praxis, it would be false to reduce the one to the other, and thus destroy their particular differences, on the pretext that they possess common elements. Hence the need to analyze the *chorismos* (difference) between the terms of the theory/praxis relationship.

First of all, we must be careful not to dissolve theory into praxis, on the basis that everything is practice, including theory (theoretical practice). Conversely, neither must we dissolve praxis into theory, on the grounds that everything is theory, including praxis (practical, or practiced, theory).

Even though it is a practice, theory does not cease for all that to be bound to other practices, thus forming an articulated system of practices. This forbids us to conceive of all practices, including theoretical practice, as equivalent on the social plane, after the manner of horses all pulling the same wagon. Such indeed is the hidden pitfall in such expressions as "theoretical practice," "intellectual work," "theory as one practice among others," and so on.

To call "thinking" a practice, then, is not false. But neither does it solve the problem of the relationship of this particular practice to others, most notably with political practice, which can be likened to the "substance" of (all) praxis—and can thus claim the title of "architectonic practice," to use Aristotle's expression. To say, for example, that theoretical practice—unlike ideological, pedagogical, or any other practice—has as its finality cognition and not some other practice, is still not an answer to the question, "What is cognition good for?"

Similarly, activities of "ideal" content and activities of "concrete" content are likewise distributed in either sphere. It is in virtue of this fact that the designations "theory" and "praxis" attach to these respective series of activities, both in current parlance and in that of philosophical tradition. Thus we might say, in the spirit of the former, that it is the "head" and what it produces that is predominant in the field of theory, whereas the "hand" and its works are more broadly represented in the field of praxis.[16]

If we must not confound the two spheres or orders under analysis here, neither must we separate them, and still less set them in mutual opposition as if we were dealing with opposing fields.[17] Such an opposition can be effectuated in two ways: either by setting up praxis against theory, or by setting up theory against praxis.

In the former case, we are confronted, once more, with an artificial, contradictory opposition between the concrete and abstract, between life and thought, between experience and science, between action and study, between objectivity and subjectivity, and so on. I have already criticized this conception, if indeed this be the name for it (see §8).

We are dealing here with a myopic theology—in fact, we might well say that it is blind. Besides being ignorant of that of which it claims to speak, it is ignorant of the contradiction under which it labors, seeking as it does to move to "acts," to "the concrete," to "things"—and remaining all the while in "theory," "the abstract," and the element of "thought" that it condemns. Such is the contradiction of self-styled realists, and practical persons, devotees of "common sense," with their abhorrence of "speculation." They make (practical) pragmatism into a "theory" of their own: but a pitiful theory, one that fails to move on from a pure transcription of an equally pitiful practice. This common, vulgar ideology, which celebrates the virtues of practice in the element of theory, and, in its desire to salvage the grandeur of practice alone, leads directly to opportunism, has already been sufficiently criticized to excuse me from spending more time on it.[18]

At the opposite extreme are those who think to possess the world by the simple fact of possessing its ideas. These are the thinkers who scorn, as illusory and ideological, all knowledge that is not scientific, and all reality not reducible to the form of a concept. Sometimes we have a genuine fetishism here, of a positivistic mold—a fetishism of the concept, whose formulation might be: whatever is *nonconceptualizable* is *inconceivable*. We have already encountered this tendency. It has been called "theoreticism," which in turn is another name for scientism.

But inasmuch as the determination of social locus is not foreign to the ideopolitical definition of a social agent, the following symmetrical correspondence is easily verified: what pragmatism is for "practical persons," theoreticism is for "intellectuals." The latter do more than simply take a theoretical position of particular contours: they adopt an attitude of life, a diffuse, general mentality. It is no wonder, then, that among intellectuals there can be a contradiction between a theoretical position and a practical position. A theoretical nonpositivism can very well coexist with an existential positivism—that is, with a pragmatism.[19]

Now, this position, too, pays the price of a corresponding contradiction. The "theoretical" renunciation of "life" can be perpetrated only within and in virtue of life itself, even if it is life suppressed or forgotten. Thus it is in virtue of the secret force of "life"—that is, of "ideology"—that positivists find it possible to assert what they assert: that science is the only thing that matters.

We have referred more than once to that element of sensitivity by which our body is rooted in the substance of the world and by which our spirit is immersed in the current of life. This rooting and this immersion are such as to prohibit an interpretation of the "breach" of science with the "vital world" (Husserl) in accordance with the material content of metaphor. It permits an interpretation of this "breach" only in accordance with its formal content of metaphor, in the sense that this "breach" transpires on the level of spirit and mind.

After all, even science is more than just a theoretical practice. It is the home of a mentality, a "spirit," which is concretized in a lifestyle, analogously as Aristotle conceived the relationship between a philosophic life and a political life. Now, this spirit entails a monopolistic dynamism, in virtue of which science thinks arbitrarily to impose its measure on the world, on existence, on being.

Hence the contempt shown by "intellectuals" and "educated persons" for popular culture and its manifestations.[20] These aristocrats of the intelligence are ignorant of, or pretend to be ignorant of, the matter of which they are made—they and their knowledge—and the limits that define themselves and that knowledge.

However, that one is abroad on the high seas of empiricism in virtue of an invocation of the "facts," "the concrete," or "life," is true only on the plane of theoretical practice and the prescriptions of its canons—that is, within the minor circle of dialectic. The same will apply to the exhortation *zur Sache* and the like, which, considered critically, smack indisguisably of sensualism.

Science is not existence. It is only one of its expressions. Science occurs localized deep within existence, which is its envelope. Further: science is a historical fact, and as such has no title to necessity or eternity.[21] Nor does science enjoy any intrinsic right to universal dominion. Science is but a form of being, perhaps indeed not of the noblest.[22]

I have already discussed, at the end of §9, the (practical) "leap" to span the gulf dividing theory and praxis—corresponding to the (epistemological) "leap" in the opposite direction, from praxis to theory.

It would be desirable to return to this dialectic to analyze some of its relationships, which I have left somewhat tentative, indeed obscure. For example, it would be worthwhile to delineate in greater detail the theory/awareness and praxis/world relationships, as well as the theory/awareness and theory/science relationships. Will they be thought of in terms of *breach*, or simply in terms of *difference*, or in terms of both at once? But these are questions I cannot study in depth here.

§61 DIALECTICAL MOVEMENT AND ITS RULES

Thus far, we have seen, first, that theory and praxis are de facto bound up with each other, and next, that they are mutually differentiated, "without mixture or confusion." I now propose to reflect on the dialectical movement between these same terms, and to define the nature of this movement in its specific rules.

When we say "dialectic," we think first of all of the ongoing *dynamic* character of the relationship between theory and praxis, whereby these terms alter in and by the very movement of that relationship. Next we think of the *conflictual*, indeed dramatic, structure of this movement, in virtue of the fact of their constitution in mutual contradiction. Finally, "dialectic" also designates for us the aspect of transcendence, of synthesis, of creation, as the effect of the dialectical process itself.

The result of this ceaseless oscillation, called "dialectical movement," is an open—ever *in via*—totalization. Thus the living synthesis is not the pure deed of praxis, without a contribution from theory. This would be only soul, or sense, or meaning. But neither does it pertain to theory alone to unify the whole. This is a unity that can only be the synthesis of both its terms, in a plural, precisely dialectical, unity. This unity is expressed in each sphere in accordance with the proper mode of each: theoretical totality or practical totality. Thus, for example, science, a particular form of theoretical totality, realizes only a relative totalization. And this is part of the very concept of science. Scientific functioning and finality can be effectuated only within a broader totality, which is precisely that of historical dialectic.

Having made these brief observations, I should now like to indicate, in as clear a way as possible, both the formal structure of (the major) dialectic, and the mechanism of its articulation in its simplest expression. To this purpose I shall attempt to illustrate each of these conceptualizations in two diagrams.

The first one, Diagram 8, is in the form of a large circle, representing praxis as a totality. Upon the base of this circle, another opens: that of theory. Of this latter, a third is born: science. Finally, we have one more circle, the fourth and last, within the preceding: that of theology.

The totality of the circles is articulated as a complex whole, as we shall see below. For the moment, however, I shall be content with demonstrating the simple mode of articulation of the so-called dialectical drive, or penchant, as well as the extremes in either direction, both of which lead to antidialectical drives. This is what I attempt to show in Diagram 9. The extreme positions on the chart—those whose thrust is labeled nondialectical—are closed, fixed, immutable totalities: the results of a mechanical, nondialectical process, a frozen movement. These totalities bear on their foreheads the mark of their closure: "-ism"![23]

What has been said about the bond uniting theory and practice is still in the order of simple description here. I have not yet embarked upon its theoretical elucidation. Hence I must move ahead a bit, and examine the complex nature of this process more closely.

I shall attempt, then, to discern the laws of the mechanism binding theory and praxis dialectically. I need only implement suggestions made above, joining them together in a synthetic and ordered formulation.[24]

Diagram 8

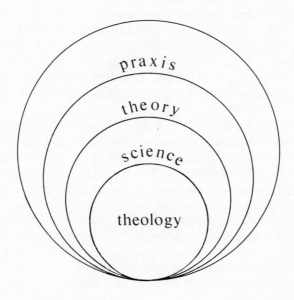

Diagram 9

dialectical drive

pragmatism	PRAXIS	THEORY	theoreticism
determinism	world	awareness	utopianism
positivism	facts	meaning	voluntarism
objectivism	object	subject	subjectivism
empiricism	experience	truth	dogmatism
realism	being	thought	idealism
etc.	etc.	etc.	etc.

nondialectical drive

1. It must first of all be acknowledged that *praxis holds the primacy over theory*. This primacy is of an analytical, not an ethical, character. It is not to be understood as one of mechanical causality, but precisely of dialectical causality. It defines how the one factor is the prime, material condition for the existence of the other. Praxis is de facto the comprehensive element of theory; as such it constitutes the space where theory is localized and defined, the space where it arises, develops, and comes to completion.

2. Theory, for its part, is a *function of praxis*. But it is possessed of its own

proper logic, to which justice must be done. Thus its involvement in praxis is distinctively its own—theoretical; its involvement is that of *symbolic intervention*. This is specifically human activity. Hence we may conclude that it is theory that confers upon action its human character—that is, its essence as praxis, by which human beings freely implement historical meaning and come to their own destiny.[25] What I am saying is: theory holds the key to the identity of praxis. There is no praxis except that borne on the shoulders of theory. Let it be noted, however, that theory is not reducible to the content of awareness, either personal or thematic: the significance of history always surpasses our human awareness of it.[26]

Having thus defined the correlative terms, theory and praxis, in their difference and in their reciprocal "relationality," we must confront the fact that this relationality may not be conceived as something smooth and pacific, as some perfect circle binding homogeneous poles. On the contrary, this relationship must be represented as a current receiving its first thrust from the side of praxis, ricocheting off theory, and returning to praxis and dislocating it—and so on, over and over again. It is in terms of such a "scansion" process, of blow and counterblow, that the dialectic of theory and practice is to be conceived. For each pole of the relationship is qualitatively distinct, and offers its own contribution to each successive provisional synthetization.

As can be seen, then, dialectic is regulated. Otherwise it would be "unthinkable," and would lead us nowhere. If it were absolute surprise, it would utterly destroy the very possibility of thought. On the other hand, the dialectical *ratio* must itself be dialecticized: otherwise it will become a *system*—a system pretending to be the key to the "mystery of history."[27] But in no case may dialectic be regarded as purely rhetorical, or practiced with the immoderation of a Hegelian language. The process is definitely a complex one, not to say enigmatic, perhaps even insoluble.[28] My modest discussion is scarcely adequate to the full extent of the problematic and its importance. But for my particular purposes, it will suffice.

§62 THEOLOGY OF THE POLITICAL WITHIN THE GREATER CIRCUIT OF DIALECTIC

If we must conceive of theology as a particular theoretical practice, we must localize it within the greater circle of dialectic. This will show the relative role it performs.

First of all, although located on the theory side, theology clearly does not constitute *a* theory, much less *all* theory. It is but one theoretical practice among a great number of others. Furthermore, in the form of a theology of the political, it is a theoretical practice having the particularity of always being the latecomer. It comes *after faith*, in virtue of the intervention of hermeneutic mediation, and also *after the "social sciences"* and their hermeneutic mediation.

It is the proper right and constitutive exigency of theology to aim at a theoretical totalization, placing everything, including politics and history, in relation to the Absolute. At the same time, the theological totalization is only *proleptic*: it is proclamation and anticipation of the End as present in history in a transcendental way. And the theoretical formulation of the pistic intent is possible only within the relativity of a culture.

One must be careful, then, not to make of this theological totalization an ideological totalitarianism that will conjure away the determinations and mediations of praxis.[29] Only in the presence of this caution will theology safeguard its right to utter a unique word whose vitality comes from outside itself—the word of salvation.

Such is the place of theology, and of the theology of the political in particular, within the greater dialectic. I acknowledge that, on this level, the network of relationships, complex even at their general level, is yet more complex. For here the issue is the interrelationship of the *lesser dialectic of the theology of the political* with the *greater dialectic of theory and praxis*.

To clarify this point, I have attempted to represent this interrelational articulation in Diagram 10, consisting of a "field" circumscribed by four points.

Diagram 10

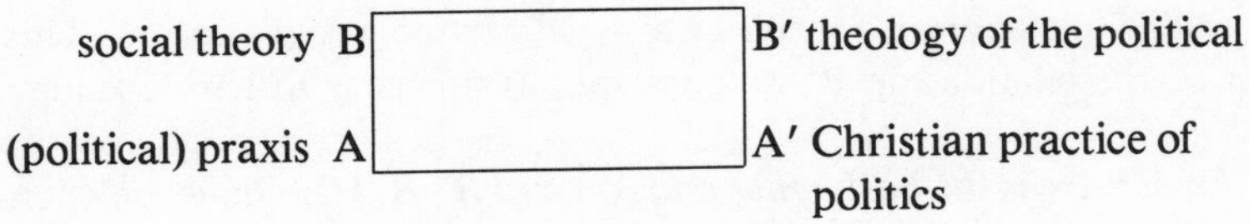

social theory B ⃞ B' theology of the political

(political) praxis A ⃞ A' Christian practice of politics

If we project a *horizontal* line through Diagram 10, cutting the rectangle in two, its content is divided into two levels: level A, that of *praxis*, and level B, that of *theory*. The spatial arrangement, as well as the letters designating each of the four terms, have their signification. They designate the fundamentality of function and primacy of praxis (A, A') vis-à-vis theory (B, B'), which is thus accorded a secondary place.

If we project a *vertical* line through the center of Diagram 10, once more cutting it in two, we obtain an axis A-B, which I shall call the *secular realm*, and an axis A'-B', which I shall call the *religious realm*.[30] Here again, the spatial distribution of the letters, and the letters themselves have their meaning: the simple letters (A, B) represent an order of realities that is given in its simplicity—the "secular realm." The letters with primes (A', B') designate the "religious" realm, which is the secular regime itself *qua* "elevated" to an order of differential signification: the supernatural order.

Using the same dividing lines—the horizontal and the vertical—the same "field" can be depicted as in Diagram 11.

My principal interest here is the situation of B'—that of the theology of the political. My purpose is to come to a grasp of any relationship obtaining

Diagram 11

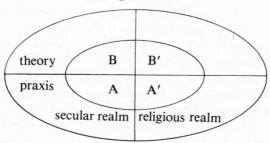

between B' and the other terms of the diagram—the relationships B'-A', B'-B, and B'-A. I shall consider these three relationships individually.

1. First there is the *vertical relationship B'-A'*. Here theology appears as the theoretical expression of the practice of Christians. We do not begin with a theology of the political *simpliciter*, but precisely with a theology of the political-*of-Christians*, or better, a theology of the *Christian practice of politics*. Thus theology is understood as having its feet planted firmly in the living, vital faith of the ecclesial community. It is only via the "detour" of A' that the theologian acquires the necessary conditions for thinking faith correctly, and for thinking the political according to faith. That is to say: it is by way of pistic, or better, agapic, engagement, including engagement in the political field, that the theologian is able to elaborate a theology at once pertinent and relevant. This being the case, the relationship B'-A' corresponds precisely to hermeneutic mediation.[31]

2. Then there is the *horizontal relationship B'-B*. Here dialectic operates on the level of theory. It is on this level that socio-analytic mediation is constituted. But, as we saw in part 1, the relationship B'-B obtains solely under the injunction of the relationship B'-A', in the sense that it is the awareness of engaged Christians that calls for the enlightenment of faith concerning praxis. That is: B' guarantees the relationship A'-B. B' then becomes a mediation of faith. A direct relationship A'-B is seen to be impracticable: it is oblique, diametrical. Bereft of mediation, it tends to complete disarticulation. It is impossible to join a qualified praxis (A') and theory as such (B). Such an attempted relationship is reminiscent of the undertaking, impossible to defend, of "engaged" Christians who, for lack of a secure theological base (B'), which they replace with purely secular schemata (B), end by losing their religious identity (A').

3. Finally, there is the *oblique relationship B'-A*. It suggests mixing all four terms at once: Christian theory and secular praxis. The result of such a questionable combination can only be an explosion! Such a relationship implies that a shortcut has been found, dispensing it from passing by way of A' (hermeneutic mediation), but it ends up in the truly absurd notion of a "secular," "areligious," "atheistic," "post-Christian" theology.

A direct relationship B'-A is as impossible to maintain as a relationship A'-B, because A will tend to pull B' into its field. A "secular" theology, in proportion as it loses the identifying references of faith (A'), can only become social theory (B)—and social theory of the worst kind, because it will be no more than an ideological substitute for the genuine social sciences.

Besides A′, another possible intermediate term for the relationship B′-A is B: so that we would have the relationship B′-B-A. Here we are dealing with socio-analytic mediation. Thus, in the relationship B′-A, or theology-praxis, we find the two essential mediations of the theology of the political: B, socio-analytic mediation, yielding the relationship B′-B-A; and A′, hermeneutic mediation, yielding the relationship B′-A′-A.

These diagrams and explanations are meant to clarify the complex network of internal and external relationships of a theology of the political. There are important mediations at stake here; they can be neglected only under pain of a loss of rigor and vitality on the part of a theology of the political. The dialectical *ratio* proceeds along routes marked out by an established code. Dialectic is neither "injected" (Hegel) nor applied (Althusser). Dialectic is practiced.

§63 WHO HAS THE LAST WORD?

I hope that my explanations have clarified the code of practice of the theology of the political. I have given only a very general sketch here, and it must be filled in and enriched. But I have striven to bring the theoretical status of the theology of the political from a confused, complicated state to one that is clearer, if still complex—from a simple and disordered, to a simplified and articulated, state.[32]

What emerges from these considerations is that the theologian's task represents a genuine challenge to thought. Second theology is still wilderness. We need only to think of its methodological complexity, and then its presuppositions in terms of a first theology, and finally, still closer to its roots, its philosophical premises in terms of a "theology at zero degrees."[33]

The difficulties of a theory, however, do not constitute evidence against the need for the theory. They are evidence against the dispositions of a thinking that is habituated to facility, and innocent of the discipline of a regulated practice.[34] It is no cause for wonder whatever, then, that so many desert this field of endeavor, or acquit themselves of its demands with a few writings hastily baptized "theological" in virtue of a singular *ex opere operato* procedure that yields its results only "if you really have faith."

The hard work required by theological practice today is not only, or even mainly, in the manifold internal mediations that it presupposes, but also, and especially, in the manifold engagements that it implies in the order of pistic experience and agapic practice—as indeed theological tradition itself shows.[35] These preconditions of theology acquire a particular urgency in our time, especially because faith is lived today in a webwork of coordinates that are both new and unprecedented, and marked off by historical confrontations that are transformed into the new locus of the exercise of the theological *logos*.

But without allowing this to constitute a pretext either for theoretical indolence or, at the opposite extreme, for theoretical impatience, we are constrained, when all is said and done, to acknowledge that the emergence of a new discourse of faith, geared to current urgencies, depends more on practical engagement than on theoretical effort, difficult as the latter may seem and be. After all, if it is true that this is precisely the terrain where faith is "lost," so also it will be here that faith has the best chances of being "found again," and of sounding forth its original word once more.

I may even say: the discourse of faith is conditioned by an even more basic eventuality—the course of history. Theology, too, takes time. One does not do the theology one would like; one does the theology one can.[36] *Summae* are possible only when a historical phase has completed its ascent. Thus it may be doubted whether we today dispose of all the theoretical, pistic, and especially historical conditions necessary to produce a genuine theology of the political. We are certainly capable of "doing theology" today, and of "doing political science" (if only recently). But perhaps we are not yet in a position to do a theology of the political, even though we may be sure of its logical possibility and its epistemological principles.

Meanwhile, the relationship between faith and politics remains the charge of the experience of Christian communities and of the religious discourse corresponding to that experience. This discourse may not be destined to rise above the plain and simple dialect of a geographically scattered and historically marginal subgroup. But the destiny of faith lies not in the future of history, but in the future of God.

Theology has a process of maturation to undergo, which will take its own time. After all, all things come at their *kairos*. But this *kairos* appears as such only to those who await its coming. Isaiah knew this all too well:

> They call to me from Seir,
> "Watchman, how much longer the night?
> Watchman, how much longer the night?"
> The watchman replies,
> "Morning has come, and again night.
> If you will ask, ask; come back again" [Isa. 21:11–12].

Summary of Conclusions

I have completed my study, and the time has come to sum up my conclusions. I shall present them in a series of theses stating my epistemological positions, whose rational justification and general articulation has been presented in the body of the text. These theses will be of a frankly epistemological nature, then, and their content will be now dogmatic, now historical. All of them, however, concern the theoretical status of the theology of the political.

GENERAL EPISTEMOLOGICAL PRINCIPLES AND APPROACH

The theology of the political is constructed on the basis of two fundamental theoretical mediations: socio-analytical and hermeneutic. The former furnishes the material object of this theology, the latter its specific means of production. Further: the (theological) theory that functions here is continuously determined by the dialectical relationship it maintains with praxis (the praxis of faith), and at the same time brings to bear its own determination of this praxis, in its proper manner—that is, theoretically. Finally, although both mediations are to be understood as falling in the category of the *medium quo* of this theology, praxis is related to it as its *medium in quo* (Preface).

PART 1

1. Socio-analytical mediation seeks to apprehend the autonomous nature of the material, or thematic, of the theology of the political—namely, the political—but always for the sake of theology (or here, with a view to the "new problematic" of this theology) (Introduction to part 1).

Chapter 1

2. Socio-analytical mediation is required by theology principally in virtue of its point of departure in, and in function of, praxis, and in a particular manner: that of a "Christian praxis of politics" (§2).
3. Socio-analytical mediation is not incumbent upon the theology of the political principally in virtue of the demands of the unity of knowledge, or social critique, or pastoral problems, or the sociology of theological knowledge (§1).
4. The traditional approach of moral theology to the social suffers from two

absences: (a) that of the objectively theological sense of social practices (on the level of the object, and therefore on that of the area of interpretation), and (b) that of the structural character of social relationships (on the level of method, and consequently on that of the area of "interpellation," or moral demand) (§3).

5. The philosophical mediation of traditional social theology, by reason of its speculative, and hence idealistic, tendency, demonstrates its insufficiency for the clarification of praxis in its concrete forms today (§§2, 3).

6. Philosophical mediation is incumbent upon the theology of the political to the extent to which political practice and theoretical practice demand it—thus, and especially, in the area of ethics (§3; see also §56).

7. Philosophical mediation is (extrinsically) constitutive of a "first theology" in the measure that it concerns the humanity of the Christian human being and the divinity of the God of Jesus Christ (§4; see also §27).

8. From a point of departure in, and beyond the confines of, praxis, contemporary culture itself demands that theology incorporate (as an extrinsically constitutive element) the new *episteme*—the sciences of the human being, including the "social sciences" (§4).

9. A theology that, since the appearance of the sciences of the social, (still) usurps their place in the cultural area can only be exercising an objectively ideological function ("ideological 1") in respect of the culture in question (§4).

10. Since the work of Marx, theology may no longer bracket the material conditions of existence, under pain of mystifying the reality of evil and unjust situations after the manner of an ideology ("ideological 2"). The theological word concerning the social enjoys credit only as "second word"—that is, only after having done justice to a secular consideration of those conditions. This is the precise function of socio-analytic mediation as (extrinsically) constitutive of theology (§5).

11. A political or social theology lacking the capacity, or its actualization, to accept analytic mediation would have to be subjected to a process of "de-theologization," as a prerequisite for its adequate "re-theologization" (§5).

12. Lest theological practice succumb either to empiricism, theoretical pragmatism, or epistemological idealism, it must be recognized as comprising two distinct, but inseparable, "regimes": one internal and the other external. The former is defined by the *autonomy* of theoretical practice, whose rules are to be respected. The latter corresponds to the *dependence* of theology on the social conditions of productivity—that is, on the economy of cultural goods, of which theological products constitute one area, and over which it is incumbent on the theologian to exercise permanent ideo-political vigilance (§§6, 7).

Chapter 2

13. The "epistemological obstacles" of a theology of the political are fundamental theoretical dispositions that impede, or even completely obstruct, the articulation of this theology, particularly in its relationship with the sciences of the social (§8).

14. All theological discourse upon the social supposes a sociological theory, either spontaneous or critical. An immediate or intuitive reading of society today involves *empiricism*, which constitutes a basic "epistemological obstacle" to the establishment of a correct theology of the political (§8).

15. The empiricist antithesis between "concrete and abstract," or between "practical and theoretical," not only forms an *in actu* contradiction, but also ignores, on the one hand, the fact that theoretical practice, and hence also theology, is genuine practice, producing the "cogitated concrete"—and on the other hand, the fact that concrete practice is always impregnated by theory (§8).

16. Among several "epistemological obstacles" to the establishment of socioanalytic mediation are: "methodological purism," which neglects the historico-cultural status of theological language; "theologism," which (mis) takes theology for a universal, even totalitarian, discourse; and especially, "semantic mix" and "bilingualism," which prevent reflection, in appropriate terms, on the specific place and function of the sciences of the social with respect to theology and vice versa (§§9–12).

17. The relationship of mediation, by way of socio-analytic mediation, between the theology of the political and the sciences of the social is not a simple relationship of juxtaposition, but one of (extrinsic) *constitution*, in the sense that the findings of the sciences of the social become constitutive parts of the theoretical process, in its generation of an adequate raw material, or material object, for the theology of the political (§13).

18. Inasmuch as, to the eyes of faith, all things relate to God, for theological practice there will be nothing that is not "theologizable" in principle. The theoretical field of the theology of the political can therefore extend to all praxis, even to a political practice declaring itself atheistic. It belongs to practical theology to produce "the theological," even at the price of a breach, or "rupture," in the form of a renunciation of explicit theological language (§14).

19. The primary *theoretical* object of a theology of the political is constituted by real situations and concrete practices, not by religious or ideo-political representations constructed of them by social agents (§14).

Chapter 3

20. Although assimilating the benefits of the sciences of the social through socio-analytic mediation, a theology of the political must at the same time safeguard the rights of the "truth of faith" against all attempts at ideologization— that is, at the "denaturing" of that faith (§15).

21. Ideological declaration fails to transcend the level of gratuitous, vacuous imputation, unless it be the result of a process of judgment. Indeed such declaration assumes its ideological content to be already established, which is tantamount to begging the question as to what constitutes the "real" that is at issue (§15).

22. The particular theology of a political practice does not degrade faith to the level of an ideology; on the contrary, it does justice to its truth, as long as it acknowledges its own particularity, in function of the "incarnational" status of faith and the consequent plurality of practices that are rendered possible by the transcendency of faith (§16).

23. Besides its neutral use to denote a complexus of forms of consciousness ("ideological zero"), the term "ideology" can be used to denote discourse organized in *immediate* (undistanced, uncritical) service of a given practice ("ideological 1"), or discourse deliberately masking the reality of an (unjust) social situation ("ideological 2"). In both cases, however, only an exercise of (analytical) critique can impart the designation "ideological" (§17).

24. From the standpoint of the real Object intended (the *significatum*), theology, by definition, is the language of the Absolute and the Transcendent. But from the standpoint of the concepts and linguistic propositions of its intention (its *modus significandi*), theology is necessarily a relative and historical language—that is, what I have called a *regional* language (§18).

25. In order to delimit with precision the theoretical status of theological language, especially in the case of a theology of the political, the distinction between the *real object* and its *knowledge* must be kept clear: each of these is autonomous in its own order and process (§18).

26. Although the classic theologies of history are orientated more toward contemplation than action, they furnish a theology of the political with an indispensable type of reflection, inasmuch as this theology must ascribe to historical practices a universal and transhistorical signification (§19).

Chapter 4

27. The constitutional relationship obtaining between a theology of the political and the sciences of the social in virtue of socio-analytic mediation can be realized only through the antecedent application of certain concrete means—in particular, those of the "deontological code" governing the interrelationships of the various disciplines. This deontological code can be condensed into two principles: that of mutual *respect* for the autonomy of each discipline, and that of a relentless *critique* of any and all unwarranted extrapolation, especially in the form of a dogmatism of thought (§20).

28. Theology must address Marxism just as it addresses any other social theory—that is, in conformity with the deontological code. Thus, as regards Marxism, it is obligated to distinguish between its *hypothetico-scientific* aspect (historical materialism), which theology is bound to respect, and its *philosophico-metaphysical* aspect (dialectical materialism), which theology can only criticize and reject (§21).

29. In choosing between the functionalist orientation and the dialectical orientation of current social theories, a theology of the political will submit to two kinds of criteria, those of a *scientific* order and those of an *ethical* order, keeping well in mind that it is the ethical criteria that will determine the selection of the scientific criteria, as indeed can be gathered from an examination of the political practices of the most conscientious Christian communities (§22).

30. As to the product of socio-analytic mediation, in terms of the material object of a theology of politics, it is to be observed that this is forthcoming from research in progress. At the same time, it will be appropriate to emphasize that it is much more important to form a *socio-analytic expertise* than to remain habitually dependent upon available analyses (§23).

PART 2

31. Hermeneutic mediation is mediation responsible for the theological *formality* of the theology of the political (Introduction to part 2).

Chapter 5

A theory can be theological only in virtue of its *pertinency*—that is, in virtue of its formal object (§24).

32. It is erroneous to apply the label "theological" to discourses in virtue simply of the fact that they adopt a "religious" topic. If they apply to their object any other mode of treatment than that of theology, they are theologically nonpertinent discourses (§24).

33. According to Louis Althusser, theoretical practice consists in a process of transformation of a given raw material (first generality) into a determinate product (third generality) according to certain definite means of production (second generality)—all on the level of thought (§25).

34. According to Thomas Aquinas, theology, like any other theoretical practice, can be said to proceed by transforming any first generality into a specific third generality by the operation of the proper principles of its second generality, which are precisely the *articuli fidei* (§26).

35. Theological pertinency, which identifies the "theologicity" of a given discourse, is constituted by the relationship of this discourse to the positivity of faith (word of revelation)—a relationship observable on the level of second generality, which is the determining instance of the process of theological knowledge (§26).

36. Both a "topical" epistemology (Melchior Cano) and an epistemology of "common experience" (Augustinianism) fall short of the imperatives of the rationality of faith, especially of those of the "Christian practice of politics" (§26).

37. To assert that "life" is a *locus theologicus* is to open the way to the most pernicious errors. This position can be defended only if "life" is understood in the sense of raw material, or else in the sense of a *medium in quo* of theology, but in no case as in the sense of a second generality or *medium quo* (§26).

38. The theology of the political is not opposed to "classic" theology, nor does it replace it. On the contrary, it presupposes it, in the moment of its second generality, to the extent that this too needs to be constituted (§27).

39. A first theology, corresponding to "classic" theology, and concerned with "religious" realities, is to be distinguished from a second theology, which treats of "secular" realities, hence also of the political. Mediations of the former are primarily philosophical; those of the latter are primarily analytical, or positive (§27 and Presentation).

40. In order to avoid both a conflict in interpretations, and a formal, vacuous harmony, it is necessary to articulate various discursive levels, presupposed in a theology of the political, according to the various loci or instances of the theoretical practice of theology. Thus the first generality of a theology of the political is constituted by the third generality of a social analysis, whereas the third generality of a first theology constitutes the second generality of a theology of the political (§28).

41. The so-called Chalcedonian dialectic is too general and formal a model for the articulation of faith and politics: first, it cannot transcend "semantic mix" and "bilingualism"; secondly, it is unable to theorize concrete situations of practice (§28).

42. The epistemological principles established by Thomas Aquinas in the question 1 of the *Summa Theologiae* is an adequate basis for a proper conceptualization of the theoretical status of a second theology and its correct articulation with the languages it presupposes (§28).

Chapter 6

43. The discourse of the theology of the political can only "speak the truth" in appropriate fashion on condition that its field of reference (its "real") has been previously established and fittingly organized (§29).

44. Inasmuch as a certain circularity obtains between method and object, epistemology is constrained to concern itself with the actual nature of the theological area itself, proposing, with a view to a second theology, a reinterpretation of the model categories of first theology through their general restructuring. Thus this *recasting* is at once the prerequisite and the effect of a sound theology of the political (§29).

45. In order to provide the foundation for the peculiar objectivity of (Christian) theology, a basic distinction must be drawn between the *reality* of salvation, or of the supernatural order, and the *consciousness* that may be had of this salvation or supernatural order. Thus the order of salvation is anterior to consciousness of it and independent of its content, be that content immediate (faith/revelation) or subsequently thematized critically (theology) (§30).

46. For the theological *ratio*, and a fortiori for the eyes of faith, no "natural order" exists as a historical realization. The "natural order" is only a conceptual construct, necessary for comprehending the gratuity of the supernatural order, which is the only order in real existence, and in which alone all human beings are constituted, whether they are aware of it or not (§30).

47. The order of salvation resolves existentially into grace or sin, according to the decisions of human freedom as expressed in concrete practices. The practice of *agape* is the appropriate and adequate practice for the assimilation of salvation as grace (§31).

48. Where the practice of *agape* in the political area is concerned, theology has the function of theoretically overcoming the break between ethical and objective structures, in such wise as to make possible the transcendence both of an individualistic conceptualization of salvation (Marx's "Robinsonized" conceptualization) and a fatalistic conceptualization (§31).

49. The *logocentric* interpretation of Christian positivity, to the extent that it prioritizes a constitutive consciousness and its (religious) expressions, fails to do justice to the nature of salvation as an objective, *sui generis* reality (§32).

Chapter 7

50. The forms of the expression of salvation, however conformed in relation to their object, admit of a diversity in relation to their functions (§33).

51. Faith is the conscious (noetic or experiential) appropriation of salvation. It is the (ever ambiguous) phenomenon of salvation in the area of personal awareness as the effect of revelation (§35).

52. Religion—or more concretely, the church—is the phenomenon of faith in the socio-cultural area. It is the emblematic realm of salvation, and hence the locus of the identification, doxological (liturgical) manifestation, and kerygmatic (missionary) manifestation of salvation (§35).

53. As social institution, the church is to be considered as a particular, autonomous sector in the social whole, and always articulated upon this whole (§35).

54. Christian identity consists in the capacity of a Christian to discover the soteriological (concretely, the christic) sense of the world and history, in virtue of the word of revelation functioning after the manner of a reading code (§35).

55. On the plane of *theoretical object*, theology is dependent on the word of revelation, which furnishes it with the principles of its proper practice. On the plane of *mode of knowledge*, however, and the linguistic expression of this mode, *religious discourse* and *theological discourse* are to be distinguished (§33).

56. The formal difference distinguishing theological language from religious language was identified by Thomas Aquinas, but without an *ex professo* treatment. Thomas, most unfortunately, posited this difference in the heterogeneous unity of what was represented by the notion of *sacra doctrina* (§34).

57. Religious language operates under the rules of everyday language. Accordingly, it is subject to the "economy of the unconscious," which is structured especially upon the mechanisms of metaphor and metonomy (§36).

58. Unlike religious language, theological language is characterized by its *criticity*—that is, by its vigilance over its procedures and operations, as expressed in an effort of analytical rigor, and in a search for a systematic organization of the intellection of the faith (§36).

59. In order for a particular language of a theology of the political to be able to operate, the simple reciprocal relationship between faith and politics prescribed by the Chalcedonian model is insufficient. Rather, the more fertile model of theoretical practice must be invoked, which makes possible the discernment in politics (first generality), from a point of departure in faith (second generality), the extent of the "incarnation" of divine salvation *in* human history (third generality: the theology of the political) (§37).

Chapter 8

60. In order to constitute its second generality, a theology of the political must refer to Christian positivity. This task can be executed in critical fashion only through an appropriate reading of the Christian writings, especially the foundational or canonical, texts of the faith. This is precisely the function of hermeneutic mediation (§38).

61. The "hermeneutic circle" is a dialectical recourse permitting the articulation of the work of interpretation while avoiding the extreme positions of "hermeneutic improvisation" and "semantic positivism." Thus the seat of sense or meaning appears not in (paired) terms, but in the *relationship* between such terms (§39).

62. The concept of the "closure of revelation" not only presents no obstacle to a hermeneutic of political intent, but is actually its basis, in the sense that the "closure" of scripture as scripture implies the opening of its message to ulterior interpretations. Thus the canonical character of scripture takes the form of a *model interpretation*, or hermeneutic paradigm (*norma normata ut normans*) (§40).

63. The relationship between gospel and politics in terms of "model of application" is marked by a mechanical or juridical, and hence antidialectical, character. Further, it leaves out of account the historical context of each of its terms. Hence it leads to an impasse, ending in the suppression of one of the terms of the relationship (§42).

64. In the concrete case of a theology of the political, the normative character of scripture does not consist in being a "master copy," to be reproduced mechanically, as the "model of correspondence of terms" tends to represent it (§41).

65. A consideration of the hermeneutic practice of the primitive community, as well as the daily hermeneutic of the various Christian communities of today, leads me to propose, as an alternative to the "model of correspondence of terms," a "model of correspondence of relationships." This model is distinguished by its concern for a basic, organic *homosemy* between past sense of scripture and present sense of historical situations. To this end, it ascribes a more important place to the living memory and creative fidelity of the interpreting community (§§41, 42).

66. The "model of correspondence of relationships" presupposes in the theologian such a "hermeneutic spirit" as will accord the praxis of Christians a primacy over the texts of scriptures as such, together with a concern for the acquisition of a *hermeneutic skillfulness* that will eschew any dependency on fragmentary analyses and particular applications (§43).

PART 3

67. Any theory, hence also theology, is concretely subject to the influence of praxis as its vital milieu (*medium in quo*). This subordination is registered on three levels: that of the theologian's social involvement, that of the historical relevance of a theme, and that of the political intent of a theology (Introduction to part 3).

Chapter 9

68. Praxis alters (theological) theory primarily in virtue of the fact that theory, like its producer, is always, willy-nilly, situated in a framework of social relationships (§44).

69. The real problem for a theologian is not that of knowing whether a theology is "engaged" or "alienated" (in its social situation), but that of determining *which* engagement to assume, *which* political position to adopt—and this on the level of theory itself (§44).

70. No univocal, direct relationship necessarily obtains between social engagement (in the sense of position) and theoretical engagement. Each of the two has its own order of proper demands, which cannot be overstepped without an inversion of orders (§45).

71. The difference between social engagement and theoretical engagement demonstrates the discrepancy, and at times the contradiction, between theoretical truth and political justice in a particular theological discourse or the work of a particular theologian (§45).

72. Although a discontinuity between theory and practice is to be admitted, a determinate social position *permits* a corresponding theological discourse— but only as to theoretical object and style. Social position does not determine the theoretical quality of a theology. This quality depends on the internal criteria assumed by the theology in question, by which alone it is to be judged (§46).

73. It is always possible to procure a correspondence between social engagement and theoretical engagement. This correspondence is effectuated through a *living synthesis* between political objective and theoretical objective, on the one hand, and on the other, between social agent and theoretical agent (§46).

74. A synthesis of theology and politics can take various forms, depending on the terms it prioritizes. Three basic models of synthesis can be identified here: (a) the "model of specific contribution," according to which the theoretical product as such acquires a political signification; (b) the "model of alternation of moments" between theoretical practice and political practice; and (c) the "model of incarnation," which implies a profound involvement of life and lot with those of the groups in question (§47).

75. In order to identify the most adequate type of synthesis, it is necessary to "dialecticize" the social data and subjective data of a given concrete situation, while safeguarding the primacy of praxis over theory, in analysis as well as in strategy (§47).

Chapter 10

76. Praxis exerts an influence on (theological) theory inasmuch as the (real) *problems* of praxis are taken up by theory under the form of (theoretical) *questions*. Thus theory has its origin in praxis. Theory is always marked by praxis, even when it effectuates a "rupture" in its regard (§48).

77. The notion of "relevance" defines the relationship of a theory to the socio-historical conjuncture that furnishes it its subjects. "Relevance" designates the system of questions proposed for reflection by a given historical moment (§49).

78. Every theology de facto treats of what it subjectively deems to have a relationship to the exigencies of its own historical moment. Thus the thematic problem does not consist in finding "relevant" subjects or themes, but in consciously deciding *which* "thematic" is of objective relevance or significance with respect to a given socio-historical conjuncture (§§49, 50).

79. In order to judge which thematic relevance ought to be assumed in theological practice, one must have recourse to judgments of experience and judgments of analysis, placing them in a reciprocal relationship (§50).

80. The meaning of the kerygma itself is not indifferent to the question of ideological resonances that that meaning can be lent by a given historical conjuncture. As a consequence, the very truth of the kerygma demands an attitude of vigilance with regard to its potential ideo-political effects (§50).

Chapter 11

81. (Political) praxis likewise exerts an influence on (theological) theory, inasmuch as theory has a role in the interplay of social interests and political strategies (§51).

82. Any theory, hence also theology, is at once disinterested and interested, depending on whether it is considered from the viewpoint of its autonomy or from that of its dependency. Accordingly, knowledge has both the rationale of *end*, for theoretical practice, and the rationale of *means* or mediation, for the higher ends of political practice (§51).

83. In a given theoretical practice, a *real* relationship between interest and disinterestedness always obtains; the former determines the latter, without thereby necessarily denaturing it (§52).

84. Inasmuch as (theological) theory is always interested—that is, politically orientated—it is of the first importance for theologians to know *which* concrete causes call for the mediation of their theoretical practice (§52).

85. In order to control the political intent of theology in the exercise of ideo-political vigilance, one must have recourse simultaneously to analytical judgments and ethical evaluations (§52).

86. In a political conjuncture torn by class conflict, theology is objectively *partial*, or classist. It is of key importance, then, to know for *which* class to "do theology" (§52).

87. Theory and practice are not situated on a continuum. A radical discontinuity intervenes. This discontinuity can be transcended only by a *leap*, such as in an act that is creative of freedom. This is the only sense in which it is true that theory is transcended by praxis (§52).

Chapter 12

88. To posit praxis as a criterion of truth implies empiricism and leads to pragmatism. It conjures away not only the theoretical problem, but the ethical one as well, which consists in asking *which* praxis and *which* theory are being referred to when this thesis is advanced (§54).

89. Theological criteriology is distinct from pistic criteriology, although they are interlinked (§55).

90. Theological criteriology is of a *theoretical* order (orthodoxy). It embraces two instances: one of a *logical* nature—namely, the cohesiveness of the system of propositions in a theology—and the other of a positive nature—that is, the conformity of the theology in question with the positivity of faith (§55).

91. The criteriology of faith is of a *practical* order (orthopraxis). It likewise comports two instances, with reciprocal ties: faith criticizes praxis in respect of its (liberating) signification, and praxis criticizes faith in respect of the historical realization of its intentionality (§56).

92. Although formally distinct from the practice of faith, the practice of theology is not really separated from it. Accordingly, the practice of faith is determinative for *ecclesial credibility*. At the same time, the practice of faith procures the rational justifications of which it stands in need by its alliance with theology (§57).

Chapter 13

93. Dialectic is to be conceived more as a basic disposition of thought than as a particular method. It consists in a permanent effort to transcend what has already been acquired (§58).

94. Two modes of dialectic can be distinguished: one in a minor key, and the other in a major key. The former operates between the constitutive terms of theoretical practice; the latter intervenes on the level of theory and practice at the heart of history (§59).

95. Where the theology of the political is concerned, the minor-key dialectic operates between the two basic mediations that constitute the theology of the political—that is, socio-analytic mediation and hermeneutic mediation (§59).

96. The major-key dialectic—that is, the dialectic operating between theory and praxis in general—presupposes a mutual inclusion (*perichoresis*) as well as a difference (*chorismos*) between its terms. These two presuppositions must be correctly apprehended in order to be themselves correctly dialecticized (§60).

97. A dialectic of theory and praxis is never realized in a purely formal manner, without any limit, but only according to the injunctions of an axiomatic: praxis exerts pressure on theory (thesis); theory, reacting, modifies praxis (antithesis); theory and praxis are transcended, and sublimated in a synthesis; and so on in that order (§61).

98. The minor-key dialectic (operating between socio-analytic and hermeneutic mediations) is situated within the major-key dialectic (between theory and praxis), which latter translates the movement of the totality of history. The former dialectic operates at the heart of the latter from a point of departure in its own autonomous principles, but remains ultimately dependent on the enigmatic determination of history itself (§§62, 63).

Notes

Works lacking full bibliographical details are listed in the Bibliographic References, p. 337.

PREFACE

1. One of the liberation theologians, Ignacio Ellacuría, has drawn up a kind of taxonomy of these postulates, with one hundred propositions: "Tesis sobre la posibilidad, necesidad y sentido de una teología latinoamericana." A global survey of the theoretical positions of liberation theology has been made by J. van Niewenhove: "Rapports entre foi et praxis dans la théologie de la libération latino-américaine." Van Niewenhove (pp. 80–208) studies the method of four liberation theologians in particular: Eduardo Pironio, J. A. Hernández, Gustavo Gutiérrez, and Hugo Assmann. My study presupposes such work of a more positive and analytical nature, and proceeds to a discussion of methodological points.

2. Artistotle, *Metaphysics*, book 2, chap. 3 (995a12–13), p. 513.

3. *In Boethii de Trinitate*, q. 6., a. 1, ad 3; see also ibid., lectio 2: "*Ante scientiam oportet inquirere modum sciendi.*" See also Hugo of Saint Victor, *Didascalion*, book 3, chap. 3 (786C): "*Scholastici autem nostri aut nolunt aut nesciunt modum congruum, in discendo servare, et idcirco multos studentes, paucos sapientes invenimus.*"

4. This is one of the great lessons of Gaston Bachelard's epistemology, to which I shall have occasion to refer later in this study. See his *La philosophie du Non*, pp. 8, 48, 72, 138; and his *Le rationalisme appliqué*, pp. 15, 29, 47–48, 104, 112–13, 135.

5. See, e.g., Raúl Vidales, "Crônica de algumas publicações recentes na América Latina sobre 'Teologia da Libertação,'" *Concilium* 96 (1974) 792–800; Hugo Assmann, *Nomad Church*, pp. 56–64; Gustavo Gutiérrez, "Movimentos de libertação e teologia," *Concilium* 93 (1974) 403–12, esp. 411–12. Another liberation theologian, L. Gera, referring to the three moments of the "scheme of reflection" adopted by the theology of liberation—seeing, judging, and action, following *Gaudium et Spes* (1965) and the Medellín documents—observes: "Up to the present, so far as I know, we do not yet have available a relatively complete and adequate study of the epistemological implications of the said schema (and object) of reflection—nor one on the nature and viability of the method it seeks to put in practice. It is one of so many tasks that remain to be carried out" ("Cultura y dependencia," p. 179). See also P. Rochette, "Théologies de la libération," pp. 82–83: "To put it simply: demanding as it may be, the important thing is to 'do' theology, and not to sidestep the crisis of its foundations through which the theological enterprise is passing in our day. A patient detour by way of the question of the identification of the discourse upon God is not a bourgeois luxury when one considers the demands of the contemporary world: it is a test of honesty and 'radicality' in the face of these demands." In this vein, after a "critical evaluation" of the theology of liberation,

which he censures for a "precipitant dogmatism" with respect to the relationship between salvation and liberation, a "tendency to prioritize horizontality," the absence both of the idea of "incarnation" and of any "theonomic reference," Rochette concludes that the "theology of liberation fails to liberate theology" (pp. 82–84).

6. "Documents de Medellín, I" (Portuguese translation), in SEDOC 1 (1968) 5, col. 667, 2nd ed.

7. For my use of the term "mediation," and especially for the expression "socio-analytic mediation," I draw inspiration from the tenor of Hugo Assmann's approach in his *Theology for a Nomad Church*, pp. 59–64, 115–19. In justification of my composite term "socio-analytic," I appeal to the positive analyses of the social sciences—the political sciences, economics, anthropology, social psychology, history, and especially sociology. I leave aside, then, other mediations, however possible and legitimate they may be: philosophical mediation, psychological mediation, linguistic or literary mediation, and so on. In the contemporary productions of liberation theology other qualifiers implying "mediation" are to be found: "critical," "scientific," "theoretical," "rational," "dialectical," or simply "analytical." These designations seem less precise than the one I have chosen and shall normally employ: "*socio-analytic* mediation."

8. The last column to the right has been added to allow space in this schema for the theoretico-practical methodology of Catholic Action: see Assmann, *Nomad Church*, pp. 63, 112–13. Leonardo Boff (*Teologia do cativeiro*, p. 28) thinks that these three steps signal a "genuine methodological revolution." See also Gera, "Cultura y dependencia," p. 179. For an example of the three moments of seeing, judging, and acting at work, see the documents: Bispos do Centro-Oeste, *A Marginalização de um povo*; and Bispos e Superiores Religiosos do Nordeste, *Eu ouvi os clamores do meu povo*—both dated May 6, 1973.

9. On the much-discussed extension of the concept of epistemology, see R. Blanché, *L'épistemologie*, pp. 29–33; also Jean Ladrière, "Sciences et discours rationnel," pp. 754–55. The tendency today is to reserve the use of the term "epistemology" for the criticism of "sciences" in the modern sense of the term, as in the works of the followers of Louis Althusser, which have appeared in the Théorie series published by Maspero (Paris) beginning in 1965. See Balibar and Macherey, "Epistémologie." For Althusser, "theory" is: "the theory within the science itself, the system of theoretical concepts on which is based every method, and every practice, even the experimental method and practice, and which simultaneously defines its theoretical object" (*Reading Capital*, p. 109); see also his *Pour Marx*, pp. 168ff.

10. This is Gaston Bachelard's distinction, which he uses, e.g., in *La Formation de l'esprit scientifique*, p. 10. Note that the expression "architectonic [reason]" appears in Aristotle, *Nichomachaean Ethics*, book 6, chap. 8 (1141b, 4–22) ["practical wisdom," in the Ross translation, p. 390].

11. Let us take as directed toward the epistemology of theology what Henry Duméry has remarked about the status of the philosophy of religion: "The conclusion is not in polemics. It is in logic. But logic demands that one know whereof one speaks—that one clearly enunciate what the formal element of philosophy is and what the formal element of theology is. Failing these precisions, an abundance of historical references does not shed more light—it creates more confusion, and occasions quite a heavy tumble as one falls short of the distinctions that seven hundred years of philosophical practice have had the merit of establishing and imposing" (*Raison et religion dans la philosophie*, p. 593). It is evident, then, that a voluntaristic or consensualistic conception of theological epistemology is out of the question.

12. See Althusser, *Philosophie et philosophie spontanée*, pp. 13-15, 55-61.

13. I am well aware of the cautions to be observed in any transposition of Bachelard's concepts from the physical sciences—their basic and specific field of application—to other epistemological areas. See the observations of Michel Fichant, "Epistémologie," esp. pp. 158-59.

14. "For it may be that in everything, as the saying is, 'the first start is the main part': and for this reason also it is the most difficult; for in proportion as it is most potent in its influence, so it is smallest in its compass and therefore most difficult to see: whereas when this is once discovered, it is easier to add and develop the remainder in connexion with it. This is in fact what has happened in regard to rhetorical speeches and to practically all the other arts" (Aristotle, *On Sophistical Refutations*, chap. 34 [183b21-27], p. 253).

15. See Thomas Aquinas, *Summa Theol.*, I, q. 1, a. 7, "*Utrum Deus Sit Subjectum hujus Scientiae*," especially in the corpus: "*Omnia autem tractantur in sacra doctrina* [i.e., theology] *sub ratione Dei: vel quia sunt ipse Deus* [first theology], *vel quia habent ordinem ad Deum, ut ad principium et finem* [second theology]."

16. As to the "novelty" of second theology, the following might be a fair statement of the situation. It has only been since the 1930s that theology has begun to take a theological interest in "earthly realities" *qua* earthly. (It was always interested in them, but only qua "religious" or "sacred.") There have been two currents of thought here: one Anglo-Saxon, beginning with F. Gogarten and Dietrich Bonhoeffer and continuing through J. A. T. Robinson to the group of American "radical" or "secular" or "death of God" theologians such as Thomas J. J. Altizer, William Hamilton, Paul Van Buren, and Harvey Cox; and the other Francophone, beginning with Pierre Teilhard de Chardin and Gustave Thils, and issuing in Vatican II with the Pastoral Constitution *Gaudium et Spes*, this document spilling over, in Latin America, into the Medellín documents, which in turn have opened the field for the "theology of liberation." At all events, we have since Vatican II a kind of detonation of the thematic universe of theology, fragmenting into the most varied, indeed contrary directions, producing, one might say, theologies *de omni re scibili et quibusdam aliis*.

In order to gather a realistic idea of the "novelty" of the "new theological thematic," one need only look at G. Baraúna's survey of articles in the 20,000 pages of the *Dictionnaire de la Théologie Catholique*, where the subjects examined are God, the soul, angels, demons, saints, worship, heaven, hell, purgatory, sin, evil, indulgences, order, clerics, the pope, and so on—with nothing about labor, the family, human love, sex, pleasure, joy, science, beauty, freedom, culture, evolution, atheism, society, the working class, economics, politics, or the like (G. Baraúna, "Transcendência/imanência," *Revista Eclesiástica Brasileira* 28 [1968] 813-14).

17. See Thomas Aquinas, *Summa Theol.*, I, q. 1, a. 3, on the unity of theology, especially in the corpus, where he maintains: "*Sacram doctrinam unam scientiam esse . . . secundum objectum, non quidem materialiter* [in the subject matter], *sed secundum rationem formalem objecti* [pertinency]."

18. Althusser defines "problematic" as "the particular unity of a theoretical formation" (cf. *Pour Marx*, p. 32); see also 62-68. See also his *Reading Capital*, 2:154-57 ("the theoretico-systematic matrix for posing a series of problems," p. 155). For this author, then, a "problematic" would be the "horizon," as it might be called, against which problems are seen and posed, and would determine the *way* in which they are posed. Thus, for our case, theology has always been concerned with politics, but today we pose this same question in another way—that is, within another problematic, the one opened up by the "social sciences."

19. See Leonardo Boff, *Teologia do cativeiro*, pp. 27–56: "what does it mean to do theology from captivity and liberation?"

20. Anyone who has read Aristotle's *Topics* or *On Sophistical Refutations* knows very well what rhetoric, or better, dialectic, is. It is the art of discussion. It is discourse upon the general or the conventional. It is the "faculty of reasoning about *any* theme put before us from the most *generally accepted* premises that there are" (*On Sophistical Refutations*, 34, 183b36–37, p. 252; emphasis added). Analytic is different from dialectic. Analytic produces demonstrative, or "scientific," lines of reasoning—not from general premises, but from first or basic principles, expressly defined.

21. The concepts of "paradigm" and "normal science" are those of T. S. Kuhn, *The Structure of Scientific Revolutions*.

22. Augustine, *De Trinitate*, book 14, chap. 1. Cf. Thomas Aquinas, *Summa Theol.*, I, q. 1, a. 2, *sed contra*.

23. Friedrich Nietzsche, *The Antichrist*, p. 182. Nietzsche, again: "The most precious truths are those that one discovers last; but methods themselves are the most precious truths" (cited by Jean Guitton, *Make Your Mind Work for You*, p. xi).

INTRODUCTION TO PART ONE

1. "*Quamvis scientia divina sit prima omnium scientiarum naturaliter, tamen quoad nos aliae scientiae sunt priores. Unde dicit Avicenna, in principio suae Metaphysicae: 'Ordo illius scientiae est ut addiscatur post scientias naturales, in quibus sunt multa determinata, quibus ista scientia utitur. . . .' Similiter etiam post mathematicam*" (Thomas Aquinas, *In Boethii de Trinitate*, q. 5, a. 1, ad 9). This order of exposition coincides with that of the articulation of the theology of the political, as we shall see in part 2.

2. The scientifically correct method, according to Marx, consists in rising from the abstract to the concrete (Karl Marx, *Para a crítica*, pp. 122–23).

CHAPTER 1

1. Reflection on these problems has become very abundant. But this reflection has not always been precise about the level and terms of the multiform relationship between theology and the sciences of the social. The best bibliography on the subject is the one published by the Instituto Fe y Secularidad, in Madrid: *Sociología de la religión: Estudio bibliogràfico*, listing 16,291 titles! For the specifically *methodological* problem of the relationships in question, see chap. 9, nos. 1 and 2, pp. 387–88, of the Madrid bibliography, where some one hundred items are indicated. I note too that, according to the annotations furnished in this bibliography for the more important works under each heading, of the eight in the category of my own work, not one is directly in line with the perspective that I have adopted, with the possible exception of the article by H. Schelsky, "Religionssoziologie und Theologie," positing certain explanatory theoretical principles along lines that I shall be following in part 2 (see p. 78 of the above-cited bibliography). See also G. Girardi, "Verité et libération: les présupposés philosophiques d'une théologie de la libération," with its fine description but lack of articulation. As terms of the "new relationships defining theology," Girardi cites five: revolutionary praxis, the economic and social system, the collective unconscious, the human sciences, and the militant Christian community.

2. This is what Jean Ladrière, for example, does so skillfully in many of his contributions, esp. in *L'articulation du sens*. See also Yves M.-J. Congar, "Théologie et sciences humaines"; F. Chapey, *Science et foi*; certain publications of Semanas dos Intelectuais Católicos under the series title Recherches et Débats (Paris, Desclée de Brouwer), such as *Science et Théologie: Méthode et langage* (no. 67, 1970) and *Chemins de la Raison: Science, philosophie et théologie* (no. 75, 1972); H. R. Rapp, *Cibernética e Teologia*, pp. 195-202, citing the work of K. Heim; G. Söhngen, "Teologia, Filosofia, Ciência." Juan Alfaro ("Teología, filosofía y ciencias humanas") is diffident with respect to any dialogue between theology and sociology; he issues a stern warning to "political theology" concerning the use of Marxism (pp. 234-35).

3. Here I may cite the dialogue that a "political theology" of German inspiration seeks to strike up with the Marxism of the Frankfurt school; see Geyer, Janowski, and Schmidt, *Theologie und Soziologie*; Dullaart et al., *Les deux visages de la théologie de la sécularisation;* Groupe de Recherche Théologique CEP, *La pratique de la théologie politique*; Edward Schillebeeckx, "La teología hermenéutica en correlación con una teoría de la sociedad." On the danger of a "new positivism" lurking in the "human sciences" in terms of a "reduction" of human beings and their "totalization" in a single particularity, so that the absolute is relativized, see Paul VI, *Octogesima Adveniens*, nos. 38-40 (in Gremillion, *The Gospel of Peace and Justice*, pp. 503-4).

4. For the problem of "pastoral" or "religious" sociology, see the bibliography cited above (chap. 1, n. 1), *Sociología de la religión*: "Sociología y práxis teológico-pastoral" (pp. 390-94), "Teología pastoral" (pp. 396-99), and "Sociología de la religión" (pp. 111-49). See also the periodicals *Social Compass* (Louvain), and *Sociological Analysis* (University of Connecticut), as well as the following global approaches: H. Desroche, *Sociologies religieuses*; M. Lefebvre, "Sociologie et ecclésiologie existentielle"; J. Labens, *La sociologie religieuse* (Paris, Fayard, 1956); *Concilium*, no. 91 (1974); the works of François Houtart, esp. "Sociologie de l'Eglise comme institution."

5. I prefer this expression, especially because it succeeds in avoiding the pitfall of the clericalism of classic "political theology" with its "Christian practice of politics"—the title of the French bishops' "Lourdes document." Concerning this document and certain others, see Bishop Gabriel Matagrin's *Politique, Eglise et foi—Lourdes 1972: Rapports et études présentés à l'Assemblée plénière de l'Episcopat français* (Paris, Centurion, 1972).

6. For the sociology of theological cognition, see Liénard and Rousseau, "Rapports sociaux et systèmes symboliques: Conditions et implications sociales des innovations théologiques et de leur utilisation"; A. Rousseau, "Le discours théologique sur la société," presenting a sociological analysis of some thirty works; G. Defois, "Sociologie de la connaissance religieuse et théologie de la croyance," an extract of the author's doctoral dissertation presented to the Institut Catholique de Paris entitled "Révélation et société" and treating of the sociological conditions of enunciation of the Constitution *Dei Verbum*; J. Merlo, "Le Pape et les idéologies," an analysis of the Encyclical *Octogesima Adveniens*; R. Costa, "Le problème des sociologies de la connaissance"; Adolphe Gesché, "Un colloque sur 'la sociologie de la connaissance et la théologie' "; and esp. J. Séguy, "Sociologie de la connaissance," where the author, after a perfectly pertinent critique of the prejudicial mixture—practiced particularly by theologians—of scientific approaches, claims autonomy for each discipline, citing the "discontinuity of language" obtaining among them, and alleging that this discontinuity rules out any "bridge" between theology and sociology (p. 107). "Interdisciplinarity, from a scientific point of

view," would thus be "strictly impossible" (p. 104). For my part, although the "dialectic" of each discipline must surely be safeguarded, I see no reason why one discipline should not be able to be articulated with another—as indeed occurs in ordinary scientific practice. The real question is concentrated in the "canonics" of this articulation.

7. I say "main approaches," because, just as it is legitimate to look for the "sociological" meaning of theological practice, so also one may do just the reverse, along the lines of a "theology of science," after the fashion of, for example, Philippe Roqueplo, *La foi d'un mal-croyant: Mentalité scientifique et vie de foi*; Dominique Dubarle, *Approches d'une théologie de la science*; Edouard Mairlot, *Science et foi chrétienne*.

8. The compound concept "socio-historical" is a concrete designation referring to a particular society ("socio-") in a particular historical moment ("-historical"). The determination is applied precisely to the concept of "conjuncture." Indeed, "the conjuncture is the very type of the collective, involuntary occurrence. The result of the principal sociological balances, it translates the life of the group at each moment of its history" (Gaston Bouthoul, *Sociologie de la politique*, p. 38). "The *political conjuncture*, or 'current moment' [is the level] constituting the synthesis of all the contradictions of a determinate society at a given moment of its development" (Marta Harnecker, *Les concepts élémentaires du matérialisme historique*, p. 172).

9. See, e.g., Paul VI, *Octogesima Adveniens*, no. 46.

10. See Leonardo Boff, *Teologia do cativeiro*, chap. 1: "the hermeneutic of the historical consciousness of liberation."

11. See Yves M.-J. Congar, *Situation et tâches présentes de la théologie:* "If the church hopes to reach the real questions of the world today and endeavors to sketch a response, as it has sought to do in *Gaudium et Spes* and *Populorum Progressio*, it will have to open as it were a *new chapter in theologico-pastoral epistemology*. Instead of beginning solely with the datum of revelation and tradition, as classic theology has generally done, theology will *have to begin here with a datum of facts and questions received from the world and history*. This is much less comfortable. We can no longer content ourselves with repeating the old—with beginning with the notions and problems of the eighteenth or sixteenth centuries. We must begin with the problems, if not the ideas, of today, as a new datum—to be elaborated, doubtless, in the light of the perennial evangelical datum, but without the benefit of elaborations already acquired and possessed in the calm of a self-confident tradition" (p. 72; emphasis added).

12. The de facto inevitability, for theology, of a "profane" analytic mediation did not escape Karl Rahner as he reflected, *post festum*, on the theoretical status of *Gaudium et Spes*: "Réflexions sur la problématique théologique d'une Constitution Pastorale." See also Rahner's *Schriften zur Theologie* (Einsiedeln, Benziger): "Zum Verhältnis zwischen Theologie und heutigen Wissenschaft," vol. 10, 1972, pp. 104–12; "Über künftige Wege der Theologie," ibid., pp. 41–69; "Die Zukunft der Theologie," vol. 9, 1970, pp. 148–57. On this same problem, see Edward Schillebeeckx, "Le statut critique de la théologie." "Theology is impossible today," says Schillebeeckx, "without the critique and contribution of the sciences" (p. 65); likewise Jean Ladrière ("La sociologie, son introduction dans la pensée catholique," p. 203): "Social theology must rely on as adequate a knowledge as possible of social reality."

13. With Claude Lévi-Strauss, I distinguish "praxis," which is the basic totality or "social activity" belonging to the infrastructure, and "practices," which are "discrete realities, localized in time and space" (Lévi-Strauss, *The Savage Mind*, pp. 129–30). Further: for my own part, I adopt, even where "theological practice" is concerned, the definition of "practice in general" given by Louis Althusser: "The entire process of the

transformation of a given, determinate prime matter into a determinate *product*—a *transformation* accomplished by a determinate human work, using determinate (productive) means" (cf. *Pour Marx*, p. 167). In Althusser, what I call "praxis" bears the name of "social practice," which, for Althusser, "comports a great number of distinct practices—namely, economic practice, political practice, ideological practice, and so on" (ibid., pp. 167-68). Althusser's conception coincides with that of Lévi-Strauss here. See also Gilles-Gaston Granger, *Filosofia do estilo* (São Paulo, Perspectiva/Ed. da Univ. de São Paulo, 1974, pp. 14, 165), where practice is defined as "a totalizing, active experience" that includes its social "context." I do not, then, take "praxis" in the acceptation of Germanic theological literature, where it usually means "pastoral practice." Thus, e.g., the well-known dictionary *Sacramentum Mundi* is subtitled, in the German edition, *Theologisches Lexikon für die Praxis*, and a Dutch periodical is called *Praktische theologie: Nederlands tijdschrift voor pastorale wetenschappen*. To my thinking, it is not basically this "praxis" that presents a problem for theology today, as we so often hear that it is—e.g., in Walter Kasper, *The Methods of Dogmatic Theology*, chap. 5; or in Guy Bourgeault et al., *Quand les églises se vident: Vers une théologie de la pratique*.

14. See the following general works, the first two with extensive bibliographies: Jean Touchard, *Histoire des idées politiques*, vol. 1; Maurice Duverger, *An Introduction to the Social Sciences, with Special Reference to their Methods*; idem, *The Idea of Politics: The Uses of Power in Society*; Marcel Prélot, *La science politique* (bibliography, p. 126); Gaston Bouthoul, *Sociologie de la politique* (bibliography of the political classics, p. 124).

15. For this distinction, see Paul Ricoeur, "La paradoxe politique," pp. 729-31. For my definitions, as well as for the expression "theology of the political," see René Coste, *Les communautés politiques*, pp. 7-11, 21-28.

16. See O. Mongin, "Quelques livres sur la politique, l'état, et l'autogestion," pp. 38-54. E. Morin says: "From the computer to coitus, everything has a political dimension now" (cited by P. Blanquart, "L'acte de croire et l'action politique," p. 12). Emmanuel Mounier's lapidary statement is familiar: "Politics is not everything: it is in everything" (*Oeuvres* [Paris, Seuil, 1962], 3:528).

17. "The concept of the political fact, . . . anterior to political science, which it serves as a basis and whose contours it shapes, not only establishes the horizon, but also defines the political reality to be studied, and characterizes as political, politically relevant, or indifferent, determinate segments of reality" (W.-D. Narr, in Gisela Kress and Dieter Senghaas, eds., *Politikwissenschaft: Eine Einführung in ihre Probleme* [Frankfurt, 1972], pp. 17-18, cited by L. Rütti, "Interpretação," pp. 455-56).

18. "The kingdom of God to come demands of the Christian community a *common appreciation*, rationally reliable (*kenntnisreich*) and realistic, of social and political life. It calls for an attitude and an activity in which the reconciliation realized in Jesus Christ may become efficacious even in revolutionary activity" (Hans Joachim Kraus, *Reich Gottes*, p. 411).

19. "If the state of domination and dependence in which two-thirds of humanity live, with an annual toll of thirty million dead from starvation and malnutrition, does not become the starting-point for every Christian theology today, even in the affluent and powerful countries, then theology cannot begin to relate meaningfully to the real situation. Its questions will lack reality and not relate to real men and women. As one speaker at the Buenos Aires Seminar [ecumenical seminar on the theology of liberation, Aug. 3-6, 1970] observed, 'We have to save theology from its cynicism'" (Hugo Assmann, *Nomad Church*, p. 54; see also pp. 123, 133-34).

20. See Jean Ladrière, "Le statut de la science dans la dynamique de la compréhension." Or again: "As has been observed in various countries, and for other sciences, more advanced than ours [sociology], scientific knowledge can keep accumulating ad infinitum, ritually, without any advance in the science, producing only confirmations and reconfirmations of old hypotheses or the accumulation of mere data, to the point of cliché and insipidity, and blocking any comprehensive syntheses" (O. Fals Borda, "La crisis social y la orientación sociológica," p. 74). Likewise Heinz Eduard Tödt, "La méthodologie de la coopération interdisciplinaire," p. 20: "If we abandon the scientific disciplines to their immanent logic, they will go on producing new and ever more differentiated paradigms."

21. For the ethico-political critique of science, see P. Roqueplo, *L'énergie de la foi*; Gérard Fourrez, *La science partisane*; Lévy-Leblond and Jaubert, *(Auto)critique de la science* (bibliography, pp. 299-310); Jürgen Habermas, *La technique et la science comme "idéologie,"* esp. pp. 133-62: "Cognition and Interest."

22. Expressions of Roland Barthes, "Introduction à l'analyse structurale des récits, *Communications* 8 (1966) 1.

23. It is recounted that Jean Daniélou, in the course of a journey to Latin America, was heard to define "liberation theology" as a subdivision of "political theology," which, he continued, was part of "social theology," which was part of "moral theology," which was part of "theology" — as simply as that! (Juan Carlos Scannone, "Necesidad y posibilidad de una teología socio-culturalmente latinoamericana," p. 356).

24. See Gerhard von Rad, *Old Testament Theology*, vol. 2, *The Theology of Israel's Prophetic Traditions*, pp. 99-125, 301-15; Max Weber, *Ancient Judaism*, p. 13: "Yahweh was a God of history; more precisely, he was a God of political and military history, a God of political destiny"; see also pp. 297-321.

25. See Hugo Assmann, *Nomad Church*, pp. 92-94. Like Juan Luís Segundo, Assmann is of the opinion that the separation between dogmatics and ethics is an ideological position, which depoliticizes "political theology" as such. This is a criticism made of Johannes Metz in *Diskussion zur "Politischen Theologie,"* Helmut Peukert, ed., pp. 279-82. On this question, see also Heinz Eduard Tödt, "Theologie der Gesellschaft oder theologische Sozialethik?"

26. In this section I present my revisions of José Comblin's criticisms of social moral theory made in his *Théologie de la pratique révolutionnaire*, pp. 25-30. Comblin's theoretical alternative, in my view, moves in the right direction. He posits, between the Bible and activity, the necessity of a mediation ("other modes of cognition"), constituted by a "natural law" that would have three components: an "anthropology," a "politico-social analysis," and a "moral judgment" (pp. 40-47). "Politico-social analysis" would consist in an "analysis of the event," or an "analysis of the historical situation" (pp. 344-45). It would correspond, then, to my socio-analytic mediation, and the other two components would correspond to my hermeneutic mediation as mediating the Bible.

27. It is instructive, for the epistemological status of the theology of the political, to examine the circumstances that occasioned publication in 1912 of the celebrated, and enormous (some one thousand pages), work of the German theologian, historian, and sociologist Ernst Tröltsch, *The Social Teaching of the Christian Churches*. Another theologian had written on the potential cooperation of the church in the solution of the social problem, in complete ignorance of the true nature of the problem—of its *social* nature, precisely—and of the capacity of the church to contribute to a resolution. This led Tröltsch to reply to the "wretched book." His reply analyzed the relationships between church and society—and suddenly we had a work on the *sociology* of Chris-

tianity. For us, this is the first lesson afforded here: the need for socio-analytic mediation. And yet, Tröltsch stayed on the level of this mediation itself: he answered a book of (social) theology with a book of (religious) sociology. This is what led Bodenstein to consider Tröltsch a "failed theologian" (Heinz Horst Schrey, "Neuere Tendenzen der Religionssoziologie"). And this is the second lesson that we may draw from the controversy: the need for hermeneutic mediation.

28. Here I am thinking of the idealizers of the "new Christendom": Nikolai Berdyaev, Etienne Gilson, Henri-Irénée Marrou, Emmanuel Mounier, and esp. Jacques Maritain.

29. See the celebrated work by Alois Dempf, *Sacrum Imperium: Geschichte und Staatsphilosophie des Mittelalters und der politischen Renaissance* (Munich/Berlin, Oldenbourg, 1929).

30. Carl Schmitt, *Römischer Katholizismus und politische Form* (Hellerau, Hegner, 1923); Wilhelm Stapel, *Sechs Kapitel über Christentum und Nationalsozialismus* (Hamburg, Hanseatische, 1932); Friedrich Gogarten, *Politische Ethik: Versuch einer Grundlegung* (Jena, Diederichs, 1932); H.M. Müller, and others.

31. Among the opposition: Ernst Wilhelm Eschmann, H. Keller, R. Grusche, Erik Peterson, and one wing of the "religious socialism" to which Paul Tillich and Karl Barth belonged. See Tillich's *Christentum und soziale Gestaltung: Frühe Schriften zum religiösen Sozialismus (Gesammelte Werke*, vol. 2 [Stuttgart, Evangelisches Verlagswerk, 1962]). But it is the prophetic figure of Barth that dominates the scene, with his consuming zeal for the purity of the revealing word that dispensed with all human mediation, even mediation of a socio-analytic type, as is so eloquently demonstrated by the celebrated Barmen Confession of 1934, of which Barth was the inspirer and redactor: "Jesus Christ, such as he is witnessed to us so abundantly in the scriptures, is the sole Word of God whom we must hear, in whom we must trust, and whom obey, in life and in death. We reject the false doctrine according to which, besides this sole Word of God, the church could and should likewise recognize, as font of its preaching, other events and powers, other phenomena and truths, than those of divine revelation" (cited by Daniel Cornu, *Karl Barth, teólogo da liberdade*, pp. 44–45). On Barth's "political theology," see also Friedrich-Wilhelm Marquardt, *Theologie und Sozialismus: Das Beispiel Karl Barths* (Munich/Mainz, Kaiser/Grünewald, 1972); E. Castro, *Die theologische Lage in Lateinamerika und die Theologie Karl Barths* (Zurich, 1956), pp. 926–37.

32. It is hardly necessary to cite here the works of Johannes B. Metz, Dorothee Sölle, Jürgen Moltmann, and others, whose theologies come to us by way of the mediation of Marxism, but that of a still very Hegelian, speculative, humanistic, one might even say theological, Marxism—rather the young Marx, or Marx as cultivated by the Frankfurt school.

33. Illustrations of (nontheological) religious language bearing on politics: "Our only social program and doctrine was that of the Trinity"—Federov, see N.O. Lossky, *History of Russian Philosophy* (New York, International Universities Press, 1951), pp. 75–80; "It is sin that loses battles"—Joan of Arc to the generals of her armies, cited by Gaston Fessard, *De l'actualité historique* (Paris, Desclée de Brouwer, 1960), 2:211; and the list could be lengthened.

34. See Georges Gusdorf, *Les sciences humaines et la conscience occidentale*; idem, "Sciences humaines," in *Encyclopaedia Universalis*, 14:767–72; Michel Foucault, *Order of Things*, esp. part 2.

35. The French Revolution was the great historical experience by which a society became conscious that it was the product of its own action, in the sense of Giambattista Vico's "Humanity is the deed of the same" (*Scienza Nuova* [1725]). See also Alain Tou-

raine, *The Self-Production of Society*, pp. 48–53: "The Birth of Sociology"; see also p. 68 and p. 4: *"Society is not what it is, but what it makes itself be."*

36. See M.-D. Dubarle, "Epistémologie des sciences humaines," pp. 177–79: "the delayed reaction of Catholic theology." On the reaction of the church to the rise of liberal societies, see E. Poulat, "L'Eglise romaine, le savoir et le pouvoir: Une philosophie à la mesure d'une politique," *Archives de Sciences Sociales des Religions* 37 (1974) 5–21.

37. One of Louis Althusser's most important theses is that Marxism is not a "theoretical humanism" but a science—a "science of history"; see esp. *Pour Marx*, pp. 225–58, "Marxism and humanism." Theology has not yet taken due account of the transcendence of the sciences of ideological humanism, not even in "political theology" circles. Alluding to this situation, Althusser writes: " 'Transcendence,' in its eschatological or authoritarian form, is still flourishing today among large numbers of theologians, some reactionary, some very progressive, from Germany and Holland to Spain and Latin America" ("Response to John Lewis," p. 45). Consider also the following two "depositions," one by a sociologist and the other by an intellectual. Y. Le Gal, referring to the classical theologians who "did" Vatican II: "These grand efforts . . . ignored the greatest cultural happenings of their era. . . . Nor can we any longer pass over in silence the tranquilizing use, in Vatican II, of these sixty-year-old theologians for the purpose of ignoring the most burning questions of the current time. . . . [Christians] are only just now emerging from humanism" (Y. Le Gal, "Déplacements dans l'Eglise: une cartographie," *Autrement* 2 [1975] 91). And the Editor of *Esprit*, J.-M. Domenach: "Show me a theology that is on the level of our culture. I know of none. Father de Lubac's or Father Chenu's was on the level of the humanist discourse of the nineteenth century . . . and those conducting a reflection on the faith today are persons formed in the human sciences, speaking a contemporary discourse, using up-to-date argumentation. They are not, properly speaking, theologians" (cited by S. Maillard, "Un langage en miettes," *Autrement* 2 [1975] 24, and by G. Morel, ibid., p. 80). Perhaps more in reaction than in response to Althusser, the Spanish exegete José María Gonzáles Ruíz has written his *Atheistic Humanism and the Biblical God*, Milwaukee: Bruce, 1969.

38. *Gaudium et Spes*, no. 62: "Theological inquiry should seek a profound understanding of revealed truth without neglecting close contact with its own times. . . . Recent studies and findings of science . . . raise new questions . . . and demand new theological investigations" (in Gremillion, *Gospel of Peace and Justice*, pp. 298–99). Besides the "liberation theologians," for whom socio-analytic mediation is standard procedure, there are others who stress a need for it: A. Manaranche, "La fe ilumina toda la existencia," pp. 54–55, 67–68; idem, *L'existence chrétienne*; J.-M. Domenach, "Pour une éthique chrétienne de l'engagement"; the entire issue (entitled "the political life of Christians") of *Autrement*, no. 2 (1975); J. Audinet et al., *Recherches actuelles*; R. de Oliveira and B. Domingues, "Conversão—Rumo novo"; Georges Tavard, *La théologie parmi les sciences humaines*, p. 131 and passim; N. Greinacher, "Praxis do engajamento político," pp. 461–63; Georges Casalis, in Metz and Schlick, *Die Spontangruppen in der Kirche*, pp. 219–20; Jules Gritti, *Foi et nouvelles sciences de l'homme*.

39. On this criticism, see Charles Wackenheim's fine study, *La faillite de la religion d'après Karl Marx*, pp. 165–90, 248–53, from which I borrow much.

40. Karl Marx, *On the Jewish Question*, p. 151.

41. Karl Marx, *Contribution to the Critique of Hegel's Philosophy of Law*, p. 176.

42. Karl Marx and Friedrich Engels, *The Holy Family*, pp. 39–40.

43. Karl Marx, *Contribution to the Critique of Hegel's Philosophy of Law*, p. 175: "Religion is the general theory of that world [the human world, a world turned inside out,

inverted], its encyclopaedic compendium, its logic in a popular form, its spiritualistic *point d'honneur*, its enthusiasm, its moral sanction, its solemn complement, its universal source of consolation and justification."

44. See Karl Marx, *Moralising Criticism and Critical Morality*, pp. 312–40.

45. Karl Marx and Friedrich Engels, "Circular Against Kriege," pp. 35–51.

46. Karl Marx and Friedrich Engels, *Sobre la religión*, p. 171. See also *On Religion*, pp. 41–42.

47. Karl Marx and Friedrich Engels, *Sobre la religión*, pp. 173–74. See also pp. 339, 354ff.

48. Karl Marx, *On the Jewish Question*, p. 169; first emphasis added.

49. See Karl Marx, *Critique de l'économie politique*, pp. 259–62: "against the young Hegelians."

50. See Karl Marx and Friedrich Engels, *L'Idéologie allemande* (Paris, Ed. Sociales, 1962), p. 46: "A true, practical resolution of this phraseology, the elimination of these representations in the human conscience, cannot be realized—I repeat—except by a transformation of these circumstances and by theoretical deductions." Karl Marx, "Letter to Arnold Ruge," Nov. 30, 1842, pp. 394–95: "I requested further that religion should be criticised in the framework of criticism of political conditions rather than that political conditions should be criticised in the framework of religion . . . for religion is itself without content, it owes its being not to heaven but to the earth, and with the abolition of distorted reality, of which it is the *theory*, it will collapse of itself" (cited by Georges Morel, *Problèmes actuels de religion*, p. 73). After all: "Surely the mystical phenomenon, like any other, is open to an attempt at scientific interpretation, at once necessary and insufficient in our perspective as Christians. But why should it flee the light of faith, to which we subject, for example, the political universe?" (Philippe Warnier, *La foi d'un chrétien révolutionnaire*, p. 123).

51. "One can be delivered from Marxism only by assimilating and transcending it" (Comblin, "Autour de la théologie," p. 529). See the entire issue of *La Foi et le Temps*, vol. 5 (1975), no. 6, devoted to the question I am analyzing; as also *Lumière et Vie*, vol. 23 (1974), nos. 117–18. Among recent theological reactions to the Marxist critique, the following are notable: Miranda, *Marx and the Bible*; van den Oudenrijn, *Kritische Theologie als Kritik der Theologie*; Refoulé, *Marx et Saint Paul*; Boisset, *La théologie en procès*. See also §21 below, on historical materialism.

To give just one illustration of the manner in which, even with an interest in current problems, one can nevertheless empty them of any intrinsic importance of their own—that is, mystify them—for want of an appropriate understanding and grasp of their "profane reality," which is precisely the responsibility of socio-analytic mediation, let me cite the contribution of the Italian Association of Moral Theologians, *Rivoluzione: magistero, teologia e mondo contemporaneo* (Bologna, Dehoniane, 1970). Here we find a bilingualism of objective reality and supernatural reality, and proposed solutions along spiritualistic lines: love, forgiveness, patience, and so on. One really wonders whether it is not indeed necessary to "de-theologize" problems, at least where a like theology is concerned! Note that my position has nothing in common with that of Péguy, who also sought a "de-theologization" of Christianity—but for the purpose of its subsequent passionate "remythologization" (see P. Duployé, *La religion de Péguy*, Paris, Klincksiek, 1965).

52. Marx's whole undertaking is, as it were, suffused with a critique of the ideological function that the sciences may exercise, from philosophy (*The German Ideology*, 1845) to political economics (*Capital*, 1867). Subsequent Marxist practice was consistent with this criticism, sometimes with grave abuses, as can be seen in the case of the Soviet biolo-

gist Lysenko: see the study by a member of Althusser's circle, Dominique Lecourt, *Proletarian Science? The Case of Lysenko*. For the critique of anthropology, see, e.g., J. Copans, ed., *Anthropologie et impérialisme*. Even mathematics and formal logic have been subjected to this kind of critique: see, e.g., R. Jaulin, ed., *Pourquoi la mathématique?* (Paris, Union Gén. d'Editions, 1974).

53. The most memorable debate was doubtless the *Werturteilsstreit*, or controversy on values, that divided the members of the Berlin *Verein für Sozialpolitik* ("Association for Social Policy"). Max Weber, a member of this association, ostentatiously broke with it, espousing a *wertfreie Wissenschaft* ("pure science," a value-free science). For this debate (and bibliography) see Ralf Dahrendorf, *Essays in the Theory of Society*, pp. 1-18. But the question is still open. By way of illustration, see the very interesting discussion between O. Fals Borda and A. E. Solari, two Latin American social analysts, the former a proponent of an "engaged sociology" and the latter in favor of a "value-free sociology" (1. Fals Borda, "Ciencia y compromiso"; 2. Solari, "Algunas reflexiones"; 3. Fals Borda, "La crisis social . . . una réplica"; 4. Solari, "Usos y abusos . . . una dúplica"). On "engaged sociology," esp. in Latin America, see the bibliography in Fals Borda's "La Crisis social," p. 64, n. 2. The same kind of debate took place between mathematician R. Godement, in favor of "the scientist's social responsibility," in *Le Monde*, July 9, 1975, pp. 15-16, and E. Labin, engineer and adviser in information/communication services, for whom "the only ethics to which science ought to be subordinate is that of its own operations," with the utilization of its results delivered over to "the responsibility of the citizenry" (ibid., Oct. 15, 1975, pp. 15-16). A similar polemic in the area of economics can be noted, with S. Brunhoff, M. Beaud, and C. Servolin on the side of a "politicized" economics (ibid., May 22, 1973), and H. Guitton, J. Lesourne, and A. Reynaud championing an "apolitical" economics (ibid., June 26, 1973), all of this material appearing in the economics section of *Le Monde*. In the area of theology, we have an excellent illustration of contrary *prises de position* that finally strangle any dialogue, in the work cited above, Dullaart et al., *Les deux visages de la théologie*, pp. 118-29: "theology at an impasse." See also H. C. de Lima Vaz, "O Ethos da atividade científica."

54. I find practically nothing in the way of specific, systematic resources for the examination of the articulation between (scientific) theory and (political) praxis—an extremely difficult problem, as may be gathered, for example, from the testimony of one of the best epistemologists of the sciences of the human being, Gilles-Gaston Granger, in his "Science pratique et pratique de la science." Louis Althusser ranks among the most rigorous and fertile theoreticians to have reflected upon this articulation. In *Reading Capital*, 1:57-59, he furnishes us with excellent theoretical materials for its constitution. He underscores the differences among the differentiated practices, and opposes "an *egalitarian conception of practice*," arguing the need to develop "a new conception of the relations between theory and practice (p. 58). We might call "Althusser I" (up until 1967) the Althusser of "autonomy," and "Althusser II" (since 1967) the Althusser of "dependence." Below, in part 3, I shall make certain criticisms of the inadequacies of his recent evolution. Jean Ladrière, in his study "Vérité et praxis dans la démarche scientifique," posits a basic principle for the articulation under consideration here, stating that scientific practice must be conceived, on the one hand, as a particular "system"—that is, as "a complex totality, relatively susceptible of isolation vis-à-vis the material around it, endowed with a sufficient degree of stability and capacity for evolution . . . in virtue of purely internal resources . . ." (p. 293), and, on the other hand, as a system "situated as well in a relationship with other systems"—among them, the "political" (pp. 301-2).

See this same author's *La science, le monde et la foi*, pp. 59–60; and *L'articulation du sens*, p. 50 and passim. See the clear, and clarifying, positions of Ralf Dahrendorf, *Essays in the Theory of Society*, pp. 13–31, 287–311. Finally, see Thomas Aquinas, *Summa Theol.*, II-II, q. 47, a. 2, ad 2: "*Quamvis dici possit quod ipse actus speculativae rationis, secundum quod est voluntarius, cadit sub electione et consilio, quantum ad suum* exercitium *et per consequens cadit sub ordinatione* prudentiae [dependency], *sed quantum ad suam* speciem, *prout comparatur ad* objectum, *non cadit sub consilio, nec sub prudentiae* [autonomy]" (emphasis added).

55. Recall A. Touraine's formula: "Sociology is neither engaged nor neutral." See the idealistic position of Raymond Aron, *Dimensions de la conscience historique*, pp. 347–67; however, the author does offer a more balanced perspective in *Dix-huit leçons sur la société industrielle*, pp. 29–31.

56. I leave aside, here, the question of scientific discovery and the birth and constitution of a theory or even of a new science. This is an intermediate region falling between an epistemology (autonomy) and a sociology (dependency) of cognition, and would fall under the competency of the history of sciences and the psychology of knowledge. After all, we know that, in a science, one must distinguish the "context of the discovery," which refers to the external (psychological, social, and so on) conditions of the science, and the "context of justification," which is located on its internal side (the side of rational construction and logical and experimental validation). See H. Reichenbach, *Experience and Prediction*; K. Popper, *Logic of Scientific Discovery*; H. G. Arana, "Investigação científica: invenção e justificação," *Klinica* (Itatiba, Brazil) 1 (1974) 9–16.

57. See Thomas Aquinas, *De Veritate*, q. 3, a. 3, ad 9: "The good can be considered under a speculative aspect," even though in themselves the good and the true coincide.

58. Recall Thomas Aquinas's distinction between the *enuntiabile* and the *res*: *Summa Theol.*, II-II, q. 1, a. 2, ad 2. Note that *res* here has an ontological, not a technical, value.

59. Althusser's paraphrase, from *Reading Capital*, 1:106. In §18, below, I shall return in greater detail to the distinction between knowledge (of the real) and the real itself (known or to be known).

60. See H. E. Tödt, *La méthodologie de la coopération interdisciplinaire*, pp. 20–28, on "big science" and "systems technology"; Philippe Roqueplo, *L'énergie de la foi*, pp. 78, 91–92, 109, etc., on the "science of science"; W. Ölmüller, "Problemas del proceso moderno"; M.-L. Roquette, *La créativité*, pp. 107–9; L. von Bertalanffy, *General System Theory* (New York, Braziller, 1968); C. West Churchman, *The Systems Approach* (New York, Dell, 1979).

61. All the great theoreticians of society have recognized the difference of levels obtaining between awareness and structure, between (subjective) intention and (objective) signification—e.g., Marx, Durkheim, Weber. This is the problem of the social "decentration of consciousness" or awareness. See Bourdieu et al., *Le métier de sociologue*, pp. 29–34: "illusion of transparency and principle of non-awareness"; François Houtart, "Sociologie de l'Eglise comme institution," pp. 65–67: "constrictions on the signification of the practices of agents."

62. See A. Grosser, *Au nom de quoi?*, pp. 229–37: "personal joys and social responsibilities." This author cites Descartes's statement that he, Descartes, unlike Galileo, would never expound in writing what he held to be the truth if this truth would prejudice religion or the state (p. 29).

63. See Althusser, *Reading Capital*, vol. 1, chap. 4, pp. 91–118: "An Outline for a Concept of Historical Time." See also Augustine: "*Etiam nos, secundum quod aliquid*

aeternum mente sapimus, non in hoc mundo sumus" (*De Trinitate*, book 4, chap. 20). On the (relative) transcendency of the human spirit vis-à-vis spatio-temporal coordinates, see Thomas Aquinas, *De Potentia*, q. 3, a. 10, ad 8; *Summa Theol.*, I-II, q. 53, a. 3, ad 3; *Contra Gentiles*, book 2, chap. 96; and esp. *Summa Theol.*, I, q. 112, a. 1, ad 1.

64. There is considerable emphasis today in Marxist circles on the notions of "in the last instance" and "relative autonomy." But it does not appear perfectly certain to me that this latter concept explains the singular situation of knowledge—which I, for my part, seek to grasp with the help of both concepts. In any case, the notion of "relative autonomy" does not seem to me sufficiently analytical. As to the notion of "in the last instance," which I frequently employ, see Henri Desroche, " 'Dernière instance' et 'premier rôle,' " pp. 153–57. We must recognize that it is Marxism that has contributed the most to setting in relief the historicity of scientific cognition and its social functions. At the same time, dogmatization of such perspectives in common-currency Marxism has led to a confusion between the two levels of autonomy and dependency. This dogmatization has been effectuated apropos of the two basic principles of Marxism: that the superstructure is a function of the infrastructure, and that praxis is the criterion of theory. We should note the efforts of Louis Althusser, Lucien Sebag, Claude Lévi-Strauss, and others, to rectify these narrow interpretations. See Sebag's *Marxisme et structuralisme*; Lévi-Strauss's works, esp. *The Savage Mind*, pp. 130–31, and *Structural Anthropology*, passim.

65. See Girardi, "Théorie et praxis dans la pensée marxiste," pp. 4–6. Economy of language prompts my use of the terms in quotation marks, recognizing the risk of the "ideological overflow" that can be latent in such notions.

66. As cited by Raymond Aron, *Dimensions de la conscience historique*, p. 113.

CHAPTER 2

1. The verb "mediate" is employed by, among others, Jean-Paul Sartre, *Critique of Dialectical Reason*. It is employed more and more frequently in Latin American theological works.

2. See Gaston Bachelard, *La formation de l'esprit scientifique*, chap. 1, esp. p. 13: "The problem of scientific cognition has to be posed in terms of obstacles. Not external obstacles, such as the complexity or ephemeral character of phenomena; nor is it a matter of incriminating the weakness of human meanings and the human mind. It is in the very act of cognition, intimately, that there appear, with a sort of functional necessity, certain recalcitrancies and disturbances. This is where we shall discover certain causes of stagnation, and even regression; certain causes of inertia, which I shall call epistemological obstacles." In my description of these obstacles I shall follow Bachelard's own modus procendi: "It is of the nature of the epistemological obstacle to be confused and polymorphic" (p. 21). Bachelard likewise notes that these obstacles always occur in pairs, as my exposition will show. In order to justify the polemical character of his descriptions, which at times approach caricature, Bachelard says: "I shall not hesitate, then, to list as error—or as spiritual nonutility, which is not far from the same thing—any truth that is not a part of a general system" (p. 11). A good illustration of the same method as applied to theology is to be found in Adolphe Gesché, "Essai d'interprétation dialectique du phénomène de sécularisation." Let us recall in passing that such a method approaches that of Max Weber's *Idealtypus*, as well as that of Marx's "middle ideal."

3. I make no claim to originality with respect to the concepts developed in this section,

which only represent certain general findings of epistemological investigations bearing on my material. See, e.g., Jean Ladrière, in many places in his writings, esp. "La théologie et le langage de l'interprétation"; Louis Althusser, *Reading Capital*, 1:34–40; Jean Piaget, *Psychology and Epistemology*, pp. 63–88: "The Myth of the Sensorial Origin of Scientific Knowledge"; Ferdinand Gonseth, "L'unité de la connaissance scientifique," pp. 58–69: ideas as simple as "datum," or "concrete fact," or "pure fact" do not constitute a priori evidence in science (p. 64). Gonseth has shown the same thing with respect to the notions of "space," "number," "truth," and "being": *Les mathématiques et la réalité*. "Historical facts" are no exception: Henri-Irénée Marrou, *The Meaning of History*, esp. pp. 301–2, 311–14. For sociology in particular, see Pierre Bourdieu et al., *Le métier de sociologue*, esp. pp. 27–49: "the illusion of immediate knowledge"; idem, *Esquisse d'une théorie de la pratique*, esp. pp. 174ff., on "habitus."

4. See, e.g., Hugo Assmann, *Nomad Church*, pp. 58–59 and passim. Note also the *desde* used twice in the title of the Spanish original of Assmann's book: *Teología desde la praxis: Ensayo teológico desde la América dependiente*. Expressions like these are very common in the works of the liberation theologians.

5. On constructionism in epistemology, see Jean Piaget, *Structuralism*, pp. 121–22. For its applications in sociology, see Bourdieu et al., *Le métier de sociologue*, pp. 51–80: "construction of the object." For theoretical practice in general, see Althusser, *Pour Marx*, pp. 186–97: "the process of theoretical practice." See also Karl Marx: "It seems correct to begin with the real, the concrete. . . . But a more attentive consideration shows that this is false. . . . The method that proceeds from general ideas to concrete ideas is manifestly the scientifically correct method. . . . The concrete comes into thought by way of a process of synthesis—as a result, not as a point of departure. . . . The method that goes from the abstract to the concrete is the method for thought that appropriates the concrete, reproduces it as concrete thought" (cf. *Para a crítica*, §3: "the method of political economy," pp. 122–23). Aristotle speaks similarly: "The natural way of [determining what relates to the principles of any branch of study] is to start from the things which are more knowable and obvious to us and proceed towards those which are clearer and more knowable by nature. . . . Thus we must advance from generalities to particulars" (*Physics*, book 1, chap. 1, 184a16–b15). It is scarcely necessary to recall that constructionism was not absent from the classic philosophical tradition—e.g., through the concept of the *intellectus agens* of Aristotle and Thomas Aquinas. The *intellectus agens* produces the concept through the operation of abstraction. See Aquinas, *Summa Theol.*, I, q. 84, a. 6. Similarly in Augustine: cognition is the "offspring" of reason— *"prolem mentis"* (*De Trinitate*, book 9, chap. 12, no. 18).

6. José Comblin ("Autour de la théologie," pp. 532–33) asserts that to take theology as a discourse subsequent to that of the sciences of the human being is to forget that the latter imply valuations upon which theology has something to say. Even bracketing the question of science and values, the concrete practice of a discipline is one thing—and here Comblin may have a point—but its position in an epistemological or political strategy is something else.

7. See Althusser, *Reading Capital*, 1:93.

8. See Jean Ladrière, *La science, le monde et la foi*, pp. 137ff., where he distinguishes "the immediate 'false' of an ingenuous attitude," and "the true immediacy of a pure bestowal" effectuated by philosophy. Along the same lines, S. Strasser (*Phenomenology and the Human Sciences*) posits philosophy in the third degree (as the "third objectivity"). In that case, theology should step back (advance) even further. Better: theology would introduce a new (joining) mediation between itself and its object.

9. Referring to this nebulous opposition, Althusser writes: "This confusion . . . not only nourishes . . . an ideology in vogue today, but threatens to lead astray into a theoretical cul-de-sac those who let themselves be captivated by the 'obviousness' of its often very considerable potential for protest. The criticism [it generates]—in the final analysis, the abstraction that wants to belong to theory, to science—is still ideological criticism: it denies (1) the reality of scientific praxis, (2) the validity of scientific abstractions, (3) and the reality of the theoretical 'concrete' that is knowledge. Wanting to be 'concrete,' wanting 'the concrete,' this presentation will appear to be 'true,' but it has already begun to deny the reality of precisely the praxis that produces knowledge! It remains in the ideology that it declares 'overthrown'—i.e., it remains not in abstraction in general, but in a determinate, ideological abstraction" (cf. *Pour Marx*, p. 190).

10. "A concrete theology refuses to make an abstraction from the experience of faith, renounces 'theologizing' from external instances" (Charles Wackenheim, *Christianisme sans idéologie*, p. 135; see also 136ff.). Wackenheim takes a position against any attempt at a theological deciphering of events and conjunctures except in the form of personal and spiritual reflection; anything else would be "ideology." See Hugo Assmann's criticism of "theological purism" in *Nomad Church*, pp. 63–64 and passim.

11. I shall return to this question below, in part 2. For the moment, consider only the following statements: Thomas Aquinas, *Summa Theol.*, I, q. 1, a. 6, ad 3: "*Ejus* [of theology] *principia ex revelatione habeantur*"; and a. 2, c.: "*Doctrina sacra credit principia revelata sibi a Deo*"; Melchior Cano, *De Locis Theologicis*, book 1, chap. 2: "*Primum stringat fidei sermonem necesse est, quicumque Christianae scholae magister esse volet.*"

12. Augustine cannot reflect as Thomas, nor can Thomas as Augustine: the "cultural positivity" of each was different. For the former, see Henri-Irénée Marrou, *Saint Augustine et la fin de la culture antique*; Yves M.-J. Congar, *La foi et la théologie*, pp. 216, 223–24, 227 (n.1). For Thomas, see the numerous studies of M.-D. Chenu, which I shall be citing, esp. *Saint Thomas d'Aquin et la théologie*.

13. An illustration of the proposition that a minimum of "profane" knowledge is necessarily presupposed by the discourse of faith: "*Credimus Dominum Jesum Christum natum de Virgine, quae Maria vocabitur. Quid sit virgo, quid sit nasci, et quid nomen proprium, non credimus, sed prorsus novimus*" (Augustine, *De Trinitate*, book 8, chap. 5, no. 7 [PL 42:952]).

14. As may be gathered, for instance, from statements of this kind: " . . . The theologian dares this: to attempt to order and interpret the manifold data of . . . belief in such wise as to gather their connections and roots as God has ordained them, and therefore as they appear in the knowledge that God has of them—to rediscover the architecture of the work of God" (Yves M.-J. Congar, *La foi et la théologie*, p. 132). Note that there have always been, in the history of theology, from its beginnings to our present day, tendencies that have rejected the application of critical reason to the content of faith on the pretext of "purity," and so on. Thus the language of faith would presumably be composed of some special semantic substance or other, and be organized by some special syntax or other—both doubtless divine?—and this has been the case with monastic theology, with the Franciscan school, with the movements of the Reformation, with the "dialectical theology" of Karl Barth, and so forth.

15. Karl Marx, editorial in no. 179 of the *Kölnische Zeitung*, where Marx is actually referring to a mixture of physics and theology.

16. See Ambroise Gardeil, *Le donné révélé et la théologie*, pp. 78ff., where he uses the term "theologism" in an equally totalitarian sense, that of the dictatorship of theo-

logical discourse—not in opposition to (another) scientific discourse, however, but in opposition to faith or religion.

17. My conceptualization of this opposition is inspired by Gaston Bachelard, *Le rationalisme appliqué*, p. 37.

18. Expressions of Henri Lefebvre, *La vie quotidienne dans le monde moderne*, pp. 53 and 110.

19. See Edward Schillebeeckx, *World and Church*, pp. 163–76.

20. See, e.g., Oswald von Nell-Breuning, in *Marx, cristianismo, luta de classes*. He shows in a very convincing manner the anonymous influence of Marxist theory on Pius XI's *Quadragesimo Anno*, and states that Pius "took the Marxian essentials and introduced them into Catholic social teaching; nevertheless, substantial differences between the two systems remain" (p. 4).

21. See M. Montuclard, "La part de l'idéologie"; M. Legrand and P. Meyers, "L'analyse socio-linguistique de deux documents pontificaux: l'encyclique 'Rerum Novarum' (1891) et la 'lettre du Cardinal Roy'—Méchanismes didactiques et structure de leur modèle idéologique," *Social Compass* 20 (1973) 427–57.

22. I am thinking here of the "political theology" of the German tradition, where the semantic mix is finer and more surreptitious. The *ideo-political positions* of the theologians of this current are in opposition to those maintained by the authors of ecclesiastical discourse. *Epistemologically*, however, their position is different only in that it is under the dominance of the logic of a "social theory," rather abstract and speculative, whose analytical presuppositions are not "up front." Inasmuch as the respective "epistemological profiles" (Bachelard) of these two currents are similar in their internal structure, they are of a piece for purposes of my considerations here. It does not belong to the jurisdiction from whose standpoint I speak to deliver certificates of good ideo-political conduct, but precisely to analyze, short of their content, the state of the rules of the formal organization of a given discourse.

23. See Montuclard, "La part de l'idéologie," p. 140: "Mixage sémantique"; Hans Zwiefelhofer, *Bericht zur "Theologie der Befreiung,"* pp. 24–25: "Vermischung der 'Sprachspiele' "; Adolphe Gesché, "Le Dieu de la révélation," who follows the method of "typologies" adopted here, and speaks of "mixed discourse," "mixture," and an "incomplete articulation" (pp. 254–59, 261).

24. The criticism I lodge here against the form of magisterial discourses corresponds essentially to that of the detailed study by J. Guichard, "Foi chrétienne et théorie de la connaissance."

25. "Seeking to preserve itself intact, official discourse only demonstrates its indifference to the practice of which it pretends to speak and its function as verbal protection in a threatened institution" (Michel de Certeau, *Le Christianisme éclaté*, p. 56). For orthodoxy, see the fundamental study, with its empirical base, of Jean-Pierre Déconchy, *L'orthodoxie religieuse*; idem, "Une tentative d'épistémologie de la pensée religieuse." For Déconchy, the doctrinal rigor of an institution is in direct proportion to its rational frailty. See also A. Rousseau, "Essai sur la function sociale de l'orthodoxie religieuse"; Jean Grenier, *Essai sur l'esprit d'orthodoxie*.

26. I borrow the term "bilingualism," with its content, from Michael de Certeau, *L'étranger*, pp. 199–203. The same author, in his "La vie religieuse en Amérique Latine," describes "bilingualism" as "the fissure in the structure of all Christian reflection today . . . between a scientific process and a dogmatic method" (p. 11). In his study "De la participation au discernement," "bilingualism" is synonymous with "syncretism," and is placed in analogy with "franglais," to be defined as a symptom of dis-

accord between ecclesiastical inquiry and current investigations. Adolphe Gesché "Le Dieu de la révélation," pp. 255–56, 261) speaks of the "danger of concomitance," and a "want of articulation." The entire no. 85 of *Concilium* (1973) is devoted to the "crisis of religious language": see esp. Edward Schillebeeckx, "O problema hermenêutico," esp. pp. 560–63, on "linguistic dualism" or a "two-language approach." For his part, the young Marx saw in this type of discourse an index of alienation: "Each sphere [the moral and the economic] suggests to me a criterion different from and opposed to that of the other . . . because each is a particular human alienation, and each represents a particular sphere of alienative activity" (cf. *Critique de l'économie politique*, p. 179).

27. This is the tendency some have observed in the work of Hugo Assmann.

28. It remains to analyze in greater detail the degree of bilingualism of the non-German productions of a theology of the political, European and Latin American. Among the latter, the following deserve particular attention: Juan Luís Segundo, *De la sociedad a la teología*; and José Comblin, especially his *Théologie de la révolution* and *Théologie de la pratique révolutionnaire*. Among European works, see Jacques Rollet, *Libération sociale et salut chrétien*; Georges Thill, *La fête scientifique*, esp. pp. 225–31, where he proposes "an interlocutionary process" between theology and science.

29. See Althusser, *Philosophie et philosophie spontanée*, pp. 28–51, where this distinction is described and utilized for an understanding of the different relationships among the various disciplines.

30. On the theoretical legitimacy of a "political theology" that would judge concrete practices and even historical alternatives (e.g., in our case, judge between capitalism and socialism), see Thomas Aquinas, *Summa Theol.*, I-II, q. 7, a. 2: *"Utrum Circumstantiae Humanorum Actuum Sint Considerandae a Theologo."* Thomas's reply to this question is that theology has the competency to judge not only of ends, but also of the *commensuratio* or *proportio* of a given act vis-à-vis its end. To objection 3, which denies the theologian the capacity formally to qualify a practice *"ab eo quod est extra ipsum* [theologian]," Thomas answers that, for the purpose of such qualification, the theologian has the right to have recourse to other disciplines—ethics, rhetoric, and politics. Am I saying anything different when I speak of socio-analytic mediation?

31. The adverb underscored is from Edward Schillebeeckx, "Le statut critique de la théologie," p. 64. Schillebeeckx asserts that the relationship between theology and the sciences is, for the former, a question of "life or death." The status conferred by him on the sciences—an equivocal one, in my view—is one of constituting "theological loci" (pp. 62–65). Still, apart from vocabulary, our ideas coincide with his and, generally, with the decisions of the Brussels Theology Congress (ibid., pp. 159–63).

32. See Feuerbach, *Manifestes philosophiques: textes choisis*: "The philosopher must introduce, in the *text* of philosophy, the stand of the person who does *not* philosophize, nay, who is *against* philosophy, who *combats* abstract thought—everything, then, that Hegel relegates to a note. Only thus can philosophy become a *universal, all-powerful, irrefutable, and irresistible force*. Philosophy may not, therefore, begin *with itself*. It must begin with its *antithesis*—with *nonphilosophy*" (p. 155).

33. Thomas Aquinas, *Summa Theol.*, I, q. 1, a. 3: *"Quia igitur sacra doctrina* [theology] *considerat aliqua secundum quod sunt divinitus revelata . . . omnia quaecumque sunt divinitus revelabilia. . . . "* And Yves M.-J. Congar comments, writing in *Bulletin Thomiste*, 1938, p. 496: "The term *revelabile . . .* like *scibile, credibile, sensibile, amabile*, is a term formed to designate a determinate order of objects—in this case, anything that can be known in the light of revelation. The equivalent is used by Saint Thomas himself, a. 4 (in the corpus): *'prout sunt divino lumine cognoscibilia.'* "

34. "Theoretical field": *"[ea] ad quae se extendat"* (Thomas Aquinas, *Summa Theol.*, I, q. 1, title).

35. Consider the works of today that remain a prisoner of tradition, of the "deposit."

36. This tendency comes to forceful expression in the works of the German current of "political theology" as may be seen, e.g., from the works listed by Henri de Lavalette, "Bulletin de théologie politique." I might add that the exploration of the political thematic from a point of departure in the themes of biblical and theological tradition has become generalized since Vatican II. The most influential German authors here are Johannes B. Metz (*Theology of the World*) and Jürgen Moltmann (*Theology of Hope*). See, further, the debates on these two works in Peukert, *Diskussion*; Berkhoff, *Diskussion*.

37. For the traditional approach, see G. Thils, *Propos et problèmes de la théologie des religions non chrétiennes*.

38. This is the direction in which the principal efforts of an "African theology," and the beginnings of an "Indian theology," are being carried on. For the former, see J. S. Mbiti, "La théologie africaine," which offers a panorama of the most important works. For the latter, see J. Dupuis, "Le mouvement théologique en Inde." The great question that might be asked about these theological endeavors, which are situated on the cultural level, is the one that emerges from a conception of society in which culture is a function of social structure—historical materialism. This question concerns the spontaneous sociology of a theological enterprise of this type—and at the same time suggests an examination of the historical scope, and indeed the objective viability, of the cultural project intended by this theological enterprise.

39. Here I am thinking primarily of Latin American "liberation theology," as well as the "black theology" of the United States and the "black liberation theology" of Africa, all of which explore the political side of Christianity. For the first, see the extensive bibliography in François Malley, *Libération*. For the other two currents, see the whole no. 120 (vol. 23, 1974) of *Lumière et Vie*; J. Peters, "Black Theology como sinal de esperança."

40. It is sometimes useful to distinguish, with Pierre Teilhard de Chardin, between "Christian" and "christic"—the former being used to denote material relative to the order of awareness of (explicit) faith, and the latter referring to the real order of salvation, independent of, and antecedent to, such awareness.

41. See Leonardo Boff, *Teologia do cativeiro*, pp. 37–38, 43–44. As an illustration, consider the attempts to theologize the Chinese cultural revolution: *Informations Catholiques Internationales* 465 (1974) 7–9; *Theological Implications of the New China* (Geneva/Brussels, Lutheran World Federation/Pro Mundi Vita, 1974); J. Cardonnel, "La Chine populaire et la foi," *Le Monde Diplomatique*, Feb. 1976, p. 21.

42. "The task and function of the theologian is so vast that no argument, no discussion, no material, seems alien to its profession. . . . The pursuit of this discipline holds the primacy in all the world. . . . Wherefore it ought not to seem strange that so few are found to be equal to such a task" (F. Vitoria, "Relección sobre la potestad civil," cited by Alberto Methol Ferré, in CELAM, *Liberación*, p. 419).

43. I reject the division of the theological field made by Henri Desroche in his *Jacob and the Angel*, pp. 124–52 ("*Sic et Non*: Sociology, Christian Theology, and the Sciences of Religion"), in virtue of the definition of its material object. The formula *omnia sub specie Dei* expresses not only the (material) *universality* but also the (formal) *regionality* (*"sub aliquibus certis limitibus"*—Thomas Aquinas, *Summa Theol.*, I, q. 1) of theological discourse. This is held as well by one of the best theologians of the nineteenth

century, Matthias Joseph Scheeben: " . . . Theology embraces all things in heaven and on earth, the natural as well as the supernatural, although the former only with respect to the latter, and hence the most sublime objects" (Scheeben, *The Mysteries of Christianity*, p. 789; see also p. 792).

CHAPTER 3

1. This expression cannot but recall a celebrated debate in the history of theology—a decisive one, and one bearing a certain parallelism to the one concerning us here. Then the bone of contention was the entry of Aristotelian *episteme* (reason) into theological discourse. One mentality, similar to the one manifesting such diffidence today when confronted with an integration of the same kind, spoke in those days of *philosophantes in sacra doctrina*. Today the diffidence would be with respect to *sociologizantes in sacra doctrina*. See Denzinger-Schönmetzer 824 (*Enchiridion Symbolorum*, pp. 267-68); Schillebeeckx, *Revelation and Theology*, pp. 155-206. See also the very interesting contribution of A. Rousseau, "L'emploi due terme 'sociologie' dans les textes du Magistère," painting a rather negative picture of sociology as the one held by the magisterium, which, we read, regards it as less than trustworthy, an antithesis to theology, "a kind of countertheology" (p. 320).

2. See, e.g., P. Aubenque, "Philosophie et idéologie"; Charles Bettelheim, *Initiation aux recherches sur les idéologies économiques et les réalités sociales*; N. Birnbaum, *The Sociological Study of Ideology (1940-1960)*; Ecole Pratique des Hautes Etudes, *Contributions à la sociologie de la connaissance*, Cahier 1; J. Gabel, "Idéologie," in *Encyclopédie Universitaire*, vol. 8; Georges Gurvitch, *Les cadres sociaux de la connaissance*; D. Vital, *Essai sur l'idéologie*; Frederick Watkins, *The Age of Ideology*; various, *Sociedade tecnocrata: ideologia e classes sociais—fim da ideologia*; the whole issue of *Convivium*, 1970, no. 1; see also Karl Marx and Friedrich Engels, *The German Ideology*; Karl Mannheim, *Ideology and Utopia*. For the case of theology, see esp. H. R. Schlette's "Boletim," *Concilium* 6 (1965); S. Breton, *Théologie et idéologie*; Wackenheim, *Christianisme*; E. Duval, "L'idéologie," offering an excellent exposition of the essential concepts relative to "ideology."

3. See esp. Charles Wackenheim, *Christianisme sans idéologie*, pp. 135-40, 214-20; Hans Zwiefelhofer, *Bericht zur "Theologie der Befreiung,"* pp. 23-30. For an illustration of how the criticism of "reduction" is formulated, see R. Pucheu, "Confession d'un paumé," p. 527; to "political theologians" who "opt for the liquidation of the church," Pucheu recommends, surely not without some justification, that they "read Machiavelli before they reduce faith to politics. He knew what politics is. The 'political theologians' do not. . . . Politics is *dura*, not *pura*. It is not dialogue, it is war."

4. The terminology "center" and "periphery" reflects an alternative interpretation (and strategy) to the phenomenon of "underdevelopment"—that of "dependency." See, e.g., Samir Amin, *Accumulation on a World Scale* (New York, Monthly Review Press, 1974) and *Unequal Development* (New York, Monthly Review Press, 1976). This same vocabulary is current with Latin American social analysts espousing the "theory of dependency," as well as with "liberation theologians."

5. Thus, e.g., Hugo Assmann, *Nomad Church*, pp. 86-105 and passim. On pages 57-58, Assmann speaks of a "nordic" or "North Atlantic" theology as exercising an ideologico-political function. See also Enrique Dussel, *A History of the Church in Latin America*, pp. 313-14. See also the following note.

6. See Juan Carlos Scannone, "El actual desafío"; but esp. Juan Luís Segundo, "Capitalismo—Socialismo."

7. In his *I Believe in Hope*, José M. Díez-Alegría notes the inconsistency that may obtain between a transcendence *proclaimed* and a transcendence *practiced*, esp. on the level of political practices. Roger Garaudy has likewise called repeated attention to this contradiction.

8. "When [the worker] says 'Jesus was a good man' he is at any rate saying more than when the bourgeois says, 'Jesus is God' " (Dietrich Bonhoeffer, *Christ the Center*, p. 35, cited by André Dumas, *Dietrich Bonhoeffer: Theologian of Reality*). "If I am lacking in love and wanting in justice I shall inevitably stray from you, and the worship I offer you will be neither more nor less than idolatry. To believe in you I must believe in Love and Justice, and it is a thousand times better to believe in them than simply to call upon your name. (See St. Bonaventure, *In Sent.*, d. 8, q. 1, q. II, concl.) Apart from them I can never hope to find you, and those who take them as their guides are on the road that leads to you" (Henri de Lubac, *The Discovery of God*, pp. 106–7; cited by Leonardo Boff, *La vida religiosa e a Igreja no processo de libertação*, pp. 88–89.

9. Thomas Aquinas (*Summa Theol.*, II-II, q. 4, a. 4) distinguishes between *fides informis*—faith without charity—and *fides informata* ("informed," or "formed")— faith animated by charity, along the lines of the Epistle of James, chap. 2. Aquinas holds that "information" of faith by charity is not per se essential in order for faith to be faith. Let us note that this is true for the *concept* of faith (orthodoxy), but not for its *reality* (orthopraxis).

10. These two dimensions are expressed most felicitously by Thomas Aquinas, *Summa Theol.*, II-II, q. 9, a. 2, ad 1: *"Licet ea, de quibus fides, sint res divinae et aeternae, tamen ipsa fides est quoddam temporale in animo credentis."*

11. Let us recall: "Actions and productions are all concerned with the individual; for the physician does not cure *man*, except in an incidental way, but Callias or Socrates or some other called by some such individual name, who happens to be a man" (Aristotle, *Metaphysics*, book 1, chap. 1, 981a15–20, p. 499). See also *Nicomachaean Ethics*, book 6, chap. 8, 1141b8–22, p. 390, as well as Thomas Aquinas, *Summa Theol.*, II-II, prologue: *"Sermones enim morales universales minus sunt utiles, eo quod actiones in particularibus sunt."*

12. See Ludwig Feuerbach: "Politics must become our religion"; Pierre-Joseph Proudhon: "Astonishingly, at the bottom of our politics we always find theology" (*Confessions*, Paris, 1849, p. 61); Karl Marx: "We transform theological problems into political problems"; Albert Camus: "Marx . . . understood that a religion which did not embrace transcendence should properly be called politics" (*The Rebel*, p. 167); and so on. Henri Desroche speaks of the "fervor of converts" with which Christians throw themselves into politics. For this whole question, see D. Hervieu-Leger, *De la mission à la protestation*, esp. part 2, chap. 3, on "transference of orthodoxy" from religion to politics; and G. Feran, "Au-delà de la gauche chrétienne," *Chronique Sociale de France*, June 1973, esp. p. 34.

13. See Paul VI: There is a "humanitarian tendency" to transform "theology into sociology" (*Documentation Catholique* 65 [1968] col. 1348). See also Leonardo Boff, "Salvação em Jesus Cristo," esp. pp. 755–57: Jesus is for "global revolution," and against the "regionalization of the kingdom."

14. See Jacques Maritain, *True Humanism*, p. 128, n. 2; p. 279, n. 3.

15. Thomas Aquinas, *Summa Theol.*, I-II, q. 21, a. 4, ad 3. The logion "Give to Caesar what is Caesar's, but give to God what is God's" (Mark 12:17) has no other

meaning. *Adoration*, as absolute gift of one's person, can be rendered only to God: "You shall do homage to the Lord your God; him alone shall you adore" (Mark 12:17; cf. Deut. 6:13). See also Ralf Dahrendorf, *Essays in the Theory of Society*, pp. 19–87: "Homo Sociologicus."

16. See M. Gauchet's penetrating article, "Réflexions sur l'état totalitaire."

17. I might cite the counsel of Buddhist wisdom, to leave aside every other consideration when your house catches fire; or again that piece of popular wisdom to the effect that an empty stomach overrides all other considerations. Here we must distinguish between the order of importance, which regards ends (wisdom), and the order of urgency, which regards means (prudence). See below, chap. 10, n. 30.

18. See 1 Sam. 15:22; Amos 4:4–5, 5:21–25; Hosea 6:1–6, 14:3; Isa. 1:10–16, 29:13–14, 58:1–8; Jer. 7; Mic. 6:5–8; Joel 2:3. As for Jesus: Mark 12:33; Matt. 5:23–34, 9:13, 10:7, 12:7, 15:1–23, 21:12–13, 23:23–25, etc.

19. I occasionally use "pistic" in the sense of "relative to Christian faith," i.e., to the New Testament *pistis*. "Believing" (adj.) inclines heavily in the direction of "religion," or "worship," and is not very apt for use in a political sense.

20. See Juan Luís Segundo, "Capitalismo—socialismo," esp. p. 788. See also the above-cited opinion of Thomas Aquinas apropos of the pertinency of a theological judgment to be rendered on circumstances or conjunctures: *Summa Theol.*, I-II, q. 7, a. 2.

21. This question is not decided solely by force of rational argumentation, but also and especially in relationships of (polemical and political) force: see Giulio Girardi, "Vers de nouveaux rapports entre marxisme et christianisme," *Lumière et Vie* 23 (1974) 185, where the line of demarcation between partisans and adversaries of liberation theology is sociological rather than theological. J. Chabert and J. Guichard say the same thing where the position of Christians with respect to Marxism is concerned (*Lumière et Vie* 23 [1974] 56).

22. "And thinking in itself deals with that which is best in itself" (Aristotle, *Metaphysics*, book 12, chap. 7, 1072b17).

23. Here we find, *grosso modo*, the two basic acceptations that Althusser claims to find in Marx's concept of "ideology" (Althusser, *Essays in Self-Criticism*, pp. 119–25, 153–61).

24. "First ideological" here has the epistemological sense given it by Althusser and his circle, esp. in Althusser, *Pour Marx*, pp. 186ff., and Fichant and Pêcheux, *Sur l'histoire des sciences*. See also L. Sebag, *Marxisme et structuralisme*, pp. 97ff. Let us observe that, in sociological parlance, the word "ideology" is also used in the neutral sense of the symbolic field, sphere, or instance in contradistinction to the real to which it refers. This would be the ideological at zero degrees— "ideological zero." The term "ideological" is also used in the sense of any practical idea that motivates an action, without prejudice to the theoretical ("first ideological") or ethico-political ("second ideological") quality of that idea.

25. M.-D. Dubarle (*Epistémologie des sciences humaines*, p. 11) employs the term "preknowledge" instead of "ideology," to point up the ambivalence of the former as not only illusion (Plato's *doxa*), but font of truth (Aristotle's *endoxon*). See also, along these same lines, J. Taminiaux, "Sur Marx, l'art, et la vérité," *Revue Philosophique de Louvain* 72 (1974) 311–27. On the Aristotelian notion of *endoxon*, see the questionable interpretation of Enrique D. Dussel, *Método para una filosofía de la liberación*, pp. 17–31. I have to admit that, in my work, the notion of "ideology" tends to be defined in terms of the ambivalent concept of "preknowledge"; but I must recognize as well that it always inclines *in malam partem*, by a kind of "semantic concupiscence."

26. See Jürgen Habermas, *La technique et la science comme "idéologie,"* pp. 133ff.; Philippe Roqueplo, *L'énergie de la foi,* pp. 63, 80 (thesis 1), 101, etc.

27. Thus ideology can be defined as a "méconnaissance" (Bourdieu), the "verosimile" (Gritti), the "evidence of common sense" (Gramsci), "that-which-is-taken-for-granted" (Barthes), the "discourse of experience" (Althusser), the "obvious" (R. D. Laing), "Öffentlichkeit" (Heidegger), "reliability" (Houtart), "credibility" (de Certeau), "plausibility" (Peter Berger), "acceptability" (Chomsky), and so on. Even in theology, Thomas Aquinas had already perceived this phenomenon of the "naturalization" of historical religious content as the result of the work of culture: *"Consuetudo autem, et praecipue quae est a puero,* vim naturae *obtinet; ex quo contingit ut ea quibus a pueritia animus imbuitur, ita firmiter teneat* ac si essent naturaliter et per se nota" (*Contra Gentiles,* book 1, chap. 2, emphasis added [apropos of the "ontological argument"]). Likewise Aristotle, *Metaphysics,* book 2, chap. 3 (994b31–995a20, p. 513).

28. The former expression is from Michel de Certeau, *Le christianisme éclaté,* p. 43.

29. We may recall the experience of so many Christian militants who entered political movements from a Christian motivation, and who ended by losing all reference to the faith, it having thus become a simple propaedeutic for political struggle. See José Comblin, *Théologie de la pratique révolutionnaire,* p. 31; J. van Niewenhove and H. Lombaerts, "Une formation pastorale latino-américaine en Europe: Réflexions à la suite d'un voyage," *Lumen Vitae* 26 (1971) 625ff.; Jean Ladrière, "Marxisme et rationalisme," p. 558.

30. See Jacques Maritain, *Distinguish to Unite,* pp. 461–63: speculative vocabulary and practical vocabulary.

31. Think of the Inquisition for Christianity, Stalinism for Marxism, and, finally, the ideology of contemporary scientificism. See L. Sebag, *Marxisme et structuralisme,* p. 170 and p. 185, n. 1.

32. Karl Mannheim, in his classic work, *Ideology and Utopia* (1929), denies that it is "possible for one point of view and interpretation to assail all others as ideological without itself being placed in the position of having to meet that challenge" (p. 74; see also p. 78).

33. Theodore Preis: "We have the absolute order to act in the relative" (cited by Georges Casalis, "Politique, foi et discernement," p. 193). Marxists generally take this sense of the "absolute." See, e.g., D. MacKinnon, "Absolu et rélatif dans l'histoire." Scannone distinguishes between an "absolute option" without a "univocally universal and eternally valid character," and an "absolutist option," which would be "sectarian or totalitarian" (*Teología y política,* p. 263).

34. In his *Metaphysics* (book 1, chap. 2, 983a5–10, p. 501) Aristotle asserts that "first philosophy" is the "most divine," in virtue of the fact of having God as subject and object.

35. Althusser has frequently cited the idealist and empiricist confusion between, on the one side, the real, the order of the real and its process, and on the other, cognition, the order of cognition and its process (*Reading Capital,* pp. 40–43, 86–90, 119–44, 155–57, 189–93, etc.). Likewise Thomas Aquinas often cites the distinction between *modus essendi* (the order of the real) and *modus cognoscendi* (the order of cognition), or between *modus mentis* and *modus rei.* For the distinction in general, see *Summa Theol.,* I, q. 84, a. 1; q. 85, a. 5, ad 3. For its applications in theology: *Summa Theol.,* I, q. 3, a. 4, ad 2; q. 13, a. 12, ad 3; q. 88, a. 2; II-II, q. 1, a. 2; *Contra Gentiles,* book 1, chap. 36; *De Veritate,* q. 14, a. 12; etc. Where analogical discourse is concerned,

Thomas always distingishes between the *significatum* (signification) and the *modus significandi* (representation): *Summa Theol.*, I, q. 13, a. 3, c. and ad 3; etc. Since G. Frege (1892), it has become usual to distinguish *Sinn* (sense, connotation, intention) and *Bedeutung* (signification, denotation, designation, or referent).

36. See, e.g., J. Dhooge, "Quelques problèmes," pp. 224–29: "Theology and Totalizing Interpretation"; Yves M.-J. Congar, "Théologie et sciences humaines," esp. pp. 124, 128.

37. A. de Waelhens, criticizing the pretension to *Voraussetzungslosigkeit*, asserts that the notion of *omnitudo realitatis* under the mode of *Vorhandenheit* (subsistence) corresponds to a circular ontology that can be entertained only at the price of forgetting that it is the human being who makes this claim ("Le mythe de la démythologization,") esp. p. 260.

38. The notion of theology as "second word" was first proposed, I think, by Rubem Alves, in his *A Theology of Human Hope*.

39. On the systematic spirit of all knowing, see Jean Ladrière, "La science, le monde et la foi," pp. 46–47, etc.

40. See Søren Kierkegaard, *Concluding Unscientific Postscript*, cited by Jacques Durandeux, *Quem é teu Deus?* (São Paulo, Duas Cidades, 1970), p. 29.

41. See Hugo Assmann, "Consciencia cristiana y situaciones extremas en el cambio social." See also Sirach 13:2, 17–19: "How can the earthen pot go with the metal cauldron? When they knock together, the pot will be smashed. . . . Can there be peace between the hyena and the dog? Or between the rich and the poor can there be peace? Lion's prey are the wild asses of the desert; so too the poor are feeding grounds for the rich."

42. J.-R. Ladmiral, in his preface to Jürgen Habermas, *La technique et la science comme "ideologie."* It would seem likely that we may assimilate Habermas's "resolute" or "resolved reason" to Aristotle's *phronesis* (*Nicomachaean Ethics*, book 6, chap. 5, 1140a25–b24), as well as to Thomas Aquinas's *prudentia* as the virtue of means and concrete applications (*Summa Theol.*, II-II, qq. 47–56).

43. See the study, considered a classic, of Henri-Xavier Arquillière, *L'Augustinisme politique*.

44. Some bibliographical indications and critical evaluations may be found in G. Thils, *Théologie des réalités terrestres*, vol. 2; F. Olgiati, "Rapporti tra storia, metafisica e religione"; G. Flick and Zoltan Alseghy, "Teologia della storia"; Hans Urs von Balthasar, *De l'intégration*; the works of Enrico Castelli, esp. *I presupposti di una teologia della storia*.

45. See Yves M.-J. Congar, "Histoire," in *Catholicisme*, vol. 5 (Paris, 1962), cols. 779–82; Jean Daniélou, "Geschichtstheologie," in *Lexikon für Theologie und Kirche*, 4:794–99. See also Paul Tillich (*A History of Christian Thought*, pp. 175–80), who states that Augustine's theology of history led to conservatism, whereas that of Joachim of Fiore bore a revolutionary stamp.

46. See Paul Ricoeur, *History and Truth*, pp. 93–97; Linus Bopp, *Unsere Seelsorge*, esp. pp. 3–4; R. Aubert, "Discussions récentes autour de la théologie de l'histoire," (extract from *Collectanea Mechliniensia*, March 1948), pp. 129–49, citing Karl Rahner in *Stimmen der Zeit* 115 (1947) esp. pp. 410–11. If we take the modern theologians who have become "classic"—Jean Daniélou, Yves M.-J. Congar, Henri de Lubac, Karl Rahner, M.-D. Chenu, and others—and analyze their theories, it becomes clear that, for them, history pretty much hovers in the abstract. Their elaborations are practically unusable for my purposes. They register not a trace of practiced socio-analytic media-

tion. In the case of Rahner, see, e.g., Louis Roberts, *The Achievement of Karl Rahner*, pp. 18–44, 58–71; F. Gobériaux, *Le tournant théologique aujourd'hui selon Karl Rahner*, pp. 54–64. For Congar, see Jean-Pierre Jossua, *Yves Congar*. As for Chenu, his great sensitivity to the "problems of the world" must be acknowledged; still, on the level of theological practice, I am forced to the same conclusion: when all is said and done, his theories are impracticable for a theology of the political. See his studies *Evangile dans le temps; Théologie de la matière; Civilisation technique et spiritualité chrétienne; The Theology of Work*. As for his view, still in a traditional mold, of a possible relationship between theology and science, see "Théologie et recherche interdisciplinaire." For the particular case of theology vis-à-vis the sciences of the social, see M.-D. Chenu, *La foi dans l'intelligence*, pp. 59–68, 371–83; idem, " 'Spiritualisme' et sociologie." A complete bibliography of Chenu's works may be found in Congar et al., *Mélanges offerts à M.-D. Chenu*, pp. 9–29. For Daniélou, see his *The Lord of History*. For de Lubac, see his *Catholicism: A Study of Dogma in Relation to the Corporate Destiny of Mankind*.

47. See Matt. 13:24–30, 36–43.

48. See Jacques Ellul, *The Politics of God and the Politics of Man*, a study in theology of history in 2 Kings, in which Ellul posits God's action and human action in relationship according to Karl Barth's principle, "the free determination of man in the free decision of God." See also Karl Löwith, *Meaning in History*, esp. p. 8.

49. This can be verified in the field of philosophical reason itself. See J. Hersch, "Sur le sens de l'histoire," esp. p. 97: "History, in order to be history, must have a meaning implying the intent of a totality." Along the same lines, see Jean Ladrière, *Vie sociale et destinée*, pp. 191–95; R. Aron, *Introduction to the Philosophy of History*; idem, *Dimensions de la conscience historique*; Léopold Malevez, *Histoire de salut et philosophie: Barth, Bultmann et Cullmann*; Henri Lefebvre, *La fin de l'histoire*; René Rémond et al., *Philosophies de l'histoire*; Jacques Maritain, *On the Philosophy of History*; etc.

50. See esp. Henri-Irénée Marrou, *Time and Timelessness* (a work inspired by Augustine) and Linus Bopp, *Unsere Seelsorge*, with its ten "laws" of history induced from ten currents of thought along the lines of a theology of history. These authors, despite the erudition of their studies, fail to get beyond generalities—owing to the fact that their interpretation of the current historical moment remains "in the indefinite," despite their will to practice. But will to practice is no substitute for practice, including theoretical practice.

CHAPTER 4

1. Thomas Aquinas already had the clear view here: "*Non pertinet ad* [sacred doctrine] *pobare principia aliarum scientiarum* [the principle of respect], *sed solum judicare de eis: quidquid enim in aliis scientiis invenitur veritati hujus scientiae repugnans, totum condemnetur ut falsum* [the principle of criticism]" (*Summa Theol.*, I, q. 1, a. 6, ad 2). On the relationship of theology with the sciences of the human being, see Adolphe Gesché, "Le discours théologique sur l'homme." José M. Gonzáles Ruíz, in an order inverse to mine and in his own fashion, has argued for these same two principles: "We have absolute need of sociologists in order to attain the objective we envisage, as also of the theologians and intellectuals of our time—that is, we need the radical detheologization of all rigorously scientific approach, and the radical descientificization of all theological approach" ("Théologie et sciences sociales," p. 295).

2. See *Gaudium et Spes*, no. 36: "Societies themselves enjoy their own laws and values which must be gradually deciphered, put to use, and regulated by men" (pp. 270–71).

3. See Jacques Monod, *Chance and Necessity*, pp. 173–80.

4. Recall "Ockham's razor": *Entia non sunt multiplicanda praeter necessitatem*. Peter L. Berger has insisted a great deal on "methodological atheism" in the context of a sociology of religion: see his "Some Second Thoughts on Substantive Versus Functional Definitions of Religion."

5. "Core" is a concept of I. Lakatos, standing for the corpus of hypotheses maintained throughout the execution of a program of investigation. See S. Amsterdamski, "L'évolution de la science," p. 37.

6. See Jean Ladrière, *L'articulation du sens*, pp. 211ff. If this is problematic even in the area of the "natural sciences," what is to be said of the "human sciences"?

7. To Albert Einstein, who had begged theologians not to theologize from a point of departure in obscure points of scientific research, Paul Tillich responded: "Theology above all, must leave to science the description of the whole of objects and their interdependence in nature and history, in man and his world. And beyond this, theology must leave to philosophy the description of the structures and categories of being itself and of the *logos* in which being becomes manifest. Any interference of theology with these tasks of philosophy and science is destructive for theology itself" (*Theology and Culture*, p. 129).

8. See Jean Ladrière's remarkable study, "Langage auto-implicatif et langage biblique selon Evans," in *L'articulation du sens*, pp. 91–139, esp. p. 135, where he posits a difference between "properly religious language" and "speculative theological language," which latter would effectuate a "bracketing of the auto-implicative aspect, but not a suppression of this aspect" (p. 136).

9. *Via longa* ("long way") and *via curta* ("short way") are expressions used by Paul Ricoeur: *Le conflit des interprétations*, pp. 10ff. Indeed, see Pascal, *Pensées*, p. 139 (n. 287): "I freely admit that one of these Christians who believe without proof will perhaps not have the means of convincing an unbeliever, who might say as much for himself, but those who do know the proofs of religion can easily prove that this believer is truly inspired by God, although he cannot prove it himself."

10. See Peter Berger, *The Sacred Canopy*, pp. 186–88. Berger's methodological suggestion is that one theologize only after and within this fact, established by the sciences: that religion is a human product. Only then would theology be able to speak its word with pertinency.

11. On the problematic of secularization, see Dullaart et al., *Les deux visages* (bibliography, pp. 251–58); Christian Duquoc, *Ambiguité des théologies de la sécularisation*; Adolphe Gesché, "Essai d'interprétation dialectique du phénomène de sécularisation"; Marcel Xhaufflaire, *Feuerbach*. See also V. Bolan, *Sociologia da secularização* (bibliography, pp. 173–74).

12. See, e.g., L. Gera's and Enrique D. Dussel's criticisms of science in *Stromata*, nos. 1–2 (1974).

13. This is the case, e.g., with the criticisms of religion by the "masters of suspicion." To the extent that theologians reject such criticisms on grounds of their scientificist character, without making an effort to distinguish illegitimate extrapolation from legitimate results (would this have been possible in that era?), theology renounced two advantages: (1) it continued to take the material for its reading from a view that had been transcended, because a new intelligibility or *episteme* had already been projected upon it; (2) to the extent that it continued to posit its discourse on the level of the *dictum*—in the

sense of the *dictum* of the *dictum* (the "re-said")—it exposed itself to the danger of involvement in the problematization of this same *dictum* introduced by the new positivity of the sciences of the human being. In my view, theology has the right to situate its discourse on a much more original level—that of (religious or pistic) being and (ethical or agapic) action, because this is its proper element—*to idion*.

14. I shall not resist the temptation to make reference to Andrew Greeley's "ten commandments" for theologians interested in sociology: "1. Thou shalt not confuse the elite and the masses. . . . 2. Thou shalt not adopt simplistic evolutionistic models. . . . 3. Thou shalt not exaggerate the speed of social change. . . . 4. Thou shalt remember that reality is grey rather than white or black. . . . 5. Thou shalt avoid the fallacious temptation of the "good old days." . . . 6. Thou shalt abstain from seeing crises where there are none. . . . 7. Thou shalt not denounce the religion of the masses. . . . 8. Thou shalt not hope for the instantaneous transformation of popular values by activity of the churches. . . . 9. Thou shalt remember that there are two kinds of statistics (good and evil). . . . 10. Thou shalt remember above all that the human personality and human society are complex" (cf. *Social Compass* 17 [1970] 277–80).

15. Jean Piaget, *Epistémologie des sciences de l'homme*, pp. 38–41; Louis Althusser, *Reading Capital*, p. 157, n. 35.

16. See H. Splengler, "Le préjugé théologique," where he shows how the antitheological presupposition, no less than its contrary, leads to false sociological conclusions.

17. This is what Augustine did with Platonism and Thomas Aquinas with Aristotelianism, and it is what "political theologians" will have to do with Marxism. See *Summa Theol.*, I, q. 1, a. 5, ad 2; *In Boethii de Trinitate*, q. 2, a. 3. See, too, Yves M.-J. Congar, "Théologie," in *Dictionnaire de la Théologie Catholique*, vol. 14, cols. 495–500: "theology and sciences."

18. Jean Ladrière: "For that matter, it is theology that is the genuine consummation of sociology, in the sense that it pertains to the former to reveal to us, in the last analysis, much more profoundly than philosophy can, the true signification of social relationships" ("La sociologie, son introduction dans la pensée catholique," p. 204).

19. See Walter Kasper, *The Methods of Dogmatic Theology*, pp. 26, 42; idem, *Dogme et évangile* (Tournai, Casterman, 1967), pp. 118ff.

20. "Liberation theologians" presuppose an analysis of the phenomenon of "dependence" as handled in Marxist tradition. We must say, however, that this relationship remains somewhat undefined and rather implicit. See the criticisms of R. Poblete, "La teoría de la dependencia," esp. pp. 213–17; Pierre Bigo, "El 'instrumental científico,'" pp. 247–70; idem, "Marxismo y liberación en América Latina," pp. 236–46. As for "political theology" of a German orientation, I have already alluded to its interlocution with the Marxism of the young Marx: see in particular the works of Marcel Xhaufflaire, esp. *Feuerbach*, esp. pp. 280–98; as well as Fernando Belo, *A Materialist Reading of the Gospel of Mark,* esp. part 4: "An Essay in Materialist Ecclesiology," pp. 241–97. See also the popular version of this work: *Uma leitura política do Evangelho.*

21. For this important distinction, see Chilean Bishops' Conference, *Evangelio, política y socialismo* (working document), esp. nos. 33 and 37; Dom Hélder Câmara, in Enrique D. Dussel, *Historia de la Iglesia*, p. 290.

Let me cite two authors who have taken a position on the question of the relationship between theology and Marxism: René Coste and Giulio Girardi. For the former, see the annotated bibliography of some of his writings in *Nouvelle Revue Théologique* 93 (1971) 1109–11, as well as his "Marxisme et théologie"; "L'Eglise et le défi du monde"; and "Les chrétiens et l'analyse marxiste." In this last article, Coste expresses himself very negatively with respect to "the Marxist impregnation" of Christian thought (pp. 21ff.). Although he does not oppose Marxism in principle as an "operative model," he sees materialism and atheism as two of its essential traits (pp. 31–38). But he avoids the question of whether these proceed from an intrinsic demand of Marxist logic or from an ideological intention or option on the part of its theoreticians. Coste's methodological propositions in his section 2, "What is a political analysis?" (pp. 26–31), seem to me too general, and not sufficiently operational.

Girardi takes another viewpoint. He remains absolutely *within* Marxism, but considerably corrects its philosophical bases, especially where materialism is concerned, holding that materialism would be acceptable as a scientific position, but not as a philosophical principle. (On this point, let me note in passing the similar position of R. Vancourt, "Idéologie, marxisme et 'dépassement' de la philosophie," pp. 49ff. Vancourt lays to the account of Friedrich Engels the hardening of Marxism as a global philosophy in the form of dialectical materialism.) Girardi, in his article "Vers de nouveaux rapports entre marxisme et christianisme," asserts: "The new instruments of which theology has need are furnished by historical materialism as a theory of revolution. Revolutionary theology, therefore, can be characterized, synthetically, as the application of historical materialism in theology and to theology. Marxism thus becomes a fecundating principle of Christianity" (p. 183). He compares this undertaking to that of Thomas Aquinas with Aristotelianism. (For this assimilation, see also José Comblin, *Théologie de la pratique révolutionnaire*, pp. 32–33; Dom Hélder Câmara, in Enrique Dussel, *Historia de la Iglesia*, p. 290.) For my part, I find that Girardi's position is epistemologically insupportable, except in the sense of socio-analytic mediation. See also other works of his, all influenced, in greater or lesser degree, by Marxist thought: *Marxism and Christianity*; *Dialogue et révolution* (Paris, Cerf, 1969); *Amour chrétien et violence révolutionnaire* (Paris, Cerf, 1970); *Christianisme, libération humaine et lutte des classes* (Paris, Cerf, 1972); "Théorie et praxis dans la pensée marxiste"; and finally, the international encyclopedia published under his direction: Facoltà Filosofica della Pontificia Università Salesiana di Roma, *L'ateismo contemporaneo* (Turin, Società Editrice Internazionale, 1967–70).

22. See Jean Ladrière, "Marxisme et rationalisme," p. 562; G. Cottier, "Valeur de 'l'analyse marxiste,'" and other articles in *Nova et Vetera*. He notes the indefinite epistemological status of Marx's work: for Marx, *scientific postulates* at times surreptitiously assume the value of *metaphysical principles*, thus engendering *petitiones principii* and thereby strangling discourse ("Athéisme et marxisme," esp. p. 356). See also the studies of Paul Valadier: "Marxisme et scientificité" (on the genuinely original concept that Marx has of "science," along the lines of the scientism of the nineteenth century); "Marxisme et chrétiens"; "Analyse politique et marxisme."

23. See Jolif, "Le temps fait beaucoup à l'affaire." Roger Garaudy underscores this point with great vigor—the importance of the test of time with respect to an idea, esp. in the matter of the tests that Christian faith may yet pass in respect of a conscious participation in social construction. If materialism—says Garaudy—is the sole theoretical principle capable of basing a scientific investigation of history, this will be decided in scientific investigation, not by ideological dogma. Likewise, if only atheism can base a consistent revolutionary action, this will be decided by the revolutionary action, not by dogmatic pronouncement. These propositions are to be found in José M. González Ruíz, *Dios está en la base*, p. 147; see also pp. 142ff: "Marxism and Christianity"; and idem, *The New Creation*.

24. It would be superfluous to cite Althusser's work here. His merit, from our view-

point, is to have effectuated a double demarcation within Marxism: first, the so-called *coupure* between *ideology* (the humanism of the young Marx, who was not yet a Marxist but a Hegelian) and *science* (the science of history, that of the mature Marx); and secondly that between *philosophy* (dialectical materialism) and *science* (historical materialism). See also the epistemological observations of Gilles-Gaston Granger on Marxist "style" (as seen in contrast with Freud's analytical "style"): *Essai d'une philosophie du style*, pp. 287–89.

25. I should like to see applied to Marxism what Sigmund Freud held of psychoanalysis: "In itself, psychoanalysis is neither religious nor antireligious. It is a nonpartisan tool that can be used by the clergy as well as by the laity, provided they use it solely in the service of the liberation of creatures who suffer" (*Correspondance de Sigmund Freud avec le Pasteur Pfister* [Paris, Gallimard, 1966], p. 47. Gustavo Gutiérrez notes that the famous Peruvian Marxist, José Carlos Mariátegui, along the line of Engels and Lenin, considered Marxism "simply a canon of interpretation," and "not a philosophy of history" (*A Theology of Liberation*, p. 97, n. 40).

26. This is observable in the work done by social scientists, such as G. Rocher, *Introduction à la sociologie générale*, 2:82–83; D. Ribeiro, *La civilización occidental y nosotros* (Buenos Aires, Centro Editor de América Latina, 1969), 1:30; "Sociologie," in *Encyclopaedia Universalis,* vol. 15, pp. 72–84, esp. 74–75, 81; *Revista Mejicana de Sociología*, 1970, nos. 3, 4; Ralf Dahrendorf, *Essays on the Theory of Society*, pp. 129–50; François Houtart, "Réflexions sur une théologie de la politique." Theologians do the same: Geyer, Janowski, and Schmidt, *Theologie und Soziologie*, pp. 101ff.; Hugo Assmann, *Nomad Church*, pp. 65–66: "The World as Conflict"; G. Girardi, *Christianisme, libération humaine*, pp. 178ff.: "from a religion of harmony to a religion of confrontation"; René Coste, "Chrétiens et l'analyse marxiste"; etc.

27. The accusation that functionalism, a very strong current in the United States (which stands to reason), is "reactionary" is a familiar one. R. K. Merton has attempted to respond to such accusations with the concept of "dysfunction": see G. Rocher, *Introduction à la sociologie*, pp. 170–74. See also the criticism of American functionalism in politics by Pierre Birnbaum, *La fin du politique* (Paris, Seuil, 1975). The dialectical or conflictual conception, for its part, has been and is held to be "revolutionary." Thus one cannot help but wonder whether the selection of either of the two conceptualizations is not basically directed by an ethico-political or ideological (class viewpoint) evaluation: see Michael Lowy, *Dialectique et révolution*, esp. the conclusion: "science and revolution."

28. For this whole series of problems, see F. Châtelet, ed., *Histoire de la philosophie*, vol. 8 (*La philosophie des sciences sociales*), esp. p. 329. J.-D. Robert reviews this book in *Nouvelle Revue Théologique*, 1974, pp. 1067–78, cautioning the theologian not to take the results of the sciences of the human being too naively as simply "scientific," for they are impregnated with ideological and philosophical presuppositions— "free choices," then (p. 1078). See the extensive work of Gilles-Gaston Granger, who ranks among those who have done the most for the scientific character of the sciences of the human being. J.-D. Robert offers a complete bibliography of Granger's works, along with a good resumé of his epistemological positions, in *Laval Théologique et Philosophique* 31 (1975) 239–63. On the status of the human sciences, see G. Gusdorf, *Sciences humaines et la conscience occidentale*; and Jean Piaget, *Epistémologie des sciences de l'homme*.

29. Let us note that an option, unlike a simple choice, may be defined as a decision "of

a piece with its own cause": Adolphe Gesché, "Mutation religieuse et renouvellement théologique," p. 296, n. 84.

30. I shall return to this dialectic in part 3. Here, see only Jean Ladrière, *L'articulation du sens*, pp. 25–50.

31. For Emile Durkheim, socialism, at its origin, is a passion—a passion for justice, for the rescue of the oppressed. The science, according to Durkheim, occurs in a second instance, and is for the purpose of supporting the initial option. See his *Socialism and Saint-Simon*.

32. The Chinese cultural revolution expressed the synthesis of these two aspects in the slogan, "red and scientific," but with the emphasis on the former: K. S. Karol, *La deuxième révolution chinoise* (Paris, Laffont, 1973), pp. 28, 36, 81.

33. See Max Weber, *Der Sinn der "Wertfreiheit."* See also José Comblin, *Théologie de la pratique*, pp. 45–47, citing Jean Ladrière, *L'articulation du sens*, pp. 141–59.

34. See Chilean Bishops' Conference, *Evangelio, política y socialismo*; Peruvian Bishops' Conference, *Justicia en el mundo* (Aug. 1971). Both documents plead for an "option for the poor." See François Houtart and F. Hambye, "Implications sociopolitiques de Vatican II": "The gospel furnishes the first criterion for responsible choices vis-à-vis the implementation of this demand [for justice]: the situation of those in need" (p. 94). The authors posit two principles of Christian reflection with regard to the political: faith, as "transethical," utopic, intent (p. 93), corresponding to hermeneutic mediation; and the need for an instrument of analysis for political practice (p. 91), for which I have recourse to socio-analytic mediation. For the choice of a Marxist conceptuality from a point of departure in the faith option, see Georges Casalis, "Politique, foi et discernement," pp. 191ff.; idem, *Idéologies de libération et message du Salut*, p. 216; Girardi, *Christianisme, libération humaine*, pp. 181–82; idem, "Teología y revolución," p. 5: here Girardi pleads for a transcendence of philosophical mediation in favor of that of the sciences of the human being, but "marked by a *prise de position*" consisting of a "passage from a dominant theology to a revolutionary theology" (p. 15). See also his "Théorie et praxis," pp. 25–27, 31–33, where the problem of criteriology remains ambiguous. It will be all but superfluous to recall, here, the movements Marxist Christians and Christians for Socialism, whose major documents are those of Santiago de Chile (April 1972) (see John Eagleson, ed., *Christians and Socialism*, Maryknoll, N.Y., Orbis, 1975) and Quebec (April 1975) (see SEDOC 8 [1975] col. 169–76). The first European congress of this movement, in Nov. 1976, occasioned a stern warning on the part of Pope Paul VI: see *Jornal do Brasil*, Nov. 11, 1976, pp. 1, 14.

35. Where Latin America is concerned, a goodly proportion of the social analysts there, at least of those with the most awareness, are to be found in the line of Marxist tradition, such as those of the "sociology of dependency" current.

36. This has been, and remains, true even at the level of philosophical mediation, as Rudolf Bultmann notes: "We must realize that there will never be a right philosophy in the sense of an absolutely perfect system, a philosophy which could give answers to all questions and clear up all riddles of human existence. Our question is simply which philosophy today offers the most adequate perspective and conceptions for understanding human existence" (*Jesus Christ and Mythology*, p. 55; see also pp. 52–54).

37. See Fernando Belo, *Materialist Reading*, pp. 277–83: "The Discourse of Powerlessness or the Theological Negation"; idem, *Leitura política*, pp. 113–18. Let us retain the suggestion implied in this notion, but not the interpretive content, which is simply unacceptable.

38. *Habitus* here has the meaning of the Aristotelian *hexis*: capability, competence,

system of dispositions, matrix of multiple acts. This sense is expressed in the celebrated Chinese maxim to the effect that a fishhook is more important than a fish. See Pierre Bourdieu, *Outline of a Theory of Practice*, pp. 167ff.

39. Some theology students apply themselves to the social sciences along with their study of theology, which suggests that the locus of theological interlocution or conversation has shifted. But it remains for this change to be registered in the corresponding "canonical locus," in terms of ecclesiastical discipline and directives.

40. See *Gaudium et Spes*, no. 62: "Through a sharing of resources and points of view, let those who teach in seminaries, colleges, and universities try to collaborate with men well versed in the other sciences" (p. 299); see also ibid., no. 44 (p. 280). For the question of interdisciplinarity in theology, see François Houtart, ed., *Recherche interdisciplinaire et théologie*; M. Renaud, "La recherche interdisciplinaire en théologie"; François Russo, "La pluri-disciplinarité"; Johannes B. Metz and T. Rendtorff, eds., *Die Theologie in der interdisziplinären Forschung*; Karl Rahner, "Die Theologie im interdisziplinären Gespräche der Wissenschaften"; F. Taborda, "Teologia e ciências no diálogo interdisciplinar," including a good bibliography. For interdisciplinarity as a general problem, see Dario Antiseri, *I fondamenti epistemologici del lavoro interdisciplinare*; Hilton Japiassu, *Interdisciplinaridade e patologia do saber*.

41. See Hugo Assmann, "Seminario: Consciencia cristiana y situaciones extremas en el cambio social."

42. Thomas Aquinas's *Summa Theologiae* seems to me to constitute the consummate type of the integration of an originally foreign mediation (*"ex extraneis argumentis"*: I, q. 1, a. 8, ad 2), that of philosophy, appropriating it in such a way, however, that it disappears within the broader theological project—this project now lending the erstwhile alien its own coloration. Aquinas himself compared this operation of the transubstantiation of philosophy into theology to the conversion of water into wine (*In Boethii de Trinitate*, q. 2, a. 3, ad 5).

43. These considerations are inspired by A. E. Solari, "Usos y abusos de la sociología," pp. 47–53.

44. "Liberdade," in A. C. Monteiro, *Fernando Pessoa: Poesia* (Rio de Janeiro, Agir, 2nd ed., 1959, p. 51).

INTRODUCTION TO PART TWO

1. J. D. Smart, *Divided Mind*.

2. See *Selecciones de teología*, vol. 13 (1974); R. Vander Gucht and H. Vorgrimler, eds., *Bilan de la théologie du XXe siècle*, esp. the contribution by Karl Rahner, "L'avenir de la théologie" (conclusion of vol. 2; also published in *Nouvelle Revue Théologique* 93 [1971] 3–28), as well as the contributions of R. Aubert and José Comblin on the situation of Catholic theology in the 20th century, vol. 1, pp. 423–531. See also Adolphe Gesché, "Bibliographie raisonné: Le problème de Dieu dans le monde aujourd'hui," in his *L'annonce de Dieu au monde d'aujourd'hui*, pp. 75–102. See further: Yves M.-J. Congar, *Situation et tâches présentes de la théologie*, esp. the bibliography on p. 11, n. 1. Let me cite one of the most sensitive witnesses to the "crisis of foundations" in theology today in France: Claude Geffré, *A New Age in Theology*; idem, "Théologie," in *Encyclopaedia Universalis*, esp. p. 1087; idem, "Les courants actuels de la recherche théologique." For its substantial coincidence, discovered a posteriori, of his views with mine, I recommend François Refoulé, "Orientations nouvelles de la théologie en France."

3. "Recasting" is the technical term used by the group "Théorie" around Louis

Althusser to signify breaches *within* a theoretical field already constituted by virtue of the "epistemological breach." The group borrows the term from F. Regnault; see Fichant and Pêcheux, *Sur l'histoire des sciences*, p. 12. In my estimation, this concept is altogether apt for designating the internal reorganization imposed upon the theoretical field of theology by the "new theological problematic," as the latter opens up a new sector of reflection: that of second theology. In his article, "Rapport sur la situation de l'incroyance en France," (*Esprit* 1 [1971] 3–15), G. Granel also proposes a "recasting" of theology—but in the sense of an intellectual effort to place the *ratio fidei* in contact with the "resources of contemporary thought," which would mean a great deal more than a simple "adaptation" (pp. 10, 12–15). Furthermore, Granel is thinking mainly of a philosophical mediation. For this mediation, see his *Traditionis traditio*.

4. Louis Althusser: "The moment of the theory of theoretical practice—i.e., the moment when a 'theory' has need of a theory of its own practice—the moment of the theory of method in general, always appears later (*après coup*), to help overcome practical or 'theoretical' difficulties, to solve problems, that, in the play of praxis immersed in its workings, are unresolvable—theoretically blind—or to counter a yet deeper crisis. . . . But science can do its work—namely, produce knowledge—for a long time without sensing the need of producing the theory of what it is doing, the theory of its practice. Think of Marx" (cf. *Pour Marx*, p. 176). See also Jean Ladrière, *La science, le monde et la foi*, p. 205; but esp. Thomas S. Kuhn, *The Structure of Scientific Revolutions*, where it is shown that the whole history of science is marked by the relationship between scientific crisis and epistemological investigation.

5. Epistemological reflection in theology is still very deficient. Priority is given to questions connected with logic and language, as I shall indicate below. As for the theology of liberation, it is returning with ever greater insistence to "questions of method." One need only examine the themes of its international congresses—that of the Escorial in 1972 and Mexico City in 1975. It seems to me that the *hic* of theology appears here, rather than in the first type of research in which the sciences of the social have no major importance. Bernard Lonergan, e.g., is satisfied with generalities when referring to praxis: *Method in Theology*, pp. 361–67; *Theologie im Pluralismus heutiger Kulturen*, esp. pp. 184–90 ("the revolution in Catholic theology"), where the question of method is posited clearly, but without any relationship to the vital questions of today, such as those of the political.

6. The function of epistemology vis-à-vis the discipline to which it refers is, perhaps, analogous to that attributed by Wittgenstein to philosophy vis-à-vis thought generally: the *therapeutic* function. See *Tractatus Logico-Philosophicus* (1921), proposition 4.112 (p. 49 in the Pears-McGuinness English translation).

7. For the scholastics' method, see M.-D. Chenu, "Scholastique," in *Dictionnaire de la Théologie Catholique*.

8. See G. Deleuze, "A quoi reconnaît-on le structuralisme?" esp. pp. 304–7.

9. Immanuel Kant: " . . . Explanations and examples, and other helps to intelligibility, aid us in the comprehension of *parts*, but they distract the attention, dissipate the mental power of the reader, and stand in the way of his forming a clear conception of the *whole*; as he cannot attain soon enough to a survey of the system, and the colouring and embellishments bestowed upon it prevent his observing its articulation or organization—which is the most important consideration with him, when he comes to judge of its unity and stability" (*The Critique of Pure Reason*, Preface to the First Edition, p. 3).

CHAPTER 5

1. See Luís J. Prieto, *Pertinence et pratique*; Jean Ladrière, "L'applicabilité des mathématiques aux sciences sociales," esp. pp. 1545–46. Descartes, in *Regulae ad Directionem Ingenii*, VIII, defines the principle of pertinency, or specificity: "*enumerationem certis limitis circumscribi atque aliquot capita disponi.*" Algirdas J. Greimas employs the concept of "isotopy" to define the homogeneity of a semantic field: *Structural Semantics* (cited by Paul Ricoeur, *Le conflit des interprétations*, pp. 77 and 94). See also Greimas, *Sémiotique et sciences sociales*, pp. 17–18.

2. "Epistemological reflection" must "deliver us from a universally nosey theology whose 'catholicity' seems to some to demand that everything get all mixed up with everything else" (S. Breton, "Logique et argumentation de convenance," p. 261). Breton recalls Aristotle, for whom a "universal science" is unthinkable, because every science must have an object of a determinate kind (p. 261, n. 33). Let me also cite Thomas Aquinas here: *Summa Theol.*, I, q. 1, a. 1, ad 2: "*Diversa ratio cognoscibilis diversitatem scientiarum inducit*"; I-II, q. 57, a. 2. This is valid for theology as well, in its quality as a (particular) "science": I, q. 1, aa. 3, 7.

3. I refer to current expressions such as "Bantu theology," "theology of Saint Francis," and even "theology of Jeremiah" or "of Paul," and so on. The content of theology has never ceased to be related to its "epochality."

4. See Thomas Aquinas, *Contra Gentiles*, book 2, chap. 4: "*Quod aliter considerat de creaturis philosophus et theologus.*" For the questions of a "philosophy of religion," see the classic works: Georges van Riet, *Philosophie et religion*; Henry Duméry, *Philosophie de la religion*; Karl Rahner, *Hearers of the Word*; Werner Jaeger, *The Theology of the Early Greek Philosophers*.

5. For "religious sociology," see the works of Henri Desroche, especially *Jacob and the Angel*, chap. 8. I might also mention the periodicals *Archives de Sciences Sociales des Religions* and *Social Compass*. See, too, the bibliography I have already cited: *Instituto Fe y Secularidad, Sociologia de la religión* (chap. 1, n. 1, above).

For "religious psychology," see the works of A. Vergote, esp. his *Psychologie religieuse* (Brussels, Dessart, 1966), and *Interprétation du langage religieux* (Paris, Seuil, 1974). See, too, the studies of A. Godin, J. Pohier, L. Beirnaert, R. Hostie, A. Plé, A. Görres, J. Durandeaux, G. Zunini, Charles A. Curran, S. Hiltner, J.-P. Déconchy. See also the review *Archiv für Religionspsychologie* (Göttingen).

On analyses of religious language, see below, chap. 7, n. 82.

6. In this sense there can be no doubt that Thomas Aquinas's *Summa* is genuinely a "theological" one. It is the horizon of articulation, the area of problematic, that decides this predicate, and here the decision is clear. That Thomas has recourse to Aristotelianism, and confers upon theology a powerful rational structure, pertains to the very character of theology as theo*logy*. Only those will be surprised who reduce theology to its *principium*: the word of faith. I have yet to discuss all this in depth.

7. It would be too much of a digression to apply here to the sciences of the human being in general what Thomas Aquinas says of "knowledge of creatures" regarding its value for a better knowledge of God: "*Quod cognoscere naturam creaturarum valet ad destruendum errores qui sunt circa Deum*" (*Contra Gentiles*, book 2, chap. 3). Here he says, among other things: "*Divinae virtuti in creaturas operanti aliquid detrahitur per hoc quod creaturae natura ignoratur. . . . Haec enim omnia* [ignorance of the world around us] *divinae derrogant potestati. . . . Sic ergo patet falsam esse quorundam sententiam qui dicebant* nihil interesse ad fidei veritatem *quid de creaturis quisque sen-*

tiret, dummodo circa Deum recte sentiatur. . . . *Nam* error circa creaturas redundat in falsam de Deo sententiam *et hominum mentes a Deo abducit, in quem fides dirigere nititur, dum ipsas quibusdam aliis causis supponit"* (emphasis added). See also chap. 69, *"De opinione eorum qui rebus naturalibus proprias subtrahunt actiones"*: in this important chapter, Thomas asserts that to refer everything immediately to God, diluting away the autonomy of "worldly" causes, has the effect not only of neglecting the utility of things *(frustra)* and thus denying the very possibility of science *("et sic subtrahitur nobis omnis cognitio scientiae naturalis"),* but also entails the devaluation of God *("detrahere ergo perfectioni creaturarum est detrahere perfectioni divinae virtutis");* and in another passage—*"detrahere ergo actiones proprias rebus est divinae bonitati derogare."* Here we have the wherewithal for basing, *in the proper element of theology* the legitimacy of the sciences of the social. As it has always been—in the encounter with Hellenism in the apostolic and patristic age, in the encounter with Aristotelianism in the Middle Ages, and in that with the "human sciences" today—it is doubtless painful for Christian awareness to have to do its symbolic universe all over again—recast it—with the help of new comprehensive syntheses, articulated under the sovereignty of revelation. The recognition today of the autonomy of social organization and evolution, while maintaining the notion of the sovereignty of God and of Christ over history, constitutes a true trial by fire for faith and for the thinking of the faith—i.e., for theology. It is not to be wondered at, then, that so few have been able to cross the *Feuerbach*, the "river of fire," to borrow Marx's play on the name.

8. By reason of the nature of its particular object, theology is altogether different from a "human science of religion," as Thomas asserts in his *Summa Theol.*, I, q. 1, a. 1, ad 2: *"differt secundum genus."* It is (epistemologically) meaningless to assert that theology can replace the "human science of religion." Yet this is what is suggested by theologians such as L. Dullaart, "Institution et légitimation"; Louis Boisset, *La théologie en procès*, conclusion; or, in the form of a question, Claude Geffré, "Théologie," in *Encyclopaedia Universalis*, p. 1087.

So much for theoretical statements. As for theoretical practice, I can cite Fernando Belo's book, *A Materialist Reading of the Gospel of Mark*. The pertinency of this work, as can be seen from the title, is that of a reading of Mark by Marx (p. 18). Its epistemological identity is difficult to locate. In my view, properly theological practice would consist in doing just the opposite—i.e., in practicing a "Markan reading of Marx"—Mark working on Marx, to paraphrase Louis Althusser in *Lenin and Philosophy*, pp. 107-25. After all, it is the "agent instance," the second generality, that defines the pertinency of a theoretical practice, as I shall explain in §25. Belo's "methodological imprecision" has not been lost on some of the reviewers of his work, such as J. Delorme, writing in *Lumière et Vie* 23 (1974) 114-18, or Yves Congar, in *Etudes*, June 1975, pp. 927-33, esp. p. 931. Finally, let me note that the fact of being Christian or of asserting the content of the faith is no substitute for the theoretical quality of one's work.

9. The challenge of Marxism to theology in its alleged quality of "Christian ideology" may not be allowed to have the effect of subsuming theology (and revelation) within the Marxist theoretical purview, at the price of a surrender of the proper difference of theology (and revelation). To consider theology (and revelation) as "ideology," and as pertaining per se to the superstructure, is itself to "play" within a particular "topic." It means looking with quite determinate lenses, and lenses with a hue of their own. In vain does Marxism proclaim itself the universal *mathesis* (see the studies cited above). For Marx's own idea of "science," see Paul Valadier, "Marxisme et scientificité"; for Marxism as "the most consistent and most radical expression of European rationalism," then

in the midst of crisis, and as "the consummate expression of modernity," see Jean Ladrière, "Marxisme et rationalisme."

But theology is not merely observable—it can do observing of its own, with its own (clear!) eyes. Thus it can enter into a relationship with Marxism by integrating the latter to itself. There is nothing to prevent the "reverse dialectic" of Marxism from being "re-reversed": see Peter Berger, *The Sacred Canopy*, pp. 175-88. To think Christianity, to reflect upon Christianity, with Marxism as a tool, in socio-analytic mediation, is possible and even desirable. But to reduce the reflection to this, and pass off its product as theology, is "selling cat for rabbit." See Jean Guichard, "Le marxisme de Marx à Mao," and "Les chrétiens face au marxisme." Guichard's basic positions are taken up and followed by Louis Boisset, *La théologie en procès*, pp. 104-6. See also G. Girardi, the works cited above, in chap. 4, n. 21. In my opinion, Christianity can only suffer a reduction if it is thought, reflected upon—as these authors seem to do—within the Marxist horizon (pertinency) exclusively in accordance with the place Marxism grants it. Why? Because the Marxist *topica* succeeds in apprehending only one aspect of religion—that of being a social product or a social factor. The meta-empirical (or divine) reference, by which religion is (self)-defined, can be comprehended by Marxist philosophy only under the form of illusion—that is, by ascribing it to the imaginary, for Marxist philosophy has no other categories for it. This is its *primum principium metaphysicum*: the extramental = matter. In my view, where theological practice is concerned, a Marxist analysis can be only a first moment, doubtless necessary, but always antecedent—as socio-analytic mediation. Theology, in order to pronounce its own proper discourse, shall have to open a horizon of its own—by its hermeneutic mediation. In this second moment, Marxist instrumentality becomes, in the proper sense of the word, nonpertinent. We have the contrary tendency (rather than system) in Hugo Assmann, *Nomad Church*, where the author carries out a sociological analysis of Christianity rather than a Christian analysis of society. Finally, let us recall, once and for all: there is no such thing as a "prioritarian discourse" that would fix the limits and the tasks of the other discourses. Each discipline establishes itself "on its own," however it can do this: see Jean Ladrière, *Vie sociale et destinée*, pp. 208-10. It would be truly an "irony of history" (Hegel) if theologians were no longer able to speak without asking permission of Marxists!

10. Here I shall use Louis Althusser's two presentations of the process of theoretical practice: *Pour Marx*, chap. 4, no. 3, pp. 186-97; *Reading Capital*, pp. 40-43. See also the concrete illustration set forth in Althusser's *Lenin and Philosophy*, pp. 60-63. For the later evolution of Althusser's thought, see the critiques and self-critiques cited below. It should be clear that I am *using* this author, and that I need not follow him wherever he goes.

11. In speaking of the epistemological status of theology, I use such terms as "theoretical practice," "discipline," "regulated [or "regular"] knowledge," and even "science" (in the classic sense of the word). The core of these designations is the concept of "rule": the "canonics" of method. For the definition of some of these expressions, see M.-D. Dubarle, *Epistémologie des sciences humaines*, pp. 9-10; Michel Foucault, *The Archaeology of Knowledge*, pp. 199-211.

12. Thomas Aquinas, *In Boethii de Trinitate*, q. 6, a. 2: *Peccant qui* uniformiter *in tribus his speculativis partibus* [natural sciences, mathematics, and metaphysics, the latter including theology] *procedere nituntur"* (emphasis added).

13. See Pierre Bourdieu et al., *Le métier de sociologue*, p. 20; Algirdas J. Greimas, *Sémiotique et sciences sociales*, pp. 9, 32.

14. Gaston Bachelard, *L'activité rationaliste de la physique contemporaine*, p. 86.

15. See Jean Ladrière, "Vérité et praxis," pp. 295–97; W. Kluxen, "Vérité et praxis de la science"; François Russo, "La science comme action et artifice."

16. Althusser, *Reading Capital*, pp.40–42. The conception is classic. Greek tradition and scholasticism agree: there can be science only of the general (science in the strict sense: knowledge of the necessary); the singular is ineffable. See Thomas Aquinas, *Summa Theol.*, I, q. 86, a. 1 (referring to Aristotle's *Physics*, book 1, chap. 5); and ibid., a. 3, *praeterea* (referring to Aristotle's *Ethics*, chap. 6). The particular can be known only through the intermediary of the universal. Reason works with concepts; it is the senses that "know" the particular, and it is "practice" that touches it—this is what Thomas holds. The real-and-concrete, the particular, participates in the process of cognition by preparing the *materia* for the concept. It is not the *tota causa* of the concept, but its material "principle," its precondition sine qua non. In a "materialistic" key, Althusser does not seem to diverge from these views. Indeed, as we study the epistemology of Thomas Aquinas, which, as we know, is inspired in Aristotle, we note a surprising basic agreement between these two authors: that of a basic materialism, a distinction between the real and cognition of the real, as well as between the respective autonomous orders and structures of these two regions, the notion of "rupture," or "breach," the *processus* from the general to the concrete and particular, cognition of the concrete real by the concrete-thought, abstraction as an operation of the mind producing the concept, and so on. For this problematic in Thomas, see *Summa Theol.*, I, qq. 84–89. For Thomas's epistemological "materialism" in particular, cf. ibid., q. 88, a. 1: "*Intellectus noster secundum statum praesentis vitae, naturalem respectum habet ad naturas rerum materialium.*" See also ibid., ad 2. Let me remark in passing that Marxism and Thomism seem to be the only two metaphysics of our time. This is the opinion of Ladrière, "Marxisme et rationalisme," p. 555, and even that of Maritain, *The Peasant of the Garonne*, pp. 98–104, esp. 102–3.

17. Althusser, *Reading Capital*, pp. 89–90.

18. Althusser, *Pour Marx*, p. 189; idem, *Reading Capital*, p. 41; Ladrière, *Vie sociale et destinée*, pp. 198–99; Maritain, *Distinguish to Unite*; pp. 202–18.

19. This radical anti-empiricist conceptualization comports a natural tendency toward its opposite—"theoreticism," or the immanentism of knowing, for which Althusser later felt he had to criticize himself (*Essays in Self-Criticism*). In this book he also criticizes the very notion of "theoretical practice," in which the term "theory," covering, as it does, science and philosophy, is seen to lead to "speculative confusion" (esp. p. 147). See the criticisms of Althusser by J-D. Robert, "Autour d'Althusser," pp. 18, 44; J. de Prin, "Y a-t-il une 'pratique théorique'?" in Adam Schaff, ed., *Structuralisme et Marxisme*; F. H. Cardoso, "Althusserianismo ou marxismo?" in his *O modelo político brasileiro e outros ensaios*, pp. 104–22, where he objects (unjustifiably, in my view) to the "metaphysical" distinction between "real object" and "theoretical object"; finally and especially, J.-C. Forquin, "Introduction," in Pierre Vilar et al., "Dialectique marxiste et pensée structurale." See also Caio Prado, Jr., *Estruturalismo de Lévi-Strauss e Marxismo de L. Althusser*.

20. See the citation from Marx in Althusser's *Pour Marx*, p. 189, n. 24 (given above, chap. 2, n. 5, p. 247).

21. See Althusser, *Reading Capital*, p. 23.

22. Ibid., p. 24.

23. Althusser, *Pour Marx*, p. 195; see also p. 167.

24. See ibid., p. 187; idem, "Sur le travail théorique," *La Pensée*, April 1967, pp. 5–6.

25. Althusser, *Pour Marx*, p. 188.

26. Ibid., p. 189.

27. Ibid., p. 187.

28. For the place of the *epistemic subject*, or knower, in Althusser, see *Reading Capital*, pp. 41–42. For verification, see his *Pour Marx*, p. 188, n. 23, as well as his *Essays in Self-Criticism*, pp. 133–34. Each of these two elements is linked to the place of the second generality as an essential component of the latter. According to Gaston Bachelard, the epistemic subject develops itself, in and through the work of cognition: see Michel Fichant, "L'épistemologie en France," p. 154. Verification, on the other hand, can be evaluated only by a theoretical jurisdiction.

29. See, e.g., Claude Bernard, *Introduction à l'étude de la médicine expérimentale* (1865) (reprinted, Paris, Garnier-Flammarion, 1966), part 1, chap. 1, for this method, set forth and closely followed by J. Fourastié, *Les conditions de l'esprit scientifique*, esp. pp. 129–51.

30. Althusser, *Reading Capital*, p. 19; see also p. 16. Thomas Aquinas, in *Contra Gentiles*, book 3, chap. 84, is opposed to the "mirror" epistemology of the Stoics, for whom the intellect would be "*sicut speculum quoddam, vel sicut pagina . . . absque hoc quod aliquid agat.*" And he goes on: ". . . *Intellectus non est sicut recipiens tantum imagines corporum, sed habet aliquam virtutem corporibus altiorem*"—observations coinciding with the modern conceptualization of Jean Piaget, for whom to know is to act.

31. Thomas Aquinas states that the theory of knowledge in general is of interest to the theologian: "*Animae potentiae* [intellective] *pertinent directe ad considerationem theologi*" (*Summa Theol.*, I, q. 84).

32. See François Russo, "Introduction," pp. 9–17. See also Casper, Hemmerle, and Hünermann, *Theologie als Wissenschaft*; Gerhard Sauter, ed., *Wissenschaftstheoretische Kritik der Theologie*; idem, *Vor einem neuen Methodenstreit in der Theologie?*; G. Söhngen, "A sabedoria da teologia."

33. For Thomas Aquinas's epistemology of theology, see: *Summa Theol.*, I, q. 1; the whole of *In Boethii de Trinitate*; and the first 26 chapters of *Contra Gentiles*. (I pay most attention to the *Summa Theol.* in my own treatment.) See the commentaries on *Summa Theol.*, I, q. 1, by A.D. Sertillanges, in *Saint Thomas d'Aquin, Somme Théologique*, vol. 1; A. Gardeil, *Saint Thomas d'Aquin: La Théologie*, vol. 1, "Prologue et Question I.*" For everything relating to Thomas Aquinas I rely heavily on the studies of Marie-Dominique Chenu, esp. his *La théologie comme science au XIIIe siècle*; but also *Toward Understanding Saint Thomas*; *Saint Thomas d'Aquin et la théologie*; *La foi dans l'intelligence*; and *Is Theology a Science?* See also the now classic introductions to theology: Jacob Bilz, *Einführung in die Theologie* (Freiburg, Herder, 1935); Gaston Rabeau, *Introduction à l'étude de la théologie* (Paris, 1926). See also A. Stolz and H. Keller, *Introductio in Sacram Theologiam* (Freiburg, Herder, 1941); Bartolomé M. Xiberta, *Introductio in Sacram Theologiam* (Barcelona, Herder, 1964); C. Colombo, "La metodologia e la sistemazione teologica"; and of course the authors already cited whom I use so often, Yves Congar, Charles Journet, Ambroise Gardeil.

34. See M.-D. Chenu, *Théologie comme science au XIIIe siècle*, chap. 5, pp. 67–92.

35. The expressions "truths of faith," "mysteries of faith," *articuli fidei*, Christian "creed," "content of the faith," Christian "revelation," "revealed truths," the "founding" or "foundational message" of Christianity, "data of faith," "Christian positivity," and others of the sort, are used equivalently here; and I prefer the last: "positivity of faith" or "Christian positivity." One might say of the "mysteries of faith," in their

capacity as second generality (*principia*) of theology, what J. Rivière said of myths: "They explain. . . . Mysteries, being inexplicable, are not directly proven. They are proven by everything that they explain" (cited by G. Gusdorf, *Mythe et métaphysique*, p. 227).

36. The *objectum quo* is also, and more properly, designated as *subjectum*: *Summa Theol.*, I, q. 1, a. 7.

37. See the Decree of the Holy Office, *Lamentabili* (1907), DS 3422 (*Enchiridion Symbolorum*, p. 671).

38. *Summa Theol.*, I, q. 1, a. 3.

39. See Leonardo Boff, *A ressurreição de Cristo*, pp. 79–81: "A tipicidade do pensar teológico."

40. F. de Saussure, *Cours de linguistique générale* (1916) (Paris, Payot, 1969), p. 26, col. 5. This assertion, as understood by Luís J. Prieto (*Pertinence et pratique*, pp.77ff., 102–3, 125–27, 145–48, 152ff.), seems very questionable to me. Prieto simply transfers the concept of "pertinence" in phonology (as in the Prague school) to the epistemology of the sciences of the human being. Instead of this more formalistic conception, I might propose another, more ontological one, with J.-D. Robert, "Pensée et 'réalités' scientifiques." See also his *Philosophies, epistémologies, sciences de l'homme*, and his *Philosophie des sciences*.

41. Thomas Aquinas, III *Sent.*, d. 23, q. 2, a. 4, ad 1. For this question, see the excellent study by Yves M.-J. Congar, "Le moment 'économique' et le moment 'ontologique,' " esp. p. 170 and n. 122; see also ibid., p. 163, n. 103, for a good bibliography on Thomas's epistemology. See also Karl Rahner, "Formale und Fundamentale Theologie" (*Lexikon für Theologie und Kirche*, vol. 4, col. 205–6).

42. *Summa Theol.*, I, q. 1, a. 7.

43. See Georges Thill's review of Gutiérrez's *A Theology of Liberation*, in *Revue Théologique de Louvain* 6 (1975) 496–502, attacking the partiality of this theology. On the other side, Segundo Galilea rightly pleads for a pluridimensional approach with a view to a precise practical activity: "Introducción a la religiosidad latinoamericana."

44. These assertions will be more precisely delineated in part 3, where I shall posit a relationship between theory and practice, between (theoretical) object and (real) thing, in the sense that the object known is the thing itself, but precisely qua known.

45. See Althusser, *Pour Marx*, p. 188, n. 23 (on the *incompleteness* of any scientific theory—Gödel's theorem). See also Leon Henkin, "Completeness."

46. In Feuerbach's terms, we should say that second theology differs from first theology on the level of *species*, and by no means on the level of *genus* or *essence*. Otherwise why call it theology? For Thomas Aquinas (*Summa Theol.*, I, q.1, a. 2, ad 2) there are indeed two genera of theology, but their distribution is: "*sacra doctrina*," and the theology that is "*pars philosophiae*." The verbal radicalism of a certain theoretical revolutionarism matters little here. Swerves in the course of theology, as in other areas, are not the result of the arbitrary choice of an eagerness for change, but the result of a whole objective process that is independent of the individual subject.

47. See Melchior Cano, *De Locis Theologicis* (1563), book 12, chap. 6.

48. The concept of "recurrence," thus understood, is part of the definition of the method of scientific epistemology as proposed by Balibar and Macherey in "Epistémologie." See the development of this concept by Fichant and Pêcheux, *Sur l'histoire des sciences*, pp. 96–114.

49. See A. Lang, *Die Loci theologici des M. Cano und die Methode des dogmatischen Beweises* (Munich, 1925), with its vast bibliography; Ambroise Gardeil, "Lieux

théologiques," in *Dictionnaire de la Théologie Catholique*; idem, *La notion de lieu théologique*; Tharcisse Tshibangu, *Théologie positive et théologie spéculative*; M. Nicolau and J. Salaverri, *Sacrae Theologiae Summa* (Madrid, Católica, 1958), vol. 1, nos. 12–17, where *loci* are defined as the sites of theological argumentation, the theologian's "thesaurus," or the fonts of theological knowledge or cognition.

50. Cano speaks of the *"perfectus absolutusque theologus"* (*De Locis Theologicis*, book 12, chap. 11).

51. According to Etienne Gilson, Cano's methodology was already out of date from the start: "La tradition française et la chrétienté," *Vigile* 4 (1931) 74, n. 1: "The Thomist school of the sixteenth century completely failed in its mission inasmuch as it opposed the Renaissance instead of assimilating it and orientating it spiritually. . . . Not only did Thomism have, in its principles, the wherewithal to do this, but it was its proper destiny to do it. . . . Perhaps it was because the reign of the commentators succeeded that of the creator," and so on. Be this as it may, this was certainly not what Cano thought. Cano sought to found a theology precisely *tempori aptior* (*De Locis Theologicis*, book 12, chap. 11).

52. It is symptomatic that, although Thomas had worked out his theory of theology referring to Aristotle's *Analytica*, and in accordance with Aristotle's paradigm of *episteme*, Cano did so referring to the Aristotelian *Topica*, by way of Rudolf Agricola and Cicero. As to Aquinas, see M.-D. Chenu, "Escolástica," in H. Fries, ed., *Dicionário de Teologia*, 4:212; H. Fries, "Teologia," ibid., 5:297–311, esp. 306–7; but esp. C. Dumont, "La réflexion sur la méthode théologique." As to Cano, see A. Gardeil, "Lieux théologiques," in *Dictionnaire de la Théologie Catholique*, vol. 10, col. 712–47.

53. We know what Cano's method can lead to: theologies à la Denzinger and the like. Curiously, along these lines, Ambroise Gardeil, with perfect logic, is led to make this proposition, at the end of his "Lieux théologiques," col. 746 (see n. 52, just above), that a kind of theological computer be created, called a "universal characteristic of the fonts of theology" (sic), or "a material theological Topica" (sic)—as if mere rigid ordering could be adequate for theology. Let me point out that this pretended scientific spirit is not without its affinity to Cano's sympathies for the Inquisition: see Gardeil, ibid., col. 736; A. Duval, "Cano (Melchior)," in *Catholicisme* (Paris, 1949), vol. 2, col. 467.

54. Congar says that reason plays a more active role in theological development for Thomas than it does for Cano ("Théologie," in *Dictionnaire de la Théologie Catholique*, vol. 15, col. 421–23). Indeed, even for classical epistemologists like Chenu, Gardeil, Journet, and others, "positive theology" constitutes only one of the moments of the integral process of doing theology.

55. An illustration: the colloquium of the Institut Catholique de Paris on "the shifting loci of theology"; see *Le Monde*, Feb. 17, 1976, p. 9.

56. Apropos of the bothersome polysemy of the notion of "place" or locus, anticipating the discussion to be presented in part 3, let me only say that this notion covers at least three distinct values: (1) *Topos* or seat of arguments for rhetorical practice; (2) epistemic position defining a pertinency; (3) (Political) situation or position of an agent in any structure, especially the social structure.

57. "The Christian left, in France, has evangelical guts, but no theological head" (C. Tresmontant, "Tâches de la pensée chrétienne," *Esprit*, July-Aug. 1965, p. 120).

58. I would not say that there is question here of "revealed concepts," as does Claude Geffré, "Théologie," in *Encyclopaedia Universalis*, p. 1090—unless their asymptotic semantic content were to be thought of as "revealed."

59. For modern investigations in the methodology of first theology, see Bernard J. F. Lonergan, *Method in Theology*, chap. 1; B. Welte, *Ein Vorschlag zur Methode*; idem, "Sur la méthode de la théologie"; Walter Kasper, *The Methods of Dogmatic Theology*; John Macquarrie, *Principles of Christian Theology*; Wolfhart Pannenberg, *Strutture fondamentali della teologia*; Eberhard Simons and Konrad Hecker, *Theologisches Verstehen*; Adolf Kolping, *Einführung in die katholische Theologie*; Zoltan Alszeghy and Maurizio Flick, *Introductory Theology*; Paul Touilleux, *Introduction à une théologie critique*; L. Guzmán, *La teología, ciencia de la fe*; Engelbert Neuhasler and Elizabeth Gössmann, eds., *Was ist Theologie?*

60. Methodological reflection on this problem is fragmentary and polemical, as, e.g., in Charles Wackenheim, *Christianisme sans idéologie*, pp. 148–52, 231.

61. See, e.g., Ignacio Ellacuría, "Método teológico."

62. See Karl Rahner, "L'avenir de la théologie," p. 25: "It would be . . . erroneous to understand political theology simply as the theology that should replace all earlier theologies by reason of a new social situation. Human beings are not reducible, adequately and in a socially apprehensible fashion, to what they are in society, through society, and for society." See also H. Lepargneur, "Les théologies de la libération."

63. Gaston Bachelard, *La philosophie du Non*, pp. 135–45; idem, *O novo espírito científico*, pp. 247–337.

64. On the possibility of knowledge of the supernatural, the metaphysical, the divine, or the theological—determinedly and typically disputed in our contemporary culture, especially in current philosophy—Aristotle, in line with Plato, and against the ancient Greek poets—e.g., Simonides—comes down on the side of the affirmative. The reason he gives is that the *nous* that is in the human being is of divine nature: *Metaphysics*, book 1, chap. 2, 982b28–983a11; *Nicomachaean Ethics*, book 10, chap. 7, 1177b26–1178a8. See Werner Jaeger, *Humanism and Theology*, esp. p. 64.

65. "Lenin said that after the content of religious language had been destroyed, in a first moment, it would be necessary, in a second, to employ certain signs of this language to assist humanity and society to realize itself. Thus the revolutionary thrust uses not only Christian discourse, but the coals of Christian hope to feed the fire of its earthly realization" (H. Breti, *Positions luthériennes*, Paris, April 1970, p. 114).

66. The *cultural* definition of the real depends on the choice made by a society: the real is what "it" is decided to be. In former times, "it" was said to be God or gods; then "it" was said to be being or beings; today, "it" is said to be the world, or things— summarizing Auguste Comte. See Peter L. Berger and Theodore Luckmann, *The Social Construction of Reality*. The scientific definition of the real is chosen by the discipline in question. The sociologist's "real" is not the psychologist's "real," which in turn is not the biologist's "real," and so on.

67. Vico's fifty-fifth "axiom" or "dignity" is significant: "Golden the passage in Eusebius . . . in which he says: *Primam aegyptiorum theologiam mere historiam fuisse fabulis interpolatam quarum quum postea puderet posteros, sensim coeperunt mysticos iis significatus affingere*" ("The Egyptians' first theology was no more than a rudimentary history, crammed with fables. But this embarrassed later generations, which began to find all sorts of mystical meanings")—Giambattista Vico, *Principios de [uma] ciência nova* (1725), p. 49.

68. See N. Lash, "A Igreja e a liberdade de Cristo." Lash is an Indian theologian working in the United States. He criticizes "Christian schizophrenia," for which "economic, political, psychological slavery" is not the same thing as the "slavery of sin." For Lash, it is the same thing, except for the *ratio*, the perspective. But unless the legitimacy

of this *ratio* is postulated, the difference remains on the level of the words, so that the same "object" will be called "exploitation" by the sociologists and "sin" by theologians, with this sole difference, that the former are doing science, and consciously, whereas the latter are doing ideology, thinking that they are doing theology.

69. Consider the justifiable uneasiness of Yves Congar in his review of Charles Wackenheim, *Christianisme sans idéologie* (*Documentation Catholique* 72 [1975] col. 596-98, as well as in Congar's book, *Un peuple messianique*, p. 191). See also H. Lepargneur, "Les théologies," p. 168. These authors say that we still manage to develop a Christian thought because we are still invested with the vitality of faith, handed down to us by a tradition, even when we criticize or deny that tradition. What will occur later, when these hidden fonts will have been exhausted?

70. See Thomas Aquinas, *In Boethii de Trinitate*, commentary on the Prologue: "The proximate efficient cause of theological inquiry is the intellect of the theologian which is, as it were, a small flame. . . . The human soul is weak, its purity is disturbed by its union with the body, its light is hidden, its powers are weak, its flight toward the heights is retarded. This is the reason that its ability can be compared to that of a small flame. This is the reason too that it does not suffice to discover the truth in such questions as those of the Trinity, unless it has been enlightened by the Divine Light. Hence in theology the Divine Light is the principal cause, and the soul is the secondary cause" (in Charles Journet, *The Wisdom of Faith*, pp. 67-68).

71. See Jean Ladrière, *Vie sociale et destinée*, p. 210.

72. To use Thomas's example, fire is considered by Christian faith "*non inquantum ignis est, sed inquantum divinam altitudinem repraesentat, et in ipsum Deum quoquo modo ordinatur. . . . Unde non est ad imperfectionem doctrinae fidei imputandum si multas rerum proprietates praetermittat*" (*Contra Gentiles,* book 2, chap. 4).

73. That theories of meaning come after theories of structure, or that meaning follows the apprehension of laws and relies on them, seems to be the epistemological strategy being more and more adopted by the "hermeneutic sciences." Thus, e.g., for Paul Ricoeur, *Le conflit des interprétations*, pp. 31-63. Likewise Stephan Strasser (*Phenomenology and the Human Sciences*) asserts that phenomenology (the third objectivity) should come after the human sciences (second objectivity, the first objectivity being "antepredicative"). We find the same position in Max Weber, *Essais sur la théorie de la science*, pp. 151-63. I may also cite Nietzsche, who, rethinking the status of philosophy vis-à-vis the new sciences, adopted the same strategy: *Beyond Good and Evil*, no. 211, p. 136.

74. For example, Yves Congar, in the final words of his *Un peuple messianique*, p. 195: "We hope that it has been understood that the dualism we maintain expresses and requires only a distinction of the levels and the specificity of the supernatural or the religious, and not a separation of these latter vis-à-vis the so-called profane. It is the Chalcedonian status once again: without separation, without confusion." See ibid., pp. 145-63, where this method is applied to the problem of "liberation and salvation today," esp. pp. 154-63. See ibid., pp. 182-95, for the matter of politics and faith; and pp. 181-82; "notes on the 'rejection of dualism.' " See, too, Congar's contribution in T. I. Jiménez Urresti, ed., *Teología de la liberación*, esp. p. 199.

75. See Paul VI, *Evangelii Nuntiandi* (1975), chap. 3, pp. 20-26: "The Content of Evangelization."

76. See the critique of the document of the Permanent Council of the French Episcopate, *Libération des hommes et salut en Jésus-Christ* (1975), by P. Warnier, in *Le Monde*, July 14, 1975, p. 15, where he deplores the "idealistic, dualistic, and . . . cen-

trist language" of the document, alleging that it "solves problems in a purely formal and abstract way, when it is a question of knowing, 'factually,' whether the church of Jesus Christ has betrayed the poor or whether it has not!" See the same sort of criticism of the same document by Hans Holstein, in his review in *Etudes*, Aug.-Sept. 1975, pp. 271–76: Holstein observes that, in chap. 2, the document has certainly followed the christological dialectic, but, had it been sensitive to a political analysis (socio-analytic mediation), it would have appealed rather to the connection between faith and socialism. See likewise A. Rousseau, "Essai sur la fonction sociale de l'orthodoxie religieuse"; analyzing the language of the French bishops in speaking of "politics," he qualifies it as a "vocabulary of metamorphosis" (pp. 215–26), in virtue of a transformation of the religious code into a sociological code and vice versa. As an illustration of the more or less dualizing approach to the model in question, besides Congar's *Peuple messianique*, I may cite Jacques Rollet, *Libération sociale et salut chrétien*; A. Dondeyne, "Jesus-Christ libère et unit," *Revue Théologique de Louvain* 6 (1975) 292–310, esp. pp. 306–9.

77. Congar's book *Un peuple messianique* bears the subtitle: *Salut et libération*. But "liberation," devoid of nearly all historical concreteness, appears to be neither challenging nor promising (*destituido de quase toda gravidade [ou gravidez]*) vis-à-vis the current situation of imperialistic capitalism. It represents an echo rather than a thematic, in Congar's book. It is not a theme reflected upon, but a reflex theme. It is not something "thought" (theory); it "thinks" among us and for us (ideology).

78. See, e.g., Gustavo Gutiérrez, *A Theology*, chap. 1, pp. 36–37, defining the three levels of liberation; likewise Hugo Assmann, *Nomad Church*, pp. 55–56 and passim.

79. On this point I am in agreement with Hugo Assmann, *Nomad Church*, pp. 45–51, esp. pp. 48–49, and pp. 111–19, where he sets in relief the material, physical content and connotation of the notion of "liberation." Without this content and connotation, discourse would simply drift with every possible current of meaning, from the most "materialistic"—e.g., in Nikita Khrushchev, *The National Liberation Movement* (Moscow, Foreign Languages, 1963)—to the most "spiritualistic," as in Hindu *moksa*, liberation in Brahman.

80. J. Remy speaks of "transcodification" as a "*conditio sine qua non* for a fruitful dialogue" between sociology and theology ("Questions de la sociologie à la théologie chrétienne," 1:211).

81. As can be seen, I am giving an illustration here of the articulation of a theology of the political reduced to its minimal formal expression—i.e., to its *concept*. My purpose is only to identify a structure whose laws must operate as well in relation to theoretical *propositions*, and even to more complex theoretical *wholes*.

82. The dogmatic bases implied in this method will be explicitated in chap. 6 and 7.

83. See *Summa Theol.*, I, q. 1, aa. 2, 7; I-II, q. 57, a. 2. By the same token, theology, besides being *science*, is also *wisdom*—but in the form of science (ibid., I, q. 1, a. 6). "*Sapientia non dividitur contra scientiam, sicut oppositum contra oppositum, sed quia se habet ex additione ad scientiam*" (*In Boethii de Trinitate*, q. 2, a. 2, ad 1.)

84. On their origin in philosophy, see *Summa Theol.*, I, q. 1, a. 1, ad 2; on their origin in the other sciences, see ibid., a. 3, ad 2.

85. Ibid., a. 3, ad. 2, and a. 4.

86. Ibid., a. 6, ad 2: "*Non pertinet ad eam probare principia aliarum scientiarum.*"

87. Ibid., a. 5: "*Utrum Sacra Doctrina Sit Dignior Aliis Scientiis,*" esp. ad 2: "[Theology] *non accipit ab aliis scientiis tanquam a superioribus, sed* utitur eis tanquam inferioribus et ancillis, *sicut architectonicae utuntur subministrantibus*" (emphasis

added). Of course, it is neither interesting nor advantageous for theology to manipulate the other sciences at will.

88. Ibid., a. 5, ad 2.
89. Ibid., a. 3, ad 1. See also *De Veritate*, q. 14, a. 8, ad 2.
90. *Summa Theol.*, I, q. 1, a. 3, ad 1.
91. Ibid., c.

CHAPTER 6

1. See Jean Ladrière, "Vie sociale et destinée," pp. 199–200; Louis Althusser, *Pour Marx*, p. 31. This is also true for theology: M.-D. Chenu, "Le sens et les leçons d'une crise religieuse," *Vie Intellectuelle*, no. 13, Dec. 10, 1931, pp. 356–80.

2. Martin Heidegger, *Being and Time*, p. 195; see also pp. 188–95. See also Jean Ladrière, "Vie sociale et destinée," pp. 209–10; Bourdieu et al., *Le métier de sociologue*, pp. 11–25, esp. pp. 11–12.

3. See Martin Heidegger, *Being and Time*, pp. 49–50; G. Granel, "Remarques sur l'accès à la pensée de Martin Heidegger: 'Sein und Zeit.' "

4. Aristotle, *Metaphysics*, book 2, chap. 3, 995a6–16 (p. 513); and ibid., book 1, chap. 3, 984a18–19 (p. 502): "As [philosophers] advanced, the very facts opened the way for them and joined in forcing them to investigate the subject." See also *Nicomachaean Ethics*, book 1, chap. 3, 1094b11–27; chap. 7, 1098a26–28 (pp. 339–40, 343). Charles Péguy contrasted "rigid methods" with "flexible methods," more respectful of the nature of their object and therefore more rigorous: *Note conjointe*, April 26, 1914, p. 51, cited by Jean Guitton, *Nova arte de pensar* (São Paulo, Paulinas, 1964), pp. 130–31.

5. Thomas Aquinas, *Summa Theol.*, I, q. 1, a. 7, *praeterea* 1; *In Boethii de Trinitate*, q. 2, a. 2, *praeterea* 1. For the "principle of formal objects," see *In Boethii de Trinitate*, lectio 2; *Contra Gentiles*, book 1, chap. 7; *Summa Theol.*, I, q. 14, a. 8, *praeterea* 3 (referring to Aristotle, *Metaphysics*, book 10, no. 9 [1058a28-b26, p. 586]). See also n. 6, just below.

6. See *Summa Theol.*, I, q. 84, a. 7: *"Potentia cognoscitiva proportionatur cognoscibili."* But on the other hand, *"objectum cognoscibile proportionatur virtuti cognoscitivae (sicut supra* [q. 84, a. 7])" (ibid., q. 85, a. 1). See also ibid., I-II, q. 57, a. 6, ad 3: *"Judicium de unaquaque re fit per propria principia ejus. Inquisitio autem nondum est per propria principia ejus."*

7. "Our faith, which having been received from the Church, we do preserve, and which always, by the Spirit of God, renewing its youth, as if it were some precious deposit in an excellent vessel, causes the vessel itself containing it to renew its youth also" (Irenaeus of Lyon, *Irenaeus Against Heresies*, book 3, chap. 24, no. 1, p. 458—cited in G. L. Prestige, *God in Patristic Thought*, pp. 83–84).

8. G. Söhngen, "Fundamentaltheologie," in *Lexikon für Theologie und Kirche*, vol. 4, cols. 456–57: "theory of theological categories (. . . one of the most important and doubtless most difficult tasks of a fundamental theology)." Without being rigidly bound to either the structuralism or the rationalism of a Bachelard, there is nothing to prevent my taking my inspiration in them for an approach to theology, while of course exercising the reservations still to be developed, as I have already noted. As to a primacy accorded to relations over "substance" in epistemology, see Bachelard's *La philosophie du Non*, pp. 27–30, and his *Le rationalisme appliqué*, pp. 33–37, 121–24 and passim.

9. Jean Guichard posits, in correspondence with the Althusserian trilogy real-ideology-science, the trilogy faith-religion-theology (in Boisset, ed., *La théologie en procès*, pp. 113, 116.

10. For this distinction, see S. Breton, "Le paradoxe du menteur," p. 533.

11. Let us note that the designation "theo-ontology," as also our conception generally, has nothing in common with the "onto-the-ology" criticized by Heidegger as being the veiled essence of Western metaphysics—an edifice of beings, with the Supreme Being, God, at the summit. See Martin Heidegger, "La constitution onto-teo-logique de la métaphysique," in *Questions*, vol. 1, Paris, Gallimard, 1968.

12. I take this opportunity to emphasize my debt to Karl Rahner in the following reflections, especially as to the question of nature and grace, and its corollary, the theory of the "anonymous Christian." For the former question, see the studies on grace in *Schriften zur theologie*, Einsiedeln, 4th ed., 1961, vol. 3. For the "anonymous Christian," see *Mission et grâce* (Tours, Mame), 1 (1962):21–22, 67–68, 101–3, 156, etc.; 3 (1965):28–31, 63–64, etc.; and esp. "Chrétiens anonymes" (*IDOC-International*, no. 20, 1970).

13. On the "supernatural order," I am indebted to Henri de Lubac: *Surnaturel*, and *Le mystère du Surnaturel*. In this same line, see Leonardo Boff, *A graça libertadora no mundo*, esp. chap. 10, pp. 135–51 (bibliography, pp. 269–73).

The expression "salvation history," with the official sanction it received in Vatican II, has become a most celebrated one. See, e.g., the collection, Johannes Feiner and Magnus Löhrer, eds., *Mysterium Salutis: Grundriss heilsgeschichtlicher Dogmatik*; or the collection, *Il messaggio della Salvezza* (Turin/Leumann, Elle Di Ci, 1965–).

14. For a general view of Paul Tillich's thought, see Carl J. Armbruster, *The Vision of Paul Tillich*; Georges Tavard, *Paul Tillich and the Christian Message*, esp. chap. 2; D. M. Brown, *Ultimate Concern*.

15. See J. Kamp, *Credo sans foi, foi sans credo*, pp. 26–36, where the author criticizes objectivity in theology; A. Dondeyne, "Un discourse philosophique de Dieu est-il encore possible?" pp. 426–28, with an explanation of the polysemic notion of "object"; Peter Berger, *The Sacred Canopy*, pp. 180–88; Claude Geffré, "Sentido e não sentido"; idem, "L'objectivité propre au Dieu révélé." In his brilliant essay, *God in Patristic Thought*, George Leonard Prestige shows that the Greek fathers employed the terms *hypostasis* and *ousia* to signify the objectivity and reality of God (chap. 7, 9), although God was essentially defined as *agen(n)etos*—i.e., as absolute and transcendent (chap. 2). Let us recall, too, Thomas Aquinas: "*Actus credentis . . . terminatur ad rem*," *Summa Theol.*, II-II, q. 1, a. 2, ad 2, where what is being discussed is the "*objectum fidei*"). Karl Barth, for his part, applied to God the idea of *Gegen-stand* to point up God's absolute transcendence. Perhaps it would not be without utility to distinguish here between *Object*, as being absolute object, anterior to objectivity and opposed to subject; and *Gegenstand*, as the object constituted as such by the subject. We would then say that, for the truth of theology, it is necessary that "God" be *Object* in order to be able to be *Gegenstand*. For this distinction, see Louis Althusser's "Note" in his translation of Ludwig Feuerbach, *Manifestes philosophiques*, pp. 14–15.

16. For this tradition, see the works of Henri de Lubac cited in n. 13, above.

17. See H. Bouillard, *L'idée de surnaturel*, esp. pp. 154, 166.

18. For this, I rely on, without following them in every respect, the "definitions" of Karl Rahner, *Mission et grâce*, 1:64–70: "concepts and distinctions."

19. Whereas for the sciences only "nature" exists, for theology only "super-nature" exists, with "nature" constituting a "remainder," so to speak—the result of an abstrac-

tion: "(super)nature." From the point of view of theology, then, there are only two kinds of science: "divine" or "supernatural" science, and "human" or "natural" science, so that, vis-à-vis theology, all other sciences constitute a single block. See Thomas Aquinas, *Summa Theol.*, I, q. 1, a. 1: *"Utrum Sit Necessarium Praeter Philosophicas Disciplinas Aliam Doctrinam Haberi."* The principle of distinction here is the formal object: the "light of reason" or "revelation."

20. "Supernatural order" (a third generality) and "mystery of salvation" (second generality) have the same signification (or reference), but not the same sense (or pertinency). They therefore seem to me not interchangeable, although they are mutually articulable. Let us also note that, for the time being, the two notions of "revelation" and "faith" enjoy the same epistemological status here—that of furnishing theology with its *principia*. I shall determine their difference at the appropriate moment, in §35.

21. On the fictitious character of the concept of "pure nature," see Henri de Lubac, *Surnaturel*, pp. 101–27, esp. p. 107; M. Gervais, "Nature et grâce chez Saint Thomas d'Aquin," *Laval Théologique et Philosophique* 30 (1974) 333–48, 31 (1975) 293–321, esp. pp. 311–21. The concept of "pure nature" has a status that Gervais defines as involving a "passing by way of the unreal" (p. 318), and he cites D. Soto, *De natura et gratia*, book 1, chap. 3 (Paris, 1549), folio 7r: *"Igitur licet nunquam fuerit . . . concipere illum tamen animo et effingere nihil vetat,* clarioris disputationis gratia" (emphasis added).

22. I join de Lubac and Rahner here. My objective is to provide the concept under discussion, as well as others, with a univocal theoretical content, to be preserved without variation throughout the discourse, in such wise as to be articulable in a theory whose end is to give an account of the truth of faith. On this level, I am engaged in an effort more hypothetico-theoretical than properly dogmatic. For "semantic constancy," see Gaston Bachelard, *La philosophie du Non*, pp. 114, 117, 121.

23. See these examples of dualism in the domain of a theology of the political: J.-M. Aubert, *Morale sociale pour notre temps* (Paris/Tournai, Desclée, 1970): pp. 42–45, creation/redemption; pp. 60ff., development/salvation; pp. 45ff., natural law/revelation. René Coste, *Les communautés politiques*, pp. 11–12, 56–61: gospel/politics, etc.

24. In accordance with the basic propositions here set forth, the distinction between "nature" and "pure nature" is, in theology, a "purely formal" distinction—the effect of a reading, not of a text.

25. See Adolphe Gesché, "Une approche du sacré," esp. pp. 154–66: "the theological distinction between 'being' and 'being hoped for.'"

26. See Karl Rahner, "Pour la notion scolastique de la grâce incréé," in *Ecrits théologiques*, 3:37–69.

27. A distinction emphasized by Juan Luís Segundo, *Teología abierta*, 1:67–73.

28. Thomas Aquinas embraces this conceptualization (*Summa Theol.*, III, q. 8, a. 3), which is a very current one. See Charles Wackenheim, *Christianisme sans idéologie*, pp. 121–22, where the same conceptualization is proposed as an alternative to the theory of "anonymous Christians," in which Wackenheim has little confidence.

29. See Darlapp, "História da salvação." Darlapp distinguishes between "general salvation history," as constituting an "athematic," and sometimes anonymous, framework, and "particular" (Judeo-Christian) salvation history, which is history as such in its transparency—i.e., as revelation history. Unfortunately, Darlapp also introduces "profane history," and then attempts, unsuccessfully, I think, to articulate the three. See, too, his collaboration on the same theme with Heinrich Fries, on the subject of revelation, in Feiner and Löhrer, *Mysterium Salutis*, vol. 1/1 in its entirety.

30. On revelation, besides the study just cited, see René Latourelle, *Theology of Revelation*, with extensive bibliography. Latourelle, unlike myself, takes revelation as salvific (concluding pages).

31. See Leonardo Boff, "Tentativa de solução ecumênica para o problema da inspiração e da inerrância," esp. pp. 656ff.

32. Cassian held that Jesus is above all "*redemptor vitae*," against Nestorius, who saw Christ as "*eruditor humani generis magis quam redemptor*" (Yves Congar, *Un peuple messianique*, p. 190).

33. On the parable of the last judgment, see Joachim Jeremias, *The Parables of Jesus*, pp. 209-10, where he proposes the hypothesis that the *Sitz im Leben* of this parable was precisely the question that Jesus was asked concerning the possibility of salvation for pagans.

Wolfhart Pannenberg interprets the dogma of the universality of salvation as referring to the salvation of pagans, in his *La foi des Apôtres: Commentaire du symbole*, pp. 105-6; *Jesus—God and Man*, pp. 260-63, 271-72.

34. See Gustave Thils, *Propos et problèmes*. This work provides us with a good *status questionis* on this whole problematic.

35. For the apologetes, see *Lumen Gentium*, no. 2. See Augustine's universalizing position on the incognito existence of the Christian religion from all time: *Ep*. 102, 12, 5; *Retractationes*, 1,13, 3. For the fathers generally, see Henri de Lubac, *Catholicisme*, pp. 179-81. For the scholastics, see Thomas Aquinas, *De Veritate*, q. 17, aa. 2-5; and, on *fides implicita*, *Summa Theol.*, II-II, q. 2, aa. 5-8, esp. a. 7, ad 3. For a modern position, consider the rejection by the magisterium of two propositions of Jansenist Quesnel as set forth in Denzinger, *Enchiridion Symbolorum*, nos. 2420 ("*Nullae dantur gratiae nisi per fidem*"), 2429 ("*Extra Ecclesiam nulla conceditur gratia*"). For a contemporary position, see *Gaudium et Spes*, no. 22: "For, since Christ died for all men, and since the ultimate vocation of man is in fact one, and divine, we ought to believe that the Holy Spirit in a manner known only to God offers to every man the possibility of being associated with this paschal mystery" (p. 261).

36. See Gutiérrez, *A Theology*, p. 76, n. 33, where he indicates criticisms of the "anonymous Christians" theory (Michel de Certeau, Maurice Bellet, André Manaranche, P.A. Liégé), and Karl Rahner's response ("Anonymous Christianity and the Missionary Task of the Church," pp. 70-96). See also Edward Schillebeeckx, *World and Church*, pp. 32-35, 103-7, etc.

37. One thinks of E. Levinas, *Totalité et infini*.

38. See J. B. Libânio, *Pecado e opção fundamental*; H. Reiners, *Grundintention und sittliches Tun* (Freiburg, Herder, 1960), pp. 47-74; Leonardo Boff, *A graça libertadora*, chap. 11, 12, pp. 152-70; P. Anciaux, *Le Sacrement de la pénitence* (Louvain/ Paris, Nauwelaerts, 2nd ed., 1960), pp. 42ff.

39. See Philippians 2:12: "Work with anxious concern to achieve your salvation." The relationship between being and doing has been admirably propounded by Jean-Paul Sartre, *Being and Nothingness*, pp. 433-81.

40. The two positions, "religio-cultic" and "ethico-prophetical," have been well characterized by José María Díez-Alegría, *I Believe in Hope*. This is also the approach taken by Leonardo Boff, *Die Kirche als Sakrament der Welterfahrung*, esp. chap. 5, 18. See likewise the conception permeating the whole of Fernando Belo's *Materialist Reading*: that of two basic symbolic systems, the "pollution system" and the "debt system" (pp. 37-59).

41. See the magisterial condemnation of the concept of "philosophic sin" (Denzinger-

Schönmetzer, nos. 2290-91). For this problematic generally, which, incidentally, so shook circles at Louvain, see T. Deman, "Péché philosophique," in *Dictionnaire de la Théologie Catholique*, vol. 12 (1933), cols. 255-72.

42. *"Opera humana possunt considerari dupliciter. Uno modo secundum* substantia *operum; et sic non habent aliquid condignum ut eis merces aeternae gloriae reddatur. Alio modo, possunt considerari secundum suum* principium, *prout, scilicet, ex impulsu Dei aguntur, secundum propositum Dei praedestinantis, et secundum hoc eis debetur merces praedicto secundum debitum"* (Thomas Aquinas, *In Epist. ad Romanos*, chap. 4, v. 4, *lectio* 1; emphasis added). Let us recall that in Matt. 25:31-46, the just as well as the unjust have failed to take account of the *salvific* scope of agapic practices. Polemical purposes will bend our reflection in the direction of the ontic dimension (the sheer reality of agapic deeds), obscuring the ontological (relating to awareness of reality),whose importance will nevertheless, at its moment likewise have to be recognized, inasmuch as salvation is never effectuated independently of *all* intentional content in the subject.

43. See Giulio Girardi, *Christianisme, libération humaine*, p. 205. For Thomas Aquinas, *fides informis*—faith deprived of the "form" of *agape*—is yet not deprived of all meaning (*Summa Theol.*, II-II, q. 4, a. 4), although, inasmuch as it does not constitute a "virtue," it is incapable of ensuring salvation.

44. Would the *specific* contribution of Christians, and therefore of "political theologians," be to "save subjectivity, threatened by power"? This is what we hear from Carlos Bravo, "Notas marginales a la teología de la liberación," esp. p. 34; Edward Schillebeeckx, "Teorias críticas e engajamento político na comunidade cristã," esp. pp. 440ff.; Giulio Girardi, "Nouveauté chrétienne"; Geyer, Janowski, and Schmidt, *Teologia e sociologia*, esp. pp. 105-7. This position is surely defensible, but if the decision is for a theology *of the political*, will it still be necessary to turn to the *private*? Would this not be to seek to "suppress" thinking that bears precisely on this area where the "private" itself is decided, albeit in hidden fashion?

45. Marx's term, to characterize the "abstract" human being, utilized as a concept by the bourgeoisie and consecrated as reality: *Capital*, book 1, section 1, chap. 1, pp. 33-34. Against an individualistic conception of salvation, see only Romans 5:12-19, as well as the work of Henri de Lubac already cited, *Catholicism*, with its meaningful subtitle, *A Study of Dogma in Relation to the Corporate Destiny of Mankind*. Here de Lubac reports Origen's conception, according to which Jesus himself could not enjoy perfect beatitude until he had handed the kingdom over to his Father (pp. 57-58, with the apposite passage from Origen's Homily on Leviticus, no. 2, in an appendix, pp. 235-40). Jürgen Moltmann speaks of "the future of Jesus Christ," the total realization of the promises: *Theology of Hope*, chap. 3, pp. 139-229, esp. 202-29.

46. Gaston Bachelard's expression, in his *La formation de l'esprit scientifique*, p. 222.

47. Where the development of an adequate political moral theory in particular is concerned, one must carefully consider the hiatus that exists between the individual and the political, between private conscience and social structures. The precepts of individual morality cannot simply be transferred to the social area as if the latter were only a homogeneous extension of conscience. Nietzsche, with his customary irony, says that such an idea is "a theory like that of free trade, taking for granted that the general harmony *must* result of itself according to innate laws of amelioration" (*Human, All Too Human*, 6:40). Let us recall the very appropriate distinction made by Max Weber between an "ethic of conviction" and an "ethic of [political] responsibility": "Politics as a Voca-

tion" (1919), pp. 110–21. For all of this, see Raymond Polin, *Ethique et politique*. In this sense, classic social morality, of which I have already stated my critique, is unequal to its object—the social—at least as the sciences of the social reveal it to us, as can be seen for example in Thomas Aquinas, *De Regimine Principum*, esp. book 1, chap. 14. The same holds true for *agape*, whose translation in intersubjective relationships is not the same as in social relationships. Here, see M. Horkheimer's criticism of "abstraction love," in "Réflexiones sur le théisme et l'athéisme," esp. p. 51: "Where love is concerned, it would be well to set forth . . . to what point love must be denied in order to be expressed, and, a fortiori, in order to be able to be imposed. Even the will never to see anyone suffer from hunger any longer, or from injustice, is still abstract—although surely more concrete than empty discourses on values, on their eternal significance, on the truth of being." For the question of a political ethics, see also §56, below.

48. See H. Gollwitzer, in *Eglise et Société*, 2:31: "There is no such thing as Christian politics, any more than there is such a thing as Christian medicine"; Paul Ricoeur, in *Les chrétiens et la politique*, p. 85: "There is no such thing as a Christian politics that can be developed without a hiatus from a creed"; P. Arroyo, "Discurso al premier encuentro latinoamericano de cristianos por el socialismo"; Karl Rahner, *Missão e graça*, 1:11–14.

49. See Joachim Wach, *Sociology of Religion*, where religion is analyzed in its three constitutive aspects: doctrine, ritual, and social organization.

50. On the "patristic method in theology," Yves M-J. Congar writes ("Schisme," in *Dictionnaire de la Théologie Catholique*, vol. 14, col. 1305): "The fathers take the biblical text just as it is, in their historical writings as in their doctrinal statements, in such wise as to be led, by the circumstances of a text, whose composition is not homogeneous in all its aspects and whose intention is neither speculative nor systematic, to make statements at which a scientifically developed theological method would not arrive."

51. This notion does not have the precise sense here that it has in J. Derrida, *De la grammatologie*. The characterization of "theological logocentrism" established here obeys the same methodological procedure that I follow generally in the present work, especially for the purpose of sketching the profile of the "epistemological obstacles" of which I speak. As always, my concern is to set in relief the traits that I consider to be open to criticism. The value of such a recourse is more heuristic than theoretical, more polemical than architectonic. In certain "theoretical conjunctures" it is perhaps the best, if not the only, means of producing some alteration in the problematic under discussion, *"sicut faciunt illi qui tortuosa lignorum dirigunt"* (Thomas Aquinas, *Quodlibetales*, III, a. 13, *in fine*).

52. See *Summa Theol.*, II-II, q. 2, aa. 3, 4; *Contra Gentiles*, book 1, chap. 3; *In Boethii de Trinitate*, q. 3, a. 1; *Compendium Theologiae*, I, chap. 1: *"Consistit enim humana salus in veritatis cognitione"*; *Summa Theol.*, I, q. 1, a. 1: *" . . . a cujus tamen veritatis cognitione dependet tota hominis salus"; In Epist. S. Pauli I ad Timotheum, I,* lectio 2: "Those who do not have the true faith cannot love God. It is their error that they love, and not God. . . . For the effect aims only at what the intelligence shows it." Against this basic position, globally and regularly maintained, it is captious to cite a few texts in which some variations are introduced, such as those indicated above in note 35.

53. See *Summa Theol.*, II-II, q. 1, a. 7; *In Boethii de Trinitate*, q. 3, a. 1. See, however, M. Seckler, "Fé," in Fries, ed., *Dicionário de Teologia*, pp. 200–201, examining the element of decision in Thomas Aquinas's doctrine of faith. The observation with which I concluded the foregoing note is applicable here as well.

54. See M. de Wulf, *Histoire de la philosophie médiévale*, vol. 2, no. 283: "intellectualism" (pp. 22–23): "No scholastic philosophy is more intellectualistic, more 'noocentric,' than that of Thomas Aquinas."

55. See the criticism of Greek logocentrism (the Apollinian or Socratic vector) by Friedrich Nietzsche, *The Birth of Tragedy*, no. 15, pp. 93–98.

56. See the criticisms of the ecclesiology of the "new Christendom" à la Maritain by "liberation theologians" such as Gustavo Gutiérrez, *Réinventer le visage de l'Eglise*; Leonardo Boff, *Teologia do cativeiro*, chap. 11. The ecclesiology of the "new Christendom" may be summed up in the proportionality: supernatural order/natural order = church/state, whereas the correct formula would be: church-society (state)/supernatural order, inasmuch as the supernatural order is not an organism apart, but the whole as interpreted and lived in the light of God's salvific plan (revelation).

57. We know, on the other hand, that the church has always rejected a duopolistic christology after the manner of the Greek heroes, half-human, half-gods. Consider how Thomas Aquinas solves the problem of the synergy of creator and creatures in *Contra Gentiles*, book 3, chap. 70, esp. in the conclusion: *"Patet enim quod* non *sic idem effectus causae naturali et divinae virtuti attribuitur quasi* partim *a Deo, et* partim *a naturali agente fiat, sed* totus ab utroque *secundum alium modum: sicut idem effectus totus attribuitur instrumento, et principali agenti etiam totus"* (emphasis added).

CHAPTER 7

1. As has been noted, e.g., by John Macquarrie (*Principles of Christian Theology*, p. 2) and Georges Tavard (*La théologie parmi les sciences humaines*, pp. 13–14), there are as many theologies as there are revelations: the former claim to be the rigorous thinking of the latter. This does not mean that all theologies are equal, for the prerequisite that there be a revelation upon which to reflect in no way prejudices the varying capacity of the revelation in question to be satisfactorily ration-alized—i.e., to sustain the critique of historical and cultural reason. On the other hand, unless one gives what is implied in a culture its due, it will be imprecise and abusive to speak, in the absolute, of "faith," "revelation," "theology," and so on—i.e., without adding the corresponding analytical predicate—here, "Christian."

2. The concept of "epistemological rupture" or breach is defined by the fact that a new organized knowledge establishes itself on its own bases, detaching itself from its theological envelope, which it sheds as part of its prehistory and identifies it as such—i.e., as ideological, as the "other" of the new science. See Gaston Bachelard, *Le rationalisme appliqué*, chap. 6; idem, *Le matérialisme rationnel*, the last chap. See also Jean Ladrière, "Vérité et praxis," p. 290. It is Bachelard's work that has given rise to a current that advances a *discontinuistic* conception of science and its history. Althusser and his group may be cited here (see the Théorie series published by Maspero, Paris) as well as Canguilhem, Foucault, Koyré, and others. By contrast, there is the more classic current—let us call it the *continuistic* one—which regards the progress of a science as the actualization of virtualities that have always been present within the human mind. In this current we may place Brunschvicg, Duhem, and others.

3. Aquinas himself posited an "epistemological breach" between sensation and the concept: *Summa Theol.*, I, q. 84, a. 6. I have already noted earlier (§25) that the "breach" between a first and a third generality is characteristic of any rigorous theoretical procedure.

4. This is what is expressed by the concept of *subalternatio*, which Thomas drew from Aristotelian epistemology (Aquinas, *In Posteriorem Analyticam*, book 1, lectio 25, no. 2; *De Veritate*, q. 14, a. 9, ad 3), and which he narrowed in order to accommodate it to the status of theology, calling it *"quasi subalternatio":* the theological science depends on the "divine science" (the word of revelation) only *ratione subjecti*, not *ratione modi* (*In Sententias*, Prologue, a. 3, solutio 2). M.-D. Chenu (*La théologie comme science*, pp. 80–85) says that this conceptual attenuation represents the partial victory of the Augustinians over the Thomists, in the direction of an intimate rapprochement between theology and faith. Without taking any explicit position respecting this inference, I prefer, on the contrary, to underscore the aspect of distance or difference introduced into theology vis-à-vis faith by the notion of *quasi subalternatio*. Such a difference can be conceived as a "quasi breach," but by no manner of means as a "breach."

I take this opportunity to cite one of the "blind alleys" into which the present investigation turned in one of its stages. In line with Gaston Bachelard's statements to the effect that all scientific truth is "rectified error" (*La formation de l'esprit scientifique*, p. 239), and that "no precision is clearly and neatly made without the history of a former imprecision" (*La philosophie du Non*, p. 72), I confess that I was tempted to determine the relationship between faith and theology in terms of the "epistemological breach," even though I knew that in doing so I would be going counter to the whole of classic theological tradition. My attempt, however, did not meet with success. I have therefore shifted the line of breach from faith vis-à-vis (theological) reason to reason vis-à-vis faith. The positive result of my frustrated attempt was an appreciation of the delicate precision of Thomas's concept of "quasi subalternation," which manages to establish on the one hand a *continuity of content*, and on the other a *discontinuity of method*, between faith and theology—which allows me to speak of a "quasi breach," or a "methodic breach," or even of a "linguistic breach." Indeed, D. Dubarle posits, for science, "two breaches": one vis-à-vis the prescientific *experience*, and the other vis-à-vis *language*. Thus, midway between the rationalist temptation à la Bouillard, and, at the other extreme, that of a positivistic "over-flight" à la Karl Barth, I take a position with Jerôme Hamer, who follows Aquinas here: see his study, "Parole de Dieu ou parole sur Dieu dans la pensée de Karl Barth." I am grateful to Jean Ladrière for having helped me extricate myself from the impasse described in this note.

5. On the *language* level, there is no pertinent difference between the word of faith (for instance, Jesus' words) and religious discourse (for instance, a homily today). The difference is solely on the level of the relationship to revealed content, where the word of faith is original and foundational, whereas religious discourse remains ever derived and founded, as indeed does theological discourse. On the linguistic level, religious discourse, including that of faith, is governed by the rules of any ideology (ideological practice), which is defined by its *immediate and direct relationship to life and practice*. See Louis Althusser, *Pour Marx*, pp. 238ff. From this viewpoint, theology belongs to the genus of "science": its language is "of the scientific type" (Jean Ladrière, *L'articulation du sens*, p. 136).

6. The theological difference is found much attenuated in the classic epistemologies that I have been able to consult, either in the sense that the word of faith is rationalized, or in the sense that theological reason is "fideized": Yves Congar, *La foi et la théologie*; idem, "Théologie," in *Dictionnaire de la Théologie Catholique* 15 (1946) cols. 341-502; Claude Geffré, *A New Age in Theology*; idem, "Théologie," in *Encyclopaedia Universalis* 15 (1973) 1087–91; Johannes B. Metz, "Theologie," in *Lexikon für Theologie und Kirche*, vol. 10, col. 62–71; G. Ebeling, "Theologie—Begriffsgeschichtlich"; Josef Ratzinger, "Theologie"; Karl Rahner, "Theology"; Karl Rahner and H. Vor-

grimler, "Teología," in *Diccionario teológico* (Barcelona, Herder, 2nd ed., 1970, col. 720-26); H. Fries, "Teologia," in *Dicionário de teologia* 5:297-311; but esp. the two following authors: Ambroise Gardeil, *Le donné révélé*, esp. p. 250 (*sacra doctrina* is homogeneous with *scientia Dei* and the *visio beatifica* [!]); and M.-D. Chenu, *La théologie est-elle une science?* pp. 22-24 (an explicit *continuitas* or *continuatio* obtains between faith and [theological] reason); "La théologie comme science ecclésiale"; *Une école de théologie*; pp. 69-77; *Saint Thomas d'Aquin et la théologie*, pp. 34-38, 42-45, 83-84, 125, 128, 155, 166, 168-69, etc.; *Théologie comme science au XIIIe siècle*, pp. 71-80. But did not Thomas himself "evolve" here, and erase the internal differences of *sacra doctrina*, as we see in his *Summa Theologiae*, I, q. 1? This reductive tendency is prejudicial to theology as well as to faith. Reservations are in order, then, when it comes to "popular theology," a "theology of the poor," and the like, argued by the adepts of "engaged" or "revolutionary" theologies. An example: B. Oliver, "Pour une théologie populaire," *La Revue Nouvelle* 62 (1975) 465-68.

7. See Michel Foucault, *The Archaeology*, esp. pp. 56-76. This author places great emphasis on the notion of *discursive practices* as the subjection of discourse to objective regularities. For Althusser, Godelier, and Marxists in general, too, ideology is and always has been structured in accordance with determinate laws. See Godelier's interview in *Lumière et Vie* 25 (1975) 52. Pierre Bourdieu has insisted on the ambiguity of the term "rule," holding that it covers the meanings of "regularity" and "regulation" (*Esquisse d'une théorie de la pratique*, pp. 171-73). Finally, the Wittgensteinian concept of "language play" likewise evokes the notion of a regularity internal to all language.

8. Here I am referring to current Anglo-Saxon language analysis, the analysis of "speech acts," championed by J. L. Austin, especially, as well as by D. D. Evans, J. R. Searle, and others, whose analyses suggest a rethinking of the status of religious language such as Jean Ladrière has successfully undertaken.

9. *"Non dicitur* [theologian] *de his quae supponit habere scientiam, sed de conclusionibus quae, ex principiis suppositis, de necessitate concluduntur"* (Aquinas, *De Veritate*, q. 14, a. 9, ad 3).

10. See *Summa Theol.*, I, q. 1, a. 4: *"Sacra doctrina . . . magis . . . est speculativa quam practica."* My distinction coincides with that of Charles Journet, *The Wisdom of Faith*, in which he sees "two different forms or states" of faith: faith as "rhetoric," to whatever extent it is "in an unpolished state," and faith as "science," when it is found "in an elaborated state" (p. 33; see also pp. 87, 186-93). The first form is concerned with its *addressees*, and therefore arms itself with a language of an *illocutionary* type; the second is concerned with scientific *content*, and adopts, to this end, an *enunciative* language. Journet notes that this distinction is to be found in Thomas, following Aristotle's *Peri Hermeneias*, book 1, chap. 4, lectio 7, nos. 5, 6 (*Wisdom of Faith*, p. 200, n. 4).

11. See Paul Ricoeur, *Le conflit des interprétations*, pp. 64-79.

12. See *Summa Theol.*, I, q. 1, a. 10, ad 1, where Thomas says that in order to staunch the hemorrhage of meanings occasioned by the polysemic character of biblical language, the theologian must articulate "spiritual" meanings only upon the objective base of the *sensus litteralis*. Only on this condition will theology stave off *equivocatio*, *confusio*, and *deceptio*, to the emolument of any effort of explanation and clarification. See also Paul Ricoeur, "Cours d'herméneutique," pp. 62-63.

13. See S. Breton, "Le paradox du menteur et le problème de l'indicible dans les énoncés de foi," pp. 519, 523. The whole article is a confrontation of the language of faith with the contributions of modern logic.

14. It is interesting to note that when Alexander of Hales posed the question—and he

was one of the first to do so—of the scientific status of theology, he solved it with the theory of the *modi* of cognition. These, for him, were of two orders: the *modus definitivus* or *argumentativus*, proper to science, and the *modus* that I would call "performative," which is divisible into submodes: the *praeceptivus*, the *exemplificativus*, the *exhortativus*, the *revelativus*, the *orativus*, and so on. The earliest discussions of the problem situated the status of theology within the second mode. But it was not long before it moved to the first. For all of this see M.-D. Chenu, *Théologie comme science*, esp. pp. 40–41.

15. See *Summa Theol.*, I, q. 1, a. 2. See also John Chrysostom, *Interpretatio in Isaiam Prophetam*, chap. 1 (PG 56:14): "The beginning of our dogmas has its roots on high, with the Lord of the heavens."

16. Thus it is that many scientists, actually rationalists, consider theology a kind of antiscience or pseudo science. See Max Weber, e.g., at the conclusion of his address "Wissenschaft als Beruf" (1919) (*Le savant et le politique*, pp. 93–98); idem, *Essays in Sociology* (1915), chap. 13, pp. 350–59, esp. p. 351; and Alain, *Propos sur le Christianisme* (Paris, Rieder, 1927), pp. 31–34. Fichte, referring to dogmas decreed in councils, spoke ironically of a "truth submitted to the ballot" (cited by H. Duméry, "Théologie," in *Encyclopaedia Universalis* 15 [1968] 1086). It is usually in a tone of derision that theological terminology is employed in intellectual circles today. For Louis Althusser ("L'Eglise en crise?") theology is nearing the end of its resources. If theology, he says, is a "theory," it is certainly not a "scientific theory," but more of an "ideological theory." It is one of the "sciences without objects," however it may summon forth "massive theoretical efforts, and the more or less rigorous production of solutions as fantastic as their object" (*Reading Capital*, p. 115, n. 11). (Frankly, on the existence of God, Althusser knows more than the theologians!) The qualification of theology as a "pseudo science" is found in Karl Marx, *The Holy Family* (1845), as well as in Ludwig Feuerbach, who lists a series of "pseudo sciences" generated by theology: "astro-theology," "litho-theology," "insecto-theology," "arido-theology," and "pyro-theology" (cited by Henri Desroche, *Jacob and the Angel*, p. 131).

17. Alberico Gentilis (1552–1608), *De Jure Belli*, cited by René Coste, *Les communautés politiques*, p. 16.

18. See M. J. Scheeben, *Mysterien des Christentums* (1865), §104, n. 1, p. 631: theology *"redet . . . aus Gott und über Gott."* Professor Vollert translates, "It is theology because what it says comes from God, and because it speaks about God" (M. J. Scheeben, *The Mysteries of Christianity*, p. 739—cited by Yves M.-J. Congar, *La foi et la théologie*, p. 134, n. 3). Rudolf Bultmann also distinguishes between speaking "of God" *("von Gott")* and "about God" *("über Gott"): Faith and Understanding*, 1:53–65.

19. For this notion, see Gaston Bachelard, *Le rationalisme appliqué,* chap. 4, pp. 77–80; and Bourdieu et al., *Le métier de sociologue*, p. 14 and passim.

20. See J.-P. Jossua, "De la théologie au théologien," *Concilium*, no. 60 (1970), supplément, pp. 55–60; Walter Kasper, "La fonction de la théologie dans l'Eglise," ibid. pp. 47–53; and generally the whole issue, devoted to the International Theology Meeting in Brussels, 1970.

21. I am thinking of the pneumatic, doxological, and "eucharistic" conception of "theology" of the Orthodox: L. Sertorius, "La théologie orthodoxe," in Vander Gucht and Vorgrimler, *Bilan*, 1:562–600; A. de Halleux, "A teologia ortodoxa," in Feiner and Löhrer, *Mysterium Salutis*, I/4, pp. 179–85.

22. M.-D. Chenu, *Théologie comme science au XIIIe siècle* (1st ed., 1927).

23. Both Martin Heidegger, for Western metaphysics, and Karl Marx, for an idealistic philosophy, have taught us that no theoretical problem solves itself, least of all by being ignored or forgotten. To get beyond it, one must real-ize it, re-trace its path, complete its questions, effectuate its *Aufhebung*—in a word, to use Marx's own expression, "get everything out in the open." For Heidegger, see *Was ist die Metaphysik?* esp. p. 8, and "Zur Seinsfrage," esp. p. 35. For Marx, see his *The German Ideology*.

24. In his *Théologie comme science au XIIIe siècle*, M.-D. Chenu shows that every step forward taken by theology to assert its theoretical status aroused reaction and resistance, sometimes violent, on the part of traditionalists, especially among the most powerful: Orderico Vital e Esmaragdo, against a grammatical critique applied to scripture (p. 9, n. 1); Rupert Deutz and Bernard of Clairveaux, against Abelard's dialectic (pp. 15–22); Roger Bacon, R. Fishacre, Gregory IX, and others, against Aristotelian *ratio* (pp. 26–32). See also Philotheus Böhner and Etienne Gilson, *História da filosofia cristã* (Petrópolis, Vozes, 1970).

25. See L. Genicot, *Les lignes de faite du Moyen Age* (Tournai/Paris, Casterman, 1951), pp. 286–91; J. Paul, *Histoire intellectuelle de l'Occident médiéval* (Paris, Colin, 1973), pp. 353 and passim.

26. See, e.g., Thomas Aquinas's epistemological masterpiece, *In Librum Boethii de Trinitate*. The whole of question 5 is devoted to tracing the lines of demarcation between natural philosophy (the natural sciences), mathematics (the formal sciences), and *scientia divina* (philosophy and theology). Question 6 studies the *method* (the "modus") of each of these three rational regions—namely, its *processus rationalis*, according to the expression employed many times by Thomas, an expression which calls to mind Althusser's "process of theoretical practice." But Thomas's final intent is to reveal the *modus appropriatus* (nonexclusive) of theological knowing.

27. See *Summa Theol.*, I, q. 1, a. 4; *In Boethii de Trinitate*, q. 5, a. 1, etc. See also Yves M.-J. Congar, *La foi et la théologie*, pp. 134–36, and 245–46, where he stresses the difference between this project of systematic rationality and that of other theologies, such as that of the Franciscan school.

28. See M.-D. Chenu, *La foi dans l'intelligence*, pp. 101–2. *Scientia affectiva* is Albertus Magnus's expression, from I *Sent.*, dist. 1, a. 4 (cited by Chenu, *Théologie comme science au XIIIe siècle*, p. 99, n. 3). See also L. Asmoros, "La teología como ciencia práctica en la escuela franciscana en los tiempos que preceden a Escoto," *Archives d'Histoire doctrinaire du Moyen Age*, vol. 9; R. Caleffi, "Relação entre arte e teologia em São Boaventura," *Convivium* 14 (1975) 13–28.

29. See the commentaries already cited on question 1 of the *Summa Theologiae*: Ambroise Gardeil, *Thomas d'Aquin*, 1:107–9; A.-D. Sertillanges, *Thomas d'Aquin*, pp. 17–18. See also Yves Congar, *La foi et la théologie*, pp. 126, 244; M.-D. Chenu, *Théologie comme science au XIIIe siècle*, p. 79. In question 1, the concept of *sacra doctrina* refers to revelation in article 1, theology in articles 2 through 8, and scripture in articles 9 and 10.

30. My chapters 6 and 7 offer a kind of theological *semantics*, inasmuch as they attempt to define the formal content of the theology: architectonic concepts of salvation, *agape*, grace, and sin on the side of the real, and revelation, faith, and religion on the side of awareness.

31. If the reader will permit me to draw the unfair parallel, Thomas's undertaking here, consisting in equivalating Christianity with *sacra doctrina*, is like Althusser's identification of Marxism with the science of historical materialism. Criticism of Thomas's theological "intellectualism" is familiar: e.g., Pierre Rousselot, *The Intellectualism of*

Saint Thomas; J. Baillie, *The Idea of Revelation in Recent Thought* (London, Oxford University Press, 1956).

32. The aporias of Thomas's thought are concentrated, it seems to me, around his logocentrism.

The heterogeneous theoretical status of *sacra doctrina* has permeated the whole history of Thomism, as may be seen from the controversies it has aroused, particularly concerning article 2 of question 1 of the *Summa*, which maintains the scientific nature of *sacra doctrina*, and where Cajetan, Serra, and others, for example, took their stand against John of Saint Thomas, Silvius, and so on: see Thomas Aquinas, *Summa Theologica* (Turin, Marietti, 1926), 1:3, n. 5.

For the Franciscan opposition, see Bonaventure, *Collationes in Hexaemeron*, 19, 7 (5, 421a): "*Apud philosophos non est scientia ad* dandam remissionem peccatorum"; ibid. (19, 14–15): "*Pessimum miraculum*: wine changed to water"—a sarcastic reference to the theoretical intent of Thomas Aquinas in a university lecture series given in Paris in 1273 (cited by M.-D. Chenu, *La théologie est-elle une science?* p. 20, n. 1). Thomas himself says: "*Illi qui utuntur philosophicis documentis in Sacra Scriptura redigendo in obsequium fidei, non miscent aquam vino, sed convertunt aquam in vinum*" (*In Boethii de Trinitate*, q. 2, a. 3, ad 5). See Edouard-Henri Weber, *Dialogue et dissensions entre saint Bonaventure et saint Thomas d'Aquin à Paris (1252–1273)* (Paris, Vrin, 1974).

For the Reformers, see, e.g., Luther's celebrated *Disputatio contra Scholasticam Theologiam* (1517) and *Disputatio Heidelbergae Habita* (1518). Yves Congar (*La foi et la théologie*, p. 238, n. 1) observes that the first Reformers reacted vigorously against the identification, tendentious in their eyes, between theology and *sacra pagina*, seeking to reserve the latter expression exclusively for the Bible.

For the humanists' critique of scholasticism, see G. Chantraigne's study, *"Mystère" et "Philosophie du Christ" selon Erasme* (Namur, Faculté de Philosophie et Lettres, 1971). See also Erasmus's celebrated letter to a Louvain theologian, Dorpius (1515), in *Eloge de la Folie et Lettre d'Erasme à Dorpius* (translated by P. de Nolhac, Paris, Garnier, 1953). M.-R. Gagnebet sums up Luther's and Erasmus's attacks on scholastic theology in his article, "La nature de la théologie spéculative," *Revue Thomiste*, 1938, pp. 574–645.

33. Martin Luther, *Disputatio contra Scholasticam Theologiam*, proposition 44.

34. Augustinian epistemology was more favorable to the sciences than to theology, considering the latter wisdom, not science, thus leaving the field open for the development of empirical inquiries. So it was in the thirteenth century at Oxford with Robert Grosseteste and with Roger Bacon. Scotus, Ockham, and Augustinians, also wrote scientific tractates. See J. Verger, *Les universités au Moyen Age* (Paris, Presses Universitaires de France 1973), pp. 95–97, 112–16.

35. Here I am thinking of modern theological currents that define themselves as "existentialist" or "revolutionary"—whereas in fact they are completely impregnated with empiricism, so characteristic of the Augustinian current—which lay claim to the most direct and immediate relationship possible with the Bible and the church fathers, complaining of the "dryness" of scholasticism, and seeking to substitute a "vital," "living" contact with "reality," with "life," with "practice," and so on and so on.

36. M.-D. Chenu's aim in *Théologie comme science au XIIIe siècle*, pp. 80, 93ff.

37. See F. Ferré, *Le langage religieux a-t-il un sens?* esp. pp. 14–16; Ludwig Wittgenstein, *Tractatus Logico-Philosophicus*, proposition 3.3 (p. 25): "Only propositions have sense; only in the nexus of a proposition does a name have meaning."

38. See G. Kalinowsky, "Philosophie, théologie et métathéorie." From this most informative and enlightening work I extract the following (all in italics in the original): *"Axiomatization . . . is actually the epistemological perfection to which philosophy and theology can—and must—attain"* (p. 168). Axiomatization is the "rigorous explicitation of all the methodological rules of a system of propositions" (ibid.). "The progression of a science in the direction of its epistemological perfection is a process of exhaustive, rigorous explicitation of all of [its] methodological rules and of their maximally precise enunciation" (p. 180). *"Theological theses are admitted in virtue of certain methodological rules, implicit if not explicit, and independently of whether or not they are conscious"* (p. 200).

39. Ludwig Wittgenstein, *Tractatus Logico-Philosophicus*, proposition 4.116 (p. 51): "Everything that can be thought at all can be thought clearly. Everything that can be put into words can be put clearly."

40. Louis Althusser, *Reading Capital*, p. 87; see also pp. 86–87: "The decisive point of Marx's thesis concerns the principle distinguishing between the *real* and *thought*. The real is one thing, along with its different aspects: the real-concrete, the process of the real, the real totality, etc. *Thought* about the real is another, along with its different aspects: the thought process, the thought-totality, the thought-concrete, etc." See also Nicos Poulantzas, *Political Power and Social Classes,* pp. 12–13.

41. Augustine's distinction, *De Trinitate*, 13, 2 (PL 42:1017).

42. See Jossua et al., *Une foi exposée*, as well as other works of Jossua. See, too, Jean Mouroux, *L'expérience chrétienne: Introduction à une théologie* (Paris, Aubier-Montaigne, 1954); idem, *Je crois en toi: La rencontre avec Dieu vivant* (Paris, Cerf, 1966); Charles Wackenheim, *Christianisme sans idéologie*, pp. 109–19; Charles Moeller, "Que signifie aujourd'hui être sauvé?"

43. Faith necessarily comports a determinate noetic content. Hence Vatican I, followed by Vatican II, refers to "two orders of knowledge" (*Gaudium et Spes*, no. 59, p. 295). See Leonardo Boff, "Ciência e técnica modernas e pensar teológico: Recolocação de um velho problema," esp. pp. 249–50. The same contribution is to be found in Leonardo Boff's *A graça libertadora*, pp. 70–85.

44. Romance languages will have to find a way of distinguishing between the scientific plane of *experimentation* and the religious plane of *experience*, perhaps by manufacturing, for the latter, a verb such as *experienciar*, instead of having to use *experimentar* for both. See Georges Thill, *La fête scientifique*, p. 278, n. 447.

45. See M. Seckler, "Fé," in Fries, ed., *Dicionário de teologia*, 2:192–214. For the distinction in question—"I believe in you" and "I believe that . . . ," see ibid., pp. 206–7, 210–11.

46. *"Da fidei quae fidei sunt. Frustra sudaverit qui coelestia religionis arcana nostrae rationi adaptare conabitur"* (Francis Bacon, *Instauratio Magna: De Dignitate et Augmentis Scientiarum*, book 3, chap. 2, no. 1; see also nos. 2ff., and chap. 4).

47. The order of things has been so disposed by God from the beginning, in virtue of the deed of Jesus Christ in history (salvific economy), that what is *decisive* for salvation (see Matt. 25:31–46) is not the cognition or noncognition of faith, but precisely the practice of faith: *agape*: "In Christ Jesus neither circumcision nor the lack of it counts for anything: only faith, which expresses itself through love (*agape*)" (Gal. 5:6).

48. See Thomas Aquinas, *In Boethii de Trinitate*, q. 2, a. 2, ad 5: *"Articuli fidei, qui sunt principia hujus scientiae ad cognitionem divinam . . . supponuntur in scientia nostra."*

49. In order to appreciate the force of the difference established by theological practice

vis-à-vis faith, we might well paraphrase Spinoza: "The concept of a dog does not bark." Thus neither does the concept of God save!

50. See Jean Ladrière's remarkable studies on "speech acts," in which he calls attention to the circumincession that is characteristic of faith. See esp. "Langage théologique et philosophie analytique"; and *L'articulation du sens*, pp. 91–139, 227–41.

51. See Wolfhart Pannenberg, *Jesus—God and Man*, pp. 106–8.

52. See E. Ortigues, *Le discours et le symbole* (Paris, Aubier, 1962). For the general problematic of the sacramental order, see Leonardo Boff, *Die Kirche als Sakrament im Horizont der Welterfahrung*, an exhaustive inquiry on the subject; Edward Schillebeeckx, *Christ the Sacrament of the Encounter with God*; idem, *Etude théologique du salut par les sacrements*.

53. See the following works of François Houtart: "Les religions comme réalités sociales"; *Igreja e mundo; The Eleventh Hour*. See also Jacques Sutter, *Comme si Dieu n'existait pas*; Gérard Defois et al., *Le pouvoir dans l'Eglise*.

54. See Benedict Spinoza, *A Theologico-Political Treatise*, chap. 1, no. 5, p. 289. Law, for that matter, has no interest in intentions, but in practices—such is the notion of Kant and Hegel.

55. Here we might recall the critique of rationalism by phenomenology, that of ideological scientificism by the currents of "counterscience," that of the primacy of conscience by Freudianism, Marxism, and structuralism, and so forth. For this problem, see M.-D. Dubarle, "Epistémologie," pp. 136–42, 161–68, 200–214.

56. See Adolphe Gesché, "Mutation religieuse," esp. p. 290, and the authors cited by Gesché in n. 52; Gustave Thils, *Christianisme sans religion?* pp. 82–83; Maurice Bellet, *Déplacement de la religion*, pp. 5, 173, 179ff., 193ff. See, too, Adolphe Gesché, *L'annonce de Dieu*, pp. 65–71.

57. See *Lumen Gentium*, nos. 10–12, and generally the whole of chap. 2. Taking simply the case of liturgy, it may be inferred, from the religious conceptualization worked out here, that liturgy develops in terms of a constitution of the human and historical moment and locus in which the divine truth of the world and of things is manifested and proclaimed, and where history and events are extrapolated to their eschatological *pleroma*: in liturgy, bread is the body of Christ, wine is the blood of the Lord, word is God's revelation, the community is the people of God, the shared meal of brothers and sisters is the messianic banquet, the human beings there present are the sons and daughters of God, and so on.

58. For the question of the specificity of Christianity, see the whole of no. 116, vol. 23 (1974), of *Lumière et Vie*, entitled "Christian identity"; the whole of no. 2, vol. 7 (1973), of *Servitium*, entitled "the 'specifically Christian' "; the whole of no. 92 (1970) of *Le Supplément*, esp. J.-M. Aubert, "La spécificité de la morale chrétienne selon Saint Thomas"; John A. T. Robinson, *The Difference in Being a Christian Today*; C. H. Dodd, *Gospel and Law*; Rudolf Schnackenburg, *The Moral Teaching of the New Testament*. As for our own problem, from the viewpoint of political practice, see Giulio Girardi, "Nouveauté chrétienne"; Edward Schillebeeckx, "Les théories critiques," pp. 56–62; José Comblin, *Théologie de la pratique*, pp. 49–54; Jürgen Moltmann, *L'espérance en action*, esp. pp. 156–59; idem, *The Crucified God*, chap. 1; Juan Luís Segundo, *Massas e minorias*. See also the ethical pragmatism of Benedict Spinoza, *Theologico-Political Treatise*, esp. chap. 14 (pp. 182–89). In sum, one might say that (explicit) Christianity consists only in a *formality*, defined by a *conscious* reference to Christ, which, on the level of practices, "only" offers new motivations: Jesus' example, his promises, and so forth.

59. See Peter L. Berger, *The Sacred Canopy*, pp. 186–87. On this problem generally, see *Foi et religion*. The difference between faith and religion, in the understanding of the dialectical theology of a Karl Barth or a Helmut Gollwitzer—i.e., as the correlate of the difference between Christianity and other religions—is, to my way of thinking, impossible to maintain. A mutual opposition of faith and religion represents a facile piece of theory with no value except for polemics. See J. Kamp, "Enseigner la religion?" esp. pp. 340–42. See also my study, "A religião contra a fé?" (*Vozes* 63 [1969] 99–116).

60. See *Lumen Gentium*, no. 8: *"Haec Ecclesia . . . subsistit in Ecclesia catholica"* (emphasis added).

61. See Wolfhart Pannenberg, *La foi des Apôtres*, pp. 133–35.

62. See Augustine, *In Galatas Expositio*, no. 28 (PL 35, col. 2125), as cited in de Lubac, *Catholicism*, p. 35. Along these same lines, see Yves Congar, *Un peuple messianique*—Congar's title being a designation found in *Lumen Gentium*, no. 9 (due, by the way, to Congar himself).

63. After the criticisms of the founders of the great religions, after the attacks of the prophets, of Jesus, and nearer to our own times, of Marx, Nietzsche, and Freud, we may rest assured of this: religious distortions are *recurrent*. Could it be that they are connected with the (historical) nature of sign itself? See the following note.

64. The fact of a barrier between the signifier and the significate has been sufficiently underscored by all of the theories of signifier, from a point of departure in linguistics and its applications. For psychoanalysis, see Jacques Lacan, "L'instance de la lettre dans l'inconsciente," J.-M. Palmier, *Lacan: Le symbolique et l'imaginaire*, esp. chap. 2: "the supremacy of the word and the signifier," pp. 43–66, which can be summed up in the basic algorithm of Lacanian theory: S/s—showing the immovable barrier separating the signifier from the significate. The same occurs in *economics*, in accordance with Marx's analyses of what he considers to be the fetish nature of trade: *Capital*, chap. 1 (pp. 13–37). So also in art, as noted by Roman Ingarden in his *The Literary Work of Art*, to the effect that, although the representative objects of a work tend to replace and subjugate the objects represented, they never perfectly coincide with them, unless they manage to deceive the addressee. Hence Jean-Paul Sartre's recommendation, in *Imagination: A Psychological Critique*, that, in order to determine the proper characters of the image qua image, we have recourse to a new act of awareness: reflection. For a more general treatment of this problematic, see also R. Laporte, "L'empire des signifiants"; F. Skrzypczak, "Le signifiant"; C. B. Clément, *Le pouvoir des mots*.

65. The elaborations of the theology of liberation move in this same direction. See Gustavo Gutiérrez, *A Theology*, pp. 149–52; Hugo Assmann, *Nomad Church*, p. 138; Rafael Avila, *Teología, evangelización y liberación*, pp. 74–79; Leonardo Boff, *Teologia do cativeiro*, chap. 11, pp. 201–19; idem, *O destino do homem e do mundo*, pp. 69–84. My viewpoint is in line with this position, although my larger objective is to "unblock" theological practice from the institutional ideology of a certain ecclesiological dogmatics here, and this from a point of departure in, and with a view to, a theology of the political. It now goes without saying, surely, that this blockage constitutes a major "epistemological obstacle" to the correct development of a theology of the political!

66. See O. Nogueira, "Ciência, pesquisa, método e técnica"; Georges Kalinowsky, *Querelle de la science normative*, pp. 170–82; Louis Althusser, *Reading Capital*, p. 39, n. 17; Pierre Bourdieu et al., *Le métier de sociologue*, Introduction, pp. 11–25.

67. On the rational, theoretical nature of theology, see my citations, above, of Thomas Aquinas's epistemology, esp. *Summa Theol.*, I, q. 1, a. 8: *"Utrum haec Doctrina Sit Argumentativa."* The response of this article could be summed up thus: *faith makes one*

think. Thomas states that theology is *rationalis* in the sense that it *"discurrit ab uno ad alterum"* (*In Boethii de Trinitate*, q. 6, a. 1); but not in the sense of apodicity or demonstration of its proper object, its *subjectum*, for this is the *"forma divina quae est ultra omnia phantasmata"* (ibid., a. 4). Theological *rationes* are not *necessariae* or *demonstrativae*, but *persuasoriae* or *manifestativae*: *Summa Theol.*, I, q. 32, a. 1, ad 2; II-II, q. 1, a. 5, ad 2: *In Boethii de Trinitate*, q. 2, a. 1, ad 5.

68. See Jean Ladrière, *L'articulation du sens*, pp. 162–65. This author defines "critique" as "a knowledge operating upon itself," and expressing itself, in the first place, in negative form, as a "questioning and dissolution of evidence"; and then in positive form, as "search for system"; and, finally, as "method."

69. See M.-D. Chenu, *La foi dans l'intelligence*, pp. 115–38. Here, as on pp. 244–49 and 277ff., Chenu speaks of the "primacy of the revealed datum." The latter is valid especially for classic theology—first theology—as contradistinguished from the empty speculativism into which, as Chenu says, baroque scholasticism fell. As for the current tasks of theology—second theology—Chenu says that there might be reason to doubt the "primacy of the datum" beyond its status of "principle." See also G. Philips, "Les méthodes théologiques du Vatican II." See also the following note.

70. *"Quando intelligimus debemus rationi, quando credimus auctoritati"*: Augustine, *De Utilitate Credendi*, 9 (PL 42:83).

71. For analyses of *religious* language, see the studies that I have cited by Jean Ladrière, upon which I depend, esp. "La théologie et le langage de l'interprétation"; "Le langage théologique et le discours de la représentation"; and "Langage théologique et philosophie analytique"; as well as his "A operatividade da linguagem litúrgica." See also W. de Bont, "La religion en tant que pensée symbolique"; idem, "La sécularisation de la pensée." Note that "discourse" and "language" *(linguagem, langage)* are equivalent in the sense in which I use the terms. Perhaps it would have been well to distinguish them in correlation with the elementary linguistic distinction between language *(langue)* and word. "Language" *(langage)* would then be the abstract system of signs, and "discourse" would be the concrete performance of this system. For this distinction, see Emile Benveniste, *Problems in General Linguistics*.

72. Ludwig Wittgenstein, *Tractatus Logico-Philosophicus*, proposition 6.41 (p. 145); see also proposition 6.4312 (p. 149): "The solution of the riddle of life in space and time lies *outside* space and time."

73. See Jean Ladrière, "La théologie et le langage de l'interprétation," pp. 262–67; Paul Ricoeur, *Le conflit des interprétations*, esp. pp. 64ff.

74. See G. Söhngen, "A sabedoria da teologia," pp. 131–38.

75. For the notion that the appropriate assent of theological signifying is constituted by symbols, not by formal concepts, see Thomas Aquinas, *Summa Theol.*, I, q. 1, a. 10, c.; Hugo of Saint Victor, *De Scripturis et Scriptoribus Sacris*, chap. 14 (PL 175:20). See also Jean Ladrière, in *Science et théologie*, pp. 14–15; Paul Ricoeur, *The Rule of Metaphor*.

76. See Paul Ricoeur, *The Rule of Metaphor*; Jean Ladrière, "Langage théologique et philosophie analytique," pp. 106–10.

77. Michel de Certeau's play on words, in his "La rupture instauratrice," p. 1213.

78. See Paul Ricoeur, *Le conflit des interprétations*, pp. 20–23, 283–328.

79. On the structuring function of these two mechanisms outside the field of linguistics, we may recall the psychoanalytic theories of Sigmund Freud in *Interpretation of Dreams* (1900); idem, *Five Lessons on Psychoanalysis* (1910), p. 36; Jacques Lacan, *Ecrits*, pp. 155–64; not to mention the structural analysis of myths by Claude Lévi-

Strauss. Before being taken up and developed by Lacan, the relating of the unconscious mechanisms described by Freud to the linguistic procedures of metaphor and metonymy was done by the Russian linguist of the Prague school, R. Jakobson: see Jean Laplanche and J.-B. Pontalis, *The Language of Psycho-Analysis*, p. 123.

80. See J.-T. Desanti, *La philosophie silencieuse*, p. 236.

81. The "licence" taken by religious language in its spontaneity clearly appears in, e.g., the Psalms. There, all mediations are abolished, as well as any theoretical discipline, and rightly so. The same occurs with "mythic" thought, e.g., in its conception of the "miracle"—God acting in such and such a place and at such and such a time (and not in another place at another time). For the latter case, see Benedict Spinoza, *Theologico-Political Treatise*, chap. 6 (pp. 81–97), and the excellent article by Paul Valadier, "Signes des temps, signes de Dieu?" esp. p. 273. For the "reification" of ideas, a typical trait of ordinary language, see Pierre Bourdieu, *Outline of a Theory of Practice*, pp. 29, 203 (nn. 48, 49); and idem et al., *Le métier de sociologue*, pp. 31, 152–53, with reference to Emile Durkheim and Ludwig Wittgenstein.

82. This problem can be approached from another direction, that of modern logic. See *L'analyse du langage théologique*; Dubarle et al., *La recherche en philosophie et en théologie*; Jacques Poulain, *Logique et raison*; Michel Combes, *Le langage sur Dieu peut-il avoir un sens?* Ian T. Ramsey, *Religious Language*; W. Pater, *Theologische Sprachlogik*; Anton Grabner-Haider, *Semiotik und Theologie* (Munich, Kösel, 1973); John Macquarrie, *God Talk*; Leonardo Boff, "Teologia e semiótica"; F. Ferré, *Le langage religieux a-t-il un sens?* (bibliography, pp. 191–97); J. M. Bochenski, *The Logic of Religion*. These authors make practically no distinction between religious discourse and theological discourse, but simply lump them together.

83. See Jean Ladrière, "Langage théologique et philosophie analytique," p. 104; idem, *L'articulation du sens*, p. 136. In accordance with what I have said in §33, above, I maintain that the "illocutionary operator" stated as "I believe [that it is true] that . . . " is operative in theological discourse only on the level of (revealed) *content*, and not on the level of the *form* of the discourse. Vis-à-vis the former aspect, theology is *ex fide*, otherwise it is not theology. Thomas Aquinas energetically insists upon the correct order of theological rationality: faith to reason, not reason to faith: *In Boethii de Trinitate*, q. 2, aa. 1 and 3; *Contra Graecos*, chap. 2; *Summa Theol.*, I, q. 1, a. 8. The same order will, by the way, be valid for the question that I shall be analyzing shortly, that of the relationship of faith and politics, or salvation and liberation.

84. A theologian's head is like everyone else's: Yves M.-J. Congar, "Théologie," in *Dictionnaire de la Théologie Catholique*, vol. 15, cols. 475–76; H. Duméry, "Théologie," in *Encyclopaedia Universalis* 15 (1968) 1087; Melchior Cano, *De Locis Theologicis*, book 12, chap. 11: *"Divina et humana ratio quod saepe dixi dissimiles non sunt nec alio haec alio ducit illa."*

85. Consider the three functions ascribed to theological *ratio* by Thomas Aquinas (*In Boethii de Trinitate*, q. 2, a. 3): *"Ad demonstrandum ea quae sunt praeambula fidei . . . ad notificandum per aliquas similitudines ea quae sunt fidei . . . ad resistendum his quae contra fidem dicuntur."* Thomas also says (ibid.): *"Oportet doctores sacrae scripturae* [i.e., of theology!] *quandoque contra philosophos agere; ergo oportet eos philosophia uti."*

86. Here I am giving the notion of "symbol" a wide, yet realistic, sense. Symbol is a reality which evokes another with which it maintains an internal relation, as indeed Paul Tillich understands. Perhaps it would be better to speak of *parabole* ("parable"), as does Yves Congar in his *Jalons pour une théologie du laïcat* (Paris, Cerf, 1954, p. 628),

or even of "analogy," with Karl Barth (*Community, State, and Church*, p. 170). The notion of "image," in Plato's sense, or, better, in the biblical sense, translates the same meaning, for it implies a participation in an intended reality that becomes partially present in the image itself: see F. A. Stein, "O matrimonio segundo São Paulo," in J. Salvador et al., *Atualidades biblicas*, p. 446. Jacques Maritain, in his *Humanismo integral*, speaks of "figure" (p. 154), "refraction." (pp. 115, 216-17). *Gaudium et Spes* (no. 38, p. 273) employs the noun "material" (material of the kingdom).

87. See Eph. 1 and Col. 1. "The world in which we live is supernatural. . . . Even before the coming of Christ, it is moved by grace" (Karl Rahner, *Ecrits théologiques*, 1:15).

88. Here we are before a particular, special case of the "classic" question in the relationship between God and the human being, grace and freedom, and so on. See the interesting "solution" proposed by Romano Guardini, "God's Dominion and Man's Freedom" (in Guardini, *The Faith and Modern Man*, pp. 27-37)—a talk given in Berlin during World War II, under the watchful eye of the Nazi state, as we read in ibid., p. vii.

89. One recognizes, in the last formula, the title of a document of the Permanent Council of the French Episcopate.

90. Objection lodged by L. Rütti, "Interpretação do lugar político," esp. pp. 447-48. But the author's alternative is unconvincing: pp. 450-51. See also Karl Marx's criticism of "speculative thinking," for which "things" are the *incarnation* of "ideas": *Critique de l'économie politique* (1844), pp. 305-8.

91. Terms borrowed from Jürgen Moltmann, *The Crucified God*. Both models espoused by Moltmann are badly chosen: they are posited in the delicate area of the church-state relationship.

92. See Thomas Aquinas, *Summa Theol.*, I, q. 88, a. 2: the realities of faith, vis-à-vis the platonic ideas, are *"omnino alterius rationis"*—i.e., neither series has anything whatever to do with the other. On this basis, we can reject the assimilation of the theological reading of history to Proudhon's "speculative method," which Marx censured as a fashion of reading historical facts "from above," from on high, from a point of departure in supposedly eternal and immutable categories, of which the facts in question would be "incarnations": Karl Marx, *Poverty of Philosophy* (1847); idem, "Letter on Proudhon to J. B. von Schweitzer," (Jan. 24, 1865). Here is a criticism valid for all idealism, Hegelian or Platonic.

93. See R. Caillois, "L'utopie négative," esp. p. 57. The "Son of Man" died on the cross "that the cross, for the most perceptive, might become a theologian": Gregory of Nyssa, *Opera*, edited by Werner Jaeger, 9:303. The paradox of the *logos tou staurou* (1 Cor. 1:18) in history, especially in politics, is the theme of Moltmann's book just cited, *The Crucified God*. The parallel between salvation history and human history fails to withstand the most elementary confrontation with the reality of the facts.

94. My term for the theoretical symbols of theology. Although these fail to apprehend their object (hence, asymptotic), at all events they apprehend the right path to their discovery (hence their conceptuality). This is Thomas Aquinas's thinking as well, as expressed particularly in his dialectic of the *enunciabile* concept and the asymptotic *res*: *Summa Theol.*, II-II, q. 1, a. 2. For this particular question, see M.-D. Chenu's excellent study, *La foi dans l'intelligence*, pp. 31-50. On this problematic generally, see Charles Journet, *Connaissance et inconnaissance de Dieu* (Paris, Deselée de Brouwer, 1969).

95. "Transvaluation"—Jean Ladrière's term in his "La théologie et le langage de l'interprétation," p. 262. In his study, "Le langage théologique et le discours de la représentation," Ladrière speaks of the capacity of theology to "metaphoricize" existential language (p. 172).

CHAPTER 8

1. See *Dei Verbum*, no. 17. For both the history and the meaning of this document, see *A Biblia na Igreja depois da "Dei Verbum"*; Bernard-Dominique Dupuy, ed., *La révélation divine*, esp. Henri de Lubac's contribution in vol. 2; P. van Leeuwen, "La révélation divine et sa transmission." For the value of Old Testament revelation, see Samuel Amsler, *L'Ancien Testament dans l'Eglise*.

2. *Dei Verbum*, no. 18.

3. For this notion, see Paul Ricoeur, *Freud and Philosophy*, pp. 20–36, 54–56, as well as his *Conflict of Interpretations*.

4. Hermeneutics, as a theological activity, obviously takes place in the element of faith, as I have said many times. What other reason could there be for assigning priority to the gospels instead of, e.g., to Pindar's odes? See, however, Paul Ricoeur, *Freud and Philosophy*, pp. 28–36, esp. 29–30. A *Christian* hermeneutics may be inconceivable on the level of *rules* of interpretation, but not as far as the *object* to be interpreted is concerned: see Ricoeur, ibid., pp. 26–27; Roger Lapointe, *Les trois dimensions de l'herméneutique*, pp. 139–51.

5. See K. Kérényi, "Origine e senso dell'ermeneutica."

6. Thus we find authors distinguishing between hermeneutics and exegesis, the former being the code of rules whose application is constituted by the latter. See Augustin Bea, "Biblische Hermeneutik," in *Lexikon für Theologie und Kirche*, vol. 2, col. 437; E. Mangenot, "Exégèse," in *Dictionnaire de la Théologie Catholique*, vol. 5, col. 1744; Rudolf Bultmann, *Jésus*, p. 213; Paul Ricoeur, *Freud and Philosophy*, pp. 8, 24, 26, etc.; as well as W. Kümmel, A. Haag, and Raymond E. Brown. For the problematic of hermeneutics and exegesis in general, see Roland Barthes et al., *Exégèse et herméneutique*; esp. H. Bouillard's article, pp. 271–83; Settimana Biblica, *Esegesi ed ermeneutica*; Gerhard Lohfink, *Exegesis bíblica y teología*; A. Haag, "Hermenêutica"; James M. Robinson and John B. Cobb, Jr., eds., *The New Hermeneutic*, esp. pp. ix–x, 1–11; Raymond E. Brown, "Hermeneutics"; and Henri de Lubac's classic, *Exégèse médiévale*.

7. It is along these lines that the "new hermeneutics" is to be situated: Ernst Fuchs, *Hermeneutik*; idem, *Marburger Hermeneutik*; G. Ebeling, "Hermeneutik"; idem, *Wort und Glaube*; idem, *Theology and Proclamation*; Rudolf Bultmann, *Faith and Understanding*, vol. 2; Lothar Steiger, *Die Hermeneutik als dogmatisches Problem*; Lortz and Strolz, eds., *Die hermeneutische Frage der Theologie*; Pierre-André Stucki, *Herméneutique et dialectique*; Jean-Paul Resweber, *La théologie face au défi herméneutique*. For the history of hermeneutics, see Franz Mussner, *Histoire de l'herméneutique de Schleiermacher à nos jours*. I am particularly indebted to Roger Lapointe, *Trois dimensions de l'herméneutique* (gathers up the most significant elements of biblical exegesis), and René Marlé, *Le problème théologique de l'herméneutique*. See also Claude Geffré, *A New Age in Theology*; H. Cazelles, *Ecriture, Parole et Esprit* (a good survey).

8. See, e.g., Jürgen Moltmann, *The Crucified God*, pp. 317–24: "Political Herme-neutics of Liberation." Moltmann defines this notion as the reflection of faith bound to the concrete of praxis (ibid., pp. 317–18). See also his "Hacia una hermenéutica política del Evangelio." Along the lines of "political hermeneutics" in the third sense, see Dorothee Sölle, *Political Theology*.

9. "Theology, to a very large extent, is a science that arises from texts: the Bible, exege-sis, tradition, the fathers of the church, the liturgy, the texts of the magisterium, and conciliar texts" (Yves Congar, "Théologie et sciences humaines," p. 31).

10. Besides Gadamer's *Truth and Method*, let me call attention to his "Rhetorik, Her-meneutik und Ideologiekritik" and his "Le problème herméneutique." For material from Gadamer, as also from Friedrich Schleiermacher, Wilhelm Dilthey, and Martin Heidegger, I am in the debt of Paul Ricoeur and his "Cours d'herméneutique."

11. Such is J. Greisch's criticism of Gadamer in Greisch's "La crise de l'herméneu-tique." See also his "La raison herméneutique."

12. See Paul Ricoeur, *Freud and Philosophy*, pp. 20–24, where he takes his distance from this conception, judging it "overly 'long' " (p. 20).

13. The distinction between *comprehension* (hermeneutics) and *explication* (science) can be considered as of purely heuristic value. It would not, then, be the designation of a dichotomy between two epistemological provinces: that of the sciences of the human being and that of the sciences of nature, as Wilhelm Dilthey sought to establish in *Le monde de l'espirit*, and as is maintained by Raymond Aron, *Introduction to the Philos-ophy of History*, and Emilio Betti, *Die Hermeneutik als allgemeine Methodik der Geistwissenschaft* (Tübingen, Mohr, 1962). Jean-Pierre Osier, in his presentation of Ludwig Feuerbach's *L'essence du Christianisme*, places the two approaches in frontal opposition, finally relegating hermeneutics to the limbo of ideology—i.e., of pseudo knowledge. But the orientation of investigations in the epistemology of the sciences of the human being appears to be in the direction of an extinction of the dualism implied here. It perceives that *interpretation* is absent neither from the purely formal sciences (see Jean Ladrière, *L'articulation du sens*, pp. 64–67, 167–72), nor, a fortiori, from the empirico-formal sciences (see Ladrière, "La théologie et le langage de l'interprétation," pp. 251–57; idem, *Vie sociale et destinée*, p. 200). For this question in general, see Ladrière, "Le rôle de l'interprétation en science, en philosophie et en théologie." On the other hand, on the part of the sciences of the human being, one registers the effort to break through a hard-and-fast line of demarcation between explicitation and compre-hension: thus Paul Ricoeur, "Cours d'herméneutique," pp. 5–6, 67, 98, 121–22, 137, etc. For his part, Jean Piaget, in his *Epistémologie des sciences le l'homme*, finds the distinction impossible to maintain (pp. 110, 114–17), asserting that the evolution of the question and current tendencies are in the direction of a transcendence of the division between sciences of nature and sciences of the human being (pp. 91–106). Along these same lines, see Claude Lévi-Strauss, "Critères scientifiques dans les disciplines sociales et humaines," and Pierre Bourdieu et al., *Le métier de sociologue*, esp. pp. 18–19.

14. Paul Ricoeur, *Freud and Philosophy*, pp. 18–19, 24–26; Ricoeur, "Du conflit à la convergence des méthodes en exégèse biblique," esp. pp. 47–51: "hermeneutics and the concept of interpretation."

15. After all, if we took hermeneutics in the third sense, so that we would consider theology to *be* a hermeneutic, it would no longer make any sense to speak of "hermeneu-tic *mediation*."

16. I have this expression, with its meaning, from Paul Ricoeur, who has generalized it from a point of departure in Martin Heidegger, *Being and Time* (1927), parag. 32, pp.

194–95. See also Roger Lapointe, *Trois dimensions de l'herméneutique*, chap. 7, pp. 121–38.

17. Of course, there are circles and then there are circles. After all, we do speak of a *circulus vitiosus*, and Heidegger himself reminded us of this (*Being and Time*, p. 194). That there is dialectic and then there is dialectic, we know from Marx and his "double reverse" on the Hegelian dialectic. Conclusion: it is not enough to dialecticize your thought; you must know how—else you do so in name only.

18. The concept of "pragmatics" is employed by R. Carnap, C. Morris, and others, to designate the use-context of an expression, the context that is one of the essential elements for the comprehension of a determinate expression, the other two being the *semantics* and the *syntax* of the same expression.

19. See *Dei Verbum*, nos. 8, 19, 21 (pp. 116, 124, 125). Let us also recall Thomas Aquinas's very strict formula: *"[it is believed] propter veritatem primam propositam nobis in Scripturis secundum doctrinam Ecclesiae intelligentis sane."*

20. *Lumen Gentium*, no. 12, pp. 29–30.

21. See *Dei Verbum*, chap. 2, pp. 114–18. Let us note that tradition, in this document, is systematically placed *before* scripture (chap. 3), in its quality of intermediary between the origin and the hearing of the word: see P. van Leeuwen, *Révélation divine et sa transmission*, pp. 18ff.; Henri de Lubac, *L'écriture dans la tradition*; Georges Tavard, *La théologie parmi les sciences humaines*, chap. 5 (pp. 107–24).

22. See Spinoza's criticisms of the unwarranted hypostatization of the word of God in the letter of scripture. For this philosopher—the founder, or at any rate one of the founders, of a critical reading of scripture—such a hypostatization is tantamount to "worshiping paper and ink." For Spinoza, scripture, like anything else, can be "called sacred and Divine" only "so long as it is religiously used" (*Theologico-Political Treatise*, chap. 12, p. 167).

23. Against the opinion of charismatics of his time, Tertullian forthrightly declares the importance of the positivity (content) of faith, with his striking formula: Christ taught *"aliquid unum et certum"*: see his *De Praescriptione*, book 1, chap. 9, nos. 3, 4. See also the study of this work by Dimitri Michaelidis, *Foi, Ecriture et tradition ou les "Praescriptiones" chez Tertullien* (Paris, Aubier-Montaigne, 1969).

24. See *Dei Verbum*, no. 9, p. 117: the mutual relationship between tradition and scripture. See also André Manaranche, *L'existence chrétienne*, pp. 190–96 ("the word of God"), 196–99 ("the words of God").

25. I take my inspiration from hermeneutic "improvisation" or "tinkering" (my neologism, *"biscateação"*) from Claude Lévi-Strauss's *La pensée sauvage* (Paris, Plon, 1962, pp. 26–47). Where Lévi-Strauss writes *bricolage*, or *bricoler*, the Portuguese translation retains the French term, because there is no precise equivalent in Portuguese. "In its old sense," observes Lévi-Strauss, "the verb 'bricoler' [was] always used with reference to some extraneous movement: a ball rebounding, a dog straying or a horse swerving from its direct course to avoid an obstacle. And in our own time the 'bricoleur' is still someone who works with his hands and uses devious means compared to those of a craftsman" (*The Savage Mind*, pp. 16–17). Lévi-Strauss is discussing the "science of the concrete," which, he says, is one of "savage" thinking (a better term than "primitive" thinking). See too his *Le cru et le cuit* (English translation, *The Raw and the Cooked*, University of Chicago Press, 1983) and *Du miel aux cendres* (*From Honey to Ashes*, University of Chicago Press, 1983). This notion suggested to Antoine Casanova, in his *Vatican II et l'évolution de l'Eglise*, an interpretation of the theology of Vatican II as "the work of a mechanic" (p. 72; see also pp. 102–4, 124–33, 146–53). According to

Casanova, the "make-do hermeneutic" of Vatican II vis-à-vis the "signs of the times" treats scripture as if it were an "inexhaustible totality . . . having an infinite aptitude for taking advance account of all problematics of earthly situations, and for answering the questions human beings ask themselves in all their various historical conjunctures" (p. 124). The celebrated scriptural "fuller meaning" would thus be brought out by present situations, leading to the discovery of this meaning in scripture (p. 133) with a view to a symbolic transcendence of real contradictions. With regard to "hermeneutic *bricolage*," see also Paul Ricoeur, *Le conflit des interprétations*, pp. 46, 50ff. [In what follows, the term "hermeneutic improvisation" translates *biscateação* (or *picaretagem*) *hermenêutica.*—Ed.]

26. This is the direction taken by the violent critique of exegete André Paul, *L'impertinence biblique*. He calls the archaeological, "exhumative," reading of the Bible "hellish." And he continues: this "incestuous, necrophiliac love-making" can only engender a dead offspring, one in which rigor mortis has set in. What we need to do, he says, is to reeffectuate the biblical act, the act that gave birth to the Bible itself as a text: we must read-and-be-read, interpret-and-be-interpreted, act-and-suffer-activity, and thus produce meaning. See also his "Pour la Bible, une anti-exégèse."

François Refoulé ("L'exégèse en question") sketches the state of the exegetical problematic today (bibliography, pp. 392–400), and pleads for an antidogmatist, plural interpretation. He adduces Nietzsche's testimony against the *in se* of a meaning "that was always there," and proposes a "perspectivism," in function of what he sees as an undeniable relationship of any reading with the reading subject, together with the supreme value of "life," above and beyond any "truth" or "sense." See Nietzsche's *The Will to Power*, book 3, no. 581; *The Joyful Wisdom*, 5, no. 374; *Beyond Good and Evil*, 1, 4 (pp. 8–9); and his letter to K. Fuchs (Aug. 26, 1886), in which he states: "That which is unjust, indeed, can be determined, in innumerable instances; but that which is just, never"—a fine motto for any theological antipositivism. Along these same lines, Xavier Léon-Dufour, writing in *Etudes* (Feb. 1974), says that the "exegete-who-tells-the-meaning-of-the-text" is a "mythic figure" (p. 285).

27. François Refoulé concludes his article just cited, "L'exégèse en question," by saying that the moment of scientific exegesis is an obligatory "passage" for any serious and, esp., any dialectical, interpretation (pp. 420–21).

28. From a point of departure in structuralism, a rather severe criticism of hermeneutics arises, to the effect that the latter pretends to dissolve structure, and proclaim its "message" without further ado, as Barth, Gadamer, and others seem at times to do. See J. Greisch, *La crise de l'herméneutique*, where he underscores the fact that no reading is the pure garnering of a sense that has been deposited there in the text: any reading is also the production of meaning, for the hiatus between past and present is "irreducible" and unhermeneutizable. See also Roger Lapointe, *Les trois dimensions de l'herméneutique*, chap. 4 (pp. 73–87): "the esthetic parameter" (which consists in the actual tissue of the text). See also Michel van Esbroeck, *Herméneutique, structuralisme et exégèse*; Paul Ricoeur, *Conflict of Interpretations*, pp. 31–63, 80–97; idem, "Signe et sens," in *Encyclopaedia Universalis*, 4:1011–15.

29. As I have already stated, this is the strategy proposed and practiced by Paul Ricoeur in the works already cited, especialy in his substantive study, "Les incidences théologiques des recherches actuelles concernant le langage," and in his "Contribution d'une réflexion sur le langage à une théologie de la parole."

30. For the general articulation of sense and structure, see Jean Ladrière, "Sens et système." The same author applies this articulation to the case of ethics, where it will

obtain between moral value and the economic order: "L'ordre économique et l'ordre éthique" (in *Vie sociale et destinée*, pp. 105-15), as well as to the case of church and world, in terms of an articulation between the faith principle and the historical moment: "La démarche interdisciplinaire," pp. 46-50. Closer to our own matter—the political—I observe the same interplay, in the form of an articulation between faith-meaning and societal structures, in Charles Wackenheim, *Christianisme sans idéologie*, pp. 183-91, which I consider the best pages in the book, and the same articulation, even more rigorously, in his "Analyse politique et foi." In the same direction, see Philippe Roqueplo, *La foi d'un mal-croyant*, pp. 214-40; idem, *L'énergie de la foi*, pp. 37-50.

31. See Paul Ricoeur, "Cours d'herméneutique," chap. 2, pp. 24ff.

32. As we know, the "savage beauty" of the biblical writings was repugnant to Jerome and Augustine, with their education in classical rhetoric.

33. See Roger Lapointe, *Les trois dimensions de l'herméneutique*, chap. 6 (pp. 103-19). Lapointe emphasizes the primacy of the present in hermeneutic work, in the sense that it is the present that, when all is said and done, arouses interest in the text. For Lapointe, the ultimate sense of scripture is to shed light on the destiny of the interpreter. It is thus that the sense par excellence is realized, the sense without which "all meanings would be without sense" (p. 119). Nietzesche, Heidegger, and Gadamer, as well as Fuchs, Ebeling, and Bultmann, all insisted on this primacy of the present, all historicism to the contrary notwithstanding. This is tantamount to saying that, in and through the hermeneutic operation, interpreters are themselves interpreted. This is one of the keys to Bultmannian exegesis, as can be seen in, e.g., Bultmann's *Jesus and the Word*, his *Faith and Understanding*, or his *Theology of the New Testament*. This "presentistic" conception of hermeneutics takes the Bible as a process that develops its immanent sense through successive readings, in such wise that the sense that these readings deliver comes to be considered as *constitutive* of the Bible itself, as Roger Lapointe says in his *Trois dimensions de l'herméneutique*, pp. 86-87. This is likewise the direction in which the notion of a *sensus plenior* looks.

34. The literary or historical sense is the *foundation* of all further sense. This is the theory of Thomas Aquinas, *Summa Theol.*, I, q. 1, a. 10, ad 1, as well as that of the fathers of the church. See, e.g., Augustine, *Sermons*, II, 7: *"Ante omnia, fratres, . . . quando auditis exponi sacramentum Scripturae narrantis quae gesta sunt, prius illud quod lectum est credatis sic gestum, quomodo lectum est;* ne subtracto fundamento rei gestae, quasi in aere quaeratis aedificare" (emphasis added). Similarly, Hugo of Saint Victor, *Eruditionis Didascaliae*, 6, 3: *"Aedificaturus ergo primum fundamentum historiae pone: deinde per significationem typicam in arcem fabricam mentis erige"* (emphasis added). Finally, Denis the Carthusian, in the introduction to his commentary on the Psalms: "Sensus vero historicus seu litteralis est fundamentum seu basis intellectuum aliorum *et ex eo solo argumentum ad fidei probationem*" (emphasis added). For these citations, see W. Frank Shaw, *Chapters on Symbolism* (London, Skeffington, 1897), pp. 37-38.

35. Ebeling says that God's word is not light to be seen, but light to see by—nor a light that blinds, but one that enlightens, clarifies. See René Marlé, *Introduction to Hermeneutics*, p. 72.

36. See R. Avila, *Teología, evangelización y liberación*, chap. 6 (pp. 61-70): "prophecy, interpretation, reinterpretation."

37. The Heideggerian thematic is in evidence here.

38. See Michel de Certeau, *Le christianisme éclaté*, pp. 17, 45-46; idem in de Certeau et al., *Crise du biblicisme*, esp. p. 51.

39. See Jean Ladrière, *La science, le monde et la foi*, pp. 179ff., esp. p. 183.

40. Gadamer, referring to pietist theology, says that *applicatio—Applikation* or *Anwendung*—is the true term of the hermeneutic process: "We are forced to go, as it were, one stage beyond romantic hermeneutics, by regarding not only understanding and interpretation, but also application as comprising one unified process" (*Truth and Method*, pp. 274–75).

41. See François Refoulé, "L'exégèse en question," pp. 406–9.

42. A very familiar definition, having currency particularly in liberation theology milieus. See Gustavo Gutiérrez, *A Theology*, pp. 6–15, 145; Leonardo Boff, *Teologia do cativeiro*, pp. 41–44.

43. For the question of hermeneutics and tradition, see *Herméneutique et tradition*, esp. pp. 129–30; Carlo Molari, *La fede e il suo linguaggio*, chap. 2: "principles for a hermeneutic of the magisterium," pp. 66–98; Oscar Cullmann, *La tradition: Problème exégétique, historique et théologique*; Yves Congar, *La tradition et les traditions*; J. R. Geiselmann, *Die heilige Schrift und die Traditionen*; Gabriel Moran, *Scripture and Tradition*; G. Eichholz, *Tradition und Interpretation*; Walter Kasper, "Tradition als Erkenntnisprinzip zur theologischen Relevanz der Geschichte."

44. See, among other works, Karl Rahner et al., *Exégèse et dogmatique*.

45. See Heb. 9:12; Gal. 1:8–9.

46. See *Dei Verbum*, no. 4; Denzinger-Schönmetzer, *Enchiridion Symbolorum*, nos. 783, 2021.

47. See 2 Cor. 3:6: "The written law kills, but the Spirit gives life."

48. See 2 Cor. 3:14–18; *Dei Verbum*, no. 18.

49. See Michel de Certeau, "La rupture instauratrice," esp. pp. 120ff.

50. On the closure of revelation, see the whole no. 125 of *Revista Eclesiàstica Brasileira*, vol. 32 (1972), esp. U. Zilles, "A Revelação acabou com a morte do último apóstolo?" and H. Lepargneur, "Qual a função da Igreja frente à Revelação?" See also what Gerhard von Rad has to say in his *Old Testament Theology*, 2:361–62, p. 361: " 'Radical openness to the future' has been rightly called the characteristic of the understanding of existence in the Old and New Testaments alike"—citing Rudolf Bultmann, *Primitive Christianity in Its Contemporary Setting*, pp. 180ff.

51. Fernando Belo, *Uma leitura política do Evangelho*, p. 62: "One of the theses that I here present, and that I believe to be a new one, is that the gospel functions as a narrative offered, among other things, to our reading (and not as 'revelation' made once and for all). . . . " In chap. 6, pp. 51–56, Belo explains that Jesus did not preach a message, he struck up a *practice*—the gospel being precisely "the story of Jesus' practice" (p. 52), and its function being to teach us to read our own practice (p. 62). See also Belo's *A Materialist Reading*, esp. p. 251: "[Jesus] never makes the reading himself; the grill is always set up so that the hearers-witnesses will *make it by themselves*" (emphasis added).

52. Gabriel Marcel distinguishes between "éclairant" and "éclairé," along the lines of Heidegger's distinction between *Sein* and *Seiende*, or Blondel's between "pensée pensante" and "pensée pensée": Marcel, *Foi et réalité*, p. 8.

53. See *Dei Verbum*, nos. 8, 19, 20, 23, 26, etc.

54. See historian Robert Wilken's very interesting book, *The Myth of Christian Beginnings*.

55. See Rudolf Bultmann, *Jésus*, p. 216. Note that this distinction must be carefully maintained in order to deal with both "hermeneutic improvisation" and "semantic positivism."

56. Bossuet's expression, cited by F. Bott in *Le Monde*, March 9-10, 1975, p. 15. Jean Ladrière speaks of a "signification detour" (*Chrétiens et politique*, p. 12). Spinoza, for his part, spoke of "doing violence to Scripture" (*Theologico-Political Treatise*, chap. 1, p. 16). Gregory the Great (PL 76:187-89) cites Prov. 30:33 as a principle of biblical reading: "Who jerks the teat, draws butter; who bites it, blood."

57. Two illustrations only: L. E. Halkin, the Belgian historian, in his article "Christianisme et tolérance" (extract from *Cahiers de "Foi et Vérité,"* Geneva, 1954), shows how, in history, scripture has been invoked to justify, e.g., the penalty of burning at the stake (John 15:6), politico-religious repression and torture (Luke 14:23), the political power of the pope (Luke 22:38), and so on (esp. pp. 13-14). For his part, G. Le Bras, in his study, "Commentaires bibliques et Droit Canon" (in Congar et al., *Mélanges offerts à M.-D. Chenu*, pp. 325-43, esp. pp. 336-43), shows how the evangelical *correctio* of Matthew 9:12-13 was interpreted and practiced in the Middle Ages under the form of *denunciatio* and *accusatio*, with court and all—and how Gratian derived a whole series of juridical norms from the Beatitudes! Surely here is the place to say, with Alan de Lille: *"Auctoritas cereum habet nasum, id est in diversum potest flecti sensum''* (*De Fide Catholica*, book 1, chap. 30).

58. Spinoza: "I confess that some profane men, to whom religion is a burden, may, from what I have said, assume a licence to sin, and without any reason, at the simple dictates of their lusts conclude that Scripture is everywhere faulty and falsified, and that therefore its authority is null; but such men are beyond the reach of help, for nothing, as the proverb has it, can be said so rightly that it cannot be twisted into wrong. Those who wish to give rein to their lusts are at no loss for an excuse" (*Theologico-Political Treatise*, chap. 12, p. 166).

59. G. W. Peck's expression, apropos of Harvey Cox's exegesis, in Jourdain Bishop, *Les théologiens de la mort de Dieu* (Paris, Cerf, 1968), p. 137. The object of criticism when it came to scholasticism's use of Scripture, this procedure has also been reproached by the practitioners of "political theology," especially the theology of liberation. See Carlos Bravo, "Notas marginales a la teología de la liberación," esp. p. 59. Alain observes: *"Machina* is the name rightly attaching to . . . any idea without a thinker. . . . Who knows? It may be the fate of any theology, the moment it is completed, to sweep over the earth like a tank on the attack" (*Propos sur le Christianisme*, Paris, Rieder, 1927, pp. 33-34).

60. See Plato, *Phaedo*, chap. 34, nos. 89-90, on "misology" and its origin.

61. Nietzsche, *Human, All Too Human*, book 1, chap. 1, no. 2, pp. 14-15.

62. Ambroise Gardeil, in his *Le donné révélé et la théologie*, maintains the central thesis of the homogeneity of the terms in his title. But the spirit in which he propounds his position, that of maintaining a thesis *against* another thesis, has prevented his own position from being "sufficiently dialectical" (Marx) for him to be able to perceive the truth of the contrary thesis (antithesis), and thus be able adequately to articulate it (in a synthesis). Gardeil, then, is astonished at the astonishment (really quite normal) of Sully Prudhomme, who, leafing through Saint Thomas's *Summa* at the end of his days, said: "How complicated all this is! How can all this have come out of the gospel, which is so simple?" (pp. 356-57).

63. For the first conception, suffice it to recall here the ideal of *Christendom*, which reached its apogee in the Western Middle Ages and which H.-X. Arquillière characterized so brilliantly in his *L'Augustinisme politique*. *Clericalism* can be understood as a prolongation of this ideal, with its typical representative, Bossuet (1627-1704), *Politique tirée des propres paroles de l'Ecriture Sainte*. René Coste, at the beginning of his

Evangile et politique, cites Bossuet, along with Leo XIII (*Immortale Dei*, 1885), Benedict XV (*Ad Beatissimum*, 1914), Pius XII, and others, as outstanding figures of this ideal.

The second conception, that of the *political impracticability of the gospel*, dates from just as far back in history as the first, doubtless from the first moments of the existence of the church community. Did Tertullian himself not say, "Nothing is more foreign to us than the Republic"? The Emperor Julian (361–63) is known to have considered the gospel, and the Sermon on the Mount in particular, an absurd, and politically pernicious, doctrine—in his estimation not even a family could be guided by it, much less a state, if indeed it was of any use even for private life: see P. Hoffmann, "Die bessere Gerechtichkeit: Die Auslegung der Bergpredigt, IV," *Bibel und Leben* 10:264–75. This question was asked with all forthrightness by the pagans who saddled Christians with the responsibility for the fall of Rome. Volusian, the Roman philosopher and aristocrat, was the spokesman of this current: "The preaching of the Christian doctrine," he declared, "is in no way suitable to the conduct of the state. Here, we are told, are its precepts: Not to render evil for evil (Rom. 12:17); if someone strikes you on one cheek, turn the other; to the one who seeks to rob you of your tunic, give your cloak as well; if someone wishes to torture you, walk twice as far with him (Matt. 5:39–41). All these maxims are catastrophic for the direction of the state. For who would put up with an enemy's taking anything from him? Who would not desire, in virtue of the law of war, to repay in an instant the one who pillages a Roman province? . . . If such misfortunes have come to this state, it is by reason of the Christian emperors, who observe the Christian religion as they can. The case is clear" (Marcellinus, "Epistola 136 ad Augustinum," PL 33:515). Such objections, by the way, were the occasion of Augustine's composing *The City of God*—Charlemagne's *livre de chevet* and the manual of politics par excellence for the whole era of European feudalism.

During the period just mentioned, practically no objections were raised. Doubts did arise, however, at the dawn of the modern era, with the rise of the modern, autonomous states. From the Reformers to the political philosophers (Macchiavelli, Montesquieu, Hobbes, Spinoza, Locke, and others), the autonomy of the state was more and more vigorously defended. Thus, Cosimo de' Medici (1519–74): "One does not govern states with Pater Nosters." We know the thinking of the champions of the Enlightenment, at the apogee of the "modern age": thus, Jean-Jacques Rousseau (*The Social Contract*, book 4, chap. 8, "civil religion") says that the Christianity of the gospel can be the religion of the human being, but not of the state. See also Denis Diderot, *Entretien d'un philosophe avec la Maréchale*, cited by Lucien Goldmann, *Structures mentales et création culturelle*, p. 109: "If twenty thousand Parisians were to take it into their heads to abide strictly by the Sermon on the Mount . . . [there would be] so many madmen that the police would not know what to do with them. . . . Our asylums are too small." Hegel, for his part, finds, instead, that the Sermon on the Mount, like the Lord's Prayer, can serve as the mystique of a whole people—but with the abandonment of effectiveness: see E. Borne, "Jésus devant les philosophes," in Jean Guitton, ed., *Jésus*, (Paris, Hachette, 1971, pp. 224–27). It will not be necessary to cite Marx and the whole Marxist tradition here (Mao, Trotsky, Che, Cabral, and so on), or Sigmund Freud (*Civilization and Its Discontents*, chap. 5), and others besides, as to the incompatibility of the gospel and social life.

Finally, let us recall that the internal paradox of Christianity, expressed in the fact that it *is* politically unrealizable, and yet at the same time *ought* to be realized, has been dramatically felt by H. Richard Niebuhr, *The Social Sources of Denominationalism*

(1929). See also his *Christian Realism and Political Problems*. Niebuhr is considered to be the "most profound American thinker of the twentieth century," and former president Jimmy Carter's "favorite theologian" (*The Times*, New York, June 20, 1976, p. 10).

64. This cannot but be a consuming theme of the whole theology of liberation. See, e.g., Gustavo Gutiérrez, *A Theology*, pp. 155–87, 263, 294–95; Hugo Assmann, *Nomad Church*, pp. 66–67 and passim; CELAM, *Liberación*, esp. the studies by J. Mejía and Samuel Ruiz González. See also P. Grelot, "Note méthodologique," pp. 89–91.

65. See Leonardo Boff, *Teologia do cativeiro e da libertação*; M. Arias, *Salvação hoje: Entre o cativeiro e la libertação*, esp. the last chapter. The Latin American Theological Meeting, in Mexico City, Aug. 11–15, 1975, took place, for all practical purposes, under the sign of "captivity."

66. See my study, "Foi Jesus um revolucionário?" esp. the bibliography.

67. Oscar Cullmann, *Jesus and the Revolutionaries*; idem, *Dieu et César*. Martin Hengel, *Was Jesus a Revolutionist?*; idem, *Die Zeloten*. Robert Eisler, *Iêsous Basileus oû Basileusas*. S. G. F. Brandon, *Jesus and the Zealots*; idem, *The Trial of Jesus of Nazareth*.

68. Some illustrations, inspired by the current initiated by Cullmann and reinforced by Hengel: Yves Congar, *Un peuple messianique*, pp. 126–29; Jürgen Moltmann, *The Crucified God*, pp. 136–45: "Jesus and Authority: 'The Rebel' "; Ignacio Ellacuría, *Freedom Made Flesh*, pp. 21–85: "The Political Character of Jesus' Mission."

69. For all the questions, I refer to Wolfhart Pannenberg, *Jesus—God and Man*, pp. 235–44: "Universal Conditioned Elements in Jesus' Activity." No less appropriate are José Comblin's observations—directly political in his case—in his *Théologie de la révolution*, pp. 236–37. As for Fernando Belo (*A Materialist Reading*, pp. 260–64, and in the popularized version, *Una leitura política*, pp. 71–75), it is my opinion that he has not correctly stated the problem at issue. His "Jesus" appears endowed with a political awareness that will enable him to practice a strategy objectively and subjectively revolutionary—whereas, in the historical conditions that were his, Jesus simply could not have had such an awareness. Let us confess, after all, that Jesus could only have been a pre-Marxist!

70. See *Dei Verbum*, no. 18.

71. See *Dei Verbum*, no. 19. It would be superfluous to cite references to the classic pioneers here—Schmidt, Dibelius, Bultmann, Dodd, and others. Let me refer only to Werner Georg Kümmel, *Introduction to the New Testament*; André Robert and André Feuillet, eds., *Introduction to the New Testament*; Oscar Cullmann, *The New Testament: An Introduction for the General Reader*; C. F. D. Moule, *The Birth of the New Testament*. This last author avers that no part of the New Testament "was an academic exercise—it was simply the response of the Spirit of God within the Church to the challenges of its environment and history" (p. 4).

72. See Wolfgang Trilling, "Legitimidade e localização da questão do Jesus histórico" (in J. Salvador, ed., *Atualidades Biblicas*), pp. 357–59: "three stages of transmission."

73. See *Dei Verbum*, no. 7. The hermeneutical status of the Old Testament is no different, as is shown with such competence and aplomb by Gerhard von Rad, *Old Testament Theology*. Note the titles of each of the two volumes of his work: *The Theology of Israel's Historical Traditions* (vol. 1), and *The Theology of Israel's Prophetic Traditions* (vol. 2). See also the very suggestive study by K. Heinen, "Glaubensüberlieferung und Neuinterpretation im Alten Testament." He shows that the crisis of the exile occasioned a

reinterpretation of the three key articles of the Hebrew faith: exodus, election, and covenant—which of course confirms the inevitable presence of the hermeneutic circle.

74. This is the sense of Irenaeus's "tetramorphic gospel": *Against the Heretics*, III, 11, 8, cited in *Dei Verbum*, nos. 18, 31. See also Oscar Cullmann, *The New Testament*, pp. 23–29.

75. As Jerome rightly observes: *"Evangelium non consistit in verbis . . . sed in sensu; non in superficie, sed in medulla; non in sermonum foliis, sed in radice rationis": Commentarium in Epistolam ad Galatas*, 1, 11 (PL 26:347A). Perhaps it would be enriching for a hermeneutic adapted to second theology to recover the patristic theory of the "spiritual sense" of the scriptures.

76. J. Kamp (*Foi sans credo*, p. 121, n. 13) finds it "artificial" to have recourse to biblical texts in the hope of shedding light on contemporary questions. To Kamp's mind, it would be better to refer to sociological analyses. Let me remark that what is missing here is the mutual articulation of the two terms.

77. Gerhard von Rad (*Old Testament Theology*) has shown that the Old Testament was constituted by way of a constant renewal of old traditions in view of new situations. This, he shows, is what the prophets did. This is also what the primitive Christian community did with the Old Testament itself—and "with an amazing freedom" (see ibid., vol. 2, part 3, esp. pp. 319–35). On the "canon of the canon," see René Marlé, *Hermenêutica e catequese*, chap. 5.

78. Besides its attention to "literary forms" and the "situation of . . . time and culture" (no. 12, p. 120), *Dei Verbum* also posits the "unity of the whole of Scripture" as a principle of interpretation. See also Karl Rahner, "L'avenir de la théologie" (p. 19), stating that the "canon of the canon" is the whole of scripture—a hierarchized whole; P. Grelot, "Note méthodologique sur le recours à la Bible dans l'étude de ce sujet," esp. pp. 81–82, 87; Yves Congar, *Un peuple messianique*, pp. 101 (n. 1), 188–89. The great problem, in my view, is how the "oneness of scripture" is to be conceived. The integral citation of whole texts bearing on a given theme, in accordance with the criteria of current "biblical theology," after the fashion of, e.g., Congar in the work just cited, is doubtless better than an arbitrary, partial selection; but even this procedure seems to stop short at a still elementary level in comparison with the demands of a genuine hermeneutics.

79. Observation of François Biot, *Théologie et politique*.

80. "The temptation of Christians is to seek to justify their practice by a gospel passage or a deed of Jesus. They appeal to violence because Jesus used violence in John 2:15–17. Or they cry for nonviolent action because Jesus preached and lived it (Matt. 26:52; 5:39). Both appeals situate the 'specifically Christian' in a false hermeneutic locus. Christian faith does not prescribe a determinate concretion, but a specific *manner* of concretion or position-taking, in all instances" (Leonardo Boff, "Salvação em Jesus Cristo e processo de libertação," pp. 762–63). I must mention Wolfhart Pannenberg's program here: the "depositivization" of scripture and of Christian positivity generally: see I. Berten, *Histoire, révélation et foi: Dialogue avec Wolfhart Pannenberg* (Brussels, CEP, 1969), pp. 45–46.

81. See J. Coppens, "Le problème des sens bibliques," with bibliography.

82. Here I should cite the semantic "bivalence" of the Greek *sema*, meaning both "sign" and "tomb." *Dei Verbum* appears to share an evolutionistic conception of meaning, one difficult to reconcile with the historical facts. See, e.g., nos. 8, 23.

83. "Those informed by scripture, by meditation on the gospel, by the liturgy, and by the life of the Christian community, will be able to find, in every circumstance, what the

life of faith should inspire in them: what they must invent at a given moment" (Jean Ladrière, *La science, le monde et la foi*, p. 214).

84. "The church, not scripture, is the spouse of Christ": J. E. Kuhn, cited by H. Fries, *L'Eglise: Questions actuelles* (Paris, Cerf, 1966, p. 23). I might add that, by reason of its quality as paradigm of interpretation, what really counts where (explicit) Christianity, or the Christian religion—the church—is concerned is real history, and the salvation occurring in that history, and not the theory of that salvation, not even its theological theory. Recall Augustine's teaching, according to which God wrote two books: the book of the world and the book of the Bible. It was because the first became illegible, by reason of sin, that God wrote the second, in order that by the second we should be able to read the first once more—in such wise that now "all creation becomes for us a revelation of God." Conclusion: the Bible was made for us, not we for the Bible: see Carlos Mesters, "O futuro do nosso passado," p. 275; idem, "Flor sem defesa," col. 375.

85. Anton Vögtle, "Révélation et histoire dans le Nouveau Testament," p. 47. See also H. Düsberg, "Il leur ouvrit l'esprit à l'intelligence de l'Ecriture (Lc 24,45)." In this same sense, see 1 Cor. 2:10–11, 7:40; 2 Cor. 3:14–17; Luke 24:48; Acts 1:4, 2:33; John 7:39, 14:15–17, 26, 16:7, 13–15, 20:21–22; Matt. 28:20, etc. José Comblin has written: "The object of theology is not simply the reconstitution of the published words of Jesus. Theology performs its entire task only when it seeks to comprehend the words of the Spirit, who applies Jesus' words at a determinate time" ("Autour de la 'théologie de la révolution,'" p. 530).

86. See above, chap. 4, n. 1. In the conclusion of his *On Sophistical Refutations* (183b40–184a10), Aristotle refers to the proverbial wisdom of teaching persons to fish before handing them the pole, and ridicules the Sophists for procedures that remind us of things like "learn Spanish in two weeks," "philosophy made easy," and the like. "For they used to hand out speeches to be learned by heart," Aristotle says, "some rhetorical, others in the form of question and answer, each side supposing that their arguments on either side generally fall among them. And therefore the teaching they gave their pupils was ready but rough. For they used to suppose that they trained people by imparting to them not the art but its products, as though any one professing that he would impart a form of knowledge to obviate any pain in the feet, were then not to teach a man the art of shoe-making or the sources whence he can acquire anything of the kind, but were to present him with several kinds of shoes of all sorts: for he has helped him to meet his need, but has not imparted an art to him."

87. See below, chap. 10, on "thematic relevance."

88. Johannes B. Metz, "La présence de l'Eglise dans la société." See also Charles Wackenheim, *Christianisme sans idéologie*, pp. 141–58: "faith as memory"; J. H. Pico, "Método teológico latinoamericano."

89. See Xavier Léon-Dufour, "Qu'attendre d'un exégète?"

90. R. Pucheu, "Confession d'un paumé," p. 532.

INTRODUCTION TO PART THREE

1. See, e.g., the reflections on the status of the notion of "praxis" in the theologians of liberation in *Víspera*, no. 29 (1972), esp. the articles by A. Methol Ferré, "Itinerario de la praxis," and M. M. Cottier, "La filosofía de la praxis." José Comblin (*Théologie de la pratique révolutionnaire*, pp. 198ff.) gives us a good *status questionis* on the problem today.

2. The question of praxis is a very complicated one. Aristotle himself found it difficult

to introduce order into this tangled universe: one need only glance at the holes and patches in his *Nicomachaean Ethics*. For praxis generally, let me cite the classic work of Maurice Blondel, *Action: Essay on a Critique of Life and a Science of Practice* (1893); as well as A. Sánchez Velásquez, *The Philosophy of Praxis*; Benedetto Croce, *Philosophy of the Practical*; and, nearer our own area, Enrique D. Dussel, *Ethics and the Theology of Liberation*; and the works I shall be citing in part 3.

3. Aristotle, *Nicomachaean Ethics*, book 1, chap. 3, 1094b11–27 (pp. 339–40). Along the same lines, see book 1, chap. 7, 1098a26–28 (p. 343), and book 2, chap. 2, 1104a1–5 (p. 349).

4. As we saw in §25, not all "generalities" are absolutely equivalent. There is a *theoretical generality*—one that elucidates: that of the concept, and of the universality that the concept guarantees; and there is an *ideological generality*—an abstract one: that of the vague, imprecise notion. The latter confounds, rather than clarifies, one's vision: this is the generality of the un-reflected-upon, the generality of commonplaces. Emile Durkheim contradistinguishes the "concept" and the "general idea" (*The Elementary Forms of the Religious Life*, pp. 480–81; *Pragmatisme et sociologie*, pp. 105 [n. 1], 203–5). Gaston Bachelard found in "generalities" one of his principal "epistemological obstacles." He contradistinguished the "ill-posited," "hasty generality," composed of "varieties," and the "constructed generality," composed of "variations": *La formation de l'esprit scientifique*, chap. 3.

CHAPTER 9

1. See Gustavo Gutiérrez, *A Theology*, p. 49 and passim; Hugo Assmann, *Nomad Church*, pp. 71–86, 119–25; M. Schooyans, "Théologie et Libération," esp. pp. 172–75, 182–83; Bernard Olivier, *Développement ou libération?*; Juan Luís Segundo, *The Liberation of Theology*; Fernando Belo, *A Materialist Reading of the Gospel of Mark*—a work claiming both to be situated (pp. 1–6) and to situate the gospel narrative itself. Note that the Latin American theologians of the liberation-theology current are completely frank in their intent to draw a clear line of demarcation between themselves and what they call "European," or "bourgeois," or "North Atlantic" theology. This *prise de position* goes so far as to imply the geo-political locus of the discourse: these theologians proclaim that they are theologizing *from the periphery*. We see this eagerness in the very subtitles of their works: Assmann's subtitle for his *Theology for a Nomad Church* (in the Spanish original) is *Ensayo teológico desde la América dependiente*; Enrique Dussel's *History and Theology of Liberation* is subtitled: *A Latin American Perspective*; and so on. The Commission for Studies of Latin American History actually undertook a series of essays in Latin American history from the viewpoint of the "poor," the "oppressed." See Enrique D. Dussel, *A History of the Church in Latin America*, pp. 3–35, 240–53, 293–305. See also a book issuing from the same circles: Eduardo Hoornaert, *Formação do catolicismo brasileiro, 1550–1800: Ensaio de interpretação a partir dos oprimidos* (Petrópolis, Vozes, 1974), esp. the Introduction, which seeks to justify the methodological option indicated in the subtitle.

2. As to the complex term "socio-historical," I shall concentrate first on the first term, "socio-"—that is, on the precise social *topos* of a theological practice. Then, when I come to analyze the *kairos* of a subject or theme, in chap. 10, I shall refer to the second term, the "-historical" factors bearing on the same practice.

3. See Torcuato S. di Tella, *Para uma política latino-americana* (Rio de Janeiro, Paz

e Terra, 1969), chap. 5: "activity of intellectuals." This author defines intellectuals as "social animals," or "producers of goods and services"—i.e., of ideas—on a par with laborers, industrialists, or bankers; see also A. L. Machado Neto, *Da vigência intelectual: Um estudo de sociologia das idéias* (São Paulo, Grijalbo, 1968).

4. As is evident, these summary statements of mine themselves presuppose a sociology susceptible of being criticized and solidly based. Such an undertaking would go beyond my present intentions. Let me merely say that I situate myself in a line that is *more dialectical than functionalistic*. For me, then, the political is not a simple function or part of the social, but rather an instance articulated with the others (the economic and the ideological), within a contradictory social whole. What we are dealing with, then, is an all-englobing ("everything is political"), and yet specific ("but the political is not everything"), dimension. For this conception, see Nicos Poulantzas, *Political Power and Social Classes*; as well as my own study "Teologia das relações Igreja-Estado." J. Rancière, writing in *Révoltés logiques*, no. 1 (winter 1975) avers: "Hence the need to maintain both propositions: that ultimately there is never a third alternative to either obeying power or resisting it—in the concrete shape it takes in each circumstance; but also that, in every instance, a struggle is waged, one of 'power against power': there is no *good* instrument, nor any apparatus that would consist of 'good power,' as the power of the proletariat or mob; as also there is no instance of nonpower." I am not in agreement, then, with a theoretical position—in its strict form—that identifies the political (as jurisdiction) with politics (as practice) and finally with the power of the state, leaving the door open to the possibility of *apolitism*. This is the direction in which a position of the type held by Max Weber leads, as he expresses it in his *Politik als Beruf* (1919). P. Blanquart has made a very clear presentation of the two orientations cited, the one as represented by Machiavelli and Freud, the other by More and Marx (Blanquart, "L'acte de croire et l'action politique").

5. See Peter Kemp, *Théorie de l'engagement* (Paris, Seuil, 1973, 2 vols.), a work that I have found to be of no use to me, although the author has promised to treat, in later works, the "current societal act" (2:156). See also Jean Ladrière, *L'engagement*, where we have a philosophical reflection for the purpose of defining the signification of "engagement" in its current usage, without any treatment of the sociological, esp. the political, aspect.

6. For example, there was the case of the "developmentalism" of theologies (actually this was a "developmentalism" of the church, and, still more fundamentally, of "Third World" governments) until the 1960s. There was also the case of the "progressivism" of theologies (in actuality a "progressivism" of the whole church) after Vatican II. Thus the program of *aggiornamento*, perfectly correct in respect of the "founding message" of the Christian faith, can signify, in political terms, simply an intelligent conservatism—e.g., as a modernization of Christian forms in view of historical changes that may be occurring. See Paulo Freire, "Educazione, liberazione e chiesa," esp. pp. 78–85; Roland Leroy et al., *Les marxistes et l'évolution du monde catholique*. As for the "theology of development," see the bibliographies in: Sodepax, *In Search of a Theology of Development*; Gerhard Bauer, *Towards a Theology of Development: An Annotated Bibliography* (with more than 1,000 titles!); Philip S. Land, "Theology Meets Progress: Human Implications of Development." For the "theology of progress," see the works of Juan Alfaro, *Hacia una teología del progreso humano*; *Esperanza cristiana*; and *Cristianismo y justicia*.

7. The ideological content of the notion of "engagement" is evinced in the "engagement" (with a vengeance!), normally, of repressive power with respect to the contain-

ment of the impulse to liberation. On the other side, under the ideological cloak of "alienation"—the correlative and opposite of "engagement"—lurks the pitfall of *political neutralism*: the idea of "alienation" allows for the possibility of a-political and u-topian positions, positions not situated in relation to society and history, respectively.

8. For the distinction between *situation* and *position*, see Marta Harnecker, *Les concepts élémentaires du matérialisme historique*, pp. 171-72.

9. "The class making a revolution comes forward from the very start, if only because it is opposed to a class" (Karl Marx, *The German Ideology*, p. 60—cited by Georg Lukács, *Existentialisme ou Marxisme?* p. 208). In other words, class is the term of a relationship. For the concept that "classes exist only in class struggle," see Nicos Poulantzas, *Political Power and Social Classes*.

10. See Pierre Bourdieu, *Esquisse d'une théorie de la pratique*, pp. 179, 200ff., 210-11, and passim; José Comblin, *Théologie de la pratique révolutionnaire*, pp. 356-62; Max Weber, *Economie et société*, pp. 481-90, 519-34: the influence of intellectuals in and on religions.

11. "We do not have a choice between purity and violence but between different kinds of violence. . . . Violence is the common origin of all regimes. . . . What matters and what we have to discuss is not violence but its sense or its future" (Maurice Merleau-Ponty, *Humanism and Terror*, p. 109).

12. Before appearing as a political resource, class struggle is a social datum. Thus the question here, too, is not *whether* to "opt for a class," but for *which* class to "opt." We may apply to theology what Giulio Girardi says with respect to the church: "What we ask of the church once more, then, is not to make 'a' class option, but to make a different one, one humanly and evangelically more just and liberating" (*Christianisme, libération humaine, lutte des classes*, p. 209.

13. I borrow my terminology here from Martin Heidegger, *Q'appelle-t-on penser?* p. 261.

14. For the time being, I am restricting consideration to the analytical moment. The dialectical moment, which reveals the relationship between the two orders at play, is reserved for the following section. This same procedure will be followed in subsequent chapters.

15. "Homology" is the "formal correspondence between specified structures" (Paul Ricoeur, *Le conflit des interprétations*, p. 40). Another definition: the "identical disposition of elements of a structural whole" (idem, "Cours d'herméneutique," p. 156).

16. For the thematic of praxis, and for the need to keep a very clear distinction between cognition and reality, between science and society, see Pierre Bourdieu, *Esquisse d'une théorie de la pratique*, p. 133, n. 17. He establishes a definite breach between *practical* cognition and cognition *of practice*. The former comes with living experience, and is nonthematizable as such; the latter, by contrast, constructs its object and demonstrates it. According to Bourdieu a mixture of these two modes in science is simply catastrophic: hence he criticizes (1) spontaneistic and populistic theologies that credit practical cognition with the magical virtues of an initiatory experience, (2) ideologies of what he styles a participating observation, and (3) even certain forms of overemphasis on terrain.

17. Louis Althusser (*Pour Marx*, p. 21) goes so far as to speak of a "flag raised and flapping in a void: 'bourgeois science, proletarian science.'" Raymond Aron, in his introduction to Max Weber, *Le Savant et le Politique*, poses the problem of the autonomy of science, and the fatal influence that that power can exert upon it (pp. 14ff.), recalling, for example, the "obscene farce" teachers under the Third Reich were obliged

to play out as they acknowledged an "Aryan mathematics" in contradistinction to "Jewish mathematics" (p. 15). I have already had occasion to note the classic case of Lysenko's "Marxist biology."

18. As a typical instance of this kind of discourse, see Jean Ladrière, *L'articulation du sens*, to which I refer so often throughout this work.

19. On the spirit, as soul transcending the corporeal organism while confined to its instrumentality *in statu viae*, see Thomas Aquinas, *Summa Theol.*, I, q. 84, aa. 6, 7; I-II, q. 2, a. 6; *De Spiritualibus Creaturis*, q. 2, ad 3, 4, 18, 19; a. 3, ad 4, 16; a. 4, ad 3; a. 5; a. 9, ad 5; a. 11, ad 12, 14; etc.

20. This was effectively Althusser's position during one period of his career: see *Reading Capital*, pp. 46-48, 110-11, 119-44. It was a position that he would later ascribe to his "theoreticist" tendency: *Elements of Self-Criticism*, esp. pp. 119-25.

21. This is what is meant by the expression "material conditions of production." For this question, see the work of Michel Foucault, G. Canguilhem, and Gaston Bachelard. This aspect is heavily emphasized by epistemologists of the Marxist tradition—e.g., A. Vieira Pinto, *Ciência e existência*. He lays out the twofold, social and historical, nature of scientific research, esp. in chapters 5, 12-14, 18, 21, 22. See also Georges Thill, *La fête scientifique*, part 2, pp. 80-93, 119-25, 156-81. For the special case of history (which is itself historical), see Michel de Certeau, *L'écriture de l'histoire*, pp. 40-57, 65-79.

22. See Pierre Bourdieu et al., *Le métier du sociologue*, pp. 95-106, and the readings, pp. 307-23.

23. See Michel de Certeau, *L'écriture de l'histoire*, pp. 78-79.

24. See Louis Althusser, *Reading Capital*, p. 47. A. Régnier gives the following definitions: "A relationship between variables x and variables y is univocal if there can be no more than one y in relationship with the same x; it is biunivocal if it is univocal in both directions—i.e., if it sets up a one-to-one correspondence between the x's and the y's" ("De la théorie des groupes à la pensée sauvage," in P. Richard and R. Jaulin, eds., *Anthropologie et calcul*, Paris, Union Gén. d'Editions, 1971, p. 272).

25. "Merely taking the locus seriously does not explain history. Nothing has yet been said about what is produced in it" (Michel de Certeau, *L'écriture de l'histoire*, p. 79).

26. See the scholastics' concept of the *intellectus agens*, borrowed from Aristotle's *De Anima* (book 2, no. 17), e.g., in Thomas Aquinas, *Summa Theol.*, I, q. 79, aa. 3, 4, 5.

27. See Gaston Bachelard, *L'activité rationaliste de la physique contemporaine*, pp. 25-27 (cited in Bachelard, *Epistémologie, Textes choisis*, p. 198): "The notion of epistemological acts that we oppose today to the notion of epistemological obstacles corresponds to those strokes of the scientific genius that is the vehicle of unexpected impulses in the course of scientific development."

28. The theoretical fortunes of the concept of "complementarity," proposed by Niels Bohr in 1927, are a matter of record. It was applied first in the area of nuclear physics, and subsequently to other areas, not excluding theology—as Yves Congar notes in his *La foi et la théologie*, p. 200. In note 2, he gives some bibliographical indications—e.g., G. Howe, "Zu den Äusserungen von Niels Bohr über religiöse Fragen," *Keryma und Dogma* 4 (1958) 20-46.

29. See the last part of Hegel's *Phénoménologie de l'Esprit* (Paris, Aubier-Montaigne, 1941), 2:291ff.

30. See Immanuel Kant, "L'idée d'une histoire universelle au point de vue cosmopolitique" (1784), 8th proposition, in his *La philosophie de l'histoire* (Paris, Aubier-Montaigne, 1974), p. 73.

31. See John 16:23: "On that day you will have no questions to ask me"; 2 Cor. 5:7: "We will walk by faith, not by sight"; 1 Cor. 13:12: "Now we see indistinctly, as in a mirror; then we shall see face to face."

32. For the *style* of the sciences, see B. G. Kouznetzof, "Style et contenu de la science" (*Diogène* 89 [1975] 55–75), where "style," as the changeable element of science, ascribed to the epistemic subject, is contradistinguished from "method," which would be the fixed element, linked with the neutrality of the scientific approach—i.e., with its content. See also the very precise approach of Gilles-Gaston Granger, *Essai d'une philosophie du style*.

33. It is disastrous to mistake passion for theory, feelings for thoughts, or tract for theology. This is the risk run by certain writings, so full of indignation or enthusiasm, whose authors choose to call them "theology." Thus, e.g., we have James Cone, *A Black Theology of Liberation*. Perhaps this may also apply to the works of Jean Cardonnel, such as *Dieu: Essai sur les pouvoirs* (Paris, Galilée, 1975). The term "theology" has been so used and abused in our day that it is like inflated currency—there is nothing "backing it up" any longer, it has lost its real correspondent. Anyone writing on anything—provided it have something to do with "religion"—can assume the title of "theologian," and no one can be found to object. This situation is symptomatic of a more general one.

34. See R. K. Merton, "Sociologia do conhecimento," p. 99: "The conceptual content of the natural sciences is not attributable to an economic base, although the 'finalities' and 'materials' of these sciences are subject to this economic base."

35. Pius XI, *Discourse to the Italian Catholic University Federation*, Dec. 18, 1937: "We might say that nothing, other than religion, is superior to the political domain, which concerns the interests of all society, and which, in this sense, is the domain par excellence of the broadest form of charity: *political charity*." Paul VI, *Octogesima Adveniens*, no. 46, p. 508: "Politics are a demanding manner—but not the only one—of living the Christian commitment to the service of others." See also *Gaudium et Spes*, no. 75, p. 311; Conferência Nacional dos Bispos do Brasil, *Exigências cristãs de uma ordem política*, no. 27.

36. Karl Marx, letter to Kugelmann, Aug. 28, 1866: "I think that this work that I am doing [on *Das Kapital*] has a far greater importance for the working class than anything I could do in *any* congress" (p. 179)—a reference to the Geneva Congress of the International, Sept. 3–8, 1866. Marx, letter to Freiligrath, Feb. 29, 1860: "I have the firm conviction that my theoretical labors are more useful to the working class than collaboration with organizations that, on the continent, no longer have any raison d'être (cited in M. Rubel, *Pages de Karl Marx* [Paris, Payot, 1970], 1:43–44).

37. For the conception of scientific research as work, see A. Vieira Pinto, *Ciência e existência*, chap. 12. Louis Althusser's notion on the (political) role of theoreticians can be situated within this first model. In a first period (until 1967 or 1968—"Althusser I") he defined (Marxist) philosophy as "epistemology"—i.e., as "theory of theoretical practice" (*Pour Marx*, 1965); but in his second period (since 1968—"Althusser II") he defined it as "polemics"—i.e., as "class struggle in theory" (*Philosophie et philosophie spontanée des savants*, 1967; *Lenin and Philosophy*, 1968; "Response to John Lewis," 1972; *Elements of Self-Criticism*, 1974; and finally, *Positions*, 1964–75). For this whole consideration, see Saul Karsz, *Théorie et politique: Louis Althusser*. See also, however, the criticisms directed at Althusser apropos of the practical consequences of his position: *Contre Althusser* (Paris, Union Gén. d'Editions, 1974), and J. Rancière, *La leçon d'Althusser*. Rancière censures the Althusserian idea of a "timeless" and "imagi-

nary" struggle on the part of theory and its "lonely heroes," whereas, when all is said and done, the game is played out in another locus than the theoretical front. This form of theoretical engagement, without ties to the extratheoretical, was also imputed to the theoreticians of the Frankfurt school by G. Lukács, in the following heated tones: "You have conveniently installed yourselves in the Hotel of the Void. Life is fine there, the service impeccable, your quarters comfortable. The great mass of clients are content with that, and never go out to look at the void. You yourselves have seen it, and have come away shaken; but this has only whetted your appetite for the good life, and comfort" (cited by J.-M. Palmier in *Le Monde*, Oct. 25, 1974, p. 21). From one point of view this resembles what "liberation theologians" criticize in the "political theologians" of Europe. One of the former has cited Emmanuel Mounier's warning in his *Feu la Chrétiente* (Paris, Seuil, 1950): "It is a mighty temptation for the Christian to sit down, emotionally moved, before lovely theological landscapes, while the human caravan trudges past with its feet on fire": E. Ibarra, "Le contexte de la théologie de la libération," p. 27.

38. This is the Aristotelian concept of *hexis*, which the scholastics translated as *habitus*: Aristotle, *Nicomachaean Ethics*, book 2, chap. 5, 1105b19–1106a12, p. 351; see also chap. 1, 1103a12-b24, pp. 348–49.

39. It would appear that the idea of the intellectual as social laborer, and, what is more, as linked with a determinate (political or productive) social practice, belongs to the theoretical and practical tradition of Marxism. Indeed, we have concrete implementations of the second model in the educational programs of "socialist" countries as, e.g., in China, with its famous "May 7 schools," where intellectuals undergo an apprenticeship in productive social work in order to come, or keep, "in contact with the masses." See K. S. Karol, *The Second Chinese Revolution* (New York, Hill and Wang, 1974), pp. 338–44. It seems to me, further, that it is along the lines of this second model that intellectuals of the "center," including theologians, see their political engagement, especially since the crisis of their social status at the time of the student revolt of 1967–68. Consider Gramsci's conception of the "organic intellectual," one linked either with the bourgeoisie or with the proletariat, a "new-type intellectual" corresponding to industrial society, and to be contradistinguished from the "old-type intellectual"—the "bureaucratic" or "ecclesiastical" or "transhistorical" intellectual characteristic of a society of farmers and artisans. See the excellent study by Maria Antonietta Macciocchi, *Pour Gramsci*, pp. 203–82. See also G. Roth, *Gramscis Philosophie der Praxis*, pp. 108–19, 136–46. As for Marx himself, let me recall only Engels's graveside eulogy, in which he emphasized two basic facets of his friend, the scientist-and-revolutionary: "Such was the man of science. But this was not even half the man. . . . For Marx was before all else a revolutionist" (*The Marx-Engels Reader*, R. C. Tucker, ed., New York, Norton, 1972, p. 604), cited by D. Riazanov, *Karl Marx: Homme, penseur et révolutionnaire* (Paris, Anthropos, 1968), p. 32. For Maximilien Rubel, Marx was more a theoretical than a political revolutionary. Let us note that Marx's practice was in the order of politics rather than economics, at least as far as directly productive work is concerned. More than anything else, he was a publicist and propagandist. Against the hagiographical oversimplifications of a Marx who brought theory and practice together ideally, we might well heed what Solzhenitsyn has written about Marx's recommendation (in *Critique of the Gotha Program*) that criminals be resocialized through productive work: "[Marx] himself had never in his life taken a pick in hand. To the end of his days he never pushed a wheelbarrow, mined coal, felled timber, and we don't even know how his firewood was split—but he wrote that down on paper, and the paper did not resist" (*The Gulag Archipelago*, p. 143, cited by J. Elleinstein, "Marx est-il coupable?," *Le Monde*, Feb. 15, 1975, p. 9).

40. Many "leftist" groups, especially those in the Maoist line (as in Godard's film, *La Chinoise*), preponderantly university types, have understood their political option in a way involving close companionship with the popular classes. I may cite the case of the "worker priests," as well as many advanced movements in the religious life in Latin America as throughout the world—e.g., the Little Brothers and the Little Sisters of Jesus, as well as so many other small religious communities living and working in the milieu of the poor. This third model is the one that has the sympathies of the theologians of liberation. For the theological and political content of this model, see Gustavo Gutiér-rez, *A Theology*, the last chapter: "Poverty: Solidarity and Protest," pp. 363–86.

41. See Giulio Girardi, "Théorie et praxis dans la pensée marxiste," pp. 31–33, 68–69, 114–22, 140ff.—where he emphasizes the notion of engagement, participation, or "taking sides," in and by theory. But the epistemological question has remained without development. See also E. Ibarra, "Contexte de la théologie de la libération," pp. 23–65.

42. Two illustrations: Marx and Sartre. As for the former, Althusser has shown how Marx's "discoveries" in the course of his intellectual odyssey were finally determined by the living, militant contact that he had with political praxis, and this according to a dialectic of real challenge and theoretical response: *Pour Marx*, pp. 67–83; *Essays in Self-Criticism*, pp. 151–61: "On the Evolution of the Young Marx." As for Sartre, he himself recounts the circumstances in which he finally grasped Marxism: "What did begin to change me was the *reality* of Marxism, the heavy presence on my horizon of the masses of workers, an enormous somber body which *lived* Marxism, which *practiced* it, and which at a distance exercised an irresistible attraction on petit bourgeois intellectuals" (*Search for a Method*, p. 18). Sartre also avers that, although he is a "traditional intellectual," he has also learned from communists that "writing is just another function" (*On a le droit de se revolter*, p. 41).

43. See Karl Marx, *Theses on Feuerbach*, esp. Thesis 2 (p. 3) and Thesis 3 (p. 4): "truth" and "reality" have need of each other.

44. Note that I am expressly treating, here, exclusively the *political* significance to be found in theological practice. I merely prescind from, without by any means denying, what has been established in part 2 as to the pertinency of theological practice, which—let it be recalled—is not the political. I call attention to this lest I be faulted for "reductionism" here in part 3.

45. Leonardo Boff, *Teologia do cativeiro*, pp. 54–56.

CHAPTER 10

1. See H. C. de Lima Vaz, "Sinais dos tempos—lugar teológico ou lugar comum?" Michel de Certeau gives the following definition of place: "the conjunct of determinations fixing the limits of an encounter of specialists, and which circumscribe to whom and of what they may speak": *La culture au pluriel*, p. 268; see also p. 303. To my mind, such a definition, besides being only descriptive, glosses over the ambiguities introduced by the term "place."

2. "The life of the church": Gustavo Gutiérrez, *A Theology*, pp. 8, 12; M.-D. Chenu, *La foi dans l'intelligence*, pp. 258–59; idem, "La rénovation de la théologie morale," *Supplément de la Vie Spiritualle* 90 (1969) 290. "The experience of Christian communities": R. Ageneau, *Spiritus* 15 (1964) and *Le Monde*, Dec. 21, 1974, p. 10. "The 'base'—the exploited, the oppressed, the poor": José M. González Ruiz, *Dios está en la base*, pp. 7–10. "The praxis of liberation": J. van Niewenhove, "Les 'théologies de la

libération' latino-américaines," pp. 90–94 ("praxis of liberation as *locus theologicus*"); B. Olivier, *Développement ou Libération?* p. 130. *Sensus fidei*: Yves Congar, *Tradition and Traditions*, pp. 317–21, 327, 337. "Church history": Congar, "A historia da Igreja, 'lugar teológico' "; Jean-Marie Levasseur, *Le lieu théologique "Histoire"* (Trois-Rivières, Ed. du Bien Public, 1960); Enrique Dussel, *A History of the Church in Latin America*, pp. 16–18. "The 'other' ": Dussel, *History*, pp. 15–16. "Lived experience": Pierre de Locht, *The Risks of Fidelity*. "Christian existence": J. Audinet, "Questions de méthode," esp. p. 81 ("thesis: 'the point of departure of the investigation is the reality of Christian existence' ").

3. "Ideological" here has the sense of "first ideological" as explained in part 1, §17. For this sense, see Louis Althusser, *Pour Marx*, pp. 44ff.; idem, *Philosophie et philosophie spontanée des savants*, p. 49.

4. Gaston Bachelard, *Epistémologie: Textes choisis*, p. 17. Aristotle, *Topics*, book 8, chap. 3, 158b16–18 (p. 215): "In general, it is safe to suppose that, whenever any problem proves intractable, it either needs definition or else bears either several senses, or a metaphorical sense, or it is not far removed from the first principles."

5. Against the empiricist illusion of an immediate reading of the sense, let us recall Augustine's lapidary statement: *"Nec respondent ista interrogantibus nisi judicantibus."* ("Nor yet do the creatures answer such as ask, unless they can judge": *Confessions*, X, 6, 10, p. 73.)

6. See Leonardo Boff, *A vida religiosa e a Igreja no processo de libertação* (a "christophany" or "theophany" among the people corresponds to a "contemplative vision": pp. 88–90, 97–99).

7. See Dominique Lecourt, *Marxism and Epistemology*, p. 192.

8. See S. Moscovici, "Le jour de fête du cordonnier." See also Karl R. Popper, *The Logic of Scientific Discovery*, which was first published in German in 1935 and has attracted so much attention over the years.

9. Of course there are the historical relapses into the majestic thrust that was Hegelianism represented by Ludwig Feuerbach with his return to sensitivity or "sensibility," Søren Kierkegaard with his return to subjective existence, and Karl Marx with his return to human history. See Enrique D. Dussel, *Método para una filosofía de la liberación*, pp. 128–55. See the very suggestive study of H. Maldiney, "La méconnaissance du sentir," in his *Regard—parole—espace*, pp. 254–321, where Hegel's "consciousness" is shown to be worldless and bodiless. Thus the world has been lost from the start. Thus sensible certitude, or the "pathetic" dimension of receptivity, which makes contact with the world, is likewise totally annulled. Still—notes Maldiney—the "I am spoken" is precisely the origin of the "I speak." Here I must mention studies in phenomenology, such as those of Husserl, Heidegger, Merleau-Ponty, Henry, Chambon, Maldiney, de Waelhens, and others, to which I shall be referring occasionally.

10. Naturally I acknowledge Karl Marx's critique here, in *The German Ideology*, and in *Theses on Feuerbach*, respecting ahistorical, static, "contemplative" conceptualizations of sensible objectivity. For Marx this objectivity is a "product of historical praxis." See Marcel Xhaufflaire, *Feuerbach*, pp. 270ff.

11. This is the classic position, as found, e.g., in Aristotle's *Metaphysics*. This is also what is shown so penetratingly by phenomenology with regard to the spirit and practice of science. See Jean Ladrière, *Vie sociale et destinée*, pp. 19–37. Ladrière writes: "The type of rationality proper to positive science is explained as founded on the structures of the world-as-lived. Scientific rationality is as it were already sculpted in bas-relief on this living, lived world. . . . Generally speaking, whatever belongs to the sphere of expli-

citation, and therefore of predication, is already present in the sphere of the antepredicative and the nonexplicitated" (p. 30). See also L. Robberechs, "La filosofía como expresión" (in *El pensamiento de Husserl*, Buenos Aires, Breviario del Fundo de Cultura Económica, 1968), pp. 52–66, where it is shown how even the "physical real" is an "abstraction" from the "lived real." M. Merleau-Ponty ("La philosophie et la sociologie") sees philosophy as present at the heart even of sociology. Criticizing the "objectivism" of the sciences, he says: "Under the collective name of science, we have nothing but a systematic arrangement, a methodic exercise . . . of the same experience that begins with our first perception." See, too, Stephan Strasser, *Phenomenology and the Human Sciences*; F. Dumont, *Chantier: Essais sur la pratique des sciences de l'homme*, pp. 211–27; A. de Waelhens, *La philosophie et les expériences naturelles.*

12. See Benoît Verhaegen, *Introduction à l'histoire immédiate*, pp. 148ff.: "La rupture épistémologique."

13. See Louis Althusser, *Essays in Self-Criticism*, pp. 119–25, "Science and Ideology," where we read of a "simple opposition between science and ideology," a "recurrent, even 'perpetual' and 'endless' opposition" (p. 122). "Every recognized science not only has emerged from its own prehistory, but continues endlessly to do so (its prehistory remains always contemporary: something like its *Alter Ego*) . . . " (p. 114). I am unable, however, to share Althusser's "theoreticist" disdain for lived experience, which he relegates to the domain of the ideological, if not of the illusory. Here let us recall Roger Garaudy, *Parole d'homme* (Paris, Laffont, 1975), p. 32: "This intellectualism of the West . . . has crucified life on the cross of the concept."

14. Gaston Bachelard's notion, in his *Epistémologie*, pp. 23–26.

15. See Martin Heidegger, *Being and Time*, parags. 7B (pp. 56–58), 44 (pp. 268–69), where it is shown that the "primary 'locus' of truth" (pp. 57, 269) is not the conceptual judgment, but *aisthesis*—perception, sensibility, in a "primordial kind of uncovering" yielding *a-letheia* (p 269).

16. Canguilhem's distinction: see Dominique Lecourt, *Marxism and Epistemology*, p. 125; Fichant and Pêcheux, *Sur l'histoire des sciences*, p. 9.

17. It does not seem to me to be too much in the way of a digression at this point to call attention to the fact that the "real" cannot be reduced to a simple "cultural construction" of an era (Peter L. Berger). It also embraces the "transempirical," or "world of God." God, as John Damascene reminds us, is that "infinite ocean of substance" within which the historical real is but an "island" (*De Fide Orthodoxa*, book 1, chap. 9 [PG 94:836]).

18. For the *conversio ad phantasmata*, see Thomas Aquinas, *Summa Theol.*, I, q. 85, a. 1, ad 4; a. 5, ad 2; III, q. 86, a. 1. This aspect has been underscored by Karl Rahner, *Spirit in the World*. See also J. Marías, *Antropologia metafísica: A estrutura empírica da vida humana* (São Paulo, Duas Cidades, 1971), pp. 15–26.

19. See Jean Ladrière, *Vie sociale et destinée*, pp. 29–31, esp. p. 29: "The rational is coextensive with the self-explicitation of the ego—that is, of experience." See also Albert Dondeyne, "Un discours philosophique de Dieu est-il encore possible?" pp. 435–36, as well as Martin Heidegger, *Lettre sur humanisme*, pp. 57ff.: the human being as ex-sistence.

20. The terms "pertinence" or "pertinency," and "pertinent" are often used as synonymous with, respectively, "relevance" and "relevant,"—e.g., by Pierre Bourdieu and Jean-Claude Passeron, *La reproduction*, pp. 18–46, where "pertinencies" are spoken of in the sense of viewpoints, conceptions, images of the world, legitimated by the dominant culture and simultaneously imposed through the educational system; or again by A.

Lalande, *Vocabulaire technique et critique de la philosophie* (Paris, Presses Universitaires de France, 11th ed., 1972), p. 219. The term "relevance" or "relevancy" is also sufficiently marked by Anglo-Saxon pragmatism for us to adopt a suspicious attitude toward it.

21. This is what we find in François Châtelet, *Logos et praxis*, p. 39: "What matter the polished stone, the slow progress of humanity, when the real question is not that of the beginning, but that of destiny! . . . If I wish to understand human beings, and understand them in order to help them, then it is less to humanity's genesis that I ought to address myself than to its worldview, its mode of existing. It is not of much interest that before human beings existed there were stones and amoebas. Today, a *cogito* interrogates itself, and finds itself interrogated. The existence of a living being has more meaning than the supposed or reconstructed life of Australopithecus." In chapter 5, section 2, on theory and praxis (pp. 179–86), Châtelet interprets the present *kairos* as a "moment of passage" (p. 180). If this is the case—the author continues—theory too must make a sides-taking decision with respect to what type of problems to approach. Through a "theory of passage" (to a classless society), Châtelet seeks to "underscore the importance of certain types of problems, sweep abstract questioning aside as empty or illusory, renounce solutions that do not involve the possibility of effective solution on the level of daily existence" (p. 180). Here let us note that the question of relevance rests on an interpretation of history. But this is a question that I cannot go into here.

22. See Louis Althusser, *Pour Marx*, pp. 51–67, where the author deals with "problematic" conceived as the "unity of an ideology," or as "the question of its questions" (p. 64, n. 30).

23. For the distinction between *question* (with its semantic chain: theory—debate—response, without connections to historical time) and *problem* (with its semantic chain: practice—struggle—solution, connected with the historical time), see Ralf Dahrendorf, *Essays in the Theory of Society*, pp. 256–78, esp. 256–57. See also Louis Althusser, *Lenin and Philosophy*, p. 35.

24. Regarding "irrelevant" theoreticians, Miguel Unamuno stated, caustically and to the point, that, "instead of looking the sphinx straight in the face, they spend their time counting the hairs on its tail" (cited in *Verdad y Vida* 126 [1974] 147). Let us also recall in this respect the observation of Friedrich Nietzsche: " . . . The knowledge of the chemical analysis of water to the sailor in danger in a storm" would be irrelevant (*Human, All-Too-Human*, p. 21). Marcel Légaut (*Introduction à l'intelligence du passé et de l'avenir du Christianisme*, Paris, Aubier-Montaigne, 1970, p. 278) writes: "In Christianity, then, one finds an abundant literary production, but one of mediocre value, together with scholarly works that, although showing a great deal of intellectuality and erudition, are stuck, with rare exceptions, on questions of detail. . . . At the same time, the real problems escape detection. . . . " The New Testament, too, treats of "empty, irrelevant questions": see the "pastoral epistles": 1 Tim. 1:6 *(mataiologian)*; 6:20 *(kenophonias)*; 2 Tim. 2:16 *(kenophonias)*; 2:23 *(moras kai apaideutous zeteseis)*; Titus 1:10 *(mataiologoi)*; and further: 1 Tim. 1:3–4; 4:7; 6:5; 2 Tim. 2:14, 23; 4:4; Titus 1:14, 3:9.

25. See Thomas Michels, ed., *Geschichtlichkeit der Theologie* (Salzburg, Universitätsverlag, 1970), and Gustave Thils's review of it in *Revue Théologique de Louvain* 1 (1970) 458–59.

26. See Louis Althusser, *Essays in Self-Criticism*, pp. 57–58: "Even speculative ideologies, even philosophies which content themselves with '*interpreting the world*,' are in fact active and practical: their (hidden) goal is to act on the world, on all the social prac-

tices, on their domains and their 'hierarchy'—even if only to 'place them under a spell,' to sanctify or modify them, in order to preserve or reform 'the existing state of things' against social, political, and ideological revolutions. . . . 'Speculative' philosophies have a political *interest* in making believe that they are *disinterested* or that they are only 'moral'. . . . Whether this strategy is 'conscious' and deliberate or 'unconscious' means little: we know that it is not consciousness which is the motor of history, even in philosophy."

27. Coexisting with its scientific dimension ("historical materialism," "science of history," "scientific socialism"), Marxism includes another side, that of a metaphysical, mystical, ethical nature—the vital atmosphere, as it were, of the former, and the secret of its attraction ("dialectical materialism," "ideology of the proletariat": Lenin's "secular religion"). See Maximilien Rubel and B. Bottomore, eds., *Karl Marx, Selected Writings*; Leon Trotsky, "The Moralists and Sycophants Against Marxism"; Albert Camus, *L'homme révolté* (Paris, Gallimard, 1951), pp. 237-51. Jean-Paul Sartre strongly emphasized the fact of an unformulated anthropology underlyingMarxism, especially in his *Critique of Dialectical Reason*, as well as in *On a raison de se révolter*: "It is absurd to think that the human being might be definable solely in terms of class. There is something else to be considered: alienations refer directly to freedom, for the only thing you can alienate is someone's freedom" (p. 342). "How can you oppress a robot? You can oppress or exploit only beings that are free in principle, but whose freedom you have sidetracked and alienated" (p. 100). See also chap. 6, pp. 94-106, esp.: "I doubt whether any society can dispense with the philosopher. Philosophy, in any society, is the understanding of what the human being of this society is" (p. 94).

28. See Raymond Polin, *La création des valeurs*, pp. 282-90: on cynicism in ethics, defined as "a philosophy of activity united in contempt of all theoretical speculation" (p. 285). See also François Châtelet, *Logos et praxis*, pp. 66-68, where the author refers to Plato's character, Callicles (see *Gorgias*, 505C), representing bad faith—as opposed to philosophical reason, represented by Socrates. The former, the person of bad faith, questions and "reduces" philosophical reason by the use of violence. One is reminded of a confrontation of the same sort between *Thrasymachus* (force) and Socrates (reason) in book 1 of Plato's *Republic*.

29. The spontaneous reaction of scientists when confronted with the dangers and threats of their own creations, now detached from them and placed at the disposition of states, is often expressed in pathetic, moving protests. But for want of an educated analysis of the structure of a determinate society, the good will they manifest flounders about in helplessness. See E. Boné, "Le scientifique chrétien et les questions d'aujourd'hui," *Nouvelle Revue Théologique* 97 (1975) 208-28. Similarly, currents of second theology, not rarely, cling to the level of sensitivity to a current problematic without moving to a systematic examination of this problematic in its structural coordinates. Hence the awkwardly prophetical tone of their indignation, of their will for change and humanization. The de facto insufficiency, at times catastrophic, of these protests of sensitivity when it comes to intelligent political action is revealed to us in the romantic "revolutionism" of petit bourgeois and desperate leftists, or in the horrified outcry of the upper-middle class scandalized by the "monstrosities" committed by "subversives."

30. There is room here for a distinction between the scale of importance and the scale of urgency. Thomas Aquinas employs the terminology, *"optimum simpliciter"* and *"optimum huic."* And he says, based on Aristotle, *Topics*, book 3, chap. 2, 118a8-16 (pp. 164-65), that doing philosophy is *important*, but earning money becomes *urgent* in a moment of need: *Quaestiones Disputatae de Malo*, q. 12, a. 1; *Quodlibetales*, I, q. 7,

a. 14. The *urgency* of reflection (upon urgent subjects) is another name for "relevance." One may also speak of whether a matter is "significant" or not. See Paulo Freire, *Pedagogy of the Oppressed*, pp. 91–95, where the author refers to popular education, and speaks of "generative themes," and a "thematic universe," consisting in the (p. 91) "complex of ideas, concepts, hopes, doubts, values, and challenges" of a given era. This notion, which Freire also refers to as "meaningful thematics," corresponds precisely to what I call "thematic relevance."

31. See Thomas Merton's beautiful pages in *Faith and Violence* (Notre Dame University Press, 1968), pp. 145–64, "Events and Pseudo-Events," where he scores the naivety of a certain "journalistic theology," remarking that "nine-tenths of the news, as printed in the papers, is pseudo-news, manufactured events. Some days ten-tenths" (p. 151). And: "Our over-sensitive awareness of ourselves as responsible for 'making history' is a grotesque illusion, and it leads us into the morass of pseudo-events. Those who are obsessed with 'making history' are responsible for the banality of the bad news which comes more and more to constitute our 'history' " (p. 162).

32. Any theology, without exception, even a "kerygmatic theology," ought to be attentive to its inevitable "political quotient." (We need only recall "evangelist" Billy Graham and other charismatic preachers.) Even when we restrict ourselves to the proclamation of "Jesus risen," it is always possible, and by no means irrelevant, to pose this simple question: *Cui bono?* To whose interest is it that Jesus be risen (in this world of interests)? As another example, we might consider what the French Jocists said of a speech a certain bishop gave: "To lump together—even in an evangelical bag—'materialism of the right' and 'materialism of the left' in a country where 'materialism of the right' is in power at the moment, is a de facto option for the 'materialism of the right' " (*Le Monde*, Aug. 2, 1974, p. 5). Thus also, in his "La Iglesia chilena ante el socialismo," Juan Luís Segundo examines the working document of the Chilean bishops, "Evangelio, Política y Socialismo" (SEDOC 4 [1972] col. 1443–76), showing that, although they explicitly deny it, the bishops cannot but take a well-defined position. This is revealed in Segundo's lexical analysis of the document. In section 3 alone, where the bishops use the expression "risks and dangers" 26 times, they use it 24 times with reference to socialism, once with reference to capitalism, and once with reference to both. Segundo then ascertains the presence, in the same section 3, of 15 terms etymologically akin to "dehumanization" or "inhumanity" (or indeed these words themselves). He finds 12 applications to socialism, 1 to capitalism, and 2 to both together. Segundo's conclusion: the bishop's ideology is *teneamus quod habemus*. One last indication: with respect to Pierre Bigo, *The Church and Third World Revolution*, one might ask, entirely apart from the author's subjective intentions, what might be the meaning, in ideo-political terms and in the context of Latin America today, of the "third way" of which he writes.

33. Peter L. Berger, *A Rumor of Angels*, pp. 24–31, 107 and passim. Berger criticizes most vigorously the modern tendency in theology to appeal to the "spirit of the age," and so on, a spirit that Berger calls a quest for "timeliness" and "relevance," arising from the need for (p. 107) being "with it," for "with-it-ness." And he quotes Dean Inge to the effect that "a man who marries the spirit of the age soon finds himself a widower" (p. 28). To the search for fads, and the concessions they involve, Berger opposes the gratuitous quest for truth. Søren Kierkegaard also scores epochality, or the appeal to the spirit of the age: see his *Armed Neutrality*. Marx himself, attached as he was to the historical present, called attention to the fact that, unlike simplistic evolutionism, it was impossible to "do a critique" of one's own era without having passed through it (*Introdução à Crítica da Economia Política*, pp. 126–27). Let me also cite Rom. 12:2: "Do not con-

form yourselves to this age but be transformed by the renewal of your mind." Finally, it
was G. K. Chesterton who said that the church was the only thing that had spared the
human being the degrading slavery of being a child of the time.

34. The better to concretize the notion of "relevance," let me cite three studies that
took up the (relevant) subject of the theological significance of the phenomenon of the
youth protests of the sixties. These contributions are at once concrete examples of relevant theology, and explicit reflections on the importance of theological relevance:
Adolphe Gesché, "Vrai et faux changement en théologie"; Michel de Certeau, *La prise
de la parole: Pour une nouvelle culture*, together with his article, "L'articulation du
'dire' et du 'faire' "; finally, L. A. Monfort, "Upsal, un symptôme: Signification théologique de la contestation des jeunes," *Nouvelle Revue Théologique* 91 (1969) 47–64.

CHAPTER 11

1. "He asks every idea, 'What are you good for?' " (Bertholt Brecht, "Elogio do
Revolucionário," in *A mãe*, cited by L. J. Prieto, *Pertinence et pratique*, p. 7).

2. Both expressions are Althusser's: *Pour Marx*, p. 19 and p. 172, n. 9.

3. The whole history of science appears to have developed out of this maxim. This
ascetic, contemplative ideal of knowledge has its grandeur. It comes to us from ancient
Greece and the superiority of theory over practice held by that culture. See Aristotle,
Metaphysics, book 1, chap. 1, 981b20–22 (p. 500): "[Other] sciences which do not aim
at giving pleasure or at the necessities of life were discovered. . . . " And chap. 2,
982b20–28, 983a10–11 (p. 501): philosophers eventually found themselves "pursuing
science in order to know, and not for any utilitarian end. And this is confirmed by the
facts; for it was when almost all the necessities of life and the things that make for comfort and recreation had been secured, that such knowledge began to be sought. Evidently
then we do not seek it for the sake of any other advantage; but as the man is free, we say,
who exists for his own sake and not for another's, so we pursue this as the only free
science, for it alone exists for its own sake. . . . All the sciences, indeed, are more necessary than this, but none is better." This ideal has been passed down by Christian tradition, with its priority of contemplation over action. See Thomas Aquinas, *Summa
Theol.*, II-II, qq. 180–82. It is still maintained today. Gaston Bachelard, in his *La formation de l'esprit scientifique*, has emphasized the perpetual self-questioning of a science, in pursuit of the indefinite progress of knowledge by means of knowledge. Much is
made of gratuity, or immanent finality, of science in our own day, in the ambit of the so-
called positive sciences as well as in that of those we call "human." In the area of the
latter, here are two particularly noteworthy testimonials: Auguste Comte: "We must not
. . . fall into the error of our time, of regarding Science chiefly as a basis of Art. . . . We
must never forget that the sciences have a higher destination still—and not only higher
but more direct—that of satisfying the craving of our understanding to know the laws of
phenomena" (*The Positive Philosophy of Auguste Comte*, 1:20). Karl Marx: "Someone who pursues a science not for its own sake—because it can be in error—but adapts it
to ulterior interests, I call debased" (*Théories sur la plus-valie*, II, cited in *Oeuvres
choisies*, Paris, Gallimard, 1966, p. 232). As for Marx, I am of the opinion that he was
conscious of the duty he had to conduct his investigations exclusively in the interest of
(scientific) truth, and not in the (direct) interest of a class, although, as he saw, the two
could coincide historically. One need only examine his two famous prefaces: the one to
Das Kapital (first edition, 1867), and the one to *Zur Kritik der politischen Ökonomie*

(1859). These texts afford us ample reason to take our distance from the Marxist thesis of today to the effect that the viewpoint of the working class is a privileged "locus of truth." Further, compare Emile Durkheim's emphasis on "the pursuit of truth for truth's sake" with the pragmatism of a John Dewey, who went so far as to oppose theory to practice: Durkheim, *Pragmatism and Sociology*, lesson 16: "Speculation and Practice." It will be unnecessary to remind the reader of Max Weber's position. See further: Jean Piaget, *Psychology and Epistemology*, pp. 121-24, where we have a like insistence on pure research, independent of any concern with practical application. Where the "positive" sciences are concerned, see Albert Einstein: "Under pain of fading away and dying out, science must not aim at practical objectives" (*Comment je vois le monde*, Paris, Flammarion, 1934, p. 40). Bertrand Russell: "The finality of science is the contemplative love of nature, and not its technological domination" (*The Scientific Outlook*, New York, Norton, 1931, pp. 261-69). There is a vigorous expression of this same disinterested, ascetic spirit in Jacques Monod, *Chance and Necessity*, chap. 9, pp. 160-80, where the radical recommendation is made that the "ethic of knowledge," summed up in the "principle of objectivity," be extended to the whole of human life, both personal and social. See also idem, "La science, valeur suprême de l'homme."

4. See the classic authors of *Wissenssoziologie*: Karl Mannheim, C. Wright Mills, and R. K. Merton. I might add here the "social philosophers" of the Frankfurt school, who have made their mark in a critique of contemporary ideology and the current "perversion of reason." See Pierre V. Zima, *L'Ecole de Francfort* (Paris, Ed. Universitaires, 1974), Introduction. Let me single out two members of this school: Jürgen Habermas, *Technik und Wissenschaft als "Ideologie"*; and Herbert Marcuse, *One-Dimensional Man: Studies in the Ideology of Advanced Industrial Society*. For the current social and political situation of the intelligentsia, see Frederic Bon and Michel-Antoine Burniér, *Les nouveaux intellectuels* (Paris, Seuil, 1971); Jean-Jacques Salomon, *Science and Politics: An Essay on the Scientific Situation in the Modern World*. For Brazil, see Wilson Martins, *História da inteligência brasileira* (São Paulo, Cultrix, 1977); for the particular case of Brazilian social scientists, see Octavio Ianni, *Sociologia e sociedade no Brasil*; Florestan Fernandes, *A sociologia no Brasil*. Finally, for the Brazilian intelligentsia today, see the series of reports in *Jornal do Brasil*, section B, May 2-5, 1977: "What is the power of the intelligentsia?"

5. See H. Carrier, "Pour une politique de la recherche dans l'Eglise," which situates the subject against a broader horizon than that of the church: the situation of "scientific policy" in the principal countries today (pp. 8-11), the relationship between science and power (pp. 11-13), and so on. See also José M. González Ruíz, *Dios está en la base*, pp. 12-25: "theology and praxis."

6. Here we have Max Weber's familiar criticisms of scientists who play the prophet from their "academic locus," the "chair" of their discipline—in other words, *ex cathedra* (*Essais sur la théorie de la science*, pp. 413-15).

7. In order to illustrate the confusion, even in scientific circles, between disinterestedness and interest, the true and the good, objectivity and justice, in science, I take the liberty of transcribing an anecdote recounted by scientist Georg Picht: "I recently attended a dinner gathering of German and American scientists, including Nobel laureates. At one point, Heisenberg turned to the great American physicist Isaak Rabi, Chairman of the Atomic Energy Commission, and said, 'We know about eighty-five percent of everything that can ever be known about [subatomic] particles. What use is it to keep building bigger and bigger cyclotrons? Wouldn't it be better to spend these huge sums on more urgent tasks?' And Rabi exclaimed, 'Oh, no! We can't put the brakes on our thirst

for knowledge!' Heisenberg: 'Well, how large should the dimensions of a cyclotron grow, then?' Rabi: 'From here to Ecuador, if they need to!' " (*Express*, Sept. 6, 1971, as well as in Picht, *L'Express va plus loins avec*. . . [Paris, Laffont, 1973], p. 360). In my view, this is a characteristic expression of positivist belief in science-the-emancipator—the belief for which the slogan "knowledge for the sake of knowledge" is the supreme good that automatically engenders all the others (cf. Wisd. 7:11).

8. See R.-C. Gesret, "Naissance de la théologie au service de l'Eglise militante des IIe et IIIe siècles," *Lumière et Vie* 14 (1965) 15–31.

9. See Yves Congar, *La foi et la théologie*, pp. 203–6, 245.

10. I know of no specific study of the ideological coefficient of the scholastic system. On the *jus dominativum*, see Thomas Aquinas, *Summa Theol.*, II-II, q. 57, a. 3, ad 2; and a. 4. See also Karl Marx, *Pre-Capitalist Economic Formations*.

11. Wilhelm Dilthey: "Where interest is concentrated, there also is the understanding sharpened"—cited by H. Haag, "A Palavra de Deus," p. 167. Karl Marx: "It is not consciousness that determines life, but life that determines consciousness" (*The German Ideology*, p. 37); "It is not the consciousness of men that determines their existence, but, on the contrary, their social existence determines their consciousness" (*A Contribution to the Critique of Political Economy*, pp. 11–12).

12. W. de Bont ("La religion en tant que pensée symbolique," p. 232) shows that interest, in science, is an adventitious stimulant, not the basis of its objectivity, and he exemplifies this with the case of the first atomic bomb: the bomb was conceived in pursuit of bellico-political interests, but it was feasible only on the basis of the atomic theory. Thus we may say, de Bont continues, that the war gave an impulse to the atomic theory, which, being further elaborated, now made it possible to "win" the war.

13. See Friedrich Nietzsche, *Beyond Good and Evil*, part 6 (pp. 119–41): "The scientist is a tool, a laborer, the sublimest slave of all—but not the end, not the outcome, not the conclusion—for knowledge, like power, is a function of the search."

14. "When society has technological needs, it thrusts science ahead rather than universities. . . . In Germany, alas, we've got into the habit of writing the history of the sciences as if they'd fallen from the sky" (Friedrich Engels, letter to Borgius, Jan. 25, 1894, quoted by Marta Harnecker, *Les concepts élémentaires du matérialisme historique*, p. 63). Let us note that Aristotle placed political activity below, and in function of, meditative or philosophical activity, and, in parallel fashion, political science in subordination to speculative or metaphysical philosophy: *Politics*, book 7, chap. 3, 1325a16–23, b14–32 (pp. 529–30); and *Nicomachaean Ethics*, book 10, chap. 7, 1177a11–b26 (pp. 431–32). Thomas Aquinas, in his commentary on the Nicomachaean Ethics, book 10, chap. 7, writes: *"Ad felicitatem speculativam tota vita politica videtur ordinata; dum pace, quae per ordinationem vitae politicae statuitur et conservatur, datur hominibus facultas contemplandi veritatem."* A like conception is not as far removed from Marxist thought as might appear: Marx himself foresaw the passage from a ("prehistoric") "reign of need" to the "reign of freedom" in "history," in which human beings would at last be able to devote themselves to all manner of creative activities.

15. "Interest" here has first a theological or structural sense, and only subsequently an ethical or subjective sense. (Subjective) "scientific disinterestedness," à la Monod, can be most "interesting" for power. For the sense of this concept, see Jean Piaget, *Epistémologie des sciences de l'homme*, pp. 315–19.

16. See Thomas Aquinas's commentary on the First Letter to the Corinthians, chap. 8, lectio 1, vv. 1–2, esp.: *"Augustinus: addite ergo scientiae charitatem, et utilis erit scientia. Per se quidem est inutilis, ex charitate vero utilis. . . . Quicumque habet*

scientiam et non modum utendi ea, habet scientiam insufficienter. . . . Scire autem contingit dupliciter, scilicet habere scientiam et uti scientia, sicut videre: habere visum et uti visu."

17. In the same sense of the articulation between wisdom (in its dependency) and reason (in its autonomy), see Jacques Maritain, *The Rights of Man and Natural Law*: " . . . The community never has the right to require a mathematician *to hold as true* one mathematical system in preference to another" (p. 17). "The State can, under certain definite circumstances, ask a mathematician to teach mathematics, a philosopher to teach philosophy. . . . But the State cannot force a philosopher or a mathematician to adopt a philosophical doctrine or a mathematical doctrine" (pp. 70–71). Reason expressed in politics may be called "architectonic reason," as it subsumes all other forms of rationality in view of the totality. See Aristotle, *Nicomachaean Ethics*, book 1, chap. 2, 1094a28–1094b2 (p. 339): Knowledge of the chief good "would seem to belong to the most authoritative art and that which is truly the master art *[techne architektonike]*. And politics appears to be of this nature; for it is this that ordains which of the sciences should be studied in a state, and which each class of citizens should learn and up to what point they should learn them." On the distinction of the two "reasons," see Augustine, *De Trinitate*, book 12, chap. 4, cited by Thomas Aquinas, *Summa Theol.*, I, q. 89, a. 9, in a distinction between *ratio superior* or *sapientia*, and *ratio interferior* or *scientia (prudentia)*, the former concerning the *rationes aeternae*, and the latter, contingent means. This corresponds to the distinction in modern philosophy between reason and understanding, the former being synthetic and the second analytic.

18. See Jürgen Habermas, *Knowledge and Human Interests*.

19. See B. Olivier, *Développement ou libération? Pour une théologie qui prend parti*; Alain Durand, *Pour une Eglise partisane* (Paris, Cerf, 1975); Jean Guichard, *Eglise, lutte de classes et stratégies politiques*, esp. pp. 171ff.; idem, "Lutte des classes et annonce du salut"; Hugo Assmann, "Compromiso político no contexto de luta de clase"; Girardi, *Christianisme, libération humaine, lutte des classes*, esp. pp. 153ff.

20. As early as 1954, Karl Rahner observed that a pastoral or kerygmatic theology was not exempt from, but rather that it demanded, greater scientificity on the part of the theologian (*Mission and Grace: Essays in Pastoral Theology*).

21. See Jürgen Moltmann's beautiful insight: "A theology conscious of its responsibility is obliged to reflect in a critical manner on the psychological and political implications of its words, its images, and its symbols. It may not simply continue to consider as adequate and neutral the institutions through which it acts, nor may it seek to preserve them at all cost, prescinding from their functionality. Each time it speaks of God, it should ask itself whether it is offering the people religious opium or an authentic leaven of freedom. This does not mean that theology must cease speaking of God and devote itself to the class struggle or the process of humanization, as many urge. On the contrary, it means that, in every word that it pronounces, it should be clearly apparent whether it speaks of the God of the crucified, or of the Baal of the nations or the idols of the heart. It should clearly appear whether it is diffusing faith or superstition. It also means that theology must have a clear grasp of which institutions and which functions are those in which it can be really operative, and in which it will remain ineffective. We may not, therefore, ask ourselves which sense—which linguistic sense—we must employ in order to speak of God. The question must be: What public efficacy, in this determinate situation, attaches to speaking of God or remaining silent?": "Crítica teológica de la religión política," pp. 15–16.

22. For the *Aufhebung* of theory in and through praxis, see R. Vancourt's excellent

study, "Idéologie, marxisme et 'dépassement' de la philosophie." Vancourt's conclusion: The theoretical explication of a reality does not, of course, suppress this reality. Thus its theoretical solution is not its practical dissolution. Example: Religion has not been abolished in virtue of having been explained by Marx. "Inversely, one may speak of the 'transcendence' of philosophy by action." This occurs when the passage is made from "knowledge to truth," from "interpreting the world to transforming the world" (p. 42).

23. Karl Marx: "*Ideas* can never lead beyond an old world order but only beyond the ideas of the old world order. Ideas *cannot carry out anything* at all. In order to carry out ideas men are needed who can exert practical force" (*The Holy Family*, p. 119). Similarly: " 'Liberation' is a historical and not a mental act, and is brought about by historical conditions, the [level] of industry, com[merce], [agri]culture . . . " (Marx, *The German Ideology*). Finally: "The weapon of criticism cannot, of course, replace criticism by weapons, material force must be overthrown by material force; but theory also becomes a material force as soon as it has gripped the masses" (*Contribution to the Critique of Hegel's Philosophy of Law*, p. 182).

24. See Jean Ladrière, *L'articulation du sens*, pp. 141–59: "the language of action"; Mao Tse-Tung, *Cinq essais philosophiques: De la pratique* (1937), pp. 1–43, esp. pp. 27ff.: "the leap from knowledge to practice"; Aristotle, as well, in the last chapter of his *Nicomachaean Ethics* (book 10, chap. 9), insists a great deal on the need for practice for the passage from theory to its execution. Just as much as "knowledge," "virtue" too, for Aristotle, is a "praxis," inasmuch as it is the action of human beings upon themselves, an act of self-creation. Psychologists—Stern, Claparède, Piaget—have long since established a "dichotomy between thought and action" (Gaston Viaud, *Intelligence: Its Evolution and Forms* [Westport, Conn., Greenwood, 1973], p. 96). See also Friedrich Nietzsche, with his conceptualization of the sovereign human being, the creator of values, or the evaluator, the "appreciator": existentialism follows these same lines, as we see in Jean-Paul Sartre, *Being and Nothingness*, pp. 433–81, "Freedom: The First Condition of Action," esp. the conclusion of the chapter, pp. 476–81.

25. What Ralf Dahrendorf asserts of sociology is valid, *mutatis mutandis* for theology: "Rich as the country of sociology with its open frontiers may be in potential, however, and as far as its light . . . may shine beyond these frontiers, its glories do not extend to practice. Sociology is theory, and no amount of 'decided reason' will set it to dealing actively with the social and political problems of our time. The verbal radicalism of those who like to see sociology and socialism confused—the silly talk, for example of theory that itself becomes practice—is pseudo-practice, the wishful thinking of people rendered politically inactive by frustrated ambition" (*Essays in the Theory of Society*, p. 275).

26. "From the logical point of view, theory guides praxis and is insuperable; it is not as if praxis, too, constituted the truth of theory" (R. Vancourt, "Idéologie, marxisme et 'dépassement,' " p. 42).

27. For this Kantian distinction, see Joseph Maréchal, *Le point de départ de la métaphysique* (Brussels, Universelle/Desclée de Brouwer, 1944), cahier III, pp. 58–59, 267–68.

28. I am paraphrasing the title of Gaston Bachelard's *Le nouvel esprit scientifique*.

29. The notion of "political vigilance" in praxis finds its correlate for theory in the notion of "epistemological vigilance" or watchfulness (Gaston Bachelard). Let me point out here that "political vigilance" is an attitude of mind adopted by many of the social theoreticians of Latin America, dealing as they do with what they term an "alienated science," and, more broadly, with an "alienated" and "alienating" culture. See the criti-

cisms of Alvaro Vieira Pinto, *Ciência e existência*, esp. pp. 246–54, 277ff., 313–21, 367ff., and 512–15; idem, *Consciência e realidade national*. In the field of popular pedagogy, see Paulo Freire, *Pedagogy of the Oppressed*; idem, *Education, the Practice of Freedom*. For philosophy, see the works of Enrique Dussel, Juan Carlos Scannone, A. Methol Ferré, S. Bondy. For the "social sciences," let me note Orlando Fals Borda, *Ciencia propia y colonialismo intelectual*; R. Stavenhagen, "Comment décoloniser les sciences sociales appliquées." For the case of Brazil, see Michel Schooyans, *O desafio da secularização*, pp. 12–16: "Brazilian studies"; and the authors cited above, in n. 4, Ianni and Fernandes. The complementary terms "critical awareness" and "naive awareness" introduced by Vieira Pinto and generalized by Freire, have become common currency. These categories are most apt for designating what I wish to say with my "political watchfulness" on the level of theory (in function of its presence in praxis). For the pair of categories mentioned, see Darcy Ribeiro, *Teoria do Brasil*, esp. pp. 130ff.

CHAPTER 12

1. See Dieter Berdesinski, *Die Praxis, Kriterium für die Wahrheit des Glaubens?* In chap. 1 (pp. 11–36), the author discusses the thinking of six theologians, all representing the *Bewahrheitungsthese*: Kerstiens, Metz, Schillebeeckx, Moltmann, Sölle, and Marsch. In chap. 2 (pp. 37–64), he analyzes the history of the term "verification" and its general equivalents. In his third and last chapter (pp. 64–121), Berdesinski confronts this thesis with the data of the New Testament and renders a rather negative verdict (pp. 122–24). Berdesinski limits his examination to the dogmatic content of the authors cited. He does not discuss their approaches. Praxis, then, cuts an empty, spineless figure. His criticism of "political theology" is limited to the horizon of thought of the authors criticized—one of idealism in the Marxian sense of the term. Neither the "political theologians" nor Berdesinski himself favors us with the slightest reference to determinate practice, nor again any recourse to socio-analytic mediation or anything remotely like it. Everything is worked out within "pure theology." This theoretical vacuum is present in the "political theologians" themselves, fly the devastating declamations about our ears as they will: "praxis, revolution, transformation, change, verification, test," and the like, and Berdesinski echoes with appeals to "freedom, peace, justice, love," and so on, followed by admonitions in the *sola gratia* style—God alone, as distinguished from praxis, human beings, freedom, and so forth.

2. See C. Dumont, "Des trois dimensions retrouvées en théologie"; Raimundo Pannikar, *L'homme qui devient Dieu*, pp. 29ff.; idem, *Le mystère du culte dans l'hindouisme et le christianisme*, pp. 159–68: "orthopraxy and orthodoxy"; M.-D. Chenu, "Orthodoxie—Orthopraxie"; B. Kloppenburg, "Las tentaciones de la teología de la liberación," esp. pp. 414–15: "heteropraxy"; Johannes B. Metz, "Precisa a Igreja de nova reformação?"; idem, *Theology of the World*, pp. 107–36; see also pp. 137–55; Charles Journet, "Sécularisation, herméneutique, orthopraxie"; Quinn and Davidson, "Theology : Sociology = Orthodoxy : Orthopraxis," with helpful indications for the English-speaking world.

3. Hugo Assmann's term, in his *Nomad Church*, pp. 74–86: "A 'Praxiology' of Liberating Faith in the World."

4. The now celebrated definition by Gustavo Gutiérrez, *A Theology*, pp. 6–15, 145; on p. 10, Gutiérrez speaks of verification by "orthopraxis." See also his "Marxismo e cristianesimo," esp. p. 260: the definition of theology.

5. For "speculative boldness," see Jean Ladrière, "La théologie et le langage de l'interprétation," p. 248, where the author uses this expression to designate what theology today seems to be missing by reason of its "intimidation" by a "scientific view" of the world.

6. See Peter Berger, *A Rumor of Angels*, chap. 3 (pp. 61–94), "Theological Possibilities: Starting with Man," where we have a new method proposed—that of "inductive faith" (pp. 71, 115), emerging from attention to the "signals of transcendence" (pp. 65, 103, 106) occuring in the empiricity of human life. See also Georges Casalis, "Théologie pratique et pratique de la théologie," esp. pp. 98ff.: "the measure of the real"; M.-D. Chenu, "Trente ans après" (*Lumière et Vie* 25 [1975] 72–77), recalling studies carried out in 1947, published in *The Theology of Work*, and proclaiming a "radical change of perspective" as the result of the introduction of the inductive method; René Laurentin, *Evangélisation après le quatrième Synode* (Paris, Seuil, 1975), pp. 141–45, esp. pp. 103–4: "new approach to Christian realities." Meanwhile, as early as the turn of the century, Ambroise Gardeil was writing: "We must lay to rest once for all the idea of an inductive theology, as exciting as it may appear" (*Le donné révélé*, p. 126).

7. Besides the study by J. van Niewenhove, "Rapports entre foi et praxis dans la théologie de la libération latino-américaine," see Xosé Miguélez, *La teología de la liberación y su método*; Roberto Oliveros, *Liberación y teología*, esp. pp. 108–10, 199–214, 390–404; Alfonso García Rubio, *Teologia da libertação*, part 3, pp. 217–73 (bibliography, pp. 275–82).

8. For scientism, see Michel Foucault's critique in his *The Archaeology of Knowledge*, part 4, chap. 6, (pp. 184–86): "Knowledge (Savoir) and Ideology"; and the devastating criticism by A. Grothendieck, "La nouvelle église universelle," presenting "the creed of scientism" in six myths.

9. See Dieter Berdesinski, *Praxis, Kriterium für die Wahrheit?* chap. 1 (pp. 12ff.); José M. Gonzáles Ruíz, *Dios está en la base*, p. 12; Jürgen Moltmann, *Diskussion zur "Theologie der Hoffnung,"* pp. 73–75. I recognize, to the credit of the "political theologians," that there is no unanimity even among Marxists and Marxologists when it comes to these famous theses. Thus on the one side we have Lucien Goldmann, *Marxisme et sciences humaines*, pp. 151–96, where we have a discussion of the theses and their evaluation as "one of the principal changes of direction in Western thought" (pp. 148–49, 164); in the same line, Ernst Bloch, "Keim und Grundlinen: Zu den Elf Thesen von Karl Marx über Feuerbach," *Deutsche Zeitschrift für Philosophie* 1 (1953) 237–61, which Charles Wackenheim follows in his *La faillite de la religion d'après Karl Marx*, pp. 256–60. On the other side, we have Louis Althusser, who situates the theses among Marx's "works of [epistemological] breach," and labels them as still very "ambiguous": *Pour Marx*, pp. 9, 26, 28, 51–57, 254–58. For this question, see also W. Heise, "Die historische Bedeutung der Thesen von Karl Marx über Feuerbach," *Einheit* 8 (1953) 1248–56; N. Rotenstreich, "Marx Thesen über Feuerbach," *Archiv für Rechts und Sozialphilosophie* 39 (1951) 338–60; F. Rottcher, "Theorie und Praxis in den Frühschriften von Karl Marx," *Archiv für Philosophie* 11 (1961) 246–311. For the general problem of the epistemological status of praxis, see M. N. Rutkiewitsch, *Die Praxis als Grundlage der Erkenntnis und als Kriterium der Wahrheit* (Berlin, Dietz, 1957).

10. On "acting in truth" (John 3:21)—literally, "doing the truth"—see Dieter Berdesinski, *Praxis, Kriterium für die Wahrheit?*, pp. 96, 109–12; Georges Thill, *La fête scientifique*, pp. 215–24; Walter Kasper, *Dogme et évangile*, pp. 62–78, and bibliography; I. de la Potterie, "Faire la vérité: devise de l'orthopraxie ou invitation à la foi," *Le Supplément* 118 (1976) 283–93; J. Cardonnel, "A verdade não se contempla: se faz," in

H. J. de Souza and L. A. Gomez, eds., *Cristianismo hoje*, São Paulo, Ed. Universitária, 1962.

11. For Feuerbach's conception of theory and praxis and their relationship, in particular for his idea of "praxis as criterion of truth," see Marcel Xhaufflaire, *Feuerbach*, pp. 189–211, 261–65. On pp. 270ff., the author presents Marx's critique of Feuerbach for his alleged *fetishization* of the *notion* of praxis without having passed by way of *real* praxis. The gulf between the two is clear. Compare, e.g., Marx's Thesis Eight (actually still empiricist)—"All social life is essentially *practical*. All mysteries which lead theory to mysticism find their rational solution in human practice and in the comprehension of this practice" (*Theses on Feuerbach*, p. 5)—with Feuerbach's statement (no less empiricist): "Science does not solve the enigma of life. What conclusion is to be drawn from this? . . . That you must move to life, to praxis. Praxis solves for you the doubts that theory does not resolve" (in Marcel Xhaufflaire, *Feuerbach*, p. 261).

12. Here I follow the Althusserian exegesis of the (not yet Marxist) writings of the young Marx, especially as presented in *Pour Marx*, pp. 229–38.

13. "Epistemological density" is Hugo Assmann's expression. See his "Compromiso político," p. 478.

14. See Spinoza, *A Theologico-Political Treatise*: "I am astonished . . . that it should be thought no crime to think with contempt of the mind" (p. 192); "Who, unless he were desperate or mad, would wish to bid an incontinent farewell to reason, or to despise the arts and sciences, or to deny reason's certitude? But, in the meanwhile, we cannot wholly absolve them from blame, inasmuch as they invoke the aid of reason for her own defeat, and attempt infallibly to prove her fallible" (p. 197).

15. "Impatience demands the impossible: it seeks to attain the end without the means" (Hegel, *Morceaux choisis* [Paris, Gallimard, 1939], 2:122). Hegel actually went so far as to set Zeno, the sophist theoretician, in opposition to Diogenes, the cynic practician: see Jean-Paul Sartre, *Critique of Dialectical Reason*, 1:19, 806. For Hegel, Diogenes is the figure of good sense, which fails to satisfy the elevated demands of reason: *Logica Major*, book 3 (last chap. cited in Hegel, *Morceaux choisis*, 1:296). As an illustration of the contradictory interrelationships between theory and praxis, see *Cristãos para o socialismo*, "II Encontro," esp. col. 173, n. 18, where "new theoretical models" of theology are set in diametrical opposition to "revolutionary practice," the latter being taken as the criterion of theological verification.

16. Besides the examples already mentioned of the ambiguous position to which I allude, I might add: "It is the acknowledgment of the fact of, and active participation in the confrontations of, the class struggle that is the touchstone of theological authenticity" (Georges Casalis, "Conclusion," in Metz and Schlick, eds., *Idéologies de libération*, p. 216). "It is *praxis* that is the basis of discernment, the 'epistemological [*sic*] principle' that enables faith to shed its light on the totality of the real" (Casalis, "Politique, foi, et discernement," p. 195). "The theology of liberation attempts to reflect on the experience and meaning of the faith based on the commitment to abolish injustice and to build a new society; this theology must be verified by the practice of that commitment" (Gutiérrez, *A Theology*, p. 307). The same language appears in Bernard Olivier, *Développement ou libération?* pp. 128–30.

17. See the studies of Jean Ladrière, esp. chap. 3 of *L'articulation du sens* (pp. 73–90), as well as "Le langage théologique et le discours de la représentation," where the author shows, as he has already done in other writings, the autonomous status of scientific theory with respect to experience, and its character as effectuation or performance and not simply representation or demonstration of nature (pp. 157–66). Thus science

appears as a particular practice, not beholden to any practice external to it, as its own empirical verification is in some manner *interior* to itself.

18. "It pertains to theology to understand itself as theology" (Jean Ladrière, "Langage théologique et le discours," p. 168). "It belongs to theology to create its proper language in function of its proper object" (idem, "La théologie et le langage de l'interprétation," p. 262).

19. I leave out of consideration the criteria of *fides quae*, which involve the question of the reasonableness or credibility of the Christian creed. I treat only of a criteriology that reflects (theory) on existence (practice), and shares in neither of the criteriologies cited.

20. If the criterion of *orthopraxis* is essential and internal to *faith* (see Matt. 7:15–27; Gal. 5:19–24; 1 John 2:3–6; James 2:14–26; etc.), *orthodoxy* is the same for *theology*. Of this there can be no doubt. J.-M. Domenach has called "orthopraxy" an "inconsistent notion," inasmuch as action cannot in and of itself be the criterion of truth, for it "supposes a value-option and a reading of history. Orthopraxy supposes an intellectual action, and can vaunt no superiority over reflection" ("L'histoire n'est pas notre absolu," p. 152). Domenach recalls the case of "progressive Christians of the postwar era, who blazed abroad their support for the Stalinist policy!" For his part, Herbert Marcuse (*One-Dimensional Man*, p. 223) recalls the collapse of the "truth" of Galileo and of the Manifesto of the Communist Party—and inversely, of the "victories" of Fascism. Max Weber (*Le savant et le politique*, pp. 175ff.) demonstrates that it is precisely from a point of departure in the contradiction of truth and failure—that revelation of the irrationality of history—that religions have arisen, and that it is upon a theodicy that they maintain themselves.

21. "Indeed, the theological system prevails that perceives integrally, and constructs more organically, the elements of God's word and human intelligence" (M.-D. Chenu, *La foi dans l'intelligence*, p. 369). "Catholic theologians today seem to agree in attributing to systematic theology, ultimately and as its principal function, that of ordering the diverse propositions of revelation in an organic synthesis" (P. Adnès, *La théologie catholique*, Paris, Presses Universitaires de France, 1967, p. 77). "The intellectual construction of the helter-skelter revealed according to scientific categories—i.e., by linking effects to causes and derived truths to principal truths . . . is the most important task of theological science" (Yves Congar, *La foi et la théologie*, p. 171). "The supreme function of theology [is] the organization of all revealed truths in a cohesive whole" (Ambroise Gardeil, *Le donné révélé et la théologie*, p. 354). "The principal function of theology is to manifest the order that exists in the truths of revelation and to show how they mutually explain each other" (Charles Journet, *The Wisdom of the Faith*, p. 54).

22. See Vatican I, Session 2, chap. 4: *"Nexus mysteriorum."*

23. See Jean Piaget, *Epistémologie des sciences de l'homme*, pp. 43–80.

24. See S. Breton, "Le paradoxe du menteur," pp. 523–25; A. Astier, *Dialogue Eglise-Monde*, pp. 84ff. There are few specific studies along this line.

25. I take my inspiration here from Jean Ladrière, esp. his articles "Langage théologique et philosophie analytique" and "Théologie et le langage de l'interprétation." See further: J.-P. Siméon, "Pensée et idéologie," *Esprit* 1 (1972) 31–43, where it is said, in effect, that one of the most solid certitudes of scientific consciousness is that the application of any criterion, whatever it be, can only be the deed of an efficacious *theoretical* process. In no critical attitude, therefore, is the critic favored with a guarantee external to the evidence of the criterion itself. Thus in order to identify the "ideological" character of thinking, the only operation we have available is that of thinking itself, which establishes its own insufficiency or its own falsity by operating upon itself. Thinking "is

verified by its own exercise" (Merleau-Ponty). Althusser has insisted one-sidedly upon this point ("theoreticism"), esp. with regard to the basing of the "scientificity" of historical materialism (*Essays in Self-Criticism*, pp. 105–6). In *Reading Capital*, pp. 56–60, he refutes the extrinsicist criterion of Engels's "unfortunate pudding." "The proof of the pudding is in the eating!" (p. 56).

26. An interesting parallel between verification in the sciences and verification in theology has been drawn by Jean Ladrière in his "La théologie et le langage de l'interprétation," pp. 255–57, where he denies that verification is uniform for every science, holding instead that it is proportioned to the nature of the object of each. Theology does not intend a given empirical reality, but the historical reality of revelation, "deposited" in the code of its founding interpretation. Given that verification is a circular process occurring within a theoretical language that is at once verifier and verified, Christian theology is measured exclusively by means of a retrospective process intending a resumption of revealed significations. And just as science "believes" a priori in the logical character of the universe, so theology believes a priori in the truth of revelation. To my view, this conception agrees with Thomas's epistemology as set forth in part 2. If the tendency to posit praxis as the criterion of truth pretends to do so with the secret intention of modeling itself on the sciences, then it should know that it is sadly mistaken. To understand verification in the form of a comparison between a theory and an empirical datum presupposes a simplistic and erroneous conception of science. Indeed, in the article just cited, "Théologie et le langage de l'interprétation," Ladrière explains that the confrontation between theory and empiry never dispenses from the theoretical instance. Indeed, the confrontation occurs between propositions: theoretical propositions and empirical propositions, the latter being themselves the *theoretical* expression of an empirical result. Doubtless theory can be called to account by experimentation. But there ever remains an irreducible margin of "faith." Indeed it was Leibnitz's "preestablished harmony" between logic and the world that filled Albert Einstein with such admiration. For him it was the wellspring of what he called the piety of the scientist, or cosmic religion (Einstein, *The World as I See It*, e.g., pp. 23, 40–47, 261–68).

27. Thomas Aquinas observes that theology is a matter of study, not virtue (*Summa Theol.*, I, q. 1, a. 6, ad 3). It can even be the occasion of sin: *"Tamen potest homo in hoc peccare"* (*In Boethii de Trinitate*, q. 2, a. 1). It would be possible to find a *"malus theologus"* who would be of less worth in God's sight than a *"sancta vetula"* (*Commentarium in Epistolam ad Ephesios*, chap. 3, lectio 5, v. 19). John Henry Newman declared that theology is an affair that is "not devotional" (cited by Ambroise Gardeil, *Le donné révélé*, p. 339). George Tyrrell was of the opinion that the theologian could have "no more faith than a pup" (ibid., p. 200). "We are better in theology than Saint Peter or Saint Mary Magdalen," he continued. "But do we have more faith, hope, more love?" (ibid., p. 339).

28. We need only turn to article 18 of Thomas Aquinas's *Quodlibetales*, book 4, where he says that the *an ita sit* of faith is a matter for religious authority, whereas the *cur ita sit* of the same faith is a matter for theological authority.

29. See Olivier A. Rabut, *Faith and Doubt*; Hans Urs von Balthasar, "Vérité et vie"; M.-D. Dubarle, "La vérification du discours de la foi." See also the following bibliographies: Adolphe Gesché, "Bibliographie raisonée: Le problème de Dieu dans le monde d'aujourd'hui," in *L'annonce de Dieu au monde d'aujourd'hui*, pp. 75–102; Nicolas Dunas, *Connaissance de la foi*, pp. 147–215. Note that, if a *rationalistic* approach to God is to be eschewed, in virtue of the radical inadequacy of human reason in respect of infinite Mystery (see Thomas Aquinas, *In Boethii de Trinitate*, q. 2, aa. 1, 3), a fortiori,

and still more vigorously, one must reject an *experimental* approach to God, which is to flirt with absurdity, and as it were to "tempt God." Thomas defines such an attitude precisely as *experimentum sumere [de Deo]," "explorare an Deus sciat,"* and the like (*Summa Theol.*, II-II, q. 97, a. 1). On the self-styled scientific proofs for the existence of God, see Ferdnand van Steenberghen, *Hidden God: How Do We Know That God Exists?* (Saint Louis, Herder, 1966, pp. 57–59, 82–118). Of God we may have at most a *cognitio experimentalis* or *ex compassione* (Denis the Areopagite): *Summa Theol.*, II-II, q. 97, a. 2, ad 2. Here, more than anywhere else, the criterion of verification is *internal*, in Pascal's sense, as also in that of Kierkegaard, who said, "There is but one proof of the Eternal One: faith in the Eternal One" (*La parole du coeur*).

30. Karl Marx himself discerned a *"schmutzigjüdische Erscheinungsform"* of praxis—a form of manifestation "sordidly Jewish"—identifiable with pragmatism. See Georg Lukács, *Existentialisme ou marxisme?* pp. 198ff., 282–90.

31. See 1 Cor., chaps. 1 and 2—not, however, that one must take the cross as a metaphysical *principle*, still less as a practical (an ascetical, ethical, or political) principle.

32. Consider Jürgen Moltmann's contribution, *The Crucified God*, where he insists on a "political theology of the cross." Here political theology is conceived as nailed to the cross of service. The cross itself becomes a "political critique." In sight of the cross, "the political social edifice no longer has any reality" (Hegel). To my view, however, Moltmann runs the recurrent risk of losing himself in the "clouds of mysticism," in virtue of an unbridled panlogist, garrulous dialectic. See also the study already cited, Moltmann, "Crítica teológica de la religión política," pp. 11–45.

33. For a critique of a short-circuited morality such as we hear expressed in slogans like "acting for the sake of acting," "creating for the sake of creating"—the morality, indeed, of the Nietzschian hero—see Raymond Polin, *La création des valeurs*, pp. 242–45; idem, *Ethique et politique*, vol. 1. Along the same lines: A. Grosser, *Au nom de quoi?* esp. pp. 62–67: "the ambiguous criterion of efficacy." "If the objective is the elimination of internal enemies and domination over neighboring peoples, fields of concentration are perfectly efficacious." Of course, "you may not be able to get away from them," says the author ironically, referring to Nazism (p. 63). And he asserts: "Only an antecedent hierarchization of finalities can lend the notion of efficacy any sense or meaning" (p. 67).

34. Max Weber (*Politics as a Vocation*, p. 41) proclaims *Distanz* a political virtue, and warns that its absence is "one of the deadly sins of every politician." Passion alone will never do. You must also have cold analysis. Maurice Merleau-Ponty, in his *Humanism and Terror*, p. 11, made his celebrated observation: "One does not become a revolutionary through science, but out of indignation. Science comes afterward, to fill in and delimit that open protest." Similarly, Mikel Dufrenne, *Pour l'homme* (Paris, Seuil, 1968), p. 56: "Who has ever plunged into the study of Marx without first having joined him in his indignation and hope?"

35. "Perhaps the greatest triumph of conservatism in the history of thought was when empirical verifiability became the criterion of truth. This was to abide by appearances, and since the datum which could be experienced was the prevailing situation, the status quo was set up as the criterion of truth and rationality. Any thought which might go beyond or transcend the status quo was automatically relegated to the catalogue of the irrational": José Miranda, *Marx and the Bible*, p. 261. See also Herbert Marcuse, *Ideologia da sociedade industrial* (Rio de Janeiro, Zahar, 1969), pp. 32–34, 94ff., where we read a critique of science as ideology, truth as verification, and pragmatism as the road to Fascism (p. 107, see also pp. 128, 146ff.). See also W. Ölmüller, "Problemas del proceso moderno," pp. 85ff.; Giulio Girardi, "Théorie et praxis," p. 103.

36. There is a rationalistic tendency abroad today that fails to recognize the possibility of an ethical rationality. Ethics is abandoned either to the caprice of individual options, as in Max Weber's position, or to the historical play of material forces, to which a kind of immanent morality is ascribed (Marxism). To reduce the exercise of reason to the horizon of empiricity, even historical empiricity, lends itself to positivism, which issues in the species of gutless morality called cynicism.

37. For the question of a rational ethics, see first of all the works of Georges Kalinowski: *Querelle de la science normative; Le problème de la verité en morale et en droit; Théorie de la connaissance; Etudes de logique déontique*, esp. pp. 237–56: "Edmund Husserl's logic of values." See also *Chrétiens et politique*, esp. chap. 4, pp. 73–96: "moral values and politics"; André Manaranche, *Y a-t-il une éthique sociale chrétienne?*; J.-M. Domenach, "Pour une éthique de l'engagement"; Josef Fuchs, *Existe-t-il une "morale chrétienne"?*; J.M. O'Connor, *São Paulo e a moral de nosso tempo*; René Coste, *Les communautés politiques*, esp. p. 43, n. 1: "Eléments de bibliographie"; G. Matai, *Morale politica*; Claude Geffré, "Y a-t-il une morale révolutionnaire?"; Jacques Ellul, *The Political Illusion*; Claude Bruaire, *La raison politique*. See also what has been said above on morality, in §§3 and 31.

38. As proposed by one of its most representative theoreticians, C. T. Kotarbinski, "praxeology" excluded, by definition, the moral question. See his "Idée de la méthodologie générale: Praxéologie," pp. 190–94; idem, "La notion de l'action."

39. See H. Bouillard, "La tâche actuelle de la théologie fondementale," esp. pp. 33ff.: "the process of verification"; Juan Alfaro, *Corso di aggiornamento teologico*, pp. 21–35: "the unity of orthodoxy and orthopraxy."

40. Charles Wackenheim, *Christianisme sans idéologie*, pp. 124–40: "faith as action." The idea of "faith" held by the author does not succeed in overcoming the dichotomy between awareness and structures.

41. See Rom. 3:19.

42. The eschatological "verification" of the truth of revelation, championed by Jewish apocalyptic, has been championed in an altogether particular manner in the writings of Wolfhart Pannenberg. See also Hans Urs von Balthasar, "Parole et histoire."

43. See *Gaudium et Spes*, no. 39.

44. See John 13:35, 17:21; Acts 4:32–35.

45. See the following contributions of Michel de Certeau: "La rupture instauratrice"; "L'articulation du 'dire' et du 'faire'"; "Qu-est-ce qu'un Congrès de Théologie?"; "Le prophète et les militaires: Dom Helder Câmara."

46. Paul Tillich (*Theology and Culture*, 159–72) recounts, in pathetic testimony, the reflections that came upon him when the Third Reich deprived him of his chair of philosophy in Frankfurt and he had to leave for the United States. And he observed: "If Hitler is the outcome of what we believed to be the true philosophy and the only theology, both must be false. With this rather desperate conclusion we left Germany" (p. 164). Then he tells of how, in the United States, his German "transcendentalism" was stalemated after every academic lecture, for someone would always ask "What shall we do?" (ibid.).

47. Hans Urs von Balthasar has underscored the connection in reality between theology and holiness. On this question, see J.-D. Torrel, "Théologie et sainteté," *Revue Thomiste* 71 (1971) 205–21 (with a good bibliography).

48. See Jean Ladrière, *L'articulation du sens*, pp. 227–41, where, by way of a general conclusion of his book, in extremely dense language, the author discusses the problem of the truth of the language of faith. Theological discourse, however, does not come in for consideration in its total difference from pistic discourse. Hence a bit of tightrope-

walking between self-realization as interior criterion of the word of faith, and "works," introduced somewhat unexpectedly as the "true criterion" of faith.

49. Here I am thinking of Martin Heidegger and his notion of the "destiny of being," and the luminous apparition of God. See J. B. Lotz, "Ni athéisme ni théisme dans la philosophie de Martin Heidegger"; Odette Laffoucrière, *Le destin de la pensée et le "mort de Dieu" selon Heidegger.*

50. See M. Velásquez, "Foi, espérance et action politique," pp. 386–87 and n. 7, on the "dialectic of inclusion."

51. See 1 Cor. 1:17–25.

52. "Der Mensch ist der Hirt des Seins" (Martin Heidegger, *Lettre sur l'humanisme*, pp. 76, 108).

53. Edward Schillebeeckx, *The Understanding of Faith*, p. 154.

54. The distinction between "problem" and "mystery" is that of Gabriel Marcel: *Etre et avoir*, p. 145; *Foi et réalité*, pp. 7–8; *Essai de philosophie concrète*, pp. 107–8.

55. Karl Rahner: "Theological speech is always inadequate, because every theological affirmation is conditioned by its *Verstehenshorizont*—hence the necessarily dialectical nature of theological language" (cf. "Theologische Erkenntnis- und Methodenlehre").

56. Let me recall here Gaston Fessard's beautiful paraphrase, in his *De l'actualité historique*, 1:23: "I am the Way, the Truth, and the Life—which I dare to translate: I am the Method for uniting Theory and Praxis."

CHAPTER 13

1. See Maurice Merleau-Ponty, *Résumé de cours*, pp. 77–87: "dialectical philosophy"; idem, *Les aventures de la dialectique*; Jean Ladrière, "Le langage théologique et le discours de la représentation," pp. 174–76: "speculative discourse as a journey through the desert."

2. It is obviously impossible to provide any other adequate foundation for the use of a dialectic than a dialectic one, as Jean-Paul Sartre has maintained in his *Critique of Dialectical Reason*. The fact is that dialectic is the only way to think the historical as issue of the rational in the contingency of the world, as Hegel suggested. Thus the Aristotelian categories are shown to be inadequate for thinking history as history. History came to awareness only with the appearance of the encyclopedists of the eighteenth century. See Gaston Fessard, *De l'actualité historique*, 1:13–25, where he considers whether Thomism can think the "historical" conceived as middle term between the "natural" (the necessary real, object of demonstrative science) and the "ideal" (the purely rational, object of the Aristotelian dialectic).

3. For a view of the whole, see P. Foulquié, *La dialectique*. In his conclusion, the author calls "dialectic" an ambiguous term, inasmuch as the common trait of all conceptions of this term is the *dynamism* of thought: dialectic is thought in motion. A historical view of the whole, with applications to the "social sciences," is offered by Georges Gurvitch, *Dialectique et sociologie*. See historical panorama, esp. since Descartes, sketched by Enrique D. Dussel, *Método para una filosofía de la liberación*. Basing himself on Levinas, Dussel attempts to transcend dialectical (Hegelian) thinking, which is that of the system of "the same," to arrive at an "analectical" thinking, whose point of departure is that it is outside the system (of "the other"—the oppressed person). Jean-Paul Sartre *(Critique of Dialectical Reason)* defines dialectic as the movement of being and knowing, determined by what he calls the human being's truth in process of totaliza-

tion. For Sartre, dialectical reason seeks a perpetual "passage beyond," in the direction of totality—a passage beyond positivistic, analytical reason, which is always partial, and, in the extreme case, false.

4. For a bibliography on the problematic of theory and praxis in general, and of praxis in particular, see Dieter Berdesinski, *Die Praxis, Kriterium für die Wahrheit des Glaubens?* pp. 168–70, a list of more than 30 titles, with emphasis on the German tradition; W. Post, "Theory und Praxis," col. 900–901, referring to 30 studies, likewise in German. See the following works: Immanuel Kant, *On the Old Saw*; Horst Stuke, *Philosophie der Tat*; Domingo G. Marques, *Ordem especulativa e ordem prâtica em Lenine*; A. de Waelhens, Jean Ladrière, J. Taminiaux, and Paul Ricoeur, in *Revue Philosophique de Louvain* 72 (1974): "truth and praxis"; B. Quelquejeu, "Les infortunes de la pensée et les prospérités de la pratique: Eléments pour l'histoire d'un mot," *Le Supplément* 118 (1976) 310–19; and R. Vancourt, "Idéologie, marxisme et 'dépassement' de la philosophie," esp. the third and last installment (1975), "Marxism and philosophies of action," where the author sets forth, critically, the principal pre-Marxian (pp. 5–16), Marxian (pp. 16–33), and Marxist (pp. 33–42) conceptions respecting the relationships between theory and praxis. Finally, see the basic study, of Marxist inspiration, by Jürgen Habermas, *Theory and Practice*.

5. Jürgen Habermas (*Protestbewegung und Hochschulreformen*, Frankfurt, 1969) has been one of the few theoreticians to have discerned this difference: "The systematic unification of theory and praxis does not produce a unification of scientific analysis and immediate preparation for political activity. Hence the demand for an institutional unification of science and planning cannot be founded on the necessity of a union between theory and praxis. These two must be separated" (p. 246). "Between science and planning, then, structural differences obtain, and these call for a clear institutional separation of the two domains. Their confusion will be to the prejudice of both. The pressure of praxis wreaks havoc on science, and political activity is led down blind alleys by a pseudo science geared directly to praxis" (p. 248) (both passages cited by Edward Schillebeeckx, "Teorias críticas e engajamento," p. 437). See also Habermas, *Toward a Rational Society*, p. 6. Herbert Marcuse writes in the same vein: *Ideologia da sociedade industrial* (Rio de Janeiro, Zahar, 3rd ed., 1969), pp. 125–41, 160–61.

6. One of the special traits of Bachelardian epistemology is its emphasis on the rationalism of modern science, as translated in a movement that goes from thought to the real and not in the opposite direction. In Bachelard, the primacy is conferred on the properly theoretical component of science. See the titles of Bachelard's works: "applied *rationalism*," "*rational* materialism," "*rationalistic* engagement," "*rationalistic* activity of contemporary science," and so forth. In his *La philosophie du Non*, p. 6, he states: one of the two metaphysical directions ought to be privileged: the one that moves from rationalism to experience." See further: Antoinette Virieux-Reymond, *Introduction à l'épistémologie*, pp. 114–17 (on Bachelard), 137–38 (appealing to Koyré); Georges Kalinowski, *Querelle de la science normative*, p. 79.

7. On the methodological circularity obtaining at every level of scientific practice, see Jean Ladrière, *L'articulation du sens*, pp. 25–50, esp. p. 49: the "circle of truth"; A. Vieira Pinto, *Ciência e existência*, chap. 3, 9, 10,11, where the author resorts to the dialectical method in order to give a satisfactory explanation of the scientific process, the analytic method having betrayed its insufficiency for such purpose.

8. Thus, prescinding from the "classist" nature of the social contraposition—intellectual work versus manual work, or free work versus servile work, or again liberal professions versus "the others"—one might well subscribe to what we read in an old

manuscript of the century of the Cluniac reform: *"Scribere qui nescit, nullum putat esse laborem: Tres digiti scribunt, totum corpusque laborat."*

9. The infinitude of knowledge is one of the aspects most emphasized by theoreticians of science: Kant, Comte, Bachelard, Einstein, and others. See Georges Gurvitch, *Dialectique et sociologie*, pp. 25ff.; Georges Thill, *La fête scientifique*, pp. 91, 160; Max Weber, "Science as a Vocation," p. 138: "Every scientific 'fulfilment' raises new 'questions'; it *asks* to be 'surpassed' and outdated. Whoever wishes to serve science has to resign himself to this fact."

10. See 1 Cor. 12:28: "Furthermore, God has set up in the church first apostles, second prophets, third teachers, then miracle workers, healers, assistants, administrators, and those who speak in tongues"; 1 Cor. 12:7–11; Rom. 12:6–8; Eph. 4:11; etc. For this question, see Paul Neuenzeit, ed., *Die Funktion der Theologie in Kirche und Gesellschaft*, esp. pp. 156–70: Norbert Greinacher, 'Theologie im Spannungsverhältnis von Theorie und Praxis"; Hans Joachim Kraus, *Reich Gottes*, pp. 77–84: on theology and its tasks today; V. Schurr, "Theologie im gesellschaftlichen Kontext," pp. 181–83 and 216–18, where we find a general view of "political theology"; finally, the entire issue no. 71 of *Lumière et Vie* 14 (1965): "theologians and the mission of the church."

11. Let us note that Western philosophical tradition has always made the relationship between theory and praxis a special subject of its reflection. Thus we have the classic conception of Aristotle, for whom the terms of the articulation between theory and practice in no way correspond to ours. Aristotle sees a neat distinction between *praxis* and *poiesis*. Praxis is a form of activity characterized by its immanence: its development is its own end—e.g., in thinking, willing, and so on. In this wise, philosophy, or any sort of theoretical activity, is praxis, in the most proper and noblest sense of the term. This is what occurs, as well, with the practice of the virtues. The activity of praxis is exercised beginning with the human being and bearing upon and ending with that same human being, be it on the level of reason or on that of the will. It is a matter of self-production, as it were. The scholastics translated *praxis* by *actio*, and the verb *prattein* by *agere*. As for the second form of activity *(operatio—poiesis)* the doctors of the church translated this by the word *productio*, and the corresponding verb—*poiein*—by *facere* or *producere*. This time we have a *transitive* activity: its finality is something other than itself. Now we are on the plane of arts and techniques. Politics, for Aristotle, is praxis, by the fact of its seizing upon the intellectual virtues *(aretai)*, in conjunction with prudence *(phronesis)*. But, like philosophy, politics can also become a manner of living, a lifestyle. Philosophy, however, for Aristotle, is superior to politics, because speculative (or mediative) praxis represents what is noblest (the divine) in the human being. See Aristotle's *Politics* and *Nicomachaean Ethics* (in the latter, esp. book 6, chap. 5; book 7, chap. 3; book 10, chap. 7–8). For this problematic in general, see Georg Picht, *Wahrheit, Vernunft, Verantwortung*, pp. 108–35: "the sense of the distinction between theory and praxis in Greek philosophy"; and pp. 135–40: "the sense of the distinction between theory and praxis in modern times"; Bruno Snell, *Theorie und Praxis im Denken des Abendlands*; Pierre Aubenque, *La prudence chez Aristotle*, with bibliography. As for Thomas Aquinas, who basically follows Aristotle, see Joseph de Finance, *Etre et agir dans la philosophie de Saint Thomas*; Jean-Yves Jolif, "Le sujet pratique selon St. Thomas d'Aquin"; C. J. Pinto de Oliveira, "D'une anthropologie à une morale politique"; but esp. H. Keraly, ed., *Saint Thomas d'Aquin: Préface à la Politique*, with bibliography, pp. 176–79. For Duns Scotus, see P. Scapin, "Liberté, Praxis et Incarnation selon Duns Scot" (Paris, Aubier-Montaigne, 1975). Here I must recall Karl Marx's famous statement: "Already the British schoolman, *Duns Scotus*, asked

'*whether it was impossible for matter to think?*' . . . he made *theology* preach *materialism*" (*The Holy Family*, p. 127). Obviously it will be impossible for me to expand on the question of contemplation and action here: it would deserve a whole study of its own.

In current usage, "praxis" means both types of activity discerned by Aristotle. But whereas for Aristotle knowledge was the praxis par excellence, for us it is knowledge generally that is contradistinguished from praxis. Primarily owing to the ideological and historical pressure of Marxism, praxis is no longer understood as its own end, *Selbstzweck*, self-finalized activity—but on the contrary, as the production of an external result. Praxis is action resulting in an effect of transformation, even in the cognitive field. It is what causes theoretical practice to be defined as "production of knowledge." The semantic reverse of the term is total, then. However, Marxists have not always succeeded in avoiding the pitfall of pragmatism or of positivism, to which an undifferentiated notion of praxis tends to lead: see Jürgen Moltmann, *L'espérance en action*, pp. 40-52. It has been proposed, therefore, to distinguish a praxis-production, in the noble sense of the term, from a praxis-fabrication, a technical action, an inferior action, one of a lower grade, one maintaining an extrinsic relationship with its object: see Ernst Bloch, *Das Prinzip Hoffnung*, pp. 321-22; Louis Althusser, *Philosophie et philosophie spontanée des savants*, pp. 40-48, 58-61. Meanwhile, it will be in order to give due credit to the young Marx, who, in his manuscripts of 1844, following in the footsteps of Hegel, understood praxis, esp. in the form of productive work, as the *Selbsterzeugungsakt* or the *Fürsichwerden des Menschen*: see G. M. Cottier, "Athéisme et marxisme: Marx," section 3: "praxis," esp. pp. 176-77.

For material bearing generally on what I have been discussing, see further: R. Vancourt, "Anthropologie thomiste et anthropologie marxiste"; E. Weil, "Pratique et praxis," in *Encyclopaedia Universalis*, 13:449-53.

12. See Karl Marx, First Thesis on Feuerbach: "The chief defect of all previous materialism (that of Feuerbach included) is that things *[Gegenstand]*, reality, sensuousness are conceived only in the form of the *object or of contemplation*, but not as *sensuous human activity, practice* . . . " (*Theses on Feuerbach*, p. 3; as well as theses 5 and 9: "sensuousness as practical activity" (ibid., pp. 4-5). Martin Heidegger, however, in his *Lettre sur humanisme*, warns against a "technical interpretation of thinking" (p. 194), which "may be compared to the procedure of trying to evaluate the nature and powers of a fish by seeing how long it can live on dry land" (p. 195).

13. See Michel de Certeau, *La culture au pluriel*, esp. part 3: "cultural policies," pp. 191ff.

14. This is what phenomenology has consistently shown, and has called "passive genesis." See Jean Ladrière, *Vie sociale et destinée*, pp. 28-29. Here it will be appropriate to recall the whole contribution of psychoanalysis. See also Julian Marías, *Antropologia metafísica*, chap. 27, p. 221, as well as pp. 58, 60, 84, 102, 167; A. Methol Ferré, "Política y teología de la liberación," p. 7; Pierre Furter, *Educação e reflexão*, chap. 2, section 5: "reflection and action." Furter (p. 28) distinguishes simple "thinking," which inevitably accompanies every human action, from "reflecting," which is a "thinking to the second power," and which permits the conscious appropriation of acting itself.

15. For the *perichoresis* under consideration here, let us listen to Hegel: "The theoretical is essentially contained in the practical; we must decide against the idea that the two are separate. . . . The will determines itself and this determination is in the first place something inward, because what I will I hold before my mind." Conversely, "a man . . . can just as little be theoretical or think without a will, because in thinking he is of necessity being active. The content of something thought has the form of being; but this being

is something mediated, something established through our activity. Thus these distinct attitudes cannot be divorced; they are one and the same; and in any activity, whether of thinking or willing, both moments are present" (*Hegel's Philosophy of Right*, p. 227).

16. Fernando Belo speaks of "The practice of the hands or charity," and "the practice of the eyes or faith" (*A Materialist Reading*, pp. 244–52).

17. Hegel: "It must not be imagined that man is half thought and half will, and that he keeps thought in one pocket and will in another, for this would be a foolish idea" (*Hegel's Philosophy of Right*, p. 226). Hegel then goes on to establish the difference, as well as the unity, between the "theoretical attitude" *(theoretisches Verhalten)* and the "practical attitude" *(praktisches Verhalten)* (ibid., pp. 226–27).

18. "The most salient feature of Opportunism is hostility to 'theory' " (Rosa Luxemburg, *Oeuvres*, Paris, Maspero, p.86; see also pp. 85–90, "opportunism in theory and in practice," as well as pp. 18–22). Note, meanwhile, that the rejection of "theory" means, concretely, esp. among youth, the rejection of empty verbalism and hollow phraseology. In reality, there is nothing more practical than a good theory.

19. It seems to me that the term "positivism" straddles two distinct practices: theoretical practice and ethico-political practice. Perhaps it would be better to speak of "empiricism" for the former and "pragmatism" for the latter. Dubarle speaks of two scientisms—the first a "scientism of doctrine," connected with Kant, Comte, and others, and the "second scientism," a "scientism of life," bound to the "ideology of the time," and opposed to metaphysics, religion, esthetics: "Epistémologie des sciences humaines," pp. 239–45.

20. See Michel de Certeau, *La culture au pluriel*, esp. parts 1 and 2; de Certeau, Dominique Julia, and Jacques Revel, *Une politique de la langue: La Révolution Française et les patois* (Paris, Gallimard, 1975). For theology in particular, see Jacques Maritain, "Le tenant-lieu de théologie chez les simples."

21. Remarking the disappearance of whole zoological groups, and the current disintegration of the great world religions as a result of secularization, Jacques Monod has called into question "the future and lot" of "objective cognition," which seems not really to guarantee anything (cited in Louis Althusser, *Philosophie et philosophie spontanée*, p. 52).

22. Inasmuch as I refer so often to Althusser's thought, I feel obliged to register here my disagreement with him, not on his properly theoretical positions, but on the value that he tacitly attributes to these positions in a spirit of what appears to me to be a certain rationalism. This emerges most clearly when Althusser is discoursing on living experience *(le vécu)*—e.g., in *Lire le capital*, 1:75–78, 145 (= *Reading Capital*, pp. 61–63, 115); and on "ideology"—e.g., in his *Pour Marx*, pp. 238–43. In my opinion, he fails to do justice to these realities. To be sure, he denies them what empiricism unduly attributes to them: scientific virtue. But he does not appear to credit them with their due. He is too little the philosopher here, remaining within the mental pale of rationalism, or locked into the narrow circle of dialectic. Here Lucien Goldmann is on the mark with his criticisms of rationalism, even "mechanism," in Althusser the philosopher (Goldmann, *Marxisme et sciences humaines*, p. 166).

23. A well-presented illustration of this articulation is to be found in Paulo Freire's consideration of conscience and revolution in his *Pedagogy of the Oppressed*, pp. 119–37. Another illustration, a more systematic one, dialecticizing horizontalism and verticalism on the fulcrum of the historical, is that of Ignacio Ellacuría, "Tesis sobre la posibilidad, necesidad y sentido de una teología latinoamericana," pp. 340–41 (section 9.4.1).

24. Although here I take my inspiration from the thinking of Marxism—where else?—I do not wish to employ its categories because their theoretical content has not yet clearly emerged. Here it will be enough to sketch the principles of this dialectic. See the very difficult study by Louis Althusser, in *Pour Marx*, pp. 161–224: "materialist dialectic." See also G. M. Cottier, "Athéisme et marxisme: Engels," where we learn that dialectic consists of the following points: (1) there is nothing absolute but movement; (2) contradiction is the wellspring of movement; (3) the world is process; and the laws of dialectic are: (a) the passage from quantity to quality; (b) the compenetration of contraries; (c) the negation of negation. Thus we perceive that Marxist materialism conceives dialectic within certain limits. Marx himself said: "The dialectical form of exposition is correct only when it knows its limits" (cited in Louis Althusser, *Positions*, p. 127); and Feuerbach: "Dialectic is not a monologue of speculation with its 'own self,' but a dialogue of speculation with empiry. A thinker is a dialectical one only in the measure that he is his own adversary. To call oneself into question—behold the supreme art and virtue" (*Manifestes philosophiques*, p. 32).

25. See Jean Ladrière, *Vie sociale et destinée*, pp. 76–79, 195–96.

26. Karl Marx: There are those who make history (praxis)—but they do not always know that it is they who are making history (theory). Nor do they always know *what* they are doing (theory of praxis).

27. Dialectic is the demummification of all system, including dialectical system. Here I am thinking of Hegel, and then of Marx, each of whom claimed to have found the key to the "mystery of history." In §19, I had something to say on what the Christian faith thinks about this mystery. On the dialecticization of dialectic, see Jean-Paul Sartre, *Critique of Dialectical Reason*; Paul Foulquié, *La dialectique*, p. 116; Werner Post, "Theorie und Praxis," col. 899; Karl Rahner, "Theologische Erkenntnis- und Methodenlehre." The last two authors assert that the conception of the relationship between theory and praxis has always been itself historical, varying in every era, and that therefore it must constantly be taken up and examined anew. If we admit that it is dialectic alone that is the key to the correct thinking of history, then we cannot think that we shall one day succeed in solving, dialectically, the "mystery of history." In solving the mystery, the thinking would cease to be dialectical. Dialectic would now be dead, turned into a system, a frozen current, as has happened with Hegelianism and dialectical materialism. If dialectic is the only way of thinking that will grasp historical intelligibility, this can be true only in the sense that it is a *systematic antisystem*. It is thus that it "solves" the problem of history; by destroying any pretension of being able to solve it, including any pretension of its own. For dialectic, history is no longer grasped in the rationale of an enigma to solve, but in the rationale of a task to execute, a work to accomplish—in a word, a creation.

28. The theory-and-praxis problem is "insoluble," according to P. Valéry (cited in Lucien Goldmann, *Structures mentales et création culturelle*, p. 79).

29. Johannes B. Metz posits the problem of dialectic in theological terms, but, for want of the necessary theoretical mediations, fails to emerge from the abstract. See his *Theology of the World*, pp. 13–104, 134–35, 148, n. 12. The subtitle of the original German edition of his work is symptomatic of the universalizing pretensions of a certain theology: "*society, politics, peace.*" After all, in theory as well, our "eyes may be bigger than our stomach," and "a bird in the hand is worth two in the bush." Let us remember here that the tendency to global syntheses constitutes precisely one of the "epistemological obstacles" cited by Gaston Bachelard—that of "unitary cognition" (*La formation de l'esprit scientifique*, pp. 83–91). Obviously this problem presents itself differently in

theology and in other disciplines. But my critique here is directed against what Bachelard himself calls a "bargain-basement unity" (ibid., p. 86).

30. For my part, I consider the correlatives secular/religious as absolutely *necessary in order to be able to think theologically*. The true problem with these categories is not of a *semantic* order, but of a *syntactic* one—i.e., of the manner of their mutual articulation. For the theoretical basis of this distinction, see chap. 6 and 7, above.

31. See J. Guichard, "Communautés de base et contexte politique," esp. pp. 97-102, where the author distinguishes the base ecclesial community as specific locus of religious and theological formation from the political party and other, similar, organizations as locus of strategic and political formation.

32. See Gaston Bachelard, *Le nouvel esprit scientifique*, chap. 6: "non-Cartesian epistemology." Here, over against the immediate intuition of "simple and distinct ideas," Bachelard proposes the notion of the *production* of the simple (the simplified) and the clear (the clarified): pp. 139ff.

33. Gregory of Nazianzus, Oratio 27, 3, chap. 13-16: "Not all . . . can philosophize upon God, far from it! For it is not a facile undertaking, nor is it for infants still creeping. . . . To whom will the task fall? To those who dedicate themselves to it with seriousness, not as if it were just one more task among others, or as if it were a hobby, or like attending the theater, or concerts, or some other recreation, or even something lower than these" (cited in Philotheus Boehner and Etienne Gilson, *História da filosofia cristã*, p. 86); Anselm of Canterbury, cited in ibid., pp. 274-75; Lacordaire, *Mémoire pour le rétablissement en France de l'ordre des Frères Prêcheurs*, chap. 4: "The *Doctor Catholicus* is almost impossible—someone who must know, on the one hand, the whole deposit of faith, the scriptures, the acts of the papacy, and, on the other, what Saint Paul calls the elements of the world—that is, everything about everything" (cited in Yves Congar, *La foi et la théologie*, p. 195, n. 2). Congar himself: "It may perhaps be impossible for a single individual to produce a complete theology, synthesizing at once the inspirations and contributions of all research" (ibid., p. 272). Erasmus, *Lettre à Dorpius*, XVII, pp. 210-11: "I hold the theological science in such high esteem that I habitually reserve to it alone the name of science. So highly do I respect and venerate [the] order [of theologians] that in it alone have I wished to be enrolled, although modesty prevents me from arrogating to myself so eminent a title; for I am not ignorant of the titles of erudition and of life attaching to the name of theologian. There is something of the superhuman in the theologian's profession *(Nescio quid nomine majus profitetur qui theologum profitetur)*." René Descartes, *Discourse on Method*, p. 43, averred that, if he wished to do theology, "it was necessary . . . to be more than a mere man." Etienne Gilson: "A theologian is not a matter of improvisation. . . . Fifty years of metaphysics do not suffice for introducing the novice to the sense of the rudiments of doctrine" (*Introduction à la philosophie chrétienne*, Paris, Vrin, 1960, p. 224). Thomas Aquinas, *Summa Contra Gentiles*, book 1, chap. 4: For theological practice, *"multa praecognoscere oportet"*: indeed, a *"totius philosophiae consideratio"* is postulated, which involves *"longum tempus," "longum exercitium," "cum magno labore studii."*

34. Gaston Bachelard shows that in the 18th century a consideration of the difficulty of a theory served to disqualify it. Science had to be easy: if it were not, this would be unjust to those of less brilliant endowments! Bachelard reports the historical case of Father Castel, who declared war on Newton for the sole reason that the latter's physics seemed to him to be too "complicated" (Bachelard, *La formation de l'esprit scientifique*, pp. 228-31).

35. See G. Cottier, "Quelques réflexions sur la situation du théologien en temps de crise."

36. See Gustavo Gutiérrez, *The Power of the Poor in History*, pp. 169–221: "Theology from the Underside of History," where, along the lines of historical materialism, it is shown that theological thought, like all thought, is conditioned by the social conditions prevailing where the thought is actually being processed; Jean-Yves Jolif, "Le temps fait beaucoup à l'affaire," esp. pp. 194–96: praxis and faith. My own position, moreover, coincides with that of Martin Heidegger: see above, chap. 12, n. 49, p. 328.

Bibliographic References

The titles of primary resources are preceded by a solid circle (•).

Albert, Hans. • *Trakat über kritische Vernunft*. Tübingen, Mohr, 1975.

Alfaro, Juan. *Corso di aggiornamento teologico*. Milan, 1973.

_____. *Cristianismo y justicia*. Madrid, Propaganda Popular Católica, 1973.

_____. *Esperanza cristiana y liberación del hombre*. Barcelona, Herder, 1972.

_____. *Hacia una teología del progreso humano*. Barcelona, Herder, 1969.

_____. • "Teología, filosofía y ciencias humanas," *Gregorianum 55 (1974) 209–38*.

Alonso, J. • "Una nueva forma de hacer teología," in Alonso et al., *Iglesia y praxis de liberación*, pp. 50–87.

_____. • "La teología de la praxis y la praxis de la teología," *Christus* (Mexico City) 444 (1972) 28–41.

_____, et al. • *Iglesia y praxis de liberación*. Salamanca, Sígueme, 1974.

Alszeghy, Zoltan, and Flick, Maurizio. *Introductory Theology*. Denville, N.J., Dimension, 1983.

Althusser, Louis. • "L'Eglise en crise?—Diagnostics," *Lumière et Vie* 18 (1969) 26–29.

_____. • *Elements of Self-Criticism, Essays in Self-Criticism*.

_____. • *Essays in Self-Criticism*. Atlantic Highlands, N.J., Humanities Press, 1976. (Includes translations of *Réponse à John Lewis*, Paris, Maspero, 1973, and *Eléments d'autocritique*, Paris, Hachette, 1974.)

_____. • *Lenin and Philosophy and Other Essays*. New York/London, Monthly Review Press, 1971.

_____. • *Philosophie et philosophie spontanée des savants: Cours de philosophie pour scientifiques*. Paris, Maspero, 1973, 2 vols.

_____. • *Politics and History: Montesquieu, Rousseau, Hegel, Marx*. New York, Schocken, 1978.

_____. • *Positions*. Paris, Ed. Sociales, 1976.

_____. • *Pour Marx*. Paris, Maspero, 1965. (English translation, *For Marx*, New York, Schocken, 1979.)

_____. *Reading Capital*. New York, Schocken, 1979. (French edition, *Lire le capital*, Paris, Maspero, 1973.)

_____. *Response to John Lewis*, in *Essays in Self-Criticism*.

Alves, Rubem. • *A Theology of Human Hope*. New York, Corpus, 1971.

Amsler, Samuel. *L'Ancien Testament dans l'Eglise: Essai d'herméneutique chrétienne*. Neuchâtel/Paris, Delachaux/Niestlé, 1960.

Amsterdamski, S. "L'évolution de la science: Réforme et contre-réforme," *Diogène* 89 (1975).

L'analyse du langage théologique: Le Nom de Dieu. Paris, Aubier-Montaigne, 1969.

Antiseri, Dario. • *Foi sans métaphysique ni théologie*. Paris, Cerf, 1970.

338   *BIBLIOGRAPHIC REFERENCES*

_____. • *I fondamenti epistemologici del lavoro interdisciplinaire*. Rome, Armando, 1972.

Aquinas, Thomas. • *In libros Politicorum Aristotelis expositio*, Proemium, nos. 1–8.

_____. • *In Librum Boethii de Trinitate*. Paris, Lethielleux, 1881.

_____. • "De Prudentia," *Summa Theologiae*, II-II, qq. 47–56.

_____. • *Quaestiones Quodlibetales*, IV, aa. 17–18. Paris, Lethielleux, 1926.

_____. • *Summa contra Gentiles*, esp. chap. 1. Turin, Marietti, 1927.

_____. • *Summa Theologiae*, I, qq. 84–89: on human thought.

_____. • *La théologie*, I, Prologue and Question 1. French translation, notes, and appendixes by H.-D. Gardeil. Paris/Turin/Rome, Desclée et Cie., 1968.

Arias, M. *Salvação hoje: Entre o cativeiro e la libertação*. Petrópolis, Vozes, 1974.

Aristotle. *Metaphysics*. Translated by W. D. Ross. In *The Works of Aristotle*, vol. 1. Chicago/London/Toronto, Encyclopaedia Britannica, 1952.

_____. • *Nicomachaean Ethics*. Translated by W. D. Ross. In *The Works of Aristotle*, vol. 2. Chicago/London/Toronto, Encyclopaedia Britannica, 1952.

_____. *Physics*. Translated by R. P. Gardie and R. K. Gaye. In *The Works of Aristotle*, vol. 1. Chicago/London/Toronto, Encyclopaedia Britannica, 1952.

_____. • *Politics*. Translated by Benjamin Jowett. In *The Works of Aristotle*, vol. 2. Chicago/London/Toronto, Encyclopaedia Britannica, 1952.

_____. *Posterior Analytics*. Translated by G. R. G. Mure. In *The Works of Aristotle*, vol. 1. Chicago/London/Toronto, Encyclopaedia Britannica, 1952.

_____. • *On Sophistical Refutations*. Translated by W.A. Picard-Cambridge, in *The Works of Aristotle*, vol. 1. Chicago/London/Toronto, Encyclopaedia Britannica, 1952 (also, in *Aristotle, On Sophistical Refutations, on Coming-to-Be and Passing Away, on the Cosmos*, Loeb Classical Library, no. 400, Harvard University Press).

_____. • *Topics*. Translated by W. A. Pickard-Cambridge. In *The Works of Aristotle*, vol. 1. Chicago/London/Toronto, Encyclopaedia Britannica, 1952.

Armbruster, Carl. J. *The Vision of Paul Tillich*. New York, Sheed & Ward, 1967.

Aron, Raymond. *Dimensions de la conscience historique*. Paris, Union Gén. d'Editions, 1961 (2nd ed., Paris, Plon, 1964).

_____. *Dix-huit leçons sur la société industrielle*. Paris, Gallimard, 1962.

_____. *Introduction to the Philosophy of History: An Essay on the Limits of Historical Objectivity*. Boston, Beacon, 1961; Westport, Conn., Greenwood, 1976.

Arquillière, Henri-Xavier. *L'Augustinisme politique: Essai sur la formation des théories politiques au Moyen Age*. Paris, Vrin, 1934; 2nd ed., 1955.

Assmann, Hugo. • "Aspetti fondamentali della riflessione teologica nel'America Latina e valutazione critica della 'teologia della liberazione,'" in Assmann et al., *Teologie dal Terzo Mondo*, pp. 37–53.

_____. "Compromiso político no contexto de luta de clase," *Concilium* 84 (1973) 473–81.

_____. "Seminario: Consciencia cristiana y situaciones extremas en el cambio social," in Scannone et al., *Fe cristiana y cambio social*, pp. 335–43.

_____. • "Teología política," *Perspectivas de Diálogo* 50 (1970) 306–12.

_____. • *Theology for a Nomad Church*. Maryknoll, N.Y., Orbis, 1973.

_____, et al. • *Teologie dal Terzo Mondo: Teologia nera e teologia latino-americana della liberazione*. Brescia, Queriniana, 1974.

Aubenque, A. "Philosophie et idéologie," *Archives de Philosophie* 22 (1959) 483–520.

Aubenque, Pierre. *La prudence chez Aristotle*. Paris, Presses Universitaires de France, 1963.

Audinet, J. "Questions de méthode," in Audinet et al., *Recherches actuelles*, 1:73–98.

_____, et al. • *Recherches actuelles*. Paris, Beauchesne, 2 vols., 1971–72.

Autrement, 2 (1975). • *Eglise: L'épreuve du vide.*

Avila, Rafael. *Teología, evangelización y liberación.* Bogotá, Paulinas/Indo-American Press Service, 1973.

Bachelard, Gaston. *L'activité rationaliste de la physique contemporaine.* Paris, Presses Universitaires de France, 1951.

_____. • *L'engagement rationaliste.* Paris, Presses Universitaires de France, 1972.

_____. • *Epistémologie: Textes choisis.* Paris, Presses Universitaires de France, 5th ed., 1975.

_____. • *La formation de l'esprit scientifique: Contribution à une psychanalyse de la connaissance objective.* Paris, Vrin, 8th ed., 1972.

_____. *Le matérialisme rationnel.* Paris, Presses Universitaires de France, 1953.

_____. • *Le nouvel esprit scientifique.* Paris, Presses Universitaires de France, 12th ed., 1973. (Porguguese translation, *O novo espírito científico*, São Paulo, Abril, 1974.)

_____. • *La Philosophie du Non: Essai d'une philosophie du nouvel esprit scientifique.* Paris, Presses Universitaires de France, 6th ed., 1973.

_____. • *Le rationalisme appliqué.* Paris, Presses Universitaires de France, 5th ed., 1975.

Balibar, Etienne, and Macherey, P. • "Epistémologie," in *Encyclopoedia Universalis*, 6:370–73.

Bandera, Armando. • *La Iglesia ante el proceso de liberación.* Madrid, Católica, 1975.

Banning, Willem. • *Over de ontmoeting van theologie en sociologie.* Amsterdam, 1946.

_____. • *Theologie en sociologie: Eenterreinverkenning en inleiding.* Assen, 1936.

Barth, Karl. *Community, State, and Church: Three Essays.* Garden City, N.Y., Doubleday, 1960.

Barthes, Roland, et al. *Exégèse et herméneutique: Parole de Dieu.* Paris, Seuil, 1971.

Bauer, Gerhard. *Towards a Theology of Development: An Annotated Bibliography.* Geneva, Sodepax, 1970.

Baum, Gregory. • "Sociologia e teologia," *Concilium* (1974) 25–33.

Bayer, Raymond, ed. • *L'unité de la science: la méthode et les méthodes (IV),* Part 1: *Travaux du IXe Congrès International de Philosophie.* Paris, Hermann, 1937.

Bellet, Maurice. • *Déplacement de la religion: Recherche sur la région réelle de la foi chrétienne.* Paris, Desclée de Brouwer, 1972.

Belo, Fernando. • *Uma leitura política do Evangelho.* Lisbon, Multinova, 1974.

_____. • *A Materialist Reading of the Gospel of Mark.* Maryknoll, N.Y., Orbis, 1981.

Benveniste, Emile. *Problems in General Linguistics.* University of Miami Press, 1971.

Berdesinski, Dieter. • *Die Praxis, Kriterium für die Wahrheit des Glaubens? Untersuchungen zu einem Aspect politischer Theologie.* Munich, Don Bosco, 1973 (bibliography, pp. 165–74).

Berger, Peter L. • *A Rumor of Angels: Modern Society and the Rediscovery of the Supernatural.* Garden City, N.Y., Doubleday, 1969.

_____. • *The Sacred Canopy: Elements of a Sociological Theory of Religion.* Garden City, N.Y., Doubleday, 1967.

_____. • "Sociology and Theology," *Theology Today* (1967) 329–36.

_____. "Some Second Thoughts on Substantive Versus Functional Definitions of Religion," *Journal for the Scientific Study of Religion* 12 (1974) 125–33.

_____, and Luckmann, Theodore. *The Social Construction of Reality: Treatise on the Sociology of Knowledge*. Garden City, N.Y., Doubleday, 1966.

Berkhoff, H., ed. *Diskussion über die "Theologie der Hoffnung."* Munich/Mainz, Kaiser/Grünewald, 1970.

Bettelheim, Charles. *Initiation aux recherches sur les idéologies économiques et les réalités sociales*. Paris, 1948.

• *A Bíblia na Igreja depos da "Dei Verbum": Estudos sobre a Constituição Conciliar*. Translated from the Italian by R. Vidigal. Bíblica, no. 13. São Paulo, Paulinas, 1971.

Bigo, Pierre. • *The Church and Third World Revolution*. Maryknoll, N.Y., Orbis, 1977.

_____. "El 'instrumental científico' marxista," in CELAM, *Liberación*, pp. 247–51.

_____. "Marxismo y liberación en América Latina," in CELAM, *Liberación*, pp. 236–46.

Biot, François. • *Théologie et Politique: Foi et Politique, éléments de réflexion*. Paris, Ed.Universitaires, 1972.

Birnbaum, N. *The Sociological Study of Ideology (1949–1960): A Trend Report and Bibliography*. Oxford, Blackwell, 1962.

Bispos do Centro-Oeste (Brazil). • "Marginalização de um povo: Grito das Igrejas." May 6, 1973.

Bispos e Superiores Religiosos do Nordeste (Brazil). • *Eu ouvi os clamores do meu povo*. Salvador, Beneditina, 1973.

Blanché, R. • *L'epistémologie*. Paris, Presses Universitaires de France, 1972.

Blanquart, P. • "L'acte de croire et l'action politique," *Lumière et Vie* 19 (1970) 12–30.

Bloch, Ernst. *Das Prinzip Hoffnung*. Frankfurt, Suhrkamp, 1959.

Blondel, Maurice. *Action: Essay on a Critique of Life and a Science of Practice*. Notre Dame University Press, 1984.

_____. • *Essai d'une critique de la vie et d'une science de la pratique*. Paris, Presses Universitaires de France, 3d ed., 1973.

Bochenski, Joseph. • *The Logic of Religion*. New York University Press, 1965.

Boff, Clodovis. "Foi Jesus um revolucionário?," *Revista Eclesiástica Brasileira* 31 (1971) 97–118.

_____. "Teologia das relações Igreja-Estado," *Vozes* 71 (1977) 5–24.

Boff, Leonardo. "Ciência e técnica modernas e pensar teológico: Recolocação de um velho problema," *Grande Sinal* 29 (1975) 243–59.

_____. *O destino do homen e do mundo: Essaio sobre a vocação humana*. Petrópolis, Vozes, 1973.

_____. *A graça libertadora no mundo*. Petrópolis, Vozes, 1976.

_____. • *Die Kirche als Sakrament im Horizont der Welterfahrung: Versuch einer Legitimation und einer struktur-funktionalistischen Grundlegung der Kirche im Anschluss an das II. Vatikanische Konzil*. Paderborn, Bonifacius, 1972.

_____. *A ressureição de Cristo, a nossa ressurreição na morte*. Petrópolis, Vozes, 1972.

_____. "Salvação em Jesus Cristo e processo de libertação," *Concilium* 96 (1974) 753–64.

_____. "Tentativa de solução ecumênica para o problema da inspiração e da inerrância," *Revista Eclesiástica Brasileira* 30 (1970) 648–67.

_____. • *Teologia do cativeiro e da libertação*. Lisbon, Multinova, 1976.

_____. "Teologia e semiótica," *Vozes* 70 (1976) 325–34.

_____. *A vida religiosa e a Igreja no proceso de libertação*. Petrópolis/Rio de Janeiro, Vozes/CNBB, 2nd ed., 1976.

Böhner, Philotheus, and Gilson, Etienne. *História da filosofia cristã: Desde as origens até Nicolau de Cusa*. Petrópolis, Vozes, 1970.

Boisset, Louis. • *La théologie en procès face à la critique marxiste*. Paris, Centurion, 1974.

Bolan, V. *Sociologia da secularização: A composição de um novo modelo cultural*. Petrópolis, Vozes, 1972.

Bonhoeffer, Dietrich. *Christ the Center*. New York, Harper & Row, 1966.

Bopp, Linus. *Unsere Seelsorge in geschichtlicher Sendung*. Freiburg, Herder, 1952.

Bouillard, H. • "L'idée de surnaturel et le mystère chrétien," in Welte et al., *L'homme devant Dieu*, 3:153–66.

_____. "La tâche actuelle de la théologie fondementale," in Audinet et al., *Recherches actuelles*, pp. 7–49.

Bourdieu, Pierre. • *Esquisse d'une théorie de la pratique*. Geneva, Droz, 1972. (English translation, *Outline of a Theory of Practice*, Cambridge University Press, 1977.)

_____, and Passeron, Jean-Claude. *La reproduction*. Paris, Minuit, 1970.

_____, et al., eds. • *Le métier de sociologue: Préalables épistémologiques*. Paris/The Hague, Mouton, 2nd ed., 1973.

Bourgeault, Guy, et al. *Quand les églises se vident: Vers une théologie de la pratique*. Paris/Tournai, Desclée de Brouwer; Montreal, Bellarmin, 1974.

Bourgy, P. • "Un colloque sur théologie et sociologie," *Evangéliser* 108 (1964) 563–72.

Bouthoul, Gaston. *Sociologie de la politique*. Paris, Presses Universitaires de France, 3rd ed., 1971.

Brandon, S.G.F. *Jesus and the Zealots*. Manchester University Press, 1967.

_____. *The Trial of Jesus of Nazareth*. New York, Stein and Day, 1968. (Popular version of *Jesus and the Zealots*.)

Bravo, Carlos. • "Notas marginales a la teología de la liberación," *Ecclesiástica Xaveriana* (Bogotá) 24 (1974) 3–60.

Breton, S. "Logique et argumentation de convenance," in Breton et al., *La recherche en philosophie*.

_____. • "Le paradoxe du menteur et le problème de l'indicible dans les énoncés de foi," in de Waelhens et al., *Mito e fede*, pp. 517–46.

_____. *Théologie et idéologie*. Lyons, Profac, 1971.

_____, et al. • *La recherche en philosophie et en théologie*. Paris, Cerf, 1970.

Brown, D.M. *Ultimate Concern: Tillich in Dialogue*. London, SCM, 1965.

Brown, Raymond E. "Hermeneutics," in Brown et al., *The Jerome Biblical Commentary*, 2:605–23.

_____, Fitzmyer, Joseph A., and Murphy, Roland E., eds. *The Jerome Biblical Commentary*. Englewood Cliffs, N.J., Prentice-Hall; London/Dublin, Chapman, 1968.

Bruaire, Claude. *La raison politique*. Paris, Fayard, 1974.

Bultmann, Rudolf. *Faith and Understanding*. New York, Harper & Row, 1969.

_____. *Jésus*. Paris, Seuil, 1958.

_____. *Jesus and the Word*. New York, Scribner's, 1962.

_____. *Jesus Christ and Mythology*. New York, Scribner's, 1958.

_____. *Primitive Christianity in Its Contemporary Setting*. London/New York, Collins/Thames & Hudson, 1956.

_____. *Theology of the New Testament*. New York, Scribner's, 1970.

Bunge, Mario. • *Ética y ciencia*. Buenos Aires, Siglo Veintiuno, 1971.

Cahiers pour l'Analyse, 9 (1968). • *Généalogie des sciences*.

Caillois, R. "L'utopie négative et la religion," *Diogène* 87 (1974) 44–60.

Camus, Albert. *The Rebel*. New York, Knopf, 1954.

Cardoso, F.H. *O modelo político brasileiro e outros ensaios*. São Paulo, Difução Européia do Livro, 2nd ed., 1973.

Carrez, M., et al. *Orientations*. Paris, Beauchesne, 1973.

Carrier, H. • "Pour une politique de la recherche dans l'Eglise," *Gregorianum* 53 (1972) 5–42.

Casalis, Georges. *Idéologies de libération et message du Salut*. Strasbourg, Cerdic, 1973.

_____. • "Politique, foi et discernement," in Metz and Schlick, *Politique et Foi*, pp. 184–210.

_____. • "Théologie pratique et pratique de la théologie," in Carrez, *Orientations*, pp. 85–105.

Casanova, Antoine. *Vatican II et l'évolution de l'Eglise*. Paris, Ed. Sociales, 1969.

Casper, Bernhard, Hemmerle, Klaus, and Hünermann, Peter. • *Theologie als Wissenschaft: Methodische Zugänge*. Freiburg, Herder, 1970.

Castelli, Enrico, et al. *I presupposti di una teologia della storia*. Milan, Fratelli Bocca, 1952.

Cazelles, H. *Ecriture, Parole et Esprit: Trois aspects de l'herméneutique biblique*. Tournai/Paris, Desclée, 1971.

CEDIAL. • *Desarollo y revolución: Iglesia y Liberación—Bibliografía*, 2 vols. and supplement. Bogotá, 1973.

CELAM (Consejo Episcopal Latinoamericano). • *Liberación: Diálogos en el CELAM*. Bogotá, Secretariado General de CELAM, 1974 (Doc-CELAM, no. 16).

_____. • "Presença da Igreja na atual transformação da América Latina," SEDOC 1 (1968) col. 641–768.

Centro de Estudos e Acão Social. • *Marx, cristianismo, luta de classes*. Salvador (Brazil), CEAS, 1970.

CEP. *See* Groupe de Recherche Théologique.

Chapey, Fernand. • *Science et foi: Affrontement de deux langages*. Paris, Centurion, 1974.

Charlier, Louis, et al. *La parole de Dieu en Jésus-Christ*. Tournai, Casterman, 1964.

Châtelet, François. • *Logos et Praxis: Recherches sur la signification théologique du marxisme*. Paris, Sedes, 1962.

_____, ed. *Histoire de la philosophie*. Paris, Hachette, 1972–73, 8 vols.

Chenu, Marie-Dominique. *Une école de théologie: Le Saulchoir*. Kainles/Tournai/Etiolle, 1937.

_____. • *L'Evangile dans le temps*. Paris, Cerf, 1964.

_____. • *La foi dans l'intelligence*. Paris, Cerf, 1964.

_____. • *Is Theology a Science?* New York/London, Hawthorn/Burns & Oates, 1959.

_____. • "Orthodoxie—Orthopraxie," in Philips et al., *Le service théologique*, pp. 51–63.

_____. • "Position théologique de la sociologie religieuse," in Chenu, *La foi dans l'intelligence*, pp. 59–62.

_____. • *Saint Thomas d'Aquin et la théologie*. Paris, Seuil, 1959.

_____. • "Sociologie de la connaissance et théologie," in Chenu, *La foi dans l'intelligence*, pp. 63–68.

_____. • "'Spiritualisme' et sociologie," in Ladrière et al., *Jacques Leclercq*, pp. 209–16.

_____. • *La théologie comme science au XIIIe siècle*. Paris, Vrin, 3rd ed., 1969.

_____. • "La théologie comme science ecclésiale," *Concilium* (1967) 85-93.

_____. *Théologie de la matière: Civilisation technique et spiritualité chrétienne.* Paris, Cerf, 1968.

_____. "Théologie et recherche interdisciplinaire," in Houtart, ed., *Recherche interdisciplinaire et théologie.*

_____. *The Theology of Work: An Exploration.* Chicago, Regnery, 1966.

_____. • *Toward Understanding Saint Thomas.* Chicago, Regnery, 1964.

_____. • "Vie conciliare de l'Eglise et sociologie de la foi," in Chenu, *La foi dans l'intelligence*, pp. 371-83.

Chrétiens et politique. Paris, Ed. Universitaires, 1974.

Clément, C.B. *Le pouvoir des mots: Symbolique et idéologie.* Paris, Mame, 1973.

CNBB (Conferência Nacional dos Bispos do Brasil). • *Igreja e política: Subsídios teológicos.* São Paulo, Paulinas, 1974.

Colombo, C. "La metodologia e la sistemazione teológica," in Pontificia Facultà Teologica, *Problemi e orientamenti.*

Combes, Michel. *Le langage sur Dieu peut-il avoir un sens?* Le Mirail: Publications de l'Université de Toulouse, 1975.

Comblin, José. • "Autour de la 'théologie de la révolution,'" *La Foi et le Temps* 5 (1975) 504-40.

_____. • *Théologie de la pratique révolutionnaire.* Paris, Ed. Universitaires, 1974.

_____. • *Théologie de la révolution: Théorie.* Paris, Ed. Universitaires, 1970.

Comte, Auguste. *The Positive Philosophy of Auguste Comte.* Translated and condensed by Harriet Martineau. New York/London, Appleton/Chapman, 1853, 2 vols.

Concilium 60 (1970), supplément. • *Actes du Congrès de Théologie à Bruxelles.*

Concilium 85 (1973). • *Crise da linguagem religiosa.*

Concilium 96 (1974). • *Praxis de libertação e fé cristã.*

Cone, James H. • *A Black Theology of Liberation.* Philadelphia, Lippincott, 1970.

Congar, Yves M.-J. • *La foi et la théologie.* Tournai, Desclée, 1962.

_____. • "A historia da Igreja, 'lugar teológico,'" *Concilium* 57 (1970) 886-94.

_____. • "L'influence de la société et de l'histoire sur le développement de l'homme chrétien," *Nouvelle Revue Théologique* 96 (1974) 673-92.

_____. • "Le moment 'économique' et le moment 'ontologique' dans la Sacra Doctrina (Révélation, Théologie, Somme Théologique)," in Congar, et al., *Mélanges offerts a M.-D. Chenu*, pp. 135-87.

_____. • *Un peuple messianique: Salut et Libération.* Paris, Cerf, 1975.

_____. • *Situation et tâches présentes de la théologie.* Paris, Cerf, 1967.

_____. • "Théologie et sciences humaines," *Esprit* 7-8 (1965) 121-37.

_____. *La tradition et les traditions.* Paris, Fayard, 2 vols., 1960-63.

_____, et al. *Mélanges offerts à M.-D. Chenu.* Paris, Vrin, 1967.

Contre Althusser. Paris, Union Gén. d'Editions, 1974.

Copans, J., ed. *Anthropologie et impérialisme.* Paris, Maspero, 1975.

Coppens, J. "Le problème des sens bibliques," *Concilium* 30 (1967) 107-18.

Cornu, Daniel. • *Karl Barth, teólogo da liberdade.* Rio de Janeiro, Paz e Terra, 1971. (French edition, *Karl Barth et la Politique*, Geneva, Labor et Fides, 1968.)

Costa, R. "Le problème des sociologies de la connaissance: A propos du document du clergé latino-américain (1966-1970)," *Archives des Sciences Sociales des Religions* 37 (1974) 43-77.

Coste, René. • "Les chrétiens et l'analyse marxiste," *Revue Théologique de Louvain* 4 (1973) 20-38.

————. • *Les communautés politiques: Le mystère chrétien*. Paris, Desclée de Brouwer, 1967.

————. "L'Eglise et le défi du monde," *Nouvelle Revue Théologique* 93 (1971) 1109–11.

————. *Evangile et politique*. Paris, Aubier-Montaigne, 1968.

————. • "Marxisme et théologie," *Nouvelle Revue Théologique* 96 (1974) 918–32.

Cottier, G. M. "Athéisme et marxisme: Appréciation," in Girardi and Six, *Des chrétiens*, 348–74.

————. "Athéisme et marxisme: Engels," in Girardi and Six, *Des Chrétiens*, pp. 201–15.

————. "Athéisme et marxisme: Marx," in Girardi and Six, *Des chrétiens*, pp. 173–85.

————. "Quelques réflexions sur la situation du théologien en temps de crise," *Nova et Vetera* 47 (1972) 99–114.

————. • "Sur la théorie de la praxis." *Nova et Vetera* 48 (1973), no. 4.

————. • "Valeur de l'analyse marxiste,' " *Nova et Vetera* 46 (1971) 173–87.

Cristãos para o Socialismo. • "I Encontro de Cristãos para o socialismo (Santiago, abril 1972): Documento Final," SEDOC 5 (1972), col. 623–32.

————. • "I Encontro de cristãos para o socialismo (Québec, abril 1975): Documento Final," SEDOC 8 (1975), col. 169–76.

Croce, Benedetto. *Philosophy of the Practical: Economic and Ethic*. New York, Bible and Tannen, 1969.

Cullmann, Oscar. *Dieu et César: Le procès de Jésus; Saint Paul et l'autorité; L'Apocalypse et l'Etat totalitaire*. Neuchâtel/Paris, Delachaux/Niestlé, 1956.

————. *Jesus and the Revolutionaries*. New York, Harper & Row, 1970.

————. *The New Testament: An Introduction for the General Reader*. Philadelphia, Westminster, 1968.

————. *La tradition: Probleme exégétique, historique et théologique*. Paris, Delachaux, 1953.

Dahrendorf, Ralf. • *Essays on the Theory of Society*. Stanford University Press, 1968.

Daniélou, Jean. *The Lord of History: Reflections on the Inner Meaning of History*. London/Chicago, Longmans/Regnery, 1958.

Darlapp, A. "História da salvação," in Fries, ed., *Dicionário de teologia*, 2:294–301.

de Bont, W. • "La religion en tant que pensée symbolique," *Le Supplément* 26 (1972) 217–42.

————. • "La sécularisation de la pensée," *Supplément de la Vie Spiritualle* 88 (1969) 5–28.

de Certeau, Michel. • "L'articulation du 'dire' et du 'faire': La contestation universitaire, indice d'une tâche théologique," *Etudes Théologiques et Religieuses* 45 (1970) 25–44.

————. *Le Christianisme éclaté*. Paris, Seuil, 1974.

————. *La culture au pluriel*. Paris, Union Gén. d'Editions, 1974.

————. *L'écriture de l'histoire*. Paris, Gallimard, 1975.

————. *L'étranger, ou l'union dans la différence*. Paris, Presses Universitaires de France, 1969.

————. • "Expérience chrétienne et langage de la foi," *Christus* 46 (1965) 147–63.

————. • "La parole du croyant dans le langage de l'homme," *Esprit* 10 (1967) 455–73.

————. "De la participation au discernement," *Christus* 13 (1966) 518–37.

————. *La prise de la parole: Pour une nouvelle culture*. Paris, Desclée, 1968.

————. "Le prophète et les militaires: Dom Helder Câmara," *Etudes*, July 1970, pp. 104–13.

_____. "Que-est-ce qu'un Congrès de Théologie? (Bruxelles, 12-17 septembre 1970)," *Etudes*, Nov. 1970, pp. 587-96.

_____. • "La rupture instauratrice ou le christianisme dans la culture contemporaine," *Esprit* 6 (1971) 1177-1214.

_____. "La vie religieuse en Amérique Latine," *Etudes*, Jan. 1967, pp. 108-12.

_____, et al. *Crise du biblicisme, chance de la Bible*. Paris, Epi, 1973.

Déconchy, Jean-Pierre. *L'orthodoxie religieuse: Essai de logique psycho-sociale*. Paris, Ouvrières, 1971.

_____. "Une tentative d'épistémologie de la pensée religieuse," *Archives de Sociologie des Religions* 24 (1967) 141-48.

de Finance, Joseph. • *Etre et agir dans la philosophie de Saint Thomas*. Paris, Beauchesne, 1943.

Defois, Gérard. • "Sociologie de la connaissance religieuse et théologie de la croyance," *Le Supplément* 112 (1975) 101-25.

_____, et al. *Le pouvoir dans l'Eglise*. Paris/Tournai, Cerf/Desclée, 1973.

de Haas. P. • *The Church as an Institution: Critical Studies in the Relation between Theology and Sociology*. Apeldorn (Netherlands), Boek- en Offsetdrukkerij Jonker, n.d.

de Lavalette, Henri. • "Bulletin de théologie politique," *Recherches de Science Religieuse* 63 (1964) 605-30.

Deleuze, G. "A quoi reconnaît-on le structuralisme?," in Châtelet, ed., *Histoire de la philosophie*, 8:299-335.

de Lima Vaz, H. C. "O Ethos da atividade científica," *Revista Eclesiástica Brasileira* 34 (1974) 45-73.

_____. • "Sinais dos tempos-lugar teológico ou lugar comum?," *Revista Eclesiástica Brasileira* 32 (1972) 101-24.

de Locht, Pierre. *The Risks of Fidelity*. Denville, N.J., Dimension, 1974.

de Lubac, Henri. *Catholicisme: Aspects sociaux du dogme*. Paris, Cerf, 5th ed., 1952. (English translation, *Catholicism: A Study of Dogma in Relation to the Corporate Destiny of Mankind*, London, Burns, Oates & Washbourne, 1950.)

_____. *The Discovery of God*. New York, Kenedy, 1960.

_____. *L'écriture dans la tradition*. Paris, Aubier-Montaigne, 1966.

_____. *Exégèse médiévale: Les quatre sens de l'Ecriture*. Paris, Aubier, 4 vols., 1959-64.

_____. *Le mystère du Surnaturel*. Paris, Aubier, 1965.

_____. *Surnaturel: Etudes historiques*. Paris, Aubier-Montaigne, 1945.

Denzinger, Henricus, and Schönmetzer, Adolfus, eds. *Enchiridion Symbolorum, Definitionum et Declarationum de Rebus Fidei et Morum*. Barcelona/Freiburg/Rome, Herder, 36th ed., 1976.

de Oliveira, R., and Domingues, B. "Conversão—Rumo novo," *ISET* (Instituto Superior de Estudos Teológicos, Lisbon), June 1972, pp. 4-10.

Derrida, J. *De la grammatologie*. Paris, Minuit, 1967.

Desanti, Jean T. • *La philosophie silencieuse ou critique des philosophies de la science*. Paris, Seuil, 1975.

Descartes, René. • *Discourse on the Method of Rightly Conducting the Reason*. Chicago/London/Toronto, Encyclopaedia Britannica, 1952. (Also, *Discourse on Method*, Indianapolis, Bobbs-Merrill, 3d ed., 1981.)

Desroche, Henri. "'Dernière instance' et 'premier rôle': A propos de l'ouvrage de L. Althusser, *Pour Marx*," *Archives de Sociologie des Religions* 23 (1967) 153ff.

_____. • *Jacob and the Angel: An Essay in Sociologies of Religion*. University of Massachusetts Press, 1973.

_____. *Sociologies religieuses*. Paris, Presses Universitaires de France, 1968.

de Waelhens, A. "Le mythe de la démythologization," in de Waelhens et al., *Mito e fede*, pp. 251–61.

_____. • *La philosophie et les expériences naturelles*. The Hague, Nijhoff, 1961.

_____, et al. *Mito e fede*. Padua, Instituto di Studi Filosofici, 1966.

de Wulfe, M. *Histoire de la philosophie médiévale*. Paris/Louvain, Alcan/Institut de Philosophie, 5th ed., 1925.

Dhooge, J. "Quelques problèmes posés par le dialogue entre sociologie et théologie pastorale," *Social Compass* 17 (1970).

Díez-Alegría, José María. *I Believe in Hope*. Garden City, N.Y., Doubleday, 1974.

Dilthey, Wilhelm. • *Le monde de l'esprit*. Paris, Aubier, 1947.

Dodd, C. H. *Gospel and Law: The Relation of Faith and Ethics in Early Christianity*. Columbia University Press, 1960.

_____. *The Moral Teaching of the New Testament*. London, Burns & Oates, 1975.

Domenach, J.-M. • "Pour une éthique de l'engagement," *Christus* 13 (1966) 466–77.

_____. "L'histoire n'est pas notre absolu," *Lumière et Vie* 23 (1974).

Dondeyne, Albert. "Un discours philosophique de Dieu est-il encore possible?," in Ladrière et al., *Miscellanea Albert Dondeyne*.

Dubarle, Dominique. *Approches d'une théologie de la science*. Paris, Cerf, 1967.

_____, et al. • *La recherche en philosophie et en théologie*. Paris, Cerf, 1970.

Dubarle, M.-D. • "Epistémologie des sciences humaines." Paris, Institut Catholique de Paris, Faculté de Philosophie, 1973.

_____. • "La vérification du discours de foi et l'expérience théologale." Paris, Institut Catholique de Paris, Faculté de Philosophie, 1973.

Dullaart, L. "Institution et légitimation: Le point de vue de la sociologie de la connaissance sur les rapports entre l'Eglise et la théologie," in Dullaart et al., *Les deux visages de la théologie*, pp. 133–53.

_____, et al. *Les deux visages de la théologie de la sécularisation: Analyse critique de la sécularisation*. Paris/Tournai, Casterman, 1970.

Dumas, André. *Dietrich Bonhoeffer, Theologian of Reality*. New York/London, Macmillan/Collier-Macmillan, 1968.

Duméry, Henry. *Philosophie de la religion: Essai sur la signification du Christianisme*. Paris, Presses Universitaires de France, 1957, 2 vols.

_____. *Raison et religion dans la philosophie*. Paris, Seuil, 1974.

Dumont, C. • "La réflexion sur la méthode théologique," *Nouvelle Revue Théologique* 83 (1961) 1034–50, 84 (1962) 17–35.

_____. • "Des trois dimensions retrouvées en théologie: eschatologie, orthopraxie, herméneutique," *Nouvelle Revue Théologique* 92 (1970) 561–91.

Dumont, F. *Chantier: Essais sur la pratique des sciences de l'homme*. Montreal, Hurtubise, 1973.

Dunas, Nicolas. • *Connaissance de la foi*. Paris, Cerf, 1963 (bibliography, pp. 147–215).

Dupuis, J. • "Le mouvement théologique en Inde," *Revue Théologique de Louvain* 6 (1975) 324–31.

Dupuy, Bernard Dominique, ed. • *La révélation divine: Constitution dogmatique "Dei Verbum."* Paris, Cerf, 1968, 2 vols.

Duquoc, Christian. *Ambiguité des théologies de la sécularisation: Essai critique*. Gembloux, Duculot, 1972.

_____. *Dieu différent: Essay sur la symbolique trinitaire*. Paris, Cerf, 1978.

Durkheim, Emile. *The Elementary Forms of the Religious Life*. London, Allen & Unwin, 1976.

_____. • *Pragmatisme et sociologie*. Paris, Vrin, 1955. (English edition, *Pragmatism and Sociology*, New York, Cambridge University Press, 1983.)

_____. *Socialism and Saint-Simon*. Yellow Springs, Ohio, Antioch Press, 1958.

Düsberg, H. "Il leur ouvrit l'esprit à l'intelligence de l'Ecriture (Lc 24,45)," *Concilium* 30 (1967) 97–104.

Dussel, Enrique D. *Ethics and the Theology of Liberation*. Maryknoll, N.Y., Orbis, 1978.

_____. *Historia de la Iglesia en América Latina: Coloniaje y Liberación (1492–1973)*. Barcelona, Nova Terra, 3d ed., 1974. (English edition, *A History of the Church in Latin America: Colonialism to Liberation [1492–1979]*, Grand Rapids, Eerdmans, 1981.)

_____. • *History and Theology of Liberation: A Latin American Perspective*. Maryknoll, N.Y., Orbis, 1976.

_____. • *Método para una filosofía de la liberación: Superación analéctica de la dialectica hegeliana*. Salamanca, Sígueme, 1974.

_____. • *Para una ética de la liberación latinoamericana*. Buenos Aires, Siglo Veintiuno, 3 vols., 1973–74.

Duval, E. • "L'idéologie," *Le Supplément* 116 (1973) 283–310.

Duverger, Maurice. *The Idea of Politics: The Uses of Power in Society*. London/Methuen, Mass./New York, Bobbs-Merrill, 1966.

_____. *An Introduction to the Social Sciences, with Special Reference to Their Methods*. London/New York, Allen & Unwin/Praeger, 1964.

Ebeling, Gerhard. "Hermeneutik," in Galling, *Die Religion*.

_____. "Theologie—Begriffsgeschichtlich," in Galling, *Die Religion*, vol. 6, col. 754–69.

_____. *Theology and Proclamation: A Dialogue with Bultmann*. Philadelphia, Fortress, 1966.

_____. *Wort und Glaube*. Tübingen, Mohr, 1965–69, 2 vols.

Ecole Pratique des Hautes Etudes. *Contributions à la sociologie de la connaissance*, Cahier 1. Paris, Hautes Etudes, 1972.

Eichholz, G. *Tradition und Interpretation: Studien zum neuen Testament und zur Hermeneutik*. Munich, Kaiser, 1965.

Einstein, Albert. *The World as I See It*. New York, Covici-Friede, 1934.

Eisler, Robert. *Iêsous Basileus oû Basileusas*. Heidelberg, Winter, 2 vols. 1929–30.

Ellacuría, Ignacio. *Freedom Made Flesh*. Maryknoll, N.Y., Orbis, 1976.

_____. • "Método teológico: Problemática actual en Europa y en América Latina—Epistemología y análisis" (presentation to the Encontro Latinoamericano de Teología, Mexico City, Aug. 1975).

_____. • "Tesis sobre la posibilidad, necesidad y sentido de una teología latinoamericana," in Ellacuría et al., *Teología y mundo contemporaneo*, pp. 325–50.

_____, et al. *Teología y mundo contemporaneo: Homenaje a Karl Rahner*. Madrid, Cristiandad, 1975.

Ellul, Jacques. *The Political Illusion*. New York, Vintage, 1972.

_____. *The Politics of God and the Politics of Man*. Grand Rapids, Eerdmans, 1972.

• *Epistemologia e teoria da ciência*. Epistemologia e pensamento contemporâneo, no. 2. Petrópolis, Vozes, 1971.

Erasmus. *Lettre à Dorpius*. Published with *Eloge de la Folie*, by Erasmus. Translated by P. de Nolhac. Paris, Garnier, 1953.

Escobar, Carlos H. • *Epistemologia das ciências*. Rio de Janeiro, Pallas, 1976.

Fals Borda, O. *Ciencia propria y colonialismo intelectual*. Mexico City, Siglo Veintiuno, 1973.

_____. • "Ciencia y compromiso: problemas metodológicos del libro 'La subversión en Colombia,'" *Aportes* 8 (1968) 118-28.

_____. • "La crisis social y la orientación sociológica: una réplica," *Aportes* 15 (1970) 62-76 (bibliographical material, p. 64, n. 2).

Feiner, Johannes, and Löhrer, Magnus, eds. *Mysterium Salutis: Compêndio da dogmática historico-salvífica*. Petrópolis, Vozes, 1972. (German original, *Mysterium Salutis: Grundriss heilsgeschichtlicher Dogmatik*, Einsiedeln/Zurich/Cologne, Benziger, 1965.)

Fernandes, Florestan. • *A sociologia no Brasil: Contribuição para o estudo de sua formação e desenvolvimento*. Petrópolis, Vozes, 1977.

Ferré, Frederick. • *Language, Logic and God*. University of Chicago Press, 1981. (French edition, *Le langage religieux a-t-il un sens? Logique moderne et foi*, Paris, Cerf, 1970.)

Fessard, Gaston. *De l'actualité historique*. Paris, Desclée de Brouwer, 1960.

Feuerbach, Ludwig. *Manifestes philosophiques: textes choisis*. Paris, Presses Universitaires de France, 1960.

Fichant, Michel. • "L'épistémologie en France," in Chatelet, ed., *Histoire de la philosophie*, vol. 8: *Le XXe siècle*, Paris, Hachette, 1973, pp. 135-78.

_____, and Pêcheux, Michel. • *Sur l'histoire des sciences*. Paris, Maspero, 1974.

Flick, G., and Alseghy, Zoltan. "Teologia della storia," *Gregorianum* 35 (1954) 256-98.

Foucault, Michel. • *The Archaeology of Knowledge*. New York/San Francisco/London, Harper & Row, 1976 (New York, Pantheon, 1982).

_____. • *Order of Things: An Archaeology of the Human Sciences*. New York, Random House, 1973.

Foulquié, Paul. • *La dialectique*. Paris, Presses Universitaires de France, 1949.

Fourastié, J. *Les conditions de l'esprit scientifique*. Paris, Gallimard, 1972.

Fourrez, Gérard. • *La science partisane*. Gembloux, Duculot, 1974.

Freire, Paulo. • *Conscientisation et révolution*. Paris, Maspero, 1974.

_____. *Education, the Practice of Freedom*. London, Writers and Readers Publishing Cooperative, 1976.

_____. "Educazione, liberazione e chiesa," in Assmann et al., *Teologie dal Terzo Mondo*, pp. 55-90.

_____. • *Pedagogy of the Oppressed*. New York, Seabury, 1970.

Freud, Sigmund. *Five Lectures on Psycho-Analysis*, in *The Standard Edition of the Complete Psychological Works of Sigmund Freud*, vol. 9. London, Hogarth Institute of Psycho-Analysis, 1957. Also, *Five Lectures on Psychoanalysis*, New York, Norton, 1977.

_____. *Interpretation of Dreams*. New York, Modern Library, 1978.

Fries, Heinrich, ed. *Dicionário de teologia: Conceitos fundamentais da teologia atual*. São Paulo, Loyola, 1970.

Fuchs, Ernst. *Hermeneutik*. Tübingen, Mohr, 1974.

_____. *Marburger Hermeneutik*. Tübingen, Mohr, 1968.

Fuchs, Josef. *Existe uma moral cristã?* São Paulo, Paulinas, 1972. (French edition, *Existe-t-il une "morale chrétienne"?*, Gembloux, Duculot, 1973.)

Furter, Pierre, *Educação e reflexão*. Petrópolis, Vozes, 1971.

• *Futuro da teologia*. Translated from the French by H.F. Japiassu, Teologia Hoje. São Paulo, Duas Cidades, 1970.

Gadamer, Hans-George. "Le problème herméneutique," *Archives de Philosophie* 33 (1970) 3–27.

———. "Rhetorik, Hermeneutik und Ideologiekritik," in *Kleine Schriften*, Tübingen, Mohr, 1967, 1:113–30.

———. • *Truth and Method*. New York, Seabury, 1975.

Galilea, Segundo. "Introducción a la religiosidad latinoamericana," in Galilea et al., *Religiosidad y pedagogía*.

———. • "Situation de la théologie de la libération," *Spiritus* 15 (1974) 297–304.

———, et al. *Religiosidad y pedagogía de la fe*. Madrid, Marova, 1973.

Galling, Kurt, ed. *Die Religion in Geschichte und Gegenwart*. Tübingen, Mohr, 1957.

Garaudy, Roger. *From Anathema to Dialogue: A Marxist Challenge to the Christian Churches*. New York, Herder and Herder, 1966.

———. *Parole d'homme*. Paris, Laffont, 1975.

Gardeil, Ambroise. • *Le donné révélé et la théologie* (1909). Paris/Seine-et-Oise, Cerf/Juvisy, 2nd ed., 1932.

———. *La notion de lieu théologique*. Paris, Gabalda, 1908.

———. *Saint Thomas d'Aquin: La Théologie*. Paris/Tournai/Rome, Desclée de Brouwer, 1968.

Gauchet, M. "Réflexions sur l'état totalitaire, sur l'impossibilité d'une société non divisée et sur les fondements de la démocracie," *Esprit* 7–8 (1976) 3–28.

Geffré, Claude. "Les courants actuels de la recherche théologique," *Supplément de la Vie Spirituelle* 20 (1967) 1087.

———. • *A New Age in Theology*. New York, Paulist, 1974.

———. "L'objectivité propre au Dieu révélé," in Geffré et al., *Procès de l'objectivité de Dieu*.

———. "Sentido e não sentido de uma teologia não-metafísica," *Concilium* 76 (1972) 783–92.

———. • "Théologie," in *Encyclopaedia Universalis*, 15:1087–91.

———. • "Y a-t-il une morale révolutionnaire?," *Le Supplément* 110 (1974) 335–42.

———, et al. *Procès de l'objectivité de Dieu*. Paris, Cerf, 1969.

Geiselmann, J.R. *Die heilige Schrift und die Traditionen*. Freiburg, Herder, 1962.

Gera, L. • "Cultura y dependencia a la luz de la reflexión teológica," *Stromata* 30 (1974) 169–227.

———. • *Teología de la liberación*. Lima, MIEC-JECI, 1973.

Gesché, Adolphe. • *L'annonce de Dieu au monde d'aujourd'hui*. Malines, 1968 (bibliography, pp. 75–102).

———. • "Une approche du sacré à partir de la théologie de l'espérance," in Gesché et al., *Heil und Macht*, pp. 149–68.

———. "Un colloque sur 'la sociologie de la connaissance et la théologie' (Louvain, 24–25 mars 1972)," *Revue Théologique de Louvain* 3 (1972) 369–74.

———. • "Le Dieu de la révélation et de la philosophie," *Revue Théologique de Louvain* 3 (1972) 249–83.

———. • "Le discours théologique sur l'homme," *Nouvelle Revue Théologique* 97 (1975) 801–19.

———. "Essai d'interprétation dialectique du phénomène de sécularisation," *Revue Théologique de Louvain* 1 (1970) 268–88.

_____. • "La médiation philosophique en théologie," in Ladrière et al., *Miscellanea Albert Dondeyne*, pp. 75-91.

_____. "Mutation religieuse et renouvellement théologique," *Revue Théologique de Louvain* 4 (1973).

_____. • "Vrai et faux changement en théologie," *Collectanea Mechliniensia* 53 (1968) 308-33.

_____, et al. *Heil und Macht: Approches du Sacré*. S. Augustin bei Bonn, Anthropos, 1975.

Geyer, Hans-Georg, Janowski, Hans-Norbert, and Schmidt, Alfred. • *Theologie und Soziologie*. Stuttgart, Kohlhammer, 1970.

Girardi, Giulio. *Christianisme, libération humaine, lutte des classes*. Paris, Cerf, 1972.

_____. *Marxism and Christianity*. New York, Macmillan, 1968.

_____. • "Nouveauté chrétienne et nouveauté du monde," *Lumière et Vie* 23 (1974) 98-121.

_____. "Teología y revolución" (notes for a course given to students at the Lumen Vitae institute for catechetics, Brussels, 1972-73).

_____. • "Théorie et praxis dans la pensée marxiste: Cours parallèle donné aux étudiants de 'Lumen Vitae.' " Brussels, 1975.

_____. "Vers de nouveaux rapports entre marxisme et christianisme," *Lumière et Vie* 23 (1974).

_____. • "Vérité et libération: les présupposés d'une théologie de la libération," *Etudes Théologiques et Religieuses* 2 (1974) 271-97.

_____, and Six, J.-F., eds. *Des chrétiens interrogent l'athéisme*, vol. 2/1: *L'athéisme dans la philosophie contemporaine*. Paris, Desclée de Brouwer, 1970.

Gobériaux, F. *Le tournant théologique aujourd'hui selon Karl Rahner*. Paris, Desclée de Brouwer, 1968.

Goldmann, Lucien. • *Marxisme et sciences humaines*. Paris, Gallimard, 1969.

_____. *Structures mentales et création culturelle*. Paris, Union Gén. d'Editions, 1970.

Gollwitzer, Helmut. *Ich frage nach dem Sinn des Lebens*. Munich, Kaiser, 1974.

_____, et al. *Eglise et société*. Geneva, Labor et Fides, 1966.

Gonseth, Ferdinand. *Les mathémathiques et la réalité*. Paris, Alcan, 1936.

_____. "L'unité de la connaissance scientifique," in Bayer, ed., *L'unité de la science*.

González Ruíz, José M. *Dios está en la base: Aproximación a una teología de la base*. Barcelona, Estela, 1970.

_____. *The New Creation: Marxist and Christian*. Maryknoll, N.Y., Orbis, 1976.

_____. "Théologie et sciences sociales," *Social Compass* 27 (1970) 294-99.

Granel, Gérard. "Remarques sur l'accès à la pensée de Martin Heidegger: 'Sein und Zeit,' " in Châtelet, ed., *Histoire de la philosophie*, 8:199-204.

_____. • *Traditionis traditio*. Paris, Gallimard, 1972.

Granger, Gilles-Gaston. • *Essai d'une philosophie du style*. Paris, Colin, 1968.

_____. • *Pensée formelle et sciences de l'homme*. Paris, Aubier-Montaigne, 1960.

_____. • "Science pratique et pratique de la science," in Granger et al., *Dialogues en sciences humaines*, pp. 55-77.

_____, et al. *Dialogues en sciences humaines*. Brussels, Facultés Universitaires Saint-Louis, 1975.

Greimas, Algirdas J. • *Sémiotique et sciences sociales*. Paris, Seuil, 1976.

_____. *Structural Semantics: An Attempt at a Method*. University of Nebraska Press, 1983.

Greinacher, N. • "Práxis do engajamento político das comunidades cristãs," *Concilium* (1973) 458–72.

Greisch, J. "La crise de l'herméneutique: Réflexions méta-critiques sur un debat actuel," in Greisch et al., *La crise contemporaine*, pp. 135–78.

_____. • "La raison herméneutique," *Recherches de Science Religieuse* 64 (1976) 5–24.

_____, et al. • *La crise contemporaine: Du modernisme à la crise des herméneutiques*. Paris, Beauchesne, 1973.

Grelot, P. • "Note méthodologique sur le recours à la Bible dans l'étude de ce sujet," in Grelot et al., *Libération des hommes*, pp. 77–97.

_____, et al. *Libération des hommes et salut en Jésus-Christ: Réflexions proposées par le Conseil Permanent de l'Episcopat à la Session pastorale de 1974*. Paris, Centurion, 1975.

Gremillion, Joseph, ed. *The Gospel of Peace and Justice: Catholic Social Teaching since Pope John*. Maryknoll, N.Y., Orbis, 1976.

Grenier, Jean. *Essai sur l'esprit d'orthodoxie*. Paris, Gallimard, 3rd ed., 1967.

Gritti, Jules. • *Foi et nouvelles sciences de l'homme*. Paris, Centurion, 1972.

Grosser, A. • *Au nom de quoi? Fondements d'une morale politique*. Paris, Seuil, 1969.

Grothendieck, A. "La nouvelle église universelle," in Jaulin, ed., *Pourquoi la mathématique?* pp. 11–25.

Groupe de Recherche Théologique CEP. *La pratique de la théologie politique: Analyse critique des conditions pratiques de l'instauration d'un discours chrétien libérateur*. Tournai/Paris, Casterman, 1974.

Guardini, Romano. *The Faith and Modern Man*. New York, Pantheon, 1952.

Guichard, Jean. "Les chrétiens face au marxisme," Lyons, *Chronique Sociale de France*, 1968.

_____. • "Communautés de base et contexte politique," *Lumière et Vie* 19 (1970) 77–102.

_____. • *Eglise, lutte de classes et stratégies politiques*. Paris, Cerf, 1972.

_____. "Foi chrétienne et théorie de la connaissance," *Lumière et Vie* 22 (1973) 61–84.

_____. "Lutte des classes et annonce du salut," in Guichard et al., *Idéologie de libération*, pp. 143–64.

_____. "Le marxisme de Marx à Mao: Théorie et pratique de la révolution," Lyons, *Chronique Sociale de France*, 1972.

_____, et al. *Idéologies de libération et message du salut*. Strasbourg, Cerdic, 1973.

Guitton, Jean. *Make Your Mind Work for You*. New York, Macmillan, 1958.

Gurvitch, Georges. *Les cadres sociaux de la connaissance*. Paris, 1973.

_____. • *Dialectique et sociologie*. Paris, Flammarion, 1977.

Gusdorf, Georges. *Mythe et métaphysique: Introduction à la philosophie*. Paris, 1953.

_____. *Les sciences humaines et la conscience occidentale*. Paris, Payot, 1966, 6 vols.

Gutiérrez, Gustavo. "Marxismo e cristianesimo," *Servitium* (Vicença) 30 (1973) 249–77.

_____. • *The Power of the Poor in History: Selected Writings*, esp. pp. 36–74: "Liberation Praxis and Christian Faith"; pp. 169–221: "Theology from the Underside of History." Maryknoll, N.Y., Orbis, 1983.

_____. • "Praxis de libération et foi chrétienne," *Lumen Vitae* 29 (1974) 227–54.

_____. "Réinventer le visage de l'Eglise." Paris, Cerf, 1971.

_____. • *A Theology of Liberation*. Maryknoll, N.Y., Orbis Books, 1973.

Guzmán, L. *La teología, ciencia de la fe*. Bilbao, Desclée de Brouwer, 1967.

Haag, A. "Hermenêutica," in Feiner and Löhrer, *Mysterium Salutis*, I/2:152–87.

_____. "A Palavra de Deus," in Feiner and Löhrer, *Mysterium Salutis*, I/2.

Habermas, Jürgen. • *Knowledge and Human Interests*. Boston, Beacon, 1971.

_____. • *Technik und Wissenschaft als "Ideologie."* Frankfurt, Suhrkamp, 1968. (French edition, *La téchnique et la science comme "idéologie,"* Paris, Gallimard, 1973.)

_____. • *Theory and Practice*. Boston, Beacon, 1973.

_____. *Toward a Rational Society: Student Protest, Science, and Politics*. Boston, Beacon, 1970.

Hamer, Jerôme. "Parole de Dieu ou parole sur Dieu dans la pensée de Karl Barth," in Charlier et al., *La parole de Dieu*, pp. 287–93.

Harnecker, Marta. • *Les concepts élémentaires du materialisme historique*. Brussels, Contradictions, 1974.

Hegel, G. W. F. *Hegel's Philosophy of Mind*. Translated by William Wallace. Oxford, Clarendon, 1894.

_____. *Hegel's Philosophy of Right*. Translated with notes by T. M. Knox. Oxford, Clarendon, 1942.

Heidegger, Martin. *Basic Writings*. New York/San Francisco/London, Harper & Row, 1977.

_____. *Being and Time*. New York/Evanston, Ill., Harper & Row, 1962.

_____. *Lettre sur humanisme*. Paris, Aubier, 1970.

_____. *Qu'appelle-t-on penser?* Paris, Presses Universitaires de France, 2nd ed., 1967.

_____. *Was ist die Metaphysik?* Frankfurt, Klostermann, 5th ed., 1949.

_____. "Zur Seinsfrage," in *Was ist die Metaphysik?*

Heinen, K. "Glaubensüberlieferung und Neuinterpretation im Alten Testament," in Turk, ed., *Zwischen Ordnung und Veränderung*, pp. 205–17.

Hengel, Martin. *Was Jesus a Revolutionist?* Philadelphia, Fortress, 1971.

_____. *Die Zeloten: Untersuchungen zur jüdischen Freiheitsbewegungen in der Zeit von Herodes I. bis 70 n. Chr.* Leiden, Brill, 1961.

Hengenberg, L. • *Explicações cientificas: Introdução à filosofia da ciência*. São Paulo, Herder/EDUSP, 1969.

Henkin, Leon. "Completeness," in Morgenbesser, ed., *Philosophy of Science Today*, pp. 23–35.

Herméneutique et tradition. Rome/Paris, Istituto di Studi Filosofici/Vrin, 1963.

Hersch, J. "Sur le sense d'histoire," in Hersch et al., *Science et conscience*, vol. 1.

_____, et al. *Science et conscience de la société*, vol. 1. Paris, Calmann-Lévy, 1971.

Hervieu-Leger, D. *De la mission à la protestation*. Paris, Cerf, 1973.

Herzog, Frederick. • *Liberation Theology*. New York, Seabury, 1973.

Hollweg, Arnd. • *Theologie und Empirie: Ein Beitrag zum Gespräch zwischen Theologie und Sozialwissenschaften in den USA und Deutschland*. Stuttgart, Evangelisches Verlagswerk, 1971.

Horkheimer, H. "Réflexions sur le théisme et l'athéisme," *Diogène* 48 (1964) 38–53.

Houtart, François. *The Eleventh Hour: Explosion of a Church*. Introduction by Harvey Cox. New York, Sheed & Ward, 1968.

_____. *Igreja e Mundo*. Petropolis, Vozes, 2nd ed., 1966.

_____. • "Les religions comme réalités sociales," in Vander Gucht and Vorgrimler, *Bilan*, 1:63–75.

_____, ed. • *Recherche interdisciplinaire et théologie*. Paris, Cerf, 1970.

_____. "Réflexions sur une théologie de la politique." Louvain, 1974.

_____. "Sociologie de l'Eglise comme institution." Université de Louvain, 1974.

_____, and Hambye, F. • "Implicações socio-políticas do Vaticano II," *Concilium* 6 [1968] 83-93. (French edition, "Implications socio-politiques de Vatican II, *Concilium* 36 [1968] 85-94.)

_____, and Rousseau, André. • *Eglise, force anti-révolutionnaire?* Brussels, Les Editions Ouvrières, 1973.

Ianni, Octavio. • *Sociologia e sociedade no Brasil.* São Paulo, Alfa-Ômega, 1975.

Ibarra, E. "Le contexte de la théologie de la libération," in Ibarra et al., *Théologies de la libération.*

_____, et al. • *Théologies de la libération en Amérique Latine.* Paris, Beauchesne, 1974.

Ingarden, Roman. *The Literary Work of Art.* Northwestern University Press, 1973.

Instituto Fe y Secularidad. • *Fe cristiana y cambio social en América Latina: Encuentro de El Escorial 1972.* Salamanca, Sígueme, 1973 (bibliography, pp. 394-414).

_____. • *Sociología de la Religión y Teología: Estudio bibliográfico.* Madrid, Edicusa, 1975.

Jaeger, Werner. *Humanism and Theology.* Marquette University Press, 1943.

_____. *The Theology of the Early Greek Philosophers.* Westport, Conn., Greenwood, 1980.

Japiassu, Hilton. • *Interdisciplinaridade e patologia do saber.* Rio de Janeiro, Imago, 1975.

_____. • *Introdução ao pensar epistemológico.* Rio de Janeiro, Alves, 2nd ed., 1977.

_____. • *O mito da neutralidade científica.* Rio de Janeiro, Imago, 1975.

_____. • *Para ler Bachelard.* Rio de Janeiro, Alves, 1976.

Jaulin, R., ed. *Pourquoi la mathématique?* Paris, Union Gén. d'Editions, 1974.

Jeremias, Joachim. *The Parables of Jesus.* New York, Scribner's, rev. ed., 1963.

Jiménez Urresti, T.I., ed. *Teología de la liberación: Conversaciones de Toledo, junho de 1973.* Burgos, Aldecoa, 1974.

Jolif, Jean-Yves. • "Le sujet pratique selon Saint Thomas d'Aquin," in Jolif et al., *Saint Thomas d'Aquin,* pp. 13-14.

_____. "Le temps fait beaucoup à l'affaire," *Lumière et Vie* 23 (1974) 184-98.

_____, et al. *Saint Thomas d'Aquin aujourd'hui.* Paris, Desclée de Brouwer, 1963.

Jossua, Jean-Pierre. *Yves Congar: Theology in the Service of God's People.* Chicago, Priory, 1968.

_____, et al. *Une foi exposée.* Paris, Cerf, 1972.

Journet, Charles. • *The Dark Knowledge of God.* London, Sheed & Ward, 1948.

_____. • "Sécularisation, herméneutique, orthopraxie, selon E. Schillebeeckx et P. Schoonenberg," *Nova et Vetera* 44 (1969) 300-312.

_____. • *The Wisdom of Faith: An Introduction to Theology.* Westminster, Md., Newman, 1952.

Kalinowsky, Georges. *Etudes de logique déontique.* Paris, Librairie Générale de Droit et de Jurisprudence, 1972.

_____. "Philosophie, théologie et métathéorie," in Kalinowsky et al., *La recherche en philosophie,* pp. 158-205.

_____. *Le problème de la verité en moral et en droit.* Lyons, Vitte, 1967.

_____. • *Querelle de la science normative: Une contribution à la théorie de la science.* Paris, Librairie Générale de Droit et de Jurisprudence, 1969.

_____. *Théorie de la connaissance pratique.* Lublin, 1960 (in Polish, with resumé in French).

_____, et al. *La recherche en philosophie et théologie*. Paris, Cerf, 1970.

Kamp, J. *Credo sans foi, foi sans credo*. Paris, Aubier-Montaigne, 1974.

_____. "Enseigner la religion?" *Revue Nouvelle* 69 (1975).

Kant, Immanuel. *The Critique of Pure Reason*. Chicago/London/Toronto, Encyclopaedia Britannica, 1952.

_____. *Idea of a Universal History on a Cosmo-Political Plan*. Temple University Press, 1953.

_____. • *On the Old Saw: That May Be Right in Theory but It Won't Work in Practice*. University of Pennsylvania Press, 1974.

Karsz, Saul. • *Théorie et politique: Louis Althusser*. Paris, Fayard, 1974.

Kasper, Walter. *Dogme et évangile*. Tournai, Casterman, 1967.

_____. • *The Methods of Dogmatic Theology*. New York, Paulist, 1969.

_____. "Tradition als Erkenntnisprinzip zur theologischen Relevanz der Geschichte," *Theologische Quartalschrift*, 1975, pp. 198–215.

Kaufmann, Franz-Xaver. • *Theologie in soziologischer Sicht*. Freiburg, Herder, 1973.

Keraly, H., ed. *Saint Thomas d'Aquin: Préface à la Politique*. Paris, Nouvelles Editions Latines, 1974.

Kérényi, K. "Origine e senso dell'ermeneutica," in *Herméneutique et tradition*, Rome/Paris, Istituto di Studi Filosofici/Vrin, 1963, pp. 129–39.

Khodoss, Fl., and Khodoss, Cl. • *Morale et Politique* (texts of Aristotle). Paris, Presses Universitaires de France, 1970.

Kierkegaard, Søren. *Armed Neutrality and Open Letter*. Bloomington, Ind./London, Indiana University Press.

_____. *Concluding Unscientific Postscript*. Princeton University Press, 1941.

Kloppenburg, B. "Las tentaciones de la teología de la liberación," in CELAM, *Liberación*, pp. 401–15.

Kluxen, W. "Verité et praxis de la science," in Ladrière et al., *Chemins de la raison*, pp. 73–88.

Kolping, Adolf. *Einführung in die katholische Theologie*. Münster, Regensberg, 2nd ed., 1963.

Kosik, Karel. • *Dialectics of the Concrete*. Hingham, Mass., Kluwer Boston, 1976.

Kotarbinski, C.T. "Idée de la méthodologie générale: Praxéologie," in Bayer, ed., *L'unité de la science*.

_____. "La notion de l'action," in Kotarbinski et al., *Actes du XI Congrès*, pp. 169–74.

_____, et al. *Actes du XI Congrès International de Philosophie*. Louvain, Nauwelaerts, 1953.

Kraus, Hans Joachim. *Reich Gottes: Reich der Freiheit—Grundriss systematischer Theologie*. Neukirchen-Vluyn, Neukirchener Verlag, 1975.

Kuhn, Thomas S. • *The Structure of Scientific Revolutions*. University of Chicago Press, 1966.

Kümmel, Werner Georg. *Introduction to the New Testament*. Nashville, Abingdon, 1975.

Lacan, Jacques. *Ecrits: A Selection*. New York, Norton, 1977.

_____. "L'instance de la lettre dans l'Inconsciente ou la Raison depuis Freud," in *Ecrits*, Paris, Seuil, 1966.

Ladrière, Jean. • "L'applicabilité des mathématiques aux sciences sociales," *Economie et Société* 6 (1972) 1511–48.

_____. • *L'articulation du sens: Discours scientifique et parole de la Foi*. Paris, Aubier-Montaigne, 1970.

_____. • "La démarche interdisciplinaire et le dialogue Eglise-Monde," in Ladrière et al., *Recherche interdisciplinaire*, pp. 45-64.

_____. *L'engagement*. Brussels, Centre National de Pastorale Familiale, n.d.

_____. • "Langage scientifique et langage spéculatif," *Revue Philosophique de Louvain* 69 (1971) 93-132.

_____. • "Le langage théologique et le discours de la représentation," in Ladrière et al., *Miscellanea Albert Dondeyne*, pp. 144-76.

_____. • "Langage théologique et philosophie analytique," in Ladrière et al., *Le Sacré*, pp. 99-111.

_____. *Language and Belief*. University of Notre Dame Press, 1972.

_____. • "Marxisme et rationalisme," *La Foi et le Temps* 5 (1975) 541-65.

_____. • "A operatividade da linguagem litúrgica," *Concilium* 82 (1973) 183-94.

_____. • "Le rôle de l'interprétation en science, en philosophie et en théologie," in Ladrière et al., *Science—Philosophie—Foi*.

_____. • *La science, le monde et la foi*. Tournai, Casterman, 1972.

_____. • "Sciences et discours rationnel" in "Sciences," *Encyclopaedia Universalis*, 14:754-57.

_____. • "Sens et système," *Esprit* 5 (1967) 822-24.

_____. • "La sociologie, son introduction dans la pensée catholique," in Ladrière et al., *Jacques Leclercq*, pp. 185-205.

_____. • "Le statut de la science dans la dynamique de la compréhension," in Ladrière et al., *Chemins de la raison*, pp. 29-46.

_____. • "La théologie et le langage de l'interprétation," *Revue Théologique de Louvain* 1 (1970) 241-67.

_____. • "Vérité et praxis dans la démarche scientifique," *Revue Philosophique de Louvain* 72 (1974) 284-310.

_____. • *Vie sociale et destinée: Sociologie Nouvelle*. Gembloux, Duculot, 1973.

_____, et al. *Chemins de la raison*. Paris, Desclée de Brouwer, 1972.

_____, et al. *Chrétiens et politique*. Paris, Presses Universitaires de France, 1974.

_____, et al. *Jacques Leclercq: L'homme, son oeuvre et ses amis*. Tournai, Casterman, 1961.

_____, et al. *Miscellanea Albert Dondeyne: Godsdienstfilosofie—Philosophie de la Religion*. Gembloux/Louvain, Duculot/Leuven University Press.

_____, et al. *Recherche interdisciplinaire et théologie*. Paris, Cerf, 1970.

_____, et al. *Le Sacré: Etudes et recherches*. Paris, Aubier-Montaigne, 1974.

_____, et al. *Science—Philosophie—Foi: Colloque de l'Académie Internationale de Philosophie des Sciences*. Paris, Beauchesne, 1974.

_____, et al. *Science et théologie*. Paris, Desclée de Brouwer, 1969.

Laffoucrière, Odette. *Le destin de la pensée et le "mort de Dieu" selon Heidegger*. The Hague, Nijhoff, 1968.

Land, Philip S. "Theology Meets Progress: Human Implications of Development." Rome, Gregorian University, 1971.

Laplanche, J., and Pontalis, J.-B. *The Language of Psycho-analysis*. New York, Norton, 1973.

Lapointe, Roger. • *Les trois dimensions de l'herméneutique*. Paris, Gabalda, 1967.

Laporte, R. "L'empire des signifiants," *Critique* 302 (1972).

Lash, N. "A Igreja e a liberdade de Cristo," *Concilium* 93 (1974) 370-80.

Latourelle, Renée. *Theology of Revelation*. Staten Island, N.Y., Alba House, 1966.

Lecourt, Dominique. • *Marxism and Epistemology: Bachelard, Canguilhem and Foucault*. London/Atlantic Highlands, N.J., NLB/Humanities Press, 1975.

_____. *Proletarian Science? The Case of Lysenko*. Atlantic Highlands, N.J., Humanities Press, 1977.

Lefebvre, Henri. *La fin de l'histoire: Epilégomènes*. Paris, Minuit, 1970.

_____. *La vie quotidienne dans le monde moderne*. Paris, Gallimard, 1972. (English edition, *Everyday Life in the Modern World*, New York, Harper & Row, 1971.)

Lefebvre, M. • "Sociologie et ecclésiologie existentielle," *Gregorianum* 52 (1971) 689-726.

Léon-Dufour, Xavier. "Qu'attendre d'un exégète?," *Etudes*, Oct. 1967, pp. 316-30.

_____, ed. • *Exégèse et herméneutique*. Paris, Seuil, 1971.

Lepargneur, H. • "Les 'Théologies de la Libération' et théologie tout court," *Nouvelle Revue Théologique* 98 (1976) 126-69.

Leroy, Roland, et al. *Les marxistes et l'évolution du monde catholique*. Paris, Ed. Sociales, 1972.

Levinas, E. *Totalité et infini: Essai sur l'extériorité*. The Hague, Nijhoff, 2nd ed., 1965.

Lévi-Strauss, Claude. "Critères scientifiques dans les disciplines sociales et humaines," *Aletheia*, no. 4 (May 1966) (also in *Structural Anthropology*, 2:288-311).

_____. *The Savage Mind*. London, Weidenfeld and Nicolson, 1962.

_____. • *Structural Anthropology*. New York, Basic Books, 1976.

Levy, Oscar, ed. *The Complete Works of Friedrich Nietzsche*. New York, Russell & Russell, 1964, 18 vols.

Lévy-Leblond, J.-M., and Jaubert, A., eds. • *(Auto)critique de la science*. Paris, Seuil, 1975.

Libânio, J. B. • *Discernimento e Política*. Petrópolis, Vozes, 1977. (English translation, *Spiritual Discernment and Politics: Guidelines for Religious Communities*, Maryknoll, N.Y., Orbis, 1982.)

_____. *Pecado e opção fundamental*. Petrópolis, Vozes, 1975.

Liénard, G., and Rousseau, A. "Rapports sociaux et systèmes symboliques: Conditions et implications sociales des innovations théologiques et de leur utilisation," in CEP, *La pratique de la théologie politique*, pp. 216-36.

Lobkowicz, Nikolaus. • "Théorie und Praxis," in *Sowjetsystem und demokratische Gesellschaft*, Freiburg/Basel/Vienna, Herder, 1972, vol. 6, col. 411-50.

Loewith, Karl. • *Theorie und Praxis als philosophisches Problem*. Marburg, Mitteilungen des Universitätsbundes, 1931.

Lohfink, Gerhard. *Exegesis bíblica y teología*. Salamanca, Sígueme, 1969.

Lonergan, Bernard J. • *Method in Theology*. London/New York, Darton, Longman & Todd/Herder and Herder, 1972.

_____. • "Pour une méthode en théologie," *Science et Esprit* 26 (1974) 275-301.

_____. *Theologie im Pluralismus heutiger Kulturen*. Freiburg/Basel/Vienna, Herder, 1975.

Lopez Trujillo, Alfonso L. *Liberación marxista y liberación cristiana*. Madrid, Católica, 1974.

Lortz, O., and Strolz, W., eds. *Die hermeneutische Frage der Theologie*. Freiburg, Herder, 1968.

Lotz, J.B. "Ni athéisme ni théisme dans la philosophie de Martin Heidegger," in Girardi and Six, *L'athéisme dans la philosophie contemporaine*, pp. 451–73.

Löwith, Karl. *Meaning in History*. University of Chicago Press, 1949.

Lowy, M. *Dialectique et révolution*. Paris, Anthropos, 1973.

Lukács, Georg. • *Existentialisme ou Marxisme?* Paris, Nagel, 1961.

_____. • *History and Class Consciousness*. Cambridge, Mass., MIT Press, 1971.

Lumière et Vie 23/117–18 (1974). • *Chrétiens marxistes*.

Lumière et Vie 23/120 (1974). • *Théologie de la libération: Les noirs ont la parole*.

Macciocchi, Maria Antonietta. • *Per Gramsci*. Bologna, Il Mulino, 1974. (French edition, *Pour Gramsci*, Paris, Seuil, 1974.)

MacKinnon, D. "Absolu et relatif dans l'histoire: Une réflexion théologique à l'occasion du centenaire de la naissance de Lénine," in MacKinnon et al., *La théologie de l'histoire*, vol. 1.

_____, et al. *La théologie de l'histoire*. Paris, Aubier, 1971.

Macquarrie, John. *God Talk: An Examination of the Language and Logic of Theology*. London, SCM, 1967.

_____. • *Principles of Christian Theology*. London, SCM, 1966.

Mairlot, Edouard. *Science et foi chrétienne: Dimensions religieuses de l'activité scientifique*. Brussels, La Pensée Catholique, 1968.

Maldiney, H. *Regard—parole—espace*. Lausanne, Age d'Homme, 1973.

Malevez, Léopold. *Histoire de salut et philosophie: Barth, Bultmann et Cullmann*. Paris, Cerf, 1971.

Malley, François. • *Libération: Movements, analyses, recherches, théologies—Essai bibliographique*. Paris, Centre L.-J. Lebret "Foi et développement," 1974.

Manaranche, André. • *L'existence chrétienne: Essai de discernement*. Paris, Seuil, 1973.

_____. "La fe ilumina toda la existencia," in Manaranche et al., *Política y fe*, pp. 49–95.

_____. • *Y a-t-il une éthique sociale chrétienne?* Paris, Seuil, 1969.

_____, et al. *Política y fe*. Salamanca, Sígueme, 1973.

Mannheim, Karl. *Ideology and Utopia: An Introduction to the Sociology of Knowledge*. New York, Harcourt, Brace & World, 1953.

Mao Tse-tung. • *Cinq essais philosophiques: de la pratique* (1937). Peking, Ed. en langues étrangères. (English edition, *On Practice*, New York, International Publishers, n.d.)

Marcel, Gabriel. • *Essai de philosophie concrète*. Paris, Gallimard, 1940.

_____. *Etre et avoir*. Paris, Aubier-Montaigne, 1935. (English translation, *Being and Having: An Existentialist Diary*, New York, Harper & Row, 1965.)

_____. *Foi et réalité*. Paris, Aubier-Montaigne, 1967.

Marcuse, Herbert. • *One-Dimensional Man: Studies in the Ideology of Advanced Industrial Society*. Boston, Beacon, 1964.

Maréchal, Joseph. *A Maréchal Reader*. Edited and translated by Joseph Donceel. New York, Herder and Herder, 1970.

_____. *Le point de départ de la métaphysique: Leçons sur le développement historique et théorique du problème de la connaissance*. Vol. 3: *La critique de Kant*. Paris, Desclée de Brouwer, 4th ed., 1964.

Marías, Julian. *Antropologia metafísica*. São Paulo, Duas Cidades, 1971. (English translation, *Metaphysical Anthropology: The Empirical Structure of Human Life*, Pennsylvania State University Press, 1971.)

Maritain, Jacques. *Distinguish to Unite, or the Degrees of Knowledge.* New York, Scribner's, 1959.

_____. *The Peasant of the Garonne: An Old Layman Questions Himself about the Present Time.* New York/Chicago/San Francisco: Holt, Rinehart and Winston, 1968.

_____. *On the Philosophy of History.* New York, Scribner's, 1957.

_____. *The Rights of Man and Natural Law.* New York, Scribner's, 1943.

_____. "Le tenant-lieu de théologie chez les simples," *Nova et Vetera* 44 (1965) 81–121.

_____. *True Humanism.* New York, Scribner's, 1938.

Marlé, René. *Hermenêutica e catequese.* Petrópolis, Vozes, 1973.

_____. • *Introduction to Hermeneutics.* New York, Herder and Herder, 1967.

_____. *Le problème théologique de l'herméneutique: Les grands axes de la recherche contemporaine.* Paris, Orante, 2nd ed., 1968.

Marques, Domingo G. • *Ordem especulativa e ordem prática em Lenine.* Lisbon, Multinova, 1969.

Marrou, Henri-Irénée. *The Meaning of History.* Baltimore, Helicon, 1966.

_____. *Saint Augustine et la fin de la culture antique.* Paris, De Boccard, 2nd ed., 1949.

_____. *Time and Timelessness.* New York, Sheed & Ward, 1969.

Marx, Karl. *Capital.* Edited by Friedrich Engels. Chicago/London/Toronto, Encyclopaedia Britannica, 1952.

_____. *Contribution to the Critique of Hegel's Philosophy of Law.* In *Collected Works,* by Karl Marx and Frederick Engels, vol. 3. London, Lawrence & Wishart, 1975.

_____. *A Contribution to the Critique of Political Economy* (1859). Chicago, Kerr, 1904.

_____. *Para a crítica da Economia Política* (1857). São Paulo, Abril, 1974.

_____. *Critique de l'economie politique* (1844). Paris, Union Gén. d'Editions, 1972.

_____. *Critique of the Gotha Program.* New York, International Publishers, 1933 (also in *Collected Works,* London, Lawrence & Wishart).

_____. *On the Jewish Question.* In *Collected Works,* by Karl Marx and Frederick Engels, vol. 3. London, Lawrence & Wishart, 1975.

_____. "Letter to Arnold Ruge," in *Collected Works,* by Karl Marx and Frederick Engels, vol. 1. London, Lawrence & Wishart, 1973.

_____. *Moralising Criticism and Critical Morality: A Contribution to German Cultural History Contra Karl Heinzen.* In *Collected Works,* by Karl Marx and Frederick Engels, vol. 6. London, Lawrence & Wishart, 1976.

_____. *Poverty of Philosophy.* In *Collected Works,* by Karl Marx and Frederick Engels, vol. 6. London, Lawrence & Wishart, 1976.

_____. *Pre-Capitalist Economic Formations.* London, Lawrence & Wishart, 1964.

_____. *Theories of Surplus Value.* London, Lawrence & Wishart, 1969–75, 3 vols.

_____. • *Theses on Feuerbach.* In Karl Marx and Frederick Engels, *Collected Works,* vol. 5. London, Lawrence & Wishart, 1976.

_____, and Engels, Frederick. "Circular Against Kriege," in *Collected Works,* by Karl Marx and Frederick Engels. vol. 6. London, Lawrence & Wishart, 1976.

_____. *The German Ideology: Critique of Modern German Philosophy According to Its Representatives Feuerbach, B. Bauer and Stirner, and of German Socialism According to Its Various Prophets.* In *Collected Works,* by Karl Marx and Frederick Engels, vol. 5. London, Lawrence & Wishart, 1976.

_____. *The Holy Family, or Critique of Critical Criticism: Against Bruno Bauer and Company*. In *Collected Works*, by Karl Marx and Frederick Engels, vol. 4. London, Lawrence & Wishart, 1975.

_____. *On Religion*. Introduction by Reinhold Niebuhr. New York, Schocken, 1964.

_____. *Sobre la religión*. Hugo Assmann and R. Mates, eds. Salamanca, Sígueme, 1974.

Matagrin, Gabriel. *Politique, Eglise et foi—Lourdes 1972: Rapports et études présentés à l'Assemblée plénière de l'Episcopat français*. Paris, Centurion, 1972.

Matai, G. *Morale politica*. Bologne, Dehoniane, 1971.

Mbiti, J. S. • "La théologie africaine," *Spiritus* 15 (1974) 307–21.

Merleau-Ponty, Maurice. *Les aventures de la dialectique*. Paris, Gallimard, 15th ed., 1955.

_____. *Humanism and Terror: An Essay on the Communist Problem*. Boston, Beacon, 1969.

_____. "La philosophie et la sociologie," *Cahiers Internationaux de Sociologie* 10 (1951) 50–70.

_____. *Résumé de cours: Collège de France, 1952–1960*. Paris, Gallimard, 1968.

Merlo, J. "Le Pape et les idéologies," *La Lettre*, Oct. 1971.

Merton, R. K. "Sociologia do conhecimento," in Merton, et al., *Sociologia do conhecimento*, pp. 81–125.

_____, et al. *Sociologia do conhecimento*. Rio de Janeiro, Zahar, 1967.

Mesters, Carlos. "Flor sem defesa," SEDOC 9 (1976) col. 326–92.

_____. "O futuro do nosso passado," *Revista Eclesástica Brasileira* 35 (1975) 261–87.

Methol Ferré, Alberto. • "Itinerario de la praxis," *Víspera* 6 (1972) 40–44.

_____. "Política y teología de la liberación" (presentation to the third CELAM coordination meeting, Bogotá, Nov. 1973).

Metz, Johannes B. "Precisa a Igreja de nova reformação?," *Concilium* 54 (1970) 459–67.

_____. "La présence de l'Eglise dans la société," *Concilium* 60 (1970) 91–101, supplément.

_____. • "O problema de uma teologia política como instituição de liberdade crítico-social," *Concilium* 6 (1968) 5–20.

_____. • *Theology of the World*. New York/London, Crossroad/Burns & Oates, 1969.

_____, Moltmann, J., and Ölmueller, W. • *Ilustración y teoría teológica: La Iglesia en la encricijada de la liberdad moderna—Aspectos de una nueva teología política*. Salamanca, Sígueme, 1973.

_____, and Rendtorff, T., eds. • *Die Theologie in der interdisziplinären Forschung*. Düsseldorf, Bertelsmann Universitätsverlag, 1971.

_____, and Schlick, Jean. • *Idéologies de libération et message du salut*. Strasbourg, Cerdic, 1973.

_____, eds. • *Politique et foi: Hommes et Eglise* (IIIe Colloque du Cerdic, 4–6 mai 1972). Strasbourg, Cerdic, 1972.

_____, eds. *Die Spontangruppen in der Kirche*. Aschaffenburg, 1971.

Miguélez, Xosé. • *La teología de la liberación y su método: Estudio en Hugo Assmann y Gustavo Gutiérrez*. Barcelona, Herder, 1976.

Miranda, José Porfirio. • *Marx and the Bible: A Critique of the Philosophy of Religion*. Maryknoll, N.Y., Orbis, 1974.

Moeller, Charles. "Que signifie aujourd'hui être sauvé?" in Philips et al., *Le service théologique*, pp. 345–73.

Molari, Carlo. • *La fede e il suo linguaggio: Saggi di teologia*. Assisi, Cittadella, 1972.

Moles, Abraham A. • *La création scientifique*. Geneva, Kister, 1957.

Moltmann, Jürgen. "Crítica teológica de la religión política," in Moltmann et al., *Ilustración y teoría teológica*.

_____. • *The Crucified God*. New York, Harper & Row, 1974.

_____. *Diskussion über die "Theologie der Hoffnung."* Munich, Kaiser, 1967.

_____. • *L'espérance en action: Traduction historique et politique de l'Evangile*. Paris, Seuil, 1973.

_____. "Hacia una hermenéutica política del Evangelio," *Cristianismo y Sociedad* 24–25 (1970).

_____. • "On Latin American Liberation Theology," *Christianity and Crisis* 5 (1976) 57–63.

_____. • *Theology of Hope: On the Ground and the Implications of a Christian Eschatology*. New York/Evanston, Ill., Harper & Row; London, SCM, 1967.

_____. et al. *Ilustración y teoría teológica*. Salamanca, Sígueme, 1973.

Mondin, Battista. • *Teologie della prassi*. Brescia, Morceliana, 1973.

Mongin, O. "Quelques livres sur la politique, l'état, et l'autogestion," *Esprit* 7–8 (1976) 38–54.

Monod, Jacques. *Chance and Necessity: An Essay on the Natural Philosophy of Modern Biology*. New York, Knopf, 1971.

_____. "La science, valeur suprême de l'homme," in Monod et al., *Epistémologie et marxisme*, pp. 13–32.

_____, et al. *Epistémologie et marxisme*. Paris, Union Gén. d'Editions, 1972.

Montuclard, M. "La part de l'idéologie dans le discours ecclésiastique sur le christianisme et le marxisme," *Lumière et Vie* 23 (1974) 132–46.

Moran, Gabriel. *Scripture and Tradition: A Survey of the Controversy*. New York, Herder and Herder, 1963.

Morel, Georges. *Problèmes actuels de religion*. Paris, Aubier-Montaigne, 1968.

Morgenbesser, Sidney, ed. *Philosophy of Science Today*. New York/London, Basic Books, 1967.

_____. ed. • *Philosophy, Science, and Method*. New York, St. Martin's Press, 1969.

Moscovici, S. "Le jour de fête du cordonnier," in Jaulin, ed., *Pourquoi la mathématique?* pp. 279–313.

Moule, C. F. D. *The Birth of the New Testament*. New York/Evanston, Ill., Harper & Row, 1962.

Mussner, F. *Histoire de l'herméneutique*. Paris, Cerf, 1972.

Neuenzeit, Paul, ed. • *Die Funktion der Theologie in Kirche und Gesellschaft: Beiträge zu einer notwendigen Diskussion in Verbindung mit Norbert Greinacher und Peter Legsfeld*. Munich, Kösel, 1969.

Neuhasler, Engelbert, and Gössmann, Elizabeth, eds. *Was ist Theologie?* Munich, Hueber, 1966.

Niebuhr, H. Richard. *Christian Realism and Political Problems*. New York, Scribner's, 1973.

_____. *The Social Sources of Denominationalism* (1929). Cleveland/New York, World, 13th ed., 1970.

Niebuhr, Reinhold. • *Christian Realism and Political Problems*. New York, Scribner's, 1953.

Nietzsche, Friedrich. *The Birth of Tragedy and The Case of Wagner*. New York, Vintage, 1967.

_____. *Beyond Good and Evil: Prelude to a Philosophy of the Future*. Translated by

Helen Zimmern. In Levy, *The Complete Works*, vol. 12. (Also, *Beyond Good and Evil*, translated by R. J. Hollingdale. Baltimore, Penguin, 1973.)

_____. *Human, All-Too-Human: A Book for Free Spirits*. In Levy, *The Complete Works*, vol. 6.

_____. *The Joyful Wisdom*. In Levy, *The Complete Works*, vol. 10.

_____. *Twilight of the Idols and The Anti-Christ*. Baltimore, Penguin, 1968.

Nogueira, O. • "Ciência, pesquisa, método e técnica," *Ciências Econômicas* (Osasco, Brazil) 3 (1968) 3-16.

O'Connor, J.M. *São Paulo e a moral de nosso tempo*. São Paulo, Paulinas, 2nd ed., 1973.

Olgiati, F. "Rapporti tra storia, metafisica e religione," *Revista di Filosofia Neoscolastica* 43 (1951) 49-84.

Oliveros, Roberto. • *Liberación y teología: Génesis y crecimiento de una reflexión (1966-1977)*. Lima, Centro de Estudios y Publicaciones, 1977.

Olivier, Bernard. • *Développement ou Libération? Pour une théologie qui prend part*. Brussels, Vie Ouvrière, 1973.

Ölmüller, W. "Problemas del proceso moderno de la liberdad y de la ilustración," in Ölmüller et al., *Ilustración y teoría teológica*.

_____, et al. *Ilustración y teoría teológica*. Salamanca, Sígueme, 1973.

Palmier, J.-M. *Lacan: Le Symbolique et l'Imaginaire*. Paris, Ed. Universitaires, 3rd. ed., 1972.

Pannenberg, Wolfhart. *Faith and Reality*. Philadelphia, Westminster, 1977.

_____. *La foi des Apôtres: Commentaire du symbole*. Paris, Cerf, 1974.

_____. *Grundzüge der Christologie*. Gutersloh, Mohn, 1976.

_____. *Jesus—God and Man*. Philadelphia, Westminster, 1977.

_____. *Strutture fondamentali della teologia*. Brescia, Queriniana, 1970.

Pannikar, Raimundo. *L'homme qui devient Dieu*. Paris, Aubier-Montaigne, 1969.

_____. *Le mystère du culte dans l'hindouisme et le christianisme*. Paris, Cerf, 1970.

Pascal, Blaise. *Pascal Pensées*. Translated by A.J. Krailsheimer. Baltimore, Penguin, 1966.

Pater, W. *Theologische Sprachlogik*. Munich, Kösel, 1971.

Paul, André. • *L'impertinence biblique: De la signification historique d'un christianisme contemporain*. Paris, Desclée de Brouwer, 1974.

Paul VI. • *On Evangelization in the Modern World: Apostolic Exhortation Evangelii Nuntiandi, December 8, 1975*. Washington, D.C., United States Catholic Conference, 1976.

Pelikan, Jaroslav, ed. *Twentieth Century Theology in the Making*. London, Fontana, 2 vols., 1969-70.

Pellegrino, U. • "Teologia e sociologia," in *Atti del XIX Convegno del Centro Studi Filosofici*, Brescia, Morcelliana, 1965, pp. 301-7.

Peters, J. • "Black Theology como sinal de esperança," *Concilium* 59 (1970) 1164-73.

Peukert, Helmut, ed. *Diskussion zur "Politischen Theologie."* Munich/Mainz, Kaiser/Grünewald, 1969.

Philips, G. • "Les méthodes théologiques du Vatican II," in Philips et al., *Le service théologique*, pp. 11-35.

_____, et al. *Le service théologique dans l'Eglise: Mélanges offerts au Père Yves Congar*. Paris, Cerf, 1974.

Piaget, Jean. • *Epistémologie des sciences de l'homme*. Paris, Gallimard, 1972.

_____. • *Psychology and Epistemology*. New York, Grossman, 1971.

————. *Structuralism*. New York, Harper & Row, 1971.

Picht, Georg. • *Wahrheit, Vernunft, Verantwortung: Philosophische Studien*. Stuttgart, Klett, 1969.

Pico, J. H. • "Método teológico latinoamericano y normatividad del Jesús histórico para la praxis política mediada por el análisis de la realidad" (presentation to the Encuentro Latinoamericano de Teología, Mexico City, Aug. 1975).

Pinto de Oliveira, C.J. "D'une anthropologie," in Pinto de Oliveira et al., *L'anthropologie de Saint Thomas*, pp. 181–203.

————, et al. *L'anthropologie de Saint Thomas*. Fribourg, Ed. Universitaires, 1974.

Poblete, R. "La teoría de la dependencia: análysis crítico," in CELAM, *Liberación*, pp. 201–20.

Polin, Raymond. *La création des valeurs: Recherches sur le fondement de l'objectivité axiologique*. Paris, Presses Universitaires de France, 1944.

————. • *Ethique et politique*. Paris, Sirey, 1968.

Pontificia Facultá Teologica. *Problemi e orientamenti di teologia dommatica*. Milan, Marzorati, 1957.

Popper, Karl. *Logic of Scientific Discovery*. New York, Basic Books, 1958 (also, London, Hutchinson, 1980).

Post, Werner. • "Theorie und Praxis," in Rahner, *Sacramentum Mundi*, vol. 4, col. 894–901.

Poulain, Jacques. *Logique et raison: L'atomisme logique de Ludwig Wittgenstein et la possibilité des propositions religieuses*. Paris/The Hague, Mouton, 1973.

Poulantzas, Nicos. *Political Power and Social Classes*. London, Verso, 1978.

Prado, Caio, Jr. • *Estruturalismo de Lévi-Strauss e Marxismo de L. Althusser*. São Paulo, Ed. Brasiliense, 1971.

————. • *Notas introdutórias à lógica dialética*. São Paulo, Ed. Brasiliense, 3rd ed., 1968.

• *La pratique de la théologie politique: Analyse critique des conditions pratiques de l'instauration d'un discours chrétien libérateur*. L'Actualité Religieuse, no. 35. Tournai, Casterman, 1974.

Prélot, Marcel. *Introduction à la politique*. Paris, Gallimard, 1964.

Prélot, Maurice. *La science politique*. Paris, Presses Universitaires de France, 4th ed., 1969.

Prestige, George Leonard. *God in Patristic Thought*. London, SPCK, 1964.

Prieto, Luís J. • *Pertinence et pratique: Essai de sémiologie*. Paris, Minuit, 1975.

Pucheu, R. "Confession d'un paumé," *Esprit* 11 (1971).

• *Pueblo oprimido, señor de la historia*. Montevideo, Tierra Nueva, 1972.

Quillet, P., ed. • *Introdução ao pensamento de Bachelard*. Rio de Janeiro, Zahar, 1977.

Quinn, G. J., and Davidson, J. D. • "Theology: Sociology = Orthodoxy: Orthopraxis," *Theology Today* 32 (1976) 345–52.

Rabut, Olivier A. *Faith and Doubt*. New York, Sheed & Ward, 1967.

Rahner, Karl. "Anonymous Christianity and the Missionary Task of the Church," IDOC-NA (New York), no. 1 (April 1970), pp. 70–96.

————. "L'avenir de la théologie," *Nouvelle Revue Théologique* 93 (1971) 3–28 (also in Vander Gucht and Vorgrimler, *Bilan*, vol. 2).

————. *Hearers of the Word*. New York, Herder and Herder, 1969.

————. *Mission and Grace: Essays in Pastoral Theology*. New York, Sheed & Ward, 1963. (French edition, *Mission et grâce*, Tours, Mame, 1962; Portuguese edition, *Missão e graça*, Petrópolis, Vozes, 1964.)

_____. • "Réflexions sur la problématique théologique d'une Constitution Pastorale," in Rahner et al., *L'Eglise dans le monde de ce temps*, pp. 13–42.

_____. *Schriften zur Theologie*. Einsiedeln, Benziger. (English edition, *Theological Investigations*, Baltimore, Helicon, 22 vols., 1961–.)

_____. *Spirit in the World*. New York, Herder and Herder, 1968.

_____. • "Die Theologie im interdisziplinären Gespräch der Wissenschaften," in Rahner, *Schriften zur Theologie*, vol. 10, Einsiedeln, Benziger, 1972, pp. 89–103.

_____. "Theological Methodology," in Rahner et al., *Sacramentum Mundi*, 6:218–26.

_____. "Theologische Erkenntnis- und Methodenlehre," in *Sacramentum Mundi*, vol. 4, coll. 885–92.

_____. "Theology," in Rahner, *Encyclopedia of Theology*, pp. 1686–95.

_____, ed. *Encyclopedia of Theology: The Concise Sacramentum Mundi*. New York, Seabury, 1975; reprint, New York, Crossroad, 1984.

_____, et al. *L'Eglise dans le monde de ce temps. Constitution Gaudium et Spes: Commentaire du Schema XIII*. Paris, Mame, 1967.

_____, et al. *Exégèse et dogmatique: Textes et études théologiques*. Paris, Desclée, 1965.

Rahner, Karl, et al., eds. *Sacramentum Mundi: Theologisches Lexikon für die Praxis*. Basel/Vienna, Herder, 1968–70. (English translation, *Sacramentum Mundi: An Encyclopedia of Theology*, New York/London, Herder and Herder/Burns and Oates, 6 vols., 1968–70.)

Ramsey, Ian T. *Religious Language*. London, SCM, 1973.

Rancière, Jacques. *La leçon d'Althusser*. Paris, Gallimard, 1975.

Rapp, H.R. *Cibernética e teologia: O homem, Deus e o universo*. Petrópolis, Vozes, 1970.

Ratzinger, Josef. "Theologie," in Galling, *Die Religion*, vol. 6, col. 775–79.

Refoulé, François. • "L'exégèse en question," *Le Supplément* 11 (1974) 391–423.

_____. • *Marx et Saint Paul: Libérer l'homme*. Paris, Cerf, 1973.

_____. • "Orientations nouvelles de la théologie en France," *Le Supplément* 105 (1973) 119–47.

Reichenbach, H. *Experience and Prediction*. University of Chicago Press, 1961.

Rémond, René, et al. *Philosophies de l'histoire*. Paris, Fayard, 1956.

Remy, J. • "Questions de la sociologie à la théologie chrétienne," in Vander Gucht and Vorgrimler, *Bilan*, 1:208–20.

Renaud, M. • "La recherche interdisciplinaire en théologie," *Revue Théologique de Louvain* 4 (1973) 491–500.

Resweber, Jean-Paul. • *La théologie face au défi herméneutique*. Brussels, Vander-Nauwelaerts, 1975.

• *Révélation de Dieu et langage des hommes*. Cogitatio Fidei, no. 63. Paris, Cerf, 1962.

La Revue Nouvelle 5–6 (1972). • *Libération, nouveau nom du salut*.

Revue Philosophique de Louvain 72/14 (1974). • *Verité et Praxis*.

Ricoeur, Paul. "Du conflit à la convergence des methodes en exégèse biblique," in Ricoeur et al., *Exégèse et herméneutique*, pp. 35–53.

_____. *Le conflit des interprétations: Essais d'herméneutique*. Paris, Seuil, 1969. (English translation, *The Conflict of Interpretations: Essays on Hermeneutics*, Northwestern University Press, 1974.)

_____. "Contribution d'une réflexion sur le langage à une théologie de la parole," in

Ricoeur et al., *Exégèse et herméneutique*, pp. 301–19.

_____. • "Cours d'herméneutique." Louvain, Institut Supérieur de Philosophie, n.d.

_____. • *Freud and Philosophy: An Essay on Interpretation*. New Haven/London, Yale University Press, 1970.

_____. • *History and Truth*. Northwestern University Press, 1965.

_____. • "Les incidences théologiques des recherches actuelles concernant le langage." Institut d'Etudes Oecuméniques, n.d.

_____. "La paradoxe politique," *Esprit*, May 1957.

_____. • "Pour une prédication au monde," in Ricoeur et al., *L'Eglise vers l'avenir*, pp. 147–56.

_____. *The Rule of Metaphor*. Toronto/Buffalo, University of Toronto Press, 1981.

_____. • "Sciences humaines et conditionnements de la foi," in Ricoeur et al., *Dieu aujourd'hui*, pp. 147–56.

_____, et al. *Les chrétiens et la politique*. Paris, 1948.

_____, et al. *Dieu aujourd'hui: Semaine des intellectuels catholiques*. Paris, Desclée de Brouwer, 1969.

_____, et al. *L'Eglise vers l'avenir*. Paris, Cerf, 1969.

_____, et al. *Exégèse et herméneutique*. Paris, Seuil, 1971.

Robert, André, and Feuillet, André, eds. *Introduction to the New Testament*. New York, Desclée, 1965.

Robert, J.-D. "Autour d'Althusser," *Archives de Philosophie*, Jan.-March 1972.

_____. • "'Pensée' et 'réalités' scientifiques: Les implications épistémologiques et noético-ontologiques de leurs rapports spécifiques," *Laval théologique et philosophique* 29 (1973) 165–86, 291–305.

_____. *Philosophie des sciences*. Paris, Beauchesne, 1968.

_____. • *Philosophies, épistémologies, sciences—leurs rapports: Eléments de bibliographie de l'homme*. Namur, Presses Universitaires de Namur, 1974.

_____. • "Les positions épistémologiques de Gilles-Gaston Granger en sciences de l'homme," *Laval théologique et philosophique* 31 (1975) 239–63.

Roberts, Louis. *The Achievement of Karl Rahner*. New York, Herder and Herder, 1967.

Robinson, James M., and Cobb, John B. *The New Hermeneutic*. New York, Harper & Row, 1964.

Robinson, John A. T. *The Difference in Being a Christian Today*. Philadelphia, Westminster, 1972.

Rocher, G. *Introduction à la sociologie générale*. Paris, HMH, 1968.

Rochette, P. • "Théologies de la libération et libération de la théologie," *Etudes Théologiques et Religieuses* 51 (1976) 79–84.

Rollet, Jacques. • *Libération sociale et salut chrétien*. Paris, Cerf, 1974.

Roqueplo, Philippe. • *L'énergie de la foi: Science—Foi—Politique*. Paris, Cerf, 1973.

_____. *La foi d'un mal-croyant: Mentalité scientifique et vie de foi*. Paris, Cerf, 1969.

Roquette, M.-L. *La créativité*. Paris, Presses Universitaires de France, 1973.

Roth, G. *Gramscis Philosophie der Praxis: Eine neue Deutung des Marxismus*. Düsseldorf, Patmos, 1972.

Rousseau, A. • "Le discours théologique sur la société," *Lumière et Vie* 24 (1975) 95–102.

_____. "L'emploi du terme 'sociologie' dans les textes du Magistère central de l'Eglise," *Social Compass* 17 (1970) 309–20.

_____. • "Essai sur la fonction sociale de l'orthodoxie religieuse. A propos du document: 'Pour une pratique chrétienne de la politique,'" *Le Supplément* 109 (1974) 199–253.

Rousseau, Jean-Jacques. *The Social Contract*. Chicago/London/Toronto, Encyclopaedia Britannica, 1952.

Rousselot, Pierre. *The Intellectualism of Saint Thomas*. New York, Sheed & Ward, 1935.

Rubel, Maximilien, and Bottomore, B., eds. *Karl Marx, Selected Writings in Sociology and Social Philosophy*. Harmondsworth, Penguin, 1965.

Rubio, Alfonso García. • *Teologia da libertação: política ou profetismo? Visão panorâmica e crítica da teologia política latino-americana*. São Paulo, Loyola, 1977 (bibliography, pp. 275-82).

Russell, Bertrand. *The Scientific Outlook*. New York, Norton, 1931.

Russo, François. "Introduction," in Russo et al., *Science et théologie*.

_____. "La pluri-disciplinarité," *Etudes* 38 (1973) 763-80.

_____, et al. *Science et théologie*. Paris, Desclée de Brouwer, 1970.

_____. "La science comme action et artifice," in Ladrière et al., *Chemins de la raison*, pp. 95-105.

Rutkiewitsch, M. N. • *Die Praxis als Grundlage der Erkenntnis und als Kriterium der Wahrheit*. Berlin, Dietz, 1957.

Rütti, L. • "Interpretação do lugar político da comunidade cristã à la luz da 'Teologia Política,'" *Concilium* 84 (1973) 446-57.

Sagrada Congregação para a Educação Cristã. • "A formação teológica dos futuros sacerdotes," SEDOC 9 (1976) col. 11-42.

Salomon, Jean-Jacques. • *Science and Politics: An Essay on the Scientific Situation in the Modern World*. Cambridge, Mass., MIT Press, 1973.

Salvador, J., ed. *Atualidades bíblicas*. Petrópolis, Vozes, 1971.

Sánchez Velásquez, Adolfo. • *The Philosophy of Praxis*. Atlantic Highlands, N.J., Humanities Press, 1977.

Sartre, Jean-Paul. *Being and Nothingness: An Essay on Phenomenological Ontology*. New York, Philosophical Library, 1956.

_____. • *Critique of Dialectical Reason*. New York, Schocken, 1976.

_____. *Imagination: A Psychological Critique*. University of Michigan Press, 1972.

_____. • *Search for a Method*. New York, Knopf, 1963.

_____, et al. *On a raison de se révolter*. Paris, Gallimard, 1974.

Sauter, Gerhard, ed. • *Theologie als Wissenschaft: Aufsätze und Thesen*. Munich, Kaiser, 1971.

_____. *Vor einem neuen Methodenstreit in der Theologie?* Munich, Kaiser, 1970.

_____, ed. • *Wissenschaftstheoretische Kritik der Theologie: Die Theologie und die neuere wissenschaftstheoretische Diskussion—Materialien, Analysen, Entwürfe*. Munich, Kaiser, 1973.

Savramis, Demosthenes. • *Theologie und Gesellschaft*, esp. pp. 104-10: "Theologie und Soziologie." Munich, List, 1971.

Scannone, Juan Carlos. "El actual desafío planteado al lenguage teológico latinoamericano de liberación," in Scannone et al., *Fe cristiana y cambio social*, pp. 247-64.

_____. "Necesidad y posibilidad de una teología socio-culturalmente latinoamericana," in Scannone et al., *Fe cristiana y cambio social*.

_____. • "Teología, cultura popular y discernimiento," *Revista del Centro de Investigación y Acción Social* 237 (1974) 3-24.

_____. • "Teologia da Libertação: evangélica ou ideológica?," *Concilium* (1974) 413-20.

_____, et al. *Fe cristiana y cambio social en América latina*. Salamanca, Sígueme, 1973.

Schaff, Adam, ed. *Structuralisme et marxisme*. Paris, Union Gén. d'Editions, 1970. (English edition, *Structuralism and Marxism*, New York, Pergamon, 1978.)

Scheeben, Matthias Joseph. *The Mysteries of Christianity*. Saint Louis/London, Herder, 1946. (German original, *Mysterien des Christentums*, 1865.)

Schelsky, H. • "Religionssoziologie und Theologie," *Zeitschrift für evangelische Ethik* 3 (1959) 129–45.

Schillebeeckx, Edward. *Christ the Sacrament of the Encounter with God*. London, Sheed & Ward, 1977.

_____. *Etude théologique du salut par les sacrements*. Paris, Cerf, 1964.

_____. • *God and Man*. New York, Sheed and Ward, 1969.

_____. • "O Magistério e o mundo da política," *Concilium* 6 (1968) 21–39.

_____. • "O problema hermenêutico da crise da linguagem da fé," *Concilium* 85 (1973) 555–68.

_____. • *Revelation and Theology*. New York, Sheed & Ward, 1967.

_____. "Le statut critique de la théologie (Communication au Congrès de *Concilium*, Bruxelles, 1970)," *Concilium* 60, suppl. (1970) 61–68.

_____. • "La teología hermenéutica en correlación con una teoría de la sociedad," in Schillebeeckx et al., *Interpretación de la fe*, pp. 159–237.

_____. • "Teorias críticas e engajamento político na comunidade cristã," *Concilium* 84 (1973) 433–45.

_____. *The Understanding of Faith: Interpretation and Criticism*. London, Sheed & Ward, 1974.

_____. • *World and Church*. New York, Sheed & Ward, 1971.

_____, et al. *Interpretación de la fe: Aportaciones a una teología hermenéutica y crítica*. Salamanca, Sígueme, 1973.

Schnackenburg, Rudolf. *Le message moral du Nouveau Testament*. Le Puy/Lyons, Xavier Mappus, 1963. (English edition, *The Moral Teaching of the New Testament*, New York, Crossroad.)

Schooyans, Michel. *O desafio da secularização: Subsídios para uma perspectiva pastoral*. São Paulo, Herder, 1968.

_____. • "Théologie et Libération: Quelle libération?," *Revue Théologique de Louvain* 6 (1975) 165–93.

Schrey, Heinz Horst. "Neuere Tendenzen der Religionssoziologie," *Theologische Rundschau* 38 (1973) 54–63, 99–118.

Schurr, V. "Theologie im gesellschaftlichen Kontext," *Theologie der Gegenwart* 13 (1970) 181–83, 216–18.

• *Science et théologie: Méthode et langage*. Recherches et Débats, no. 67, Paris, Desclée de Brouwer, 1969.

Sebag, Lucien. *Marxisme et structuralisme*. Paris, Payot, 1964.

Segundo, Juan Luís. "Capitalismo—Socialismo, *crux theologica*," *Concilium* 96 (1974) 776–91.

_____. • *The Liberation of Theology*. Maryknoll, N.Y., Orbis, 1976.

_____. *Massas e minorias na dialética da libertação*. Petrópolis, Vozes, 1976. (Spanish original, *Masas y minorías en la dialéctica divina de la liberación*, Buenos Aires, Aurora, 1973.)

_____. • *De la sociedad a la teología*. Buenos Aires/Mexico City, Carlos Lohlé, 1970.

_____. *Teología abierta para el laico adulto*. Buenos Aires, Carlos Lohlé, 1966.

Séguy, J. • "Sociologie de la connaissance et Sociologie des religions," *Archives de Sociologie des Religions* 30 (1970) 91–107.

Sertillanges, A.D. *St. Thomas d'Aquin, Somme Théologique.* Paris/Tournai/Rome, Desclée, 1925.

Settimana Biblica. • *Esegesi ed ermeneutica: Atti della XXI settimana biblica.* Brescia, Paideia, 1972.

Shiprey, F. A. • "The Relations of Theology and the Social Sciences According to Gabriel Le Bras," *Archives de Sociologie des Religions* 10 (1965) 79-93.

Simons, Eberhard, and Hecker, Konrad. *Theologisches Verstehen.* Düsseldorf, Patmos, 1969.

Skrzypczak, F. "Le signifiant: Introduction à une problématique du signe," *Chronique Sociale de France* 1 (1972) 75-87.

Smart, J. D. • *The Divided Mind of Theology.* Philadelphia, Westminster, 1967.

Snell, Bruno. • *Théorie und Praxis im Denken des Abendlandes.* Hamburg, Universität Hamburg, 1951.

Social Compass, 17/2 (1970). • *Sociologie et théologie—Sociology and Theology.*

Sociedade tecnocrata: Ideologia e classes sociais—fim da ideologia. São Paulo, Documentos, 1968.

Sodepax. *In Search of a Theology of Development: Papers from a Consultation on Theology and Development Held by Sodepax in Cartigny, Nov. 1969.* Geneva, Sodepax, 1970.

Söhngen, G. • "A sabedoria da teologia adquirida através do caminho da ciência," in Feiner and Löhrer, *Mysterium Salutis*, I/4, pp. 111-78.

_____. "Teologia, Filosofia, Ciência," in Feiner and Löhrer, *Mysterium Salutis*, I/4, pp. 142-49.

Solari, A. E. • "Algunas reflexiones sobre el problema de los valores, la objectividad y el compromiso en las ciencias sociales," *Aportes* 13 (1969) 6-24.

_____. • "Usos y abusos de la sociología: una dúplica,"*Aportes* 19 (1971) 42-53.

Sölle, Dorothee. • *Political Theology.* Philadelphia, Fortress, 1974.

Spinoza, Benedict. • *Theologico-Political Treatise*, in vol. 1 of *The Chief Works of Benedict de Spinoza.* New York, Dover, 1951.

Splengler, H. "Le préjugé théologique," *Archives de Sociologie des Religions* 27 (1969) 37-50.

Stavenhagen, R. "Comment décoloniser les sciences sociales appliquées," in Copans, ed., *Anthropologie et impérialisme*, pp. 405-30.

Steiger, Lothar. *Die Hermeneutik als dogmatisches Problem: Eine Auseinandersetzung mit dem Ansatz des theologischen Verstehen.* Gütersloh, Mohn, 1961.

Strasser, Stephan. • *Phenomenology and the Human Sciences: A Contribution to a New Scientific Ideal.* Duquesne University Press, 1974.

Stucki, Pierre-André. • *Herméneutique et dialectique.* Geneva, Labor et Fides, 1970.

Stuke, Horst. • *Philosophie der Tat: Studien zur Verwirklichung der Philosophie bei den Junghegelianern und den Wahren Sozialisten.* Stuttgart, Klett, 1963.

Le Supplément 118 (1976). • *Orthodoxie et orthopraxie.*

Sutter, J. *Comme si Dieu n'existait pas.* Brussels, Epi, 1973.

Taborda, F. • "Teologia e ciências no diálogo interdisciplinar," *Revista Eclesiástica Brasileira* 34 (1974) 824-39.

Tavard, Georges H. *Paul Tillich and the Christian Message.* London, Burns & Oates, 1962.

_____. • *La théologie parmi les sciences humaines: De la méthode en théologie.* Paris, Beauchesne, 1975.

Tempo Brasileiro 28 (1972). • *Epistemologia.*

Thill, Georges. • *La fête scientifique: D'une praxéologie scientifique à une analyse de la décision chrétienne.* Paris, Aubier-Montaigne, 1973.

Thils, Gustave. *Christianisme sans religion?* Tournai, Desclée, 1968.

_____. *Propos et problèmes de la théologie des religions non chrétiennes.* Tournai, Casterman, 1966.

_____. *Théologie des réalités terrestres*, vol. 2: *La théologie de l'histoire.* Paris, Desclée de Brouwer, 1949.

Tillich, Paul. *A History of Christian Thought.* New York/Evanston, Ill., Harper & Row, 1968.

_____. *Systematic Theology.* London, SCM, 1978.

_____. *Theology and Culture.* New York, Oxford University Press, 1959.

Tödt, Heinz Edouard. "La méthodologie de la coopération interdisciplinaire," in Tödt et al., *Recherche interdisciplinaire.*

_____. "Theologie der Gesellschaft oder theologische Sozialethik?," *Zeitschrift für evangelische Ethik* 5 (1961) 211–41.

_____, et al. *Recherche interdisciplinaire et Théologie.* Paris, Cerf, 1970.

Touchard, Jean. *Histoire des idées politiques*, vol. 1. Paris, Presses Universitaires de France, 1959.

Touilleux, Paul. *Introduction à une théologie critique.* Paris, Lethielleux, 1967.

Touraine, Alain. *The Self-Production of Society.* University of Chicago Press, 1977.

_____. • *Sociologie de l'action.* Paris, Seuil, 1965.

Tröltsch, Ernst. *The Social Teaching of the Christian Churches.* New York, Harper, 1960.

Trotsky, Leon. "The Moralists and Sycophants Against Marxism," in *Their Morals and Ours: Marxist versus Liberal Views of Morality. Four Essays by Leon Trotsky, John Dewey, and George Novack.* New York, Merit, 1969.

Tshibangu, Tharcisse. • *Théologie positive et théologie spéculative: Position traditionelle et nouvelle problématique.* Louvain/Paris, Publications Universitaires de Louvain/Nauwelaerts, 1965.

Turk, H.J., ed. *Zwischen Ordnung und Veränderung.* Düsseldorf, Patmos, 1973.

Valadier, Paul. • "Analyse politique et marxisme," *Projet*, June 1974.

_____. • *Essai sur la modernité: Nietzsche et Marx*, esp. chap. 4. Paris, 1974.

_____. • "Marx, Nietzsche, Freud et la Bible," *Nouvelle Revue Théologique* 98 (1976) 784–98.

_____. • "Marxisme et chrétiens," *Etudes*, Oct. 1975, pp. 365–78.

_____. • "Marxisme et scientificité," *Etudes*, May 1976, pp. 713–26.

_____. • "Signes des temps, signes de Dieu?" *Etudes*, Aug.-Sept. 1971, pp. 261–79.

Vancourt, R. "Anthropologie thomiste et anthropologie marxiste," *Mélanges de Science Religieuse* 31 (1974) 145–75.

_____. • "Idéologie, marxisme et 'dépassement' de la philosophie," *Mélanges de Science Religieuse* 30 (1973) 3–39, 31 (1974) 49–81, 32 (1975) 3–42.

van den Oudenrijn, Frans. • *Kritische Theologie als Kritik der Theologie: Theorie und Praxis bei Karl Marx—Herausforderung der Theologie.* Munich, Kaiser, 1972.

Vander Gucht, R., and Vorgrimler, H., eds. *Bilan de la théologie du XXe siècle.* Tournai/Paris, Casterman, 1970, 2 vols.

van Esbroeck, Michel. • *Herméneutique, structuralisme et exégèse.* Paris, Desclée de Brouwer, 1969.

van Leeuwen, P. "La révélation divine et sa transmission: Développement de la doctrine au Concile Vatican II," *Concilium* 21 (1967) 11–22.

van Niewenhove, J. • "Rapports entre Foi et Praxis dans la Théologie de la Libérationlatinoaméricaine." Doctoral dissertation in religious sciences, Université des Sciences Humaines, Strasbourg, 1974 (bibliography, pp. iii–xx).

_____. "Les 'théologies de la libération' latino-américaines," in Ibarra et al., *Théologies de la libération*.

van Riet, Georges. *Philosophie et religion*. Louvain/Paris, Nauwelaerts, 1970.

_____. • *Problèmes d'épistémologie*. Louvain/Paris, Publications Universitaires de Louvain/Nauwelaerts, 1960.

Velásquez, M. "Foi, espérance et action politique," *Lumen Vitae* 28 (1973).

Verhaegen, Benoît. • *Introduction à l'histoire immédiate: Essai de méthodologie qualitative*. Gembloux, Duculot, 1974.

Vico, Giambattista. *Principios de ciência nova*. São Paulo, Abril, 1974.

Vidales, Raúl. • *Cuestiones en torno al método en la teología de liberación*. Lima, MIEC-JECI, no. 9, 1974.

Vieira Pinto, Alvaro. • *Ciência e existência: Problemas filosóficos da pesquisa científica*. Rio de Janeiro, Paz e Terra, 1969.

_____. *Consciência e realidade national*. Rio de Janeiro, ISER, 1961.

Vilar, Pierre, et al. "Dialectique marxiste et pensée structurale," *Cahiers d'Etudes Socialistes* 76–81 (Feb.-May 1968) 7–31; and Paris, *Etudes et documentation internationales*, 1968.

Virieux-Reymond, Antoinette. • *Introduction à l'épistémologie*. Paris, Presses Universitaires de France, 1972.

Vital, D. *Essai sur l'idéologie: Le cas particulier des idéologies syndicales*. Paris, 1971.

Vögtle, Anton. "Révélation et histoire dans le Nouveau Testament: Contribution à l'herméneutique biblique," *Concilium* 21 (1967) 39–48.

von Balthasar, Hans Urs. *De l'intégration: Aspects d'une théologie de l'histoire*. Paris, Desclée de Brouwer, 1970.

_____. "Parole et histoire," in Charlier et al., *La parole de Dieu*, pp. 233–46.

_____. "Verité et vie," *Concilium* 21 (1967) 77–84.

von Nell-Breuning, Oswald. *Marx, cristianismo, luta de classes*. Salvador (Brazil), CEAS (Centro de Estudos e Ação Social), 1970.

von Rad, Gerhard. *Old Testament Theology*. vol. 1: *The Theology of Israel's Historical Traditions*; vol. 2: *The Theology of Israel's Prophetic Traditions*. New York, Harper & Row, 1962 and 1965.

Wach, Joachim. *Sociology of Religion*. University of Chicago Press, 1964.

Wackenheim, C. • "Analyse politique et foi," in Metz and Schlick, *Politique et foi*, pp. 158–67.

_____. • *Christianisme sans idéologie*. Paris, Gallimard, 1974.

_____. • *La faillite de la religion d'après Karl Marx*. Paris, Presses Universitaires de France, 1963.

Warnier, Philippe. *La foi d'un chrétien révolutionnaire*. Paris, Fayard-Mame, 1975.

Watkins, Frederick. *The Age of Ideology*. Englewood Cliffs, N.J., Prentice-Hall, 1964.

Watté, P. • "Un savoir en mouvement vers l'interdisciplinarité," *La Revue Nouvelle*, Jan. 1971, pp. 44–55.

Weber, Max. *Ancient Judaism*. Glencoe, Ill., Free Press, 1952.

_____. *Economie et société*. Paris, Plon, 1971.

_____. *Essais sur la théorie de la science*. Paris, Plon, 1969.

_____. *From Max Weber: Essays in Sociology*. New York, Oxford University Press, 1958.

_____. *Politics as a Vocation*. Philadelphia, Fortress, 1965. (Also, "Politics as a Vocation," in *From Max Weber*.) (French edition in *Le Savant et le Politique*.)

_____. • *Le Savant et le Politique* (introduction by A. Aron). Paris, Union Gén. d'Editions, 1959. (German original, *Wissenschaft als Beruf* [1919] and *Politik als Beruf* [1919].)

_____. *Science as a Vocation*. Indianapolis, Bobbs-Merrill, 1956. (Also, "Science as a Vocation," in *From Max Weber*.) (French edition in *Le Savant et le Politique*.)

_____. *Der Sinn der "Wertfreiheit" der soziologischen und ökonomischen Wissenschaften* (1917–18), in *Gesammelte Aufsätze zur Wissenschaftslehre*, Tübingen, Mohr, 2nd ed., 1951.

Weil, E. • "Pratique et Praxis," in *Encyclopaedia Universalis*, 13:449–53.

Welte, Bernhard. • "Sur la méthode de la théologie," in Welte et al., *L'homme devant Dieu*, 3:303–17.

_____. • *Ein Vorschlag zur Methode der Theologie heute*. Freiburg, Herder, 1965.

_____, et al. *L'homme devant Dieu: Mélanges offerts au Père Henri de Lubac*, vol. 3: *Perspectives d'aujourd'hui*. Paris, Aubier, 1964.

Werneck Sodré, Nelson. • *Fundamentos do Materialismo Dialético*. Rio de Janeiro, Civilização Brasileira, 1968.

_____. • *Fundamentos do Materialismo Histórico*. Rio de Janeiro, Civilização Brasileira, 1968.

Wilken, Robert. • *The Myth of Christian Beginnings*. University of Notre Dame Press, 1980.

Wittgenstein, Ludwig. • *Tractatus Logico-Philosophicus*. Translated by D. F. Pears and B. F. McGuinness. Atlantic Highlands, N.J., Humanities Press, 1972.

Xhaufflaire, Marcel. • *Feuerbach et la théologie de la sécularisation*. Paris, Cerf, 1970.

_____. • *La "théologie politique": Introduction à la théologie politique de J. B. Metz*. Paris, Cerf, 1972.

Zwiefelhofer, Hans. • *Bericht zur "Theologie der Befreiung."* Munich/Mainz, Kaiser/Grünewald, 1974.

Index

Compiled by William H. Schlau

Other Orbis Titles . . .

SALVATION AND LIBERATION
In Search of a Balance Between Faith and Politics
by Leonardo and Clodovis Boff

After an introduction to the basic propositions of liberation theology, the authors discuss their stance on the relationship between faith and politics, salvation and liberation. The expositional chapters are rounded out by a lively, imaginary "conversation" among a parish priest, a theologian, and a Christian activist confronting the challenges posed by the present social reality in Latin America.

"The book serves well to introduce the reader to the theology of liberation while at the same time being self-critical and adopting a needed historical perspective. Recommended for undergraduate and graduate libraries that desire to stay abreast of one of the century's most significant religious and theological movements." *Choice*

no. 451-8　　　　　　　　　　128pp. pbk.　　　　　　　　　　$6.95

FAITH AND IDEOLOGIES
Vol. 1, Jesus of Nazareth Yesterday and Today
by Juan Luis Segundo

The first of a five-volume liberation Christology that considers how the church should interpret Jesus against the background of oppression and despair in Latin America. As an anthropology, not a theology, this work sets the stage for the Christological discussion to follow. Here Juan Luis Segundo analyzes various aspects of human existence, such as trust in life, religion, dogma, science, Marxism, and social development in industrial and Latin American societies, in terms of faith and ideology.

"Segundo has in this book excelled all his previous work."

The National Catholic Reporter

no. 127-6　　　　　　　　　　368pp. pbk.　　　　　　　　　　$14.95

THE HISTORICAL JESUS OF THE SYNOPTICS
Vol. 2, Jesus of Nazareth Yesterday and Today
by Juan Luis Segundo

In his monumental 5-volume series, *Jesus of Nazareth Yesterday and Today*, Juan Luis Segundo attempts to place the person and message of Jesus before us all, believer and unbeliever alike. He shakes off the christological dust of previous centuries so that we can hear the words that Jesus spoke. Having set forth his terms and methodology in Volume 1

(*Faith and Ideologies*), Segundo, in Volume 2, develops a novel approach to a classic theological pursuit—the quest for the historical Jesus.

Drawing upon his solid grasp of contemporary New Testament scholarship, Segundo explores the meaning of Jesus' parables as well as his proclamation of the kingdom of God, as they are recorded in the synoptic gospels. The result is insightful and challenging exegesis, which enables the reader to see Jesus of Nazareth "as a witness to a more humane and liberated human life," whose message of effective love is imbued with both religious and political significance. This book is essential reading for scholars and advanced students in religion.

no. 220-5   **240pp. pbk.**   **$9.95**

THE HUMANIST CHRISTOLOGY OF PAUL
Vol. 3, Jesus of Nazareth Yesterday and Today
by Juan Luis Segundo

For Juan Luis Segundo, the first eight chapters of Romans "embody the most complete and complex synthesis offered by Paul about the significance of Jesus Christ for the human being." This groundbreaking exegesis focuses chiefly on Paul's treatment of sin, faith, and the impact of their interaction on human existence. Segundo reveals new elements in Paul's christology that help us to see the central problem of our contemporary situation: "the creation and maintenance of structures and power-centers that are bound to block all effective forms of loving our neighbors in either the public or private sector."

"As a political scientist sympathetic to the theological argument of the liberationists, I have been worried by the naivete of much of their political analysis. Segundo's exploration of Romans is provocative and exciting. Paul's apparently 'apolitical' approach is shown to be extraordinarily relevant to our times. . . . A book to be read and pondered."
David Skidmore, University of York, England

no. 221-3   **256pp. pbk.**   **$14.95**

WHO DO YOU SAY?
Jesus Christ in Latin American Theology
by Claus Bussmann

How do Latin American liberation theologians understand Christology? German theologian and biblical scholar Claus Bussmann attempts to answer this question, "mainly by calling the Latin American authors themselves to the stand." Liberation Christology, he believes, challenges Northerners to reconsider theology's role in a divided world.

no. 711-8   **192pp. pbk.**   **$9.95**

THE PRAXIS OF SUFFERING
An Interpretation of Liberation and Political Theologies
by Rebecca S. Chopp

This book provides a comprehensive framework for understanding Latin American liberation theology and German political theology. Rebecca Chopp locates these theologies in their respective historical, theological, and ecclesiastical contexts. In the process of analyzing four representative theologians (Gustavo Gutiérrez, José Míguez-Bonino, Johann Baptist Metz, and Jürgen Moltmann), she demonstrates that these "two distinct voices" within the paradigm of liberation theology offer a new interpretation of Christianity as a praxis of solidarity with those who suffer.

"If I had one book to recommend as a general introduction for adoption as a textbook in courses on political or liberation theology, then it would be Rebecca Chopp's *The Praxis of Suffering*. The clarity and depth of her analyses are unsurpassed."

Francis Schüssler Fiorenza,
The Catholic University of America

"There will be many readers who learn for the first time from this book how crucial liberation theology is for the future of our churches." *M. Douglas Meeks,*
Eden Theological Seminary

no. 256-6 **192pp. pbk.** **$12.95**

THE IDEOLOGICAL WEAPONS OF DEATH
A Theological Critique of Capitalism
by Franz J. Hinkelammert
Foreword by Cornel West

A devastating critique of the capitalist system and official religion's role within it.

"Fortunately or unfortunately, in order to think, pray or love one must at least be alive. In order to be alive one must eat. In order to eat, one (or at least some) must work. It is as simple as that. But to discover the relation between the way we work and eat and the way we think, pray and love is not so simple. Franz Hinkelammert, Latin American by adoption and merit, economist by profession and vocation, theologian by vocation and passion, has explored in depth this relation and has shown that what we often take for granted as 'objective economic facts' hide and consecrate a whole understanding of human life and social reality—a 'spirituality' of life or a 'spirituality' of death.

"This book is complex and illuminating, cogent and provocative. The economist will be challenged to acknowledge the 'religion' underlying his/her economic theories; the theologian, to discover the economic relations hidden in her/his theological musings. Theologians or economists who aspire to be serious and honest about their work cannot dodge the challenge represented by this book." *José Míguez-Bonino*

no. 260-4 **320pp. pbk.** **$17.95**

THE CHURCH OF THE FUTURE
A Model for the Year 2001
by Walbert Bühlman
Epilogue by Karl Rahner

For the first time in its two thousand-year history the Catholic Church can truly claim to be a "universal" church. No longer solely the church of the Latin West, it has become the church of six continents, a world church in which the peoples of the Third World predominate. Such a fundamental shift in the church's awareness of itself is perhaps more radical in its implications than the Second Vatican Council. From his long experience of mission, Walbert Bühlmann focuses on the development of the church in Africa, Asia, and South America and indicates how the church as a whole can—in preparation for meeting the third millenium—benefit from the new values and forms of Christianity emerging from the South.

no. 253-1   **256pp. pbk.**   **$10.95**

CONSTRUCTING LOCAL THEOLOGIES
by Robert J. Schreiter
Foreword by Edward Schillebeeckx

The proliferation of diverse theologies, particularly in the southern hemispheres and among the marginalized peoples of Europe and North America, has shifted theological attention to the way cultural circumstances shape our response to the Gospel. Against this background, Robert Schreiter focuses on a set of problems common to all Christians: how to be faithful both to the contemporary experience of the Gospel and the received tradition and how to go about creating contextual expressions of Christian belief.

". . . the most perceptive, innovative, and balanced treatment of the subject to date."

Louis J. Luzbetak, S.V.D.
author of The Church and Cultures

no. 108-X   **192pp. pbk.**   **$8.95**

COMMUNITIES OF RESISTANCE AND SOLIDARITY
A Feminist Theology of Liberation
by Sharon D. Welch

In this remarkable exposition and extension of liberation theology, feminist theologian Sharon Welch uses the methodology of French philosopher Michel Foucault to describe how black, feminist, Latin American, and other liberation theologies have emerged from a new understanding of truth and a new form of community that challenge the West's dominant modes of thought and action. Liberation theology for Welch diverges sharply from traditional theology by measuring the truth of Christian faith not by its correspondence to something eternal but by its fulfillment in history, by the actual liberation of the oppressed and the creation of communities of peace, justice, and equality.

"A passionate and poetic book, which strikes a new chord in theology both in style and substance."

Harvey Cox
author of Religion in the Secular City

no. 204-3   **112pp. pbk.**   **$7.95**